Henry Edwards Huntington

Huntington in 1913.

JAMES THORPE

Henry Edwards Huntington

A Biography

UNIVERSITY OF CALIFORNIA PRESS

BERKELEY   LOS ANGELES   LONDON

For Betty

The publisher gratefully acknowledges the contribution
provided by the General Endowment Fund of the
Associates of the University of California Press.

Photographs reproduced by permission of the
Huntington Library, San Marino, California. Figure 15,
photo of William E. Dunn, reprinted courtesy of Frank
Wheat. Figure 29 reprinted by permission of the Art
Division of the Huntington Library.

University of California Press
Berkeley and Los Angeles, California

University of California Press, Ltd.
London, England

Library of Congress Cataloging-in-Publication Data
Thorpe, James Ernest, 1915–
   Henry Edwards Huntington : a biography / James
Thorpe.
      p.   cm.
   Includes bibliographical references and index.
   ISBN 0-520-08254-0 (alk. paper)
   1. Huntington, Henry Edwards, 1850–1927.
2. Capitalists and financiers—United States—Biography.
I. Title.
HG172.H86T48 1994
338'.04'092—dc20
[B]   93-11228
                                                 CIP

Printed in the United States of America
9 8 7 6 5 4 3 2 1

The paper used in this publication meets the minimum
requirements of American National Standard for
Information Sciences—Permanence of Paper for Printed
Library Materials, ANSI Z39.48-1984.

CONTENTS

TO THE READER

I HOPE THAT YOU ENJOY this book. I enjoyed writing it, despite the fact that it took me over four years to go through all the manuscript sources, even after I thought I knew a good deal about the subject. And then another two or three years to think about what I had read and to write the book.

I am interested in Huntington for a lot of reasons, and I hope that some of them will appeal to you. He played a crucial part in the primary development of Southern California and in setting it on a course it has followed ever since. He was the greatest American book collector of all time, and one of the great art collectors. He devoted a major part of his thought and his wealth to establishing an independent research institution with the high ideal of benefiting people by increasing human knowledge and culture. He acted on his basic belief that books and art and the beauty of nature can enhance human life and improve society. He was an interesting and appealing human being. He was an unassuming, retiring man of modest talents and limited academic training. He lived a quiet life but achieved a great deal and was, almost against his will, widely acclaimed as one of the most famous Americans of his time. On the private side, it is possible to get to know him well as a human being, and perhaps as something like a friend, because of the rich abundance of all kinds of available materials that reveal the private life of his feelings, his thoughts, his motives, his actions, and his relationships with other people.

I have tried to tell the story of his life in this book, including what he did and what he was like. An author of a biography is necessarily an interpreter if he is confronted by such a great mass of material that he has to choose which to emphasize, which to include, and which to leave out. I have made these necessary choices as fairly as I knew how, without any wish to try to make Huntington appear more interesting, more exciting, or more anything else than I could honestly perceive him to be.

I hope that readers will be sufficiently involved in this book to respond to what I have written and that you will react with your own personal feelings. Some of you will want to make further judgments about what Huntington was like in one specific circumstance or another or what he should or should not have done on a given occasion. Please feel free to do so. Many kinds of additional opinions are possible. I hope that my presentation offers a sound basis from which you can reach any further conclusions that you think are needed.

SOURCES

This biography is based on a reading and study of a vast quantity of manuscript material. Huntington was himself careful to keep his letters, notes, and other records; several of his family members (particularly his mother, his sister Carrie, and his daughter Elizabeth) were assiduous savers; and his private secretaries preserved his papers and all sorts of material about him. As a consequence, we have an incredibly rich written account of his life, as preserved in correspondence, notes, journals, and a variety of other documents. And we also have a full record of the ephemeral reminders of his daily activities, like invitations, menus, children's letters, clothing lists, table seating diagrams, programs, lists of books and art he wanted, travel itineraries, gift lists, and the like. He had trusted business associates in charge of his many companies, and they—along with the secretaries and bookkeepers— were very particular to keep full company records, including correspondence, ledgers, and financial reports.

Fortunately, the great majority of this material is preserved at the Huntington Library. The core of it consists of two hundred boxes of cataloged letters and related papers, comprising some twenty-five thousand items and covering all periods of Huntington's life. This is a treasure trove of riches that illuminate the central aspects of his life. In addition to these boxes are some one hundred fifty large lots of uncataloged (and uncatalogable) material; in all, they include millions of pieces of paper. One lot, for example, has eleven boxes of book bills from 1892 to 1927. The records of some fifty companies in which Huntington had a major interest are also present. There are nearly two hundred scrapbooks or large boxes of clippings about him or his interests. His personal finances are recorded in fifty volumes or boxes of ledgers, journals, accounts, and balance sheets. There are some five hundred original maps, mostly of Southern California, as well as the surveyors' field books and notes for them. And so forth. The Huntington photograph collections have more than a thousand pictures of him and many thousands of other images relevant to his life.

These core holdings have been enriched by various other papers relating to the life of Huntington. His sister, Caroline Huntington Holladay, and her descendants made early and late additions, including crucial diaries and journals and early memorabilia. Among later additions of great importance are the separate Metcalf Papers, centering around Huntington's favorite daughter, Elizabeth Huntington Metcalf, and consisting of twenty-six boxes of correspondence and forty-two scrapbooks and twelve boxes of clippings and memorabilia. Other collections at the Huntington Library of significance to the life of Huntington are the Patton Collection, the Shorb Collection, and the Hale Papers. The extensive institutional archives contain a large amount of material directly relating to Huntington, literally thousands of letters and papers. Soon after his death, a systematic effort was made to collect the reminiscences or recollections of persons who knew him, and the result was about fifty documents, some of considerable length and some of vital importance.

One large collection of value not at the Huntington Library is the Collis P. Huntington Papers, deposited at Syracuse University by Archer Huntington's widow and available in a microfilm edition. Its one hundred and fifteen reels contain about a hundred and fifty thousand letters and sixty-five thousand pages of legal and financial records, all of which I have examined; among them are materials of vital importance to understanding Henry E. Huntington. Also available at Syracuse are the Arabella Duvall Huntington Papers, three boxes—mostly of a business nature—on two reels of microfilm, which I have also examined. I have also, of course, used the printed sources that touch on Huntington's life and his work or that help to solve problems about his activities.

Now that human communications are carried on so largely by means other than the preservable written word, it is hard to imagine that biographers of future private persons will ever again have at their disposal—or be confronted by—such a wealth of relevant material as there is about Henry E. Huntington. Or that readers can have such rich sources on which to base their understanding.

ACKNOWLEDGMENTS

I have been fortunate to do the study and writing that culminated in this book while at the Huntington Library. In that friendly context I have been surrounded by sympathetic persons. So many people have helped me in my efforts to get at and understand the details of Huntington's life that I must express my gratitude to them—fellow members of the staff and fellow readers—only in this general way. Members of the Huntington family have also been supportive, two grandsons in particular: the late David Huntington went to great pains to collect and share important materials, and Edwards Huntington Metcalf has been especially generous with manuscripts and friendly counsel. Robert Middlekauff and Robert Skotheim read each chapter as I wrote it and gave me the benefit of their thoughtful reactions. I am deeply grateful for all the generous help I have received in trying to deal adequately with this important subject.

James Thorpe

One

IN 1840, ONEONTA WAS a village of several hundred persons. It was in this place, nestled in the Susquehanna Valley in Otsego County of central New York State, that Henry Edwards Huntington would be born and grow up.

His parents—Solon Huntington and Harriet Saunders—were married on June 4, in Harriet's hometown of Burnt Hills, Saratoga County, New York, near Schenectady. They set out in a carriage to select an area in which to make their home. They found Oneonta an attractive place, with apple orchards, pastures, fields, and hemlock woods around the village, which was essentially a prosperous farming community. It looked like a good place to live, bring up a family, and go into business. There, in October, they bought a house and farm on Chestnut Street.

Oneonta was about one hundred fifty miles northwest of Harwinton, Connecticut, where Solon had grown up, and about a hundred miles southwest of Burnt Hills. The two families united by this marriage were proud of their ancestors.

The Huntingtons included, for example, several persons who had been prominent in public affairs during and after the American Revolution, then hardly more than half a century in the past. Benjamin Huntington (1736–1800) was a member of the Continental Congress and later a judge; Jabez Huntington (1719–86) was a graduate of Yale and a general during the war; Jedediah Huntington (1743–1818) was a graduate of Harvard, a general, and a member of the court-martial that tried Major André. Best known of all was Samuel Huntington (1731–96), who was a signer of the Declaration of Independence, president of the Continental Congress for two years, chief justice of the supreme court of Connecticut for ten years, and governor of Connecticut for ten more years, all in a life span of sixty-five years and without a college education. Their common ancestor was Simon Huntington, who immigrated from England in 1633 with his wife and five children. Simon died of small pox en route to Boston, but his wife, Margaret, carried on effectively; she moved to Connecticut, raised their children, and soon remarried.[1]

Although Henry Edwards Huntington was seven generations removed from Simon, we need to remind ourselves that he was only three generations after Samuel ("the Signer")—that is, Samuel was of the generation of our Huntington's great-grandfather and had been dead only fifty-four years when our Huntington was born. These facts about his ancestors were of interest to our Huntington, and he later hired a professional genealogist to search out the facts about his early forbears for the benefit of the Huntington Family Association.

His mother's family was also proud of its ancestors. Harriet's mother, Sally Edwards Saunders, was a descendant of theologian Jonathan Edwards, and they were careful to perpetuate the Edwards name with its aura of intellectual and spiritual distinction; they named one of their children Henry Edwards, as did their daughter Harriet. Her father, Henry Saunders, was the leading physician in the area of Burnt Hills. The family relations between Harriet's parents ran to the formal style. This is a conversation reported on an occasion when husband Henry was preparing to perform a small operation on wife Sally. The wife: "Dr. Saunders, I think I am going to faint." The husband: "Mrs. Saunders, I am very glad of it. You will then not feel any pain." She pulled through quite well.[2]

Dr. Saunders was also properly prudent. When Solon Huntington sought to marry Harriet, Dr. Saunders wrote to reliable persons in faraway Connecticut for an opinion of Solon. From the firm of Curtiss, Candu and Stiles in Woodbury, Connecticut, he received a full account: they had known him for many years and had business dealings for ten years and have always found him honest, honorable, and prompt to meet all his engagements and think whatever he may state to you you may have the fullest confidence in. His character in this part of the country is without a blemish as far as we know and has always been industrious and economical and has (we think we can safely say) in ten years accumulated property to the amount of ten thousand dollars and probably more.

Solon was honorable and industrious, but he was not very articulate when it came to the expression of feelings. His extant letters to Harriet before their marriage are limited to details of his business travel. Once he says to her, "As you know I am such a miserable writer and hate to write—you will probably excuse me for not writing sooner." He was in Wolcottville, New York, and she was in Burnt Hills, where they were to be married in ten days. The most personal he gets is to conclude that same letter by saying: "You may expect to see me at Burnt Hills by the first of June. I shall come out with my own conveyance. Yours &c Solon Huntington."[3]

The families gathered together in Burnt Hills for the wedding. Solon's younger brother, Collis, made the trip in order to be present. Harriet was nineteen years old, bright, lively, well-read. Solon was twenty-eight, solid, reliable, full of business. He had gotten his money by making silver tableware and selling it throughout the local area. His father owned a small carding mill (antiquated and not very successful) to prepare cotton or wool fibers for spinning. Collis had assembled clocks and made a living by peddling them and other goods by horse and wagon. The pattern of making and selling had long run in the family; even Samuel the Signer had been apprenticed to a barrel maker at the age of sixteen and spent five years learning that trade before deciding to "read the law."

Solon had decided to further his business career after marriage by settling down in one place and opening a general store. So, in November 1840, soon after they had chosen their house in Oneonta, he bought a lot near the center of the village and contracted with a builder to erect for him a store of quarried stone with three stories and a basement for $1,450.

Their house was on Chestnut Street, a wide roadway with trees on both sides. It had been an old "Indian trail" through the area, and occasional Native Americans were still to be seen. There were only two other houses on the street; the Huntington house had been built in 1832 by Timothy Sabin to replace a log house.

Their residence was an imposing two-story frame house of fourteen rooms, including eight bedrooms; it had three halls, a basement (or cellar, as they called it), an attic, two barns, and plenty of land. Here they brought up their children, and here they lived in the same house the rest of their lives—for the father, fifty years; for the mother, sixty-six years. A stable family life, and a situation for a stable childhood.

Although the area had been occupied by white men since before the American Revolution, the township of Oneonta had been formed only in 1830. It began to prosper after the construction of a main road, the Charlotte Turnpike, through the village in 1834. This road was hardly a major artery; it went from Catskill to the southwest part of the state. The arrival of the stagecoach was for a while the biggest public event of the day, for which the boys had to stop their quoits game in the street. Oneonta continued to be an isolated small town until, and even after, the railroad came in 1865 and connected it with Albany. By 1850, when Huntington was born, its population had grown to 1,792 (938 males and 950 females, all white, according to the census), and by 1870, when he had just left, to 2,588.

Soon after the Huntingtons occupied their big house on Chestnut Street, they began to fill it with children. On August 7, 1841, their first was born, a daughter named Leonora. In the course of the next twenty years, they had six more children, with Henry Edwards born in 1850.

It was a very close family, both within itself and with grandparents, aunts, uncles, and cousins. An excerpt from a letter from Harriet to her sister Marcia, written on October 27, 1850, gives a glimpse into their family life. At this time, they had only four children, the youngest being the eight-month-old Henry Edwards, who was usually called "Edward" or "Eddy" in the family:

> My dear Sister
>
> It is a very rainy Sunday, and I do not know how I could pass away the time any more pleasantly than writing to my much loved sister. Picture to your imagination Solon in the pantry wishing for honey,

Ellen [Solon's youngest sister, age fifteen] on the settee behind the stove reading the latest news, Leonora [age nine] in the large arm chair eating apples, Howard [the oldest son, almost seven] & Edward on the floor, Howard trying to instruct Eddy in drawing the little wagon, the occupant being little Georgie [age three]. He [Eddy] has got so that he can push the wagon backwards and forwards with a considerable regularity. Howard has concluded to let baby [Eddy] taste of his apple, but you needs must know he had [to] get the wash rag and make sundry revolutions around his face before he could consent to his tasting.[4]

Harriet was a lively-minded and affectionate person, and all of her children were delighted to have her as their mother. "She was a woman of the gentle type," it was later said of her, "living that she might make home and mother terms of much meaning to her loved ones."[5] Solon was more a man of business than a homebody, but the sons were often allowed to drive with him by horse and wagon to visit the farms he owned in the area.

Another glimpse of their family life is contained in a letter that Harriet wrote in 1857 to her brother Howard and his wife, Georgia, who had just had their first child, a son. By this time, Solon and Harriet had six of their seven children:

Well, my dears, how does the appellation of Father & Mother sound? Strange, no doubt, but nevertheless perfectly natural. Georgie, I was very sorry you made such a great mistake in having a boy, as I had made great calculations on having a little Hattie. But never mind, Sis—better luck next time. I suppose Howard thinks boys are a far preferable article. Well, some folks are just so foolish. I think if he could see our little boys go from one mischief to another he would get enough of male gender. Mother has written every particle of news, I believe. But I do not care. I can write if I have no news—I can convert news out of chaos.[6]

Chaos, of course, meant those little boys, including Edward, going from one mischief to another all around the house.

Solon and Harriet's last child came four years later, in 1861, when

Edward was eleven. She was named Caroline (Carrie for short), and she had a place of special importance in the life of their family, particularly for Harriet and most of all for Edward.

Their family was complete with the seven children. Henry Edwards was the middle child, born on Wednesday, February 27, 1850. He had one older sister, Leonora, the firstborn, and two older brothers, Howard and George Darwin; he had one younger brother, Willard, and two younger sisters, Harriet and Carrie.

Families often had many children in the nineteenth century, of course, and a good many died. Solon and Harriet were luckier than many: only three of their seven died young. By the time Edward was ten years old, he had lost three siblings: Harriet or "Hatty," named for her mother, had died at the age of two; George Darwin, named for Harriet's brother, at four; and Howard, named for another brother of Harriet's, at sixteen. These deaths were important in shaping one set of Edward's essential feelings.

The death in 1860 of Howard, the oldest son, just on the threshold of manhood, brought a special sadness to the family. Howard was quiet and unassuming, ready to do a kindness for anyone, liked by everyone, of a meditative cast of mind; he liked to stand and marvel at the evening star as an example of the mystery of God's handiwork. Later, Edward's younger brother, Willard, wrote:

> I have heard my mother say that sometimes when she is looking at this star, it is with a feeling that she is in the presence of my brother who died so long ago.
>
> The morning that Howard's spirit took its flight to another world, the summons came with the earliest indication of the dawn and the silence of the room seemed more pronounced owing to the solitary notes of a robin just outside the window, announcing the advent of another and to the dying boy a greater day. How natural is it then even at this late period, that the early morning notes of the robin should carry with them so mournful a significance to our mother.[7]

Howard's coffin and remains were placed for viewing on two supports in the parlor near the front door, and then taken to the burying grounds.

Death occasioned family letters of sympathy. In the Huntington and Saunders families, these letters were often three or four pages long, thoughtful discourses on how to deal with deep affliction and on the nature of God's providence. When Solon's brother Joseph died in 1849, Mary, the oldest sibling of Solon, wrote four-page letters on behalf of herself and their mother to each of the siblings asking them all to consecrate themselves anew to God. When little Hatty died in 1855, letters came to Solon and Harriet from many relations. Harriet's father urged her to "exercise fortitude and resignation" in the loss of "dear little Hatty." Even Collis wrote from California about his "heartfelt sorrow when I learned of the death of your little Hatty, for I remember her as a sweet little child and it must have been very hard for you to have given her up."[8]

Sometimes the other siblings were also addressed in the letters. When Ellen Huntington, now sixteen, wrote to her brother Solon and Harriet about the death of George Darwin in 1852, she devoted two pages to the fact that he was now with God. Then she went on to address the two older children, Leonora and Howard: "You and Howey must be good children and love one another because you do not [know] how soon Death will call for you and you will want to meet little brother in that 'Happy land' which you sometimes sing about."[9]

The transience of human life was brought home forcefully as a part of human experience. One had to learn how to come to terms with death and to respond adequately to it. I expect that the experience of death, and the way that his parents, relatives, and friends reacted to it within the system of belief that they shared, had a bearing on the early establishment of one or two of Huntington's central traits. One was that, throughout his life, his very strongest feelings were always ones of affection for family members. Another was his drive toward accomplishment, to make the most of his life.

Growing up in Oneonta in the 1850s and 1860s offered many pleasures. We are fortunate that Edward's younger brother, Willard, kept an account of the activities of the children in that family, and we know a lot of the ordinary details of their childhood from his *Oneonta Memories and Sundry Personal Recollections of the Author,* published in 1891.[10]

In the summer, children gathered wild strawberries up Silver Brook Road. Then they swam in the Flume, with its cool water and shady area, with one gentle bank good for the younger children and one deep pool into which older boys dove from the bank to recover pieces of white marble from the bottom of the stream. Another good swimming place was at the Dam. There were many places to fish: the rivulet behind the Main Street stores was handy, while the rocky portion of Silver Brook was more adventuresome. Playing ball was popular, either One Old Cat or Two Old Cat, depending on how many boys were around; and croquet was introduced into Oneonta in the 1860s. They enjoyed kite flying in good weather and bonfires in the evenings.

In the autumn, boys competed with one another to see who could gather the most chestnuts from the trees in the area. They hammered the trees with clubs to bring chestnuts down; if the burrs were open, they climbed the trees and shook the branches; as a last resort, they poked around on the ground with a stick in search of those few valuable nuts hiding among the dead leaves. They made jack-o'-lanterns with ogrish faces and sharp, pointed teeth; some they put on the tops of fence posts, others they thrust into the faces of unsuspecting passersby. Active indoor games like I Spy kept the blood in circulation on cold evenings.

In the winter, there was plenty of skating on Frog Pond (only a few steps away), Grove Pond, or, best of all, Mill Pond, with its long run up to the Cove near Barn Hill. Some took the long trip to the Plains Lake. There was sliding on any steep incline, notably the one in front of the First Baptist Church. And snowballing: boys chose sides, stood in parallel lines, and threw at those on the other side; a boy who was hit had to change sides and throw at his former comrades.

In the spring, older boys and girls went out on the slopes around the village, as soon as the ground was dry, in search of early wildflowers; there were many on Solon's land between Laurens Road and Babcock Hollow Road. Another popular excursion was to go to the Rocks and climb around the dry crevices among them; sometimes a boy might find a card left there by a girlfriend.

In most seasons, one could try to throw a stone over the steeple of the First Baptist Church. Or, after the railroad came, crossed pins could be put on the track to be mashed into a pair of miniature shears. A lucky boy or girl might be allowed to ride in the locomotive while the engineer was switching cars in the Oneonta rail yard. Those, like the Huntingtons, whose parents had a big barn could spend happy hours playing Hide and Seek or jumping from the overhead scaffolds into the loose hay below. In the hemlock woods outside of the village, however, children had to be careful not to disturb the rattlesnakes living there.

There were chores to do. It was the job of the Huntington boys to keep the wood box in the kitchen full, and the hired woman, Rebecca, always seemed to use a lot of wood in cooking. In summer the boys had to take the cows to the pasture down below the orchard in the morning and bring them back in the evening—often after a search to find the strayed animals. The hired men did the milking, however, and brought the milk to the cool, spacious cellar. Solon had more than twenty men working for him on his various nearby farms.

And there was school. In the winter, the children had to get up before it was light and have breakfast by lamplight, as gas had not yet come to Oneonta. For most of his schooling, Edward was sent to the District School, a public school where there were about seventy-five pupils at three levels of instruction, the Primary, Intermediate, and Senior departments. Part of the time, Edward went to the small private school that Miss Sullivan ran in one or two rooms of her own house on Dietz Street; she had left the District School to try this arrangement, but she gave it up after about five years and went back to teaching at the District School. The main subjects taught at both places were reading, spelling, grammar, geography, arithmetic, and U.S. history, along with Latin grammar, French, botany, philosophy, and astronomy—all taught out of textbooks prepared for school use. One school bill has been preserved for the Huntington children, for the term September 14 to November 27, 1857, when Leonora was sixteen, Howard thirteen, and Edward seven. For Leonora and Howard, the cost was $4 each; for "Master Eddie Huntington, Primary Dep. $2.00."[11]

The Huntingtons had a lot of books in their house. Solon and Harriet were devoted readers, and so were their children. One of Edward's childhood books has, remarkably, been preserved. It is a colored picture book of fourteen pages entitled *Aunt Effie's Rhymes for Children,* published in New York in 1856. It contains half a dozen stories in verse, mostly about animals and children who act like well-bred adults, all highly moral. The caption to one of the pictures illustrating "Dame Duck's First Lecture on Education," for example, asserts, "But well-bred ducks walk in a row, straight—one behind another."[12]

Books were important presents in the Huntington family. Notice what gets first mention among the gifts in Harriet's whimsical account of the visit of Santa Claus to their home in 1856, when Edward was six, written to her brother Howard and his wife, Georgia: "Santa Claus made us his annual visit last eve and was gratefully received. At his exit, he left Books, ribbons, gloves, nuts, candies & cakes, &c, &c—which made the little ones jump for joy. What a generous old fellow he must be, and what a large bag he must have!"[13]

Edward was eager to learn, as we can see from the beginning of a letter he wrote to his sister Leonora on June 8, 1862, while he was visiting his grandparents in Burnt Hills and going to school there briefly. It is touching testimony to his belief, at the age of twelve, in the power of books:

> My Dear Sister
>
> As I have not written to you since I have been here, I will now take the opportunity. I am getting along very well with my studies & everything else. I intend to go through my grammar tomorrow and then commence it again next day, for I intend to go through again and again. For I want to learn to talk correctly, as I have not learned yet, but I will learn by the time [I] get home. For I do want to learn to speak by the time I get home.[14]

He early developed the habit of fixing his mind on doing something and persevering until he had done it.

The family went to the Presbyterian Church in Oneonta, and the children stayed on afterward for the Church School. Church provided social events, such as picnics, ice cream socials, and strawberry festivals, as well as religious instruction and guidance. Daily school began with a general assembly for prayers and music—and Edward kept a little note-book of short sentences from scripture, one to a page, like sermon texts. This is one example: "Commit thy works unto the Lord and thy thoughts shall be established. Prov XVI.3." On the first page of the book there is this full inscription: "H. E. Huntington Esq / Oneonta / Otsego Cty / N.Y." Presumably the self-important inscription of a teenager.[15] But the book as a whole is witness to the expression of a fundamentally moral outlook.

The Huntingtons entertained many family guests at their house, and the varied personalities of the visitors certainly added to the flavor of the household and its impact on the children. Harriet's mother was a frequent visitor, and she sometimes stayed two or three months at a time, in the hope of getting rid of her "low spirits"; it usually worked, and she would go home to Burnt Hills with a sense of renewal. Dr. Saunders wrote frequently in the 1860s to their children about his anxiety concerning his wife's gloominess, and he expressed his appreciation to Harriet for her help. In 1864, he wrote to Harriet that "I think her now as gloomy as I have ever known her to be, so much so she takes but very little management of her household concerns, which makes it very unpleasant for all of the family."[16] Apparently, Dr. Saunders could only advise his wife to "look on the bright side of the picture, I think it more pleasant than the dark side."[17] But Harriet and the Huntington household could bring her out of her depression, at least temporarily. When Dr. Saunders himself came to Oneonta, the grandchildren held him "in great awe" as an "aged and greatly respected physician and a man of highly informed mind."[18]

There were also visits to their grandparents' home in Burnt Hills. The Saunders property had features of interest to the Huntington boys: an immense ancient elm tree, a conspicuous sundial, a brook that ran through their property with a rustic bridge over it, and a spot nearby that was a good place to fish. It was not an easy trip from Oneonta, and Harriet preferred to have a relative accompany her children. But in April 1862, Edward made the trip alone, at the age of twelve, with his mother's warning ringing in his ears that he should write her on arrival. Here is his letter, written in ink. Since it is the earliest letter by him that I know about, I reproduce it in full:

Dear Mother

　You know that you told me to write the next day after I got here. But Uncle Darwin said that he would write so that you would know that I got here safe and sound, and he said that I could write today. Well, I will not talk about writing. Now I would like to know how you all are, and how you get along with your work. I suppose Grandmother is there: I met the stage on the way but did not know that Grandmother was in it. Uncle Charles has come here and while he has gone up to Aunt Marcia's I am writing to you, and Leonora and Will and Carrie. Does she walk, and has she got the measles? Why don't you write? (Say hey!—are you bashful?) Come, write and tell me how you are, and all of you—Leonora, Rebecca. I had a pleasant ride of 8 miles on the lake, and I got here just in time, for that was the last time that they were going. You told me that I need not write a very long letter at first. So, good morning!

H E H

P S—Write soon[19]

Edward put a brave front on separation. When Dr. Saunders wrote to Harriet about the visit, he fulfilled the gruff male role by saying only that "Edwards is well and enjoying himself well."[20]

　The other grandmother, Elizabeth Vincent Huntington, was a different sort from the depressive Sally Edwards Saunders. Her presence delighted her grandchildren. "She was a woman of beautiful disposition," Willard wrote, "and I can truly say I never saw a frown on her face." She came to Oneonta from Harwinton, Connecticut, for long visits, in part to be away from her irascible husband. After he died in 1860, she and Ellen—then twenty-five, and soon to be married—moved to Oneonta and lived for several years just down the street in Collis's house, which was noted for the profusion of lilacs in its yard. When she left in 1866 to be with another daughter in western New York State, Willard wrote that "her departure was a sad one to every member of her family living in Oneonta—both old and young. She was much beloved by her grandchildren and would entertain them by the hour with story and verse of the days of her childhood in far-away Connecticut."[21]

For the most part, the people of Oneonta had to create their own entertainment. A few houses had music. The Huntingtons owned a piano and had it tuned twice a year, at $1 per tuning, and also a violin, which had cost them $4.50.[22] There was also music at the church, along with sermons and the occasional visiting speaker.

A few public events engaged the interest of nearly everybody. One was the public exhibition and drill of the volunteer fire department, with the members—all of them neighbors and friends—dressed in their bright uniforms. They pulled the hand engine to a cistern. There they dropped a suction pipe into the water and by great physical exertion pumped the water until it shot out of the nozzle high into the sky, to the delight of all the small boy spectators.

Another occasional event was General Training with two regiments of state militia after the Civil War under the command of Major General S. S. Burnside, an Oneonta resident. They drilled on the river flats by the village, and the event attracted all the young boys and an immense crowd from the rural areas.

The Fourth of July was a more spectacular occasion. It began with a cannon salute at sunrise to arouse the citizenry (especially small boys), firecrackers in the morning, music by the West Oneonta Band and speeches during the day, and an elaborate public fireworks display in the evening at the foot of Chestnut Street, near the Huntington house.

The coming of the circus was also a great event. Immense posters appeared in public places in advance announcing the pleasure and instruction that the populace was sure to derive from the spectacles. The circus traveled by horse and wagon and set up on Solon's land near Church Street. The village boys met the circus at the outskirts of town and escorted them, with their blaring music, to the place where their canvas city went up.[23]

On one of these annual occasions, in the late 1850s, Edward had his first experience as an entrepreneur. He related the event nearly fifty years later to a close friend:

My first great speculation was when I was eight or nine years old, and a circus came to Oneonta, my childhood home in New York.

I hired a man to build a shed where I could sell candy, peanuts, and lemonade.

When I contracted for my supplies, I arranged with the sellers to take back what I did not sell.

As I opened my sales, a farmer came along with a barrel of cider and began selling next to my place.

I met this competition by purchasing his cider from him at ten cents a gallon, and then I sold it at five cents a glass. He had only a board from which to dispense his goods, while I had a cool, comfortable booth.

When I had paid my bills, I had what looked bigger than anything I ever since have made—eight dollars and fifty-five cents![24]

One public event that occurred in the course of Huntington's childhood in Oneonta stands out from all the rest in the impact it made on the people of the area: the coming of the railroad to Oneonta. A celebration in honor of the event was held on August 29, 1865, to commemorate the formal opening of the Albany and Susquehanna railroad line from Oneonta to Albany. Several citizen committees had decorated the whole village with banners and flags and inspirational mottoes and flowers, and the people thronged in from every direction for the great affair. A special train from Albany brought the governor, the lieutenant governor, and assorted judges and other dignitaries to Oneonta; it was met at the depot by four companies of state militia from the Forty-First Regiment, with General Burnside and his staff in attendance. After a dinner at the two hotels, everyone went to the churchyard of the First Baptist Church for many speeches, band music, firing of cannons, and much cheering and waving of handkerchiefs until the special train left to return the officials to Albany at 4:00 P.M., when the others turned toward home too.[25]

The community had great expectations for the future of Oneonta: it would become big and prosperous and the center of an important and bustling section of the state. The coming of the railroad was taken as a symbol of the town's bright future. Enthusiasm is the most contagious of all public qualities, especially if it is in favor of something one would like to see happen. And who at the time would think to oppose this kind of progress?

Edward, a village boy of fifteen, was presumably absorbed into the mainstream of these expectations. The railroad symbolized progress and improvement, and it would remain an auspicious symbol for Edward for all of his business life. Rail transportation was the central means by which he became rich and powerful, by which he was the main instrument in helping large areas to fulfill their hopes and ambitions, by which he could be a generous benefactor of the public.

The great expectations for Oneonta were never fulfilled. The population increased only modestly, even after the railroad repair shops were later located there. However, it may be that these expectations were fulfilled in a different way and in a different place by the later life of a resident who was only fifteen years old at the time of this enthusiasm.

After Solon built his stone store in Oneonta, he began to fill it with general merchandise. As the printed billhead said, the company was a "Dealer in Foreign and Domestic Dry Goods, Groceries, Hardware, Boots and Shoes, Hats, Caps, Crockery, &c. &c." Solon liked to keep a lot of irons in the fire. He soon began to go about in the area and buy small farms, often mortgaging one property to acquire another. The preparation of his many deeds, indentures, and mortgages over the years gave good business to the local lawyer.

In 1842, Collis—Solon's brother, twenty-one years old and nine years his junior—decided to come to Oneonta after years as a traveling peddler. He worked for two years in the store as a clerk and then as an outside seller and buyer, until in 1844 Solon and Collis formed a partnership to own and operate the store. Their agreement dated September 5, 1844, was to run for five years; each contributed $1,318.64 toward their common stock.[26]

These business matters, and those that followed, are an important background for understanding Henry Edwards Huntington. In the first place, his active business career developed out of the practice, principles, and vision of his father and uncle. In the second place, and more important, his uncle became a kind of surrogate father for him around the time the young man reached the age of twenty, a capacity in which the uncle served for the remaining thirty years of his life.

Right after the partnership agreement was signed, Collis, then twenty-three, married Elizabeth Stoddard, known as Libby, of Cornwall, Connecticut, who was twenty-one and two years younger than Harriet. The young couple bought a house in Oneonta at the corner of Chestnut and Church streets—just down the road from Solon and Harriet—and the business and family life of the two Huntingtons began to be integrated.

When the news of the discovery of gold in California came to Oneonta in late 1848, it excited some citizens to want to go and get rich. Collis was one of them, and Solon was not. At last Collis and five other young men from Oneonta, including several associated with the store, decided to make the trip and try their luck. Each had to provide his own funds; Collis managed by exploiting his own resources and by borrowing $3,000 from Solon, who had to mortgage his house to get the cash. On March 10, 1849, they rewrote their partnership agreement, extending it for three years from the original termination date of 1849 to 1852. The revision provided that Collis try trading in California for six months on behalf of the partnership and return to Oneonta if the work was less profitable than it was at home. Solon and Collis would thus continue to be partners both in Oneonta and in California.[27] Elizabeth was to stay at home.

On March 15, 1849, Collis and his companions set out from New York with a stock of merchandise to go by way of Panama to San Francisco and then to the gold country. The trip, filled with difficulties, took five and a half months, including almost two months in Panama waiting for a ship to get them to San Francisco; it was during this waiting period that Collis—as he was happy to brag later—increased his cash resources from $2,000 to $5,000 by "trading." After reaching California, they settled in Sacramento. Their first years there would have driven any ordinary man back to the safety of his home and family. Collis had to survive illness, uncertainty of supply and demand, primitive living conditions, terrorism, a psychotic assistant, and indifferent business success.[28]

One letter from Collis in Sacramento to Solon in Oneonta, written on June 17, 1850, sums up his experience to that time and epitomizes a basic principle of living that young Edward later came to share:

> I have suffered much in this country, much in sickness and much in health. And how could it be otherwise? How can one leave for four of the best years of his life his nearest and dearest friends, and a quiet home, a loved and loving wife, without looking back with bitter regret on those joys that we have left behind for something which (if obtained) is doubted by many whether it does not bring more grief than joy.
>
> But let it pass! I shall stay until I have satisfied myself and all others concerned that I have done the best that I could under the circumstances. And then I hope to return to my family and friends, and then spend many happy days. Satisfied with myself—whether I return with much or with little—that I have done my best, and therefore shall be satisfied. God speed the time of my return![29]

For Collis, then, the paramount principle was to do the best you can do in your situation and then you can be satisfied with yourself, whatever the results. The instrumental principle is that you have to trust your own judgment, rather than the opinion of others, about the value of the results you are trying to achieve. And the ultimate goal is a happy retired life with family and friends.

Collis felt optimistic enough to go back to Oneonta later in 1850 for a visit and to return to Sacramento with Elizabeth and her younger sister Hannah. They were faced with several more years of severe problems, including a disastrous fire that destroyed his store and most of his merchandise in November 1852. Elizabeth gave full details of it to her sister-in-law Phoebe Huntington Pardee and—being made of the same stern stuff that Collis was, at least so long as she continued in good health—explained why they would not give up and come home: "We will stay and try to get up again. We have succeeded once and may again. You know that Collis is not the one to be easily discouraged."[30]

Earlier that year, Collis had told Solon he was about ready to sell out; but he persisted, and by 1854 things were going fairly well and the store was making some money. Their legal partnership formally ended in

1852, and they came to terms on a settlement—with Collis getting the Sacramento goods and Solon the Oneonta goods—while continuing to work closely together.[31]

Collis still owed the original $3,000 to Solon, who kept pressing him for his money; Collis kept putting him off. The New York merchants who supplied them with goods were also pressing both Collis and Solon for payments past due. Instead of paying, they used the financial tactic of debt leverage later employed so successfully by Edward, using borrowed money to finance new acquisitions. Collis bought considerable California real estate and built four houses to rent; Solon bought stock in the Albany and Susquehanna Railroad Company and a good deal of land in Grant County, Wisconsin, and started, with Jacob Dietz, a company to manufacture carriages. It was only in August 1856 that Collis began to pay off his debt to Solon. By then, affairs had improved considerably for Collis.[32]

California had a special charm for Collis, one to which the rest of the Huntington family was not entirely immune. Even when prospects looked dim, Collis urged Solon to come to California. "The time for making fortunes in a day in California has past," he warned Solon on June 28, 1851, "but I think when things get settled here there can be more money made than in the Old States for some years to come." Solon didn't want to go. On May 31, 1853, Collis wrote that "you may send Howard [Solon's son, now age twelve] out to California to me if you are [of] a mind and I will bring him up in the way he should go," whatever that might have meant. On January 3, 1856, Collis urged Solon to give up finally on Oneonta:

> I think Oneonta must be a very poor place to make money, as so few meet with success there. And I would advise you to sell out everything there and come to California, or go to Kansas. And I should give California the preference, as I am sure that you could make plenty of money in this country—or almost anywhere except Oneonta.

Solon still wanted to keep his family in Oneonta, and on December 19, 1856, Collis made one last appeal to him:

I had sometimes thought—and even now think—it would have been better for you to have come to California, for various reasons. In the first place, we have the best climate in the world, and as good land as the sun ever shone on. . . . I am sure that merchants do better in this State than in almost any other, and I am sure that we have less failure. . . . I have no doubt but if you was out here with a few thousand dollars that you could lay it out in land that in a few years would be worth from five to ten times what you would have to pay for it at this time. And I think it would be better for your family.[33]

It is interesting to notice that the central arguments Collis used—climate, business success, increase in land value, and family well-being—were the same texts from which Henry Edwards Huntington preached as he extolled the charms of California during the last thirty years of his life.

Solon was resolute: he and his family would stay in Oneonta. But Solon's fortunes did not flourish. The store and the carriage company were not notably successful. After the termination of his partnership with Collis, Solon sold three-fourths of his interest in the store to three colleagues.[34]

In 1862, Solon went to Wisconsin to supervise his property there and was away about eight months; he wrote infrequently, and Harriet and the family were troubled by his silence. Her letters to him are filled with news and longing: "I had a letter from Eddie tonight." "Shall I buy a set of kitchen chairs for $3 so as not to have to use the living room chairs in the kitchen?" "If Solon wants to bring me a present when he comes home a nice family Bible would be what I should like above everything else." "Willie talks about your coming home and wants me to count the days."[35] The venture in Wisconsin was not particularly successful, either. By 1865, Solon had pretty much retired from the store, and for the remaining twenty-five years of his life he was occupied in managing the properties he owned in and around Oneonta.

On the other hand, during this same period, Collis's fortunes changed dramatically. The turn for him had come in the late 1850s. Then in the 1860s, big things happened: the incorporation and construction of the Central Pacific, the government land grants and subsidies, the incorporation and construction of the Southern Pacific, and much political and financial manipulation. As a result, Collis became rich and powerful, a major voice in the control of an incipient industrial empire.

In the later 1860s, Collis mostly worked out of New York, and toward the end of this period he and Elizabeth bought a house at 65 Park Avenue. They had not been able to have children of their own, and in 1862 in Sacramento they adopted Clara, the one-year-old daughter of Elizabeth's sister Clarissa, whose husband, Edwin D. Prentice, the owner of a grocery store there, had died the year before and left his wife with four little children to support, which was more than she could manage. The adoption of Clara was informal, but Collis and Elizabeth treated her entirely as if she were their own child; in fact, it was not until she was a teenager that Clara learned that Collis and Elizabeth were not her birth parents. One of Clara's older siblings was Mary Alice Prentice, of whom we shall hear much more in due course. Sixty-five Park Avenue was a place for the Oneonta Huntingtons to go in New York where they would be cordially welcomed.

Edward completed the schooling that was offered in Oneonta when he was seventeen. There is a tradition, vaguely remembered by his sister Carrie in her old age, that he wanted to leave school at thirteen, but his mother got him to continue. As soon as he had finished, he went to work as a clerk in the hardware store in Oneonta, a job he held for two years. Many years later he gave an account of this experience to a newspaper reporter in Los Angeles: " 'When I was 17 years old I worked in a hardware store in Oneonta, N.Y.,' he said reminiscently. 'I worked for nothing. However, I got a salary when I informed the owner of the store that I was going to quit in order to better my prospects.' "[36]

But even after he got a salary he felt that he had to leave home. As he wrote to his mother soon afterward, "I am getting to that age that I do not like to feel dependent on anyone."[37] He left with a sense of affection for his family and friends there and for Oneonta as the place that was his home. Throughout his life he kept coming back to see his family and friends. Over the years, his children also spent long periods with him there.

In his later years, small incidents would trigger warm remembrances of his childhood. Ethelwyn Doolittle, a schoolteacher in New York City, wrote him once about her father, Irwin Doolittle, who had grown up in Oneonta and known Huntington. He replied, "I remember very well the good times I had with your father in Oneonta in my boyhood days. That was a very happy time of my life, and it has given me much pleasure to keep in touch with everything that has happened in Oneonta."[38]

After Harriet died in 1906, Huntington gave the family house and land to the town of Oneonta to be the public library and a city park. When Lincoln L. Kellogg, an attorney in Oneonta, long afterward wrote him a letter of appreciation for the gift, Huntington replied, "Oneonta always had, and always will have, a tender spot in my heart. My memories of it as a boy are most pleasant, and it gives me much pleasure to feel that the Library and Park are being used and appreciated."[39]

Two

TOWARD INDEPENDENCE
1869–1873

EDWARD TOOK HIS FIRST step toward independence in the autumn of 1869, when he left home. It was a relatively modest step. He went about a hundred miles, to Cohoes, New York—a few miles north of Albany, on the Hudson River—to work in the hardware store run by the husband of his older sister Leonora. She was twenty-eight and had married Bradley W. Foster of Winslow, Maine, the year before.

Even though Edward was still with family, he was very lonely. Soon after he got to Cohoes, in a letter to his mother, he said:

> I have been wishing just now that I could be home. How I wish it! More, so that we could all be together on the Sabbath. Our church is not finished yet, and it will probably be some time before it is finished. But it does not seem like our church at home, and I probably shall never see any church that does seem so. I have been to Church and Sunday School today, and it rained so that there were not many out. And I probably should have attended this evening had there been any preaching. As there was none, I stayed at home.[1]

He was restless in Cohoes. After about four months there, he wrote to Harriet that he was "sick and tired of Cohoes" and gave as his reason what must surely rank among the world's great rationalizations: "One main thing is the water. I cannot get a clean, decent drink of water here.

I presume likely that I do not drink a quart a week. The more you seem to drink, the more thirsty you are."

There was another reason, of course. He wanted to move on with his life. New York City sounded better to him: "I want to go to New York. And still I do not know if I should enjoy myself either." And then he came to the crux of his thinking: "It is time that I was looking for another place. Perhaps I can find one down there. If I can, I think that I shall go there—or almost anywhere else out of Cohoes." "Looking for another place" meant taking a bigger step toward independence.

In fact, he was all ready to go. Since mothers are usually interested in their children's wardrobes, he gave the crucial details: "I have got a new pair of pants. I got a black pair this time. I shall have to get a new pair of drawers and a few other little things. And my overcoat is not fit to wear. But I do not think that I shall get a new one this winter, as it is getting so late in the season."[2]

A week later he was in New York. He arrived on February 23, 1870, and went straight to "Uncle Collis's place." Though Leonora had given him careful directions as to how to get to 65 Park Avenue, she had feared that the country mouse would get lost, but he made it without any difficulty. Collis was not at home, having gone south for a week, but Edward was invited to stay. He spent his first afternoon in New York climbing up inside the steeple of Trinity Church "and had a very fine view of New York & surroundings."[3]

He found his younger brother Willard in residence and going to school at 58 Park Avenue, right across the street from Collis's house. As Willard, age thirteen, proudly wrote to little sister Carrie, age nine: "I go to the best School in the United States—the Murray Hill Institute. Miss Hammond says so. It costs Uncle 1 thousand dollars a year." Willard also rode horseback every afternoon in the park.[4]

Edward stayed on at Collis's house for a month or two while he looked for a job. He asked Collis for advice but kept looking about on his own, searching for a place in a hardware company, the one line of work he knew something about. Finally, he got a job at Sargent and Company at 70 Beekman Street in Manhattan. Sargent was a wholesale hardware company, a manufacturer, and an agent for other manufacturers.

Edward had tried there before, and had returned to talk with Mr. Sargent once more to see whether any vacancy had developed. Nothing at all, said Mr. Sargent. The only available position was one caused by illness, for a porter to move heavy merchandise. "That suits me," said Edward, and he took the job. Soon a vacancy for an order clerk occurred, and he was given the position, in which he had to wear "very ordinary clothes."[5]

Collis had not been keen about his taking a job with Sargent, but Edward took it anyway. Edward wrote his mother that "there was no other opening for the present, and I wanted to get in some place soon, as it was getting lonesome here doing nothing." He was not sure what his wages would be: "They generally pay three dollars per week for beginners, but I think they will pay me more on account of having the good will of Uncle Collis." Collis told him it would be better to accept no salary at all rather than take $3 a week.

In any event, he wouldn't earn enough to pay his board, which was $7 a week at a boardinghouse run by Mrs. Walker at 71 Henry Street in Brooklyn. He paid fifty cents a week extra for his laundry and went on the ferry to Manhattan (sixteen tickets for twenty-five cents). The boardinghouse occupied a four-story building, with dining room and kitchen on the first floor, parlors on the second floor, and bedrooms on the top two floors. Edward was pleased with his plainly furnished, medium-sized room on the fourth floor. The other boarders were "all very pleasant people, and I think they try to make anyone feel at home, and I like it very much."

He worked from eight in the morning until six in the evening, and Mrs. Walker put up his lunch for him. Sargent and Company was only a ten-minute walk from Collis's offices at 54 William Street (later he moved to much more capacious quarters at 23 Broad Street). When Edward had finished eating his lunch, he often walked over to see Collis for the remainder of his free hour.

He expressed regret to his mother that he would not be able to save any money. (Of course saving money was the mark of prudent economic behavior.) "But the prospects are good," he added optimistically, "for learning the business, and that is the principal thing for the present."

Edward went to Henry Ward Beecher's church on Sundays (often with Collis) and very much enjoyed Beecher's sermons. He also went to the Sunday School, but he decided not to "unite with the church at present," though he attended all the meetings regularly.

Edward's first account of his life in New York characteristically expressed his interest in and his concern for family members in Oneonta. He asked about his father: "Is Father working as hard as usual? I do wish that he would not have so much business on his hands, yet he probably will never see the time when he will not be busy." He also had advice for his grandmother: "I think that if she could get out pleasant days it would be good for her." And his little sister: "Kiss Carrie for me"—an exhortation he repeats in many of his letters. And he remembered his friends: "I have a great many acquaintances in Oneonta that I think a great deal of. Give them all my best respects—I don't think I have many enemies there."[6]

So life went on for him in New York. For nearly a year he learned the business from the position of an order clerk (in very ordinary clothes) in a wholesale hardware company. He saw a lot of buying and selling, and trading between those who had goods and those who wanted goods. He didn't take any of his wages for several months and lived on his savings, an occasional gift from his parents, and an occasional twenty-dollar bill from Collis: "I do not like to get money from him," he said; "it seems like begging. Yet I do not think he would like it if I were to leave here—he seems so willing to help me all of the time." But with regular outgo and irregular and small income, he could only fall behind. In due course, he owed his landlady for four weeks, and he had to accept gifts from Collis. But accepting money made Edward feel dependent—a feeling he did not like.[7] When Harriet asked Edward what he had said to Collis when he took the money, Edward replied, "I did nothing but thank him. Yet I think that if I get any more, I shall get it with the understanding that I shall pay him back."[8] Edward felt the financial pinch personally. "I tell you, Mother," he wrote to Harriet, "I have to live close here."[9]

Edward was caught in a dilemma. He wanted to be active, to learn a business with a future, to be gainfully employed, to be independent. Yet he felt that he must defer to Collis's judgment, and he was entirely aware of Collis's ability to help him. Edward thought of leaving Sargent for a more hopeful prospect. He wrote Harriet on July 5, 1870, about consulting Collis on the matter:

> I asked him what he thought about staying to Sargent & Co., and he said that I had better stay a while yet. For it would be worth more to me to work for nothing here than to work for twelve dollars per week up in the country. He said that he was thinking about what he should do for me, and told me not to be in any hurry. I think that Uncle will do what is right with me if I try to help myself.[10]

An interesting job possibility had come up in June. A "vein of cement" had been discovered in Virginia, and Collis sent an expert down to evaluate it. "If it turned out well," Edward wrote to Harriet, "that if I thought I could take charge of it, that he would like to have me go down there. . . . Uncle says that if it is a good vein, that there will be considerable money in it. I think from what he said that he would give me a chance in there."[11] Alas, the report was negative; the man "got back and said that the cement did not amount to much, as it would not set."[12] He had to keep on learning his trade and "not to be in any hurry."

In the meantime, he spent most Sundays with Collis and Elizabeth and little Clara, now ten years old, at 65 Park Avenue, as well as some evenings. Often Collis took Edward and others for a drive in the park on Sunday afternoons. Many other family members visited. Harriet and Carrie, age nine, were invited once or twice a year, as well as Edward's sister Leonora, and Collis's sister Ellen and her husband, Edwin, and Elizabeth's sister Mrs. Hammond and her son Scott, as well as cousins like Ed Pardee. I assume that it was here that Edward met his first wife, Mary Alice Prentice, now age eighteen, who was Clara's older sister and a niece of Elizabeth's. There is, however, no evidence I know of as to when they first met. Edward always enjoyed his time at 65 Park Avenue. When he called on Collis at his office on Saturday, July 2, 1870, he was delighted that Collis asked him to come and spend two days with them to celebrate the Fourth of July. "You know that I could not refuse so tempting an offer," he wrote Harriet, "for I always have such a pleasant time up there."[13] Later, he wrote Harriet that "Uncle and Aunt are both very kind to me; and if anyone appreciates it, I think that I do. I feel so thankful tonight to feel that I have so many friends, the more so because I do not feel that I am so deserving of them."[14] Occasionally he spent a weekend with his aunt Ellen Huntington and her husband, Edwin Gates, in Elizabeth, New Jersey, and they were always glad to see him. "I see Edwards now and then, not so often as I would like to though," Ellen wrote to Harriet. "I guess he is getting along very well. I hear from him often as he is often in the office."[15] Edwin had given up preaching and was now a kind of trusted office manager for Collis in his New York offices; he doubtless reported to Ellen about Edward's frequent visits to the office.

Edward continued to enjoy Henry Ward Beecher's sermons, and the Sunday School. "If there is anything I enjoy, it is the hour of prayer," he wrote to Harriet.[16] There was a kind of moral strictness, deriving presumably from the heritage of his family, his culture, and his religion, that was often evident in Edward's attitudes both at this time and throughout his life. He repeatedly deplored the fact that his uncle Howard Saunders drank and felt that Howard should join the Temperance Society: "It seems strange that he cannot be a sober man."[17] Edward was critical of his cousin Edward Pardee because he did not save any money ("I think that he had better be saving his money for he may need it in the future") and because Ed Pardee objected that Collis did not buy enough goods from him ("It would be just robbing the road to be buying goods of Ed when he could buy them cheaper").[18] He responded to his mother's pleased comment about the fact that Hattie Ford, in Oneonta, had a lot of beaux with a rather sour rejoinder that "I do not think that it looks very well, and I should not think that Mrs. Ford would allow it. I think she does not care much who she keeps company with."[19] Poor Hattie!

In the course of Edward's year in New York, several matters occurred that further showed the unity of the family. Scott Hammond drowned in West Virginia while on a C & O construction party. Scott was the son of Elizabeth's sister Hannah, who had gone to Sacramento with Elizabeth and Collis and there married Daniel Hammond, who had gone with Collis from Oneonta and worked in the store in Sacramento.

Scott was only sixteen when he died, and Collis had planned further schooling for him. On receipt of the news, Collis and Elizabeth returned to New York immediately from a visit in western New York State; the funeral was held at 65 Park Avenue, with many family members present, including Edward, and letters of sympathy from many, including Harriet, who couldn't come. Mrs. Hammond was shattered by the death, and family members rallied to her support. "Uncle has done all that he could do for her," wrote Edward.[20]

Another family death was the passing of the mother of Solon and Collis—the woman of "beautiful disposition" who never had "a frown on her face." She died of pneumonia on March 1, 1871, at age eighty in Warsaw, New York, where she had been living with a daughter. Almost all the children went to Warsaw for the funeral and burial in a plot paid for by Collis. It was an emotional and religious occasion for them. Ellen, the youngest child, wrote to Rhoda, one of the oldest, of their mother's "kind words and deeds and all her patient struggles to keep her own head above water and to teach her children to do something and to be something in those dark days of her early life."[21] Those were "dark days" that Solon and Collis doubtless shared with her, and in which they gained patience and courage from her.

A different family matter was the education of Willard. After his time at the Murray Hill Institute, Collis arranged and paid for him to attend Dr. Fitch's School in Norwalk, Connecticut, after clearing the matter with Solon and with Willard.[22] Collis was generously and about equally helpful to all of his nephews, though in some ways, as we shall see later, more consideration was given to Willard than to Edward. Willard was thought to have a special talent, like their deceased brother Howard. Ellen wrote to Harriet about him: "Willie, the wild boy, I should like to see him. What is he doing now-a-days? I do hope you will hide books away from him. He makes me think of a candle with too large a wick. You know they burn very fast but not very long. . . . I came across some of his scribblings which he left here. . . . They reminded me so much of the little scraps Howard used to leave up at the cottage. Howard is a long way ahead of us all now I trust."[23]

One theme that runs through Edward's letters during this year is affection for members of his family. In June 1870 he wrote, "I thank you, Mother, for the interest that you take in me, and you may rest assured that that love is returned. For I think that if I ever amount to anything I owe it all to my parents and my God." His separation from his parents led him to feel and to express his affection: "I tell you, a boy knows how to appreciate Father & Mother when he gets away from home." Later, he frequently made comments like "How I wish I could be at home with you!" and "How I should like to be at home now!"[24]

But he could not be at home. He was on the first stage toward trying to "amount to something" and toward his own independence. It is a little ironic that we learn about much of his progress from the same letters to his mother in which he said, "One favor I ask of you, that is do not show my letters to anyone unless it is Father."[25] But perhaps it is all right. We read them now at a great distance in time from him, and without any effort to control his independence.

The break came for Edward in April 1871. Collis owned a company that ran a sawmill in West Virginia, and he needed someone to manage it. Would Edward like to take on the job? He would. The break was not a big one, so far as family relations went. Edward set out from New York on April 17 in the company of Collis, Elizabeth, and a relative of hers. They went to Guyandotte, West Virginia, and stayed at a hotel a few miles from the new town of Huntington, named for Collis and incorporated only two months before. His cousin Mary Emmons was also staying at the hotel; her mother was a sister of Elizabeth's, and her father, Delos Emmons, was in charge of Collis's Central Land Company, which owned five thousand acres in the vicinity. Edward's sister Leonora and her husband, Bradley Foster, had already moved to Huntington—where they were to live the rest of their long lives, into the 1920s—with Bradley working for Collis's real estate interests. The first thing Edward did was borrow the local doctor's horse and ride over to see Leonora and Bradley.[26]

After a few days in Guyandotte, the others went home. Edward moved on to nearby Coalsmouth and threw himself into his new job. His work was to see that the mill was effectively productive in making railroad ties from trees that were cut in the area—up to thirty-five miles away—and brought to the mill mostly on the Coal River. The mill had a foreman and twenty-five or thirty workmen. "My position is a responsible one," he wrote to his mother, "as Uncle says that he depends on me to keep the mill supplied with logs and to see that everything goes on all right at the mill." With a day and a night shift, they were sawing three hundred logs a day. Although the company owned a good deal of forest land in the area, Edward had to buy much of the timber from private owners. He traveled extensively in the area by horseback and was fortunate to be able to buy from Colonel Sam Early, the brother of the late Confederate General Early; Colonel Early was, wrote Edward, "about as full of his jokes as any man can be," but he owned a large tract of forest nearby, and he was willing to sell timber so that the company could save its own trees for the future. For his work, Edward received a salary far beyond the $3 a week that he had earned in New York; he was given from $1,500 to $1,800 a year, a horse, and traveling expenses.[27]

He also received advice from Collis on how to be a businessman. Collis employed several forms of control in managing "his properties." First, he knew his subordinates well and insisted on loyalty and hard work. Second, he required frequent reports to him, particularly of financial results. And third, he sent frequent personal letters to his subordinates, appraising their results and giving them directions. Collis had hardly arrived back in New York before he began to send his characteristic letters, often written in his own hand, to Edward. On May 18, 1871, he told Edward which waterways to run logs on and how to raft them to the mill. "Write me often," he concluded, "how you are getting on and how the mill is doing, how many ties are made from time to time, and any other information that you think would interest me. I hope you will watch out for the Company interest, and see that not a dollar is wasted that can possibly be saved."[28] Careful accounting and reporting, and frugality of operation: these were principles of business management that Collis regarded as crucial. He communicated them to his twenty-one-year-old nephew in this his first business venture, and they were to become crucial for him too.

Collis also checked on his properties in person. In August 1871, he and Elizabeth stopped in West Virginia on their way back to New York from California. Collis spent a day or two with Edward and learned firsthand about the progress of the mill. Willard, now fifteen, was also with them; he had been invited to go with them to California. He had had to "lose a little school" to go, but, as Edwin Gates wrote to Solon, "the knowledge of men and things and the experience he would gain in making this trip would probably more than compensate."[29]

This was Edward's first time away from New York State. He very much liked the new country, and he felt more healthy than ever before in his life. He also liked the people, whom he thought of as southerners but "as good Rebels as you can find anywhere." They struck him as being very hospitable and cordial. One family wanted him to come and live with them without any payment, but they lived too far from the mill; he compromised by going to their house for tea every Sunday evening. A banker in Charleston told him that "whenever I come to Charleston I must make his house my home." One day as he was going to the mill, "a little boy came up to me and said that his mother wanted to see me as she was saving some ice cream for me. The day being hot, of course I accepted the invitation." Although he had never seen the woman before, he knew her husband well; "they have a very nice place, and are very nice people." And the ice cream was good.

The language of the area was strange to his ears. "The ladies here use some very queer expressions," he wrote to his parents, "such as 'mighty hot', 'right smart cool weather' &c." The food was also strange to his taste. "There is not one Southern woman out of a hundred that knows how to cook," he wrote. "We hardly ever have any tea here. It is coffee, morning noon and night; yet I do not drink it, as I can always get good milk. They always have hot corn cakes and bacon on the table—and, in fact, everything is hot. The greatest wonder to me is that they do not heat the water that we drink."

He boarded with the family of the Presbyterian minister, Mr. Edward Ells, for $4 per week. He slept in his office at the sawmill: "I bought a single bedstead, mattress, pillow, and 2 sets of sheets for $12.50. Do you not think that reasonable? And I save 50¢ per week by it."[30]

Within a couple of months the rumor got around that Edward was seriously involved with the Ells's daughter. His sister Leonora, in Huntington, became exercised and wrote Harriet to tell her the bad news:

Mother, do you know that our Edward has a lady-love in Coals-mouth? Daughter of the clergyman with whom he boards. Probably he has written you about it. Be sure to tell me when you write. They say he is very much devoted to her—that accounts for his going there to board. I never have been able to learn of what denomination the minister is, with whom he boards. He does not pay attention to questions in the letters written him. I can't bear the thought of so young a boy as he marrying. He was going to be a bachelor. I hope his sweetheart is not like the majority of Southern girls; for if so, she would be a very helpless wife.[31]

There was a wedding, all right, but Edward was a groomsman in it, not the groom. Miss Minnie Ells was married, a little more than a week after Leonora's letter, to a friend of Edward's, Dr. Henderson. Edward's heart was already drawn in another direction, as we shall soon see.[32]

In this new environment, Edward was lonely, even among hospitable people. He missed his family, and he missed Oneonta. "Most of all," he wrote on September 4, 1871, "I wish that I might be home. I do not know when I have had such a longing to see Oneonta once more as I have had this morning." He was eager for letters. "I should like to hear from Father," he plaintively wrote, but quickly excused him for not writing: "I know that he always has so much business on hand that it is almost impossible for him to do so." He asked Harriet to send him pictures of herself and Solon, of Willard and Carrie; but he had to ask several times before they were all sent. When Carrie's arrived at last, he wrote to his mother, "Tell Carrie I thank her very much for her picture, and that I look at it very often." He continued to ask, in most of his letters, that his mother give Carrie a kiss for him. He added, "I have yours and Father's picture framed and hanging up in my room" in the sawmill. Collis also sent him a picture of Clara; later, Mary Alice Prentice sent him her picture, and he asked her to send one to his mother.[33]

Edward found comfort in the church during this period. In May 1871, he became a regular member of the Sunday School, and in September he "united with" the church. His religious feelings began to surge with something like enthusiasm. In August, he wrote to his mother, "You may rest assured that I never close my eyes at night without praying that my dear Father may be brought to Jesus, and I have faith to believe that that time will come when he will be rejoicing in the love of him that died that he might live." Before joining the church in September he wrote: "Dear Mother, you must pray for me that I may never be a reproach to the cause of Christ. The Church here is small, but I hope that the Holy Spirit may fall on this people and result in much good. Such is my earnest prayer." In October, he summed up his religious and family feelings when he wrote:

> You know not what comfort I take in thinking that I have Jesus for a friend. Oh, that I might be more like him is my constant prayer. It makes me feel very sorrowful when I think of how little I am doing for him, and how many blessings he is constantly bestowing on me. And if any good does come from me, it will be through the influence of my dear Mother. Oh, my dear Mother! You little dream how dear you are to me or how I long to see your good kind face again.

This theme of unworthiness is repeated in many of his letters. In January 1872 he reported to his mother:

> We have had communion today. How I wish that you might have been with me—to taste the broken body and the spilt blood of Jesus. I am so unworthy that I sometimes think that if we thought ourselves worthy we should certainly not be in a fit state of mind to partake of those emblems. Oh pray for me, Mother, that I may ever be found working for Jesus and doing all that I can for the upbuilding of his kingdom.[34]

Edward's life in West Virginia, in both Coalsmouth and St. Albans, went along for the first year in a relatively routine way, with him working, riding about arranging to buy timber, overseeing the operation of the mill, getting to know this new world and these new people, and gradually becoming independent.

One event, in the summer of 1871, was out of the ordinary. The governor of West Virginia made a visit to the area. He came on a pleasure trip with a party of some twenty state officials. They had heard of the sawmill and wanted to see it, so Edward had the honor of entertaining the party and showing them the mill.[35]

In January 1872, he was at last able to take some time off and go home to Oneonta for a short visit with his parents. Edward felt apologetic about the brevity of his stay at home. "I should have liked to have stayed with my dear Mother a time longer," he wrote her from New York on January 31, 1872, "but circumstances would not permit. For you know, my Mother, that anyone attending to business must be punctual if they succeed. I know that you would sacrifice anything and everything for your children, and that is another reason I should have liked to have stayed at home longer."

He went back to West Virginia by way of New York and stopped for a few days at 65 Park Avenue to consult with Collis. As usual, there was a lively group of young people in attendance, including Mary Alice Prentice, called Mary, who was making a visit of several months with her Aunt Elizabeth and her sister Clara. Edward and Mary had been seeing one another and had been corresponding; regrettably, none of their letters have survived. We know of this stage of their relationship only from references to Mary and their correspondence in letters that Edward wrote to his mother.[36] Then, on April 7, 1872, Edward told his mother that he and Mary were engaged to be married. "Mary knows that you know of our engagement," he wrote. "But you and Leonora are the only ones who do know of it except Father, and of course I expected you to tell him."[37] Edward had just turned twenty-two, and Mary was twenty. It was to be a long engagement of a year and a half—they were not married until November 17, 1873—and many events were to happen during that time.

In the late spring and early summer, the rivers sometimes rose to the flood stage in West Virginia. Soon after he got there, Edward wrote to Collis about this risk to their timber on the river, and Collis acknowledged that they might lose some logs at first but in due course would probably learn how to deal with the problem.[38]

In the latter part of May of 1872, the Coal River began to rise. As Edward reported to his mother on May 20, "we had a flood on the Coal

River. I had most excellent luck with my timber, as I had six or seven thousand dollars worth of timber in the river, and did not lose a single log!"[39] But there was a much worse flooding in June, and his experience in dealing with it proved an intense episode and a vivid memory for him. He wrote about it to his mother on July 1, 1872:

> Right after I finished your letter last Sunday, Coal River commenced to rise, and I had a hard fight with it until Thursday night. I presume likely I had fifty rafters of timber in the river and did not lose but one log. I have been very fortunate indeed with my timber this year. There have been great losses here. Some parties have lost three and four thousand dollars worth. Everyone here said that it was impossible for me to save a stick of my timber. But I showed them different. Before I got through, I got but nine (9) hours sleep from Sunday morning to Thursday night. But I did save all my timber, and the inhabitants say that it is something that has never been done before.[40]

He had reason to brag a little. He had lived up to his principles by meeting an emergency with very hard work and self-sacrifice, and he had been successful.

In the meantime, another problem was brewing that he was not prepared to meet. Collis was becoming restless with his ownership of the sawmill, and in the spring of 1872 he began saying that he wanted to sell it. He told Edward, "I had rather sell as I have about as much business as I want," and "I have so many things to attend to that I had rather sell it."[41] Collis reckoned that he had about $20,000 in the mill, and he wanted that much for it; he would take one-third cash and the other two-thirds in one- and two-year loans at 10 percent interest. Collis tried for about nine months to sell it, and he urged Edward to seek a buyer. Although he reduced the cash requirement to $5,000 and offered to shade the overall price, there were no takers. In the meantime, the country was entering a severe recession following the panic of 1873, and money was scarce. But at last a buyer appeared—General Richard Franchot, a Civil War veteran, for a time Collis's chief resident lobbyist in Washington for getting the votes in Congress, and a man who had managed to accumulate substantial funds for himself. General

Franchot was interested in buying the mill for his son, S. P. Franchot, who had just graduated from Union College. The Franchots came to St. Albans to look the property over.[42]

On March 11, 1873, Collis wrote to Edward that the Franchots had closed the deal to buy the mill for $20,000: $5,000 in cash and the balance in lumber. "You have the option," Collis said, "until the middle of May to take one half (½) interest in the mill. I know but little about the mill, and do not know just what I may have for you to do, and can not advise you in the matter. If you have made up your mind as to what you want to do, you had better telegraph me at once."[43]

What to do? Collis had been sending mixed signals to Edward on this matter for a couple of months. On January 2, 1873, Collis said he had told the Franchots, "I thought you [Edward] would like an interest in it but that I wanted you for something else." On January 18, 1873, he expressed confidence in the mill: "I have little doubt but that if we should stock up the mill and make up our minds to run it for the next five years that it could be made to pay largely." But he ended that same letter by saying, "Let me know as soon as you well can if you want half of it with F. You can take it [i.e., Collis would lend Edward the money] although I would rather you would stay in my interest to attend to other matters. But it is likely you could make more money out of the mill."[44]

What to do indeed. Edward could hardly turn down the offer of the half interest without repudiating his uncle's judgment and being timid; he could hardly accept it without acting contrary to his uncle's specific or vague wishes. He accepted the offer of a half interest. It turned out to be a much riskier venture than any of them had reckoned, with two inexperienced young men who didn't know one another in a partnership financed by their elders, with little or no capital, and during the most notable business recession in a period of forty years.

The partnership of "Huntington & Franchot" began right away. Their printed letterhead bore both their names in the upper corners and declared that they were "Manufacturers of All Kinds of Lumber" in St. Albans, West Virginia. Young Franchot also moved in with Mr. and Mrs. Ells as a boarder, and we are fortunate to have a letter of April 18, 1873, only a few weeks after the partnership was formed, from Mrs. Ells to her sister in Schenectady about her two boarders.

"I have Mr. Huntington's board for my spending money," she wrote. "Out of it ($6.00 per week) I clothe Annie, Eddie and myself and my two girls [i.e., servants]. Mr. Huntington is not going to leave us, but is settled here probably for years. He and the 'new boarder,' Mr. Franchot, have bought the mill. I do not want any boarders but them, and with them our family is delightful for they are just like two sons."

Mrs. Ells was more impressed by Franchot than she was by Huntington:

> Mr. Franchot is superior in some things to Mr. Huntington ["in many things" she wrote first, then substituted "some" for "many"]. He is thoroughly educated (a graduate of Union College), polished, refined, a strong Episcopalian, belongs to a first rate family. His father, Gen. Franchot, has paid us a visit and seemed delighted that his son had a home with us. He [the father] is a man of wealth, has been U.S. Senator [actually, Congressman from New York for two years]. The young man we are charmed with; he is very handsome, large and fine looking. I never saw Edward [her husband] take to a young man as much.

It is interesting to notice that she did not choose to rave about Edward, although he did have *some* of the qualities she admired in Franchot—at least his uncle was "a man of wealth"—and perhaps other qualities as well.

She thought that the two young men would be successful with the mill: "The prospects of the young men are fine; they already have an order from California for a quarter of a million ft. of oak lumber. It is such a great thing for this place to have them here. I sent Edwin today their card and one of our St. Albans papers, in which honorable mention is made of them."

She was so delighted with them that she treated them like members of her family: "I believe I am as proud of them as their own Mothers. I wash & iron and mend for them and put their clothes away, just as I would for my own sons."

She enjoyed the evenings more now. "Mr. Franchot is a very pleasant reader and reads aloud to Annie and me in the evenings." It may be that she saw young Mr. Franchot, even on very short acquaintance, as a potential son-in-law. In fact, he and Annie were later married.

Mrs. Ells was more impersonal about Edward: "Mr. Huntington will be married after awhile and bring his wife here, perhaps this fall. He says he thinks married people ought to keep house, but he had as leave board with me as keep house. He seems much more interested in our church now he is settled. I hope we will have one built this summer."[45]

Edward made two trips away from St. Albans in 1873. In June he went home to Oneonta for a brief visit. In November he went to Newark, New Jersey. There, on November 17, he and Mary Alice Prentice of Sacramento, California, were married at the home of Mr. and Mrs. Horace H. Seaton at 857 Broad Street. Mrs. Seaton was Mary's aunt, a sister of her mother and of Collis's wife Elizabeth; Mr. Seaton, Elizabeth's nephew by marriage, had gone to California in the 1850s and had worked at the Huntington store in Sacramento.

By the time the young couple, ages twenty-three and twenty-one, returned to St. Albans to begin their married life, Edward had made two big steps toward independence: he had married, and he had become half-owner of his own business.

Three

THE NEW FIRM OF Huntington & Franchot had a lot of needs to fulfill before it could get started. Edward knew one way to meet those needs—through his own hard work. His new wife wrote his mother that he had been working so hard that he was too weary to write his weekly letter home: "For the past two or three weeks he has had much to do; although never idle, he has been quite harried and when night comes is very tired and glad to rest." She would be glad when they ended boarding and moved into a house so that "I may ever strive to make his home cheerful and bright and that when weary and tired it will seem like a haven of rest and with the true loving wife's welcome it will be indeed Home Sweet Home."[1]

Each of the partners had put up $2,500. Franchot's was supplied by his father, who simply sent a check to Edwin Gates, who managed Collis's accounts, and also had him sell some of his Wells Fargo stock.[2] Edward had to scratch for his contribution. Collis kept an account for Edward—as he did for various family members and friends, rather like a private banker—and it had $1,224.10 in it at the time of the sale of the mill. Gates used that amount first to reduce the interest-bearing note of $2,500 to Collis that Edward had signed.[3]

Problems arose immediately. The lumber they shipped to the C & O railroad to begin to pay off the rest of their debt was rejected. Collis wrote them that half of the lumber in their first shipment had large, hollow, black wormholes in it and was rotting; it was of no use to the railroad.[4] Collis thought that they had understated the value of the lumber in the inventory when they bought the mill, and that their later statements were several times incorrect.[5] Sales continued to be slow for a year, the buyers of lumber did not always pay promptly, and the firm was constantly in need of capital. Edward kept getting permission to "draw on" Collis until Collis finally told him that he had no more money to lend. Franchot sold his Wells Fargo stock.

One episode of trying to borrow money was so vivid for Edward that he told of it many years later; it became the substance of a sermon by the Reverend Robert Freeman in the Pasadena Presbyterian Church and was later printed as a pamphlet. In this account, Franchot went to the banker in St. Albans to borrow $3,000 for the firm and was turned down. Then Edward, without hope of better success, presented himself to the same banker with the same request:

> "Why, certainly, Mr. Huntington."
> "But why? Surely there is some mistake. My partner saw you yesterday and you refused."
> "No mistake at all. My action only means that whatever money I lend for your firm will be made as a loan to you personally."

The banker had seen Franchot "occasionally the worse for liquor," but Huntington's "conduct warranted faith in his honor." Thus was born a pretty moral for a temperance sermon.[6]

Huntington & Franchot continued to operate for about a year in all, but never with much success. Collis began to complain that, even after a year, they had not sent him the money for the lumber on hand when they had bought the mill; it was supposed to have been paid as soon as they sold the lumber. Also, that they should make a regular monthly payment on their notes to him, which they had not been doing. Collis was further concerned that Edward might default on his debts, a thing that Collis abhorred. "There will be a good time come some time," Collis advised Edward, "and the only way is to hold on and pay out nothing that you can avoid."[7]

Edward went into business on the side by opening a general store, and this act displeased both Franchot and Collis. And it did not bring in any revenue.[8] Edward and Mary had moved into their house in May 1874, and Franchot complained bitterly that they kept buying "luxurious furnishings" with money that ought to have gone into the business, and that Edward had deeded the house to his wife to separate it from the property of the partnership.[9]

In June 1874, the young men agreed, in mutual distaste, that they did not want to continue their partnership. Over the next few months, several dozen letters flew back and forth between Edward and Collis, between Franchot and General Franchot, between Collis and General Franchot.[10] Both of the older men were surprised and greatly disappointed. Collis thought that the young partners ought to try harder to stick it out together: "It seems strange to me," he wrote to Edward, "that you and Franchot cannot get on together as I have always thought him an honest and enjoyable young man."[11] General Franchot told Collis that "all of this is mortifying to me and annoys me. I think it is a piece of boys play. Nonsensical and simply shows that they are not equal to the business. I am disgusted with such damn foolishness." And also: "I think they both should be spanked into manly business habits."[12] Franchot wrote his father that "HEH has taken into his head to act mean, and I can do nothing."[13] The older men both took a high moral view in writing to the younger men. Collis told young Franchot that "there is evidently something between you and Edward Huntington that I do not understand. I have full confidence that neither you nor my nephew will do a dishonest act, and that you will work together so long as is necessary to protect the interests of your creditors and your own honor."[14] General Franchot thoroughly approved of what Collis had written. "I only desire," he wrote Collis, that "[my son] shall be honorable and just. He is young and must work and make up his losses."[15] It apparently did not occur to these moralists that the original sin in the whole enterprise lay with the two older men in deciding to put together two young men—without knowledge of the business, experience, or financial resources—and throw them into a capital-intensive undertaking during a severe recession and a money panic.

Edward's mother was worried about whether her son had behaved properly and whether he was discouraged. He gave her a detailed account of the episode, assured her that he "did not deal unfairly with Franchot in any way," and guaranteed that he would never be discouraged unless he "lost health, friends, and the last rag on my back." "Thank the Lord," he added, "I have got a little spunk in my disposition. And I imagine that the more I think that I have need of it, the more I will have." He was frankly disappointed by Collis's behavior: "I do not think that Uncle Collis has done what he could for my interest. I do not know as I ought to say it, for perhaps he has done what he thought best." (And of course you shouldn't be critical if that were the case.) He concluded his account with these words, all underlined:

> End of it
> say no more about it
> for I don't like to think of it.

He continued his letter more cheerfully with family news, beginning with, "We are very pleasantly situated in our new home, and Mary is one of the best of wives and housekeepers." He wished that his parents could visit them in the coming winter, "but I really do not feel that we could afford it." Mary added a page at the end: "I hesitate whether it is prudent to add to Edward's letter, for I am fearful that his letter is so unusually long that it will really shock." But she proceeded with the news and then said, "I cannot refrain from saying once again that we are indeed truly happy in our new home, and enjoying it more fully each day. It would be a punishment to go back to boarding. It makes me feel eager to be a good housekeeper, as Edward seems pleased with my feeble efforts. I shall strive to improve."[16] Comforting words to send to a devoted mother at that time.

It took considerable time to terminate the partnership because of its financial entanglements. They first considered whether one of the partners should buy out the other. The first agreement was that Franchot would buy out Edward. Since Edward's share had a negative value because of their debts, he had to find money to cover his share. This was not easy.

One of Edward's expedients was to turn his library over to Franchot in lieu of cash. We are fortunate to know the details of this transaction concerning a great book collector's first library through the memoirs of Franchot's brother, N. V. V. Franchot, who was in St. Albans for a visit of three months at the time and was also boarding with Mr. and Mrs. Ells. Edward had paid $1,700 for the books, and "in the settlement of the partnership they came into the possession of my brother." The books were kept by Franchot, and then by his widow, who died in 1935, and then by their son. In 1937, the Franchots listed the eighteen titles (108 volumes), that included such authors as Ruskin, Dickens, Lowell, and Whittier. It is a suggestion of the kinds of books that Edward was buying before he was twenty-four—sets of modern popular classics, and recent books of history, poetry, and fiction. It is plain that in buying books he was acting as a reader, not as a collector. He liked his books, even from the beginning. In his later years, he often expressed regret that he had had to part with these books, acquired in the years of his early manhood.[17]

The sawmill still had to operate as a partnership, at Collis's insistence, even under ambiguous ownership. There were endless squabbles between Huntington & Franchot on the one hand and Collis on the other during the summer and early autumn of 1874 with respect to lumber that the sawmill was to supply to the Huntington Elevator and Transfer Company: they disagreed as to whether the orders had been countermanded, the lumber approved by an inspector, the bills properly drawn. The upshot of it was that Collis refused to pay for the lumber and refused to allow Huntington & Franchot to draw on him any further.

The sawmill was in a desperate situation. But that "little spunk in his disposition" of which Edward had spoken to his mother did indeed increase to meet the need. On October 11, 1874, he wrote to Collis with more than a little spunk about his feelings about himself, Collis, and their relationship:

> Your favor of the 7th received, and I cannot half express the pain it gave me to think that you should misconstrue my letter and accuse me so unjustly of things that you know (or ought to know) to be false. I know that you mean to do nothing but what is for my good, and I have ever given up to your judgment. There is no other man that could have

induced me to resume my business connections with Franchot but yourself. My feelings have never been toward him what they should be, and it is against such as F. that I have ever been warned against. He is, however, doing better now than he has been doing heretofore.

You say you think that I have too little confidence in other men to make my business an entire success. Perhaps I have. I am not very old, but then what little experience I have had teaches me that if you have too much confidence in your fellow man, in ninety-nine cases out of a hundred it will ruin you. Of course it is not _my_ experience—I did not mean that—but it is what I have been taught by others. And I think that you have had some hand in my instruction. Perhaps I have misconstrued your meaning when you have been talking with me. If so, I humbly beg your pardon.

You seem to think that I have so many errors that I should not think that you would be willing to trust me with your property. If you wish the property today, or any time within six months, if you will give me a receipt in full of all demands, I will give up everything that I have in the world and take a fresh start in some new field. And I am sure that there is more than enough to pay up all my indebtedness to you, and leave you a very fair margin besides. . . . I do not want you to think that I am an ungrateful cuss just because I have written as I felt. For I assure you such is not the case. And I shall always remember what you meant to do for me. Mary joins with me in love to all.

Your affectionate Nephew,
H. E. Huntington[18]

This letter seems to be a fair picture of the man at this time: appreciative of kindness, thoughtful, and tactful, yet independent, assertive, fair-minded, not to be run over. With a full measure of spunk in his disposition.

A little later, Edward wrote (on behalf of the firm) a more impersonal response to Collis's letter of October 7, with exact details about the lumber that had been furnished. He allowed himself to conclude with a sharp rap on Collis's knuckles: "If anyone tells you that we have outside business, they tell that that is untrue. But then it seems to us as if you would believe the evil of us rather than the good. Therefore it will do us no good to even try to excuse ourselves."[19]

Huntington & Franchot continued to limp along. They had further disagreements with purchasers, such as H. C. Parsons, president of the St. Cloud Power Company, about the acceptance of their shipments. On February 1, 1875, they formally offered to sell the mill and property to Collis—in a letter written for the firm by Franchot—at their cost of $28,273.59, under an arrangement by which "the loss will fall where it rightly belongs, upon us and not upon you. We respectfully submit this proposition, trusting that you will see fit to accept it."[20] He did not see fit. By the middle of April 1875, the firm was desperate for money. Edward gave his note for $2,200 to the firm to close out his interest.

In June, Collis was at last willing to take over the mill. Edward was to stay on and manage the properties, with a monthly salary of $50 from Collis. Later that month, Edward shut down the mill and bought out Franchot's operating interest with another note for $1,000. By September, he had become restless and wrote to Collis, "I am very anxious to be doing something better than I am now doing, and think that I could do well merchandising here if I had the money to go ahead with."

He turned to a typical Huntington enterprise—running a store—but he would have to stock it: "I could not think of asking your assistance after what you have done for me were it not for the fact that you said that when I wished to go into business again to let you know and you would try and do something for me." He had worked out the financing: "With about four thousand dollars, I think that I could make twelve hundred dollars per year besides expenses. And if you could loan me that amount, it would be a very great help to me and place me under lasting obligation." There was an equally acceptable alternative: "If there should be a situation open wherein I could get a good salary and fill the position, it would suit me as well."[21]

Collis responded immediately that he could not make the loan because he did not have the money. Edward replied that he "was very sorry that you could not loan me the money, but of course could not expect it if you did not have it to spare." He added that, if Collis should have, in the winter or spring, "any money that you could spare, it would be a great accommodation to me if you would loan it to me." He was equally eager for a job: "You know that I am not particular what the work is as long as it is honorable. Please let me know if you can what the prospect would be at some future time."[22] (As the Captain says in *King Lear*, "If it be man's work, I'll do't.")

Edward did not get an immediate answer, and in the meantime another possibility had come up. On December 6, 1875, he wrote to Collis that "I have just received a letter from home in which Father is very anxious for me to come home to assist him in his business. Now if I should go home, after I had become posted in his affairs I should hate to leave him even if I could do better." So what were the prospects for other positions? "If it is good, please tell me so. If you think there will be no chance for me, do not hesitate to tell me that. I do not want you to think that I am looking to you for anything for relation's sake, for such is not the case. But if you think that I could be useful to you, and you could help me on in the world, that is the way I wish you to look at it." He concluded by putting their relationship in terms of open friendship: "I write for advice. In my writing plain and to the point, do not think that I have an unkind feeling, for it is just the opposite feeling I have for you. And I shall not soon forget your kindness for me in the past, and I think it is always better for friends to be candid with each other."[23] A remarkable letter for a young man of twenty-four to write to the much older and richer relative on whom he had been dependent.

Collis responded right away that the job outlook was bleak: "As yet I have not seen any opening for you, and as matters are shrinking so much it does not look as though I should have one such position for you, as you would desire." He thought well of the possibility in Oneonta: "Your Father needs someone to assist him in his business, and if Willie does not care to take hold with him, it may be the best thing for you to do." There were no hard feelings: "I fully appreciate the spirit of your good letter. And if I had such a position as you would like, I should be glad to give it to you."[24]

The possibility of going back to Oneonta had its own problems. Edward asked his father what his salary would be, and the answer was $900 per year. "Of course I could not go there," he wrote Collis, "as that is really less than I get here, considering the cost of living." He was troubled that Collis may have been misinformed about him: "I feel confident from what I have heard lately that there has been influences working against me. Or, in other words, certain parties have been working against me, or trying to influence you against me."[25]

The decision about moving was held in abeyance for a little while. In the meantime, Mary and Edward had their first child, in St. Albans, on February 11, 1876. They named him Howard Edwards—Howard, after Edward's older brother who had died, and after his uncle, Howard Saunders; Edwards, after his father and his maternal grandmother's family. In April, Mary, her mother, and the new baby went to Sacramento on passes supplied by Collis to give Mary a rest after an illness and to spend the summer there.[26]

Edward continued to supervise the properties in and around St. Albans. He rented the hall over the store to the Masonic Lodge for $100 a year and the little house by the mill for $4 a month, and saw to repairs and maintenance. After several months of effort, Collis finally leased the mill in May for a year. Then Edward left St. Albans to return to Oneonta, stopping in New York to consult with Collis.[27]

Edward had spent about three years of his life in and around St. Albans, trying to manage the sawmill. The results had been notably unsuccessful. He had made no progress in establishing a career, he was at least as poor as he had been when he went there, and his relations with his Uncle Collis—the one person who could help him move along in the world—had been strained almost to the breaking point. He had given hostage to fortune by having a wife and a child, with whatever joys or sorrows they might bring him. Thus, at the age of twenty-six, he returned to Oneonta.

When Edward returned to Oneonta in May of 1876 to live and work, a number of important changes had taken place since he had set out for Cohoes and New York City in the autumn of 1869. He had made a transition from the youth of nineteen to the man of twenty-six with a wife and child. Carrie was now an adolescent of fifteen. Willard, who had been sent away to good private schools by Collis, was almost twenty and back at home, ready to act the part of a man. They were the only children in residence, since Leonora and her husband, Bradley Foster, were, of course, living in Huntington, West Virginia.

Willard had, in fact, assumed a man's role in the family structure. He had started to list and arrange Solon's mortgages and properties, and in January 1876 he had begun to take charge of Collis's Oneonta property, consisting of several houses and stores. He was given close directions in his management: he must, for example, get at least $20 a month for the vacant store, and $15 a month for Collis's house.[28]

There was not very much work that pressed itself on Edward's attention when he got to Oneonta, but he continued in this situation for five full years. His basic job was to see that Solon's farms and houses were rented to advantage; to collect the rents; to deal with delinquents by persuasion or if necessary by legal means; to take care of taxes, repairs, maintenance; and to maintain accounts and general oversight. Solon was in reasonably good health—he was to live fourteen years more, until 1890—but he had become increasingly inactive in any form of business; other people had to look after his affairs.

Six months after Edward arrived, Collis formed the impression that Willard did not care to continue his responsibility for Collis's properties, and Collis invited Willard to come to New York and "stay awhile" at 65 Park Avenue: "Please request your Brother Edwards to attend to the business that you have had charge of for me on the same condition that you have attended to it, and report quarterly as fully and correctly as you have done."[29] So Edward got this extension to his work, almost by default, and without being asked directly.

Edward carried on all of his work conscientiously. He bought new account books to register the property and the financial transactions, recording for each the acreage, cost, incumbrances, improvements, and current value. He bought and sold property for his father and for Collis. As usual, Collis's directions to him were particular, stipulating whether a tenant could be allowed to close up a doorway or not, what the minimum rent could be for each of his properties, and the like. The balance of borrowing had long since reversed itself between Solon and Collis, and by 1878 Solon was indebted to Collis for more than $30,000. Although Solon had a good many pieces of property, they were not very valuable, ranging in worth from a few hundred to a few thousand dollars. Collis wondered whether the property was worth as much as his mortgages on them; when he sold some mortgaged property "that I took of your father," he wrote Willard, I "got about one third of what it cost, but think I made a very good sale."[30] Edward's work was routine and gave little scope to original thinking. But at least it was a job.

Edward made a few business trips away from Oneonta: to Wisconsin to see to the property there, to New York to consult with Collis, and to Huntington, West Virginia.

Huntington family affairs flourished in Oneonta. Edward and Mary had their second child, a girl, on February 2, 1878. They named her Clara Leonora: Clara in honor of Mary's mother and sister, and Leonora in honor of Edward's older sister. Their third child, another girl, was born in Oneonta on February 8, 1880, and they named her Elizabeth Vincent after Edward's paternal grandmother (the one with the "beautiful disposition"); she was born after a very short labor, and before the doctor arrived—though he got there twenty minutes after he was called—with the midwife officiating.[31]

Mary was involved in responsibility for household affairs, especially since Harriet was often away visiting family. Several times Mary had to hire and train new servants. As she wrote to Harriet, "I hope you will think well of my care of everything. I have tried to the best of my ability to do what was right; and if there have been errors, it has been through accident or the carelessness of the girls." She felt lonely. "I have so often longed for your counsel and advice," she wrote to Harriet. "I have no one at all (that is female) to talk matters over with, and there are so many things I want to do this Spring." Sometimes she felt discouraged, and she communicated that discouragement to those around her.[32]

She devoted loving attention to her children and to their activities. "Howard is full of mischief as ever," she wrote to Carrie, "and what he don't think of Clara will. I wish you could see how cute Clara is. She almost walks." When Harriet was away, she was assured that Howard had not forgotten her, "as he talks to your picture a good deal." She told Harriet jokes about Howard, age three. "When Miss Stair called at the door last eve—she is an old maid you know, and wears specs—Howard rushed to the door when the bell rang and put his arms right around her and looked up in her face and says, 'Grandma! Book!' She looked very stiff and says, 'Indeed! I suppose he thinks I'm his Grandma because I wear glasses.' I thought under the same circumstances you would not have resented his innocent prattle." Then, another day "when some man called at the door and asked him for his Grandpa, he says 'Barn!' And when the man turned away, he shut and locked the front door and marched back upstairs." After the birth of their third child, Mary wrote to Carrie that "a dear little girlie has come to live with us. She will be quite a girl by the time you return. I am so undecided what to name her. Have thought of naming her after your Grandma Huntington, 'Elizabeth Vincent,' and calling her 'Bessie' for short. How would you like that?"[33]

Sometimes her concern for her children carried her to the edge of emotional disturbance. When Howard was one and a half, she and Edward left him with Harriet in Oneonta while they made a trip to West Virginia, stopping with Ellen and Edwin Gates in New Jersey en route. "I came pretty near turning back at the Depot, but you see I braved it through," Mary wrote to Harriet. "I should never have left the little precious lambkin." In New Jersey, she sat "for two hours at the front window watching for the postman, as Edward went over to New York this morning and said if there was any word from you, he would send it right over by mail." She needed to hear about Howard right then: "I felt so sure I should get some news of my precious loved one that I am awfully disappointed and sad, but hope that I may yet hear before the day closes, as it does not seem as though I could wait until tomorrow. I am longing so for my baby this afternoon, and oh! that I could step in and see the little pet!" She begs Harriet to "let me hear as often as you possibly can" and "please tell me all about Howard. . . . You must kiss my own darling boy and tell him his Mama does love him if she has to all appearances deserted him. I look at and kiss his picture very often. I know that you will all be good and kind to him."[34] They were, and he flourished, despite his mother's concern. (He did not have a "nervous breakdown" until he was just over thirty-five and beyond his mother's care.)

Edward and Mary made a visit to New York now and then; this especially pleased her mother, who wrote to Collis that "Mary and Edward had a splendid visit at 65. I am glad she did, for she needed the change—wish she could spend the summer with me." Mary had some spunk in her disposition too: once, when Edward had stayed longer in New York by himself than planned, she sent a telegram to Collis at his office saying, "What detains Edward? Is he sick?"[35]

Mary's principal interests beyond her family seem to have been social activities and clothes. Her letters are full of news of parties she attended, people who had come to call, even a party that she had not been invited to. She occasionally went with a friend to an evening event, such as a band concert, while "Edward stayed with the little folks." She was especially pleased when Edward told her that she must be sure to "receive" on the next New Year's Day. "What do you think," she jested to Carrie, "of such levity and indulgence for an old lady?"[36] By then she was twenty-six years old.

Clothes are also a recurrent topic in her letters. She was bemused as to what dress to make for Mrs. Johnson's party: a soft, thin wool in a light shade, or an organdy over pink or blue with silk or satin and lace on the outside. She asked Carrie's opinion as to which would be prettier. She sent Harriet a sample of the silk for her newest evening dress, and she frequently asked Carrie to shop for her in New York to find, for instance, some brocade in light blue or pink for $1 a yard. She was envious of Mary Pardee's "very pretty new garnet cashmere dress" with a bonnet and new cloak to match.[37]

So far as Edward is concerned, one other development of great importance began during this period: the entangling of the relations of Edward and Willard with their Uncle Collis. In order to understand some features of Edward's later life, it is important to see the changing relations between Willard and Collis. Collis had always shown an interest in both brothers, and the parallel of the two was doubtless not lost on Edward. Before 1876, he had given Edward the ill-fated job of managing the sawmill; he had sent Willard to private schools and taken him to California for a visit.

Willard thought of himself as a person of talent, especially as a writer, and he had shown some of his efforts to Collis, who sent them to a newspaperman for an opinion. The reaction was mixed: the writer was judged to have good powers of observation and could excel in description, but he "would do well to avoid all attempt at fine writing, such as using big words, and long, roundabout phrases where short ones would do."[38]

Willard stayed in New York for a while after Collis invited him for a visit. Collis then showed a strong preference for Willard by sending him to San Francisco, at the age of twenty-one, to work in the Southern

Pacific headquarters there. This was not a position that had just become vacant, and Collis could as easily have sent Edward there a few months earlier when he suggested that he accept the offer to help his father in Oneonta. During the next four years, Collis and Willard wrote letters back and forth to one another, at least once a month, sometimes more often. There are more than two hundred pages of their letters for this period preserved in the Collis P. Huntington Papers.

Collis's letters were interested and cordial. Most of all, he wanted to instruct Willard in railroad and business practices. He often commended Willard for his work: "Your views as expressed in your two last letters are very clear and very sensible" (February 9, 1880); "I am glad to learn that you are looking after our interests there so well" (March 31, 1880). Collis gave Willard advice on many aspects of his behavior. He should, for example, live and board at a prominent hotel, even at a cost of $80 a month, in order to meet important businessmen; Collis would make his salary $100 a month more than the living costs, plus an extra $30 a month to leave in his account to save (October 18, 1879). He should also spend time with A. N. Towne, as "there is no one you could learn more of as to railroad business than of him" (January 26, 1880). And Collis approved of Willard's intentions to join the Pacific Club: "It depends entirely upon yourself whether you will be helped or harmed by the association there" (August 14, 1880).

There was, however, a darker tone that became increasingly recurrent. Willard wanted to go to Tucson during the winter, and Collis objected on the grounds that he had too much to do and learn in California (November 5, 1878). Two years later, Willard suggested that he take a trip around the world, but Collis objected on the grounds that it was "much more important that you stay in California until you get a full knowledge of our business there; and perhaps at some future time you may make the trip connected with some business that can be combined with pleasure" (October 11, 1880). Charles Crocker complained to Collis that Willard tended to look too much on the dark side of things, and Collis warned Willard "against seemingly doing anything that Mr. Crocker or Mr. Stanford would object to" unless an important point was at issue (December 14, 1880).[39]

Willard took over a leadership role in the family. When it came time for Carrie to consider college, it was he who helped her settle on Elmira College after suggesting Vassar and Mount Holyoke as other possibilities; it was he who sent a check for $165 for the expenses of each term; and it was he who advised her about her conduct at college with such words as "mingle with the other girls freely," "acquire confidence in yourself," and "avoid flirtation," this last underlined.[40]

Willard quickly got a feeling of self-importance after he established himself in San Francisco. He wrote his mother that "if I am ever a very rich man, I intend to make the latter days of some of my relatives [his elderly aunts] the brightest in their lives. I am ambitious & fond of power, but the regard I have for my kinspeople is held paramount of all." He was plainly thinking of following in Collis's footsteps: "I want to perpetuate a name made famous by my uncle throughout the continent, in a manner that will in every way redound to its greatest honor, and I want its integrity to remain without a blemish in the opinion of my fellow man." He recognized that he had a big job in front of him, but his sense of a barrier "preventing my advancement is now rapidly dissolving as intimacy with my business increases." Willard was interested in Edward's son Howard, now age three and a half, because he thought that Howard was "of the temperament I possessed when very young." Accordingly, he told his mother that he hoped "you will all encourage his self reliance and esteem. This advice in some instances would be dangerous in its entirety, and perhaps Howard is not as I was."[41] If he was, Willard intimated, then he had a special talent that was to be encouraged.

In 1880 and early 1881, Edward was spending periods of time in New York working in Collis's office, then going back to Oneonta. On July 20, 1881, Edward wrote from Oneonta to Collis in New York: "If there is nothing for me to do in New York for three or four days, I can work to advantage slicking up things here. But this work of course is not of much importance, and as I do not wish to be away for one moment when I am needed there, I will return on the first train after hearing from you."[42]

Collis had another job in mind for him. Three months earlier, he had written to Willard that "your brother Edward is at my house; I think of sending him to Virginia."[43] Collis used the word "Virginia" loosely to include West Virginia, Kentucky, and Tennessee. In fact, the job was in Tennessee and Kentucky. Edward was to be in charge of laying a line of railroad track.

Edward set out on August 10, 1881, for Paducah, Kentucky, where he was given a letter of introduction by Holmes Cummins, general counsel of the Chesapeake, Ohio and South Western Railroad Company, to Dr. J. N. Wardlaw, the district manager in Ripley, Tennessee. The letter testified that Edward was "to take charge of the work of completing the line of railroad from Trimble to Covington. Mr. C. P. Huntington, of the Chesapeake and Ohio RR, is now the President of our road and is the Uncle of the bearer of this. . . . Mr. H. E. Huntington will be with you for some time. You will find him a pleasant gentleman as well as a responsible man in business."[44]

Edward started off alone on his new venture. Mary and the children stayed in Oneonta until he could get the work under way and make living arrangements for them.

He could look forward to the future with hope, but he could not look back at the preceding years with any general satisfaction.

Four

WORKING ON THE RAILROAD

1881–1885

EDWARD SPENT THE NEXT four years in railroad construction work in western Tennessee and western Kentucky. His work extended from Memphis in the southwestern corner of Tennessee to Covington in the northwestern corner of Kentucky, just across the Ohio River from Cincinnati.

On August 10, 1881, he went from New York to Paducah, Kentucky. He reconnoitered from there into western Tennessee for a few days, taking walking trips with the staff engineer over the route that the line was to follow. Within two weeks he had made a contract for the delivery of ties for the first eight miles of track, and he had a work crew consisting of a foreman and twenty-four men. They began by leveling the ground and laying track on August 23, 1881, at Trimble, Tennessee—where Edward had taken up residence—and they worked southward to Dyersburg, Tennessee, a distance of about twenty-five miles. In the first four days, they laid 1,515 feet of track. A week later, Edward made a close inspection of the route all the way south to Memphis, a distance of another hundred miles, to see what kind of work would be involved in the heavy grading and building of trestles. It had been a dry season, and he was eager to get the track laid in the bottomlands before the rains began in earnest in December. Collis had set July 1, 1882, as the time by which he wanted the whole line in operating order, and there was no time to lose. For the next couple of months Edward rarely went to bed

55

before midnight, and he said that he was working harder than he ever had in his life.[1]

This was a foretaste of the next four years. He moved around a lot: in Tennessee, he lived in Trimble, Dyersburg, and Memphis; in Kentucky, Paducah and Louisville. His family was with him only about half of the time, and then in rented furnished houses or boardinghouses. The rest of the time, they were in Oneonta or in Sacramento with Mary's mother.

When Edward got into the railroad business, it was still a relatively new industry, but it had already reshaped the economic face of the nation. It had made its start in the United States about 1830. Most of the early lines were laid first in the northeast, then in the southeast, and then to the west, with the first transcontinental line completed in 1869 and three more by 1885. There was great public enthusiasm for the extension of the lines in the expectation of commercial and human advantages to the areas traversed, and state and federal subsidies were often offered for laying track. This stage of the transportation revolution in the United States led to a great increase in national wealth and in particular to the private wealth of the entrepreneurs who were involved in its development, either directly or indirectly.

By 1880 there were ninety-three thousand miles of track in the United States, and in the decade that followed—Edward's first in the business—that amount almost doubled, constituting what turned out to be the greatest era of railroad building. Railroading was a capital-intensive and highly speculative industry, with almost all of the operating companies owned by private corporations. The initial capital funds came from the issuance and sale of stocks and bonds, mainly through financial houses in New York. Continuing financial needs were met by further issuance of bonds, by assessments on the stockholders, by recapitalization, mergers, bankruptcy, and reincorporation, all of which were common in those volatile years of a business that was full of risk and opportunity, and marked by fraud and corruption.

Edward's initial role in railroading was modest. His official title was Superintendent of Construction of the Chesapeake, Ohio and South Western Railroad Company. The company was a small feeder line controlled, like many other such companies, by Collis, who was also the official president. Edward's job was rather less important than his title might suggest, and several other officers had a higher place in the hierarchy: General John Echols was the vice-president with overall responsibility; N. Monsarrat (succeeded by Robert Meek) was the general manager, later styled general superintendent; Dr. J. T. B. Hillhouse was the chief engineer; and Holmes Cummins was the general counsel.

Edward's job was actually something like supervisor of foremen: he hired the foremen and the workmen, got their supplies and equipment, and checked on their results. He also reported almost daily by letter or telegraph to Collis in New York; the other officers also reported regularly to Collis and told him of their progress and problems. Collis liked to tell everybody individually what to do; he was a distant hands-on manager. His strategy in dealing with Edward and his other subordinates was relatively simple: they were directed to buy it cheaper than the price they had mentioned, to get through with the job before the projected finish date, and to stop wasting money and other property. At the same time, they were enjoined to be scrupulously honest and assiduous in protecting the rights of employees and the public. If his subordinates asked Collis a question to which he did not have a ready answer, he always told them that they were on the ground and he was not, and that they ought to be able to decide themselves what was best. With their advantages, the implication was, they had better get it right.

Edward was doubtful of an organizational structure in which the principals all reported independently to the absent proprietor. Within two weeks of his arrival in Kentucky, he wrote to Collis and asked him to clarify the responsibilities of the chief engineer and himself: "Please write Mr. Hillhouse and myself explaining as definitely as you can our relative duties so that we may work understandingly. I do not wish him to think that I assume any responsibility that I should not and know that he feels the same towards me. But (as you know) it is always best to commence with a good understanding. And I know that we shall work in great harmony."[2]

No explanation was forthcoming from Collis, yet they did work in harmony. In due course, however, various tensions arose that caused Edward considerable pain. In less than a year, Hillhouse wrote to Collis and objected that Edward "had a grand misconception of the extent of his independent authority" with respect to the actual field work. "Surely, Mr. Huntington, you understand Ed's nature well enough to know that in the exercise of any authority pertaining to any work, he cannot stop at any point." Hillhouse said he didn't want to annoy Collis with the matter and he had "made several protests to him [Edward] personally, in a friendly way; which he would not allow; saying that he was only acting to an extent of authority with which you had invested him." Hillhouse touched a sensitive spot when he went on to say that "with any other man I should have pressed the point to an issue; of course you must understand that considering his relationship to yourself, I could not do so, as I naturally supposed that he had a better conception of your wishes than anyone else would."[3]

Collis replied immediately to disclaim any favoritism and to turn the matter into a personal issue. "You are entirely mistaken," he wrote, "when you think that because of any relationship between me and the other party, there will be any discrimination in his favor against yourself. I should only fear that the reverse would be the effect, although I would endeavor that that should not be."[4] But he said nothing about defining areas of responsibility or limits of authority. Hillhouse responded that "it was farthest from my thoughts to hint or insinuate in the slightest degree, that you had or could make any discrimination in favor of a relative. My complaint was entirely against H. E. H. himself, who I thought had assumed (not been delegated) too much authority on this work." Hillhouse's basic complaint was reluctance "to be held responsible for things that usually come under a Chief Engineer's control and are referred to him, but about which I have had nothing to do. As long as this point is understood, I have nothing to complain of."[5] Collis did not respond, and the problem blew over.

General Echols also saw management problems. He very politely requested Collis to send communications about "the management of the road" through him rather than directly to the officer principally concerned in order to "improve the discipline and organization."[6] But Collis continued to write directly to the subordinates. And later he did no more than regret the "rift" that had come between Edward and General Echols on this issue.[7] Through it all, Edward was left in the awkward position of trying to do his job without quite knowing what the limits were. In fact, Collis thought that a little friction was not always a bad thing. He wrote to Edward on July 6, 1883, "I notice there is a little friction between you and Phillips in relation to some of these matters; but that is well enough, for anything that keeps you both trying all the time to see how well you can buy supplies for the Company is hardly to be regretted."[8] Personal relations came after business efficiency.

Edward was beset by many other practical problems that made his work difficult. He was rarely able to get the locomotives and flatcars that he needed to haul ties and equipment. "I am not able to do anything on account of not having motive power," he wrote to Collis. "My laborers are getting very much demoralized, and I fear I cannot keep them together. Many of them are now leaving." He had a hard time getting laborers at $1.00 a day, then $1.10, and then $1.25 for the twelve-hour day, which ran from 6:00 A.M. to 6:00 P.M., with an hour off to eat in the middle of the day. Then he had to deal with a strike for an advance of twenty-five cents above the $1.25 wage, and more than a hundred of his men left. "I told them," he wrote to Collis, "that we were paying as much as we could and if they could not work for that they had better go. I knew that if we did accede to their demands that there would be no end of trouble that we might have hereafter." Edward's continued pleas for locomotives and flatcars had not been met, and the workmen had been idle: "I think that if we could have had motive power here so that I could have kept them at work, we would have had no trouble, as I think that nothing breeds mischief as much as idleness."[9]

Another difficult task was getting sleeping tents for his work force, and wood ties and steel rails at the right time and price. Edward was able to keep his sense of humor even when supplies were hard to obtain. He answered his Uncle Edwin Gates's question about steel rails by telling of his frequent inquiries of the fabricator and adding that "the matter is now in the circumlocution office, and I hope (if my life is spared) I may hear from them again."[10]

Many anxieties arose from trying to satisfy Collis. Edward was directed to write a separate letter on each topic he treated, so on October 27, 1881, he wrote five letters to Collis. An immediate objection came back from Collis because they had been "sent in five separate envelopes which cost in stamps fifteen cents besides the cost of envelopes; when they could have been put into one envelope and two stamps would have brought them."[11] Collis had earlier objected to Edward sending him a regular telegram from Memphis instead of a night letter: "It was hardly worth while for you to telegraph me as it costs money, and unless there is some better reason than this for the expenditure of money it should not be expended."[12] Edward was undaunted and replied that he had hoped to get an answer the same day so that he could leave Memphis: "As my time just at present is worth three or four times what that telegram amounted to, I thought that was the best thing I could do. I fully appreciate the importance of keeping down the expenses and think that when you look over my work you will find no reason to disapprove my management."[13]

Collis was extremely careful about expenditures. He constantly exhorted Edward and all of his other subordinates to save money, and Edward reassured him over and over again that "he had been careful about that from the first," that he had received "one hundred cents worth of work and material for every dollar paid out," that he used "every endeavor to secure a large equivalent for every dollar expended," and so on.[14] Collis was almost obsessively concerned about small expenditures. For example, he complained by letter to the manager of the Willard Hotel in Washington about the amount he had been charged for claret, to the plumber in New York about his labor charges, to the veterinarian about the charges for the care of an animal that had died, and to his physician about the cost of travel expenses. Most responded to his objections with polite explanations, but some, like the physician, suggested that, if Collis doubted his fairness, "I shall not care to continue treatment [of you]."[15]

Under his uncle's scrupulous direction, Edward kept his primary task, of laying the track through to Memphis, moving along on the schedule that Collis had prescribed, and the first train went over the line on July 11, 1882. There was still more to do to finish up the job, however. There was grading along the right-of-way to be finished, trestles to be filled in, and cuts to be ditched. It was not until the middle of November that Edward felt this work was complete and disbanded his work force.[16]

When he was nearly finished, he wrote Harriet, on October 20, 1882, that "I received an encouraging letter from Uncle C. P. H. about my work here, which was very gratifying to me. I have never worked harder than I have on this work, nor had more to contend with. And I cannot tell you how gratified I am to know that he appreciates it. And I feel fully repaid for my labor."[17]

Regrettably, the work did not hold up well. The next spring General Echols made an inspection trip over the line, from Paducah to Memphis, and he wrote to Collis that he found "the new part of the road"— the part that Edward had built—"in a very bad condition in consequence of the late wet weather. Many slides are occurring in the cuts, and it is evident that a good deal of work will have to be done to get the road in proper condition. The earth cuts will all have to be sloped"— some slides were entirely covering the tracks. "The trouble is becoming so serious that we will have to organize an independent force to attend to it, as it is beyond the power of the ordinary section forces to control it. I presume that this probably will come under the head of 'Construction.' "[18] Edward had done his inexperienced best under constant pressure for early completion at minimum cost, but the result was not very successful.

In the meantime, Edward had gone on to western Kentucky. For the next couple of years he was fully occupied in a number of railroad jobs, at a salary of $350 a month. He supervised the grading and building of the railroad shops in Paducah. He acted as purchasing agent; General Echols wrote Collis that "he is a very good trader, and then we will know that everything is correct."[19] In addition, Collis had Edward make studies of his properties that were in trouble. Edward spent time on the railroad and mill property in Lincoln County, Mississippi, on the Illinois Central Railroad.[20] And he went over the whole Louisville, New Orleans & Texas Railroad from Memphis to New Orleans to try to find out how work could be expedited and at less expense.[21]

I have begun these pages on Edward's life during the early 1880s with a brief account of his work, because he looked on work as his primary activity. But his primary emotions were always reserved for his family.

Edward's family had stayed in Oneonta when he went to western Tennessee in August 1881. After two months, he felt that his work was well enough in hand to have them join him, and he wrote to Collis about the advisability of going to Oneonta for them. Collis replied with family understanding: "You can do as you think best about coming home. I think myself it would be well for you to come home and get Mary and the children, as I am satisfied they would be happier with you than they would be in Oneonta; although, as I understand, everything is pleasant for them there."[22]

So in the latter part of November, Edward went to Oneonta and brought his family, including a servant girl, to Tennessee. They went on the riverboat to New York and stopped for a few days with Collis and Elizabeth at 65 Park Avenue. "Mary wrote that the children were real good," Harriet reported to Carrie. "Said Collis made the most of Howard, Elizabeth of Bessie, and Clara of Clara."[23]

Then they proceeded on Collis's passes to Paducah, Kentucky, where Edward left his family for a week while he went back to work in Tennessee. Edward found a comfortable boarding place for them all in Dyersburg, Tennessee, and they were reunited there early in December. Mary, after eight years of marriage and with three little children, was back living the kind of life she had earlier repudiated, in boarding-houses, for the sake of Edward's work.[24]

In January 1882 they were able to get a furnished house, but then Howard and next the littler children began to suffer from illnesses. Mary began to have attacks of chills and fever. The parents attributed the illnesses to the climate of western Tennessee and Kentucky. After they had endured their illnesses for a couple of months, Edward wrote Collis that Mary and the children had been sick most of the time since they had been there, "and I fear that I shall have to send them to a different climate."[25]

So at the end of April 1882 Mary and the children went—again on passes supplied by Collis—to Sacramento to commence a long visit to her mother. There they flourished. In the summer, Collis and Elizabeth came to Sacramento, and Mary wrote an eight-page account of the reunion to Harriet back in Oneonta. When Collis and Elizabeth and their adopted daughter Clara (Mary's sister) arrived, the adults insisted on waking up Mary's children: "They looked sweet in their night gowns," wrote Mary. "They all kissed them and made a great deal of them except [the elder] Clara, who stood by the bed and never offered to kiss them or speak to them. Both Uncle and Aunt thought they did not look as well as when they left New York and thought Howard looked very poorly." Since Clara was later to be the occasion for a serious disagreement between Mary and Edward, it is worth reading a little more about Mary's reaction to her sister at this time. The next day they all went off on a trip and tried to get Mary's mother, Mrs. Prentice, to go,

> but she would not on account of Clara—the latter is so <u>hateful</u>. She has a pet dog with her—she lavishes any quantity of kisses on it, lets it eat out of her spoon and drink out of her glass—and then to think she would not <u>kiss my darlings</u> and would scorn to <u>drink out of a cup</u> <u>their sweet lips had touched</u>. God help me not to think or feel wicked thoughts about her. She may yet long for little ones to love her. She will certainly be punished sometime for this <u>cruel</u> treatment to us all.

Mary went on to say that she hoped Collis and Elizabeth would see Edward on their way back to New York: "I am so anxious to know what he is going to do. Ed Pardee said he thought Uncle would want him down there two years longer. How I can ever be reconciled to such a long and cruel separation I do not know."[26]

Willard continued to work in the Southern Pacific office in San Francisco, but he lost favor further with Collis. First, Willard suggested that he would like to come east in the autumn of 1881 to see his friends; he assured Collis his work would not suffer from an absence of some weeks. Collis was offended at the suggestion. "I had supposed," he replied, "that you were working in so that you could hardly leave there anytime without detriment to the interests partially under your charge. I know it is very nice to go every year to see one's friends. Still, it is a long journey, and not particularly necessary. I have been in business for myself 46 years this month, and do not think I ever took 6 consecutive days out of it for pleasure, either in visiting my friends, or anything else disconnected with business."[27] Later that same autumn, Willard became engaged to Marie Louisiana Ream, age eighteen, an attractive young woman of an affluent family, her parents deceased, of the Roman

Catholic faith. Willard wrote the details to Harriet and asked her to "notify all parties"; in giving this news to Carrie, Harriet said, "in my opinion he should have done it himself, but you know his eccentricities." He did tell Collis himself and got back a scorching reply: "I could have heard nothing from you that would have given me more regret than what you have written me. I regret very much that you should engage for your wife a Roman Catholic. If this engagement of yours could be honorably broken off, I have no doubt it would be the best thing for both you and the young lady that could be done."[28]

Willard chose to go against Collis's suggestion, and the marriage took place in San Francisco on February 23, 1882. When Collis, Elizabeth, and Clara went to San Francisco in August of that year, they were met by Willard and Marie; Marie wrote a twelve-page account of their meetings to Harriet. Marie said, "I tried to look my sweetest by looking crosseyed and showing all my teeth, but failed in the attempt. Mr. C. P. H. looked scared, and I worse than that. He said he was pleased to meet me, and I could only re-echo his words. Mrs. C. P. kissed me and said she was so (emphasizing the so) glad to meet me. Clara came next; she kissed me and gave me a very cordial welcome, much to my surprise, as I expected from all accounts to find her very haughty. Mr. C. P. H. did not address a word to me. Mr. Pardee said it was owing to embarrassment."[29]

Willard continued to displease Collis. The next winter he wrote Collis—on Pacific Club stationery—that he had been out on the Market Street Railway line several days ago to see how the work was progressing. Collis almost blew up: "If I were living in the City of San Francisco, as you are, and was Vice President, as you are, I should see the work every day." He told Willard to go there every morning and every evening, and thereafter write his business letters from the office, not from the Pacific Club. Later in the same year, Collis summed up his uncertainty about Willard's future success in business. "Let me tell you frankly," he wrote, "that to do this you will have to change very widely your ideas and methods of business."[30]

In the meantime, Edward was having a long bout with malaria in Tennessee. On August 18, 1882, he wrote to Collis that "I have been feeling very poorly for the last month, was laid up for a few days with malarial fever, and have not regained my strength yet. In fact, have been growing weaker each day for the last few days, and have just concluded that I will get away from business for a few days and try to recuperate." He had moved his office to Memphis to be nearer his work, and he assured Collis that everything was in good shape for him to leave for ten days. He concluded, "Do not say anything to Mary about my sickness, as it would worry her and do no good." General Echols, who also had an attack of malaria, wrote Collis about Edward's illness: "Mr. Edward Huntington has been overcome by the malaria of his region, and has been quite sick for some days past. I saw him in Memphis the other day, and noticing his condition, urged him to go away for a little while, as I was afraid that unless he did, the consequences might be serious to him." So Edward went to Oneonta to recuperate. General Echols concluded that "he has displayed, I think, remarkable energy and good sense in the transaction of his work in Tennessee and about Memphis."[31]

The separation of Edward and his family stretched out to half a year. In October 1882, Mary wrote to Carrie that "I have been so long away from my Beloved that my first duty and desire is to be with him this winter. And he, too, is very anxious to see his family. Just think: it will be six months when we get back. A long time, is it not?" She concluded by reporting that, in preparation for her return, she had her "black brocade fixed over with velvet and a new dark red suit."[32] Edward had already written to Collis for passes, saying, "I am very desirous of having Mary and the little ones home again, and she feels the same way."[33] So, on November 22, 1882, Edward went to St. Louis to meet Mary and the children and bring them home.

It was a good reunion. But on December 1, Edward had another attack of malaria, with violent chills.[34] The maid, too, suffered frequent illnesses. And in February 1883, Mary discovered—to her consternation—that she was pregnant again. She wrote about the secret to Harriet: "I assure you it is with a heavy heavy heart that I tell you. It was such a terrible surprise. I am so dreadfully sick all day long. And it happens under such unpleasant circumstances, for Edward says he cannot tell anything about where he shall be." She asked whether she and the children could come to Oneonta for the birth in October—

eight months away, so she had a wonderfully quick awareness of her pregnancy—and stay until after Christmas: "Edward says to do whatever I want to. It will be another long separation from him, though he could run up to see us once in a while." The baby was neither planned nor welcome. "Edward is as sorry as I am about it," and she toyed with the idea of abortion: "If it was not wicked, I should be tempted to get rid of it, but I cannot look to God for his blessing and help with that thought in my heart. But I do think it is cruel, when I am not strong and it seems as if I never had a chance to gain my strength." She felt dreadfully lonely there in Tennessee "amongst entire strangers," and "if I were to die, there would be no one to attend my funeral." She asked Harriet to think it over and let her know soon whether they might come: "Should I come home it would be unpleasant to meet my friends under the circumstances—mortifying to me—but that seems to be least of my worries." Harriet wrote across the top of the letter, "Poor child! What a hard time she had!"[35]

Collis heard of the illnesses, and he wrote Edward saying, "I think you would do well to send Mary and the children to Oneonta." Later he wrote, "Am sorry to hear that the little ones have been sick and that you have had the chills. Take them up to Oneonta and that climate will drive out the chills pretty quick."[36] What faith they had in the climate of central New York State!

Of course Harriet welcomed Mary and the children to Oneonta. Edward and Mary's fourth and last child, Marian Prentice, was born there on October 3, 1883.

At the same time there was a death in the family. Just two days after the birth of Marian, Collis's wife, Elizabeth, died, after a marriage that had lasted thirty-nine years. Together they had gone from poverty and obscurity to great riches and prominence. Elizabeth had been ill for more than a year with cancer. Confined to the house for most of her illness, she was bedridden for the last four months. A month before her death, Collis wrote to an old and dear friend, Abbott Robinson, about his feelings for her: "I cling to the hope that we may yet see her moving about in her usual health and spirits. You little know how much I miss her cheerful face about the house. When I allow my thoughts to dwell upon the future—and I realize the terrible Possibility that the grave face of the doctor indicates—an inexpressible feeling of loneliness comes over me, and I cannot bear to see this shadow over my home grow steadily larger and larger. It is some relief to work."[37]

Several developments during these years signaled a change of direction in Edward's life. Perhaps the one that had the most important repercussions was a new way of dealing with money. He began to accumulate some capital and to take the first tentative steps toward making it appreciate.

His salary had ranged from $50 to $350 a month during a period of ten years, and not always in the upward direction. Although he was modest in expenditure, frugality alone does not usually produce important sums of money.

Edward learned his first lesson in accumulation soon after his arrival in western Tennessee. He set up a commissary to supply the basic needs of the hundred or so men who made up the construction crew. He cleared a profit of $5,000 during the first year of his operation and continued this money-making activity throughout his time in railroad construction. He sent a draft for $1,300 to Collis on September 18, 1882, and another for $5,000 on January 15, 1883, for credit to his account and to invest for him "as you think best." Collis suggested some Big Sandy railroad bonds (6 percent bonds at ninety-five, with an effective yield of 6.3 percent); he always suggested bonds in his companies to people who sent him money to invest. Edward thought that was perfectly satisfactory. "Do as you think best with it," he repeated. "I had the money and thought it best to send it to you as I was doing nothing with it here. I am in no hurry to invest it, if you think it would pay to wait awhile."[38]

Edward also made some small beginnings in finding other ways to make his money grow. He talked with Ely Ensign about buying stock in the Ensign Car Works, and he succeeded in buying thirty-five shares. He also put a little money in Chesapeake and Nashville stock and began thinking about joining a group to buy some land in western Kentucky.[39]

Another development for him was the beginning of his involvement in negotiations between public and private agencies and the companies with which he was associated. In Memphis, for example, he called on members of the city council in June 1882 to get them to agree that rubble pavement was just as satisfactory as block pavement and that the company would not be charged any wharfage because of certain benefits that were coming to the city.[40] The railroad graded beside the tracks that were used by two oil companies, in order to get more business; he wrote to Collis that "as Josh Billings says, 'The best time to set a hen is when the hen is ready'—so it seemed to me that the best time to arrange with these parties was when they were ready."[41] Edward was sent to Paducah to talk with individual property owners and get them to sign waivers not to hold the railroad responsible for damages.[42] Later, he was sent to Louisville to get releases from property owners there, and Collis was pleased with the results: "You have done very well—it takes quiet, judicious work to accomplish such things."[43] He was later sent to Bourbon County, Kentucky, where he successfully defeated a scheme inimical to railroad interests. His expenses of $2,195 in accomplishing the task were shared by several roads.[44]

Edward had to cope with a couple of emergencies during this time. On December 1, 1882, he was involved in a train wreck near Paducah in which several cars were thrown over an embankment and down twenty-five feet because of an unlocked switch. All the passengers were injured, but no one was killed. The conductor, who should have been in charge, "was very badly bruised but no bones broken" and the other official "was out of his head." Edward took charge of the situation, sent the injured on stretchers to the nearest town, stayed with the train, and gave information to the newspapers and a full report to the company's chief legal counsel.[45]

The other emergency involved another train wreck in January 1885. Solon and Harriet had been visiting Edward and Mary (who had moved to Louisville); while Edward and Solon were making a short trip on the train, a lamp in the toilet exploded and set a coach on fire. Solon was seriously burned about the hands and face and could not escape from the car. Edward rescued his father. As the paper reported, "Mr. Ed. Huntington worked manfully trying to get his father from the burning coach, and succeeded after the old gentleman had been severely burned on the red-hot stove. Young Huntington had to make his escape by a window, 12 by 16 inches, and he did it with credit, even taking his plug hat with him." Harriet reported that Edward "was slightly burned in trying to rescue his father," but Solon's burns were terrible and required the care of a doctor for several weeks.[46]

One other event that was to have an important effect on Edward was the marriage of Collis and Arabella D. Worsham. The service took place in New York at ten o'clock on Saturday morning, July 12, 1884, in her house at 4 West Fifty-fourth Street. The ceremony was performed by the Reverend Henry Ward Beecher, to whom Collis handed an envelope containing four thousand-dollar bills. Arabella—Belle, as she was called by her friends—was about thirty-three, and Collis was sixty-three. They had known one another for nearly twenty years. She had a son, Archer, who was fourteen years old at the time of the marriage. Collis had also known several other women during the last years of his first marriage; there are a number of letters of obscure import among his papers from young, unattached, female friends, like Kittie Bushnell, who wrote that "if you should ever lose interest in me, it would almost break my heart."[47]

Edward had admired his Aunt Elizabeth. Now he had a new aunt, about his own age, with whom he was to have many things in common.

In the latter part of 1884, Edward saw that he needed a job with a clearer future, and he asked Collis what possibilities he could offer. There are two versions of the answer.

One is an appealing account given by Theodore Irwin, a friend of Edward's from Oneonta:

> C. P. H. Edward, how would you like to be a railroad president?
> H. E. H. Of what railroad?
> C. P. H. The Kentucky Central.
> H. E. H. What's the matter with it?
> C. P. H. It's no good.
> H. E. H. I'll take it.[48]

It is appealing because it makes Edward appear somewhat bold and adventuresome, a potential leader. It is not surprising that it has been repeated with pleasure.

The other account, rather more drab, is based on the correspondence. From it, we learn that Edward was thought of as quite inexperienced in railroading. And railroading, like many other occupations, was then a sort of guild into which one had to earn membership. It begins with Collis's reply on September 20, 1884, to Edward's inquiry: "I do not know just where to place you at this time. If you had some little more knowledge of operating railroads, I could give you the position of Division Superintendent somewhere on some of our roads. I did think some of having you take the Kentucky Central and giving Mr. Bender the Superintendency of the Chesapeake, Ohio & South West road; but I am afraid you have not sufficient experience to handle the property, and it is one of the most difficult pieces of railroad to manage that I have."[49]

Collis turned the matter over in his head and finally raised the question with C. W. Smith, the general manager of the Kentucky Central in Richmond. Smith thought well of the appointment of Edward:

> Notwithstanding H. E. Huntington's experience in the practical operations of railways has been quite limited, particularly in transportation matters, if it is your desire that it should be done I have no objections to giving him the position to be vacated by Mr. Bender, provided he comes to us prepared to conform to our rules and regulations and is willing to give the necessary close attention to the duties of the office. I think quite well of him and believe he has the ability to make a good Superintendent.[50]

A few days later, Smith added that Edward should be put on the job at once: "I will give the matter such attention as to insure its success. Besides placing him with a first class Chief Train Dispatcher, who is politic and an earnest worker, either Mr. Ryder or myself will be on the ground as much as may be necessary to insure smooth working and beneficial results."[51]

On March 26, 1885, Collis offered Edward the job. He sent a rather cool invitation:

> Mr. Bender leaves the Kentucky Central on the 1st of April and we want somebody to take his place. If you would like it and think you

can handle the property, I am willing to have you try, although I must get better results out of it than I have had for a long time before it will be satisfactory to me. If you think you would like to try it, telegraph me. But before you go on the road I shall want you to come here [New York] and see me.[52]

Edward accepted, and on April 10, 1885, C. W. Smith put out a printed notice for the Kentucky Central Railroad Company announcing that "Mr. H. E. Huntington has been appointed Superintendent, with headquarters at Covington, Ky.," effective April 21, 1885.[53] Edward would receive a salary of $300 a month: the $200 that the other division superintendents of the C & O received, and an extra $100 to be added privately in Collis's New York office and charged to other accounts.[54] Thus began a new chapter in Edward's life.

Five

RUNNING A RAILROAD
1885–1892

THE KENTUCKY CENTRAL was not a very promising railroad. C. W. Smith, the general manager, thought it had numerous fundamental disadvantages. His opinion was that it would continue to have limited prospects unless they could extend it across the Ohio River and have a terminal in Cincinnati.[1] More than a year earlier, Collis had considered declaring bankruptcy on the Kentucky Central and putting it into the hands of a receiver.[2] However, he expressed this view only to Edwin Gates, his confidant and brother-in-law, and not to Edward.

On the day that Edward was formally installed as superintendent, April 21, 1885, C. W. Smith went from Richmond to Covington to see that all was in order. He wrote to Collis, "I am pleased to report that notwithstanding his inexperience in detail railroading, I am inclined to believe he will prove to be a good man."[3]

Edward had been on the job for just a month when Collis wrote that he had been there "long enough now to begin to know something of the property and to get some impression concerning its earning power and the general outlook for its future. Please let me have your views about it."[4] Three days later he urged Edward "to spend some pleasant Sunday in examining the ground between the two roads [the Kentucky Central and its adjacent division] and then give me your view as to cost, &c, of making connection. What would be the cheapest and best line?"[5] Perhaps that was a good way to spend "some pleasant Sunday" —

Edward was alone, as Mary and the children were in Oneonta, having earlier been visiting at 65 Park Avenue.

Those pleasant Sundays were interrupted right away by a strike. The earnings on all the divisions of the railroad had been poor. The decision had been made in New York that all railroad employees in each division should have a 10 percent pay cut, and a strike was the response. The freight brakemen on the Kentucky Central were particularly aggressive, and the city council of Paris, Kentucky, was persuaded to appoint fifteen special police to "guard our property," as Smith wrote to Collis, "and help keep trespassers off our grounds."[6]

Collis was sorry to hear of the strike by the employees and urged Edward "to be very careful in your treatment of them, as of course they have their rights, which should be in all cases regarded. I have sometimes feared you might be a little arbitrary in your dealings with the men." The road had been running at a loss: "I think if this state of things was fairly understood by our employees" the pay cut "would be looked at in a rational way and they would be willing to sacrifice something towards keeping the wheels rolling." Collis's principle was that "of course the policy of the Company must be controlled by the owners. At the same time, the employees should be met in a kind and fair spirit and their demands acceded to so far as the Company can afford to do so." Four days later, Collis assured Edward that "I am satisfied you have done the best that could be done under the circumstances. I hope things will work better hereafter. I think if the employees of the road really knew how little the road is earning they would be satisfied with what they are getting." Collis kept repeating to Edward one of his fundamental principles of management: if employees are given a careful explanation and understanding of the facts, they will recognize management's actions as rational and just and agree with what management is doing.[7] This high-minded principle was surprisingly effective in Collis's time, and its moral essence found a place in Edward's thinking.

The strike ended, but earnings did not improve. By September, the Kentucky Central had the worst earnings record of any of the divisions; by December, Collis was thinking of selling it to the mortgage holders.[8] On January 6, 1886, Collis told Edward that he had decided to have the

Kentucky Central declared bankrupt and to have Edward appointed as receiver: "We do not expect any special change in the management of the road. Of course back salaries of employees, if any, due, will be paid as is the custom in such cases."[9] The lawyers did their work, and later in January 1886 the court appointed Edward as receiver of the Kentucky Central Railroad, and he continued to operate it as before.[10] Then on December 22, 1886, the court appointed Edward as master commissioner to preside over the sale of the Kentucky Central to the highest bidder, with a minimum price of $1.5 million.[11] On April 23, 1887, Edward sold the property for $1,505,500 to a group acting for Collis, though he complained privately that the Louisville and Nashville (L & N) had run up the price for the rolling stock. The holders of the old bonds in due course received $177.73 for each $1,000 bond.[12] In June, a new road was formally incorporated in Kentucky as the "Kentucky Central Railway Company," as opposed to the old "Kentucky Central Railroad."[13] Through all the changes and reorganization, Edward continued to run the railroad. And he was, throughout, deeply involved in the process of reorganization and was in frequent touch with Collis's chief legal counsel, Charles H. Tweed, on getting the details right.[14]

In December 1890, Collis sold the Kentucky Central to the L & N, effective January 1, 1891. For it, he received $4 million of 4 percent L & N bonds, with $6.9 million of L & N stock as collateral—a neat profit on the turnaround, even though the $4 million of L & N bonds were probably worth only about $3 million at market value.[15]

Edward continued to run the railroad until it was effectively taken over by the L & N. He began as superintendent and became receiver and finally vice-president and general manager. Throughout his six years with the Kentucky Central, Edward followed his natural inclination for hard work with daily reports, conferences, visits, trips, and constant problem solving. Occasionally the matters were not of a routine nature: in 1887 attempts were made to wreck the Kentucky Central trains by placing obstructions on the tracks. Edward called in the Pinkerton detective agency; they caught the culprit, who was given a jail sentence.[16]

The following anecdotes will help convey a picture of his daily business life. The railroad owned a steam ferry, the "Maggie May," used to cross the Ohio River at New Richmond, just east of Covington. The ferry captain, G. W. Henderson, reported directly to Edward. Many passengers complained to Edward that Henderson was often late and would not wait for people. Henderson replied, "They hant any body kicking but the agent he goes over some Days and orders to ferry boat to weate till he comes back wee cant wate on him when wee have passengers on they hant any boat but what will Detain a person some times wee are ready early and late." Henderson sent Edward weekly reports of receipts, all the bills for expenses, many questions (like how much to charge for delivery of coal across the river), and innumerable other problems.[17] The ferry was one of Edward's responsibilities, and he handled it and all the rest of them with expedition and good humor.

A second revealing episode occurred when Edward was receiver of the Kentucky Central. He called into his office C. L. Brown, the long-time general freight agent of the railroad. Brown found Huntington there with several other officials of the railroad and thought he was going to be offered coffee and biscuits. Here is the way the newspaper reported the event:

> Mr. Huntington opened at once by saying: "Mr. Brown, I have kept my eye on your proceedings of late, and have arrived at the conclusion that I will be compelled to give you your time." The shock of surprise caused the popular Freight Agent to grow suddenly weak in the knees as he stammered, "Why— why— I had— no idea; you will tell me, at least, of what I am guilty."
>
> "Well," said Mr. Huntington, "for one thing, you have been keeping extremely late hours." There was a merry gleam in the Receiver's eyes as he said this, but the disconsolate Charlie could not see for the gathering mist as he thought of his many years spent in the service of the Company and of the late hours he really had kept in promoting the interests of the new road.
>
> "Yes," continued Mr. Huntington, "I am resolved to give you your time, and here it is." With these words he handed Charlie, instead of the expected discharge, a magnificent gold watch bearing his monogram. Coffee, biscuits, "goneness", and everything else were forgotten in an instant, and at that moment it is safe to conjecture C. L. Brown was the happiest man in town.

The watch was presented as a memento of the valuable services rendered by Mr. Brown, and he took this peculiar method of surprising him.[18]

These six years were an important period in Edward's life as a businessman. He undertook the construction of a principal bridge across the Ohio River, a major project that required his attention for several years. He also acquired two skills of the greatest importance for his career. One was how to analyze a business operation, to spot its strengths and weaknesses, and to make the necessary decisions about its future. The other was how to accumulate considerable sums of money. Since such matters deserve fuller treatment, I will come back to these topics later in this chapter.

Edward, Mary, and their children occupied a series of furnished houses during the period with the Kentucky Central. First they lived in Louisville, Kentucky, at 321 East Jacob Street, and then in Covington, Kentucky, where they paid $60 a month rent. Later they moved to Cincinnati, first in the Walnut Hills area, and finally in the Mount Auburn district, at a rental of $125 a month. In Cincinnati they went to the First Presbyterian Church, renting two pews, and they placed three of their four children in private schools, at a cost of $200 a year for each child.[19]

Fortunately, the inventory of their possessions in these moves in 1885 and 1886 records Edward's books. Almost ten years earlier he had given up his first library as part of the financial settlement with his partner Franchot. In the meantime, he had accumulated a new library. He bought books wherever he could find them. In Cincinnati, for example, he bought from Robert Clarke and Company and had them mail him a few books even after he had left Cincinnati and moved on to San Francisco.[20]

Part of his new library was another collection—much like the one he had lost—of sets of the works of standard authors. It included Dickens, Scott, Shakespeare, James Fenimore Cooper, Poe, Meredith, Longfellow, and a host of other novelists and poets, mostly of the nineteenth century, for a total of 265 volumes at a cost of $725.

The other collection was larger, containing 1,644 volumes and costing $4,094.16. It too had standard nineteenth-century writers (Jane Austen, Emerson, Scott, Dickens, Ruskin, De Quincey, Kingsley, Lever, Charlotte Brontë, Reade, Tennyson, Shelley, Byron, Thackeray, Lamb, Macaulay, Coleridge, Poe), but it also contained a good sample of somewhat earlier writers (Samuel Johnson, Pepys, Pope, Bacon, Shaftesbury, Defoe, and more Shakespeare). A number of foreign writers (Balzac, Molière, Schiller, Erasmus, Montaigne) were also included, along with some specialty items (like Percy's *Reliques,* Chapman's *Homer,* Aesop's *Fables,* Hakluyt's *Voyages,* Josephus, Webster's *Speeches,* and Greek myth).[21] Edward was not yet buying rare books or collectors' copies but rather books that he wanted to read and to have around him in his house.

He was not home much, however. He had the use of a private railroad car and traveled a great deal on the lines and to Chicago, New Orleans, New York, and Oneonta. Family letters offer some pleasant glimpses of him when away from home. Marie Huntington, Willard's wife, wrote Harriet of seeing him at 65 Park Avenue; one evening they had a game of whist with Collis and Marie as partners against Edward and Belle. Marie happily reported that she and Collis won, and that the next "morning the first occurrence of any note was the presentation of a rose to yours truly from C. P. H." It was on that same visit that Marie and Willard's daughter Edith, age two and a half, made such a hit with the family. Belle "thought her lovely. She would jump Edith up on the table in the library and say to C. P. H., 'Collis, do look at those lovely eyes and cute mouth!' C. P. H. called or rather named her 'Polly Ann.' Clara thought she was lovely, and Archer [age fifteen] said when he grew to be a man who knows but she might be his wife. I feel proud to think I have had so many offers for her hand."[22]

Collis and Belle usually traveled in their private car, the *Oneonta,* with an extra car for servants. Edward sometimes met them en route and went part way, to New Orleans or Chicago, say, with them. On one of their trips, to Mexico City, Edward went as far as Durango, Mexico, where a celebration was held to honor Collis for having recently completed a railroad line to that city. Carrie, who was present, told Harriet that "the people can't do enough for him," the president of Mexico having sent his secretary of state, a special train, a band, and soldiers to welcome them. Carrie and Edward "went out on a little shopping but found everything closed in honor of the celebration. However, he has sent you a souvenir that I think you will like. It was made in Durango and will show you a specimen of their work." She concluded with this significant comment about Edward: "I never saw him have such a good time before. He left our party last night, and we all miss him ever so much." He was thirty-nine, she was twenty-eight, they were the closest of friends, and we can imagine other presumably happy occasions when they were together. "I never saw him have such a good time before. . . . We all miss him ever so much."[23]

Edward did not go with them all the way on their frequent trips to San Francisco. On April 1, 1890, for example, he met them in Huntington, West Virginia, took Carrie home to spend the night with his family, and the next day went as far as Chicago with the group before turning back.[24]

Nor did he go with them to Europe in the summers of 1887 and 1889. Belle, Collis, Archer, Carrie, Clara, and their several companions and servants were on the first voyage, which was a thorough sightseeing and museum trip to England and France. Collis told his brother-in-law, Edwin Gates, that "we have had a fairly good time since we left, and all the family have been well, and I believe have enjoyed themselves as well as it was possible to do on a junketing journey of this kind." He came to the essence of his own feeling about "vacations" when he concluded, "I must say, however, that I get more real solid satisfaction, I think, spending my nights at Throggs Neck [their summer place in Westchester County] and my days at the Mills Building [his offices in downtown Manhattan]."[25] Edward came to share this feeling, in his own terms.

The feature of the 1889 trip to Europe—with nearly the same cast of characters, except Carrie—was the wedding of Clara, Collis's adopted daughter and Mary's sister, to Prince Hatzfeldt of Wittenburg in the Brompton Oratory (Roman Catholic) in London. She settled on the prince, who was widely described in the popular press as dissipated, extravagant, debt-ridden, and a professional fortune hunter, after one or two other proposals, and Collis did some hard bargaining with the prince before fixing the size of the fortune for her marriage settlement.[26] This topic was to become a bone of contention between Edward and Mary after Collis's death.

On August 11, 1890, Edward's father, Solon, died at the age of seventy-eight. He had been relatively inactive for about fifteen years, after a career that had included running a general store, making carriages, and finally farming and handling real estate. The Oneonta newspaper concluded its obituary by saying that "Mr. Huntington was known in this community as a man of sterling integrity, of great perseverance, prudent dealings, industrious in his habits; and a natural leaning to free-handed justice made him respected by all with whom he came in contact."[27] The children all attended his funeral, Edward from Cincinnati, Leonora from Huntington, Willard and Marie from San Francisco, and Carrie from Oneonta. Solon's estate was modest, about $25,000 in bonds and a little real estate. Edward was chosen to handle the estate, and the other three children signed a power of attorney for him to hold all the property and pay the income to Harriet.[28]

He had already been handling her finances, actually, sending the income to her, and adding money of his own as needed. He had earlier reassured her about finances when his own funds were quite limited. "I want you to use what money you want to," he wrote her, "whether the interest is enough or not. Now, my dear Mother, I want you to feel at perfect liberty to call on me for money whenever you want it."[29]

Harriet's dependence on Edward was for more than money. At the end of a visit by Edward in Oneonta a few months after Solon's death, she lamented his departure and expressed the fear that she could no longer see him very often. He replied: "I am very sorry that you felt so badly when I left, and hope you will not feel this way, as I feel sure that we shall see as much of each other as heretofore. I shall return in a few weeks and will then see you again. And Belle says that she will bring you to California with them next year if you will come." He ended the letter "with a heart full of love for my Dear Mother, I remain as ever, Your affectionate son, Edward."[30] As it turned out, Harriet did spend the winters in California for the rest of her life, among her family and loved ones.

One other personal quality of Edward's began to become evident during this period—his capacity for strong and enduring friendships with persons outside of his family. W. L. Baldwin worked as Edward's secretary in Cincinnati for a year or so until he developed tuberculosis and went to Colorado Springs for a cure. He wrote many warm, friendly, witty letters back to "Mr. Huntington," whom he admired profoundly. The letters came about once a month; once after a longer interval, he wrote that "maybe you thought that someone in authority has ordered me to get off the earth, but I assure you that such is not the case; and even had it been, I should have made an almighty vigorous kick about obeying."[31] He felt on good enough terms with Edward to tease him as they wrote back and forth to one another. On hearing that the Kentucky Central had been sold, he wrote that "if you have to rustle for a job and spend your hard earned savings before getting one, just come to the Springs and I will pay your board bill till you get something."[32]

Another friend from this period was Epes Randolph, the chief engineer on the project of building the bridge across the Ohio. They admired each other immensely and formed a close friendship that lasted the rest of their lives.

This pattern of friendship developed in the years that followed. Edward formed one or two or three close friendships during each period of his life. They were always with men, and his closest friendships were with business associates and colleagues. Beyond his immediate family, he relied deeply on these friends most of all. And they relied on him.

The building of a railroad bridge over the Ohio River, from Covington, Kentucky, to Cincinnati, Ohio, occupied Edward's main attention for almost three years in the late 1880s. He began to assume principal responsibility for the project in the spring of 1886, and he continued that oversight until after the first train went across the bridge on Christmas Day, 1888.

This was not the first bridge across the Ohio in the area. The great suspension bridge for pedestrians and vehicular traffic had opened in 1866 after ten years of hard work, and there were other bridges as well. But the bridge Edward was involved in had a special importance for his railroad in that it provided a terminal in Ohio and greatly enhanced the railroad's value to a potential buyer. Collis had told Edward that he was eager to dispose of the Kentucky Central, and all of his other railroad properties east of the Mississippi, and it took remarkable zeal to complete this bridge so that the purpose could be accomplished on Collis's schedule.

Following the model he had used in building the Central Pacific Railroad, Collis established a contracting and building company to build the bridge, lay tracks, and do other construction. Edward had responsibility for it. During these years there was about one letter or telegram a day to the company from Collis and his associates in New York, with queries or directions. In April 1886, Edward was directed to get a charter for the bridge by buying up an old company for $2,500 or less; "try to get it for $500," he was told, then "run up to Frankfort and get the name changed." "If you have some bright lawyer, who is not too expensive, I think it would be well for him to attend to this matter." The next move was to buy the necessary right-of-way; Collis felt that it certainly need not cost the $105,000 asked and directed Edward to try for $75,000: "$80,000 seems a very high price to pay for the right of way there; but if that is the best you can do, we shall have to pay that. Do the best you can." He also exhorted his nephew to hurry up with bridge building while the days were long.[33]

That summer trouble arose with the citizens of Covington, some of whom opposed the bridge. Collis gave Edward a short course in public relations. The trouble, Collis said, was all being caused by "a few hostile persons" with "a manufactured opinion to prejudice the people." Edward's job was to "educate the people as to the real benefit and advantage this improvement will be to their city; then you will have no trouble in passing an ordinance allowing us to go through Covington on the time chosen by ourselves." Collis sent a letter to the chairman of the Citizens Committee in Covington for publication, and he urged Edward to get supporting letters from the governor and the U.S. senators; Edward succeeded, and Collis gravely commented that "such letters cannot help but do good."[34] The ordinance was passed.

The next difficulty was that the contractor who was building the bridge for them was too slow and expensive. Collis told Edward to get rid of him by making it unpleasant for him, either by creating unpleasantness between the contractor and Epes Randolph, their chief engineer on the project, or by writing that Randolph would quit if the contractor stayed. With another contractor, $200,000 to $300,000 could be saved.[35] They got rid of the contractor.

In the summer of 1887, Edward was formally appointed superintendent of construction under a resolution passed by the board of the Contracting and Building Company: "Resolved that H. E. Huntington of Covington, Ky be and he is hereby appointed Superintendent of Construction of this Company and that he is hereby charged with the supervision of all of the work now under construction, including the railroad between Ashland and Covington, Kentucky, known as the River Line, and also the bridge of the Covington and Cincinnati Elevated Railroad and Transfer and Bridge Company across the Ohio River, and the approaches thereto."[36]

As soon as Edward was appointed, he was urged to get the remaining foundations in. "I am disappointed at this," wrote Collis, "as it seems to me they should all have been in by this time. Please see that work on all the foundations is commenced immediately."[37] Later, he said he was fearful that Edward was "not pushing the work there with as much energy as you ought. They should work night and day on the Bridge."[38] And Collis wanted a telegram "every three days about the progress on the Bridge."[39]

But hopes were frustrated by a big flood on August 26, 1888, which swept away the uncompleted channel span. Of the 3.5 million pounds of iron in that span, 750,000 pounds went to the bottom of the Ohio River. The company responded by working even harder, using two hundred men on a night shift.[40]

Edward felt that Collis was dissatisfied with his efforts. Collis responded with a rather qualified denial: "You speak in the last part of your letter as though you thought I was dissatisfied with you. I have no doubt you have all the time done what you thought was the best thing to do, and I am not by any means certain that you have not been right; but, as I have said, the work has seemed to move with extreme slowness, and I hope that now it will be completed at the earliest day possible." A few days later Collis followed up this message with yet one more exhortation, setting forth another of his principles of success: "Nothing short of great energy, I am satisfied, will complete the bridge this year; but it can be done if all is done that can be done to accomplish it."[41]

A final obstacle arose in the form of an injunction obtained by hostile citizens against completion of the bridge. Collis told Edward to do what he could to "brush it away." His advice was an instructive account of his values: "As you know, I am very much averse to paying any blackmail, still if this is a case where something of that sort will relieve us of difficulties, I think it would be better to pay a little than to have the completion of the great Bridge delayed."[42] How Edward responded to this invitation to dishonesty we do not know. There is no record of any payment to brush away the injunction. The bridge was completed in the year. Collis's advice to Edward was, on almost all occasions, highly moral, even when it was sometimes in conflict with Collis's earlier practice. Collis told Edward, for example, to "be very careful not to use any money in the purchase of votes, as that is a thing I never allow to be done for anything, however much it may be for my interest financially."[43] (Certain United States senators and congressmen who had helped to pass various bills touching the transcontinental railroad must have turned over in their graves at this reflection.)

The bridge was 5,320 feet long. On December 25, 1888, the first train went across it, consisting of a locomotive, a tender, and six flatcars. The flatcars were full of men who had worked on the bridge; in the tender were Edward, Epes Randolph, M. E. Ingalls (president of the C & O), and some other railroad officials. "Mr. Ingalls' usually placid face broke into happy smiles; Huntington looked pleased; Randolph's swarthy complexion was all aglow." A few days later the first passenger train went across the bridge, and a dinner was held at the Queen City Club in Cincinnati as a tribute to Collis in appreciation from the city of Cincinnati. Edward was present, and Collis "gave a graceful speech."[44]

The financial records of Collis's railroads were as full and complete and exact as any careful accountant or auditor of the time could hope for. Edward learned the art of financial analysis during his years of running the Kentucky Central, and he turned this knowledge to his advantage throughout the rest of his business career.

Each disbursement and receipt was supported by a voucher approved by Edward, and a daily journal recorded all financial transactions. All transactions were organized in ledgers by account. Proposals, estimates, agreements, leases, and contracts were systematically filed after they had been seen by Edward, along with all incoming and outgoing correspondence, canceled checks and check stubs, receipts of all kinds, weekly and monthly payrolls, accounts payable and receivable, and so forth. The primary documents that constituted a record of the business all passed under his eyes. He learned to review at a glance this mass of documentary material—literally thousands of items each month—and to spot what seemed out of line. Since the company was grossing about $1 million a year, there were some worthwhile figures in the various categories to keep track of.

The bookkeepers provided him with weekly and monthly analyses of operations, which covered gross receipts, expenses, and net earnings. They were broken down by department and type of cost (payroll, construction, maintenance, and the like) and by source of income; and they gave comparative figures for the preceding week or month, or for the comparable period in earlier years. More elaborate annual analyses and balance sheets, which gave comparative figures for the preceding year, were prepared by the company auditor and given to Edward to review.[45]

Reports on projects that were under way—like a bridge, trestle, or rail line—were presented in graphic form. They were called progress profiles, and they revealed at a glance what part of the work had been completed and how much in each time period. Collis thought they were a little unnecessary and objected to having them prepared "if they cost any money."[46]

However, such analyses were congenial to Edward. His mind was analytical and methodical. He kept little notebooks in which he carefully recorded such things as his expenses and his accounts, and how much money had gone to each of their children.[47] More than that, he was a great keeper of lists, which he made out, usually in pencil, on odd pieces of paper and kept for future reference. Some were financial, citing payments he had made, or securities he owned and their yield. Later, the lists ran to books he had bought or wanted to buy and art works he had acquired or was interested in. So far as I know, he never made reminder lists.

Collis reviewed the Kentucky Central financial records in his office in New York, and he did not hesitate to question items that puzzled him.

For example, he asked Edward why he was paying ten cents a pound for wool waste when it was costing only seven cents a pound on the other roads.[48] In his review of a bill for fish plate springs, a device used to secure a nut in laying track, he noted that they had been

> charged at $35.00 a thousand, $3.50 per 100, or 3½¢ apiece. I have had one weighed, and it weighs 3 ounces, or considerably less than a quarter of a pound, which would be something over 14¢ a pound for the springs. Now I am buying steel fish plates for our Mexican road at something less than 1½¢ per lb.; so that I am inclined to think there must be some mistake somewhere about the cost of these springs. Besides, I don't think they are of much value in holding the nut. I notice that 120,000 have been bought for the K. C. and 90,000 for the C. O. & S. W. road, which is all news to me, and I will close by saying, 1st, that the price of them is 3 times what it ought to be; 2d, that we don't need them at all; and 3d, that I don't want any such important orders given for new things for our roads without being first informed of it myself.[49]

More often, Collis simply raised questions: What is this cement to be used for? Why are there so many bridge vouchers for timber, so much beyond the estimate? "I am surprised at the amount of your drafts on your Attorney account. What was this money used for? Please send me a detailed statement." Additional rails called for seemed more than were needed, but were all right if Edward thought them "important and necessary." What did Edward get from Rogers for the money paid him? "Perhaps I ought to understand your letter, but I do not."[50]

Sometimes Collis spotted the need for further details, as with the contract for a water line. The specifications for it were incomplete, and Collis went into great detail to outline the additional features that should be included in the contract.[51]

Edward was forthright in responding when he thought that Collis's observations were ill-timed or unfair. Collis complained, for example, about the large number of accidents on the Kentucky Central and declaimed that action should be taken to reduce the number. Edward responded that "the interval of time between this accident and the former one was just one year to the day, showing a remarkable freedom from the common run of such like damage to rolling stock. The matter of prevention of accidents is receiving careful attention on this Road."[52]

From responding to Collis's innumerable queries and complaints, Edward developed the ability to evaluate businesses through financial analysis. He also developed two other applications of this analytical skill. One was through personal examination of the physical properties involved. This practice he had of course begun when his primary responsibility was railroad construction, or looking after the Oneonta real estate of Solon and Collis. Now that his scope was broader and his facilities for travel and examination more extensive, he could devote more of his attention to looking at the properties and bringing his experience to bear on their problems and potentialities. He was pleased to be asked to examine the physical properties of the Chatteroi Road and the Kentucky Union railroad to see what their strengths and weaknesses were.[53] This view, by a sharp-eyed observer, could add a new dimension to the vision of the people in Collis's office in the Mills Building in downtown Manhattan.

Edward was also developing his ability to "size up" people. He mixed with colleagues at all levels of endeavor, laborers, foremen, middle managers, top executives, and owners of the property. He got along with people and was well liked. And he learned to make astute judgments about the capacities of those with whom he came in contact.

Edward came to share Collis's skill at financial analysis, but he went beyond Collis in his skill at personal examination of properties and at estimating the contributions that people were capable of making.

The other general skill that Edward was developing during this period was the art of making money grow. He had already gone through the first phase of saving a little out of whatever he earned and the second phase of investing his savings to get some return on his money.

In this third phase, he took steps toward learning how to accumulate larger sums of money. He began to buy and sell securities, particularly the stocks and bonds of companies that he was associated with or knew a good deal about. For example, he bought a thousand shares of C & O stock on October 12, 1885, and he continued to buy shares at prices of three to twenty-five cents a share. From time to time, he sold some shares and took his profits. In May 1890, for example, he sold five hundred shares at $25 a share, for a net profit of over $10,000.[54] (Of course he had to be nimble to sell when the C & O was not in one of its two bankruptcies.) Similarly, he accumulated Kentucky Central stock in small lots, beginning in 1885 and continuing over the next five years. On December 15, 1890, Edward was listed as the owner of 2,265 shares of the stock, out of about 65,000 issued and outstanding; thus he would have received, as his pro rata share of the L & N bonds, more than $100,000 in face value.[55] He made smaller investments in various other companies, such as Elizabethtown, Lexington & Big Sandy, Canda Manufacturing, the Short Route, South and North Alabama, even the Northern Railway of California. Most of his buying and selling was insider trading, based on some special knowledge, but it was also bold and astute. His basic security account was maintained in Collis's New York office; he had a cash credit of $27,000 at the end of September 1891 at 6 percent interest, though often it was a debit balance, also at 6 percent, from the purchase of securities. The German National Bank of Cincinnati also gave him, free, a large safe-deposit box for his personal use. By the end of this period, his net worth in securities was over $600,000. On March 1, 1892, he owned thirteen securities and several bank deposits; in all, they totaled $637,087.37. He had debts of $27,444.11—including $17,351.30 in his account with Collis—and a net balance of $609,643.26. He had taken good advantage of the flourishing business conditions of the 1880s.[56]

Like Collis, he was reluctant to advise anyone else about what securities to buy. On December 18, 1891, he answered a query from a friend in Louisville by saying, "I have always made it a point not to advise anyone as to investments, as, in case they should turn out poorly, I should feel under the circumstances responsible for the loss."[57] For his mother and others who needed money to spend, he took the cautious approach and bought bonds.

The other step he took toward the accumulation of large sums of money was buying and selling land. In 1886, he bought some lots in Clark County, Texas, jointly with John D. Yarrington, Belle's brother and a fellow superintendent on one of Collis's railroads.[58] In Kentucky he had learned how to estimate the current and future value of land and how to use an agent to buy land quietly without raising the price level. In 1886, he bought a number of lots in Covington, Kentucky, and sent the deeds in for his New York account to the value of $16,000.[59] He owned land in Covington under the name of the Central Covington Land and Improvement Company; when he moved away, a little of it was not sold and in 1903 lawyers were still trying to straighten out the problems of ownership.[60] When Collis was purchasing Kentucky land in 1890, Edward gladly accepted an offer of a share in it: "I would like to have an interest with you in these lands, as I had already sent out parties to purchase for me."[61]

This strategy of investing by buying and selling land was to open up almost endless possibilities for Edward in the future.

By 1891, the interesting opportunities for Edward in the Kentucky area had pretty much come to an end. The Kentucky Central had been sold and the new management was getting ready to take it over. The construction of the big bridge and its approaches and the small rail lines in the vicinity had been completed. And Collis had declared his intention to dispose of all of his railroad properties east of the Mississippi and to focus his interest on California. If Edward was to continue to be a business associate of Collis's, the natural thing would be for him to go to California in some capacity or other.

An early decision to this effect was made by the newspapers. On July 7, 1891, Cincinnati papers published a report that Edward was to become general manager of the Southern Pacific Railroad on September 1, 1891, with headquarters in San Francisco, at a salary of $50,000 per year. On July 9, the *San Francisco Examiner* repeated the story on the basis of a telegraphic dispatch from Cincinnati. They added an interview with Charles F. Crocker, one of the principal owners of the SP, who said that he knew nothing about it. Crocker's further (and temperate) remarks are of interest as an early view of Edward from the San Francisco Bay area before he had ever been there:

> The H. E. Huntington mentioned is a kinsman of C. P. Huntington. He has for several years been the manager of C. P. Huntington's rail-

road interests in Kentucky and Virginia and has been very successful with them. Mr. Huntington has a high estimation of his ability as a railroad manager and has spoken to his associates of the Southern Pacific [Crocker, Stanford, and the Hopkins interest] of him as if he valued his services very highly. Except as C. P. Huntington's manager he has never been very well known in the railroad world. It is the general opinion among those who understand the situation of affairs at Fourth and Townsend streets [the SP headquarters] that A. N. Towne, who has so successfully filled the position of General Manager, would be the last man with which the Southern Pacific Company, and particularly Mr. Huntington, would wish to dispense.

On July 14, Edward directed the following letter to the editor of the *Examiner,* which they printed to "set at rest a rumor that has been perturbing the vicinity of Fourth and Townsend streets for some time past": "Please correct statement in the Examiner of the 9th that I shall accept a position with the Southern Pacific Company on September 1st. There is not a particle of truth in the report. H. E. Huntington."

Rumors and false reports often have a life of their own, and a considerable amount of cleanup work remained for Collis to do in order to keep the peace. He wrote to A. N. Towne on July 14 to reassure him that he was pleased with Towne's work, that Towne would not be supplanted, and that the idea of a $50,000 salary was preposterous. He went on to speak of his future plans for Edward: "My nephew is now manager of some roads that I have on this side of the Mississippi which I propose to sell and being a very valuable man and very much younger than myself—for that matter yourself—I have thought that he might be made very useful in California and if he ever should come out there— although as yet no arrangements have been made for him to do so—I hope he will prove a valuable man to the owners of the property and a pleasant companion to all the officers of it, if he ever should go out." Although expressed with the utmost vagueness, Collis's intentions for Edward's future were doubtless clear enough to Towne, as they presumably were to Collis.

Collis wrote several other letters to principal persons in California. He wrote a long letter to Leland Stanford on July 18 to reassure him that he would never take any important action without consulting the directors. He ended by saying that "my nephew, both mentally and physically, is a very able man, and for his years and experience is I believe as good a railroad man as I know; but he has not had sufficient experience to take the place of either Mr. Towne or Mr. Stubbs." Collis sent a full copy of this letter to Towne and another copy to the *Examiner*, where it was printed on August 2. He also wrote fully on the subject to W. H. Mills, the head of the SP land department, on July 18, to Stubbs, the SP traffic manager, on July 25, and to the editors of the *San Francisco Wave* on July 30.

Collis also wrote to Edward in Cincinnati on July 22 and enclosed "a clipping which I have not read, but have seen others of like tenor. One or two of the papers seem to have got their information in Cincinnati. Of course no particular harm has been done, but I would rather there would not have been so much said about it as it is premature and would be in the way of doing hereafter what we might all think it was best to do."[62]

Collis was successful in quieting the anxieties in San Francisco. In the course of the following winter, the decision was made privately that Edward should in fact go to California. On February 17, 1892, Edward wrote from Cincinnati to his cousin Henry Saunders in Oneonta that "I have decided to make my future home in California and will leave for there about the first of the month. I shall not, however, take my family there until late in the Spring."[63]

And so it happened. Edward was in California by April 1892. The directors of the SP met on April 6, and the following printed announcement was issued by that company in San Francisco on April 20, 1892:

NOTICE

Mr. H. E. HUNTINGTON is hereby appointed First Assistant to the President, representing him in his absence, and with such special duties as may be assigned to him from time to time by the President.

His office will be at Fourth and Townsend Streets, San Francisco, California.

C. P. HUNTINGTON
President.[64]

Six

GOING TO CALIFORNIA
1892–1894

IT WOULD BE HARD TO IMAGINE a more difficult position than the one Edward came into in April 1892 as first assistant to his uncle Collis, the president of the Southern Pacific Company in San Francisco. The company was the largest and most powerful business enterprise in California, and it was the object of intense admiration and violent antagonism. The four principal owners of the company had come to be generally hostile to one another, and the main officers of the company aligned themselves with one or another of the owners and extended the antagonisms throughout the staff. The newspapers and magazines kept the reading public fully informed of the doings in the headquarters building at Fourth and Townsend streets, especially of rumors that could be made to suggest wrongful or blameworthy acts.

The Southern Pacific Company was the holding company for steam railroads such as the Central Pacific, Southern Pacific, and other smaller lines and for various other operations, like a land company. By 1892, the corporate enterprise had—after many vicissitudes—attained a state of wealth and power, following thirty years of construction, development, manipulation, and corruption on the part of the owners. The Central Pacific, formed in 1861, succeeded—after almost unbelievable problems with financing, labor, politics, and disharmony among the owners—in completing its part of the transcontinental railroad to join the Union Pacific at Promontory Point, Utah, in 1869. The owners averted disaster in the 1870s by expanding their lines, buying small and large railroads—including the Southern Pacific in 1868, before its lines had even been built—and refinancing their properties. By 1877, they had a monopoly on transportation in California. They controlled 2,340 miles of track, or 85 percent of all the railroad lines in the state, and all the important lines in the San Francisco and Los Angeles areas. By the 1880s, their railroads had opened up a large part of the state for agricultural and commercial development, and the operations had become financially successful. The owners became very wealthy. To centralize control and increase their power, they formed the Southern Pacific Company in 1884 and 1885 as a holding company for their many enterprises and incorporated it in Kentucky as presumed protection against local political attack.

When Edward came to San Francisco, of the principal original owners—Collis, Leland Stanford, Charles Crocker, and Mark Hopkins—two had already died (Hopkins in 1878 and Crocker in 1888). But their interests were kept together and represented, in the case of Crocker by his son Colonel Charles F. Crocker, and in the case of Hopkins by his widow, who died in 1891, and her second husband, Edward T. Searles. In actuality, the Hopkins interest was controlled by two New York lawyers, Thomas H. Hubbard and Thomas E. Stillman, who were friendly to Collis.

Leland Stanford had been the president of the Southern Pacific Company since it was organized in 1884, while being at the same time U.S. senator from California. He had been governor from 1861 to 1863 and was often still referred to as "Governor." Collis felt that Stanford had put politics and personal ambition above business, and he managed a meeting of the principal owners in 1890 in which he contrived, with the help of the Hopkins interest, to have himself elected president in place of Stanford. There were various smoldering animosities from the past, notably Collis's feeling that Stanford had shown at least bad faith in allowing his name to be put before the Republican caucus for the post of U.S. senator—and then chosen by the state legislature, according to their discretion and in accordance with law—over A. A. Sargent, an earlier incumbent, who was sure that he had been promised the railroad's support.

On assuming the presidency in 1890, Collis issued a long statement that included promises that were taken to be derogatory allusions to Stanford. "In no case will I use this great corporation," announced Collis, "to advance my personal ambition at the expense of the owners, or put my hands into its treasury to defeat the people's choice and thereby put myself in positions that should be filled by others."[1] Virtually every newspaper in California made a big story out of the statement and pontificated on the subject in editorials. Harrison Gray Otis of the *Los Angeles Times,* for example, sent a telegram in his usual bombastic style to his correspondent in San Francisco, Colonel J. H. ("Jayhawker") Woodard saying, "Huntington bomb shell is a stunner. The strongest utterance of the decade. Give us big letter traversing the ground completely."[2]

Stanford was incensed and demanded an investigation. Charles F. Crocker prevailed on Collis to write a retraction, and Collis prepared a sort of sententious apology that received little notice. A measure of public peace was restored, but the underlying resentments continued to fester.[3]

When Collis was elected president in 1890, Charles F. Crocker was elected first vice-president; A. N. Towne, the general manager, was made second vice-president; and J. C. Stubbs, the traffic manager, was made third vice-president. All of them were made directors of the company. It was to them and to W. H. Mills, head of the SP land company and nephew of Mark Hopkins, that Collis mainly addressed himself in letters from New York to try to put the company in the order he thought it should have.

A few passages from this correspondence suggest the situation in the SP headquarters in 1892 and just before that time. Collis wrote to Towne that Crocker had been "weak and vacillating and I do not propose to let him stand in the way of the future prosperity of the great properties that I in part control."[4] To Mills he said that "perhaps Mr. Crocker is doing as well as any young man will do brought up as he was by a rich father. He seems always to be anxious to get away early in the afternoon to the Clubs and, as I am told, leaves the Club for other places soon after the shadows of night have covered the city; but in that I suppose he only follows the example of his illustrious progenitor."[5] Later Collis told Mills that he thought Crocker was putting out articles against him, and Mills later told Collis that Crocker was in a conspiracy to incite political problems against the company, and he doubted Crocker's mental health.[6]

Crocker also objected to Collis. He complained that Collis had leased a piece of property for half of what he could have gotten and referred to Collis's "constant complaint that no one on this side makes a good bargain. I ask you in all seriousness, if the continuation of such practices will not prove detrimental to our interests, as showing that there is no one here with authority to transact business, for my usefulness is gone when people understand that if they cannot get what they want from me, they may always rely upon you."[7] Later, Crocker wrote to Collis objecting to the extension of the Mexican railroad: "I have invariably raised objections to the construction of this extension, and have told you that I could not be persuaded to withdraw these objections."[8] Collis replied, "I can hardly say that I am surprised [by your objection] for I do not remember any work of considerable importance since the death of your father that you have not opposed. [You oppose] I think more from habit, than from reason."[9] When Crocker ordered Mills to terminate the SP subsidy to the *Bulletin* and the *Call* on the grounds that they were attacking Stanford, Mills appealed to Collis, who sent a telegram to Crocker not to stop the subsidy without the approval of the board and the president; Crocker replied with an irate letter to Collis refusing to allow his money to be used to slander him and Stanford.[10]

Difficulties had also developed between Collis and Stanford. Earlier, the Stanfords had felt very close to Collis. When their beloved son died in Florence in 1884, Stanford immediately cabled Collis in New York: "Our boy after an illness of three weeks left us this morning for a better world."[11] And Mrs. Stanford had earlier turned to Collis for support when her husband had shown signs of illness, saying, "I feel there is no one aside from his own family who is more tenderly attached to him, and no one who appreciates what the loss of his services in the future would be to all parties most intimately connected than yourself."[12] Now, after 1890, things were different.

Collis wrote to Towne that he and Stanford "have never had any particular disagreement about business. He is no business man, as we all know; a very pleasant man to meet in board meetings and has always done just about what I wanted to have him, as he knew himself that he was not giving the business the attention that I was and that I was perfectly acquainted with all the details of it."[13] Stanford though "politically bad" was "not a fool" and was popular in corrupt circles; "all the press that is venal and all the people in the State who are venal—and there are certainly more than I wish there were—would like to have Gov. Stanford at the head again; for money filters through his business affairs with as little notice or knowledge on his part of its waste as water through an old cullender."[14]

Toward the end of his second year as president, Collis summarized his views on the SP and politics, and on Crocker and Stanford, in a letter to W. H. Mills:

> When I was elected President, the Company was so impregnated with rotten politics that it is hardly to be expected that I would in the two years of my incumbency be able to extricate it entirely from the evil influences which had so firm a hold on it; but I am doing it as fast as I can and think I have great reason to feel encouraged that there has been so much done and to feel that the time will soon come when we will be able to steer entirely clear of these political complications. Mr. Crocker is weak. Mr. Stanford is politically bad, although there are many good things about him, but he is so controlled by his ambition for place and power that I have little hope of ever getting him disconnected from the very worst phases of American politics. I do believe that I will get the railroad out of it and I will get out of the Company all those who are disposed to use offices as political caucus rooms, or the influence of the road to put themselves and friends into places that they are unfit to fill. You little know how strongly I feel upon this subject.[15]

Collis had support from friends who felt as he did about Crocker and Stanford. Ben C. Truman, for example, was blunt. After quoting Crocker as saying that Collis was condescending toward Crocker, and that Stanford was decent and dignified while Collis was not, Truman said of Crocker, "I would like to thrash the sore-eyed, small-brained, contemptible cur."[16] In another letter, Truman concluded that "if I could not make a living I would kill myself, but I would kill that son of a bitch Fred Crocker first."[17]

The other side had its public say also. J. M. Bassett, a former division superintendent of the SP and supporter of Stanford, wrote a series of signed letters, some of them addressed to Collis and all of them published in Bay area papers. Here is a typical excerpt from his letter in the *Oakland Enquirer* of July 31, 1891. Collis

is cold-blooded, grasping, avaricious, soulless, and in the attainment of his ends, unscrupulous, but he gets there. It is due something to himself, but largely to those of his associates with whom he has quarreled that he is so unpopular both with his employees and the public generally. He might redeem himself, but as he has neither the disposition nor the inclination, it is not at all probable that he will.

The uniform bad luck which has attended the Company since the day Huntington was elected president, has soured and embittered him, and created in the minds of many stockholders the impression that retributive justice is camping on his trail.[18]

Bassett and others kept up the attack. In 1892, Bassett told Collis, in a published letter, that "you are, by nature and inclination, disqualified from discharging your job. You have changed the position of the company from a fairly good one to one of the most generally detested and universally execrated of all corporations on the face of the globe. Your employees openly fear you and privately hate you."[19]

The spirit of dissension that prevailed among the owners was mirrored, by controversy and ill will, among the company officials. For example, A. C. Hutchinson, the head of the Atlantic Division based in New Orleans, complained to Collis that Stubbs—the third vice-president, based in San Francisco—always rode roughshod over his subordinates.[20] And Stubbs complained to Collis that the general managers were not carrying out his orders and were consulting directly with Collis.[21]

The California newspapers and magazines entered the fray with a vengeance. Their feature stories, cartoons, and editorials often had Collis as the main target. They made special fun of his dramatic performances in his appearances before congressional committees, and mocked him as the "millionaire without a memory." Ambrose Bierce used his spectacular skills against Collis, as in his witty piece including a letter from C. P. Buntington to the Chairman of the Committee on Buntingtonisms of the Grand Jury of San Francisco.[22] These antagonisms are summed up in Frank Norris's *The Octopus: A Story of California* (1901) and in the writings of popular historians, who for decades presented the SP and its owners as models of corruption and greed.

The true story was actually much more complex. But it is clear that when Edward arrived in California in April 1892, he entered a situation fraught with dangers for the nephew and surrogate of the president of the Southern Pacific.

When Edward first came to California, he traveled with Collis in his uncle's private railroad car. They followed the southern route through New Orleans and San Antonio and made an overnight stop in Los Angeles. J. DeBarth Shorb was an old friend of Collis's, and they spent the night in the San Gabriel Valley at Shorb's house on the San Marino Ranch. It was Edward's first night in California, and he was charmed by the house and the setting. "I thought then," he said later, "that it was the prettiest place I had ever seen." He was entranced by the beauty of the San Gabriel Valley, and he stood there drinking in the loveliness of the whole scene.[23]

There is a double irony about this experience. First, it was this exact area in the San Gabriel Valley that had specially appealed to Collis's first wife, Elizabeth, and where she had wanted to buy a place; in fact, S. J. Ross of San Gabriel offered Collis eighteen hundred acres with orange trees, vineyards, and walnut groves for $250,000 in 1877 to fulfill Elizabeth's wish, but Collis did not buy.[24] The next year, Shorb—who wanted "to free myself of debt and get some rest"—offered Collis his San Marino Ranch, including an oak grove of two hundred acres, for Elizabeth; but again Collis did not buy, though he responded that "I do think your country has some of the finest places on the face of the globe."[25]

The second irony is that it was this same San Marino Ranch that Edward himself bought ten years later. And the site of the Shorb house in which he spent his first night in California became the site of the mansion that he erected, now the Huntington Art Gallery.

But this experience in 1892 was a one-night stand, and the travelers were off the next day for San Francisco. The annual meeting of the directors of the SP on April 6 "passed off pleasantly and without friction" as Collis reported to Edwin Gates back in New York. In the election of directors, Edward took the place of Willard, thus supplanting his younger brother as a director of the SP.[26] Willard had earlier been eased out of his office in the headquarters building in favor of Stubbs; Crocker wrote to Collis that Willard had very little to do after the consolidation of several companies of which he was secretary and that he spent hardly any time in his office but followed his personal interests outside the building.[27] Edward felt some loyalty to his brother, however, and declined the offer that Collis made him of taking Willard's place as director of the Market Street Railway and some other smaller companies.[28]

On April 23, Collis had his annual dinner for the principal officers of the SP at the Palace Hotel in San Francisco. This was his fifth such event, and there were eleven courses and eleven wines. Edward and Willard were both present, Mills served as toastmaster, and Collis gave a speech about how to treat those who are "under you"—in a word, justly.

Collis stayed only a few weeks in San Francisco before he and Belle returned to New York. Soon he finalized the purchase of his first residence in San Francisco, and on May 2 he bought the magnificent Colton house on Nob Hill at California and Taylor streets. That is, he bought it in his wife's name and directed that the down payment of $77,500 be paid out of her account with the SP, with the balance of the $275,000 price coming from her resources also.[29] (Doubtless Collis was aware of and not troubled by the irony of buying the mansion built by his ex-associate David Colton, who had been involved in shady dealings for Collis and whose widow Collis had shortchanged. The candid "Colton Letters" to Colton from Collis and the other associates had discredited the railroad and its owners when they were printed in 1883.) In New York, Collis was busy supervising the construction of his own pretentious mansion on Fifty-seventh Street and Fifth Avenue, though the many suggestions by him and Belle were mainly annoyances to his architect, George Post.

Edward was left on his own in San Francisco, but Collis was always at hand with an advisory letter or telegram. If no specific instructions were needed, Collis was ready with a high principle in the form of a cliché or a moral. On June 2, Collis wrote to Edward, "I have nothing special to write but I am glad you are out there, as you will find plenty to do. There is very much to do, but it will be necessary for you to make haste slowly: in other words, to be very sure of everything before you move." Edward replied in kind: "As yet I do not find my time very fully occupied, but presume that I shall soon get into harness."[30]

On the same day that Collis told Edward that he had nothing special to write, he wrote him another letter asking Edward to take an active part in local politics on behalf of the SP. He urged Edward to talk with W. W. Stow, an SP lobbyist in Sacramento, and with Mills and Towne; "these three have my entire confidence." He concluded, "We are out of politics, but not so far out as to see the demagogues and 'heelers' destroying our property, without making an effort to save it. In short, we expect to fight the spoilsmen." Edward did have several talks with Stow, and in writing to Collis he mentioned the public mistrust of the SP; Collis flared back with the indignation of the just man accused of injustice: "I note what you say of the people of San Francisco—more particularly the press—crying out against the Railroad. They are always crying out against something and some of them are almost continually making efforts to tear down some proper and legitimate interest; but so long as we conduct our railroad business as we have heretofore, I am sure they will not be able to harm us to any considerable extent."[31]

The political discussions went back and forth among Edward, Stow, Mills, and Towne. M. H. DeYoung, with his *San Francisco Chronicle* and his thwarted political ambition, helped to create dissension by his demands and his objections to Stow and others. So it went for several months.[32]

At last, in November 1892, Edward told Collis that he did not want to act for the company in political matters: "As I told you, I am not familiar with, nor fitted for that kind of work. I do not want you to think that I wish to shirk any duty, but believe it is best that Mr. Mills, or someone else who is well acquainted with most of the members of the Legislature should attend to this matter."[33] About this time Collis finally set a salary for Edward: "I have written to Mr. Smith [the SP treasurer], by the way, to pay you $10,000 a year salary from September 1st."[34] It was the largest salary he had ever made.

Edward had made a good impression on his associates even when dealing with work that he did not feel himself fitted for. Soon after Edward had bowed out of the political work, Stow wrote to Collis that "H. E. Huntington is a very level headed man—very much more of a man than I at first supposed him to be. He is well spoken of by every one with whom he comes in business contact. You did a wise and good thing for the S.P. when you placed him in the San Francisco office."[35] Edward did not himself speak well of all with whom he came in business contact. He wrote to Collis soon after his arrival that "I don't like to speak disrespectfully of our first Vice President [Crocker], but think that for a fool he 'takes the cake.' I often regret that you did not do what you first intended to [i.e., have him be only a director], as I believe that the Company is damaged every day by his connection with it. I am getting along very well with him, but learn nothing from him." Collis responded that "I do not quite understand him, but I hope you will work pleasantly with him and very likely you will get along better. I think that frequently he says no because he simply does not understand the thing. Do the best you can with him."[36]

Mary and the children had come to San Francisco before the summer of 1892. Housing was scarce and expensive, and they stayed for almost a year at the Hotel Richelieu at a cost of a little over $500 a month for room and board. Finally, in June 1893, Edward and Mary bought a family house that served their needs. It was at 2840 Jackson Street, on the northeast corner of Jackson and Broderick, on a lot 115 by 120 feet, and comprised three stories with twenty-four rooms. The ballroom was forty by fifty feet, with a parquet floor and decorated ceilings; the wainscoting in the dining room was natural oak. It had recently been built by Herman Hyneman, a Frenchman who decorated and furnished the house with chairs, couches, and carpets that were described as "sumptuous." It was a fine house, though not nearly so pretentious as the house Belle and Collis had bought the year before. Edward paid

$50,000 for the furnished house—$10,000 of it in cash, with the rest in notes, endorsed by Collis and Towne and payable over the next year. In July 1893 they moved in, and Edward immediately sent his new home address to Collis for its business relevance: "I write you as you may wish to send important telegrams to the house Sunday, or at night." Their friends in Cincinnati sent them a barrel of the choicest of cut glassware, carefully packed; the newspapers noted that doubtless "during the coming season there will be some pleasant gatherings in the new Huntington mansion. Mrs. Huntington dispensed an agreeable hospitality in her old home in Cincinnati, and she will certainly take advantage of the opportunity to entertain here which the debut of her daughter and the possession of so admirable a house will afford." But not with the help of the choice cut glassware. Edward opened the barrel on the afternoon of its delivery: "He found just two glasses. All the rest of the costly and handsome present had been broken."[37]

In the meantime, Edward was meeting new people and traveling around California. He went to Los Angeles in July 1892 with two railroad associates and met with a group of thirty businessmen. "It seems to me," he reported to Collis, "that if our people could mix a little more freely with the business men, it would be a good thing for the Company." He hoped that Collis would "have time to spend a few days in Los Angeles & vicinity, as I believe it would do us good for you to meet those people." And a branch road to Riverside was desirable, he thought. In the next month, Edward reported on the number of fruit trees in Los Angeles County and the commercial advantage of extending their lines in Southern California.[38]

He also made a trip in July 1892 to Santa Cruz on a special train with a group of other railroad officials. The local paper was ecstatic about Edward's impact on those he met. The trip through the Santa Clara Valley, over the Santa Cruz Mountains, and through Powder Mill Canyon was especially enjoyed "by Mr. Huntington, who, unlike the others, had never seen this part of the country which is now his home. Mr. Huntington, whose residence was in Cincinnati until March last, came to California then, and has now brought his family, expecting to reside permanently in San Francisco." There was a beautiful lunch, and the leading citizens came to meet the guests, "who wield so powerful an influence in all matters pertaining to the welfare of the State." In particular, "Mr. Huntington won golden opinions from his new acquaintances; his fine face and figure would make him conspicuous in any assemblage, while his frank and genial manner gave an assurance that closer acquaintance would surely crystallize into hearty friendship for the man himself without reference to the high position he holds." There were toasts, and when it came time for Edward to respond, he did what he always did out of modesty or shyness, or a sense of weakness in this department—he designated a colleague to respond for him, even if only to express "Mr. Huntington's pleasure in meeting so many friendly faces here."

The paper also devoted its editorial in the same issue to their "first impressions" of Edward as "not the kind of man who will need to be 'naturalized' to be a thorough Californian." He was seen to possess, naturally, "that force and breadth of character we are pleased to designate, as to an extent distinctive of true Californians, and as a citizen he is destined to be an invaluable acquisition to our commonwealth." Having made him a "true Californian," the editorial went further in an estimate of his future achievements: "Californians may count upon the fact that when they have to deal with H. E. Huntington, affairs will be in the hands of a gentleman with a broad grasp, of inherent strength of character, sound judgment and regard for the right. Mr. Huntington is certainly a man well qualified to cope with practical problems."[39] (A mother could hardly have said it better—or more sincerely.)

Edward made an occasional little trip with Mary and the children. In June 1892, they went to Monterey and stayed at the Del Monte Hotel; in February 1893 they went with the Mills family for two weeks to Los Angeles and Riverside; Mills took his secretary along "for the purpose of writing some matters for publication which I have not time to write" in San Francisco.[40] Edward went back to Southern California again in March with S. T. K. Prime, an authority on crop reports, a keen observer of the rural scene, and a person well informed about California. Back in San Francisco, Edward became a member of the Pacific Union Club in June 1892 for professional reasons.

Through most of his life, Edward had spells of illness often described as "bad colds" that lasted a week or two or more. He would have to stay in bed or at home for at least a few days before he could resume work. In January 1893 he suffered from a severe attack that lasted several weeks and troubled his colleagues; Mills and Stow each wrote to Collis about the illness, and Collis asked them to try to get Edward to "take care of himself." Collis himself wrote to Edward on January 14 that "I have telegraphed Mr. Schwerin [an SP official] to see that you take care of yourself. I think you are a little careless sometimes and I thought it would be a good idea to have a good man like Schwerin take care of you. Still, you can assist him very much in this matter, which I hope you will do." On January 25, Mills was still concerned about Edward, who was "much better, but he is far from well," as Mills wrote to Collis. "His sickness is a serious thing to the affairs of the Company. He is acquiring a very intelligent view of things. He has a clear head, which he keeps level under all circumstances, is not disposed to get into a panic, and hence his counsel in great emergencies is worth something." On Friday, February 3, Mills sent Collis a telegram that Edward was "far from well" but that he was leaving on Monday, February 6, for Southern California. In response, that same day Collis sent Edward another fatherly admonition: "Don't be so foolish again as to go out to work before you are able to do so." The physician told Mills, who reported it to Collis on January 12, that Edward "had been threatened with pneumonia" and that he might have some affliction "of the heart, which is operating against his speedy recovery."[41]

Just what kind of illness this was we do not know; presumably, it was some kind of viral attack. It is well to bear in mind that he had had these attacks periodically from the time of his youth, and that they continued for the rest of his life. He had another attack toward the end of the year. In the latter part of November, he was confined to his bed for almost two weeks. On December 2 he was feeling better but found "that I will have to 'favor' myself a little for a while." Nevertheless, he was planning to leave on December 7 or 8 for a ten-day trip "over the lines."[42]

Edward created a notable impression on many of his business associates. Within his first couple of years in California, there was great enthusiasm for him and, so far as I have been able to discover, no hostility. He got along well with Mills, Towne, Stubbs, Stow, Crocker, and DeYoung. Mills, for example, wrote to Collis on January 18, 1893, that it would be "a fortunate day for the Southern Pacific Company when Mr. H. E. Huntington has large influence in the management of things here. He has notions that a great instrumentality of transportation can be wielded in such a way as to make itself signally useful in the growth of a country and in the development of its industrial resources, and make itself popular and of profit to the proprietors." In May, Mills wrote Collis that "Mr. H. E. Huntington himself is the best man for your affairs that you have ever had in California. There is a manliness about him that people recognize at once, and an absence of the timidity which leads some of your men here to exaggerate all dangers and to incur expenses prompted by unjustifiable apprehensions."[43]

Collis felt complete confidence in Edward. The governor of California, H. H. Markham, wrote to Collis that "I wish you would intimate to me, confidentially, to whom I can confer as your representative," and Collis replied that he should consult with his nephew, H. E. Huntington: "If you do not know my nephew, I would like to have you become acquainted with him. I am sure you will be pleased with him, as I know he will be with Gov. Markham."[44]

Sometimes the praise for Edward came from further away. The *New Orleans Daily States* for December 11, 1892, commended his appointment in San Francisco and quoted S. F. B. Morse, the passenger traffic manager in New Orleans, as saying that Huntington "is a splendidly equipped railroad official—in every department."[45] The *Los Angeles Times* for May 2, 1893, credited Edward with the SP's more aggressive new policies in extending its lines. "The younger Mr. Huntington is known to be enterprising, ambitious, shrewd and capable, and his friendly feeling for the State has already been made evident heretofore. He has evolved some new prospects, which if sanctioned by those in higher power, will add to the glory of the Company and benefit not only that corporation but certain sections of Southern California as well." The story concluded that "even the Southern Pacific now has faith in Southern California."[46]

The year 1893 was very difficult for Edward, the SP, and the entire business community. It was a year of perhaps the worst financial panic that the United States had ever experienced. And the economy suffered from a major depression for the rest of the decade.

By June 1893, money had become very tight in San Francisco as well as in the rest of the country, and banks were failing. Edward was in constant conference with Crocker and Stanford about handling the company finances. They stopped all building and other optional expenses, and the three of them agreed that they needed all the money they received and could borrow locally simply to pay their bills and wages. They could send no money to New York to pay the interest on bonds and other indebtedness. As a result, the company could not pay the July 1 bond coupons and some additional bills. Toward the end of July, it fell to Edward to try to persuade the railroad employees to wait until August 15 for their pay. First the men in Sacramento agreed; then those in Bakersfield, which Edward considered the "hotbed" of problems; and finally those in Los Angeles "after a little trouble." On July 26 Edward sent a telegram to Collis telling of the success. In June, Collis had begun negotiations with Speyer and Company in New York for a line of credit of $5 to $10 million—with good collateral, 6 percent interest, and a commission—to see them through the panic. Banks were closing everywhere, and many railroads failed—the Philadelphia and Reading in 1893, and in 1894 the Erie, Northern Pacific, and Union Pacific.[47]

Collis urged his relatives, such as his nephew Willard, "to get out of debt as soon as you can and then keep out." Willard was not able to follow this advice, as he had gone deeply into debt to buy large tracts of undeveloped land from the old Spanish land grants near Paso Robles, Paso Robles Springs, and San Luis Obispo. One tract was four miles long and would require eleven miles of fencing. He wrote Harriet that he had had to pay only $17.50 an acre because he had bought so much, and that he expected to make $100,000 on one tract in five years, $200,000 in ten. His expectations were dashed by the panic and depression. He was unable to raise money by selling, and Collis reluctantly lent him another $10,000 to tide him over temporarily. But he was gradually forced to give up his land.[48] Willard soon afterward also lost his SP salary, at Crocker's insistence; Collis wrote Willard on May 9, 1894, to tell him that his salary would end with that month.[49]

Leland Stanford died in the midst of the panic, on June 21, 1893, and Mrs. Stanford wanted cash to settle his estate and pay off his bequests. She refused to sign any notes for the company or to use her portion of the company's securities as collateral for essential loans. Crocker also refused to allow his portion of the securities to be used as collateral. At the worst point in the panic, Crocker resigned as president of the Pacific Improvement Company, which held the securities that represented the major wealth of the four associates and their ownership of the SP. Edward was elected in his place. On July 14, 1893, Edward reported the facts succinctly to Collis: "Crocker resigned as President of the Pacific Improvement Company yesterday and I was elected President. I did not like to do this at the present time, but probably it is just as well."[50]

The panic also had a personal impact on Collis. The architect kept writing Collis about progress on the New York house; painters and contractors had completed their work, had not been paid, and needed their money. Collis thought about offering the unfinished house for sale at $1.5 million, but he was able to hang on and not sell it.[51]

The panic continued through the summer and autumn of 1893. The SP was on the verge of insolvency. The biggest topic in the company correspondence was how to borrow money to pay off debts and interest, to meet wages, and to pay current accounts. Financial affairs were at their worst in July and August; gradually, by December, they had improved.[52]

Edward had promised his mother that he would see her at least once a year, and he was sorry that Collis was not coming to San Francisco in the spring of 1893 so that he could bring her with him. He wrote Collis that he felt he must go to Oneonta to see her; "while I can not spare the time to leave here, I feel that it is a duty that I owe her." He hoped "to have her with me much of the time" in San Francisco when they got a house.[53] He left for Oneonta on April 25, and Collis asked him to come to New York for two or three days of consultation. By the middle of May, Collis was urging Edward to get back to San Francisco, as "there are important questions coming up there every day."[54]

Soon after Edward returned to San Francisco, he began to consolidate the street railways in San Francisco. The SP owned the main one, the Market Street Railway. The "consolidation" amounted to arranging through interested financiers to take over the next largest one, the Powell Street system, and to put them under a single management, with Edward in control. This they succeeded in doing. The newspapers regarded the result as "a big victory for H. E. Huntington and the Southern Pacific" though not necessarily a victory for the public, since the merger constituted the "formation of a gigantic monopoly which will have it in its power to dictate absolutely to the systems remaining independent."[55] It was about this time that Edward was first elected a director of Wells Fargo and Company.[56]

Edward came in for unfavorable attention of a more amusing nature in October 1893 when he said, in an interview in the *San Francisco Examiner,* "I have frequently said 'Godspeed the day when we shall have a competing line in San Francisco.'" The public perception was that the SP had thwarted every effort of other railroads to have a terminal in San Francisco. The *San Francisco Daily Report,* which had long favored a competing road, devoted an editorial of mock praise to the comment. "Gracious!" it began. "How we have misjudged that man! Henceforth we shall welcome H. E. Huntington as a friend and ally." The spoofing was carried on through the news story, with heavy fun being made of his wish for Godspeed. A multitude of examples was presented, like this one: "Hereafter when the Southern Pacific financiers in London and in New York and Boston step in to prevent the lending of money for building a competing road in California, we shall not be suspicious. No indeed—that is simply the Huntington way of wishing Godspeed to the enterprise."[57]

In December 1893, it became necessary to elect a president of the Central Pacific Railroad to take the place of the late Leland Stanford. Crocker had been first vice-president, but he declined to be considered for the top job and suggested Edward, who was duly elected on December 7. The major San Francisco papers gave a good deal of space to the story, and they all praised Edward. The *Chronicle* said that he "is on the most friendly footing with all the directors, and it is pretty safe to say that, largely through him, there is a much friendlier feeling among the various representatives of the Southern Pacific than existed at a time not so far distant as to have been forgotten." The *Call* lauded him for having organized the corporate headquarters and for being "a cautious, affable gentleman, in the prime of life [forty-three], and . . . not a 'dummy' financially. He possesses in large degree the faculty of getting results from his subordinates, but is never harsh or unnecessarily severe in his treatment of them." The *Examiner* took this election as a sign that "he will continue to be advanced to higher positions in the greater corporation, the Southern Pacific Company, as opportunity offers" and that he was, according to railroad men, slated to succeed Collis as president.[58] This was heady praise for a person who had been with the company for only about a year and a half, and in an environment that included much dissension.

Edward did not continue long as president of the Central Pacific. First, Crocker announced to Collis that the principal owners must discontinue their active business association and make a financial settlement among themselves. Then the foreign stockholders of the Central Pacific strenuously objected, through the London office of Speyer and Company, to the SP dictating policy for the Central Pacific. Speyer also expressed serious doubt about the financial strength of both railroads, and of Collis's personal financial situation; Speyer declined to handle any more of their securities under the current situation.[59]

Edward resigned as president of the Central Pacific in March 1894, and both he and Crocker resigned as directors. Isaac Requa, the head of the Oakland Bank of Savings, was elected to succeed Edward as director and president. It was an uneasy and unstable situation, and the newspapers took a grave view, the *Daily Report* editorializing that a receiver might have to be appointed for the SP.[60]

One danger was averted in April 1894. Representatives of the four principal owners of the SP met in San Francisco and agreed to work together and sign notes for financial support of the company. Gates was especially glad to hear this news because of the impact it would have in securities circles. Collis said it had been easy to accomplish: "We all got together and in a few minutes agreed to do what everybody knew before would have to be done."[61]

A different danger soon arose in the form of a national railway strike. The General Managers' Association of all twenty-four railroads centered in Chicago had begun in the late 1880s to try to gain uniform control of the economic status of all their employees, and Eugene V. Debs created the American Railway Union in response. When George Pullman discharged a large part of his sleeping-car company employees in May 1894 and reduced the wages of the remainder by 20 percent, a strike resulted. The Pullman Company closed its shops, and the union declared a boycott against any railroad that used cars made by the Pullman Company.

The strike commenced on June 23 in Chicago; by June 27, it had reached San Francisco. Edward sent a telegram that day to Collis: "I think we should make a fight to the finish and there is no doubt in my mind but what we shall succeed." The same day Collis sent a hardfisted telegram to Towne, commencing with his usual high principles and giving orders as to how to handle the strike:

> You know how much I would sacrifice to sustain our employees in any of their legitimate rights, so I hope you will explain everything to them fully, and if they then refuse to take out the cars, discharge every man who so refuses, and have it understood that the men so discharged will never again have a place with our Company. In this matter give no uncertain sound, as there will be no change from this order.

The next day, the union ordered a general strike against the SP. On June 29, Collis sent an optimistic telegram to Edward: "We will come out of this trouble all right. Think they will not keep us tied up much longer."[62] It was a poor prediction.

Also on June 29, the SP put its case before the public in a three-thousand-word letter signed by Edward and published first in the *San Francisco Examiner* and then in several other papers, and in a circular issued and distributed by the SP. He began by asserting that "a public journal is the only medium through which the truth may be known, right public opinion formed, and exact justice established." He argued that the boycott by the union of railroads using Pullman cars was unfair to the railroads and to the public interest; he drew analogies to a union whose members made locomotives or wagons or produced fruit and who prevented their product from being used or transported by all railroads. He raised the threat that the entire railway system of the United States might be put under the control of the coercive demands of any tiny factory, that perhaps the union might refuse to allow newspapers that had a labor dispute to be carried by the railroads, or that they might forbid railroads to transport individuals who were obnoxious to labor organizations. In short, the boycott was unfair, he argued, and it substituted force for law, and violence for peace and safety.[63]

Edward's letter did not receive a favorable reaction in the newspapers. The *Examiner*, in an editorial entitled "Mr. Huntington's Non Sequitur," declared that the trouble with this argument was that it was totally irrelevant. The *San Francisco Call* editorialized that the managers of the SP had "so narrow a sense of their legal and moral obligations to the public as to choose to serve the Pullman Company rather than to serve the public."[64]

The situation quickly got worse. Troops were called out on July 1 and 2, and there were riots on July 2 and 3. On July 2, another long letter signed by Edward was published in the *Examiner* and other papers, this one a little shorter at eighteen hundred words. It was filled with gratitude for the consideration given his earlier letter, praise for SP employees, an appeal to the community for sober thought, and an argument against making concessions to the union on unjust grounds.[65] This letter did not generate favorable editorial reaction; in fact it seemed to provide another opportunity for venting pent-up hostility. The *Call* objected to the parallels drawn in his letters: "It is with such hair-trigger arguments as this that the local manager defends the railroad policy which has temporarily paralyzed the industries of this State. The Southern Pacific has once again demonstrated its unfitness to perform the service of common carrier, except, possibly, in competition with a competing system under public control." The *Oakland Times* said that the "railroads are taking exactly the position, which Mr. H. E. Huntington argued so ably against in his statement of the 'railroad's side.' The railroads are asserting exactly the same pernicious and destructive principle which they denounced as so unjust."[66]

On July 2—the day on which his second letter to the newspapers appeared—Edward dispatched a long telegram to Collis urging him not to send any more conciliatory messages to Towne. "We are going to break this strike," he said, and "I have about all I can do to hold him [Towne] up now." He reported that Fillmore wanted to take back all ex-employees who reported for duty, but Edward was strongly "opposed to taking back those men that have burned our bridges and destroyed our property. . . . We ought not to take a step backward and make such concessions that we will hereafter regret them. . . . Five battalions of U.S. Artillery go from San Francisco to Los Angeles tonight."[67]

The next day, Edward sent a telegram to Collis that a mob of fifteen hundred or two thousand people in Sacramento had broken into the SP yards, captured a train, and switched the cars about. The National Guard was ordered out, and the troops en route to Los Angeles had reached Bakersfield.

The strike dragged on for a couple of weeks. Collis peppered Edward with advisory letters and telegrams from New York, Westchester, and Washington. On the whole, his advice was to phase out all union men from the company. Edward replied in kind; in one long telegram, in code, he asserted that "it is evident that in order to protect Interstate Commerce from strikes, the Government must afford to the railways adequate police protection," and he suggested that Collis try to get legislation enacted that would require all engineers, firemen, brakemen, conductors, and switchmen to get a U.S. license after examination and prohibit them, like soldiers, from leaving their posts, banding together, or striking.[68]

SP employees were told to return to work by 4:00 P.M. on July 6 or consider themselves terminated. At a mass meeting in San Francisco on July 7, resolutions were passed against the SP. On July 11, an SP train was derailed by the removal of a rail and tie on a trestle near Sacramento, and five people were killed. Harry Knox, the leader of the Sacramento strikers, was arrested on July 13. Edward was personally threatened with bodily harm. A man named A. J. Collins was heard to say that he would cut H. E. Huntington to pieces; he took to following him from his home on Jackson Street to his office and tried to force his way into the office. The SP detectives on the job caused Collins to be arrested.[69] Things were much worse in the Chicago area, and the intervention of U.S. troops ordered by President Grover Cleveland raised serious questions in what was thought of as a critical struggle between capital and labor.

The California newspapers found one or two episodes in the strike amusing. Mrs. Leland Stanford had to ask permission of the strikers to be allowed to travel in her private car on the SP. The *Oakland Times* reported the permission as follows: "Mrs. Leland Stanford:—You may ride in your own car over your own road, with your own attaches, partaking of your own food, in order to reach your own home, with my permission. 'Czar' Debs."[70] Similarly, Edward needed to go by rail from San Francisco to Sacramento to negotiate about the movement of fruit. He had to get the permission of striking switchman Harry Knox, chairman of the mediation committee of the American Railway Union, and the *San Francisco Examiner* reported that " 'it is getting down to cases when a magnate has to ask permission of a poor switchman to travel on his own road,' said Knox, who knows a joke when he sees one."[71]

When the *New York Tribune* reviewed the strike in California, it took the position that the SP policy was to avoid bloodshed, and it made favorable reference to the fact that

> H. E. Huntington, in several open letters to the newspapers, defined the Southern Pacific ground so clearly that no one could fail to understand it. He put it plainly that surrender to the demands of the Railway Union would be practically turning over to this union the running of the railroad, as on any trifling pretext it could tie up the entire system. His letters had a marked influence on public sentiment.[72]

There was further violence in California, however. On July 13, as Edward reported by telegram to Collis, an SP switch engine in the Sacramento yards with "regular soldiers" on board was stoned and fired on by strikers; the "soldiers returned the fire, killing two strikers, mortally wounding one and capturing thirteen who are now in the guard house."[73] The next day, Edward reported that a mob at Oakland took a fireman off his engine.[74] But the strike was in its last stages, and within a week the union called off the strike in California.

On July 21, Edward sent Collis his reflections about the strike. "The fight is won," he said, "and I may say at this time that we have not made a move I regret or would I change any orders that we have given. . . . I regretted this strike very much." Only about 5 percent of the engineers and conductors went on strike, and "the balance have been in full accord with us." Their leaders "have been in the office here most of the time during the strike and have been constantly sending telegrams and letters to the members of their orders to stand by the Company and do their duty." Everybody, he said, now understood what the SP policy would be whenever "the laborer attempts to dictate our policy." The labor unions had "received a check, and I believe that this strike has injured them very much."[75]

The strike was a difficult time for Edward. He was, in effect, responsible for the day-to-day decisions that had to be made on behalf of the railroad. The violent acts during the strike were centered in Northern California, and they swirled around him. He became a public figure held in mixed esteem.

Seven

EDWARD'S FIRST THREE years in California following his arrival in 1892 were full of tensions and problems. He was buffeted by public hostility toward the Southern Pacific, internal dissension, the financial panic, and the railway strike. He also developed a great deal as a businessman and manager during that time. He might have hoped that the next years would be peaceful and quiet, but they presented new problems, challenges, and disappointments.

After Edward had been in San Francisco about three years, he set down his reflections on what he had tried to accomplish during that time. These thoughts took the form of a three-page, single-spaced letter, written to Collis in his stilted formal style. "I hesitate to write what follows herein," he began, "but in view of the strenuous efforts I have manifested to produce economical results, consistent with sound business policy, I feel justified in putting some figures before you compiled from actual results from operations, which I think will interest both yourself and your associates." His first effort had been "to produce every possible economy that did not interfere with the maintenance of the highest efficiency of the property." Neither his economies nor his many innovations had been popular. There were problems in getting people to accept new circumstances, but now "people have gradually become accustomed to the new conditions and have accommodated themselves accordingly." A comparison of operating results for the forty months ending July 31, 1895, with the preceding forty months showed good progress: the SP was operating 9 percent more miles of roads and carrying 4 percent more revenue car miles and 15 percent more freight and passenger miles, all for 3 percent less operating expenses, and this was with cost per revenue train mile down 7 percent. Edward did not claim all the credit: "Changes in conditions, resulting from natural exigencies, have brought about a large proportion of this reduction," but "unceasing vigilance and unswerving determination to curtail expenses to the minimum, must necessarily have had some bearing in helping to bring about this excellent result."

Next, he gave his thoughts about the effect on the SP of the railroad strike of 1894. He saw important gains from the strike. Before that time, "there was a natural feeling of timidity on the part of our people, to engage in any conflict with labor" for fear of a strike and heavy financial loss: "But now this uncertain feeling is entirely dispelled, and since we know just what we can do, labor and corporate interests are daily getting closer."

Finally, he discussed the popularity and unpopularity of the railroad. He associated attacks on the railroad with business depressions. He blamed "intriguing demagogues" who tried to make "political capital" by seeking out "some scapegoat to blame for their distress" and choosing the railroad. He looked to the future with confidence: "We seem to be entering upon an epoch of renewed prosperity on this coast, and with better times will come a better feeling that will place behind us all these petty and illiberal animosities, and then the railroad will have an even chance."[1]

Edward devoted himself during the next few years to running the SP and trying to make it bigger, better, and more profitable. As Collis's representative, he had the major voice in operating decisions. He and Crocker had an uneasy truce; Crocker did not always like what Edward did, but Collis had control so long as he had the support of the Hopkins-Searles interest. Collis spent a small part of his time in San Francisco: usually he was there once or twice a year for a couple of months each time, though sometimes a year and a half would go by without his presence. In the meantime, Edward spoke for him, but they were in frequent contact by letter and telegram.

Edward traveled a great deal on company business, mostly in California, but also to Oregon, Texas, and Mexico, once or twice a year to New York, and occasionally to New Orleans, Cincinnati, and Chicago. He was always on the lookout for rewarding directions to extend SP lines and fruitful ways to increase freight and passenger traffic. He made full use of his earlier experience in planning and laying track. In January 1897, for example, he took a thirty-mile trip by horseback with a member of the SP engineering department to consider building a line between Mojave and Randsburg to serve a new mining area.[2] Some were real Wild West adventures. Once he went to Ray, Arizona, near where some copper mines were being developed, to consider running a branch line there. He spent the night at the mining camp: "At breakfast the mining manager boasted of the peaceful nature of his camp. Just as he spoke, two shots were heard, then more." The whole male population dashed by, "every man shooting at two figures who were trying to reach the shelter of a nearby ridge of rock." One was killed by a charge of buckshot, the other by a bullet through his head. " 'Verily, this surely is a peaceful camp,' remarked Mr. Huntington." It was only two gamblers who had been to the bar and were shooting up the town.[3]

Edward made many trips around California: for example, he left San Francisco on December 27, 1898, for Southern California, returning on December 31; then he was off again on January 5, 1899, for Los Angeles, returning January 8. Often the trips were longer and more elaborate. On January 6, 1898, he left San Francisco to spend a week in Southern California, then returned to San Francisco. On January 26, he left for the East: on February 2 he was in Cincinnati, on February 14 in New York, and on March 11 he arrived back in San Francisco; four days later, on March 15, he left once more, this time for New Orleans.[4]

In San Francisco, Edward had to work in an increasingly disharmonious situation. In the first place, the representatives of the other owners of the SP expressed considerable hostility toward Edward, in part as a way of expressing their hostility toward Collis. As Edward replied to a letter from Collis about the disaffection of the Stanford and Crocker interests, "I would expect nothing less from Mrs. Stanford; in fact, she will never stop fighting me as long as I am here, or you are alive. Her actions would indicate that she will do any and every thing possible to injure you and yours." He went on to say that "the work of intrigue and undermining is now and has been going on ever since I first came here, both on the part of the Crocker and Stanford interests, and Douty is now the most formidable, as he is supposed to represent Gen. Hubbard [the Hopkins-Searles interest]. He does not hesitate to say things likely to prejudice people against me and the moral support of the General makes him bolder, as he seems to feel more secure in his position than I do in mine."[5] Collis disposed of Mrs. Stanford simply by saying that she was "a disagreeable, pestiferous, old woman, and I do not think there is any hope of her being any better than she is, while she lives, and probably she will live some time to annoy her betters."[6] Edward reviewed for Collis once more, with sadness, the nature of Mrs. Stanford's hostility, and that of the Crockers, and the hope that the time would come "when General Hubbard and Mr. Stillman [Hubbard's associate in representing the Hopkins-Searles interest] will get a correct understanding of this situation. Nobody is telling them of any good that I accomplish, but my enemies are very careful to impress them with their criticisms."[7]

The internal dissension continued. Edward told Collis: "I do not object to any sort of fight so long as it is in the open, but it is difficult to meet those who attack one secretly, when you are given no opportunity to answer the complaints; hence I thought possibly my presence here might be a bone of contention between yourself and associates, and that matters might move along more smoothly if I were not here. . . . You have little conception of this sort of work that is going on here."[8] Edward was discouraged by the situation. He had earlier told Collis,

> My inclination for sometime has been to resign and this is one of the
> things I wished to talk with you about. I am not sure but that it
> would be better for you if I did, although the discordant element
> would fight anyone who would attempt to follow a progressive policy.
> I have endeavored to conciliate the other interests in every possible
> way, but in vain, hence I am getting very tired.
>
> Yours affectionately,
> H. E. Huntington.[9]

Collis's reaction was generally supportive of Edward on the high moral level of the rightness of his actions, but not in any practical way. "If you keep right on in the way you have been doing," Collis wrote to

Edward, "I think it will be right with everybody; if it is not, it will be right in itself, and that will be a great satisfaction to you, as it will to me."[10]

There was also a great deal of bitter criticism of Edward in the *San Francisco Examiner,* particularly in a series of long feature articles entitled "Why the Railroad Is So Unpopular." In the first article, Edward was epitomized as "that dumb and smiling trickster, the nephew. . . . The control given him by his uncle makes him believe that as Premier he must make all men feel the weight of his power. Apparently bluff, hearty, good-natured and frank he is actually suspicious, cold, domineering and secretive." Edward, it said, had demoralized the railroad by his system of internal espionage: "A stenographic report of his conversation would be as amusing as a page from 'Alice in Wonderland,' or the 'Book of Nonsense.' He will tell you what he has done and repeat the sentence a half-dozen times, prefacing each repetition with 'I say I did. I say I did.'" The first article concluded by saying:

> Altogether it is safe to say that no man better constituted to
> drive business from the road, create trouble at home and make
> enemies abroad can be found in the railroad employ than Mr.
> H. E. Huntington.
>
>   The reason for turning the light of calm analysis on this man is that
> he is the resident head of the most powerful corporation in the State,
> the one that most intimately affects every person living within its borders, and this great railroad he has organized into a Bureau for the
> Creation of Enemies.[11]

The attacks continued for several weeks in March and April of 1896. A few excerpts will have to serve: "H. E. Huntington is a big man, physically, and a well-looking man. But the Old Guard insists that he is small in things both big and little. There is a general belief that his chief object in life is to suspect men of wrongdoing. He can center more hate than a white horse can center fire in a battle."[12] And again: "He is a very small man rattling about in a very large place. Some of the tricks he has resorted to to get rid of men whom he did not like are contemptible."[13] Even Edward's residence came in for attack, described as "a big, costly house, that might be a cross between scrambled eggs and a wedding cake. The house may be taken as a fair expression of the personality of Mr. Huntington—cranky and crabbed, but pretentious and vulgar."[14]

Columns of "humor" were also devoted to Edward. In one, for example, Blinker Murphy told in dialect how he first talked Collis into giving Edward a salary of $1,000 a month so he could run around a little and then got him to raise it to $1,500 to get him out of debt.[15]

W. H. Mills wrote Collis about the attacks on Edward in the *Examiner,* and Collis replied in his usual lofty tone: "As to the Examiner's pursuing H. E. Huntington; of course, I know nothing about it; and I suppose he will not care much about it. I certainly do not care anything about their talk about me, for anything from their tongue or pen cannot harm honest people."[16]

Edward gradually took greater responsibility for the street railway system in San Francisco, especially after he became president of the Market Street Railway following the death of C. F. Crocker in 1897. He concerned himself with new construction, extension of the lines, and the conversion to underground electrical power. He came in for further attacks in the newspapers because of the injuries and deaths caused by the trolleys. One full-page story featured a large picture of Edward in the middle of the page with a skull and crossbones over his head and the caption: "H. E. Huntington: The Man Who Is Responsible for It All."[17] A warrant for his arrest was served on him as the person responsible for the deaths, and he had to appear in police court to defend himself.[18]

One other extended public attack on the railroad came during the period 1894 to 1899—the agitation, particularly in San Francisco, against the funding bills under consideration by the U.S. Congress to resolve the loan of some $28 million to the Central Pacific between 1865 and 1869 in the form of thirty-year U.S. 6 percent bonds to complete the transcontinental railroad. While it was Collis rather than Edward who was under personal attack, Edward was deeply involved in trying to settle the problem. There were endless claims, counterclaims, congressional bills, and Supreme Court opinions until the matter was finally settled in 1899 by a reorganization of the Central Pacific and

Southern Pacific, the issuance of new securities, and—with the help of James Speyer and Company—an agreement for repayment to the government.[19]

Edward was most deeply involved from 1894 to 1897. A funding bill was before Congress to resolve the issue; it was strongly supported by Collis and strongly attacked in San Francisco. At a mass meeting in San Francisco in May 1894, a committee of three was elected to go to Washington and oppose the bill; another meeting was held on June 19, 1894, in which the railroad was denounced, and a telegram was sent to President Grover Cleveland on June 29. Adolph Sutro, the mayor of San Francisco, was the moving spirit in these agitations, and there was a tremendous amount of publicity against the funding bill—and against Collis and the railroad—in newspapers, pamphlets, and broadsides. Of the sixty-four broadsides, nine pamphlets, two hundred stamped envelopes with different printed messages on them, and dozens of newspaper feature stories and cartoons that I have seen, the following will have to serve as examples of what confronted Edward as the Huntington in residence during these three years.[20] One cartoon, under the title "Pity the Sorrows of a Poor Old Man," showed Collis in rags addressing Uncle Sam: "I know I owe you $65,000,000; let me have another $65,000,000 and we will call it square."[21] Another showed Collis as a pelican fishing for congressmen in a pool, using dollars as bait; the caption says "Collis Pelican Huntington Expects to Catch Some Fish. Bait That He Thinks Will Catch the Fish."[22] The stamped envelopes addressed to senators had such printed messages as "Huntington Wouldn't Steal a Red Hot Stove," "Huntington Believes All Men Are Corrupt," and "California's Protest Against the Funding Bill." Sutro's slogan was "The Octopus Must Be Destroyed," and many broadsides and pamphlets embroidered the theme with such statements as "Down with the Octopus" and "Evil Influence of the Octopus."[23]

In the meantime, Collis was busy in New York and Washington. He sent telegrams to Edward in San Francisco on January 22, 1896, asking him to "get some of the best men you can" to "telegraph to the Washington Post as much as you can that is favorable to the railroad and damaging to Adolph Sutro, Doyle and others of that ilk." Four days later, in another telegram to Edward, Collis said, "Letters published in

Washington Post having excellent effect. Let them come right along." And on February 3 Collis said, "Interviews are doing great good in Washington for almost every member of Congress reads the Post."[24]

Collis then summoned Edward to New York and Washington, where he stayed for two months. He became ill during the time and lost over thirty pounds. When he got back to San Francisco, on April 4, 1896, he reported optimistically to the *Examiner* on the prospects for the funding bill: "I do not think there is much doubt that the Funding Bill, as a means of adjusting the present Government debt of the Central Pacific, will be passed at the present session of Congress." He expressed his opinion that it was "a fair bill, no matter from what standpoint you look at it."[25] His optimism was unfounded: the bill was defeated, there was widespread rejoicing in San Francisco, and the governor proclaimed January 16, 1897, as a legal holiday in honor of the defeat of the funding bill.[26]

Edward had spent a lot of effort on a losing cause, and he had to go back to Washington in June 1897 to help lobby for a new bill. The final resolution of the problem in 1899, with the reorganization of the railroads and new securities and loans from bankers, left behind a memory of hard work, ill will, and failure. From the point of view of business, these years in San Francisco had not been happy or rewarding. Collis was temperamentally capable of ignoring temporary defeats in the prospect of ultimate victory. Edward had to learn how to share this ability.

Edward's family was at last together in their own home at 2840 Jackson Street. Family activities began soon after they moved in, in 1893. The girls began to have music lessons: Clara took piano with Mrs. Heimberger and mandolin with Samuel Adelstein; Elizabeth, called Bessie, took piano with Emil Barth. Through the rest of the decade, the children continued their music lessons, as well as riding and language lessons. Edward joined the Burlingame Country Club in 1893 for family reasons, and they rented a pew for the family in the First Presbyterian Church in San Francisco.[27]

They began to have guests. The newspapers reported an "entertainment" they gave for seventy "ladies and gentlemen" on April 18, 1894;

for the occasion, Mrs. Waldo Richards, a performer from the East, gave "some of her brightest and cleverest" readings and recitations for an hour and a half, including dialect pieces in Scots, Irish, and "Negro"; James Whitcomb Riley's "Naughty Boys"; and a chapter from Ouida's *Under Two Flags*.[28]

In the winter of 1894–95, Harriet began annual visits to California, staying with Edward and Mary and returning to Oneonta in May. Edward's family also made regular visits to Harriet in Oneonta. In June 1895, Mary took the girls to Oneonta, stopping in Covington on the way; Howard did not go, as he had already started working on October 1, 1894, at the age of eighteen, in the engineering department of the SP in Arizona. In the absence of his family, Edward was invited for dinner by several neighbors. In the middle of July, he went East "to bring my family home," as he said; he joined them in Oneonta for a short visit, and they returned together to San Francisco.[29]

When Harriet had to travel without Edward, he did what he could to facilitate her trip. Here is a letter he wrote on SP letterhead on May 9, 1896:

> Conductors,
> Southern Pacific Company and Connecting Lines.
>
> Gentlemen:
>
>   The bearer is my mother, Mrs. H. S. Huntington, journeying eastwards, accompanied by two ladies, but without gentleman escort. The ladies may need some information while en route, and if you could favor them in any way, without interfering with your other duties, it would be a kindness to them, for which I would be thankful; or if you would point out places of interest along the road to them, that is places of more than ordinary interest, it would also be appreciated.
>
> Yours truly,
> H. E. Huntington[30]

The social life of Edward and Mary centered around members of the family, and secondarily around his business associates. Things picked up when Collis came to San Francisco for a stay. Edward had taken full responsibility for preparing Collis's house at 1020 California Street for occupancy. Literally hundreds of telegrams and letters went back and forth between Edward and Collis in 1895 and again in 1896 covering all the details: plumbing, painting, wallpaper, refinishing of floors, carpeting, installation of a furnace, putting up of picture mouldings, and so forth.[31] If either of them was ever wise enough to consult with his spouse on any of these matters, it is certainly not inferable from their communications. Edward himself checked and reported on all the work. Later, after an interior repainting, he had to hang all the pictures. Collis and he both had strong opinions about how to hang pictures in order to create the best effect, and they were equally particular. Collis, after giving his own thoughts to Edward about the hanging of individual pictures, concluded by saying, "You can judge yourself as well as I can, how they should be hung." Edward, in writing to Collis about the results, expressed delight about the effect of raising the Verboeckhoven just a little: "You cannot imagine how much the change improves the appearance of the gallery."[32]

Collis expressed appreciation to Edward for all the trouble he had taken about the house. Edward replied, "I assure you it is no trouble, but on the contrary, it is a pleasure for me to feel that I can do anything for you, more especially when it is in the line of doing something that may contribute to your personal pleasure or comfort."[33]

The new house enabled Collis to hold his annual dinners for the principal SP officers at home. On May 5, 1897, after a lapse of three years, Collis entertained 120 guests at a white-tie occasion. Edward was given the tricky task of deciding who would be seated where, and he also ventured to include some representative conductors and train engineers. The party was described in the paper as "one of the most elaborate affairs ever seen in San Francisco," with vocal music and a band between toasts. It began at seven and lasted till after midnight. A few select women dined upstairs in an overlooking room behind a screen, where they could hear but not be seen. Collis delivered a speech on the glories of California.[34]

When Collis came to San Francisco for a visit in 1895, Belle wanted to see the railroad offices. Edward called for them early, and here is the newspaper account of the event:

On the way down to the office in the morning nephew Huntington escorted his relatives to a Powell-street car at Powell and California streets. He intended to transfer at Market and Powell and travel by a Market-street car to the railroad building. The nephew is one of a very few men in the city who has a street car pass. A new conductor happened to be in charge of the Powell-street car by which the trio traveled. The conductor had recently been taught the strict rule of never permitting any one to ride who did not pay cash, produce a proper transfer or show a genuine pass. So when H. E. Huntington said to him as the car started down the hill from California street to Pine, "Pass No. 2, and these two are with me," pointing to Mr. and Mrs. Huntington, the new conductor replied in a suspicious tone of voice, and yet politely, "Let me see your pass, please."

Young Huntington flushed a little while he went into his pocket and got out his pass for the inspection of the conductor. He did not say a word, but the uncle laughed heartily at the evident discomfiture of his young relative. Then in all seriousness the magnate said, "Edward this little experience should be a lesson to you. That conductor is all right. He is here to do his duty, and you must set him and other people on the road a good example by complying with the rule of showing your pass. That conductor is made of the right sort of stuff."[35]

Soon after Collis had left for the East, both he and Edward were made the subjects of a couple of the humor columns of Blinker Murphy. In the first one, "'I've had to keep my trap shut for the last few weeks,' said Mr. 'Blinker' Murphy, 'but now that uncle has gone I can shoot off my bazoo occasionally. Collis would insist on a-doing all the talking himself when he was here. The nephew tried to chip in a couple of times, but he got sat down on hard. Uncle was a little bit fidgety, and we're all kind of glad he's a-pulled his freight.'" In the other one, Blinker and Edward were visiting the zoo, and Blinker sent Edward over to look at the baby elks and the deer so that Blinker could talk: "'H. E. is always a-chipping in when conversation is a-going on,' Mr. Murphy explained as young Mr. Huntington wheeled away. 'Uncle Collis told him to shut up two or three times when he was here, but it's hard to break one of them Eastern chaps from a bad habit. Anyhow he's got sense enough not to come back until he knows I'm through a-talking. He's got some brains, has the nephew.' "[36]

When Collis and Belle were in residence in San Francisco—along with her companion, Carrie Campbell, and his private secretary, G. E. Miles, and a full complement of household servants—there were dinners back and forth and many evenings together. Then in 1896 the California family grew when Carrie—Edward's younger sister, now thirty-five, and the person who was probably his best friend—married Edmund Burke Holladay, known as Burke, a thirty-four-year-old lawyer whose father's family was prominent in the San Francisco Bay area and whose mother's family, the Ords, had been longtime Californians. The wedding ceremony took place on February 25 at noon in the drawing room of Collis and Belle's new house at 2 East Fifty-seventh Street in New York, with many relatives, including Edward and Harriet, present. Uncle Collis gave the bride away, and the ceremony was followed by an elaborate breakfast. Their wedding trip included a visit to Boston and then went west from New York in the private car *Otsego* by way of New Orleans (with a tour by Baron Natili and S. F. B. Morse), San Antonio, El Paso, Los Angeles (with a trip up Mt. Lowe), and back to San Francisco on March 23.

Carrie and Burke first occupied a separate wing of his parents' house on Clay and Octavia; Burke took a position as a lawyer for one of the Huntington companies, and the social intercourse greatly increased for Edward and Mary. On May 8, Edward and Mary held a large reception at their house in honor of the newlyweds; Herr Anton Schott sang for the gathering. The Sunday following Carrie and Burke went to church with Edward, Mary, and Harriet, and on May 12, Edward and Mary gave a large formal dinner at their house "to meet Mr. and Mrs. E. B. Holladay." And "a beautiful dinner" it was, Burke wrote.[37]

A further family event of great moment for Carrie and Burke, and involving Edward, took place on Monday, April 25, 1898. In his diary, Burke wrote:

> Caroline and I went down to 1020 California in time for a 7 o'clock dinner with Uncle Collis and Belle and Edwards, Mr. Miles and Miss

Campbell. We were to go afterwards to see "some pictures," they said. Belle came down to dinner in a black suit and hat. After dinner we all (except Miles) got into Clay St. cars and rode out to Buchanan. There they got out and led us to No. 2215 Buchanan, which was all lighted up. Uncle Collis rang the bell and at the same time opened the door with a key. We walked into the parlor and stood, waited a minute. Then looking at Carol, Belle said, "Well, the family doesn't seem to come. You had better do the honors, Carrie. For this is your house:— this house and all that is in it."

We went all about the house, and found it furnished beautifully from top to bottom. Edwards had been working all day putting up beautiful pictures in the parlor and rooms—pictures which C. P. had sent up from 1020—besides arranging all the furniture and pictures already there. Everything seemed to be in the house. We were carried away with astonishment and delight. It is the gift of Carrie's Uncle Collis who with Edwards has been over all the town for weeks to find the right home.

The next day, Burke went to work and from there straight to the new house and found "Edwards, and Uncle Collis and Belle all there. Edwards had been at work all the afternoon and had unpacked most all of the boxes of books and placed them on shelves." The next day, "We made the place our home by sleeping there."[38]

When Carrie and Burke had their first child, a girl, all the members of the family were delighted. Edward wrote an affectionate letter to Burke that "it is a nice provision of nature that this bit of humanity should come into the world and jostle so many hearts." He told how Collis had boasted that he and Belle were the first to get the news, and that it was a red-letter day. Edward asked what name they had in mind for the baby. "For my share," he added playfully, "I would ask you how Edwardina strikes you? You cannot say it is common, certainly."[39] They named her Helen Huntington Holladay—and their other child, born in 1898, Collis Huntington Holladay.

Edward and Mary came to see Carrie and the baby frequently as soon as visits were allowed. Mary brought whipped-cream pudding for Carrie, and Edward was allowed to give Helen her bottle the second time she had one.[40]

Edward did a lot of business traveling, as we have seen, but he also traveled extensively with his family. In the autumn of 1896, Clara entered school on Riverside Drive in New York. In September 1896 Edward stayed on in Oneonta with their youngest daughter Marian after Mary had returned to San Francisco. He wrote her warmly: "My Darling Wife, I was very glad to receive your long letter and to know that you arrived safely." He gave the news about Marian, and said, "Oneonta looks beautiful and I wish I lived here." Friends like Ed Pardee he cherished—"I wish we might always have him near us." And he concluded, "With very much love I remain, Your affectionate Husband, Edward."[41] In a later letter to him in San Francisco written from the Adirondacks, Mary began "My dear Husband," gave news of all the children, and concluded "Ever yours, Mama."[42] Edward was in New York in the latter part of November 1897, and he spent Thanksgiving with Archer and his wife Helen, who wrote to Carrie that "we had all the family here on Thanksgiving. Edwards too. What a nice fellow he is! We have all enjoyed having him here so much."[43] The next year Mary spent two months with the children in Oneonta in the autumn of 1898. The most extensive trip took place in the summer of 1897, however, when Mary spent two months traveling around Europe with their oldest daughter Clara, age nineteen, while the two younger children stayed in Oneonta. Clara wrote to Harriet about being seen off on the *Brittanic* in New York by Archer and Helen and "of course Papa. Hated to leave him worst of all, and I do wish he could stay with you for awhile."[44] In London, Mary and Clara met Collis and Belle and lunched with the family.[45]

Edward and Mary had an active social life while in San Francisco, particularly with Carrie and Burke. When Edward was alone, he often went to their house for breakfast and walked to work with Burke, returning to their house for dinner.[46] Mary was one of the seven lady patronesses of the cotillion club La Jeunesse, which met three times a winter for debutantes with a dance, music, and midnight supper.[47] Edward was made a member of the exclusive Bohemian Club in 1895.[48] There was also some disorganized fun. A newspaper reported in the winter of 1898 that their third child, Elizabeth, now age eighteen, "after summoning several of her boon companions, ousted the cook from his honored position, and, with her comrades, took possession of the kitchen. Each girl prepared one dish, and then they all fell to and devoured the repast. It was such fun that they all declare they will do the same thing this winter and invite in their young masculine friends to enjoy the feast with them."[49]

Howard, after six years working in the SP engineering department, first in Arizona and then in California, decided at the age of twenty-four to go to college for a professional education. He chose Harvard, passed the entrance exams satisfactorily, and supplied an acceptable bond to the president and fellows of Harvard College to guarantee that the charges for his board, room, tuition, and damages to the buildings would be duly paid. His two bondsmen were H. E. Huntington and Collis P. Huntington; both listed their "profession or occupation" as "Railroad Manager" and both gave their firm as "Southern Pacific Company."[50] Howard lived in Hastings Hall in plain circumstances at a cost of $10 per week; his father had reimbursed him for the cost of furnishing his room, which was $67.[51] Edward prudently asked a lawyer cousin in Boston how much money Howard should be given for his expenses; the answer was, "I have made some inquiries and find that he could live very well his Freshman year on $1200—and be very amply provided for on $1500."[52] The newspapers marveled that Howard, who was "heir to the greatest wealth of any freshman at Harvard," should live such "a simple, democratic life that excites the wonder and admiration of all."[53]

That style had been bred in his bones.

In the later nineteenth century, illness and good health were standard topics in family letters. Collis had frequent bad colds, Harriet had occasional spells of illness, Edward and Mary's girls had strong attacks of one thing or another. But there were two members of the Huntington family whose health frequently occasioned serious concern. One was Edward, whose problems continued through the decade and gave concern to nearly everyone—his mother, wife, uncle, secretary, children, sister, cousins. Edward himself tended to minimize his health problems. To his mother he brushed illness away by saying, "I have had a hard cold but it is better now." And to Collis he wrote, "While I have been under the weather a good deal this summer, I think perhaps Mary is unnecessarily alarmed."[54]

As soon as Edward left San Francisco for the East in January 1896, his private secretary immediately ventured to write to Collis and express his deep concern about Edward's health: "If you will permit me to make a suggestion, it would be that he should take a good rest, as he has not been looking well for sometime back, and he has been working very hard ever since I have been with him. He needs the rest badly and we can get along here for a while." Collis did succeed in keeping Edward there for a short time, and Collis's private secretary wrote to his counterpart in San Francisco that "H. E. is feeling much better. . . . I fancy the rest he is having is exactly what was needed." But it did not last. Collis later wrote to Edwin Gates, "I am worried about Edward, who I wish was strong."[55]

Reactions about his health came from all directions. Carrie, while in Los Angeles with baby Helen and Edward, wrote Burke that "Edwards is feeling badly today" so they had to cancel their program. Cousin Harriet Douglas wrote Edward, "I hope that you are feeling better than when you came to Oneonta." And Archer wrote Carrie from New York: "I am glad to hear that H. E. is doing better. Have a good sisterly eye on him every ten or twelve minutes and remember us to him." His daughter Clara wrote from Amsterdam, while on her European trip with Mary, to Harriet that "in Papa's letter he said he was feeling well, and then Uncle Ed writes that he looks dreadfully, so that we don't know what to think about him. If he will only take some regular exercise it would benefit him a great deal."[56]

"Regular exercise" was recommended to him by various people as the source of his health salvation. "I am very glad that you are feeling better than you have," wrote Collis, "and that you are out of doors more than you have been. I think for a year or two you should stay out in the open air as much as you well can." Collis's private secretary gave Edward more detailed directions: "How is your health? I hope it is much improved over what it was when I last saw you. You need, in my opinion, a regimen of steady exercise. As few men will take it systematically, the best thing for a man doing business is to walk much, because walking is an exercise always accessible. He who walks much is paced by health, while he who sits much has disease for a caller." Edward responded that "I am walking considerably every day—part of the time, walking from my house to the office mornings and walking some every evening."[57]

The other member of the family with recurrent health problems was Belle. Soon after she and Collis were married in 1884, his references to her in his letters usually alluded to her poor health. She suffered from what he called neuralgia and, at first, from chronic pain in her teeth. She tended toward obesity, and there are many references to her losing weight: she reportedly lost forty-five pounds in 1896; Helen Gates told Carrie that Belle had lost another twenty pounds in the autumn of 1897; and in the next year Collis wrote Edwin Gates that Belle "has lost a good deal of her flesh, but everybody seems to think it an improvement."[58]

Her most debilitating problem was her poor eyesight, however. By 1895 she had been to many specialists in the United States and in Europe to try to stem the onset of blindness. A resumé of the situation in 1895 is contained in a letter from Collis's private secretary, George E. Miles, when they were in Brussels back to Edwin Gates in New York:

> You know about Mrs. Huntington's eyes. Visits to different oculists have left her much depressed and practically hopeless, although the last doctor,—in Utrecht—a celebrated specialist, told her that with conscientious care she could retain her vision for many years, that is, what she now has; for it can never be improved. Nobody talks before her about her eyes and I hope when you see her you will say nothing of my letter, which is of course confidential. I am very sorry for her, particularly because her enjoyment of life is so largely dependent upon things visible and perhaps more than anything else upon books.

The family members were always concerned about her vision and tried to be optimistic. Two years later, Archer's wife, Helen, wrote to Carrie that "her eyes are certainly no worse than they were a year ago and I think they are a little better."[59]

Belle was often "under the weather." From London, Collis wrote to Gates in New York that "all are well, except Belle, who has been under the weather, I might say, ever since we reached London." Harriet wrote Carrie in 1896 that "Belle was not at all well. She has constant and terrible headaches. Edward Pardee brings the same report and says her left eye looks very bad. I do feel so sorry for her." Once on a train trip from Washington to New Orleans she had a bad "neuralgic headache." Miles wrote to Gates from New Orleans that "all the way from Washington she suffered greatly and has kept to her room entirely. Her finger has pained her constantly but we had Dr. Mada of this city meet us on arrival and his treatment has been somewhat more radical than Dr. Coley's [in New York], with good results so far. Mr. Huntington at one time contemplated turning back, but now it looks as if we should proceed to Galveston in the morning."[60]

Edward had collected his first library, of some one hundred volumes, in the 1870s when he was about twenty-four. Mostly sets of recent fiction, poetry, history, and popular classics, he lost this library to Franchot in the settlement at the termination of their partnership (see chap. 3). In the 1880s he began to buy books for another library, in all about fourteen hundred volumes, again mostly sets of standard authors, with some foreign writers and a few specialty books (see chap. 5).

In San Francisco in the 1890s he devoted a good deal of attention to buying books, and his focus began to change. It is instructive to see how he proceeded. First, he got to know book dealers, went to their shops regularly, examined their stock, and talked with them. In San Francisco, the dealer he found most congenial was William Doxey, whose shop was at 631 Market Street. Doxey's shop was a popular meeting place for young writers and intellectuals during its short life in the 1890s. Edward went there frequently to talk with Doxey and buy books. A note from Doxey, dated July 21, 1898, hints at the nature of their relationship:

> Mr Huntington
> My dear Sir
>
> I am very desirous of making a sale to-day and if there are any books I could sell you I would give you a good bargain—I should be glad if you could drop in at lunch time.
>
> Yours truly
> Wm Doxey[61]

Edward did "drop in" frequently. Doxey imported current books from his native England, picked up interesting collections when he could, and published a few things himself. His most memorable publication was probably *The Lark,* a fine little magazine edited by Gelett Burgess and others and containing "The Purple Cow," which lasted only for the years 1896 and 1897; Edward bought a set for $9 in July 1897, and then two more sets later in the year. Doxey also published thin volumes called Lark Classics, and Edward bought a copy of the *Rubaiyat* in this series in 1898, and two more copies later.[62]

Edward bought many types of books from Doxey, ranging from Sir Edwin Arnold's *Poems,* Poe and Balzac to Chambers's *Encyclopedia.* There are twenty-eight bills from Doxey extant for Edward's purchases during the period 1894–98. Generally, he bought six books a month from Doxey at $10 to $15, not including the occasional purchase of a set for $25 or $50.

Edward patronized a number of other booksellers as well. In San Francisco, he shopped with D. P. Elder, as well as with William K. Vickery, the Dodge Brothers, and John J. Newbegin. In New York, he mainly went to Henry Miller's shop, conveniently located at 65 Nassau Street.[63]

During this time Edward began to avail himself of the knowledge of booksellers and to move from buying sets of standard authors to buying individual books of interest. Also during this time we first hear of his keen interest in reading aloud from the books he had recently purchased—a practice he continued for the rest of his life. The journal of S. W. Holladay, the father of Burke, who was then engaged to be married to Carrie, tells of such an incident on Christmas Day, 1895. Mr. Holladay had lunched that day with Edward and Mary and their family in San Francisco, with thirteen at the table. "Then most of them went to matinée," wrote Mr. Holladay, "leaving H. E. & his mother & me: & I stayed till after 4 examining his rare books & heard him read a poem of Edw Arnold most beautifully."[64] Edward had bought his copy of Sir Edwin Arnold's poems from Doxey on July 7, 1894, for $3.50.

Edward began to think of books as good presents. Before Carrie was married, her mother offered to pack up her effects in Oneonta while

Carrie was getting ready for her wedding in New York. Carrie was delighted and wrote her mother in early 1896 with exact directions as to where her things were: "In the case by your room door is the set of Bulwer that Edwards gave me for Christmas. . . . Then there is a large picture book of Cathedrals and a century book of engravings that Edwards gave me, I believe in the parlor."[65]

Edward kept conscientious records of his books. In the 1890s he made two handwritten lists, and both are extant. In the first, he listed all of his books, in pencil, on twenty-six half sheets of yellow paper, giving author, title, number of volumes, binding, and cost. Then he copied the list over (with some changes), in ink, on nineteen full sheets of white paper. By now his library contained some 315 titles in sixteen hundred volumes; it had cost him about $5,000. He had numerous sets of standard authors (Thoreau, Hawthorne, Sterne, Swift), with a few off the main track like T. L. Peacock, Landor, Cowper, and Crabbe. There were many sets of historical works (Hume, Macaulay, Bancroft, Parkman), foreign authors (Hugo, Schiller, Molière, Goethe), classical authors (Plutarch, Virgil, Plato), reference works, and an increasing number of specialty items (Verne's *Exploration of the World*, à Beckett's *Comic History of Rome*, Lavater's *Essays on Physiognomy*, Mary Shelley's *Frankenstein*, Taylor's *Holy Living and Holy Dying*, *Uncle Tom's Cabin*, St. Augustine, *Ben Hur, Lamia*, and Froissart's *Chronicles*).[66] They were not "rare books" in the ordinary sense of the term, but Mr. Holladay called them rare (doubtless following Edward's lead), since they had to be hunted down in shops that catered to specialized readers.

It was also during this period that we first hear about Edward's interest in buying art. In 1897 he bought half a dozen pictures from Jules Musfelder at a cost of $140; they were presumably decorative pieces for his residence.[67] But in the same year he bought two English watercolor paintings from the catalog of Parsons of London: *Warwick Castle* for $350, and *Iffley Mill, on the Thames* for $325.[68] The next year, he bought jades in San Francisco, for $250 each.[69] He also began to collect books about art. In the lists that I have just described, he recorded the following books: *Selected Pictures of Great Britain*, four volumes, at $75; *Art Treasures of America*, ten volumes, at $50; *Masterpieces of French Art*, ten volumes, at $25; *National Portrait Gallery Lon-*

don, two volumes, at $5. These books offer a clue as to the direction of his art interests at this time.

When Edward came to California in 1892, San Francisco was the state's major city. In 1890, its population had been about 300,000, and that of the state 1.2 million. Talk had long circulated in the SP headquarters about the coming importance of Southern California. Charles F. Crocker, for example, had repeatedly urged Collis to have the railroad buy land around Los Angeles and lay more tracks there. In 1887, he urged the purchase of the 120,000-acre San Joaquin Ranch, later known as the Irvine Ranch, available for $1,250,000. "The most promising locality for investing in low priced lands at present is in the San Fernando Valley," he wrote: 60,000 acres at $30 an acre, or the Porter Ranch at $25 an acre. Or near Santa Barbara for $100 an acre, or the Posas and Simi ranches near Ventura for $5 an acre.[70] Collis did not want to buy any of these particular properties; his own agenda featured building railroads in Mexico and a port at Santa Monica. But he was enthusiastic about all of California. From San Francisco in 1888 he wrote Gates in New York: "Things in California are very flourishing. In fact, I have never seen the State looking anything like as well as it does now. Business is good everywhere."[71]

Enthusiasm, belief in California, and high expectations for the Los Angeles area in particular pervaded the SP headquarters in San Francisco when Edward arrived. He traveled all over the state and made a careful study under the guidance of William Hood, the SP's chief engineer. He went back again and again to the Los Angeles area. In 1890, Los Angeles had a population of fifty thousand, one-sixth that of San Francisco, but up from eleven thousand in 1880. The San Gabriel Valley had a special appeal for the SP executives because of its extensive citrus groves and vineyards and the railroad business they might generate. In 1893, the SP bought the property of the Rapid Transit Railway Company, including its line through the San Gabriel Valley from Los Angeles to Monrovia, and a franchise to go to Pasadena. "The main line," reported the *San Francisco Examiner,* "runs through the very richest portion of Southern California, the best part of the San Gabriel Valley . . . lined with wineries and orange-packing houses." The story concluded that "H. E. Huntington, who represents President C. P. Huntington, it can be reliably stated, intends to leave no vantage ground untouched in Southern California, for he has made a thorough study of this part of the State and has become an enthusiast as to its prospects and resources."[72]

In 1894 and 1895, Edward arranged for the SP to extend its line to Pasadena and build a depot there. He personally chose the route, attained permission from the city, and bought the land.[73] In 1895, Edward and M. H. Sherman made a plan to build, as co-owners, the Pasadena and Altadena Railway, a four-and-a-half-mile double-track line to connect the railway in Pasadena with the Mt. Lowe Railway in Altadena.[74]

Edward was also in evidence elsewhere around the Southland. A committee of citizens of San Bernardino petitioned him to build a line to their town.[75] The papers in San Diego watched Edward's movements for hints that he might extend the line in their direction: "Mr. Huntington is a progressive, enterprising and energetic man, whose perception is keen, and he can see the great and grand future in store for Southern California, and he is working hard to secure for his Company a goodly portion of same."[76] When he arrived in Los Angeles in a private car, the newspapers hailed him as "a distinguished visitor"—the account of a visit with him by a reporter is a pleasant vignette:

> The private car, Sacramento, belonging to H. E. Huntington arrived in this city yesterday afternoon bearing its owner, the assistant to the president of the Southern Pacific company, on board. The car was visited by a Herald representative shortly after its arrival and was cordially greeted by Mr. Huntington. He was sitting in the cool compartment in the after end of the car that serves the purpose of an office and had just dismissed a visitor when the reporter appeared upon the scene. "The object of my trip," said he, "is mainly one of pleasure. I like to ride over the road and it is a pleasure for me to revisit Los Angeles."[77]

In San Francisco, Edward's interest in Southern California was described as "the hobby of the nephew . . . to protect the Southern Pacific against the Santa Fe's competition in and around Los Angeles. This fact explains why the nephew suggested and the uncle approved of double-tracking the main line between Los Angeles and Shorb station, building a branch line to Pasadena, and doing other track work in Southern California." But when it came to extending the line to San Diego, "Huntington Sr., it is understood, informed his young relative that under present circumstances he was playing with fire."[78]

Edward came to be more and more highly regarded in Los Angeles. Here is a complete editorial about him published in the *Los Angeles Express* for November 6, 1897:

> Mr. H. E. Huntington, who has recently been spending some time in this city, represents the new guard in the Southern Pacific, as opposed to what is known as the old guard, or the adherents to the Stanford-Crocker interests as opposed to Mr. C. P. Huntington. It is a very lucky thing for the stockholders and those financially interested in the road that the change was made that placed the younger Huntington in power. Whatever may be said about the Huntington influence, it cannot be denied that it has transformed the Southern Pacific from a very wild, woolly and western road into, as far as discipline and business goes, one the equal of the best managed Eastern lines, and this has largely been done by H. E. Huntington, the nephew. Twelve and fifteen years ago the line was run in a go-as-you-please manner. There was little discipline among the employees. Conductors would lounge about among the passengers, and chat and smoke with them. Trains might start on time, but it was rarely that any attempt was made to bring them to their destination on the minute. If he has done nothing more for the road than remedy these faults, Mr. H. E. Huntington would merit the gratitude of the owners and the patrons of the line. He has shown himself to be considerable of a railroad man, and if his life is spared it is on the cards for him to go still further. He has one quality which all of his associates in the management do not possess, and that is politeness.[79]

Edward gradually associated himself more with the Los Angeles area. He joined the California Club, the premier social club at the time; he kept in close touch with J. DeBarth Shorb by visits and frequent letters;

he wrote detailed reviews to Collis of possible new rail lines in the area; and he began to contribute to civic causes, giving, for example, the largest donation ($5,000) to the proposed Los Angeles Convention Hall.[80]

Most important, he formed a syndicate, of which he was the majority stockholder, to acquire and reorganize the street railway system of Los Angeles. This was a desperately risky undertaking, as a quick sketch of earlier efforts in the area will reveal. The first street railway in Los Angeles, in 1874, had been a single car drawn by a horse. The first electric street railway began to operate in 1887, when three small companies became the Los Angeles Cable Railway Company, which went bankrupt in 1893 with a loss of $3.5 million. By 1895, twenty-seven out of twenty-eight street railway ventures had collapsed. The Los Angeles Railway Company was incorporated in 1895, and it was this company that Edward and his syndicate took over by buying the stock from the bondholders in 1898.[81]

A little earlier, the papers noted that Edward was in Los Angeles, but "that gentleman, with the retiring disposition and modesty of the family, was indisposed to have his presence known." His presence boded well for Southern California, the reporter assumed: "If H. E. Huntington is here it is in line with some work of benefit to Southern California, as well as to the Southern Pacific, for this portion of the land has no more ardent supporter, and no one with more confidence in the future, than young Mr. Huntington." The reporter asserted that it was entirely due to Edward that Los Angeles had a "superior suburban and country railway service to that of San Francisco," and he would have done even more "had it not been for the more conservative policy of C. P. Huntington, who had to restrain his more impetuous nephew on this subject."[82]

Shortly before the takeover, Edward reinspected the lines. The newspaper reported:

> H. E. Huntington did a heap of street car riding yesterday. He commenced at Spring and Fourth streets and rode over every foot of the street car tracks of the city from start to finish. . . . Mr. Huntington learned more about the city than he ever knew before from this excursion, and it will make him firmer than ever in his belief that this city

is the best place in which to invest money and live that there is on the coast. Mr. Huntington, whenever he can get away from San Francisco, always jumps in his [railway] car and comes to Los Angeles, and loafs about here or Santa Monica. He is stuck on this country, and does not care who knows it. Mr. Huntington will be here some days yet, and some startling developments may result from his visit that have not been hinted at yet.[83]

The takeover of the Los Angeles Railway Company was announced in September 1898, but it took about two years to complete the reorganization, deeds of trust, mortgages, and acquisitions. A total purchase price of about $5 million was involved, though most of it was paid for by mortgages. Edward put a large amount of his own cash into the enterprise; the value of his account with the Pacific Improvement Company, the holding company for the SP and its associates, went down from almost $300,000 to $66.30 in December 1898.

In the end, the company owned most of the street railways in the Los Angeles area except for the LA Traction Company, called the Hook Lines, and two small independents. Edward was the president and the majority stockholder. A substantial minority was held by three investors from San Francisco, I. W. Hellman, Antoine Borel, and Christian de Guigne. Collis held a small minority position.

Edward had become a principal personage in Los Angeles.

In the period 1895–1900, the top management of the Southern Pacific underwent several changes that had an important effect on Edward's authority and on his sense of self-esteem. The company was so loosely run that it could not respond promptly and effectively to these changes. As a result, the management was left in a state of near chaos, suffering from infighting and jockeying for position by the major players.

The first blow was the sudden death of A. N. Towne, the general manager and second vice-president, on July 16, 1895. Edward was in Nebraska, on his way East to bring his family back, when he got a telegram from Crocker reporting the death and advising him to continue on his journey. But Edward returned immediately to San Francisco.

Many of the newspapers expressed the view of the *San Francisco Chronicle* that "H. E. Huntington wants to succeed to the vacancy created by the death of Mr. Towne, and that the ambition had been growing on him for several years." The *San Francisco Examiner* assured its readers, "It is generally believed that H. E. Huntington will be given the Vice-Presidency and continue his present duties of representing his uncle on the coast." On the other hand, the same paper confidently asserted that nobody would be put in Towne's place because of "H. E. Huntington's greed of power, his dislike of giving up anything."[84] After a month of newspaper speculation, J. A. Fillmore, the general superintendent of the SP, was chosen to succeed Towne as second vice-president, and Julius Kruttschnitt was made general manager, though rumors continued for the next year or two that the owners had agreed to make Edward the second vice-president.[85]

A more important readjustment was necessitated two years later when Charles F. Crocker, the first vice-president and representative of the Crocker interest in the company, collapsed at dinner and died on July 17, 1897. Edward very much wanted to be made first vice-president, and he wrote a private letter by hand to Collis in London to urge his case: "It is not necessary for me to say that I would like to be elected to fill the vacancy. But I think it is to your interest as well as mine that this should be done. It would certainly place me in a position where there would be no doubt as to my authority, as often there is at present with the other officials of the company."[86] Collis responded that he had written to General Hubbard, and advised Edward to write him also and say, "You feel it would be better for the Company to have you be in a position of that kind, for it would give you a status that you really do not have as Assistant to the President." Collis suggested, as an alternative, that Edward might be made president of a subsidiary company, the SP of California.[87] Edward immediately wrote a private letter to General Hubbard asking that he be elected vice-president to enable him "to accomplish much more in the interest of the Company than under existing conditions."[88]

A retired assistant general superintendent of the SP, R. H. Pratt—who had also been a very close associate of Towne—ventured to write Collis after the death of Crocker, suggesting that the disharmony among the high SP officials was created for sinister purposes but that Edward, whom he knew only casually and had not consulted, was innocent of any involvement in it. He told his story so that any new appointments following Crocker's death would be made with this knowledge. Collis sent Pratt's letter on to Edward, and Edward replied to Collis with something like a self-estimate, understandably somewhat weighty in style, of his own accomplishments with the SP. This letter shows us clearly what he valued most in what he had done. "I felt sure the time would come," he wrote, "when those I am striving to please, through practical and profitable results produced in the handling of this property—that is, in so far as my prerogatives extended—would put aside those petty calumnies, born of envy and jealousy, and, I might add, through misconception, and judge me from the standpoint I have endeavored to occupy." He admitted that people would form different views about how to expand profitably. "I believe I can say, with some pride," he continued, "that every mile of railroad built by my suggestion, has been of great profit to the Company, as I have been very careful to reach out into heavily producing fertile sections." In a word, his accomplishment had been to increase the profitability of the SP through his choice of extending the lines.[89] These several letters did not have much weight, I think, in settling the appointment issues, because Collis had an overriding concern to placate his fellow owners of the property.

There was another job to fill—that of the presidency of the Market Street Railway, a position that Crocker had held. Edward wrote Collis about that job too, saying, "I have practically managed the executive affairs of the Market Street Railway. I am now Vice President and apparently in line for the Presidency." But, he concluded, "in all these matters, please let it be understood that I do not wish you to do anything for me that will tend to embarrass you in any way, as I would prefer to forego everything."[90]

There was a long wait before the appointments were settled. In the meantime, Edward had become discouraged about his role. On October 28, 1897, he wrote to Collis, "The fact of the matter is my position here has become so hampered, owing to restrictions, that it is getting to be purely clerical; so much so that I can hardly do justice to myself, or to the Company, in my efforts to produce satisfactory financial results." Collis replied comfortingly that "no doubt that is true for the time being, but I think things will improve." He had been talking frequently, he reported, with George Crocker, Charles F. Crocker's younger brother and the new, and inexperienced, representative of the Crocker interest. Collis thought that he and George Crocker would "get near together" and "there will not be the friction that there has been heretofore."[91]

There were meetings among the representatives of the principal owners in the autumn, and an arrangement was worked out to which they could agree. The plan was duly approved by the board on December 2, 1897. General Hubbard was made first vice-president and George Crocker second vice-president of the SP. Edward was made president of the Market Street Railway Company. In short, Edward failed to get what he most wanted and was given what he did not much care about. The *San Francisco Examiner* sourly commented that Edward's "work in the Bureau of Creation of Enemies has given so much satisfaction" that he was given the presidency of the Market Street Railway as a reward; "in his new position he will have many opportunities to display his unique powers."[92]

The changes in alignment were not finished. In 1898, Collis wrote to Edward asking him, at the suggestion of General Hubbard, to resign as president of the Pacific Improvement Company so that they could appoint George Crocker to the job.[93] On January 17, 1899, Edward resigned as a director of the SP, and on April 6, 1899, he resigned, "for reasons that are quite satisfactory to myself," as assistant to the president.[94] A power struggle was going on behind the scenes. The other three owners were threatening not to vote for Collis as president of the SP because they felt that they had too little voice in the management of the company, and they claimed that Edward ran it in an arbitrary manner. Collis responded by trying to conciliate the others, especially George Crocker.[95]

The San Francisco newspapers had a field day at the expense of Edward, as evidenced by the headlines: "Huntington's Nephew Shorn of His Power," "Nephew Huntington Turned Down to Please the Crockers," "More Harmony Will Prevail: Few Regrets Over the Nephew's

Retirement," "Sacrifice on the Altar of Mammon: Uncle Shatters His Nephew's Ambition to Gain Harmony and Please Money Lenders." And so it went for about ten days. Edward adopted a reserved attitude when interviewed: "I resigned from that position in order to have more time to devote to many important private affairs." Even George Crocker came to his defense: "Stories of my alleged antipathy to Mr. H. E. Huntington are ludicrous. We are all the best of friends, and the Stanford interests are quite in accord, notwithstanding all these statements to the contrary."[96] But Edward was deeply hurt by the experience, and G. E. Miles, Collis's private secretary, wrote to Edwin Gates in New York on April 19, 1899: "I must say I am sorry for him, for he has done much and his talents in the way of construction and trading are strong and effective."[97]

The game was not over, and wily Collis had another play. He arranged for his investment bankers, James Speyer and Company, to begin buying out the Crocker and Stanford interests, and he negotiated a price that those interests were glad to accept. In September 1899, the buyout began, under the management of Speyer, and leveraged by debt against the corporation through the sale of bonds by Speyer. As soon as news of this plan was published, the newspapers rushed to report that Edward would resume his old job: "Huntington in Exile Is Slated for Old Honors: Nephew to Reascend the Throne" and "The Nephew of Uncle Will Soon Be Here: H. E. Huntington Coming Back to His Old Place."[98] Friends and colleagues wrote to congratulate him. B. A. Worthington, in Kruttschnitt's office, said that "no one could have laboured more zealously, more continuously, more conscientiously, or with a stronger determination to produce the best results at minimum cost for the benefit of the owners of this property as a whole, than yourself, and I can stand sponsor for the statement that the business was always transacted from the highest incentives of personal honor and integrity—a quality for which you deserve the utmost commendation, as it is a beautiful example for subordinates."[99]

Events moved more slowly than the news. Edward returned to San Francisco on October 21, 1899, with his mother and his daughter Clara, refused to be interviewed on arrival, and spent the evening at home with his family. Edward was in a quandary, as he wrote to Collis: the department heads were asking for his directions, George Crocker had moved out but had not resigned, and he did not know what his role was in the business. Collis replied in the usual friendly, comforting tone he adopted when he did not know what answer to give: Edward should give advice to the department heads and "continue to do the business in your modest, quiet way, as is your custom." Collis offered his great panacea: "You had better use your own judgment." Collis could not hurry the financial matters, he added, but once they had gotten rid of the Crockers and the Stanfords, he and Hubbard "would work in perfect harmony."[100]

The investment bankers soon began to tell Collis how to manage the SP. Collis sent a telegram to Edward on November 15 saying that Speyer wanted the board to be composed mainly of people in the East and to meet in New York, to have a new person as first vice-president in San Francisco, and for Edward to work as assistant to the president. Edward replied the same day by telegram saying that he could not, with his experience, accept the position offered him, and that there would be no use in his remaining in San Francisco with a first vice-president in place. "Why not leave me out of the question entirely?" he concluded.[101]

Speyer received a report about the unpopularity of both the SP and Collis and asked Collis for his response. He gave it in the form of a twenty-four-page typed letter in which he presented his own self-serving version of the history of the CP, the SP, the role of each associate, and the sources of unpopularity.[102]

The San Francisco papers, in the meantime, were reporting "Huntington's Nephew Once More in Power" and "Plum for Huntington: Collis' Nephew Appointed Acting President."[103] An appreciative letter came to Edward from E. P. Ripley in Chicago, the president of the archrival railroad, the Atchison, Topeka, and Santa Fe. It had not been easy to do business with the SP since Edward was not in an official position, wrote Ripley, but Hubbard had told him that Edward would soon have a proper position: "I was very glad to hear it, and now take pleasure in congratulating you on the result. It involves no disrespect to others to say that, on the whole, our dealings with you have been satisfactory, both in the spirit in which they were entered into and that in which they were subsequently carried out." Edward sent a copy of this letter to Collis, who replied that he was still negotiating with Speyer.[104]

Edward and Kruttschnitt were ordered to leave San Francisco on December 21 (a great time to leave home!) to go to New York for consultations. The rumor mill kept grinding, but not much happened. George Crocker had left, though he did not submit his resignation until February 28, 1900. Edward returned to San Francisco in March in his own private car on the same train that brought Collis, Belle, and their entourage. Edward resumed his work with the SP, and at the annual meeting of the board in April 1900 he was elected a director and second vice-president; all the other directors from California—Kruttschnitt, Stubbs, and three others—had to step down to make room for new directors from the East, as chosen by Speyer.

Edward's tenure as second vice-president did not last long. In June, Collis and Speyer bought out the Hopkins-Searles interest, deposed General Hubbard, and elected Edward to take his place as first vice-president, with Charles H. Tweed, Collis's New York legal colleague, as second vice-president.

Edward had achieved his desire at last, and conveyed the news in a letter to Carrie on June 14, 1900.

> My Dear Sister
>
> I am just about to start south. I have just received a telegram from Uncle informing me of my election as First Vice President of the Southern Pacific Company. I know you will be glad to hear it.
>
> Your affectionate Brother
> Edward[105]

More than a dozen long newspaper stories announced Edward's election as first vice-president, and they were all laudatory. They agreed that Edward would undoubtedly succeed Collis as president. This reflection from the *San Francisco Examiner* for June 15, 1900, is typical: "There is not the least doubt that the elder Huntington is now in a position to say who shall be his successor in the Presidency. The mantle will, no doubt, in due time fall upon the shoulders of his favorite nephew, and so a Huntington will be at the head of the corporation, so both uncle and nephew fondly hope, for years to come."[106]

The question in June 1900 of Collis's successor was timely, as it turned out. On August 13, Collis was having a holiday at their vacation house, Pine Knot, at Raquette Lake in the Adirondacks. With him were Belle, their companions, secretaries, and servants. That day Collis dictated seven business letters to his secretary, five of them to Edward. On the same day, Edward dictated ten business letters to Collis while on the train in Texas.[107] On the evening of August 13, Collis suffered from heart failure, and twenty minutes later he was dead.[108]

Edward's train was in San Antonio when the news reached him. He turned around and made a record-breaking trip to get to New York in time for the funeral. It was held on August 17 in the drawing room and library of the house at 2 East Fifty-seventh Street, with about twenty family members present.

At fifty years of age, Edward was no longer "the nephew" or "Young Huntington."

Eight

WHEN COLLIS DIED, AN era of Edward's life came to an end. Collis—
"Uncle Collis," as he was usually called in the San Francisco newspapers—had been the most important and influential person in Edward's life up to the time he was fifty years old. Collis was the most
prominent and wealthy member of the family. He had been Edward's
employer and immediate superior for nearly thirty years, almost all of
Edward's working life. And Collis was a dominant personality in all of
his relationships.

Two days after Collis's funeral, Edward told his mother privately
about his grief at the death of his uncle:

> This is such a blow to me. I knew that he was getting old, but still I
> thought he might be spared to us for many years. He was so strong.
>   No one can ever fill his place in my heart. Oh, Mother, you can
> never know what he was to me. So kind, so good, and with such a
> true heart.
>   Uncle had wired me twice to come to Pine Knot, and I was going
> later. Oh, how I wish I might have been with him the last few days.[1]

His feelings—the heart—were crucial to how he saw this unique
relationship. It may seem odd to us that Edward should use these

expressions to his mother when they could be taken as detracting from his regard for his own father, who had been dead just ten years; but they both doubtless recognized the truth of what Edward had written.

Edward received more than a hundred letters of sympathy from friends and colleagues after Collis's death, and he answered each one individually. This sample of excerpts from his responses will offer some further sense of how he felt about Collis:

> He was to me friend, uncle, father—everything that stands for affection and unvarying goodness of heart. (To H. W. Garrow, Houston, August 20, 1900)

> Your letter finds me in much trouble and grief over the death of the best uncle a man ever had. I am simply broken up over it, and business of every kind seems to me secondary and, in a way, of no importance while I am trying to pull myself together. (To Herman Shainwald, San Francisco, August 20, 1900)

> I have never experienced a shock such as the announcement of my uncle's death gave me, for he was to me everything that was good and kind and great. (To E. P. Ripley, Chicago, August 22, 1900)

> However and wherever I may be called upon to carry out his wishes or his policy as I can fairly interpret it, I shall feel it the highest of my obligations to try as best I may to meet what would have been his wise and far-reaching plans. (To George Foster Peabody, New York, August 30, 1900)

> To say that I was shocked at the news of my uncle's sudden death expresses very faintly what my feelings were. I cannot even yet realize that I shall see his cheerful, kindly face no more. (To I. W. Hellman, San Francisco, September 4, 1900)[2]

Friends, colleagues, and family members also grieved for Collis. Belle suffered greatly. At the funeral in their living room, she was able to control her grief—as a niece reported to Harriet—only through the aid of medication administered by Dr. Coley "to quiet her nerves" and by sitting between Archer and his wife, Helen; at the interment in the mausoleum she stayed behind after the others had left: "It was terrible for her to leave Uncle there."[3] Two days later, Edward reported to Harriet that "Belle, poor woman, is almost heartbroken. I can do so little to comfort her. Who can?"[4] Harriet wrote to Carrie that "my heart aches for dear Belle. I do want to see her more than I can tell. I have her in my heart a great deal of the time, nights as well as day. Give her my dearest love."[5] On the four-month anniversary of the funeral, Belle wrote to Carrie that "I find it very hard to realize that I shall never see or hear that dear face and voice again. Time as yet has helped me very little, but I get through the days one by one."[6] After Collis's death, Belle wore black in mourning for him, and she continued to wear black exclusively for the remaining twenty-four years of her life. She made a number of major philanthropic gifts during that period, and every one of them was made as a memorial to Collis, even after she had remarried.

This perception of Collis is strikingly different from the Collis portrayed in newspapers of his time and by popular writers, as a corrupt and wicked man who made himself rich at the expense of the government and the public. When Collis died, the *San Francisco Bulletin* wittily suggested that the *Examiner* would have to cut its staff in half because it was "deprived in one sudden merciless stroke of its biggest, best, most dearly prized target"; "in this hour of its sore distress, of its all but unbearable misfortune, the sympathy of the people of California must go out to the *Examiner*."[7]

There were doubtless many ways to perceive Collis. Our concern is to try to gain, in more detail, a sympathetic view of him in order to comprehend a little more clearly the nature of Collis's influence on Edward.

J. O'H. Cosgrave portrayed Collis in two verbal impressions and an editorial in the issue of the *San Francisco Saturday Wave* for August 18, 1900, the day after Collis's funeral. The sketches depicted Collis as a hard worker: he was at the office from nine in the morning until after six in the afternoon; he cleared his desk by the end of the day and answered every note that came to him, and he often had business engagements at home after dinner. He was always approachable, however, even in the midst of dictating letters. He was entirely democratic and never failed in patience and good humor: "He was a fine talker, full of humor and anecdote. He spoke his mind freely and wittily and few subjects there were he could not illuminate with a pregnant phrase." Strict in business and a sharp trader, he was nonetheless "truly generous, charitable, and tolerant." He had a wonderful memory and could recall every mile of his railroads and the full details about his business transactions. "He was fast in his friendships and loyal to his friends. . . . He took a broad interest in the development of the negro race in the South. . . . He had an insight into the future that might be called prophetic. . . ." A lover of books, he kept a set of Crabbe's poems in his desk and read from it to his friends. His main hobby was paintings, which he bought "because they appealed to his personal taste. He became a real connoisseur. It was Mr. Huntington's custom after breakfast to go into the art gallery and spend an hour with his pictures. There he received the men he wanted to talk with intimately. Nothing pleased him better than to find some one with a soul for color and art to whom he would show the treasures of his collection. . . . History may do him tardy justice. He has served the state beyond all measurement, and time will not efface from the hearts of some strong men, a tender memory of this brave, loyal, rugged old man, who, with those he loved, was as gentle as a child, with those he trusted, as constant as the sun."[8]

At the dedication in 1887 of a chapel that Collis had built in Harwinton, Connecticut, as a memorial to his mother, he said that being "born poor was the reason, at least in part, of such success as I have been able to achieve. It was long years ago when I said to myself that what ought to be done could be done, and that success in life only meant labor with honesty of purpose, and an intelligent economy; but I think most of the joys in life come from doing good to others, in helping to raise those who fall, those who are below us to come up a little higher."[9]

Collis was fond of pithy sayings. His favorite (to judge by the number of times he used it) was "what ought to be done could be done." Many others also had to do with work: "All honest work is honorable work," "Never allow any social obligation to interfere with a business engagement," "I don't work hard—I work easy," and "What you do in life, do it with honesty of purpose."[10]

Collis objected to anything that reflected adversely on honest labor. He disliked Edwin Markham's "The Man with the Hoe" because in the poem working men were called "brothers of the ox." Collis wrote a letter to the *New York Sun* on July 26, 1899, anonymously, and offered a prize of $700 for the best answer to the poem, to be called "The Man without the Hoe," in praise of the true dignity of manual labor. Although the offer did not generate any great poems, it did occasion a response from Markham that it was a ruthless society that had blasted the laboring class and betrayed the rights of the people.[11]

The Huntingtons were a close family, and Edward had been on familiar terms with his Uncle Collis all of his life. When Carrie was making her scrapbook for 1898, 1899, and 1900, she wrote the following inscription on the front flyleaf: "The names of C P and H E Huntington are so intimately connected as renders it impossible to give each separate notices."[12] In thinking about the relations of Collis and Edward, it is well to remember these close family connections along with the more formal business relationship between them.

A few examples suggest something more of the nature and spirit of their daily business relations, particularly in the last few months of Collis's life. Collis made daily suggestions to Edward about details. He wanted Edward to increase the salary of Charles Harlan, a minor employee of the SP, from $135 a month to "at least $150 a month" because an influential Washington friend had asked for "an improvement."[13] One of Stanford's executors asked Collis to help him with his oil interest in the San Joaquin Valley, and Collis told Edward: "He is an honest fellow and a gentleman, and I hope you will treat him well and do something for him, if it is not to the detriment of the Southern Pacific Company to do so."[14] Edward received a barrage of such letters from Collis, and he tried to do what Collis wanted.

Sometimes Collis's general suggestions to Edward were phrased as high principle: "I am glad to see the work is progressing steadily, and I hope it will be completed so that we shall not be compelled to disappoint the people along the line by vexatious delays."[15] That is, press the work more vigorously along on the coast line construction. Or this principle of advice, made stronger by its negative import: "We want to be very careful to give our patrons the best service we can possibly afford to give. I think frequently we operate bad roads with cars in bad condition, which costs us more than it would to keep everything up in good order and run trains on exact time."[16] Edward seems to have received and acted on the suggestions with cheerfulness and good humor.

There was, however, an element of deviousness about Collis. He sent Edward a memorandum he had written himself praising the SP and Collis on their building plans and their interest in California. He suggested that Edward get some Californians to sign it and then have it published in California. He even suggested a "tall and fine looking" young man, whose name he couldn't remember, who had something to do with the right-of-way at Lompoc; "it is just such a letter as he could write, and no one would think anything of it. Perhaps he would sign it."[17] When Collis wanted to pacify Adolph Spreckels, the prominent San Francisco manufacturer, he sent Edward two letters about Spreckels: one of them was to show to Spreckels, in which Collis urged Edward to be fair with Spreckels, and to get into accord with him: "I think perhaps he is sometimes a little tenacious about his rights; but some people say I am so, when you know I am not; but I come so near to it, I suppose, that I can sympathize with my friend Spreckels, even if he is a little more so than I am." In the other letter, Collis explained that the former was written "to show it to Spreckels" but that actually he meant "pretty much all I say in it."[18]

Collis also proposed a devious solution to the problem of building a railroad across the Great Salt Lake. He wrote Edward: "By the way, do you have to get the consent of the State to cross Salt Lake? and do you propose to put in any draw-bridge? It would be well to consult Mr. Herrin [the SP public affairs counsel] about this; but my own impression is that I would go on driving sticks in the water without saying anything to anybody about it; and if they bring us up we can fix it with the authorities afterwards."[19]

Edward did not always follow Collis's suggestions. When Collis told him to get a new man without fixed views to advise on consolidating the SP properties in Houston, Edward firmly declined. He already knew what to do, he told Collis, and outlined his plan.[20] When Collis told Edward to let J. O'H. Cosgrave, of the *Wave*, handle the SP illustrations and picture work, Edward objected: they had had a very satisfactory man for twelve or thirteen years, and it was not fair to replace him.[21] Collis suggested to Edward that they hire J. P. Brown to help the SP in public matters. Edward demurred and said the less they had to do with Brown the better. Collis then went into a lengthy discourse in which he suggested that people were prejudiced against Brown and he wanted to "do him justice"; Edward responded that "if he had his just deserts, he would be in jail."[22]

Once in a while, Edward volunteered views that ran counter to Collis's practice. About the work of the legal department, for example. "I think," he wrote to Collis, "that our attorneys should spend more time in endeavoring to find out what can be done, rather than what cannot be done, as they now appear to do."[23]

In their daily dealings, Edward is revealed as eager to carry out the instructions given him. But it is also apparent that he had an independent mind, that he was prepared to present opposing views, and that he declined to follow instructions he thought were wrong.

The most striking feature of Edward's behavior at this time was, as with Collis, his love of hard work. He was generally the first person to arrive at work in the morning and among the last to leave. If the job required his presence late or to the exclusion of other routines like sleeping, he put work first. If he had worked especially hard, he sometimes made a point of telling others—like Collis—what he had done. Otherwise, Edward was modest about his achievements and self-effacing about his good qualities.

He had a strongly practical turn of mind. He delighted in dealing with physical objects, like railroad tracks, depots, houses, utilities, and land. And he was a builder by inclination. Not content to form a conclusion until he had personally examined the objects involved, he paid special attention to the people who were active in the operations. He learned to analyze an activity by reviewing the operating results, and he became quite adept at it.

Edward had somewhat wider interests than Collis did. Collis said of himself, "I am a railroad builder, and not, as you know, a speculator in land; in fact, in all my railroad building I have let pass millions of dollars that could have been made if I had invested in farming lands and town sites. I have done very little of it, for the reason that all my money has been invested and all my time spent in the building of railroads, and I am in that position to-day."[24] Edward was a railroad builder, too, and more involved with ties, track, and design than Collis ever was. Edward was also a railroad operator, which Collis was only at second hand. Edward was also actively interested in solving the problems involved in the establishment of towns and cities, like providing water and electricity, interurban transport, a free press, and good government. He was not a bold, imaginative entrepreneur eager to open up an entirely new realm but rather a wise, thoughtful developer who tried to make his work beneficial to people as well as to his companies.

Like Collis, Edward had a deep love of family and a continuing concern for his relatives. He kept in touch with them and helped those who needed assistance. In his immediate household, there were mixed feelings among the parents and children. He and his wife, Mary, were not particularly compatible: his main interest was his work, and he was away from home a great deal of the time; her main interests were clothes, social activities, and travel. (Much later, he said that he had never had a happy married life.) Edward did not spend much time with their children, and he shared very little in their growing up. He came to be very close to his son Howard after they began to work together, when Howard was in his late twenties. There was always a special bond of affection between Edward and Elizabeth, his second daughter, but he was never close to the other children, Clara and Marian, and they came to resent it. All the children turned mainly to their mother for comfort, support, and affection.

Edward was a friendly, agreeable person. He was courteous and amiable to everyone, including the employees in the most menial jobs in his businesses. He liked to maintain tranquil relations among all his colleagues; when there were disagreements, his practice was to smile and try to see if peace could not be restored. But he had a strong sense of independence and a feeling of obligation to do what he thought was right; he never, so far as I have seen, allowed a decision to be reached that he did not think right. Nor have I seen an example of deviousness in his dealing with people or problems. Although he was often involved in lobbying activities with state legislatures and Congress, there are no suggestions of corrupt or illegal dealings with elected officials or others.

His interest in books was wide and sincere. Although he had no more than a rudimentary public school education, he was a lifelong reader and buyer of books. From about the age of twenty-one, he was always in the process of building a collection of books, and it became increasingly interesting as he went along. On the other hand, Edward was just beginning to buy paintings, and his early purchases were of works popular at the time. Collis was already in the big league of art collectors, owning a Vermeer, a Velazquez, and the works of other notable painters. There is an interesting parallel between Edward and Collis in their impulses to collect books and art and in the results they achieved.

Edward and Collis were both bright, largely self-educated, perceptive, thoughtful, concerned about other people. Collis had a dramatic flair and some guile; he enjoyed interacting with groups of people, telling anecdotes, and making speeches. Edward was relatively quiet, modest, and straightforward. He would rather listen than talk. He was emotionally stable and poised in his reactions. Both of them enjoyed living.

Nine

IN 1900, EDWARD WAS FIFTY years old. The next ten years were the most complex of his career. He followed new courses, achieved new successes, and responded to critical changes in his life. Collis's death, the termination of his promising career with the Southern Pacific, and the end of his marriage profoundly altered his life and influenced the directions he took in the future.

Collis's death was reported in over one hundred newspapers across the United States. The main topics of interest were the value of his estate—with the estimates, offered with great confidence, ranging from $35 to $80 million—and who would succeed him in the presidency of the Southern Pacific. When the will was made public six weeks after his death, attention focused on the great wealth that was to come to H. E. Huntington; $33 million was a common estimate of his inheritance. He was also the expected choice to be SP president.

Collis's last will and testament was signed on March 13, 1897, nearly three and a half years before his sudden death.[1] He gave virtually all of his estate to relatives. Charles H. Tweed, his friend and lawyer, was given a legacy of $100,000, as was the Hampton Institute; the Chapin Home in New York received $25,000. All the rest went to twenty-two relatives: his widow, son, and daughter, and his sisters, nephews, and nieces. Harriet received $50,000, Willard $50,000, and Carrie $20,000.

Archer got $200,000 (plus reversionary rights to all of his mother's trusts and legacies), and Clara, Collis's daughter, received $1 million. There were no bequests to the children of the nieces and nephews. Belle received the major part of the estate: she was given lifetime possession of the furniture, jewelry, paintings, and houses; a $500,000 trust; half of the residue of the estate before the trusts and legacies were distributed; and two-thirds of the Southern Pacific stock. Edward was to receive one-third of the Southern Pacific stock and the residue of the estate after the distribution of all the trusts and legacies. As it worked out, Belle and Edward received almost the same amounts as residual legatees.

Belle, Edwin Gates, and Charles Tweed were the executors. They promptly prepaid $700,000 inheritance tax in order to save 5 percent, which led the *Portland Oregonian* to observe gravely that "the life and death of Collis P. Huntington teaches us how thankful we should be that we do not have to pay a $700,000 inheritance tax."[2] When the executors filed the appraisal of the estate in the surrogate's court in the County of New York in 1902, the gross estate was reported as $35 million, with a net estate of $28 million after expenses and charges. The property (real estate, art, and so on) in which Belle had a life interest was valued at $2.5 million, her share of the SP stock at $8.7 million, and her trust and residual share at $5.8 million, for a gross total of $16 million, and net of $15.8 million after taxes. For Edward, the SP stock was valued at $4.4 and his residual share at $4.9 million, for a gross total of $9.3 million, and a net of $8.8 million after taxes.[3] When the executors filed their legacy return with the Internal Revenue Service in 1903, the same figures were used.[4]

The actual value of what Belle and Edward received from Collis's estate was probably a little larger than these figures, in view of the common practice of minimizing appraisals in order to minimize taxes. The SP stock, for example, which was appraised at a total of $13 million, was in fact sold for $22.3 million within five months of Collis's death.[5] From this sale, Belle received $15 million rather than her $8.7 million appraisal, and Edward received $7.4 million rather than his $4.4 million appraisal. The literal shares were therefore $19.8 million for Belle after leaving out the property in which she had only a life interest and $11.8 million for Edward. It would probably be reasonable to estimate the real value of Collis's estate at about $50 million, with Belle's part on the order of $20 to $25 million (again leaving out her life interests) and Edward's share at about $12 to $15 million.

The will did not fill everyone with joy. Some relatives were touched with envy at Edward's good fortune, and the San Francisco newspapers reported local gossip about the smallness of the bequests to Willard and Carrie and about the fact that the sister and brother of Clara (Princess Hatzfeldt) got nothing.[6] The person most disaffected, however, was Clara at receiving only $1 million. She and Prince Hatzfeldt came to the United States in April 1901, hired lawyer Joseph D. Redding, and gave all signs of planning to contest the will, despite the fact that the will contained the usual provision that anyone who contested it would forfeit all rights under it. This threat disturbed Edward, since Clara was his wife's sister, and a controversy might have had deep emotional consequences. He wrote from New York to his mother in San Francisco that Prince Hatzfeldt was in town "and Clara comes this week, presumably to make trouble." Willard affiliated himself with the Prince, and Tweed refused to pay Willard his legacy until Edward insisted.[7] A week later Edward wrote to Carrie that "Clara Hatzfeldt arrived yesterday and was coming up to number two [East Fifty-seventh Street] to lunch today. Of course she is over here for no good purpose, but I imagine if they want to fight they will get all they want" in the way of a fight.[8] After another week he told Harriet that "I have written Mary that I may cable her to come home" from Europe:

> Clara Hatzfeldt is here and intends to bring suit against the estate, claiming that by a contract she shall have a daughter's share of two thirds, the other third of course going to Belle. Redding has by some unaccountable means persuaded Mrs. Prentice [Clara's mother] to sign a paper in which she makes statements contrary to what she has told many people. As you know, she has said to everyone that she never gave up Clara and never would. I wish you and Carrie to write me just what she had said to you or either of you in relation to the subject. It is for this reason that I want Mary to come home. Do not mention this matter to anyone but Burke and Carrie, and caution them not to mention it.[9]

Clara arrived in New York on April 21, 1901, and rejoined her husband. Her plan to contest the will became a cause célèbre in the newspapers and was reported in more than two hundred stories.[10] Both sides felt that the case turned on whether Clara had been legally adopted by Collis and Elizabeth or Belle. Careful searches were made of legal archives in Sacramento, New York, San Francisco, and even in Richmond, Virginia, but no adoption record was found; both sides stoutly denied that they had caused any searches to be made. Clara, her husband, and their lawyer went to San Francisco in June and then to Sacramento to visit her mother, who had earlier said that on Clara's wedding day "my daughter will be buried. I never expect to see her face again." Mary did not figure in these dealings, and she did not come back from Europe; the newspapers described the sisters as "estranged" with "bitterness between them," and "the Princess has asserted that she knows nothing of such a sister."

No suit to overturn the will was ever attempted. We do not know what went on between Edward and Mary in the course of this uncertainty. In any event, a settlement was made by which Clara received an additional $1 or $2 million, which was represented as coming out of the increase in the value of securities since Collis's death, but which actually came out of the residue of the estate that would otherwise have gone to Belle and Edward. Clara and her husband went back to Europe to begin spending the money.

Clara's visit was memorialized in some doggerel *vers de société* in the *New York Town Topics:*

> Sweet Princess Hatzfeldt is replete
>   With effervescent glee;
> She came her rival heirs to greet
>   With due pugnacity,
> But H. E. H. has anteed up
>   Plunks in a lordly bunch;
> The Princess therefore now can sup,
>   As well as dine and lunch.[11]

Collis's bequest changed the public's perception of Edward. He had already been thought of as well-to-do. His net worth in securities had increased from about $600,000 when he came to San Francisco in 1892 to about $1 million before Collis died in 1900. He had been making some $27,000 a year in salaries from the SP and the Market Street Railway, and he had been investing and reinvesting his funds in income stocks, speculative stocks, and bonds; he was only just beginning at that time his career in the ownership of electric railway lines in Southern California, and the results had not yet begun to show up on his balance sheets.

Immediately after Collis's death, a full analysis was made of Edward by J. A. Fowler, vice-president of the American Institute of Phrenology. It was printed in dozens of newspapers, with a sketch of Edward's head, divided into parts with a caption for each part. His forehead showed intuitiveness, perseverance, and energy; the base of his brain revealed executive force; his eyebrows indicated perception and memory; his eyes, acuteness; his nose, analytical powers; his jaw, endurance; and his chin, deliberateness. The caption read, "So great is the interest in what will become of the millions left by C. P. Huntington that Phrenologist Fowler gives a complete character sketch of Henry E. Huntington." It was a long, long sketch, the headlines of which will perhaps satisfy our curiosity: "Can Triple Huntington Millions. Well Fitted to Succeed His Uncle and Continue Many Projects. Healthy Organization. Grip Firm and Enthusiastic. Heart Beat and Pulse Steady." Special emphasis was laid, in the story, on the fact that Edward was destined to *triple* Collis's millions.[12]

Within six months of Collis's death, Edward was described in the San Francisco papers as having a "colossal fortune" of $33.6 million from Collis and $2.3 million of his own, and it was conjectured that the total of about $36 million "may be somewhat under the true figures." Sums like these were repeated over and over again; I have seen about a hundred clippings expressing awe at Edward's "enormous fortune."[13]

It is difficult to make fun of wealth, as envy keeps breaking in. But some newspapers had a go at it. Edward was called "the $25 million Huntington" and his brother Willard "the $50,000 Huntington." Their daughters were also handled a little roughly: Edward's three daughters were called "the rich Misses Huntington," worth $6.5 million each, while Willard's daughter, Edith, was brushed off as "the pretty Miss Huntington."[14] On another occasion, Edward's daughters were described as "not good looking but interesting girls."[15]

After the settlement of Collis's estate, Edward began to be spoken of popularly as a magnate, a Really Rich Man, one of those in the stratosphere among the Vanderbilts and the other "very rich people who are different from the rest of us." Edward's poise had carried him through numerous setbacks in his career, and it now carried him through financial success. He paid no overt attention to his sudden fame. But it would be hard to believe that it did not have some effect on his outlook.

We speculate most readily about those things that threaten us. The San Francisco papers had thus begun guessing who would succeed Collis as president of the Southern Pacific if he were to die. The newspaper clippings to which I shall refer have—like all that I have already cited and those that I will later cite—a special relevance in that they are from Edward's own files or scrapbooks, prepared by his secretaries for his information. We can be reasonably sure that he read them himself and was affected by them in one way or another.

The papers had Edward as their unanimous choice for president in the middle of June 1900, after Collis had bought the Hopkins-Searles stock and Edward had been made first vice-president.[16] They all expressed certainty that he would in due course become president, and this certainty extended to New York, where the headlines of the *Sunday Telegraph* reported that the "Future Looks Bright for Favorite Nephew. Mantle to Fall on Him. Not Much Doubt That He Will Succeed to the Presidency of the Southern Pacific."[17]

After Collis died in August 1900, the guesses became more diverse. The majority still thought Edward, but some thought Charles H. Tweed, a few thought Edwin Hawley, and some thought it would be an easterner who was president of some other railroad.[18] The editorial writers generally favored Edward, however. In the *Arizona Daily Star,* a long editorial asserted that

> while there is much speculation as to the coming president of the
> Southern Pacific company, if Arizona had a voice in making the
> choice it would be for that peerless railroad man and good citizen,
> Mr. H. E. Huntington, for he is not only the peer of any railroad man
> in the United States, but is a man of the strictest integrity of character,

stands for everything that is good, a gentleman whose presence and influence is always for the right, as he has light to see and understand the right. The STAR hopes to receive the news of the election of Mr. H. E. Huntington as president of the Southern Pacific Company.[19]

The editorial writer of the *Los Angeles Daily Times* strongly favored Edward on the grounds "that he is inclined to more liberal ideas in railroad management than were possessed by his uncle, and that he would be more inclined to give more weight to the wishes and interests of the people served by the system."[20]

Newspapers also received letters to the editor on the subject. Denis Kearney wrote to the *San Francisco Bulletin* on August 16, 1900, to tell of a conversation he had had with Collis a couple of months before on the subject of buying SP stock. Collis had favored purchases. " 'But Mr. Huntington, suppose you die, what then?' 'Why there's Ed,' replied Collis. 'No better boy ever lived. He's been with me for twenty-eight years. He knows a thing or two about railroading. I'll trust him.' " Mr. Kearney concluded that Collis must have made arrangements for Edward to be his successor.[21]

There was also a little scheming going on behind the scenes. J. C. Stubbs sent a confidential telegram to Edward saying that William F. Herrin, the chief counsel of the SP and a prominent San Francisco attorney, was ready to go to New York if he could help "in a certain matter which we all desire."[22] Edward wrote to Herman Shainwald in San Francisco and told him that a letter to D. O. Mills, a member of the presidential selection committee, "as to what you and other business men think of me might be of much benefit to me."[23] Edward received at least one letter of congratulations on his selection; he replied with a smile in his prose: "I am afraid that it is not unlike reading one's own obituary: it is pleasant to have your friends speak nicely of you, but you are not dead yet. In short, I have not been elected president. Thanking you all the same."[24] M. H. Sherman wrote to Edward that Epes Randolph "is very anxious, so are we all, that you accept of the presidency of the Southern Pacific Company, which we all believe you can have, if you want it."[25]

In fact, James Speyer and his banking colleagues were in control.

Charles H. Tweed was chosen as chairman of the SP, and the selection committee for president consisted of Tweed, D. O. Mills, and James Speyer. In October 1900 they selected as president Charles M. Hays, the general manager of the Grand Trunk Railway of Canada. It was said that this choice was made at the instance of Sir James Rivers Wilson of London, a leading foreign investor in Speyer's activities. Edward, as a major stockholder, was consulted about the selection; he approved, though he had never met Hays. The papers were full of this news for ten days.[26]

Then the rumor mill began to churn out explanations as to why Edward had not been chosen. First, it was because Speyer had insisted that Edward live in San Francisco and Edward declared that he intended to move to New York "whether he got the presidency or not." Then the argument ran that Edward was against paying dividends to the SP stockholders, and the bankers insisted on a return.[27]

The most intriguing (and elaborate) rumor was that Belle and Tweed had cooperated with Speyer to "freeze the nephew out of the presidency." Speyer reportedly told Edward that "he was too young and inexperienced to handle the finances and general policy of the company" and that "Mrs. C. P. Huntington and Charles H. Tweed are said to have coincided with the Speyers in this estimate of the nephew." Edward showed "both his bitter disappointment over the loss of the place and his keen surprise that the widow and attorney of his uncle should so readily side with the Speyers against him. . . . 'But why did he show keen surprise over the attitude of the lady and the lawyer?' is the blunt questioning remark of some friends. And the latter go on to quietly gossip that the nephew and the widow were never very warm friends, and the New York lawyer never liked the nephew's attempt to be the 'whole thing' during the lifetime of the uncle."[28] It is impossible now to know what basis there was for this rumor. We can at least presume that it was a rumor read by Edward and recorded in his memory as well as in his files.

In November, Edward returned to San Francisco from New York, where he had mostly been since Collis's death in July, to an SP job that was now inconsequential. He returned to New York in December for conferences with Tweed and Hays, but he was back in San Francisco in time for Christmas with his family.

Hays arrived in San Francisco in late December to take over as president. Many functions were held at which he was the guest of honor. The Manufacturers and Producers Association of California had a banquet at the Palace Hotel in San Francisco on January 18, 1901, with 220 of the most prominent citizens present, but not Edward. Other groups in Oakland, Los Angeles, and elsewhere honored him. He was described as "popular": he spoke well, was friendly, shook hands all around, and made a good impression.[29]

Rumors had floated around since November 1900 that the Huntingtons were selling their SP stock. Various buyers were mentioned: Vanderbilt, J. P. Morgan, Speyer, Harriman. On January 31, 1901, Belle and Edward entered into an agreement with Kuhn Loeb and Company to sell their stock (432,700 shares) for about $22 million, with one-third to be paid in cash on February 11 and the other two-thirds (with 4 percent interest) by July 10, 1901.[30] It was an advantageous deal for Belle and Edward. The price worked out to about 51½ a share, well above what had been the recent market price. There had been a contest for control of the SP, and Speyer lost out to E. H. Harriman's Union Pacific, which bought the Huntington stock through Kuhn Loeb and thus gave effective control of the SP to Harriman.[31]

Thus concluded Edward's career in steam railroading—but not quite. In April, he allowed himself to be reelected a director of the Southern Pacific. He explained it to his sister Carrie: "You of course have seen by the papers that I have been elected a director of the SP. I do not, however, expect to take an active part in the management. Mr. Harriman was anxious to have me remain on the board, and I consented."

He had been president of the Market Street Railway since 1897. In late 1901 he sold his stock to a Baltimore syndicate. When the deal was consummated in April 1902, his last substantial investment in San Francisco had been closed out, but not his interest. When San Francisco was struck by the severe earthquake and fire on April 18 and 19, 1906, Edward went into action. He was in Los Angeles at the time, and he immediately offered a lead gift of $10,000 to a relief fund being proposed there. On April 20 he went to San Francisco, assessed the damage, and established a special fund to help professional men such as doctors and lawyers replace their lost libraries and instruments. He contributed $30,000 to the fund, got three prominent San Francisco professional men—including a justice of the California supreme court—to administer it, wrote an appeal that was published in all the Los Angeles papers, and arranged for three professional men in Los Angeles to solicit contributions to the fund.[32]

By 1900, Edward had spent eight years as a San Franciscan in effective control of the operation of the Southern Pacific. He certainly had wanted to succeed Collis as president. When the settlement left him out, he was bitterly disappointed. After about 1902, he was left with no major professional commitment in San Francisco, free to follow a new line of work.

From 1900 to 1906, Edward's family life was fragmented. Edward was at home very little; he lived and worked mostly in New York and Los Angeles. Mary and the three daughters were also frequently away from home; they took several long trips, including one to Europe for almost a year, and they spent the summers in a rental house north of San Francisco or in Oneonta or in the Adirondacks. Three of the four children were married during this time and started their own families at widely separated places. For a man to whom the idea of family was crucially important, this period was marked by a breakup in the structure of his immediate family.

Right after Collis's death, Edward stayed in New York for about five months working with Gates and Tweed in the first stage of settling the estate. He knew the business side better than the others did, and at his office at 23 Broad Street in New York he spent his full time in advising and writing letters relating to the estate. For the next several years, Belle was often with Archer and Helen, mostly traveling or living in Europe, and not available for consultation. Edward first lived at the Hotel Netherland and then took a suite of rooms at the Metropolitan Club on the corner of Fifth Avenue and Sixtieth Street. "My rooms at the Club are looking very comfortable," he wrote to his mother. "They have just been repapered and I send you samples, as you may want to see them. I shall also bring the books from my room in S.F. so that when I am here I can have a place that seems a little like home."[33] It is interesting to note that he felt books, or at least *his* books, made a place seem like home. As he wrote his mother on a Sunday, "It is sunny here, and I shall spend the day in my room reading. We have a nice library in the Club."[34] His daughter Elizabeth was glad that he had settled at the Metropolitan Club "because I thought it was so much more homelike. Still, I hope you're not going to be away so much a year from now. When you take some of your pictures [from the San Francisco house], don't take that etching of a woman with two cupids framed in gold with an eagle at the top—that's my pet picture in the house and do love to look at it so."[35]

Still, he felt lonely, especially on Sundays, when he was on his own. A revealing insight into the way he thought about himself is contained in a Sunday letter to Elizabeth, written in the Metropolitan Club: "This is a beautiful day—too nice to be in the house. But some way or other, when I am in my room, I am averse to leaving it, especially Sundays. I like to walk in the Park, but it is always so crowded on fine Sundays. And I do so dislike crowds: I prefer to be alone with my books. I do not think I am unsociable in my disposition, and I love my friends. But all my love goes out to a few, and not to the great masses."[36] Those few were, first of all, his family. His children missed him. Marian wrote him rather plaintively after her eighteenth birthday on October 3, 1901: "I should like to be with you on that day, and next year we must surely manage it, for the last three years you have been away."[37]

Edward began to spend increasing amounts of time in Los Angeles. At first he stayed at the Van Nuys Hotel at Fourth and Main streets. After the Pacific Electric Building—"the Huntington Building," at Sixth and Main streets—was finished in 1904, he took an apartment in the Jonathan Club, which occupied the top two floors of the building. Sometimes he spent the nights with his friends the George Pattons at their house next to the Shorb Ranch. "It is a delightful, pleasant place to visit," he wrote Elizabeth. "They are so congenial. It seems almost like home for me to be there, as I seem to be like one of the family."[38]

His own family was often scattered about during these years. Howard was at Harvard studying science and electrical engineering. Early in 1901 Mary took the three girls on the first of their several European trips. They went to London, Paris, Florence, Venice, Berlin, Frankfurt, Dresden, and other places.

They visited picture galleries, churches, and theaters, played tennis and attended concerts, shopped for clothes and furs, went automobiling in France with Belle and Archer—both of whom were arrested for speeding—and wrote a lot of letters home. The letters to Edward from his daughters were always affectionate and appreciative. "Oh father dear, I am so happy," wrote Elizabeth. "I wish you could realize how much pleasure you are giving me. I don't deserve it one bit. Only my love can repay you—double." And later: "It seems I give very little in return for your nice letters, but I love you just as dearly and oh so much."[39] Edward wrote to each of his children regularly—though not as often as they wished—and always with warmth and affection. "My Darling Daughter" was his usual salutation, and his close was "Your Affectionate Father"; that same spirit filled the body of his letters to them. He also wrote to his mother about once every two weeks, but she generally grumbled about the infrequency of his letters and his failure to answer all of her questions.

Mary and the girls spent a month at Bad Neuheim so that Mary could take the cure for her "intense nervousness," as Clara described it to Edward.[40] "Mother seems to be better," wrote Elizabeth to her father. "The doctor said it was a very good thing she came when she did. I think a month's treatment will do her good till she can get here again next year."[41]

There were trips and holidays every year, but Edward never went with them. Sometimes he was in Oneonta or San Francisco with a child who had stayed behind. Mary wrote long, chatty letters to any child who was not on a trip. Her main topics were the hotels, the food, the beauty of the sights, their schedule, the weather, shopping, letters received, concern for relatives at home, and how glad she would be to get home. The letters were always affectionate and cheerful; she never referred to Edward except as a source for funds.

Edward was generous with them financially. In addition to paying all their expenses for trips and holidays, each daughter was given a letter of credit for $1,000 for a trip abroad beyond the regular expense allowance of $150 or $200 a month. There were also extra gifts, like $500 for birthdays, $1,000 for Christmas, $1,000 for wedding gifts for a sibling, and the amounts needed for trousseaux. Mary received about twice as much as the children on these occasions, plus payment for all household costs and about $5,000 a year for personal expenses. About half a dozen of Edward's or Mary's elderly relatives received regular monthly allowances of $50 or $100 from him.

In 1901, while his family was in Europe, Edward began thinking about buying a family house in Los Angeles. He considered the O. W. Childs house, with eight acres of handsome grounds, and the T. D. Stimson residence, in an elegant neighborhood. His daughters—then about twenty-three, twenty-one, and eighteen—got wind of the idea and sent inquiries and opinions to him from abroad. "What is this I hear about your looking at houses in Los Angeles?" wrote Elizabeth on October 7. "Surely you are not going to move there?" And Clara, on November 6: "What's this we hear about a house in Los Angeles?" On November 9, Elizabeth wrote again: "I hope you won't move to Los Angeles till spring. But then nothing is settled, so we are still perplexed. I suppose we'll be out of doors more there, and everyone says it's a lovely house." And on November 17, she wrote more tellingly: "We are of course curious to know whether our home is to be in Los Angeles or in S.F. But just so you will be with us to have a little more home life I do not much care where we live. Marian is quite cut up because she has lately so depended on her friends." Howard also conveyed his grave opinion from Harvard on November 18: "I suppose now that your electric railway interests are confined chiefly to Southern California, that you may make Los Angeles our home. If so, I hope the change would be beneficial to you."[42] Edward did buy the Childs house, and he had new carpeting installed; but he never lived there, nor did he try to establish it as the family home.

In the spring of 1902, after nearly three years at Harvard, Howard felt he had had enough academic training. He had received a technical education, completed the final courses in math and physics, and had in addition been assistant editor of the *Harvard Engineering Journal* and a member of the Harvard Union and various clubs. He felt, at age twenty-six, out of sympathy with undergraduate life, as the social fun struck him as childish. He sought the "full and hearty consent" of his father to leave Harvard and "go into business again" and grow with his work.[43] His father gave that consent. Howard left at the end of the academic year and went to Los Angeles, where he was given the job of assistant general manager of the Los Angeles Railway. Howard hoped to be helpful to his father. As he wrote to his grandmother Harriet, "Father's pleasure seems to be in his work very largely, but I hope in time to be of material assistance to him."[44]

The first of the Huntington children to marry was Clara, the oldest girl, called Peggy by her sisters. She and Gilbert Perkins were married by Bishop C. H. Brent in Trinity Episcopal Church in San Francisco on April 30, 1902, with an elaborate wedding breakfast for three hundred guests at the Huntington residence afterwards. Edward gave the bride away, and Howard came from Cambridge to serve as best man. Gilbert, a graduate of Princeton and the son of a judge in Kentucky, was in the bond department of a New York brokerage firm. Clara and Gilbert had met at Lake Mohonk in the Adirondacks a year and a half earlier. Edward made a particular effort to get to know Gilbert in New York once he was told of Clara's serious interest in him. He wrote to Carrie that "Clara is out with her young man, and I expect she will marry him sooner or later. I am not pleased, but really can find no fault with him. He is a gentlemanly, honest fellow. I had a very plain talk with him that he must first show what he could do for himself before he could ever expect any assistance from me."[45] After their marriage, Clara and Gilbert lived in New York, and Clara's departure from the family was a shock to her sisters and her mother. "I do not allow myself to think much about it; I find myself getting pretty blue at times," wrote Mary to Elizabeth. "I don't believe I shall ever get used to Clara's living so far away from us. I sometimes think it must not be. Then I realize I am absolutely helpless in the matter."[46] Before the preceding Christmas, Elizabeth had written to Edward that "this will be the last Xmas together for a long time, with Clara living in the east. Makes me sick when I think of the family breaking up. But I would not, under the circumstances, have it different."[47] But it turned out to be hard for her. Later she wrote to Edward from San Francisco: "I don't think we could stand the house without someone to fill it. With you and Howard and Clara away it is so lonesome at times."[48]

Two years after Clara's wedding, Mary and Marian were invited to stop and see Clara—who was ill, with a nurse—and Gilbert on their way to Europe, but it was not a happy visit. Mary wrote to Elizabeth that "Marian and I are full of tears most of the time, and wish so much that we had stayed at home. In fact, things are just a bit annoying, as Gilbert wishes your Father to come there and visit them, and seems to infer that it would be pleasant all around if I was not here just now—as he thinks Clara should not be annoyed in any way."[49] So Mary and Marian moved on. Elizabeth, in reporting this episode to her fiancé, was not very sympathetic toward her mother or Marian.[50]

The next to marry was Howard, the oldest child and only son. After returning from Harvard and taking the job as assistant general manager of the Los Angeles Railway in Los Angeles, he shared his father's five-room apartment in the Jonathan Club. When the general manager of the Los Angeles Railway, John A. Muir, died suddenly in January 1904, Howard was promoted to the position, at the age of twenty-seven. Epes Randolph said that "he has shown great earnestness, industry, and capacity in all the work he has undertaken." And he was the only son of the principal owner. Still, he wrote to his grandmother that he had not expected the promotion. "Much to my surprise," he wrote her, "I was selected as General Manager of the Los Angeles Railway. It is a great honor, surely. I think I am taking up some of the detail work that Father was attending to during Mr. Muir's illness, and I hope to be able to take more of the load off of Father's shoulders as time goes on. So I do not think you need worry."[51]

Edward had despaired a little that Howard would ever marry. "He goes from flower to flower," Edward wrote to Elizabeth, in a figure redolent of an earlier age, "but he does not pick any. I presume he thinks they are all park flowers and is not allowed to take them. I first think he is a little sweet on one, and then another, but doesn't seem to care much for any. So I guess he will be an old bachelor, which I would prefer to his marrying anyone of the Helen Wagner type, who would be totally unfit for him."[52]

Edward need not have despaired. Howard soon met Leslie Thayer Green of Berkeley when she was in Los Angeles visiting her relatives Mrs. Harry Bixby and Mrs. Ernest Bryant. He began to make frequent weekend visits to Berkeley. Their engagement was announced in May 1905, and they were married on the evening of August 16, 1905, at her parents' home with 150 guests present—including all of Howard's immediate family, with Elizabeth and Marian as bridesmaids—for the ceremony and supper in a "floral bower." Harriet could not be there, but she sent for her wedding gift a piece of her own handwork, a "beautiful corset cover" that thrilled Leslie and that caused Elizabeth to write to her grandmother, "That corset cover you sent to Leslie was so sweet and dainty—we couldn't see the stitches and wondered how it stayed together. It was fairy-like work, and Leslie almost cried with joy and shows it with the greatest pride. I have almost decided to get engaged myself just to get one."[53] One newspaper columnist took the wedding as an occasion for making a little fun: "Young Huntington, I hear, is a chip off the old block; that is, he possesses all those fine qualities that endeared the elder Huntington to Uncle Collis, qualities that insure success in the commercial world. It is always business before pleasure with young Huntington. Indeed, so devoted to business has he always been that it is considered surprising that he should be willing to lose that time to get married."[54] He was willing to lose that time, and also to go to Europe for a four-month honeymoon.

Less than a year later came the marriage of Elizabeth, who was called Betty by her mother, Bridget or Lizbeth by her sisters, and Peter by some of her girl friends. Her engagement to John Brockway Metcalf, called Brockway, of San Francisco had been announced in December 1905. Elizabeth had accurately predicted what her mother would want to do. As she had written to Brockway two months earlier: "Mother's chief delight is shopping. Turn her loose in a shop and she is perfectly happy. I expect she will have ducks helping me with my trousseau." They had a busy time, as the wedding took place only three months later, on the evening of March 6, 1906, in the drawing room of the bride's home before a hundred intimate friends and relatives—including all the immediate family—with Marian as Elizabeth's only attendant. The house was elaborately decorated with flowers, and the downstairs supper room was filled with fruit blossoms. The father of the groom had been secretary of commerce and labor in Theodore Roosevelt's cabinet. The young couple—she was twenty-six and he thirty-one—were very popular, and they received dozens of warm and affectionate letters of congratulation from friends and relations, who thought them an ideal pair. Elizabeth's mother said, with surprising candor, "We know he hasn't any money and that he is not handsome—but what do such things amount to?" She felt that Brockway had "more character in his little finger than most men have in their whole bodies. I think he will make a fine, considerate, thoughtful husband—which is the greatest thing in the world."[55] Marian wrote to Harriet that "he is one of the most considerate and unselfish men that I have ever known, and any girl could safely trust her happiness in his hands."[56] The couple spent their honeymoon of several months in Japan.

Edward established a trust fund of $250,000 for each of his children as a wedding present. The children were delighted, declared that they would not allow themselves to be spoiled, and accepted their presents as a challenge to help them be productive and worthwhile people. As Elizabeth wrote to Brockway, "Did you hear? Did Daddy tell you? He is such a dear, I sat down and cried for sheer joy of loving him so much. And, as I told him, I would always try to be worthy of such a Dad—and you will, too, won't you, dearest? He is going to give me for a wedding present just what he gave Howard and Clara. I believe (but am not sure) it was $250,000—which means about $800 a month interest, doesn't it?"[57]

Edward also tried to reestablish his family in Southern California. His children and their partners came for frequent visits to Los Angeles, and Edward took them on extensive trips, by trolley and by car, around the Southland. It was a happy time for all of them. He set aside three choice lots in Pasadena and offered to build houses on them for his children. Clara and Gilbert accepted, as did Howard and Leslie. Elizabeth and Brockway chose to stay in San Francisco, and Marian never married. Later he built a house in Pasadena for his sister Carrie and her family. The reestablishment was only a partial success, however.[58]

For Edward, a happy marriage was the essential way to a happy life. Over and over again, he spoke of happy marriage as his greatest desire for his children. When Clara was considering marriage, Edward told her, "I want most of all to see all my children happily married."[59] And when Elizabeth was engaged, he said, "My greatest desire is to see my children happily married."[60] He rejoiced in the prospect of a loving marriage: "I cannot tell you how much pleasure it gives me," he wrote to Elizabeth, "to know that so much love and sweetness has come into your life. Cherish and guard it, my Daughter, for it is all there is in life worth living for. Wealth and all that it can bring is nothing in comparison, for without love in the heart, life is not worth living. But with it, it becomes a fountain of everlasting happiness, peace, and sweet content."[61]

There is an undertone of apprehensiveness in some of his praise of married life. Of Clara and Gilbert, he said, "I hope the marriage will be a happy one. If it is, it will make her life such a happy one. If not, I had rather see her laid in her coffin. Let us all hope that her life will be all that she pictures it."[62] He also had an anxiety about what might happen if the couple proved not to be congenial, or if one of them proved selfish. "I cannot tell you how happy I hope you will be," he wrote to Elizabeth the month before her marriage, "for I feel that you and Brockway are congenial. If a person is happily married, life is just beginning. You must both be patient with each other and give up to each other. When one always gives up to the other, it is very apt to make the one given up to very selfish. My dear child, I don't think it is necessary for me to advise you, for you are so self-sacrificing. But you will be happier if you do not carry it too far. I speak knowingly and feelingly."[63] He apparently kept brooding on this kind of risk in marriage, and a week later he wrote once more about the importance of giving up to one another, but not too much: "Of course I know it is a pleasure to give up to one we love. But it is not best to do so always, as it naturally makes the one given up to very selfish and at last unreasonable. And will be sure to cause much unhappiness."[64]

Edward made a good many statements that expressed, in a guarded way, that his own married life had been unhappy. His mother's birthday letter to him when he became fifty-five concluded with the thought that "I ask our Father in Heaven every day and night that he will be pleased to spare your life and health and grant you many happy days yet. You have had many sorrowful ones, but I trust your last ones may be the happiest ones." In his response, Edward thanked her for being "helpful, I cannot say how much, to take much of the bitterness of my life out of it. I expect on the whole I should consider that I am not worse off than the average, and I hope (as you say) I may have many happy days before me. At least I hope to have, and believe I will have."[65] To Elizabeth, he had been a little more open when, in giving his view of himself, he wrote, "Every one has some burden to bear, and I often wish they were more evenly distributed. But no one can shift their own to another—each must bear his to the end. This should be done without publishing it on the bulletin boards, and fences of the highway. More especially, when the chains that bind them were forged by themselves. I keep my own counsel and endeavor, in a dignified way, to make the best of the situation."[66] It seems evident that this burden, these chains, and the selfishness and unreasonableness were his view of his own marriage.

A climax was reached on March 22, 1906, when the marriage of Edward and Mary was dissolved by divorce. Mary brought the action, charging desertion. The hearing was held in San Francisco in the court-room of presiding judge Thomas F. Graham. Mary entered on the arm of her brother, Edward H. Prentice; she was represented by attorney W. C. Van Fleet. Edward was not present; he was represented by attorney Peter F. Dunne, along with Edward's friend William E. Dunn from Los Angeles. Mary was called to the witness stand and gave the following testimony:

Q. Has Mr. Huntington been living with you for the last six years?
A. No, sir.
Q. Has he maintained with you any marital relations during that period?
A. No, sir.
Q. Do you know of any reason for that course on the part of Mr. Huntington?
A. What is that?
Q. Have you ever given Mr. Huntington any reason for his course in refusing to maintain marital relations with you?
A. I don't think so.
Q. Has he ever, since he went to Los Angeles, provided a house for you there and asked you to occupy it with him?
A. He has not.
Q. Has he refused to resume the marital relations which he held with you prior to the time when he went to Los Angeles?
A. Yes, sir.

Her brother was also called to the witness stand and "he testified to the fact in his knowledge that the parties in the suit had not maintained conjugal relations for the past six years." He was not asked how he knew.

William E. Dunn was asked whether he had any questions on behalf of Mr. Huntington. He had none. The judge concluded the hearing and signed the decree for the divorce. The proceedings had taken seven minutes and thirty seconds.

The hearing had begun at 9:30 A.M. Mary was "habited in an unpretentious pearl gray suit, with lavender gloves. A moderate hat supported a heavy veil that almost obscured her features." After the hearing, she went with her brother to the docks and boarded the Pacific Mail liner *Korea*. Marian joined her there in the stateroom reserved for the two of them. A large group of friends joined them at 11:30 A.M. to congratulate her on the divorce and to wish them bon voyage. The stateroom was filled with flowers, and one friend brought Mary "a huge bunch of violets and lilies of the valley." Women kissed her, and men shook hands with her. There was "an air that was distinctly congratulatory; to all of which she responded with the happiest of faces." There was "no sign of embarrassment or displeasure." The ship sailed at 1 P.M., taking Mary and Marian to Japan, where Elizabeth and Brockway were on their honeymoon.[67]

In the financial settlement between Edward and Mary, she received a trust fund of $2 million in a portfolio of twelve bonds. The house in San Francisco was already in her name, and she had some $300,000 in other funds. They had no community property.[68]

There was considerable speculation in the newspapers and among their friends as to the reason for the divorce. The main reaction reported among their friends was surprise. The rumor was repeated over and over that Edward had for five years tried to get her to join him in Los Angeles and that she had always refused because of her "aversion to the Southern city." The other main speculation was that they had fallen out over the claim of the Princess Hatzfeldt to a greater share of Collis's estate, with Edward feeling that Mary had espoused her sister's cause with improper vigor. There may be some basis for either or both of these thoughts, but I have not been able to find it.

The conclusion drawn by their friends was that the divorce was occasioned by their "absolute incompatibility" and that the final reason was a mystery. It was recalled that Edward had stayed at the family house when Elizabeth and Brockway had been married just two weeks before the divorce, and it was said that Mary's "manner toward him was cold—almost scornful." It was also reported that the four children had equal affection and devotion toward each of their parents. "Absolute incompatibility" is probably as close as we can come in attributing a cause to their divorce.[69]

One remarkable document remains, however, and it gives Edward's own deep feelings about his married life. It is a letter, quoted here in full, that he wrote on the very day of the divorce and mailed to his daughter Elizabeth in Yokohama.

My darling daughter

Before this reaches you, you will undoubtedly have learned of the separation of your Mother and myself. I can never tell you how much I regret that this cloud should come into your life, but I hope it may have a silver lining. As you of course know, we have been very unhappy for years, and getting more so as the years went by. The step taken seemed inevitable, and the sooner it was taken the better it would be for all concerned. I think we shall <u>all</u> be much happier after the clouds pass over, and that peace will come to us. Nothing could have been worse than it has been, and I felt like a wanderer on the face of the earth, without home or a place to lay my head. I think now I shall build a home where my children can come when they desire, and that many happy days will come to me and all mine. I have never talked with you about your Mother's and my relations. You could not but see, however, how unhappy I have been. But no one can ever know how much I have suffered. I would liked to have talked the matter over with you, but thought best to keep the matter from you as long as possible and not to mar the first pleasure of your wedding trip, and thought it only fair to give your Mother the opportunity to speak to you first, which I presume she will do before you receive this letter. You can never know, my precious child, how very dear my children are to me, and how much I regret that I have not been able to make your lives happier. I can only say I have done my best. With a heart full of love for my dear child

I am always
Your affectionate
Father[70]

This extraordinary letter makes plain the depth of his unhappiness in his marriage, his suffering, and his loneliness. But it also reveals a great deal about him as a human being and about his values: his abiding affectionate belief in family and children, his wish to be fair, his hope to recover the lost happiness of family life. And his optimistic faith that the future could be made better than the past.

Ten

EDWARD FREQUENTLY EXPRESSED his sense of optimism about what the future held. The newspapers, reporting the opinion of his close friend Epes Randolph, commented: "Henry E. Huntington is a sure cure for the blues. 'I have had a long talk with Mr. Huntington and, say, it would do you good to talk with him. He is one of the most optimistic men in America, and his optimism is infectious.' "[1]

There was nothing Edward felt more optimistic about than Southern California. He seems to have fallen in love with the area on his first visit in 1892. He thought of it as an earthly paradise that combined beautiful scenery and ideal climate. In 1908, he recalled that "when I first went to California, years ago, I traveled east, north, and south from one end of the state to the other, even going off the beaten paths by team and studying every section carefully. I came to the conclusion then that the greatest natural advantages, those of climate as well as every other condition, lay in Southern California, and that is why I made it the field of my endeavor."[2] In 1910, he summed up his experience by saying: "All that was necessary to capture me was my first visit to, and study of Southern California. You come here, and you are conquered. That's the whole situation."[3]

This may have been love at first sight, but the love affair lasted for the rest of his life. Whenever he returned from a trip away, he told the waiting reporters, as in 1905, that he "was glad to be breathing the air of

Southern California again" or, in 1908, that "this is the finest country in the world out here. You can't say too much in its favor."[4] Or, in 1910, " 'There's nothing like this Southern California anywhere else in the world,' he said, as he let his glance rest on the fleeting scenery of orchards and vineyards and groves. 'Nothing like it in the world! And the world is finding it out. I do not know how big Los Angeles is to become. No one does. But I do know that it is to be the most beautiful city in the country, and that it will be the one center for all that is beautiful and worthwhile in the country.' "[5]

Development did not begin in Southern California until long after the northern part of the state had reached maturity. In 1860 the population of San Francisco was a little over fifty thousand—nearly twice as much as the entire population of Southern California; about four thousand people then lived in Los Angeles, still a quiet Hispanic pueblo. In the next forty years the Southland began to grow. Citrus production commenced on a large scale in the 1870s, and a petroleum industry made a start soon afterward. New rail lines connected Southern California directly with the East, and the railroads waged a vigorous propaganda campaign to get easterners to come out, buy land, and settle in the area. The boom of the 1880s in Southern California resulted in the establishment of some sixty new towns before it collapsed into a recession. But prosperity returned in the 1890s, and in the ensuing decade the population of Los Angeles doubled from 50,000 to 100,000. (In San Francisco, it went from about 300,000 to 350,000 in the same period.)

The theme of the beauty and attractions of Southern California recurs throughout his letters to his family and friends as well as in his public utterances. From New York he wrote to his daughter Elizabeth that "we have had nice weather here, but not as nice as Southern California, for that is the best in the world."[6] From Los Angeles he remarked, "I feel as if I could remain here all my life and never leave"; "Los Angeles and Southern California are the playground of the United States perpetually."[7]

The beauty of the area, its climate, and its charm led Edward to predict a great future for it. In 1903, on returning to Los Angeles from New York, he said: "There is no limit to the possibilities of this favored section. It can't be kept down—it's too good. And this impression is rapidly gaining the possession of the minds of all classes and conditions throughout the East."[8] In 1905 he stated, "before many years it will be the largest city in the West" and "one of the great centers of industrial energy in this country."[9] In 1909, he went so far as to predict that "within twenty-five years Los Angeles will be the center of civilization."[10]

In February 1902, the Los Angeles Chamber of Commerce had an elaborate banquet—described as "brilliant"—with three hundred guests and several speakers. Edward was invited to speak but declined because of business engagements in San Francisco. Instead, he sent the following telegram, which was read to the gathering:

> It is not possible for the finite mind to predict the future of our beautiful and prosperous city. Much, but not too much, has been said of our climate, but after all it is not climate that makes a city, but its people, and we have the best people from all parts of the world. With these two factors and the wonderful resources of our City of the Angels, it can never be said, as it was of some New England settlements, with their equally good people, that "it was a good place to be born in." Los Angeles is a good place to be born in, to live in, and to die in. People who come here come to stay and are glad they came. It is needless to say, I believe, that the future of Los Angeles is more promising than most people can possibly realize.
>
> H. E. Huntington

According to the newspaper account the next morning, "the reading of the Huntington telegram evoked long applause."[11]

As he became better known in the community, he could offer the reassurance that the community wanted. In 1905 the people of Santa Barbara were glad to hear that "Mr. Huntington predicts that next winter will be the greatest tourist season in the history of Southern California, and Los Angeles will continue to draw the thousands of persons of wealth who in the winter months are seeking a climate such as can not be found anywhere else."[12] In 1908, businessmen in Los Angeles were happy to be told in an interview that the panic was over and prosperity had returned; in an editorial, the *Los Angeles Examiner* could say that "the most important piece of news in today's newspaper is the interview with H. E. Huntington. You know the sort of worker he is. Read what Huntington says. Prosperity has already returned! Look prosperous! Act prosperous, and be prosperous!"[13] In 1910, Edward summed up his view of the opportunities offered by Los Angeles in a short essay which began, "To talk about the opportunities in Los Angeles and Southern California is to talk about what every man knows or should know. It is because of the opportunities of the country and its beauty that I am here. There are opportunities at every hand."[14] One may wonder whether his own convictions lay behind these expressions of optimism, which sound so much like chamber of commerce boosterism. Much earlier he had made his response to such an implied question: "Well, I'm investing my money here and I have generally found that when a man backs his opinion with his coin he has set convictions about the matter in hand."[15]

In those days, before managed press conferences and manipulated photo opportunities, we can hope to get from an interview a relatively undistorted view of what the interviewer perceived. When Edward was interviewed in 1905 by a newspaper often hostile to his undertakings, he was challenged by the report that the extension of his trolley lines would soon reach outer space:

> H. E. Huntington's characteristic smile and a new suit of summer gray were as bright as the sunlight Friday morning.
> "I am not going to build to the moon," he asserted, the smile fading for just an instant—for even millionaire railroad builders and land owners can be annoyed by other people's extravagant claims for them. "They seem to think I'm going to build to the moon but I'm not," he repeated and now the smile broke again.
> No one can hear Mr. Huntington speak of Los Angeles and not be convinced of his sincere interest in the city and pride in it, aside from the money-making possibilities. He is a money-maker, of course, but he has a pride in his work that doesn't seem to be measured by dollars.[16]

Edward's principal competitor for trolley systems in Southern California was E. H. Harriman, who controlled the SP and the Union Pacific, and who was certainly the leading factor in railroads in the United States at the time—with far more power and much more money than Edward. Harriman belittled Los Angeles in an interview at the Raymond Hotel in Pasadena in 1909:

> Almost angrily, he replied to the hackneyed question as to what he thought of Southern California. Straightening with a jerk in his chair, and pushing back his hat, he fairly snapped: "Why don't you get out in the world and see something beyond your little circle here? I would not belittle Southern California. She has accomplished much, and will do still greater things. With that river turned in here, Los Angeles should control everything in this neighborhood. Isn't Pasadena owned by Los Angeles? It ought to be, and probably will be. But you take your map and study it. What do you know of Mexico? You certainly believe in yourself out here. I tell you that Los Angeles may some day need a country to migrate to. Study your map."[17]

Edward had already studied his map, been over the area, analyzed the situation, and concluded that this was the place for him. And for business.

Edward managed his businesses in four principal ways. He evaluated his property by means of detailed, personal inspections. He knew his key managers and top employees and kept in touch with the general attitude and well-being of everyone in his employ. He kept track of the exact financial details of the operations of every company of which he had considerable ownership. And he set a standard of hard work for all of his associates, colleagues, and employees to follow.

A concern for details characterized his oversight of day-to-day operations. He felt, as had Collis, that if the owner watched the details, then everybody in the organization would follow suit, thus enabling the owner to pay attention to the big matters. Edward was also a conscientious list maker. He made—and kept—his pencil notes about nearly everything: his securities (their cost, current value, income), the details of the capitalization and indebtedness of each of his companies, and the like.[18] These business practices served Edward well in his first decade in Southern California.

Edward's greatest business achievement was, I believe, the establishment of the electric street railway system in Los Angeles and the surrounding areas. He had taken the first step in 1898 when a syndicate of which he was the major participant bought the ailing Los Angeles Railway Company, the principal street railway company in the area.

Electric street railways had gotten under way in many parts of the world in the late 1880s, and they quickly began to replace horse-drawn cars. By 1900, there were some 8,000 miles of track in the United States; in 1898, the Los Angeles Railway had about 50 miles.[19] The track and equipment were in bad shape, the service was poor, and the company was losing money. In 1900 and 1901, Edward launched a bold and ambitious program of what the managers called "betterments"—of improving what they had and of building new lines and extensions. By November 1910, the area had—in all of the companies—918 miles of track, of which 350 were in the city of Los Angeles and 568 were interurban. The number of street railway cars and other pieces of equipment, depots, and employees had risen proportionately. In 1910, it was regarded as the best street railway system in the world.

Edward's program for betterments was carried on vigorously by new construction and by acquiring small companies. In 1900, he was considering new lines to South Santa Monica (10.25 miles), to San Pedro (22.25 miles), from Long Beach to Santa Ana (20 miles) or to Santa Ana via Whittier (31.75 miles), from South Pasadena to Monrovia (9.5 miles), and from Pasadena to the Old Mission (3.5 miles)—a total of 97.25 miles. In 1901, he commenced construction in the hope of laying 100 miles of new track that year. As the program moved along, he obtained a franchise from Monrovia in April, and began the line from South Pasadena to Monrovia in June, at a cost of $10,281.70 per mile.[20] He made his first acquisition on June 1, 1900, when he bought the Mt. Lowe Railway—including the cable incline of thirteen hundred feet, the electric plant, Alpine Tavern, the Chalet, and the observatory, all the pet idea of Professor T. S. C. Lowe and a major tourist attraction in the Los Angeles area.[21] The small Los Angeles and Pasadena Electric Railway Company was acquired in 1902.[22]

This burst of activity required more money than the Los Angeles Railway Company had or could borrow, and in 1901 Edward formed another corporation, the Pacific Electric Railway Company—into which several companies were merged—to build and operate urban and interurban electric railways in the Los Angeles area, with a projected total of 452 miles of track.[23] In the initial subscription for stock, Edward put up about $100,000 out of the total of $140,000, for a 70 percent ownership; bonds were issued as needed to cover construction costs, and additional assessments were made on the stockholders to satisfy other cash requirements.

The speed of construction was remarkable. By the end of April 1902, the electric cars were running to Redondo, twenty-one miles away, and from Redondo to Santa Monica.[24] Simultaneously, Edward "came out with a plan so magnificent in scope that it would scare an ordinary trolley line promoter," according to a long front-page story in the *Los Angeles Times:* he had acquired the land for a four-track line to Long Beach, with cars to run fifty to sixty miles per hour. The *Times* said: "Huntington is in a hurry. Property along the line of the road has advanced enormously in value. Land that could be bought a few years ago for a very small figure is now bringing $500 an acre. Several men have made fortunes out of it."[25]

The story about the completion of the line to Monrovia tells us a good deal about how they could work with such speed, and why and to what effect. The *Los Angeles Times* reported on February 25, 1903:

> Monrovia, Feb. 24—With a force of 300 men, the Pacific Electric Company extended its line through the Duncan orchard this afternoon in about three hours. Shortly before 12 o'clock not a man was in sight, but a few minutes afterward a train arrived with a small army and soon the dirt began to fly in great shape. Two rows of orange trees were cut down in a jiffy, and several plows were started to make the ground ready for the ties. Soon the shovelers had their work done, the ties were laid, and rails strung across them. By 3 o'clock the steel bands extended through the orchard and across Mayflower street. The holes were dug and poles set up before sundown.
>
> The right of way through this orchard had been in litigation several months, and only this morning the company received an order of court to proceed with the work. The company did not let the grass grow under its feet before commencing operations, as it apparently wished to get through before a restraining order could be issued.

Every citizen is rejoiced that the road is at last completed into Monrovia.

A regular half-hour service is to be started Sunday, with a round-trip fare of 40 cents.[26]

The Pacific Electric ran a full-page ad on Saturday announcing the opening of the new line the next day, with service every twelve minutes. "Go see what a beautiful country is opened up," it urged, "by this new line of the Pacific Electric Railway through Arcadia and Baldwin's Ranch to the enterprising city of Monrovia." It also called attention to the special Sunday services to Mt. Lowe, Long Beach, and the San Gabriel Mission.[27] Hundreds of visitors flocked into Monrovia all Sunday long: "The road is another monument of the work being done by Mr. Huntington in Los Angeles County and emphasizes the fact that his word can be counted on." He had said that he would build the line if they would get him the right-of-way and a place for a depot; they did, and "thereupon Mr. Huntington began grading the line from Alhambra to Monrovia."[28]

Edward had hired splendid managers for his companies. His old friend Epes Randolph was persuaded to leave the Arizona division of the Southern Pacific—despite a lung condition that benefited from the Arizona air—to become general manager of the Pacific Electric, and John A. Muir resigned as superintendent of the Southern Pacific to become general manager of the Los Angeles Street Railway Company. The SP tried to keep Muir, who had been with that company for thirty years. "I shall give up my present employment with regret," he said, "but the position with Mr. Huntington makes me a permanent resident in Los Angeles, where my children are being reared, and where all of my interests are located."[29]

As usual, Edward worked harder than anyone else. He was the first one at the office in the morning and the last one to leave at night. His mother begged him not to work so hard. "Do, my dear boy, take time to sleep," she wrote him. "You are working altogether too hard." Later, he wrote her—in a letter that would fascinate only a mother—of a two-day wagon trip he had taken to look at sites for a dam: "Had breakfast at half past four then rode till eight o'clock that night had breakfast next morning at half past four and rode all the next day." Her reply (to a son of fifty-five, from a mother of eighty-four) was an exhortation against his work habits: "I do not think you are doing right by overworking yourself. . . . My dear Edwards, you will most surely break down. . . . I beg you to stop off short, for your families sake and mammas."[30]

His associates were busy trying to keep up with him. A series of private letters in 1903 between his secretaries in Los Angeles and his secretaries in New York gives glimpses behind the scenes: "I find Mr. Huntington at the office every morning at half past seven now, and I suppose if I got here at seven I would also find him here." One lamented that he was having to work sixteen hours a day and wished he were in New York, "where we can keep proper hours." "Mr. Huntington keeps me jumping around on a dozen different matters, but I am trying to do the best I can, and, personally, think I am succeeding pretty well." "Mr. Huntington is very shy in giving details of transactions, and all I get is what I can pump out of him or someone else." "There is a good deal of talk about Mr. Huntington running his trolley lines through to Frisco. It looks a little like hot air, but I would hardly be surprised if such a thing did happen within the next year or two, would you?"[31] You learned not to be surprised at anything that "Mr. H." attempted. And his subordinates fully expected him to succeed.

One institution did not want to see him succeed—the Southern Pacific Company. SP had lines in and around Los Angeles for steam railroads, and the company tried to protect its position as a carrier of passengers and freight against the incursions of the electric railway. The struggle was seen as a "war" between Harriman and Huntington, despite their denials. In April 1902 Harriman came with his staff and his children to Los Angeles for a summit meeting with Huntington. There was a trip in a special PE car around the city, a fancy luncheon for the principals and key associates at the California Club, a visit to Catalina Island, a trip up to Mt. Lowe with a luncheon at the Alpine Tavern, a dinner at the Van Nuys Hotel, and an evening for everyone at the theater. Edward "led his guests in, and he led them out, beaming on them, attentive to every comfort." After the show, "Mr. Harriman again fell behind the rest, but Huntington extended a hand to him and led him forth through the curious crowd in the lobby." Throughout this visitation, it was felt that "H. E. Huntington is doing the honors in a princely manner." The meetings were amicable, Edward showed Harriman his development plans and reassured him that they would avoid competing with the SP, especially in carrying freight, and the tension eased off for a while.[32]

But not for long. The passenger fares on the trolleys were lower than those on the stream railroads; it cost a third less to go by trolley from Monrovia to Los Angeles.[33] And the electric railway got franchises from San Pedro to bring the traffic from the wharves—a control area that the SP had earlier abandoned and now wanted back.[34]

In 1903 Harriman and the SP were again threatening to muscle into the street railway business in Southern California by taking over the Los Angeles Traction Company—the "Hook Lines" that W. A. Clark had acquired in April in collaboration with Harriman—and by building further lines. In April, Edward wrote to his friend A. B. Hammond, "I am having a pretty stiff fight with the Sou. Pac. but think I shall win out." Harriet knew of his problems and wrote him on Easter Sunday, April 12, 1903, that "I sincerely hope and pray that you may win your case, as so far as I can see, it is just that you should win. It seems to me that all the Los Angeles people should uphold your cause, as you have done so much for the place, in bringing prosperity to the place. I feel that you must come off conqueror at last. It may take a long and hard fight. I hope it will not wear out your strength, and I pray daily for you, and many times a day."[35]

In May Edward went to San Francisco, and he and Harriman worked out an elaborate compromise by which the Pacific Electric would acquire a couple of small street railway companies, several rights-of-way and land owned by the SP, and a major part of the franchises and property of Los Angeles Traction. Harriman and Huntington would each own 40 percent of the Pacific Electric stock, with the other 20 percent owned by the Hellman minority interest. The Los Angeles Railway was not involved and continued to be under Edward's control. At the end of the business session, Harriman is reported to have said, "Huntington, what's the matter with our taking supper together tonight?" Huntington replied, in his characteristic way: "It's a good idea; I say it is a good idea." The compromise was advantageous to Edward.

The San Francisco papers carried headlines like "Huntington Wins Fight with Rival. Harriman Surrenders to All the Demands Presented. Agrees to Withdraw from LA Street Railway Competition." Edward returned to Los Angeles, and in his next Sunday letter to his mother he could say, "I have won all my battles and expect to start east soon. Have been up to Mt Lowe today and walked from the end of the road to Echo Mountain."[36]

Right away Edward announced plans to expand the street railways, and the newspapers were taken by the $30 million he proposed to spend. "The magnitude of the proposition puts it quite out of the mental reach of the ordinary individual," the *Los Angeles Times* allowed, and so the newspaper included a big map showing operating and projected lines.[37] To facilitate work, the Los Angeles Interurban Railway Company was organized with 100,000 shares of common stock, 99,950 of which were owned by the Pacific Electric; the other 50 shares were owned by ten individuals, 5 shares each.[38] The Los Angeles Railway Company, with Edward as president and Howard as general manager, had 117 miles of track; the Pacific Electric Railway, with Edward as president and Epes Randolph as general manager, had 157 miles of track; and the Los Angeles Interurban, with Randolph as president and general manager, had 78 miles of track, for a total of 352 miles of track at the beginning of 1904.[39]

By mid-1904, the total had gone up to 439 miles.[40] The expansion continued, with the new lines running in almost every direction, to Huntington Beach, Whittier, Pomona, San Pedro, Newport, Sierra Madre, Covina, Watts, Redondo, and a dozen other places. A visitor from Washington, D.C.—a visitor whose son, Lawrence Clark Powell, was later to have an important role in the book world of Southern California—wrote back to his wife, early in 1904, that "I have not seen a city so honeycombed by trolley lines as this is. They seem to run on nearly every street and they extend all over the surrounding country for miles. Some of the country lines run the cars a mile a minute."[41] A piece of newspaper fun commemorated the expansion in a more jocular vein:

Count that day lost which ere the setting sun
Sees not a beach resort or trolley line begun.

Writing in anticipation of a new line, a contributor to a suburban paper wrote a poem entitled "Make Way for the Trolley," which began:

> Oh, how jolly that will be,
> Riding on the trolley![42]

Communities were eager to have the electric railway run through their towns. Public subscriptions were often taken up to provide free land for a right-of-way and depot in order to induce the railway to build a line to or through their areas. This practice, common in the 1870s and 1880s in the East, was encouraged by the railways. The citizens of Whittier took up a subscription in late 1904 and were delighted with the results when the line was opened in 1905. The testimony "was all on the side of the Huntington road, showing that its introduction had brought prosperity to the business houses, a vast increase in the number and desirability of population, and a rise in values of realty in and around Whittier." The story was the same in Monrovia. "The universal verdict of every citizen whom I met or heard from was the same," wrote a newspaper reporter, "that the electric road has been, is and sure to be in the future 'the making of Monrovia,'" where bank deposits had increased 50 percent, the population had increased by twelve hundred to three thousand, 130 new buildings had been erected, every store employed more help, and retail business had increased by 50 percent.[43] In one year, the population of Huntington Beach rose from seventy-five to six hundred, and the town "began to throb and pulsate with newness of life. . . . But let us not forget to give credit where credit is due for this marvelous growth. Without the great Pacific Electric double-track line, Huntington Beach might have remained a cow pasture."[44] Likewise, Newport Beach "springs into life at magic touch of trolley," and Watts moved "from a ranch to a city with a population of 1600 in fifteen months."[45] It was the same in Santa Ana: the arrival of the electric line was "the greatest thing that ever happened" to Santa Ana; floats, banners, bands, and a banquet were offered to "H. E. Huntington and his lieutenants"; and "the attitude so far exhibited by the Pacific Electric toward the people of Santa Ana is worthy not only of remark, but of commendation."[46] When the trolley finally reached Pomona, bands played, crowds assembled, and the papers declared that "Pomona discards her swaddling raiment," that "the baby-city of Pomona is no more," and that the coming of the trolley marked "the date of a new and big Pomona," which they hoped might grow in five years to a population of twenty-five thousand.[47]

The effect of the expansion of the trolley lines on people's well-being was also praised. The electric railway system prevented that "tendency to crowd the population into narrow confines" and made it possible for people to live in a place of their choice and taste, with their own houses and their own property. The result was described as "the most unique and charming expanse of citified country and countrified city known anywhere on the footstool, with an everywhere ramifying trolley system as the bond of union." Moreover, it made neighbors of everyone in Southern California. "Improved transportation facilities are among the greatest civilizing and broadening factors" for society, it was urged. "In the hurry and rush of business few of us stop to consider what an important factor the enterprise of Henry E. Huntington has been in advancing the social interests of Southern California."[48]

People rode on the cars in great numbers, even in the first five years of the expansion program. On the Fourth of July 1905, well over 100,000 people traveled to holiday spots, when the total population of Los Angeles was about 150,000. Thirty thousand went to Venice, 20,000 to Long Beach, 2,000 to Mt. Lowe, and so forth. (The fare was fifty cents for a round-trip to the beach.) On New Year's Day 1906, the Pacific Electric carried 76,375 persons from Los Angeles to Pasadena—without accident or confusion—to see the Rose Parade.[49]

All of this expansion required a great deal of cash at a time when funds were scarce and the money markets were centered in distant New York. The minor panic of 1903 and the major panic of 1907 made it more difficult to raise capital for new construction through the issuance of bonds or by short-term borrowing. For a time, Edward had recourse to assessments on stockholders to finance the expansion. This tactic displeased his minority stockholders in San Francisco—I. W. Hellman, president of the Union Trust Company and other banking establishments, and his broker associates, Antoine Borel and Christian de Guigne. In May 1904, when Edward was in New York, Hellman wrote to Howard, the Pacific Electric manager in Los Angeles, and told him not to spend any further money beyond earnings; Edward was incensed and replied sharply to Hellman about this improper intrusion into "the management of the property."[50] Hellman and his associates objected strenuously to the assessments, and a few months later they offered to sell their interest. After consulting with Harriman, Edward bought out the minority interest. Hellman explained that the expansion "required more ready money than I could spare from my affairs as a banker. I never go into debt. I never speculate." Several years later, Hellman explained further that it was that principle of not going into debt "that made me withdraw from Mr. Huntington's railway enterprises. Mr. Huntington is a great business man, and railway men cannot carry out their projects without borrowing money. I am a banker, and I could not continue to be a banker if I went into debt. When I reached my limit of cash I simply called a halt and sold. Mr. Huntington was absolutely correct, and events have proved him so. I think I was correct as well."[51] The upshot was that Edward was able to buy out the minority interest.

In 1906, the struggle between Huntington and Harriman for control of the street railways in Southern California broke out again. The truce effected in 1903 had been an uneasy one. In March 1906, each side resumed the offensive. Harriman bought the Los Angeles Pacific Railway from General M. H. Sherman and W. A. Clark. This railway owned about 180 miles of track, including a crucial line and franchise through Hollywood to Santa Monica, which Edward had not tried to compete with because of his friendship with Sherman; Edward regarded the sale to Harriman a breach of trust and friendship on Sherman's part. The purchase put Harriman in a position to expand his lines and thus challenge Edward's control of the trolley traffic. In retaliation, Edward had E. W. Gilmore gain a franchise—as though for George Gould and the Western Pacific—from the Los Angeles City Council for entering the city along the riverbed; the mayor vetoed the franchise, and when it was revealed that it was actually intended for the Pacific Electric, there were public meetings and general discontent about the stratagem.

The struggle was considered a railroad war between the two men and a crisis for Edward, who went to San Francisco accompanied by Howard, George Patton, and William E. Dunn to confer with Harriman. Events were given full publicity; for the last ten days of March alone there were eighteen long newspaper stories treating the "war."[52] Further flurries occurred in December 1906. The editorial writers tended to favor Huntington. "Mr. Harriman cares nothing for Southern California," wrote one, "except as a revenue producer to swell the enormous investments that he represents, whereas Mr. Huntington's heart and soul are wrapped up not only in his splendid Southern California enterprises, but in Southern California itself." Wrote another, "It is to be hoped that the people of Los Angeles will think long and hard before they will forsake an old and tried friend (Henry E. Huntington) for an old and tried enemy (the Southern Pacific)." Wrote a third, "It is a battle of giants and well worth witnessing, but my sympathies, as far as Los Angeles and Southern California are concerned, are entirely with Mr. Huntington. H. E. is a builder; E. H. is a gambler."[53]

The struggle did not end until May 1907, when Harriman gave up his competitive efforts—under pressure from lack of funds and involvement with the Interstate Commerce Commission—and allowed Edward to continue his control of the street railways. The threat of a recurrence did not end until September 9, 1909, however, when Harriman suddenly died. Edward was asked to comment, and he wrote for publication the following letter, which gives a clue to what he valued in a fellow businessman:

> Mr. Harriman's death cuts short a career the future of which was hardly calculated, so great were its possibilities foreshadowed by the achievements of past years. He was probably the greatest organizer of his time, rapid in decision and action and with a mind like a flashlight. I knew him well for many years, during which we were associated in railway business, and I am glad to say that our relations, personal and official, were always harmonious and friendly. I much regret his untimely end.
>
> H. E. Huntington[54]

Edward faced a number of increasingly pressing problems in the operation of the street railways in this crucial decade. The Los Angeles mayor and city council were encouraged by some citizens and by one or two newspapers, particularly Hearst's *Examiner,* to take steps to control the street railways. In 1904, franchises for the operation of railways over a given route—awarded by open bidding at auction—were limited to twenty-one years, a change which created a furor. W. E. Dunn appeared before the city council and declared that Huntington would build no more lines with so short a franchise, as it was insufficient to pay off the cost of construction.[55] A demand for free transfers between the different street railways became increasingly vociferous, and one election for mayor turned on this issue.[56] The street railways were sometimes accused of illegally carrying freight when their franchise did not authorize them to do so, and there were complaints that the fare of five cents was too high in relation to the low cost of the franchises.[57] In the spring of 1906, there were months of agitation in favor of "owl cars" for late-night riders; in September, Edward authorized all lines to run hourly cars after midnight to accommodate late workers, and many people congratulated him and the newspaper that had urged the step. Fred L. Boruff said, "I believe in giving Huntington everything he wants. He has done more for Los Angeles than any other one man and he will do more yet."[58]

The city council passed an act requiring the companies to sprinkle or oil the streets on which their trolleys ran in order to prevent the noxious dust that it was feared might cause an epidemic of diphtheria, and in due course the police department issued warrants for the arrest of all directors of all railway lines for operating trolleys without laying the dust.[59] In 1907, warrants were issued for the arrest of H. E. Huntington and the motormen for operating trolleys that were not equipped with adequate fenders; Edward appeared in police court and pleaded not guilty; in due course the fender ordinance was repealed.[60] There were many complaints about the congestion caused by the large number of trolleys filling the busiest downtown streets; P. A. Ladini presented a comic petition to the Los Angeles Board of Public Utilities asking that the city abandon some streets (like Sixth Street from Spring to Main) and deed them "to the Huntington interests" for use as switching yards, as they were too dangerous for all pedestrians other than acrobats.[61] Accidents on the trolley system became an increasing source of public complaint. From 1906 to 1910, each month about three to four hundred accidents were reported and two people were killed. The causes were, in descending order: riders getting on and off before the cars stopped, vehicles running into the trolleys, collisions, and pedestrians and bicyclists being struck by trolleys. The *Los Angeles Examiner* made a particular issue of accidents and regularly published a box on the front page with a running total for the previous year or two.[62] One man, Joseph W. Stark, threatened to kill Huntington because he had been injured on his bicycle; he shadowed Huntington for several days before he was apprehended and sent to the county hospital.[63] The constant attacks on Huntington by the *Examiner* led other papers to reflect that "one of the proud boasts of the San Francisco 'Examiner' is that it 'drove Henry E. Huntington from San Francisco.' The Los Angeles 'Examiner', owned by the same individual, is now engaged in a campaign which is likely to lead to similar achievements as to Los Angeles"—though the writer hoped that this result would not come to pass.[64]

The most serious threat that the railway system faced during this period was strikes called by the labor unions. Edward's experience in San Francisco in 1894 with the violent American Railway Union strike against the Southern Pacific had led him to develop strong anti-union feelings in the course of the bitter months when he was trying to break the strike. There were several threats of strikes against the street railway companies in Los Angeles, in March and April of 1903, in the spring of 1904, in 1906, and once more in 1910. Edward was firm in his opposition to the unions, which he considered the work of selfish agitators and outside troublemakers. He stated his position in some impromptu remarks made late in the evening of April 24, 1903, while checking on the progress of the railway operations on the corner of Second and Main streets in Los Angeles.

> We have no quarrel with any unions and care little what such bodies are doing, so long as they do not interfere with our work. If our workmen would organize a mutual benefit union, they would meet with no opposition from the railway companies. The trouble is that the unions are not organized for benefit, but for trouble. This is well illus-

trated in the present instance. The union was organized last night; tonight the members of their own volition are out of a job. I object to unions because they are harmful to the men themselves. Not one man in ten who joins a union does so of his own volition. They are driven to it through fear, and trouble follows.[65]

None of these threats of strikes resulted in violence or serious work stoppages. The companies fired those few men who ventured to join the union, and they called on the police for protection in continuing their operations. But the threats troubled Edward.[66]

Edward was certainly anti-union, as were almost all major employers of his time. But he was not antilabor. Throughout his career he was known for his sincere interest in the views, wishes, and welfare of all of his employees, especially those whose work was menial. He was always on the lookout for ways to improve the lot of the people who worked for his companies.[67] His general feelings about his employees is summed up in a letter he wrote on December 11, 1902—well before there were any threats of strikes against his electric railways in Los Angeles—to the Committee of Trainmen of the Los Angeles Railway Company to thank them for a leatherbound testimonial they had given him in appreciation for voluntarily increasing their pay scale:

> I appreciate it as an unexpected and spontaneous expression of your friendliness. It is the duty of every employer to endeavor to treat those whom the fortune of life has made his employees, with as exact a measure of fairness and justice, as the limitations of human nature and intelligence permit, and such has been and always will continue to be my own determination. It is my earnest wish, moreover, that between yourselves and the owners of the Los Angeles Railway Company there may always continue the friendly feelings that your thoughtful gift indicates you have for myself, and which I reciprocate in full measure. I am, gentlemen, with cordial thanks and good wishes for a Merry Christmas and Happy New Year,
>
> Sincerely yours
> H. E. Huntington[68]

This raise in the pay scale was one of three general increases that Edward gave the street railway employees between 1902 and 1909. Each raise involved several thousand people and cost the company about $200,000, even though the company was not making money on its operations at the time. After the raise in 1906, a group of three hundred employees called on Edward and offered him a resolution of gratitude and a testimonial to the "peace and good will" between the employees and the officers. Edward had to respond, despite his disinclination to make speeches. He said: "If I was obliged to earn my living by speech-making I would have to take up a subscription to keep out of the poorhouse. Boys, I thank you for what you have done."[69]

The story of the raise was carried in papers all over the United States; editorials praised Huntington and asserted that "the public approves and is more than ever convinced that the street railways of Los Angeles are in good hands."[70] Locally, the motormen and conductors took up a subscription and raised $165 to buy and engrave a silver loving cup to present to Edward in appreciation for the raise. They decorated the car barns with greens and with a photograph of Edward mounted between flags; five hundred of them gathered to present the cup to him. "Mr. Huntington was overwhelmed by the gift and enthusiastic greeting accorded him, and declared that he did not have the words at his command to express his gratitude." He said, "I want to thank you men for the service you have rendered the company." He went on to say that when he was complimented on the service, "My answer always is, 'It is because my employees are gentlemen.' I feel that you are and I want to tell you I am proud of you."[71]

Edward made other efforts to benefit his employees. He gave the carmen a collection of over a thousand books, including "volumes of practical worth as well as selections of high-class fiction," which he installed in a library room for their benefit.[72] He extended the recreation space in the car barns to include a lounge, a room for games and billiards, and an assembly room for debates and concerts. He built a gymnasium for their use.[73]

It would be common now to brush off these tokens of concern for employees as a form of paternalism that was in fact self-serving and selfish. I do not believe that this was the case with Edward. He was naturally friendly and generous, and his instincts drew him toward being helpful to people. He seems to have felt something like an obligation toward those who worked for him, and he wanted to respond as best he could to them. Moreover, his responsiveness to the needs of others was unusual in the context of his times, when big business generally had the upper hand over labor and entrepreneurs were mainly responsive to big rewards or pressing threats.

By 1910, rumors had been floating around for several years that Edward was going to retire from the street railway business. In November 1910, an elaborate deal was consummated by which Edward and the Southern Pacific finally resolved their divided roles in the control of the street railway companies in the Los Angeles area. This deal, which had been under discussion with Harriman before his death in September 1909, gave the Southern Pacific sole control of the Pacific Electric and made SP the owner of all the interurban lines. Edward was given sole ownership of the Los Angeles Railway, which took over all the local and city street railways.[74] The latter was reorganized and incorporated on November 7, 1910, as the Los Angeles Railway Corporation, with $20 million in capital stock all owned by H. E. Huntington, with Edward as president, Howard as vice-president and general manager, and W. E. Dunn and Albert Crutcher as directors. Right away they gave free transfers for use on all their lines.[75]

After the deal was announced, speculation about it followed. Had Huntington been the winner? The conclusion drawn was yes, because he flashed his "ten-million-dollar smile" when asked about it. Had he been coerced into making the deal? "Not in the slightest degree," he responded. "You should know me well enough to understand that if a man tries to make me do anything by holding a club over me, what he wants will never be done." Would he reduce his interest in Southern California? "Nothing but the Great Reaper will ever detach me from Southern California. I am here to stay as long as I live, and my interests, both personal and material, will remain exactly henceforth as they have in the past."[76] Would he retire completely on January 1, 1911, as announced? From the management of the interurban lines, yes, entirely, but he would devote some of his attention to the Los Angeles Railway.[77]

Some were sad to see control of the interurban lines pass out of

Edward's hands. One paper wrote a long editorial on the subject entitled "A Calamity," which began:

> It is with great regret that Los Angeles witnesses the passing of the control of the interurban electric lines into the greedy hands of the Southern Pacific railroad. Mr. Huntington has been one of the foremost factors in the development of Los Angeles and its tributary territory. He has had a sublime faith in Los Angeles and unfaltering confidence in its future. Mr. Huntington is its builder and to the courage and foresight he displayed Los Angeles owes a large share of its prosperity and much of the confidence wherewith it has reason to view the future.

The conclusion was that "a calamity has befallen Los Angeles in this change."[78]

The year 1910 was a time to sum up the achievements of the preceding ten years in the creation of the street railway system. "The career of H. E. Huntington needs no greater eulogy than that he has done more for this city in railroad building than all others combined." When he arrived in Los Angeles, there was a total of only about 50 miles of tracks in the whole area; now there were 350 miles in the city and 568 miles interurban.[79] In the *Los Angeles Financier,* Sam W. Wall, in an article entitled "Huntington: What He Has Done and What Failed to Do," asserted that "the railway system has for years been the one agent most effective in the advancement of the city, no doubt; it has spread before the constant throng of visitors here the panorama of beauty which surrounds the city, thus offering a constant invitation to remain and make a home here; and it has helped to make the acceptance of that invitation easy and natural."[80] "All over the world," the *Examiner* declared, "Los Angeles is known as being the best equipped city in the world in the matter of street car service."[81] Edward's development of the street railways was a work of philanthropy, according to the *Los Angeles Times:* "His far-seeing mind has caused cities to take on new life, given transportation at a minimum cost to communities that were in need of same, made it possible for men of moderate means to erect and own homes of their own, made it possible for people to live in suburban homes and do business in the city with no more loss of time in going to and fro, than if living in the city."[82]

Edward had earlier said that "the electric railway is the pioneer of the young and growing city just as the steam road of the past was the pioneer of the State."[83] He took deep pride in, but not credit for, the development of the street railways. When he was interviewed on the subject in May 1910, he said: "It has been a wonderful growth, when you come to think of it. The lines have expanded, and we now do more business from the Pacific Electric station at Sixth and Main than the combined business of the twelve other leading cities in the United States, in which suburban street car service is operated."[84]

Edward loved Southern California for its climate and natural beauty. He expressed this love in his attraction to the land. His impulses to build, create, and make money led him to a vast enterprise of acquiring, improving, and using the land of Southern California.

Edward's brother Willard was also attracted by land. In the 1880s and 1890s he acquired large amounts of property near San Luis Obispo and north of San Francisco. He financed his purchases by borrowing from Collis, and when Collis died in 1900 Willard owed the estate several hundred thousand dollars. He continued to borrow from Edward to finance his operations and had to sell off parcels to meet his debts. After Willard died in 1914—when the chauffeur ran off the road near Oneonta and Willard was thrown down a steep embankment—his estate was of very little value.

Edward managed his interest in land much more successfully. He organized or took over a large number of land-holding companies. The first major ones were the Los Angeles Land Company (1901), the San Marino Land Company (1901), and the Huntington Land and Improvement Company (1902), this last being used as his major personal holding company. With the aid of the principal real estate agents in the area he began buying land in both large and small tracts. By 1903 he had bought, in downtown Los Angeles alone, sixteen parcels, including the Childs property and the Nadeau tract, at a cost of about $1.1 million. He also acquired some large properties outside of Los Angeles between 1904 and 1906, mainly toward the beaches: Downey Ranch

(Palos Verdes), Dodson Ranch (San Pedro), Brand Ranch (Glendale), Campbell-Johnston Ranch (Pasadena), Hammel and Decker Ranch (Venice), Northam Ranch (Long Beach), and Newport Beach properties, totaling in all more than eight thousand acres and costing several million dollars.

He also began to buy land in the San Gabriel Valley, the areas of Pasadena, San Marino, South Pasadena, and Alhambra, and other places toward the east. By 1903, he owned in this area over two thousand acres—including the El Molino, Shorb, Titus, and Winston ranches and the property of the San Gabriel Wine Company—at a cost of about $1 million, and by 1905 he had added another five hundred acres, including the Oak Knoll tract, Rosemead Ranch, and some lesser pieces. In the estimate of the secretary of the Huntington Land and Improvement Company, Edward owned about three-quarters of the present city of San Marino, half of South Pasadena, a third of Alhambra, and a large part of Pasadena south of California Boulevard and east of Marengo.[85] The press reported that he "continues to buy property in small bits and large ones at South Pasadena, and the natives are beginning to count on their fingers the number of months that must elapse before he owns the town."[86] The "natives" of other communities in the area doubtless felt the same way, but the reaction to his buying of land in their places was, almost universally, delight.

These rapid acquisitions led him to form additional companies to run his land operations. In the next couple of years, he extended his holdings with the San Gabriel River Improvement Company (1905), Huntington Redondo Company (1905), Naples Company (1905), Naples Extension Company (1905), and Rodeo Land and Water Company (1906). Each company was responsible for a specified area or group of areas: it kept records on acquisitions, subdivisions, prices of tracts and lots, and sales. A great many of his companies had "Improvement" in their titles, including the Huntington Land and Improvement Company, the Redondo Improvement Company, the San Gabriel River Improvement Company, and others. Their holdings were "unimproved" land—raw land without structures on it—and we would perhaps call them development companies. But "improvement" had a deeper meaning for Edward, who was entirely convinced that their work would *improve* the lot of the individual, California, and society in general.

Edward managed his properties astutely. His four best friends at this time were his son Howard, Epes Randolph, George S. Patton, and William E. Dunn. The first two were railroad men, and they were given the main responsibility for the operation of the street railway system. The latter two were lawyers and gave him guidance in all of his business activities.

Patton was Edward's first close friend and confidant in Southern California. Patton was born in Virginia in 1856, went to college and studied law there, came to Southern California in 1878, and was admitted to the bar in 1880; in 1884 he was elected district attorney for Los Angeles County and married Ruth Wilson, the daughter of Benjamin D. Wilson, the first mayor of Los Angeles and the owner of Lake Vineyard Rancho—which covered a good deal of the western San Gabriel Valley—through whom he gained a substantial amount of property. James DeBarth Shorb owned the adjacent property, also from Wilson, including a house that he had named San Marino, which figures in the Huntington story; Shorb and Patton were double brothers-in-law, as they had both married daughters of Benjamin D. Wilson, but Shorb died in 1896 and Patton lived on until 1927.

Patton's first Huntington contact had been unhappy. He was an ardent Democrat and in 1894 was the party's nominee for election to the Congress; Collis, an equally ardent Republican, made a special point of supporting Patton's opponent, who won the seat. But when Edward came to Southern California in the late 1890s he found the Pattons the nearest thing to family. Edward stayed with them, was friendly with their son—who eventually became the famous World War II general—consulted frequently with Patton, and came to rely on his advice. In 1903, Patton accepted the formal position of general manager of the Huntington Land and Improvement Company, with general supervision over all of Huntington's other land companies as well. He and Edward were in constant contact. They discussed policies, procedures, and the details of improvements; Edward made the final decisions, though they were almost always in general agreement, and Patton put them into effect with great skill and decisiveness.

Patton decided to retire in April 1910. He wrote Edward that it was "absolutely necessary that I should give my entire attention to my personal affairs." With reluctance he severed "a connection which has been so agreeable to me from beginning to end, that I take this step with sincere regret" but at the same time "looking forward to many years of personal association and friendship."[87]

Edward then turned to Dunn and persuaded him to agree to be general manager of the Huntington Land and Improvement Company and associated activities. Dunn was born in Michigan in 1861, studied law at Ann Arbor, was married in 1883, and came to Los Angeles in 1885. He was appointed Los Angeles City Attorney in 1890 and then elected to that office for the term 1894–98. In 1899 he formed a law firm in association with Albert Crutcher and John D. Bicknell; it had several changes of name, but soon became the long-lasting Gibson, Dunn, and Crutcher. When Edward came to Los Angeles, he availed himself of their services, though he also consulted his friend Henry O'Melveny. Edward was always careful to get detailed legal advice on all of his major steps, as Collis had done before him. Edward turned to Bicknell, for example, for advice about organizing and reorganizing his companies; he took pains to learn exactly what was possible and advisable under California law.[88] But it was Dunn—"Billy" Dunn he was generally called, or "Boss Billy" by those who thought he had too much power in local politics—in whom Edward had the most complete and absolute confidence. " 'Billy' Dunn was the most unselfish man I have ever known," Edward said. "I trusted his judgment when I would hardly rely on my own."[89] Dunn was probably the closest friend Edward ever had beyond his immediate family. Dunn stood for him in the divorce proceedings in 1906; he played, as we shall see, a key role in Edward's later crucial activities, and his legal outlook had an effect on their shape. Dunn was friend, adviser, and trusted chief deputy.

The hectic pace of Edward's land purchases continued throughout this ten-year period. He bought a great many other large ranches, but he also bought hundreds of small pieces of property, ranging in size from residential building lots to parcels of a few acres.[90] It got so that every time he visited an area the rumor began that he was planning to make extensive purchases of land there. Nearly every location in the

Los Angeles area was rumored to be the place for his next acquisition: San Bernardino, Whittier, San Pedro, San Diego, Pomona. Typically, "the moment that it was whispered about the streets [of San Bernardino] that Mr. Huntington was in town, predictions of some announcement were frequent."[91] And nowhere were these rumors stirred more frequently than on Catalina Island; every year brought the assurance that he was about to buy, or had bought, this gem of the ocean from the Banning brothers and would convert it into the world's finest amusement park.[92] Even those places in which Huntington had shown no interest could conclude that "it will be only a short time when he will be a big factor in and around Santa Monica."[93] If no new rumor was circulated in two days, it roused fear: "Can it be that he is losing interest in Southern California?"[94]

From Arizona, headlines assured the readers that Huntington "Will Grab Them All": "It is not unreasonable to suppose that in the course of a few years, the nephew of C. P. Huntington will own Southern California. Anything that is for sale, Huntington is after, and it is all for sale—so there you are."[95]

From Ventura came a similar report: "It is all Huntington, Huntington. One hears nothing else. If he secures possession of all the land he is said to be after, why Huntington will have such a slice of the county as to make him virtual owner of the county."[96] And in the conservative *Los Angeles Times,* under the heading "A Magic Name," readers were told that "there was a wild-eyed rumor on the real estate Rialto, a few days ago, that Huntington had purchased all the unimproved real estate in Southern California."[97]

Whenever Edward returned to Los Angeles after a time away, he was besieged by newspaper reporters with questions about his plans for future land purchases. These questions irritated him, because one of his fixed principles, as he told one reporter, was that "I never talk about things I am going to do until they are done."[98] To another reporter on the same day he said, "I decline to tell my plans. I have been lied about in all parts of Southern California, and my name has been used by reckless real estate speculations to boom property all the way from Santa Barbara to Mexico."[99] To another on the same day, when his patience was wearing thin, he said, "I have no new plans for a development, and as that statement may not be believed, you might add that a syndicate is being formed by me for the purchase of all the churches in Southern California, that being the only property, according to general report, that I have not yet secured."[100] And to yet another on the same day, when asked about the truth of a rumor after his patience had worn out completely, he replied, "Would you believe it if you should hear a well-founded rumor that I was about to build a railroad to the moon and open up mines of green cheese there?"[101]

Real estate agents hurried to get a piece of the action, and many tried to use the Huntington name as an inducement to get the public to buy land. The Carlson Investment Company of Los Angeles ran a large ad in 1905 under the heading "BUY Where Huntington Buys! Is Good Advice to Follow." They reported that "H. E. Huntington bought from us 22 blocks through the center of the Pasadena Villa Tract. And he has also bought all around the Pasadena Villa Tract. 'Go and do likewise' is our advice."[102] The Alhambra firm of Northrup and Peck had its business envelopes in 1906 printed, in red, with a large design of eight flags—each with a Huntington property named on it, like "Huntington's Oak Knoll Tract" and "Huntington's El Molino Ranch"—around a circle with the legend "Follow the Flag of H. E. Huntington's Investments in the Beautiful San Gabriel Valley" and concluding, in the middle, "To Alhambra: The Center."[103]

Editorials advised readers to buy property. The *Los Angeles Examiner,* in 1909, asserted that "Now Is Always the Time to Buy a House" and assured readers, "You can get your piece of land and whatever you pay for it will probably come back to you fourfold within a very brief period. Mr. H. E. Huntington, one of the best informed men on the valuations of land in Los Angeles and its vicinity, says that there is not an available piece of land within fifty miles of this city that will not grow by leaps and bounds within the next few years."[104]

These great expectations led to considerable land changing hands. Edward was selling as well as buying, and he made a good deal of money from his sales. The Childs property in downtown Los Angeles— the area bounded by Hill, Main, Eleventh, and Twelfth streets—for which he had paid $250,000 in 1902, he sold for $2.5 million in 1907.[105] Sometimes he turned a quick profit; in the middle of March 1905 he bought 189 acres on Santa Fe and Slauson avenues in Los Angeles for $114,000, and by the end of the month he sold it for $150,000.[106] In 1906, he got $160,000 for two pieces of downtown property for which he had paid $35,000 two and a half years before; a real estate dealer sagely remarked that "Mr. Huntington is a speculator as well as an operator in real estate, and frequently buys for speculative purposes. This is, perhaps, one of his speculative deals."[107] The buying and selling of downtown property was amusingly described in one paper as if it were a football game, with Huntington the captain of the team that wins the game: "The onlookers are swarming over the field, kicking, punting and passing the ball, falling on it as well as over themselves." They didn't realize that the game was all over and that Huntington had won. "Many of you who waited too long had better sneak home now, or you will be jammed against the fence, as the game down on Los Angeles and Seventh streets is over. Mark my words, Captain Huntington is now calling off his players. The exits are being closed."[108]

Sometimes Edward felt he sold too cheaply. After he had agreed to sell his friend A. B. Hammond a piece of downtown property for a certain sum, he wrote him, "By the way, after I told you you could have the property I got to thinking the matter over and what a fool I had made of myself—as usual."[109]

Most of Edward's attention, however, went to subdividing larger parcels of land and selling building lots. In the year beginning April 7, 1902, over a hundred tracts in the Los Angeles area were subdivided into 5,475 lots, and twenty-six hundred frame houses were built on them at an average cost of $2,000 each.[110] Edward's companies were the major factor in this activity throughout the decade. Most of the lots were in the range of $300 to $500 for half an acre, but a few—like those in the Oak Knoll tract in Pasadena—were as high as $5,000 an acre with a minimum building restriction of $10,000 to $15,000 for the residence (and no oil wells permitted).

Some of the early developments were in places like Whittier and Pomona, which became popular as the street railways reached them. As Edward wrote to Patton in 1905, "We all know by experience and the history of properties in and around Los Angeles what effect railway communications have in increasing land value."[111] Edward caused the street railways to be extended to all areas where there was an immediate or potential need for them, and not mainly to areas where he had or could buy land. Since the greatest part of the habitable land in Southern California seemed desirable for having "railway communications," almost any prime property that he acquired was likely to increase in value as the railways were naturally extended.

Edward turned his attention to beach properties during the latter half of this decade. He bought, subdivided, and sold a good deal of land in Newport Beach, Huntington Beach, Manhattan Beach, Alamitos Bay, and other coastal areas near Los Angeles. In 1904, he bought five miles (six hundred acres) of ocean frontage at Newport Beach, and additional property at Huntington Beach and Alamitos Bay.[112]

His activities at Redondo Beach—forty minutes by street railway from downtown Los Angeles—serve as an example of his development work at its most frenzied. When someone suggested he buy property in Redondo, he followed his usual pattern of making a personal inspection. "When I studied the place," he said, "and saw its attractions, the beautiful topography it possessed, those terraces rising in harmonious degrees from the sea, I determined that it presented such features as should make it the great resort of this region." He rode through the shaded avenues of the village and over the many knolls overlooking the community. "I made a careful study," he added, "and became satisfied."[113] It was the beauty of the place that brought him to the buying point. "The beauty of Redondo cannot be realized until it is seen. It is a revelation to me," he said, "and it will be a revelation to others to know that almost at the gate of Los Angeles has been sleeping for nearly a score of years one of the most picturesque villages in all the world."[114] Early in July 1905, Edward bought the Redondo Improvement Company, which owned four thousand lots in Redondo—almost all of the property that constituted this small seaside village—for $1 million; at the same time he acquired the Los Angeles and Redondo Railway. A week later he bought the 1,010-acre Downey Ranch along the ocean front that stretched between Redondo and San Pedro.

His purchase was reported in the newspapers on Friday, July 7. Edward announced that he would make improvements at Redondo, including a large modern bathhouse. Over the next ten days the papers, even those as far away as the *New York Sun* and the *Washington Post,* were filled with stories about the glorious future of Redondo. Edward had a sales office set up in Redondo, and so did everyone else who owned property there. Right away people began to hurry to Redondo to get in on the ground floor. A special rail fare was offered of twenty-five cents from Pasadena, and the crowds of buyers increased.[115]

On Sunday, July 9, Carrie and Burke Holladay, who were visiting Edward in Los Angeles from their home in San Francisco, were taken by Howard to Redondo to see the activity. Edward was already there. On the following Thursday Burke wrote a long letter from San Francisco to Harriet, who was in Oneonta, to tell her of their adventures and of her son Edward. He began with some reflections he had had on the way to the beach:

> On Friday last, it came out in the Los Angeles papers that Mr. H. E. Huntington had bought the entire town site of Redondo, from the Redondo Land Co., and that he would offer it for sale. And Oh! What a change! In the twinkling of an eye, immediately the people of Los Angeles rushed in droves to Redondo to buy! buy! buy! Every [trolley] car was loaded, and with a deck of straphangers added. Every 3d man had his nose buried in the map of Redondo, and all talking about trade & real estate.

When Burke, Carrie, and Howard arrived in Redondo, they saw buying and selling going on everywhere. They found

> a swarm of people in and around a selling booth or building where Edwards had his real estate men sitting at a table with map spread out. The crowd, I say, not only filled the house but spread out across the street. Those who wanted to buy of him made their way as best they could to the table, gave each his name, indicated his lot. Name, lot, block & price were taken down on a list, and in time the list was passed over to others, who made out the contract to purchase and received ⅓ cash down. And so fast did the buyers come that the agents were kept at it without a pause, some buying a number of lots, others entire blocks, to the amount of a couple of hundreds of thousands of dollars a day. And out on the streets were real estate agents, and wild-

eyed speculators, men and women. So those who had bought first hand in the booth had no trouble selling again for an advance, often in a few hours, or even minutes.

Burke was astounded by the eagerness of the buyers and the prices they were willing to pay:

> The name of Huntington had done it all. Pieces of land, bought two weeks ago at $1,500, sold for say $4,000 and again for $6,000. One piece of land which Edwards told the real estate man was worth $15,000—and at which he laughed—was two days later bought by that same man for $22,000. Well, as I said, it was Sunday when we got there, but the sales were going right along as if it were a weekday. And every candy and popcorn booth, every seashell and curio store, was ornamented by a large sign: "Real Estate."

Burke and Carrie were with Edward, who was enjoying the action but willing to take a brief break for lunch:

> After seeing the sales go merrily on, Edwards, Carrie, and I went to Mr. Ainsworth's [an early resident of the area] and had luncheon with him and his wife. Then went back and watched the boom again. Edwards couldn't keep away, and much of the time stood or sat by his agents, smiling and helping the good work along.

Edward had been there on Saturday as well as Sunday. They went together back to Redondo on Monday—"no longer the 'Dead Town,' but now 'Redondo the beautiful.'" The boom "came as a surprise even to" Edward and delayed his departure for the East. Burke saw the public eagerness to buy as a tribute to confidence in Edward's judgment:

> I never saw or heard of so sincere and unanimous a compliment to one man's judgment as this sudden and absolute change of opinion about Redondo. A place which was for years condemned as not desirable, in one hour is changed to the most desirable spot known. And not scores but hundreds of people with money are madly struggling to get each a small piece.[116]

The newspapers agreed that it was "the magic of Huntington's name" that explained the public eagerness to buy. "There is no safer leader than he to follow in business enterprise, as experience has proved."[117] Edward read the newspaper accounts about Redondo with interest. He sent his mother a long clipping about the activities at Redondo on that Monday when he and Burke and Carrie were there together; he addressed the envelope himself and enclosed only the one clipping, about the crowds in the town and the fast sale of lots, without any other message.[118]

Edward disliked it when the selling turned into a boom, and said publicly, "I am surprised at and deprecate the speculative condition that exists at Redondo. . . . A boom is something that I detest. It is bad for me and bad for Redondo." He set prices for lots on his schedule and refused to raise his prices, even when the buying became frenzied. "I have not deviated a dollar from the schedule. My friends have told me I was foolish not to make the money that others are making, but my feeling about a boom is such that I won't do it. And, further, I cannot afford to, for I do not propose to allow anyone the right to say that I took advantage of such a situation."[119]

His lots sold well. The average lot price was about $500 in 1905; some went for $300 to $400, some for $750, a few for $1,000. Many people bought groups of lots, and some whole blocks. The supply was not exhausted, however, and in 1909 the Redondo Improvement Company still had many lots for sale.[120] Edward carried out the development promised for Redondo by building a gigantic bathhouse to accommodate two thousand bathers at one time, with three large pools, a continuous flow of heated seawater, sixty-two tub baths (plus Turkish baths, needle showers, and massage rooms), and thirteen hundred fifty dressing rooms with ten thousand bathing suits and twenty thousand bath towels, all of the structure lighted in the evening by seven thousand incandescent bulbs. A big party marked the beginning of construction, and six thousand people came on the first day it was opened.[121]

Edward made money on his lots in Redondo. Probably he could have made more, but, he stated, "one of my fixed principles is not to try to make all the money."[122] He kept schedules of selling prices for all of his properties: sometimes he authorized the agents to "shade the prices" a little, and occasionally he raised all of the prices in a given area by a certain percentage. For South Pasadena, for example, he gave notice on November 22, 1908, that all the prices would be raised by 10 percent on January 1, 1909.[123]

He was glad to see other people make money also. He wrote to Patton, in connection with working out an agreement with a Mr. Collins for some Newport Beach property, that "my impression is it might be well to accept his proposition, although no doubt he will make a great deal of money out of it. That, however, I don't object to."[124] Even if he lost out in making a deal, he felt that "there is always one consolation in a disappointment of this kind. We can do something else."[125]

His fundamental idea of letting other people make money too is a key to his behavior as a trader:

> I have always felt that the true business policy was never to play for the whole stake; by that I mean, never try to get out of any kind of property all that you think you could get if you held on.
> For instance, I bought one piece here for $58,000; I was in New York and I received a telegram offering me $150,000 for it. I figured what it stood me in, with interest at 5 percent, and I said to my bookkeeper, "That property is worth $250,000, but let it go."
> Sure enough, the man who bought it sold it in less than a year for $250,000.
> But instead of losing, I made by the transaction. For with the $150,000 I got for it I bought other property; more of it because it was cheaper. And that property is now easily worth over $500,000.[126]

There was one other reason he did not try to maximize his profit: "I could have made a whole lot more money out of this country than I have done if money-making had not been tempered with real affection for this region."[127] He was a lover of Southern California before he was a businessman of Southern California.

Edward's main business activities during the period 1900 to 1910 were the street railways and land companies in the Los Angeles area. However, his business interests were much broader. On November 1, 1907, he personally controlled a total of twenty-three companies in Southern California; beyond the railway and land companies, they included a number of gas and electric companies such as the Pacific Light and Power Company, water companies like Alhambra Water Company and Marengo Water Company, and manufacturing companies such as Alfred Dolge Manufacturing Company.[128]

He also owned or controlled a number of companies outside of his local area. For example, in 1904 he owned thirty-six independent telephone companies worth several million dollars in Texas, Arkansas, Louisiana, and Oklahoma, including those in most of the largest cities.[129] And in the period 1908 to 1910 he bought a number of other telephone companies in Texas and in Oakland, California.[130]

But his major investments were in Southern California. The public utilities were of special importance to him and to the development of the area. In 1901 he was involved in the project of bringing water from Kern County and building a reservoir to store it, and in 1902 he parleyed some of his lesser holdings into the formation of the Pacific Light and Power Company to supply electric power and, after it was reorganized in 1908, gas and water as well. Edward and his associates owned 51 percent of the company. W. G. Kerckhoff was installed as president, and he and Edward worked in harmony. Edward frequently urged Kerckhoff to press ahead. "My idea," he wrote in 1904, "is that we cannot afford to lag behind the procession and should rather keep always a little ahead of it." He was also keen about giving the best service to their customers: "Our aim should always be to give better service than anybody else does. While this may cost money in the beginning, it will be very profitable in the end."[131] Edward continued his active interest in public utilities. When the Los Angeles City Council proposed, in 1910, to require a reduction in electricity rates from nine cents to seven cents per kilowatt hour, Edward wrote an open letter addressed to the "Citizens of the City of Los Angeles" and published it in all the papers; he argued that such a reduction would jeopardize the prosperity of the area by harming local corporate securities in eastern and foreign markets and thus preventing the borrowing necessary to extend their lines and services. The beginning of his letter reveals a good deal about his attitude toward himself and the community:

> I fully expect that among those who do me the honor of reading this letter, there will be a few who will give me credit for thinking only of my private gain in expressing my views publicly upon the question of the rates of public utilities companies. However, I sincerely hope that most of you will feel that the question of the great good of the City of Los Angeles, and its general prosperity, is of far more importance to yourself and to me, both from a financial and a civic standpoint, than the very small comparative gain to be made by the proposed reduction of rates.[132]

His interest in "the great good of the City of Los Angeles, and its general prosperity" led him to try to encourage manufacturing. In 1903 he began to build a model town in the area that is now Alhambra. He hired a businessman from the East, Alfred Dolge, to run the factories, and called the town Dolgeville. It was laid out like a park on four hundred acres, with factories to make felt, a business district, and a residential district. Edward envisioned a series of such towns around Los Angeles, each for one kind of manufacturing.[133] He wrote Patton in 1904 about his motives: "California is well advertised for tourists along the flower garden, climate, scenery, and 'big tree' line: but very little is done to impress people with its advantages industrially except in the direction of fruit raising, etc." He wanted to attract "a fine class of industrial people" from the East and from Europe "to come to Southern California and settle in a business that would help the State commercially speaking and socially as well. . . . One reason why I am anxious to have the Dolgeville enterprise prove an actual success and a substantial one, commercially speaking, is on account of the example it would exhibit to the world."[134]

Alas, Dolgeville did not succeed, despite his continued support and encouragement. Alfred Dolge proved to be a slick operator who promised a great deal but delivered very little. Edward had to reorganize the company in 1908 and once again in 1910 as the Standard Felt Company, when Dolge and his relatives were all forced out. Edward cut his losses and allowed the company to die out after a few years.[135] Although he did not lose much money, it was one of his few business mistakes in this decade. Others were his ill-advised attempt to get the riverbed franchise through an agent, his failure to take decisive action to prevent street railway accidents that caused loss of life, and his long absences from Los Angeles during the periods of intense expansion. In the case of Dolgeville, he was taken in by a fast-talking fraud. But Edward's idea was an interesting one, and it could have materially altered the makeup of Los Angeles had it succeeded.

Edward began to receive some national recognition as a businessman and appeared in the *Directory of Directors*. By 1903, he was a director of thirty-eight companies, and by 1905 the number had increased to sixty-one. In a sense, these figures are meaningless, since they include small subsidiary companies. But the newspapers made a good deal of the list and noted that in 1906 he stood sixth on the list with sixty directorships. (John D. Rockefeller, who had a *lot* of money, was number one.) As companies were reorganized, Edward's directorships went down, to forty-nine in 1909.[136]

But his financial assets kept rising. His business operations during this decade required large amounts of money, as he made acquisitions of $1 million here, $2 million there, and $3 million yonder. He was masterful in the way he leveraged his funds through the use of debt. Virtually all of his securities—stocks and bonds—were in use all of the time as collateral for short-term loans and notes. His purchases were usually paid for by a series of short-term notes, payable at, for example, six-month intervals over the course of the next several years. His secretaries kept exact records of cash requirements and sent him every four months a list of which loans and notes were coming due, which could be renewed, which were to be paid off, and which were available for use as collateral.[137]

He studied the financial arrangements of each company with great care and understanding. For example, like an investment analyst or banker, he made ten pages of notes on the financing of the Safety Insulated Wire and Cable Company. But the money at risk was his own.[138] He was involved in a lot of substantial securities transactions in the range of $300,000 to $1 million. On March 17, 1903, he turned over

1. Edward's parents, Solon Huntington and Harriet Saunders Huntington, in their early married years.

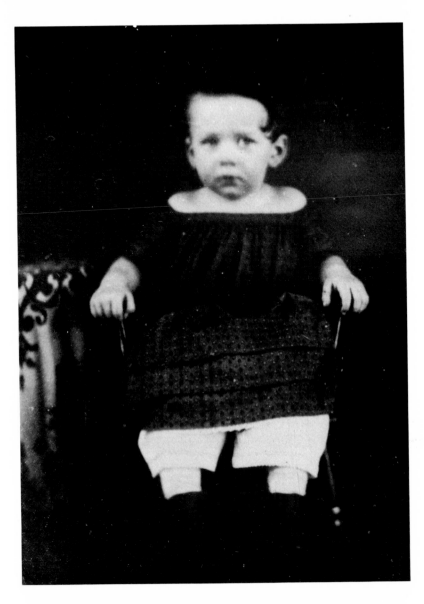

2. (*Above*) Edward under the age of two.

3. (*Opposite, above*) The family residence in Oneonta, where Edward was born and lived until the age of nineteen.

4. (*Opposite, below*) A country scene sketched by Edward in his adolescence.

5. Edward at the age of eleven.

6. (*Opposite*) Mary Alice Prentice and Edward around the time of their marriage in 1873.

7. Huntington residences in San Francisco in the 1890s. (*Above*)
Edward's home at 2840 Jackson Street. (*Opposite, above*) Collis's
home at 1020 California Street.

8. (*Opposite, below*) Edward during his years in San Francisco.

9. (*Above*) A family gathering in Oneonta, alongside the Huntington residence, about 1900. Edward is standing, between his four children. His mother (with a shawl over her head) and his wife are seated on the bench in front, with three other relatives.

10. (*Opposite, above*) A card game at the C. P. Huntington vacation house in the Adirondacks. Collis is wearing his black skull cap, and Arabella is across the table from him. The other two players are Carrie Campbell, on Arabella's left, and Jeanie Sherrill, on her right.

11. (*Opposite, below*) Edward and Collis on a street in San Francisco in the 1890s.

12. The four Huntington children as young adults in San Francisco: Howard (*opposite, above*), Elizabeth (*opposite, below*), Clara (*above, left*), and Marian (*above, right*).

13. Edward (in dark coat and hat) on an inspection trip over the lines.

14. Edward at a baseball game with Los Angeles Railway employees. Edward is in the center wearing a straw hat. Howard, in a bowler, is next to him.

15. Edward's closest business associates and friends: William E. Dunn (*above*) and George S. Patton (*below*).

16. (*Above*) Edward's dominance over Southern California as portrayed in the *Los Angeles Evening News,* October 16, 1905.

17. (*Below*) Edward represented by the *Los Angeles Daily Times* as a great builder and benefactor of Southern California.

February 27, 1917.

Messrs Sotheby Wilkinson & Hodge

Dear Sirs

      I hereby confirm the purchase by me of the Library, known as the "Bridgewater Library" of the Right Hon. The Earl of Ellesmere, London, as described in the printed Catalogue and check list of said Library for the sum of one million dollars ($1,000,000.00) in United States Coin or its equivalent, payable as follows:

      Upon delivery of the first one half of said library, the sum of $250,000.00 in cash and a promissory note for the sum of $250,000.00 payable in two (2) months from said date of delivery. The balance of said purchase price, $500,000.00 to be paid upon delivery of the second one half of said Library in two (2) notes of $250,000.00 each, payable respectively in four and six months from the date of delivery of the first half of said Library. Delivery of Books to be made at the Lincoln Safe Deposit Company, 42nd Street, New York City and a receipt given subject to treir proving correct according to check lists.

      All risks of insurance are to be assumed by me from the time of delivery of said books at the Lincoln Safe Deposit Company.

      It is understood and agreed that a reasonable time will be allowed to check the collection with catalogue and check lists.

      It is further understood and agreed that if a portion of said library is lost in transportation, the price to be paid is to be reduced proportionately for the remainder.

Accepted.

18. The original agreement to purchase the Bridgewater Library in 1917 for $1 million.

ten thousand shares of B & O stock and twenty-seven hundred shares of Colorado Fuel and Iron for $1,293,077.24, and on October 8, 1904, he sold five thousand shares of U.S. Steel for $446,412.50.[139]

Occasionally he ran close to the edge. The financial panic of 1903 was very difficult for Edward, who had to delay his payments as long as he possibly could. He wrote Patton to "go slow in your disbursements for the time being," and his secretary wrote Edward "I am in hot water again" in trying to cover the floating debts.[140] But he squeezed by without damage. The panic of 1907, although more serious, did not harm him, as his financing was by then on a more solid basis. His enterprises were well situated for the period of great economic growth that followed during the next decade. He had extended himself to the maximum possible during the tight period and was prepared to profit during the more prosperous times.

His financial successes depended on his basic strategy of aggressive expansion through debt-financed acquisitions and reorganization. He was an entrepreneur who sought to put money into activities with long-term promise and profitable side effects. He combined the theory of thinking big and running risks with the practice of frugality, saving, and investing cautiously. The possibility of the success of that strategy depended on being in the right place at the right time, and Southern California was certainly one of the right places to be during the first decades of the twentieth century. Had he been in another place or in another time, he might have used another strategy. He liked to make money.

In 1900, Edward's net assets were about $1 million, and he received in all $12 to $15 million from Collis's estate over the next several years. His assets rose very well during the decade. We can follow the course of his financial fortunes by comparing his year-end balance sheets. We need to keep in mind, however, that these figures often, for various accounting reasons, do not necessarily represent the full current year-end market value of his assets and often in these cases understate them somewhat.

The balance sheets record a multiplicity of details. On December 31, 1910, for example, his pictures were carried at $190,466.13, his books at $196,824.93, his tapestries at $577,364.43, and his furniture at

$392,838.24. And it is recorded that on December 31, 1902, he owned whiskey in warehouse to the value of $816.87 and by December 31, 1907, he owned $1,062.48 worth of that commodity, though he drank little of it himself.

At the end of 1902, his total net assets were recorded at about $15 million. There was a slow increase during the difficult financial years, and at the end of 1908 he was worth about $21 million. Then the figures increased dramatically, to about $30 million at the end of 1909. By the end of 1910 they had soared to $55 million, thanks to the reorganization of the street railways, by which $20 million was recorded for his ownership of the Los Angeles Railway. So at the end of this decade the businessman had accumulated total assets worth at least $55 million.[141]

Eleven

HERO OF SOUTHERN CALIFORNIA
1900—1910

IT IS A TRUTH UNIVERSALLY acknowledged that, in the expression of affection, one party has to make the first move. Edward expressed his love of Southern California first, as we have seen. Over and over again he spoke of his joy in being in Southern California, his preference for it over all other places in the world, his appreciation for its beauty and its climate, and his belief in its great future. Very soon his affection came to be reciprocated.

His enthusiasm for Southern California was accompanied by his remarkable successes there in the first decade of this century. His enthusiasm and his successes attracted many people, including those who were important and those who were not. They also wanted to believe in and share the future of Southern California. Edward's words and actions expressed their own hopes and aspirations. His enthusiasm contributed to his role as a leader, despite his personal modesty, his unassuming manner, and the lack of a public relations staff. Gradually he came to be held in a kind of heroic esteem.

This chapter traces public opinion in Southern California about Huntington. The public viewed him first with respect and appreciation, then with admiration, and finally came to regard him as a hero. He became a mythic figure for the people of Southern California. This progression took place with speed and decisiveness, and it had important effects on Edward's life.

The first concrete evidence the people of Southern California saw of Edward's interest in their region were his improvements of the Southern Pacific lines in the 1890s and his formation of a syndicate, with himself as the principal investor, to buy in 1898 the Los Angeles Railway with its fifty miles of track and the Pasadena Railway with its forty miles.

Edward's involvement in the area was greeted with enthusiasm. He was warmly welcomed as "a rich man," and his expenditure of "millions of dollars" in the improvement of Southern California was described as being "of inestimable advantage to this region."[1] Even San Franciscans began to be a little envious. "He took hold of the Los Angeles railway system," reported the *San Francisco Wave* in 1900, "when it was losing money and its bonds were far below par. Within a few months he had converted it into a profitable property. Its equipment is now as fine as any line in the country, and the service is admirable." Once having broken into encomium, the story goes on to praise Edward as a human being. "Personally, Mr. Huntington is a man of agreeable personality and of a simple and cordial manner," it began. "He is quite without the pretension and affectation which so many men of importance consider proper attributes of their dignity. He is very approachable, quick of decision, and a true friend of his friends. An excellent administrator, he has been successful in building up a large private fortune."[2] This last particular gave him his first attraction. This story was copied in many other papers. The *Oneonta Star*, a loyal hometown newspaper, gave it full page-one treatment, with a picture of the native "in whose success every acquaintance here takes interest and pride."[3]

As the electric railways were extended around Los Angeles, local admiration for Edward increased. By 1902, a six-column article with photo appeared entitled "Henry Edwards Huntington: A Study" and signed "S. T. C." for Samuel T. Clover (not Coleridge). It came to this conclusion: "Los Angeles is to be felicitated and warmly congratulated because of this enthusiastic citizen she has forever hypnotized." Would he leave San Francisco to make Los Angeles his permanent home? "Of that there is not the least doubt. He intimates it in every action, every speech." And what sort of a man was he? A rich man, yes, but a human person too: what was most notable about him was "his remarkable self-poise, his unaffected modesty of demeanor, his democratic habits, his quiet humor." He had "a large firm hand that suggests strength, breadth and grip, and a mobile mouth." He had "dancing eyes. The blue iris emits a sparkle that indicates a playful spirit for which one is not unprepared when the mobile mouth is in action and a chuckle of enjoyment follows a humorous suggestion that has aroused the risibilities of his hearer." He "loves to banter with friends, but always in a good-humored, jovial way that proclaims a kind, considerate heart"; and he could "take without wincing his share of the banter." In short, he struck the writer of this article—and others who observed him at this time—as an admirably humane person.[4]

In the short period from 1902 to 1905, admiration for Edward broadened and deepened in Southern California. "What has Huntington done?" asked the Los Angeles Daily Journal rhetorically in 1903. After replying that the answer would fill many volumes, it was summarized in the statement that "his street railways have probably done more for the upbuilding and betterment of the city, than any other one project that has been accomplished for many a long day."[5] That feeling was shared all around the area. The Riverside Daily Press maintained in an editorial that "H. E. Huntington is certainly Riverside's good angel," and another paper in the same community declared that "the sentiment at present is certainly, 'There is nothing too good for Mr. Huntington,' and whatever favor he asks of the city trustees or the citizens of Riverside will be granted if it is possible under any circumstances to do so."[6] They felt the same way down in San Pedro. An editorial under the title "A Master Mind" in the News began by asserting that "there are some big things doing in Southern California these days—bigger than this section has ever known before." There was "no difficulty in selecting the one enterprise which most plainly points to a master mind. . . . The Huntington electric railroad system in conception and in the details of its construction is one of the masterpieces of human industrial achievement."[7]

As Edward proceeded with his railway construction, he had the support of the public. "There is no question," began an editorial in the Los Angeles Express in 1903, "that a kindly spirit exists in the community toward the big enterprises in which Mr. Huntington is so largely interested." A few days later another editorial in the same paper asserted, in connection with Edward's application for city rail franchises, that "it is to be hoped that no unjust or unreasonable obstacles will be placed in the path of Mr. Huntington's progress, which, in this instance, we believe to be identical with that of Los Angeles. . . . The development of Los Angeles has been greatly advanced by the enterprise and investments of H. E. Huntington," and the further "effect upon the future of this city will be still more signal."[8]

Even in its early stages, there was recognition that the railway construction would have a significant effect on the region. In 1904, an editorial in the *Los Angeles Herald,* under the title "Development by Trolley," observed that "it is astonishing the effect electric railway building has had on this portion of Southern California, and as the Huntington system is only fairly in its initial [stages], marvels are ahead."[9] Later in the same year, the *Los Angeles Times* devoted an editorial of two and a half columns to "Huntington" as "a power in the community in which he lives, respected, esteemed, admired and pointed out as one American citizen whom vast riches could not ruin." He had asked himself, "How can I make my wealth benefit the community and the state?" Was he succeeding? The editorial responded:

> Ask any one of the thousands who daily enjoy the pleasures, the up-lifting, rejuvenating elixir of a day at the beaches or in the near-by hills; ask the business men of Los Angeles who live in the suburbs or the outlying residence sections of the city; ask the thousands who travel in comfort and speed within the city limits and between Los Angeles and our scores of suburbs, adjacent towns, pleasure resorts and points of interest; ask the business men who are thriving because Los Angeles is thriving under the marvelous development which our network of railroads has been largely instrumental in bringing about—ask these people what Henry E. Huntington has achieved, and you will receive an answer which, if Huntington could hear it, would warm his heart and thrill him through and through. No record of the wonderful development of Southern California during the past three years would be complete without the name of Henry E. Huntington as one of the most important factors of that development. Such distinguished success will be continued in the years to come, to the everlasting benefit and honor of Los Angeles, of Southern California and of the name of Huntington.

The editorial concluded that "it was a fortunate day for our city when Mr. Huntington selected it for his field of operations; and now, when all the world is marveling at the wonderful progress we have made in so short a time, it is only fair, just and right to publicly recognize and applaud the man who has been so large a contributor to our bounding prosperity."[10]

Not only editorial writers felt that Huntington had a major concern for the area. Alfred G. Walker, who began working as a clerk for Huntington in 1903 and ended as president of the Huntington Land and Improvement Company, said in his reminiscences that Huntington "was a great man, loved and respected by all who worked for him. He was interested primarily in the development of Southern California, and the welfare of her people."[11]

The beauty of the trolley system was often spoken of, and this attribute was also credited to Edward who, having "not forgotten that which appeals to the eye," caused California poppies to be planted along some of the lines and rose beds along some of the others.[12] "A ride on the Electric Cars from Monrovia to Los Angeles," for example, "can be enjoyed by lovers of the beautiful. The varying scenes of landscape composed of orchards, vistas and beautiful homes, extend along this drive. These little gems of scenery looking toward the giant mountains which border on the north, awaken the true sentiment of beauty in one's consciousness."[13] And the *Los Angeles Times* printed a long editorial called "Along the Golden Foothills" on the glories of taking a ride on the electric street railway: "Nature beckons, beckons. The mountains call, the hills shout, and the vales cry to us to come out and behold their splendor of color and the wealth of beauty in which they are robed."[14]

Before 1905, Edward's work in Southern California was coming to be known across the country. The syndicated column "New York Letter" for January 17, 1903, by John Marthol, devoted a long paragraph to Huntington as "conspicuous in western cities" as a very successful "electric traction man," and this paragraph was widely reprinted.[15] The *Chicago Star and Record-Herald,* in a story about Southern California in 1905, maintained that "Mr. Huntington is the most public-spirited man in Los Angeles, and one might say in California."[16] The *New York*

Globe in 1904 wrote glowingly of the Southern California trolleys, speeding along between rose beds at seventy-five miles per hour: "The people of the east do not know what a first-class electric railroad is. The Metropolitan system in New York is a go-cart compared with the Huntington system in Southern California. To H. E. Huntington belongs the credit of building up the largest and most original system of electrical transportation known." This glowing testimony was reprinted in various papers in Southern California.[17]

By 1905, Edward's place in Southern California was secure. The *Los Angeles Graphic* remarked the change in popular attitude toward him: "Privileges which the City denied Mr. Huntington some three years ago, although he was willing to pay $150,000 for them, are today granted him almost without protest and certainly without price. No more marked or complete reversal of public opinion has ever been evidenced in Los Angeles." And a month later the same paper concluded that "the enterprises of Mr. H. E. Huntington and his associates, involving the investment of some $50,000,000 in this city and its vicinity, have undoubtedly advanced the progress of Los Angeles at least ten years; the development of Los Angeles has been commensurate with the development of Mr. Huntington's projects."[18]

The *Los Angeles Times* featured Edward in their special midwinter number in 1905 and described his work as "Notable Achievements of a Great Captain of Industry."[19] And the *Los Angeles Financier* thought that Huntington should be thanked because Los Angeles was "at its flood tide of success"; "he has placed the city ten years ahead of its natural growth."[20]

This public feeling about Edward was fully shared by individuals who knew him privately. Brockway Metcalf visited Edward, his future father-in-law, in Los Angeles. After traveling around the area with him, he wrote to Elizabeth, "Don't wonder that he is so wrapped up in Los Angeles. Think I would be too if I were in his place and had really made the place, as he has done."[21]

What most residents of Southern California wanted during the first decade of this century was growth. They got it. And they attributed it largely to H. E. Huntington and his enterprises.

Growth showed itself in many different forms. Population growth—the most obvious—was usually taken as proof of the general recognition of natural advantages and a sign of progress and prosperity. The city of Los Angeles had been growing rapidly, from 11,183 in 1880 to 50,395 in 1890 to 102,479 in 1900. In early 1902, Edward was formally asked by James McLachlan of the U.S. House of Representatives to give his committee an estimate of the population in 1920. Edward responded, on February 1, 1902, with the figure of 500,000.[22] This must have seemed an absurdly high estimate. That the population would quintuple in twenty years! One could have laughed all the way to the Census Bureau. The figure turned out to be 576,673. In 1905, when the population was probably on the order of 175,000 to 200,000, Edward was asked, in the course of a newspaper interview, to prophesy the long-range possibility. He responded that the population would reach one million during his lifetime.[23] He was probably right, but he died in 1927 before the 1930 census could make it official, at 1,238,048.

There was intense public interest in Los Angeles in its population, its ranking among other cities, and its rate of growth. Between 1900 and 1907, Los Angeles was estimated to have increased in population from 102,479 to 290,000; in the process, its size had passed that of Minneapolis, Kansas City, Louisville, Indianapolis, Denver, Toledo, Columbus, and Omaha. It had the fastest growth rate of any major city.[24]

In the 1910 census, the population reached 319,198, and Los Angeles jumped from thirty-sixth to sixteenth place in size among U.S. cities; the increase was so phenomenal that, according to Stoddard Jess, vice-president of the First National Bank in Los Angeles, "the suspicion of the Census Bureau has been aroused as to the correctness of the count."[25]

Another measure of growth is the value of real property. The market for real estate was very active in Los Angeles in 1902, and even more so in 1903. The headlines of the *Los Angeles Sunday Herald* for January 11, 1903, epitomized the situation: "Values Grow Firmer. Confidence in Los Angeles Real Estate. Trend Is Higher and Active Demand Prevails." The same paper gave a similar account of construction activities: "January a Rattler. Pace in Building Exceeds Former Epochs."[26]

The assessor's official figures on property values tell a story of tremendous growth during this decade. Values went from $97,161,112 in 1900 to $169,269,166 in 1903 to $521,945,364 in 1910—an astounding increase of 428 percent in one decade.[27]

Bank clearings and building permits also told the same story—that the economy was expanding, that prosperity was increasing, that the future looked bright.

It was common to attribute this growth to the expansion of the street railway system. Even in the early years of the expansion there were editorials like one in the *Los Angeles Herald* in 1903, entitled "Los Angeles Should Never Forget," which began, "Neither the people of Los Angeles nor their official representatives should lose sight of the fact that the city owes its phenomenal expansion chiefly to the street railway service. Without that service the residential circumference would now probably be distant only a mile or two from the business center."[28] In 1904, the *Los Angeles Times* asserted that "no one thing has contributed so largely or so permanently to the industrial upbuilding and financial strengthening of the heart of Southern California as the development of electric railways and extension of interurban transportation lines in the region contiguous to Los Angeles."[29] The feeling was even stronger in the communities that had been integrated into the metropolitan area by the street railways. The headlines of a story in the *Long Beach Daily Press* in 1904 presented that view: "Electric Roads a Factor of Growth. Strong Presentation of the Huntington System in Building Up That Back Country Without Which There Is No Permanent Prosperity."[30]

During this period, the Los Angeles street railway system was thought of as Huntington's invention, and he was given full credit for its contribution to the growth and prosperity of Southern California. In 1905, the *Los Angeles Herald* reported that "there is no man in Los Angeles who has done so much for the city, in as many ways." In the next year the same paper maintained, in an editorial, that "for its distinction as the American city having the best street and interurban railway service, Los Angeles is indebted to H. E. Huntington"; moreover, in the few years since Huntington had come to Los Angeles, "the doubling of the city's population and the trebling or quadrupling of its property values within that period are due, as every citizen knows, to Mr. Huntington's vast investments."[31] Earlier, the *San Francisco Evening Post* had lamented his departure for Los Angeles: "Mr. Huntington took his millions, went to Los Angeles and transformed the metropolis of the South, which was on the eve of a severe commercial depression. There is no question that Huntington has practically transformed the southern part of the State. Ask any citizen from Los Angeles and he will tell you that Huntington saved the country down there in the hour of its greatest need."[32] Huntington's name could be used to support any good cause, provided you began with some general truths about him. Francis Murphy, "the noted temperance lecturer," in a speech in 1904 in Glendale maintained that "Mr. Huntington is a great benefactor. He has done more for Southern California than, perhaps, any other man, and for this we must honor him. His success is due largely to the fact that he keeps whisky out of his Company, and if you people want to make this pretty valley a garden spot it is for you to keep whisky as far away from you as possible."[33]

Harry Chandler of the *Los Angeles Times* wrote admiring letters to Huntington in New York, praising him for all he had done for Southern California: "Your enterprises have done more than anything else to build up the country and to make it attractive to tourists and home-seekers; and they realize also that a large part of all the development is either a direct or indirect result of your aggressive railway building operations."

Edward replied from New York with deep appreciation for Chandler's sentiments. "I must confess," he wrote, "that the progress and prosperity of Los Angeles and its environs is quite a hobby of mine. I feel myself vitally interested in it, as I indeed am and must be—proud of it, in fact. . . . I don't want any undue credit for the part I may have taken in the development of that section of our Country; but I do want to be known as one of the good people who are responsible for it, who believe in it, and who are ready to pin their money to their faith every time."[34]

People in positions of power in Southern California were not slow to offer tributes to H. E. Huntington, even when he was only an occasional visitor and a permanent resident of San Francisco.

On January 11, 1902, forty principal citizens of Los Angeles made him the guest of honor at a banquet. The original idea had been to limit the group to twenty, but response was so strong that the number was doubled, and the organizers said that it could have been a hundred if they had not strictly limited the number. The banquet was "in appreciation of the interest which Huntington has shown in this part of the State, and was given in furtherance of the desire to meet him and bring about a closer mutual acquaintance between him and the men who do things in Los Angeles. There was no further significance to the event except their desire to meet Mr. Huntington and make him feel at home." Even so, it was judged to be "probably the most elaborate semipublic function ever held in this city." There was an "elegant menu" with six wines, including Chateau Yquem and Mumm's Extra Dry. Nearly everybody—including the mayor and all the prominent citizens—spoke in the course of the evening, but Edward had to retain his seat and be the "mute target for the many bouquets which were cast his way." Edward "seemed to have a supreme appreciation of the welcome which was extended to him."[35]

A similarly elaborate event took place in Riverside at the opening of the Glenwood Hotel on March 20, 1903. A large and distinguished crowd was present, including Howard, Burke Holladay, and W. E. Dunn. The affair lasted four hours, and there were about ten speeches presented under the guise of toasts. A proper toast began the evening: "Gentlemen, here is health and happiness to Henry E. Huntington, the friend of Riverside and of Southern California." The Reverend E. F. Goff then described him as "a man firm as a rock whose firmness is virtue, but responsive as a child to sympathy, friendship and love. A man with great business interests claiming his attention, but whose affections center about his home, who loves flowers, birds, art and literature. A man whose thoughts are not so engrossed in earth that his eyes wander to the distant mountains when the light of the coming glorious day falls." Major Frank C. Prescott of Redlands began with the salutation "Hail, Lord Huntington and Princess Riverside" and declared that "in the true sense he *is* Lord Huntington of Southern California." Dr. Walter Lindley said that the refrain of the song they were to sing was "Henry E. Huntington has cast his lot among us, and the marching of prosperity is breaking upon Southern California." General

M. H. Sherman, who had built the first electric railway in Southern California, said that "Mr. Huntington had done more for Southern California than any other one man who had ever come here." And so it went in praising their guest of honor.

Edward bowed his acknowledgments to the speakers and to the group. Billy Dunn responded for him with a little speech that was reported as follows:

> The ruling passion in the Huntington family is work. In a recent conversation with me, Mr. Huntington said of his son, who is present here with us tonight: "I am not particular about the vocation Howard may choose, but I want him to be noted as a worker. That is the best fame I can ask for him."
>
> If I had Mr. Huntington's wealth, my idea of the best way to spend my time would be to cut coupons in the morning, play golf in the afternoon and whist in the evening. Mr. Huntington says his idea of life is to see things grow, to see something doing. His uncle, C. P. Huntington, was the pioneer in the things that make for permanence in California. When H. E. Huntington came here ten or twelve years ago, as his assistant J. A. Muir said then: "The Southern Pacific now has one man who loves Southern California." And from that time to now he has shown his unfailing faith and unfailing loyalty towards Southern California. He is what they call in Los Angeles the very best thing they have had since the boom busted.[36]

Burke Holladay, Edward's brother-in-law, wrote about the event to Harriet and told her that "if you could have heard the volumes of fine things they said and kept saying about your boy for four solid hours, you would have seen the proudest time of your life."[37]

There were various other tributes in the next couple of years. The Fresno Chamber of Commerce tendered a banquet to him in May 1903, with seventy business leaders present. In November 1903, Whittier held a banquet for five hundred people in his honor, and in February 1904 he was feted in Santa Barbara with an elaborate dinner. In Fresno, a newspaper reporter tried to interview him in his hotel room before the dinner while he was struggling to put in his cuff links: "Not even a railroad magnate can be expected to look pleasant on such an occasion. But Mr. Huntington did. He smiled. He has a peculiar smile. The corners of his mouth go upward and his lips form a crescent—when he's largely amused, it's almost a half moon. He is a big, husky man, with lots of life in his body and a glow of health on his cheek. Although he has little more than a fringe of hair and his close trimmed mustache is white as snow, he doesn't look the fifty years [fifty-three, actually] that he certainly is."[38]

On the evening of June 21, 1905, the members of the Jonathan Club in Los Angeles gathered for a reception in honor of Huntington, their president. (He was also president, at the same time, of the other fashionable men's club, the California Club.) The reception was held in the "handsome clubrooms" encompassing the top two floors of the Huntington Building to give all the members "an opportunity to personally greet the one man responsible for the remarkable success of the club." Huntington stood at the entrance and received, then mingled with the members in the rooms. It was an " 'at home' in a good American democratic fashion, without flub-dub of speeches or conventionalities." The affair "was purely informal, Mr. Huntington being the center all evening of the homage of the club members, more than 250 of whom were present."[39]

Perhaps the most elaborate affair in honor of Huntington was a dinner given by a group called Citizens of Southern California at the Hotel Maryland in Pasadena on October 3, 1906, as an "expression of appreciation by Southern California of the work and achievements of the man." There were five toasts, speeches by U.S. Senator Flint, Congressman McLachlan, and former Governor Markham, a nine-course dinner with various wines, a color scheme in pink and green—because they were thought to be Edward's favorite colors—carried out to the minutest detail "even to the miniature trolley cars formed in ice cream and to the delicate pink rose petals in the finger bowls," and nine pieces of music played. The eight-page program included a photograph of Huntington, a two-page biographical sketch, a map of "the greatest electric railway system in the world," a gold seal with Huntington's name embossed on it, and a gold ribbon for a tie. The toastmaster began the evening with a set of jokes, amid much laughter. "When Mr. Huntington laughed, the whole room laughed with him. There was no man present who enjoyed the event more than he, and there are few men can laugh with such wholeheartedness." Following the toastmaster's introduction the whole room rose with "thunders of applause" that lasted several minutes. Huntington rose and they sang "For He's a Jolly Good Fellow" while he smiled and even joined in. Then he bowed right and left, and said, "Gentlemen, I thank you from the bottom of my heart." The reporter commented, "It was all that he said, but somehow he said it in a way that made the simple, brief words stand out in the record of the evening." Then Billy Dunn again made a fuller response on his behalf.[40]

There were a number of other tributes and banquets in Edward's honor. One was the Pasadena Board of Trade banquet in May 1907, with six hundred participants. Another was the Long Beach Chamber of Commerce dinner in June 1909, with seventy-five guests; the mayor of Long Beach "declared that Mr. Huntington had done more and was doing more for Southern California than any other man," and Billy Dunn in his reply "declared that Mr. Huntington appreciated the approbation of his fellow-men more than he did the proprietorship of the Pacific Electric." In June 1910, the Good Government organization gave him a banquet in Alhambra with two hundred seventy on hand and presented him with a loving cup "in recognition of his work in the upbuilding of Southern California and especially Alhambra."[41]

Not all the tributes were entirely solemn. At the Jonathan Club's Christmas party in 1905, the members gave Edward a huge red stocking several feet long, containing a small trolley car and a 37½ carat "diamond." "It was clear white, and who would be so cynical as to carry a Christmas present to a jeweler for further examination?"[42]

Between 1906 and 1910 Edward came to be thought of as the most important contributor to the development and prosperity of Southern California. On January 1, 1906, a full page of the *Los Angeles Times* was devoted to him under the title "Henry E. Huntington, Captain of Industry, Southern California." He was the "one man who stands preeminently in the front rank and is the leader, the magic of whose name identified with any enterprise is sufficient to start something in any direction in any line of worthy endeavor. . . . His name is a household word throughout Southern California, and is associated with all that means progress, development and prosperity."[43]

The term "captain of industry"—or "foremost among the captains of industry of the Golden West"—was endlessly applied to him. "The name of Huntington" was not only "a household word" but was "synonymous with big things of public interest."[44] Southern California had "needed courage and inspiration. These came with the man of the hour—Henry E. Huntington. A man whose civic pride is most highly developed, he is bound to further the interests of the section in which he resides. When he came to Los Angeles for permanent interests in the latter years of the nineteenth century, a new and mighty era of development was begun for this section."[45] To no other man was "the phenomenal advancement of Los Angeles and Southern California due so much. . . . Mr. Huntington's work has been of inestimable value. As a citizen and business man, he has not only the respect of his thousands of employees, but of the entire community. All wish him continued health and prosperity, for to him, indeed, does Los Angeles and Southern California owe a deep debt of gratitude which it will require a lifetime of the present generation to pay."[46]

In the next couple of years, this view of Huntington grew and spread. Asked "Who is Southern California's most representative citizen?" a man "prominent in the municipal and other activities of Los Angeles" replied, "There's no doubt as to the answer to your question in the mind of any well informed resident of Los Angeles. Henry E. Huntington is the man. He has not only pinned his faith to this section and put his money into it, but he has aided wonderfully in directing the expenditure of other capital toward the upbuilding of Southern California."[47]

His fame spread around California. "Throughout the State," it was claimed, "he is universally admired for his ability, and San Francisco will never cease to regret his removal to Los Angeles."[48] Even the *Los Angeles Examiner* agreed that "his ability and worth are recognized throughout the State, and San Francisco has not ceased to deplore his departure from that city several years ago to devote his energies to the upbuilding of Los Angeles and all the surrounding southland."[49] The newspapers in Los Angeles continued, with glee, to reiterate the claim that the *San Francisco Examiner* had boasted about driving Huntington out of the Bay area. "Los Angeles owes a debt of gratitude to the San Francisco *Examiner* for this act," said the *Los Angeles Graphic.* "One Henry E. Huntington is of more real value to a community than all the Hearst papers ever established or to be established, rolled together and multiplied by a hundred. He is constructive by instinct and training—they are destructive. That Henry E. Huntington has done more, directly and indirectly, for the material development of Los Angeles than any factor that can be named will be readily conceded."[50] Even the San Francisco papers agreed. The *Argonaut* ran a long editorial about him under the title "San Francisco's Loss," with the plaintive reflection as to "what might have been for San Francisco but for the removal of this one man."[51] The *San Francisco Evening Post* also wrote ruefully about Huntington: "If H. E. Huntington of Los Angeles, to whom, more than to any other factor, the growth of that city is due, should be a reader of our daily newspapers, I can imagine his smile of satisfaction at having been so wise a great many years ago as to leave this city of fraternal affection, and to take his money and his brains to a community which has a little better appreciation than we seem to have of the value of progressive railroading."[52] The *San Francisco Chronicle* at least published a letter from Professor T. S. C. Lowe (of Mt. Lowe fame and the cog railroad up it) with its "thanks to Henry E. Huntington, who had the foresight and enterprise to carry through the stupendous undertaking, now acknowledged the greatest single-handed electric railway builder."[53]

Huntington's fame spread beyond California as well, with stories in such diverse journals as the *Outing Magazine* and *Leslie's Weekly.*[54] The *New York Commercial* devoted a full column with picture to a study of his personality in 1905, and there were occasional paragraphs about him in the New York *Town Topics.*[55] The *St. Louis Daily Globe-Democrat* devoted a three-column story with picture to Huntington in 1906, during the presidency of Theodore Roosevelt. "And who, it may be asked, is this man Huntington?" the story asked, and quickly answered. "Put that question to a Southern Californian and he will smile a pitying smile. Why not ask who is Theodore Roosevelt or John D. Rockefeller? . . . For Henry E. Huntington is distinctly and emphatically 'it' in the delectable region known to the world as Southern California."

Though people rushed to get in on anything he supported, the story said, he was not a speculator: "He is that rare combination of dreamer and builder—a cool, conservative business man, who sees visions and proceeds to make them realities. That all of his enterprises are of a more or less public nature and contribute enormously to the development and general prosperity of Southern California may or may not be due to public spirit on his part; but the fact remains that, unlike most successful financiers, he is remarkably public-spirited, and no public movement of magnitude is considered properly launched unless his name is at the head or somewhere mighty close to it."[56]

Despite his visibility, his private life and personality remained a mystery to most Southern Californians. "No one is mentioned oftener in the public prints, and no name carries with it the magic that clings to his. Yet in Los Angeles almost no one outside his immediate circle knows him." Moreover, there was no man in Los Angeles who "as little seeks to be known." Reporters tried to overcome this ignorance by interviewing him and describing him for their readers. To one *Los Angeles Herald* reporter in 1905 he seemed "a most genial gentleman and so pleasant that his smile almost won't come off." A question by the interviewer "made Mr. Huntington smile. And how delightfully he does smile. . . . His geniality is the most unexpected and conspicuous quality of the man."

"A large man, of big proportions" continued the article, "he is as gentle of voice and as quiet in ways as he is great physically." Six feet tall, two hundred pounds, "his hair is gray, soft, fine and thin. He has light blue eyes shaded by heavy gray brows—eyes that twinkle and laugh and yet that are full of character. His face is ruddy and full; a stubby mustache—clipped close, though it looks as if he chewed it— shadows a rather large mouth that is cut in a straight line. His chin is firm and full of the emphasis of determination." In dress, "he usually wears gray clothes and a black string tie. He is not conspicuous in his attire in any way, but looks exceedingly well groomed and high class— there is, in fact, that tinge of the patrician that comes only by nature, and no amount of polish can put it on."

The reporter, like many other observers, tried to infer his character from his behavior. "Mr. Huntington is active to a marked degree.

When talking, he emphasizes his words by gestures, and he has a habit of jumping up and walking about, standing much when he talks, and speaking rapidly. Yet his voice is soft, and even when stern one can perceive the laugh back of his strongest words." Moreover, "few men have less of the poseur about them. Mr. Huntington is just what he is, and he doesn't ask anyone to be anything else toward him, nor does he try any pose to others. . . . When one talks with him, one sees the blue eyes fixed directly on him, piercing, but yet kindly, and the words come clearly, yet modulated. The eyes have great depth, and they see much that the voice doesn't ask."

In his business, he was "a fine reader of men" and had surrounded himself "with gentlemen." Every door in his huge office building had "Walk In" posted on it. "Courtesy greets one everywhere; one wonders at this no more after seeing and talking with the head of it all."[57]

Edward was much in demand to greet visiting dignitaries. In 1909, eighty members of the American Street Railway Association arrived with their president, Senator J. F. Shaw of Boston. Edward gave them a special two-day tour in three private trolley cars over the entire rail system from Redondo to Mt. Lowe: "Long before the party returned to the city, the millionaire electric builder had captivated the visitors, resolving the trip into a Huntington 'lovefest,' so charmed were all by the personality and magnetism of the traction magnate." They were all "much impressed by his detailed knowledge of the railways and of Southern California in general. 'Why, he has personal knowledge of everything going on here and remembers every fact connected with it,' said the superintendent of one of the Massachusetts interurban systems. 'I never saw such a mental grasp.'" Mr. Shaw concluded that "Los Angeles has the greatest interurban electric railway system in the world," and his colleagues heartily agreed. "'You should be proud of H. E. Huntington,' said Mr. Shaw, 'for the system he has built, more than anything else, has made Los Angeles the great city it is today.'"[58]

When this first decade of the century ended, residents of Southern California expressed pride in the progress and prosperity of their area and attributed much of their success to Huntington's enterprises. "The career of H. E. Huntington needs no greater eulogy than that he has done more for this city in railroad building than all others combined."

Another source judged him to be "a true philanthropist indeed, to whom the thousands of dwellers in Los Angeles and vicinity owe a lasting debt of gratitude." Or, finally, the way chosen to begin a summation of a story on "H. E. Huntington, The Man: A Master Builder and a Believer in Southern California in the Truest Sense" was simply to say that "a history of the progress of Los Angeles and vicinity during the past twelve years or more would be largely a history of Mr. H. E. Huntington."[59] A recent scholarly business history of the Los Angeles area during the early years of this century concluded that "Henry Huntington must be remembered as the entrepreneur who envisioned and then established the modern contours of metropolitan Los Angeles."[60]

Our need for heroes sometimes carries us into the land of myth. When H. E. Huntington first came to Southern California, he was perceived as a rich man who had boundless confidence in the future of the area. As he embarked on the development of an electric railway system that would join the various parts of the region together, he was thought of as a modern-day frontiersman. He was described in 1906 as "a type of the American builder of today" who had brought "the new spirit of progress" to the area.[61] His coming to Southern California was described in 1907 in terms that befit the arrival of a hero: "At the most critical time Los Angeles has ever known, when everything needed a head, a man with power to take hold of and control the various interests, Henry E. Huntington appeared. In his own hands he took the transportation facilities, the real estate proposition and many other minor matters needing development." He became "the natural manager and promoter of these interests." He used "not only his name and influence but his money as well" to "develop and populate each place." This is why "the marvelous changes that have come to Los Angeles owe more to Mr. Huntington than to any other one factor for their existence," and consequently "there is no man in town better known or more respected than Mr. Huntington."[62]

Huntington's enterprises were generally understood to be his personal activities. Their work was perceived as being done not so much by the companies as by Henry E. Huntington personally. For example, the

Corona Courier told its readers in 1904 that "Henry E. Huntington has commenced the building of his Santa Ana branch in his immense system of electric railroads. Mr. Huntington can't hurry up this line too quick for the people of this valley." The *Anaheim Gazette* told of "Mr. Huntington building twenty-two miles of electric railway in Orange County." The *Los Angeles Record* was pleased to report that "a shift was made Tuesday in the Huntington family of railroads."[63] Almost always, you said that you were traveling on "Mr. Huntington's lines" or "the Huntington lines." And after the Pacific Electric Building on Sixth and Main streets was completed in 1904, it was almost universally referred to as "the Huntington Building."

If you had a problem with a Huntington business, you told Mr. Huntington. Like the wicked practice of women occupying the seats on the front platforms of the street railways, the only areas where city law allowed smoking, thus preventing men (the only smokers, of course) from exercising their natural rights. Hence a letter entitled "Mr. Huntington, Attention!" which was published in 1910 in the weekly *Los Angeles Spectator:* "Now, Mr. Huntington, this is addressed directly to *you.* Thousands of men in Los Angeles, of whom I am one, object to having women crowd in the front seats while other parts of the car are not used. Men cannot smoke on the rear platforms and it is galling to see innately selfish women capture all the front platform seats, while there are plenty of vacant back platform seats. . . . Now, Mr. Huntington, I am asked by hundreds of smokers, to request you to give us some relief" by putting up signs reserving the front section for smokers "free from intrusion by thoughtless and selfish women."[64]

The myth of Huntington as the hero is most readily seen in the popular cartoons and verses about him. One drawing, captioned "Henry E. Huntington: The Modern Colossus of Roads," showed Huntington over a map of the Los Angeles area, holding the strings to his various railroads:

> He's the modern Colossus of Roads,
> A magical bearer of loads,
> And passengers grin when his cars they get in
> To ride to their country abodes.

The real estate sharp never fails
To follow the Huntington "trails";
He knows it means much to be in close touch
With the one who can stimulate sales.

Los Angeles finds it no task
In the light of his friendship to bask;
He's a man of affairs Who Does and Who Dares—
What more could the critical ask?[65]

The *New York Evening Mail* portrayed him in 1905 holding the Newport News Shipbuilding and Drydock Company under one arm, three
scrolls—of power companies, railroads, and California interests—under
the other, and standing with one foot on the Los Angeles Railway and
the other foot on the Pacific Electric. It was followed by sixteen lines of
doggerel, concluding, "His varied interests you can hardly number, /
And yet nobody ever saw him lose."[66]

The activity in Huntington's office in Los Angeles was depicted in a
cartoon showing his door with a dozen clues to what is going on inside
in the form of such phrases as "Double Track to Redondo!," "New City
Lines!," "Extension to Covina!," and "New Tracts to Be Opened!" Four
lines of verse below concluded, "But in his wake, as sure as fate, performances are done, / Which is reason why the wise ones cry: 'Keep watch
on Huntington!' "[67]

The presentation of Huntington to the public also took the form of
little jokes. One paper offered him the following New Year's wishes for
1906: "To Henry E. Huntington, the captain of industry of Southern
California, may you live forever, have a trolley line for every road, a car
for every neighborhood, never an accident, and every seat filled on
every trip."[68] Another allowed that "for Mr. H. E. Huntington to
accomplish all that an admiring public is crediting him with accom-
plishing would require a thousand legs, as many hands and arms, and at
least a hundred heads."[69] One paper for January 17, 1906, gave a futur-
istic news report for "twenty-five years from tomorrow," January 18,
1931: "Henry E. Huntington announces that the opening of his new
floating sky amusement park will be deferred until Saturday." The
report also placed the population of Los Angeles beyond the ten million

mark with property values of $40 billion, and advertised a one-day round-the-world air service for $7 with six meals.[70] One joke of serious substance was a forty-line poem recited at the Jonathan Club High-Jinks on January 1, 1907, entitled "The Name of 'Huntington.'" Here is the last stanza:

A toast to him who makes the land
  Bloom fair, where sterile fields once lay;
Whose ready tact and willing hand
  Hath builded well for us today.
Whose links of steel bind town to town,
  And stretch from mountain unto sea;
Who well has earned the victor's crown
  Of Progress and Prosperity.
    A toast to this proficient son—
    Our able leader—HUNTINGTON![71]

Sometimes the dangerous mode of irony was attempted in trying to make a hero of Huntington, as in the illustrated monthly Los Angeles magazine, *Pictorial American,* for July 1907. Under the heading "Henry E. Huntington Accused," the article said, "'I accuse' this person of being the chief cause of the growth and prosperity of this city and contiguous territory and that his activity, broad gauge ideas, liberal views and spirit of fairness has resulted in greater benefits to this country and its people, than the efforts of all the other resident capitalists combined." The piece concluded that "the eyes of the world are upon him. He is the modern Napoleon of Finance, but I accuse him of being honest and the greatest benefactor Los Angeles and Southern California have ever known."[72]

A popular anecdote that sums up the myth of Huntington was often repeated in 1906 and 1907. Here is the version that attorney Frederick G. Hentig told as "a true story" to the Los Angeles city council on October 1, 1906:

A man and 6-year-old daughter were out for a [trolley] car ride. While on the car the child asked:

"Papa, who owns all these cars?"

"Mr. Huntington," replied the parent.

An hour later father and child were seated at the water's edge and the child was digging in the sand.

"What place is this, papa?" the child asked.

"Huntington Beach."

"Who owns it?"

"Mr. Huntington."

A few minutes later the child looked into her father's face and asked: "Who owns the ocean?"

"God," he replied.

The child pondered a moment, then asked:

"But, papa, how did he get it away from Mr. Huntington?"[73]

In other versions of the anecdote, the parent is sometimes the mother, the child is sometimes the son, and stops en route include the Huntington Building and Huntington Park.[74] What is constant is the glorification of H. E. Huntington as a hero of Southern California.

Twelve

WORK DOMINATED EDWARD'S life until he reached his fifties. His energetic ways had become legendary in Los Angeles. A characteristic story about him in 1905 was headed "Street Railway Magnate Is a Strenuous Worker. H. E. Huntington Gives His Subordinates an Example of Industry." Shortly after nine o'clock one Monday morning, a subordinate asked, "Has Mr. Huntington arrived at the office?" "Lord, bless you, yes," was the reply. "Mr. Huntington has been here this long time and already has gone through a half day's work."[1] He continued to arrive early, leave late, and work on Sunday, and it was observed with high seriousness that "men who love their work are wrapped up in it. They never know the passage of time. Huntington is one of them."[2] His habits were not welcome to some of his employees, however, who were afraid that they were expected to go and do likewise. There was a certain relief when he left for New York. Sometimes a little mild fun was ventured, as in the reflection that "back East only three men's work await Mr. Huntington at each trip. Therefore it is expected the jaunt will prove a delightfully restful spell for the railroad official." Or that he "Goes East to Freshen Up" by taking a large box of documents along, "intended to relieve the monotony of the magnate's stay in the East."[3]

As we have seen, by 1910 he had become a highly successful and wealthy businessman and a mythic figure in Southern California. A crucial change of direction was taking place in his interests, however.

He was gradually moving away from his active role as a businessman in electric street railways, land development, and utilities into what was called "retirement." He did not cease to be "a creator, a builder, [who] is only happy when his activities in that direction have full play," but he had found a new focus for his building impulses.[4] He began to move from business to nature, books, and art. In this chapter I would like, first, to fill out the sense of what he was like as a human being during this time by giving a brief account of some of his activities that were not directly associated with business or with trying to make money. Then for the new directions. He became increasingly preoccupied with "the ranch" and its development into a series of gardens featuring interesting and rare forms of plant life, as well as a residence for himself in the midst of a lot of natural beauty. At the same time, his interest in art and books deepened as he moved beyond amateur status to become a sophisticated collector of national importance.

Edward made a strong impression on other people. On the occasion of his first visit to Seattle in 1902, the reporter who interviewed him said that "in person Mr. Huntington is tall and rather portly in build, with a face in which an expression of keenness of perception and good humor are rather oddly but pleasantly blended. During his conversation he has a habit of fingering a pair of eyeglasses, which are used as a sort of baton with which at times to emphasize his remarks."[5] He was always conservatively and neatly dressed, having bought his clothes in New York from Brooks Brothers, paying such high prices as $70 for a regular suit and $63 for a sack suit.[6] When he spent a day inspecting the railway property at Huntington Beach in the company of three other Pacific Electric men, it was observed that "Mr. Huntington is a man of marked personality. He has a strong face, and he was the merriest one of the four. He laughed and chatted and evidently is a man who believes in living as he goes along."[7]

His smiling had been observed as "a give-away sign" by the hostile San Francisco papers; "don't believe a word young Huntington says when he is smiling"—but they were not so suspicious of him in the Southland.[8] One evening after watching Huntington and Dunn play dominoes at the California Club, a reporter asked Edward, "Is blocking the science of this game?" " 'No, winning,' quickly responded Mr. Huntington, with a playful twinkle in his eye that would make even a little child feel friendly and at its ease."[9] Little children were, in fact, interested in his comings and goings; his nine-year-old niece Helen Holladay reported by letter to her father, Burke Holladay, that "Uncle Edward is going to start for New York Sunday."[10] The impression he made on his contemporaries is evident in this comment about him by his friend Frank A. Miller to William Crewdson in London: "You will find him a very courteous, broad minded, straightforward business man. I hope, when you come to America again, that you will call on him, for I am sure you will enjoy knowing him."[11]

He continued to have periods of uncertain health. In 1902, Elizabeth wrote him that "we were all so worried about you and now so glad you are feeling better." In the next month, she admonished him about his way of dealing with sleeplessness: "You were a very bad man to take so much stuff to put you to sleep. Never, never do it again. If I thought you would, I would never rest easy again."[12] In the autumn of 1907, he was unwell for a couple of months and went to Oneonta to recover. Many newspapers reported that he was on the verge of a physical collapse or a nervous breakdown and that the financial world was alarmed over his condition. The truth of the matter seems to have been that he had overworked for too long, needed a period away from work, and was finally persuaded by a stomach disorder and an automobile accident to take a rest.[13]

His mother also had misgivings about his health. In 1902 she wrote to him in Los Angeles from San Francisco and said, "I dreamed last night that your Aunt Marcia came here and said you were very sick so I am going to write and ask you. So please answer if you are well."[14] Another dream was communicated directly to him in 1907 by his older sister Leonora; in this dream "the drama of life" was being played, with the actors all members of their family. "Brother Edwards seemed to be the director of it all," she wrote, "and as the last actor (sister Carrie) passed off the stage, Edward came to me and these were his words to me.

Now make of the leaves of Lethe, a boat
And in it place our little Mother

And sail away to the Isle of Love
For Love is Life and Life is Love.

Then the curtain fell, and the lights went out. Wasn't that a <u>strange</u> dream."[15]

Their "little Mother" had, in fact, died the year before. She had, as usual, been spending the winter in California with her children. At the time of the earthquake and fire in April 1906, she was with Edward in Los Angeles. Before returning to Oneonta, she stopped by San Francisco for a couple of weeks with Carrie. There, at the age of eighty-five, she suffered a serious heart attack. Edward hurried from Los Angeles and was, with Carrie, constantly at her bedside for the last several days of her life, when she was in and out of consciousness. She said farewell to her family and begged to see her favorite granddaughter, Elizabeth, who was returning with Brockway from their honeymoon in Japan. It was claimed that Harriet kept herself alive by sheer willpower in order to see Elizabeth; when the ship reached port in San Francisco, Elizabeth came straight from the dock to her bedside for a last good-bye. During the three days before she died, Edward copied down, on two sheets of Jonathan Club stationery, everything that she said, and he kept these notes for the rest of his life. Since Harriet meant so much to Edward, and since this final parting was important to him, it seems desirable to reproduce her words, in the exact form in which he recorded them, with his own lineation and his own minimal punctuation. (If one wanted to read them in the way that Edward presumably heard and remembered them, it would be with suitable emphasis on key words and with pauses, like reading verse.)

The first sheet, undated, has these notes:

It is so queer so queer
a drink of cold water would
be so nice
Certainly I know you Carrie & Edward
Let me go home and stay there
More patience more patience
How wonderful how beautiful

Dont feel so so badly for I am
so happy
I dreamed I was gone They
Would bring me back I didnt
Want to come

The first entry on the other sheet of notes, headed "Sunday morning June 24, 1906," is a breakfast interlude:

Grape fruit. Grape fruit. Grape fruit.
Oh it is so good. The best of all
I am so grateful. so grateful
Where did you get it?
Who sent it to me? (Carrie & Edward)
Can I have all I want
Who knew I liked it so well
(We all knew)

The next entry, dated June 24, carries on the theme from the day before, of her death:

I thought I was gone he came
to meet me   his head
He took me in his arms and
carried me home and then I
came back there is a heaven
Oh to be at peace with Jesus
rest. rest. rest.

The entry for June 25 continues the earthly side of this theme with just one statement:

The only thing in the world I
want is rest

And the first entry for June 26 is equally simple:

Love. Joy. Peace. Pardon.

The final notes, dated "night of June 26th," are her last thoughts:

> (To Dr Trask) Dont bring me back
> again Promise me you will
> not. I want to go
> It is cruel to bring me back
> I would not do it if any
> one begged me not to
> will you put me in the coffin
> in the morning. I am cold now
> When will we start? (No Mother
> we are going to take you to
> Oneonta when you are better
> The garden is looking beautiful
> now)
> Dont talk to me about the garden
> I want to go home (meaning Heaven)

She died at 8:15 the next morning. Edward, Carrie, and Burke took her remains in a private railroad car to Oneonta. There, other members of the family joined them for a funeral service in her home on Chestnut Street, where she had lived for sixty-six years, and she was interred next to Solon in the Huntington family plot in the Oneonta cemetery on July 5, 1906. Edward returned to Los Angeles.[16]

Death was not a stranger to Edward. Just two years before, his close friend John A. Muir, general manager of the Los Angeles Railway, had died in Los Angeles, and Edward was at his bedside daily after Muir was stricken. On the last day, "when Mr. Huntington entered the sickroom, he was overcome and almost fainted at the sight of his close friend and business associate lying within the shadow of death. He spoke to Mr. Muir, and was at once recognized." But then "as Mr. Huntington turned to go the tears coursed down his cheeks, and he almost broke down."[17] The event made such a deep impression on Muir's niece that she wrote him fifteen years later about her perception of his feelings: "It seemed to me then that you were yourself deeply touched and I thought you must have had a high opinion of my uncle."[18]

Edward supported his friends in time of trouble. In 1907, when he heard that Burke was ill in San Francisco with pneumonia, he asked to go and join Carrie. But she declined because the illness was not serious. "Of course I would have been glad to have you with me," she wrote him, "and I am more than glad that you were willing to come."[19]

As a prominent person in Los Angeles, he received numerous letters asking him to invest in schemes to get richer quicker, and occasionally letters threatening bodily harm if he did not pay a large sum of money before Saturday.[20] A less threatening and longer-running drama was the Woman in Black, who claimed to have been married to Edward when she was a child in Ohio:

> At the age of 18 years of age I was married to a man named Henry E. Huntington, whom I believe is the railroad magnate. The marriage was most peculiar. I was called to the parlor of our house [in Avondale, Ohio] one day by my father. There was a man, named Huntington, and with him was an elder of the Mormon church. His name was Randolph, I believe. My father told me I had been promised to this man from babyhood, and that he had claimed his promise. I was immature, and knew nothing of the ways of the world, so I stood up and was married, and after that my husband took the certificate and went away. I waited for him for several years and then I went to Texas with my sister.[21]

She pressed her claims on Edward for a couple of years. When he was away in New York, she would go daily to his Los Angeles office in the Pacific Electric Building, sit at his desk, call in employees and announce, "I am President of the Los Angeles Railway Company during Mr. Huntington's absence and while he is gone I will attend to any business you may have with the company."[22] She also caused some consternation by showing, just at the time that Howard and Leslie were to be married, a marriage license for herself and Howard that she had had issued in San Bernardino, though she and Howard had apparently never seen one another.[23] At last she was taken into custody, placed in a sanitarium, and then later in a state mental hospital where she died of cancer in 1908 at the age of thirty-nine, still dressed in black, still claiming that she was Edward's wife, and still maintaining that she had won a prize for having the second smallest foot of any woman in the United States.[24]

A different unpleasantness occurred late in 1906. A rumor circulated that Edward and Mary were going to remarry one another. Carrie, in San Francisco, wrote to Edward in New York that "an Examiner reporter came here last week about the reported reconciliation of Mr. and Mrs. H. E. Huntington." With a sense of relief, she concluded that "as nothing came out in the paper I think he gave it up."[25] Not everybody gave it up, however. A couple of weeks later the *New York Town Topics* devoted a long passage to the fact that "heads are close together and tongues are wagging in Los Angeles exclusive circles over the possible re-marriage of H. E. Huntington, the railroad millionaire, and his former wife." The writer assumed that there had, in fact, been a reconciliation between the two and speculated as to its cause: that their children and grandchildren loved them equally, that Mrs. Huntington had thought it over after receiving much adverse criticism for such actions as her presailing party in her stateroom immediately after the divorce decree had been issued, and that they had had "embarrassing attention" from their friends.[26] But it was only a rumor, and they continued their separate lives.

His separate life led him to some playful acts, like smuggling two cats across the country in his Pullman drawing room in 1910. When a friend, Otheman Stevens, knocked on his door en route, he hesitated before admitting him. "'I thought at first you were the conductor,' he said, 'and I have two good reasons for not admitting conductors without warning.' . . . He got down on the floor of the room and reached under the seats and pulled forth two imperial Angora cats. 'Those are the two reasons,' he explained. 'Against the Pullman rules, you know, to have animals in the cars. See those two suitcases?' And he winked just as he might have done when I. W. Hellman sold out his railway interests." They were suitcases outside but comfortable traveling cages inside. "'I got these cats for the ranch—THE ranch,' he said. 'A home without a cat is no home, and these are the most royally bred cats I could buy.' One was black and one was white, and they were beautiful. Then the cats began to fight and Mr. Huntington again got down on all fours and chased them from corner to corner until he captured them and had them safely placed in their suitcases." He got them to the ranch all right, but he had a lot of scratches on his hands when they all arrived.[27]

Some further understanding of what Edward was like as a human being at this time can be gained from reviewing a representative sample of the nonbusiness activities that he was interested in. Automobiles, for example. In 1903 he gave a trophy to the Automobile Club of Southern California to be awarded to the winner of the annual race; they chose to call it the "Huntington Challenge Cup."[28] He was active in the Good Roads Association. When it was beginning in 1907 he said, "I want to give my hearty endorsement to a movement toward better roads in this end of the state, particularly for the reason that I think it is one of the principal elements on which the future prosperity and success of this section depends." Later in the year, he urged that politics be kept out of the project and concluded that "the proposed highway improvements form one of the most important works ever undertaken here. The future success of the county, in a great measure, depends upon good roads."[29] He made his personal contribution to good roads by building, at his own expense, Huntington Drive—a splendid roadway, one hundred feet wide, connecting Los Angeles and Pasadena by the side of the trolley line. It was begun toward the end of 1904 and finished in 1906. It was universally praised as far better than roads built by the county, "a road, honestly and permanently built" and it was "a text for a dozen sermons." Of course "no one but Mr. Huntington could afford to spend money in this way."[30]

He was also keenly interested in aviation. He was active in forwarding the international Aviation Week held in Los Angeles in January 1910. In 1909, as president of the California Aviation Society—the governor of California was first vice-president—he had a major hand in planning the event, which was to call attention to the current state of the science of flying by bringing famous aviators and balloonists from all over the world. Edward contributed $50,000 toward the prize money, and the people of Los Angeles matched his gift. The event was a smashing success. There were dozens of participants, including a French contingent headed by Louis Paulham, as well as Glenn Curtiss and the famous New York balloonist Clifford B. Harmon. The "week" lasted for ten days in different locations throughout the Los Angeles area; each day featured flights by airplanes, dirigibles, and balloons. Visitors came from all over, schoolchildren were given holidays, and some forty thousand people watched each event. Each flight was measured for speed, distance, and altitude, with distances varying from 150 yards to 10.75 miles, and altitudes from 150 feet to 4,165 feet. Paulham won the biggest prize—$10,000 for the longest cross-country flight, and $3,000 for altitude. Curtiss won $3,000 for speed. Edward was invited by Harmon to take an aerial journey with him in the balloon *New York,* "but the tempting offer was declined by Mr. Huntington, who explained that he had promised his business associates that he would remain upon terra firma while the flying machines are soaring in Los Angeles during the next ten days. Mr. Harmon expressed himself as greatly disappointed because he will not be able to have Mr. Huntington in a tour of the skies. 'Mr. Huntington cannot know how much he has done for this country until he realizes the joys of a balloon trip,' said the New York enthusiast." There was a barrage of stories each day in the newspapers, and the news penetrated to such places as Aurora, Illinois, and Madison, South Dakota. "If the airship is destined to put the railroads and the trolley cars out of business," the *Los Angeles Times* wrote, "it doesn't seem to worry Mr. Huntington. There is a good deal of sporting blood in this neck of the woods, and 'H. E. H.' has again given evidence that he has his share of it."[31]

He also agreed, in 1906, to head another extravaganza—a world's fair to be held in Los Angeles in 1915 and billed as a "Universal Peace and Commerce Exposition." When he accepted the presidency, the newspapers were ecstatic. It "means success spelled in capital letters," said the *Los Angeles Evening News.* "The reputation he has gained of never having been interested in a losing proposition added more strength to the proposition than the average man can comprehend."[32] But it did not succeed, and 1915 turned out to be a bad year for an exposition on the theme of universal peace.

Edward was also actively interested in furthering education. He took part in 1905 in discussions looking to the formation of a women's college in the Pasadena area. There were extended correspondence on the subject, meetings—at one of which Edward was elected a trustee of the college—and an effort to settle on a location. But unfortunately nothing came of the project.[33] Edward was also deeply involved in 1910 in the campaign to persuade the state legislature to establish a university comparable to Berkeley in the Southland. A committee of a hundred prominent citizens was formed, with Edward as chairman, to map out a plan to present to the legislature. They pointed out that only a tiny fraction of Southern California high school graduates could afford to go to Berkeley, which was only for the wealthy and accepted six times as many students from the northern counties. Ten thousand signatures to this petition were obtained in the first three hours, and two sites were offered for the university—one hundred acres near San Pedro through Edward's interest, and one hundred acres north of Inglewood overlooking the Santa Monica beach resorts.[34] The success of this effort was also delayed. But Edward's interest in his friend Charles F. Lummis's attempt to form the Southwest Museum was more fruitful; he offered Lummis his choice of four valuable pieces of property, each of about twenty acres, and Lummis selected one and built the museum on it.[35] And Edward was eager to encourage the local public schools. When a proposal was made in 1909 to issue Los Angeles school bonds, Edward led with a subscription of $10,000 and sent a letter to citizens commending the idea; his signed letter was published in facsimile in the *Los Angeles Examiner,* with his portrait, as the most persuasive way to get others to support the project.[36]

Edward's generous inclinations were shown in many ways. The president of the Santa Ana Chamber of Commerce and the captain of their Columbia Club called on Edward in December 1905 to ask for a free car to carry the members of the club to Pasadena on New Year's Day. He agreed without a moment's hesitation: "'I have a warm spot in my heart for the Columbia Club,' said Mr. Huntington, as he gave the order, 'and want to show the boys that I appreciate them.' And Santa Ana will certainly appreciate Mr. Huntington's action."[37] When the circus came to town in 1907, the *Examiner* arranged to give free tickets to all children under the age of ten to a matinee performance. Edward offered free transportation to all children who had *Examiner* tickets, and the paper printed the thanks of the children: "Mr. H. E. Huntington: We, the children of Los Angeles, think you are a good fellow and we are glad to accept your invitation to ride to the circus free in your cars. We wish you would come with us and we would show you how thankful we are."[38]

The public interest was also involved in his establishment, in 1906, of a wild animal park on Mt. Wilson near the Alpine Tavern. He had several acres fenced and a cementlined lake created in the center. Two bears, one cinnamon and one black, were the first occupants; a herd of mountain goats was soon added, and then twenty deer—which he asked to have captured in the mountains near Riverside—were moved to the park.[39]

Edward was a lifelong Republican, but he generally tried to avoid political involvement. He did agree in 1908 to be a presidential elector from the state of New York, as his legal residence was still Oneonta; and he duly cast his vote for William Howard Taft in the Republican victory over William Jennings Bryan.[40] In 1910, it was suggested that a deputation of citizens might call on him to ask him to be U.S. Senator from California to succeed Senator Flint. At the suggestion, "it threatened to rain Angora cats for a moment. 'Don't you dare suggest such a thing,' he said. . . . I am out for enjoyment and fun, not for sorrow and disaster."[41]

To pursue "enjoyment and fun" he would have to ease up on work. Everyone close to him had been urging him to do so for years. His mother, his children, even his secretaries took the occasion whenever they dared to urge him to cut back his hours and become less preoccupied with business.

A more powerful incentive to change focus came from within himself, from his other interests—nature, books, and art—which were becoming stronger and stronger. By 1905, the rumor was persistent that he was thinking about giving up his active role in the management of his street railway companies.[42] Soon it was noticed that he was not going to his office in Los Angeles in the afternoons. When he was in New York, his visits to his office there became more and more irregular. Finally, in

November 1908 he told an interviewer for the *Los Angeles Examiner* in New York that he was planning to give up active management of his railway interests. " 'I began working when I was 17 years old,' said Mr. Huntington to-day in the private library of his apartment at the Metropolitan Club, where he makes his home in New York. 'I have been hard at work ever since and I believe I am entitled to some rest and playtime. Why shouldn't I take it? I have fixed my sixtieth birthday as the time for my retirement from business and that will be in February, 1910.' " He went on to say that he would devote his attention to "experimental horticulture" on his ranch near Los Angeles and to his books and art.[43] This announcement was widely copied, in papers in San Francisco, Fort Wayne, Seattle, Kansas City, and a dozen other places. The next day the *Examiner* printed a followup under the title "Should a Man Retire at 60? Too Young Says Banker. World Can't Spare Him." They based their story on interviews with four bank presidents in Los Angeles, all under the age of sixty. Two of the four said no, one said yes if he wants to, and one said it all depends.[44]

The announcement continued to create repercussions in the months that followed. In December, it was the basis for discussion in papers in Quincey, Illinois; St. Joseph, Missouri; Jackson, Michigan; and Des Moines, Iowa. In January 1909, readers in Albany, New York; Saginaw, Michigan; Sedaha, Missouri; Gloversville, New York; and Logansport, Indiana, knew all about it.[45] There were grave editorials in 1908, referring to his plan as

> an ideal close to one of the most ideal business careers of public men in the United States. . . . This will make Mr. Huntington's life almost a living epic of modern commercialism, and will prove that commercialism in its highest sense, reaches out for something higher than mere material profit. . . . It is eminently fitting that, in the closing years of his life, he should settle down to enjoy himself in the very midst of the scenes which he may be said to have created, with the aid of bountiful nature.[46]

Even before his retirement, he said, "I made up my mind a few years ago that when I arrived at a certain age I would give up active business employment, in order to devote all my time to doing things out in the open. And I am carrying out that resolve, and shall continue to do so, right here in Southern California. I never was happier than I am at this time." The reporter concluded that "probably there is no better contented man anywhere at this time than Henry E. Huntington."[47]

When the appointed time for his retirement came in 1910, he did in fact give up his active business career. To Otheman Stevens, the same reporter whom he had told of his plans in 1908, he said in 1910: "I don't know anything about work; you remember I told you some time ago that when I became sixty I intended to retire from work? You printed it at the time and my friends all laughed at it and said I would never do it. But I have." He added, "I only work for enjoyment now, and I am having it. . . . You will not catch me around my office, though, for I am thoroughly in earnest about making this the play time of my life."[48] After returning to Los Angeles from a seven-month stay in New York, he said, "I do not think I was in my New York office twenty-four hours all told during the entire time I was away, and I do not expect to be in my office here very much during my stay."[49]

Doubtless most people assumed that when Huntington gave up his active business work, he would simply rest. He said, "I have retired from business and am busy enjoying myself. I am building my house. You know I have always been building, and I like it."[50]

He was busy with other things as well and enjoying all of them. There were, however, two major activities that gave him increasing pleasure and that had led him from his business affairs: the ranch, where he was building gardens and a residence, and the world of books and art, which involved building his collections.

Edward's main source of "enjoyment and fun" in Southern California was what he called "the Ranch," the heart of which was the Shorb property, at the center of which was the Shorb house, where Edward had spent his first night in California in 1892. The Shorbs had called the house and ranch San Marino, after the name of the plantation of Shorb's grandfather in Frederick County, Maryland, which had in turn been named for the small republic in northeastern Italy.

On January 2, 1903, Edward bought the Shorb Ranch from the

Farmers and Merchants Bank of Los Angeles; the bank had taken it over in the settlement of the estate after the death of J. DeBarth Shorb in 1896. Edward paid $239,732.74 for the 501.89-acre property. At the same time, he bought the Winston Ranch of 162 acres contiguous to the south, and then half a dozen other pieces adjacent to the Shorb Ranch; the result was a ranch comprising more than eight hundred acres (at a total cost of $655,000), which he sometimes called Los Robles Ranch.[51]

But it was the Shorb property that engaged his special attention and provided ample scope for his active interests. It enjoyed a beautiful situation. The San Gabriel Mountains loomed across the north and east horizons. Only a few miles away to the north, in what was then called the Sierra Madre, Mts. Wilson and Lowe rose to five thousand feet; their changing colors and rugged splendor were sharply outlined against skies of blue and soft gray. To the east, Old Baldy stood serene at ten thousand feet; capped with snow through most of the winter months, it dominated the scene. A fertile, rolling valley of fruit groves and grain fields lay to the south, with the Whittier Hills and the San Bernardino Mountains beyond. This vista stretched around the Shorb house and sparkled in air that always seemed clear. When Edward took his friend Otheman Stevens to the site, Stevens wrote that "we stood drinking in the beauty of the San Gabriel Valley, forming a panorama of serene loveliness at our feet."[52] In 1910, it was asserted that the house on this spot "occupies the most sightly location in Southern California, and from its spacious verandas a vista of entrancing splendor can be had."[53]

The Shorb property had been developed only slightly between the time that the house was built in 1878 and when Edward bought it in 1903. Pepper trees had been planted around the house, and there was a barn, a pigeon coop, a tennis court, and a greenhouse. To the north, there were native oaks in a large field, and to the northeast an extensive pasture. An open reservoir in the southeast corner with a capacity of four million gallons was used to irrigate the orange groves to the south; there were two smaller reservoirs in the west canyon. A small grove of apricots stood north of the house, and one of oranges and one of olives lay to the southeast. These improvements were in the central part of the ranch, the part that is now the 207-acre grounds of the Huntington Library, Art Collections, and Botanical Gardens. The entire Shorb Ranch, with its five hundred acres, was thus about two and a half times as extensive as this central part, and the peripheral acreage was an important part of the scene that so charmed Edward. It included eighty-seven acres of oranges, thirty-three acres of lemons, thirty-nine acres of figs, eighty-three acres of pasture, and undeveloped portions with native oaks and undergrowth.[54]

Edward began visiting the Shorb Ranch soon after he bought it, at first going only on Sundays and holidays when he was in Los Angeles. Then he began to spend afternoons there, "working at details of road making and planting, and generally enjoying himself."[55] In 1904 he wrote to his daughter Elizabeth, "I was out to the ranch yesterday doing some grading and slept at Mr. Patton's last night."[56] To his mother he wrote, "I am doing some grading on the Shorb Place. You know I can't well live unless I can be grading somewhere." And he added, as a corollary of his grading activities, "This is a beautiful day—so peaceful, so calm, so restful."[57]

Walking around the ranch soon became a principal pleasure for him: "Whenever he can get away from the duties of his desk he can be found wandering about the noble property, inspecting the trees and directing the laborers in the vineyards and orchards." It was a place of rest and joy for him: "When he is weary he goes to San Marino. When he wishes to show some friend a decided honor he drives him to San Marino."[58] He would say to a visitor, "Come, let me show you my grove of live oaks and the vista that I will have from the house toward the mountains." George Patton said, "It is hard to get him to talk business when he is here—he is simply reveling in the sunshine and this big acreage." One day when Edward did not come back to Howard's house for lunch, Howard's wife said, "I guess he has forgotten all about hunger over there on his ranch."[59]

Once or twice a week he spent the night at the next-door home of George Patton, his closest friend at the time and the general manager of his holding company. The head gardener would see him on the ranch at six o'clock in the morning inspecting the area; after a good walk, Edward would return to the Pattons for breakfast.[60] During a period of several years he walked over the ranch with Patton and decided where the roads and paths should go. He enclosed the five hundred acres with a fence and planned walks and roads through the property in a way that would preserve the trees and the natural views. "The work of laying out nine miles of drives on the 500-acre estate has been one of Mr. Huntington's principal recreations during the last three or four years," wrote the *Los Angeles Sunday Times* in a story in 1908 that covered the whole front page of the real estate section and included five pictures. "He and Mr. Patton have tramped over every inch of the property with great bundles of lath under their arms, scheming out roads, dodging about trees, Mr. Huntington always jolly, and Mr. Patton complaining that he used up six pairs of shoes." Edward was very particular about the effect that the roads should create: "Mr. Huntington's knowledge of good curves on a railroad layout has come into good service in laying out these park roads. They are as natural as though they had been worn by use, as roads are sometimes naturally worn through a woodland. There is nothing forced or set anywhere in the scheme." They were, and remain, full of the charm of the wild, natural world.[61]

Most of all, he hated to see a tree cut down. It was jestingly observed that he must have had the soul of a wise and good Brahman who feels that chopping down a tree is one of the greatest crimes a man can commit. He had given orders, it was claimed, that a railway track had to go around any tree that was in the way. A little episode was used to dramatize his love of trees:

> It is whispered in Los Angeles that a tree with wide spreading branches stood directly in the path of a right of way.
> "Has H. E. been here?" asked the engineer in charge.
> "No, I don't think he has," was the answer.
> "Then he knows nothing about this blessed old tree, eh?"
> "I guess not."
> "Well, chop her down."
> Down went the tree. But an engineer dug out the roots, split the tree into kindling wood, burned it, and buried the ashes, and his heart stood still when H. E. Huntington went over the line through fear that he possibly might have known of its existence.[62]

He loved to share the improvements on the ranch with his family. When his sister Carrie was visiting him in March 1903, he took her "in his buggy for a long drive through his Pasadena place" and then for lunch at the Pattons, as she enthusiastically reported to their mother.[63] He took his daughters Elizabeth and Clara to ride around the ranch in his automobile; he drove out so frequently that Clara's husband, Gilbert, teased Edward afterward "by asking him if it had disappeared in the night." Elizabeth, who resented Gilbert's teasing her father, went with Edward alone for a ride around the ranch and reported to her husband that "the air was great."[64] Later, when Carrie and her husband arrived in Los Angeles together, "Edwards took us at once in his auto and we went out to the old Shorb place," Burke wrote in his diary. "We went through 7 miles of drives on his 500 acres."[65]

Edward was full of ideas on how to landscape to enhance the natural beauty of the ranch. While out of town in 1904 and 1905 he conveyed his wishes in dozens of letters and telegrams to Patton. "THINK AS SOON AS POSSIBLE BETTER HAVE LUPIN PLANTED ON HILL FRONT OF HOUSE" read the text of a telegram of December 31, 1904.[66] On January 3, 1905, he asked to have "a few almond trees in your planting of fruit trees" that were to be put in east of the stable.[67] Two weeks later he asked Patton to plant China umbrella, Siberian crab, and Japanese fern trees.[68] The next week he sent two pages of questions and directions specifying the kind of bamboo he wanted near the reservoir, which shrubs to move from the Childs place, and how to get black bass for the reservoir from the state fish commission.[69] In February he asked to have the largest palms taken down from the olive drive near the packing house and moved to the ranch between the tenant house and the stable.[70] He gave detailed directions about where to place fences, where to put up a corral for horses, and which trees to remove. His interest was also visual. Here is the complete text of a letter to Patton of March 3, 1905: "My dear Patton: When the barley is up a few inches I wish you would have some photographic views taken of the Los Robles Ranch and send them to me. Have the pictures of good size."[71]

Both Edward and Patton took great interest in rain. Patton wrote Edward on December 23, 1904, that "we have had a slight shower of rain and indications good for a heavy rain the near future." Edward's immediate reply on December 28 was, "How near? As you are such a good weather prophet I know the rain is bound to come." Patton responded with this telegram on December 31: "TWO INCHES ALREADY STILL RAINING LIKE H. HAPPY NEW YEAR." A little over a month later, Patton joyfully reported 7.25 inches of rain in five days, with "some gullies on the hillside where Lippia was planted." Edward gravely responded, "I would have the gullies filled and replanted with Lippia." Two months later Patton was upset by the damage caused by 4.56 inches of rain, but Edward replied that "we can afford to stand the damage" because of "the great benefit that will result from the rain itself."[72]

In early 1904, Patton hired Douglas S. Durham as head gardener for Edward's ranch, and Durham engaged laborers to carry out the work that was directed. Unfortunately, Durham was not a success, and Patton fired him in 1905 for passing a worthless check, for which he was convicted and jailed.[73] Patton then hired a twenty-six-year-old New Englander with a farm background who had recently moved to California. His name was William Hertrich, and he was to serve as head gardener for the rest of Mr. Huntington's life, and twenty-one years beyond. Edward did not, at first, know who Patton had hired and wrote him saying, "What, by the way, is the name of the new man? I may want to send him some printed matter from time to time."[74] Hertrich turned out to be reliable in hiring and supervising men and carrying out the garden plans, but it was Huntington who decided how the ranch was to be developed, what gardens there should be, and what plant material should be acquired. It is probably not surprising that Hertrich and several others who worked closely with Huntington—such as George Ellery Hale, A. S. W. Rosenbach, and Lord Duveen—portrayed themselves in their valuable personal recollections as more controlling figures in his activities than the correspondence bears out.[75]

The first major gardening project was the development of the Lily Ponds to occupy a wash or narrow ravine that detracted from the beauty of the landscape. Edward consulted first with Ernest Braunton, garden editor of the *Los Angeles Times,* who prepared, in 1906, a preliminary sketch of five ponds with lilies to be planted in redwood boxes. Within a month Patton had Mr. Marsh work out the details and the construction began. Edward got in touch with E. D. Sturtevant of Hollywood, a specialist in water plants, and Sturtevant revised the plans and provided all "the best plants required for the ponds."[76]

Edward was always on the lookout for plants as he traveled around. He went several times to the nursery of Miss K. O. Sessions in San Diego; he bought a full carload from her in 1907 and another carload in 1908.[77] He was especially interested in palms, cycads, and tropical plants; he bought twelve palms and fifteen cycads from W. A. Manda and Company of South Orange, New Jersey, for just under $5,000 in 1909, and a thirty-foot *Cocos plumosus* palm from M. J. Perrin of San Diego.[78] In 1909, he moved two thirty-foot palms from his garden in San Francisco to the ranch. He had planted them in the 1890s, but the fire following the earthquake of 1906 had stripped them completely, leaving only bare and blackened stems. Within three years they had put out new growth, and Edward valued them because they had lived through the fire. Six men worked for two weeks boxing them—each weighed ten tons boxed—and loading them on freight cars for their trip to the ranch.[79] He had set aside four acres of sloping ground near the Shorb house for palms, and that area ultimately became the Palm Garden.[80]

Edward showed the ranch to Ed Fletcher, a fellow director of the South Coast Land Company, and Fletcher thought that he had "the making of as beautiful a place as can be made in California and I shall be more than happy to have the privilege of helping a little in the collection of your plants and trees." Fletcher obtained wild white lilies, hollies, a "beautiful wild shrub" that he called *Cneridium dumosum,* pink and white azaleas to grow under the oak trees, and various other plants.[81] On a visit to the Hotel del Coronado in San Diego in 1908, Edward admired the bougainvillea and asked the manager for some cuttings; the manager sent a dozen slips by mail and added that "I have not sent you more, as they grow so rapidly and cover so much space"— but he would gladly send more if they were wanted.[82]

Edward was specially interested in tropical fruits and wanted to carry on horticultural experiments on the ranch to develop new products that could be introduced into the California fruit industry. Hertrich had built a nursery and lath house large enough to accommodate fifteen thousand plants. One of Edward's first experimental efforts was the avocado, which was not widely cultivated in California. In 1905, he brought a pocketful of avocado seeds from the Jonathan Club (some from avocados he had eaten himself, some given to him by the chef) and asked Hertrich to try to grow them. The chef of the club later supplied more seed, and within three months Hertrich had three hundred plants growing in pots. When they were several feet tall, they were planted in an orchard, twenty-five feet apart, and by 1907 seven acres were devoted to avocado trees. This was regarded as the first avocado orchard in Southern California; Edward took great delight in showing it to visitors, and many of the trees are still standing.[83]

Edward's interest in the ranch had almost no limit. He agreed with Hertrich to start a cactus garden in 1906 near the reservoir area, and in 1909 he hired Dr. A. C. Houghton, a cactus expert, to complete the installation.[84] Edward asked Hertrich to keep him up to date on progress at the ranch while he was away; on October 26, 1908, he said, "I would like to have you write me once a week, giving report of work done during the week and of anything else which you think may be of interest to me."[85] He sent Hertrich seed that he acquired on his travels: "I will send you a few Horse Chestnuts that I picked up and wish you to plant them. Also some seed of the Mountain Laurel. I don't know whether it will grow from seed or not or whether the seed are ripe."[86] Like a collector, he valued the rarity of the things on the ranch. When Hertrich moved some unusual rock from the ranch into Howard's yard, Edward objected:

> I wish you would be careful before giving things on the Ranch away
> to consult me about it, as it sometimes happens that I would much
> rather give something else away than the particular thing given. I
> notice you put in Howard's yard some of the rock you got from Santa
> Cruz, which is of course all right, but I would rather have given him
> many times the value of it in something else. We had the only kind of
> rock in that part of the country and to scatter it around makes it com-
> mon. This is written just as a caution for the future, the point of
> which I know you will at once see. If outside people want things, all
> you need to say is that you do not feel authorized to give anything
> away without my authority. Of course you understand the kind of

things I refer to—such, for instance, as have a value to me on account of rarity, &c., like the rock above referred to, unique plant specimens & the like.[87]

By 1910, the gardens on the ranch had been widely recognized as an important development for Southern California. George Patton told Edward, "I wish to say that I think you are making what will be the most magnificent and stately private estate in the United States."[88] Dozens of newspaper stories summed up what had been accomplished, praising the rare and exotic plants from all over the world and the beauty of the results. Few stories failed to mention some large sum of money that Huntington had reputedly spent on plant material, or that he had had forty gardeners at work for several years. Huntington himself was usually pictured as tramping around the ranch, looking at the progress of the plantings, and talking about other rare plants that he wanted: "Huntington, the man of business, was sleeping, while Huntington, the lover of nature, reveled in care-free happiness."[89]

While all the improvements were being made to the grounds of the ranch, Edward was thinking about a residence from which to enjoy all this beauty.[90] At first, he considered renovating the Shorb house, which was a useful but not very attractive wooden structure built as a two-story house, with a third story added in 1887. In 1904 and 1905, he began to think about tearing down the Shorb house and replacing it with a new structure. He had E. S. Strode, an engineer with the Pacific Electric, make pencil sketches of floor plans and elevations to embody his wishes—a very large two-story house with a ten-room attic and a full basement containing a bowling alley, gymnasium, and wine cellar. In the meantime, Howard and Clara decided that they wanted to live in the Oak Knoll area, and Edward agreed to have houses built for them. After checking with friends and business associates, he chose Myron Hunt, of Hunt and Grey, as the architect. The work went well in 1906 and 1907, and Edward decided to go forward with his own residential plans. In 1906 he had Hertrich, under Hunt's guidance, begin to demolish the Shorb house; the lumber was used to build six four-room cottages for those working on the ranch. In the meantime, he was talking with Hunt about the style of house he wanted—fireproof, of reinforced concrete, with stucco finish and plenty of light, the major space being reserved for his library. Or as Hunt recalled it, a "library with a few rooms about it." Early in 1908, he sent Hunt his "rough sketch of the house which I think I shall build at Los Robles (Shorb Place), although I have not fully decided to do so. I would not want any material changes made in the plan but would be glad to have you make any suggestions that occur to you." He went on characteristically to give a page and a half of details, including the height of the bookcases and type of paneling. At first glance, Hunt thought that "it looked like a hotel plan," but by putting the corridor inside to get more light and suggesting a few other changes—like moving the bowling alley to a separate building—Hunt and Edward agreed, in the course of three interviews, on "the philosophy of the house" and Hunt had the basis for making working drawings.[91]

Excavation began in the autumn of 1908, by hand, with the use of horses, plows, and wagons; workers removed eight thousand cubic yards of dirt to a depth of twelve feet; six thousand yards of the poorer soil were added to the Cactus Garden. Construction itself took only a little more than a year; the total cost was $453,606.68, and Hunt and Grey closed their account in September 1910.

Edward was intimately involved in the plans. When he was out of town, he was sent weekly reports of progress and photographs, and he was quick to suggest changes.[92] "I do not care for onyx mantels," he wrote to Hunt and Grey, "but want plain, simple mantels, and baleasted hand rail of mahogany instead of iron. Dispense with columns in drawing room."[93] When green was suggested for the finish of some rooms, Edward replied with a little Huntington jest: "The two drawing rooms are to be finished in white and grey (not Hunt & Grey) and the dining room about the same, but they are not to be green."[94] Two small pieces of evidence suggest that Arabella was involved in the planning. Myron Hunt made several visits to New York to go over the developing plans with Edward at the Metropolitan Club, and on several occasions they took the floor plan to the Fifth Avenue house of Arabella and consulted with her.[95] And Duveen, in writing to Edward about the color of paint for the small drawing room, said the two tones of gray would carry out "the character of the room in the photograph approved by Mrs. Huntington."[96] Her role seems small, however, in comparison with the extended, elaborate, and detailed control that Edward exercised over almost every aspect of the project.

During construction, Edward spent a great deal of time on the site when he was in town. Charles E. Richards, the general contractor, recalled that "Mr. Huntington made a daily practice of going to the work about ten o'clock in the morning and usually staying, without lunch, until the men quit. He knew most of the workmen by name after a short time and it was 'Good morning, Harry' or 'How do you do, Bill', and most of the men formed a decided attachment to him and this loyalty was evident in all the construction." Moreover, he "seemed familiar with the smallest detail, knowing where and how every fixture was to be located, and if he found an error he would say, 'My memory may be wrong but I thought <u>there</u> was the place for that outlet, but I may be wrong, look it up.' Invariably he was right. . . . If the workmen on the scaffold dropped a tool and Mr. Huntington was near he quickly picked it up and handed it back to the workmen without even a word. His presence was always an inspiration to the workmen."[97]

Hunt also commented on Edward's presence on the job and his habit of talking with the workmen:

> As the work progressed, Mr. Huntington would come around and watch the men work. There was one old fellow in particular in whom Mr. Huntington became very much interested, probably because he could keep up a continuous stream of talk on philosophy or any other topic that might be brought up and yet do his work too. Mr. Huntington would sit on a keg and the old mortar-mixer would talk on. One day a load of material was brought when there were not sufficient men on the job to handle it. Mr. Huntington immediately pitched in and helped. The workmen were greatly impressed by this.
>
> Mr. Huntington derived much pleasure from talks on the back platform with conductors or on the front platform with the motormen while he was riding to town. He would get suggestions or opinions on the system or just exchange a few words with his men. They loved him and respected him for it.[98]

Two serious problems arose in the course of the construction of the house. First, Edward purchased five massive eighteenth-century Beauvais tapestries—for $577,000, not the $1 million reported in the papers—from the Rudolph Kann Collection in January 1909, through Duveen, and wished to have four of them mounted on the walls of the library room.[99] (As to the purchase price, "Mr. Huntington knew he was getting gypped on them," recalled Myron Hunt.[100]) The construction of the house was so far along that structural changes would have been almost impossible; Hunt breathed a sigh of relief when he found that he could make space for them with only minor alterations of the corners, though it meant giving up more than half of the book space. The other problem concerned the wood carving for the interior finishing, which was made in London and Paris by White Allom and Company on a subcontract from Duveen, at a cost of $160,000. It was all shipped to California in lead cases inside large wooden boxes. They arrived late one afternoon, and Edward asked the general contractor to have some men stay after hours to open the cases so that he could see the carving. Alas, the lead cases had been broken on the top and deep water was standing in the bottom. The carvings were ruined, but the general contractor said that "Mr. Huntington expressed no disgust or disappointment by word or look. He was a true sport."[101] White Allom had to send men from England to rebuild the damaged work.

When the house was finished in 1910, it was widely described in the newspapers as "a Palace" or "a palatial estate." All of its grand features were described and their virtues extolled. But the main topic was Huntington's enjoyment of the process and the result. "To see Mr. Huntington hobnobbing with the carpenter, the mortar carrier, the bricklayer and the plumber is a visual treat," one reporter observed. "He is enjoying the building of that house as no owner ever has before."[102] Later, another reporter visited the house in the company of Myron Hunt and saw Huntington in his shirt sleeves helping to reassemble an antique marble statue: "Tenderly, almost lovingly, the volunteer artisan handled the tablet that bore the head of a grinning satyr." Myron Hunt laughed and said, "No owner ever had half so much joy in the building of a house as Henry E. Huntington has found. His son, Howard, once confided to me that he thought his father really took more interest in seeing a tile nicely adjusted than he did in the biggest engineering undertaking on any of his roads."[103]

The world looked on with wonder and delight when "this man of commanding affairs shook the weight of his millions from his shoulders, cleared his brain of the webs of finance, and tasted of the real life, and found its savor sweet."[104]

The nature of Edward's interest in books and art changed radically during this period. He had always been a devoted reader and a buyer of books (as we have seen in preceding chapters, especially chap. 7). Beginning with the purchase of sets, he had moved in the 1890s to individual volumes of special interest to him, bought from many booksellers, and accumulated a library of several thousand volumes. In art, his purchases had been modest, mostly decorative pieces, watercolors, and jades; but he had also bought large, comprehensive, illustrated volumes about British, American, and French art.

In this decade, his activity as a collector of books and art increased to a remarkable degree. He changed from a modest collector of material of general interest to a relatively sophisticated collector whose interests extended to rare material of international importance. He did not become a collector of national prominence during these ten years, but his actions were moving him in that direction. We can trace the stages by which this change came about.

From 1901 through 1905, Edward stepped up his book buying. He recorded the cost of his purchases during this period on the back of an envelope, which he characteristically saved. He reckoned his book purchases at $61,180.91, his picture purchases at $3,079.05, and his furniture purchases at $4,214.46.[105]

He was buying books from many dealers. Some of the books were a bit different from his earlier purchases. For example, on June 11, 1904, he bought seventeen interesting books for $346 from John Skinner's Book Store in Albany, New York. They included Bishop Burnet's life of the Earl of Rochester (1680) for $5, Izaak Walton's life of Bishop Sanderson (1678) for $7.50, the 1613 edition of Montaigne's *Essays* for $50, the 1561 edition of Chaucer for $100, the 1678 edition of *Paradise Lost* for $27.50, and good early editions of Daniel, Spenser, Jonson, Cowley,

Waller, and many others. While they are not quite "rare" books, they are books that any collector in the field would be glad to own.[106] He also continued buying standard editions. He got from Houghton Mifflin a complete set of the Riverside Press editions, and from Dodd Mead, Brentano, and others he bought the complete editions of Trollope, Poe, Whitman, Longfellow, as well as Prescott's *Works* (twenty-two volumes for $275) and *Great Events by Famous Historians* (twenty volumes for $400). He was willing to pay $1,000 for the Aquarelle edition of Nattier, the court painter under Louis XV.[107] And he read his books. When he found a defective volume in his Trollope, he complained to Dodd Mead, the publisher:

> Gentlemen:
>
> In looking over a set of Trollope in my library, I have discovered that one of the volumes is, so to speak, a dummy. The book is one of a set published by you in 1892, is in cloth and entitled "The Warden— The Chronicles of Barsetshire"; being Vol. 1 of 13 volumes. It contains the Introduction; then the first 8 pages of Chapter First, repeated over and over again for a third of the thickness of the book, all the rest being blank leaves. Of course this spoils my set and I would ask if you cannot give me a perfect volume in exchange for this one?
>
> Yours truly,
> H. E. Huntington[108]

Isaac Mendoza, a dealer in New York, led Edward to make his first en bloc purchase. In January 1904, Mendoza had bought the Charles A. Morrogh Library, a collection of about a thousand titles in several thousand volumes: it included illustrated books, choice sets, and first editions of recent works. It had, for example, some sixty volumes with Cruikshank illustrations, and a like number of Kelmscott Press books, many books on bibliography and book collecting, and a good gentleman's reading library of recent English, American, French, and classical literary and historical books from Catullus to Oscar Wilde. In March 1904, Mendoza called at Huntington's office at 25 Broad Street in New York to try to interest him in buying the entire library so that it could be kept together. He was rebuffed by the secretary, who emphatically informed him that Huntington "had no books, and wanted no books." Moreover, he was in a directors' meeting. Mendoza asked if he could see Huntington the next morning. The secretary said he "did not think so, as Mr. Huntington was a very busy man, and not accustomed to receiving peddlers." Indignation got Mendoza nowhere, but he appeared the next morning, sent in his card, and was ushered into Huntington's private office. As Mendoza remembered the occasion, "Mr. Huntington received me cordially, asked my business, which was stated briefly." He showed immediate interest, went with Mendoza to his shop, looked at the whole library, asked about the Cruikshanks and the Kelmscott Press books, and inquired as to the price. Fifteen thousand dollars, which Huntington immediately agreed to. "It was all done so quickly, it was hardly believable, but Mr. Huntington was an individual who appreciated good things, and made up his mind instantly that this Library was worth purchasing." Every day for the next several weeks Huntington came to Mendoza's shop in a hansom cab and carried the books, in leather bags, to his rooms at the Metropolitan Club.[109]

Later in 1904, he also bought the John A. Morschauser Library of some four thousand items from Mendoza. This collection included standard editions of the most important English and American writers, many of them extra-illustrated and in fine bindings.[110]

During this period, he continued to buy the individual volumes he wanted to read. His commitment to reading is central to a description of him published in Los Angeles in 1905:

> H. E. Huntington is a man of simple tastes, given much to reading, and to such amusements as may be found in an evening with his friends at the California Club, where he goes occasionally to engage in a game of dominoes or bridge. He is extremely temperate in his tastes, as he does not smoke and rarely indulges in any alcoholic beverages. He is a constant reader and his private library here contains some five thousand volumes, while his apartments at the Metropolitan Club boast a handsomely appointed library of great value.[111]

Edward's purchases of art objects continued on a modest scale from 1901 to 1905. From S. and G. Gump in San Francisco, for example, he bought a few paintings and watercolors, a mahogany card table, and a marble chair, and he carried on an extensive correspondence with them about various paintings.[112]

He picked up the pace in 1906 and 1907. By Edward's reckoning—on the back of that same envelope—he spent $124,945.65 for pictures and $42,100 for rugs during those two years. He began to look at pictures in New York at William Schaus's shop, and at M. Knoedler and Company. He bought several paintings by Israels, and looked at paintings by Corot, Daubigny, and Reynolds.[113] He began to think about art objects for the house that he was planning to build, and he bought a dozen large silk carpets from H. H. Topakyar in New York.[114]

He continued making book purchases from an increasing variety of dealers, who introduced him to the wiles of the trade. N. P. Chapin of New York, for example, told him that he could make the price of a book "as low as it possibly can be handled to you" and asserted that he was better than other dealers: "Your man Mendoza was inquiring about this set today but could not get the option on it." And again, "I can offer as close figures on rare & valuable works, as any dealer in N. Y. C., having 25 years in this business." In one postscript, he said, "I have no rent to pay for stores &c"—nor for stationery either, apparently, as he wrote on Astor House paper.[115]

In the spring of 1906, Edward asked his secretary, G. E. Miles, to catalog the books in his rooms in the Metropolitan Club. Miles found the job congenial but difficult: "It is somewhat like putting a boy to work counting pies—it's hard to keep from taking an undue interest in the pie itself." Edward replied, "I knew you would get great pleasure in cataloging the library" and added a permission dangerous to give a cataloger, that he could "read a little also."[116] Miles did complete the catalog in October 1906: it ran to 275 pages and listed 5,505 books. Nearly everyone who called on him at the club commented on the fact that his books were scattered everywhere in his rooms—on the desk, on chairs, on the floor—and that he had to move the books around to make room for a guest to sit down.

Basically, this was his reading library. Most of these books had been recently published, from about 1890 to 1905. He had sets of recent editions of the most important American, English, and European writers, and he read them: among Americans, Hawthorne, Thoreau, Twain, Franklin, Harte, Irving, Lincoln, Stowe, Jefferson; among English, Shakespeare, Smollett, Richardson, Sterne, Lamb, Macaulay, Dickens, George Eliot, Kipling, Stevenson; among Europeans, Dante, Montaigne, Balzac, Maupassant, Flaubert, Dumas, Hugo, Goethe, Heine, Turgenev. He also had sets of selected works in exemplary types, like the *British Poets*, Bell's *British Theatre* (thirty-two volumes), *Great Artists* (thirty-two volumes), *Old Dramatists, American Statesmen,* and *World's Best Orations.*

There were a good many out-of-the-way books in his collection, like the Count de Grammont's *Memoirs of the Court of Charles the Second,* Ernest Thompson Seton's books with animal drawings by the author, Gilbert à Beckett's comic histories, W. W. Skeat's Clarendon Press edition of Chaucer, Francis Hopkinson Smith's works, and the New York Social Register. It was not a collection of "rare books" in the usual sense: the presence of Pope's *Of the Characters of Women* (1735) may be a modest exception.

There were many examples of fine printing in the collection, like the Kelmscott Press books; many illustrated books, by Hogarth and Cruikshank especially; many limited editions on large paper, or Japanese vellum; and many books about books, like A. W. Pollard's *Early Illustrated Books,* the Grolier Club *Catalog of Early Printed Books,* DeBury's *Philobiblon,* DeVinne's *Historic Printing Types,* and *American Book-Prices Current* for 1902 and 1903.

A little further sense of the books may be given by mentioning that the collection included an 1883 edition of *Alice's Adventures in Wonderland* with the Tenniel illustrations, John Muir's *Picturesque California and the Region West of the Rocky Mountains* (1888), and Milton's *L'Allegro* and *Il Penseroso* (1855) with etchings by Birket Foster.[117]

Several themes are apparent from a review of the collection. One is the emphasis on American and British literature and history and their European backgrounds and parallels. Another is Edward's interest in books as objects of beauty. A third is art as exemplified in and by books. There is little focus on rare materials or manuscripts. It is a bookish man's collection, one with which a person could spend many a long evening. Shortly after Christmas 1907, Edward wrote from the Metropolitan Club to Elizabeth in Berkeley: "Christmas has come and gone and it was a happy one for me even if I had my turkey all by my lonely. I wish I had been with my children, but as I could not be I made the best of it and really spent a very pleasant evening surrounded by my old friends (my Books) which give me so much comfort and pleasure, and I am never at a loss to know what to do with myself."[118]

The collection was always changing and increasing. In 1907 Edward bought the Schneider Library from Miss Juliet Brown, who was acting on behalf of the estate. His manner of buying it revealed his increasing experience with sellers. Brown approached him several times over a period of two or three years and claimed the value of the library was $100,000. At last she asked him to make an offer for it. He agreed, on two conditions: that it should be accepted or declined within thirty minutes, and that if it were declined she should never offer it to him again. She agreed to the conditions. He offered $25,000, and she accepted it within the prescribed thirty minutes.[119] He obtained a collection of five hundred titles that included sixteen incunabula (one of which was a splendid copy of the Nuremberg Chronicle of 1493), fifty books of the sixteenth century, more than fifty of the seventeenth century, eighty-five from the eighteenth century, three hundred from the nineteenth century, more than a dozen illuminated manuscripts beginning with the thirteenth century, and four hundred fifty Hogarth engravings bound in three folio volumes. The manuscripts and the early printed books in this collection were harbingers of Edward's future acquisitions.

The pace of Edward's buying quickened once more in the years 1908 through 1910. In art, he increased the amount he would spend for objects. In 1909 he bought, as I have mentioned, *The Noble Pastoral*—five Beauvais tapestries from designs by F. Boucher for $577,000 through the Duveen Brothers, from the Rudolph Kann Collection, for his new house.[120] In April 1909 he bought Romney's *The Horsley Children* and Lawrence's *Portrait of Mrs. Robins* from T. J. Blakeslee of New York for $30,000; the year before he had bought the Raeburn portrait *Sir William Miller (Lord Glenlee)*.[121] In 1910 he bought French furniture from Seligmann for $150,000.[122] And in 1909 and 1910, from the Ehrich Galleries in New York, he bought Lawrence's *Duke of Wellington* for

$13,500 and also Reynolds's *Holy Family*.[123] In December 1910 he purchased a dozen items of furniture, including a Chippendale tapestry suite, from Partridge, Lewis and Simmons of New York for $87,500, besides a good many vases, clocks, plaques, and lesser pieces.[124]

Edward was proud of his favorite pieces and enjoyed showing them off. When the national railway officials visited California, Edward told them: "I don't want you to miss seeing five tapestries that I have at my new home. They were once the property of Louis XV, and I have never seen anything that I like quite so well."[125] When he was talking later about his paintings, he said of Romney's *The Horsley Children* that "I think this is my favorite of the pictures I have acquired" because he specially admired it as a happy and charming childhood study; the reporter concluded that "unlike many wealthy art collectors Mr. Huntington buys only pictures that please him" and "not especially because they are rare or expensive, and irrespective of the blandishments of art dealers."[126]

Edward accumulated substantial numbers of books from 1908 to 1910. During these years, however, he became increasingly sophisticated as a collector. He had learned a good deal about books from William Doxey in San Francisco in the 1890s and from Isaac Mendoza in New York in the first decade of the twentieth century. He learned even more from the Philadelphia bookseller Charles E. Sessler and from the New York dealer George D. Smith.

Sessler began to sell him books about 1907, and Edward bought a number of relatively inexpensive items—eighteenth- and nineteenth-century caricatures, fiction such as Dickens and Henry James, and art books. Sessler was a well-established, knowledgeable dealer, and Edward enjoyed going over books with him and discussing them. Sessler used to bring a box of books to New York once a week, usually on Tuesday mornings, and spend most of the day in Edward's office at 25 Broad Street. Instead of lunch, Edward sent out for chocolate bars from a nearby newsstand so they would not have to interrupt their time with the books. In 1909, Sessler asked Edward to write him a testimonial, and Edward sent a letter containing this paragraph, which suggests a good deal about the writer, the spirit of his mind, and his feeling for books and people:

I am glad to say that my dealings with you in books during the last few months have been very satisfactory to me, and I imagine equally so to yourself. The books I purchased from you were what I wanted for my particular purposes, and while, of course, I paid you too much for some, I got a good many at figures quite acceptable to me and I had not the time to go shopping about for better bargains. When I paid you the tall prices, I felt at the time that I owed it to you as a tribute to your linguistic ability and your transcendent qualities as a salesman of literary commodities, both of which used to excite my sincere admiration. If I never run across a worse man than yourself to deal with, I certainly deserve congratulations, and if you always find as good a customer as myself, you will never want for the necessaries of life.

Sessler posted this letter in the rare book room of his shop and kept it there for many years. Edward continued to buy books from him for the rest of his life.[127]

The most considerable bookseller with whom Edward began to deal at this time was George D. Smith of New York. Smith was perhaps the preeminent American bookseller of his time, and Edward chose to have Smith represent him at auctions. The first important sale at which Edward made substantial purchases was the Henry W. Poor sale, in five parts, from November 1908 to April 1909. Smith bought over a thousand lots for Edward, at a cost of about $30,000. Edward got a number of caricatures and many early printed books at prices that now seem ridiculously cheap: Elzevir Press books from $1.25 to $10, and Aldine Press books from $1 to $20. Edward's dealings with Smith were very satisfactory, and Smith continued to act as his agent at auction sales until Smith died in 1920.

Edward was also studying books about books. In 1910 he added to his bibliographical collection the catalog of the E. Dwight Church Library (in seven volumes, compiled by George Watson Cole) for $250, and that of the Robert Hoe Library (in fifteen volumes) for $225; these catalogs foreshadowed his later great acquisitions.[128] He also bought from Smith, in November 1908, a copy of a book about collecting rare books: W. Roberts, *Rare Books and Their Prices* (1896). He read this book with care, annotated it, and wrote in the margin the names of twenty-five authors or notable books mentioned in the text. His first entry was the Gutenberg Bible and his last Thomas Hardy. The first eight noted are all incunabula, and the remainder are English writers. All of them were later objects for his collecting.[129]

By 1910, his collection of books had achieved a modest renown. "His library is known by all and admired by all bibliophiles," reported the *Los Angeles Examiner,* but "by reason of its owner's great modesty, is unknown to the general public."[130] But he "delights in having an appreciative book lover call on him, and it is then the railway magnate opens up his cases and brings forth some jewel in his splendid collection and exhibits it to the visitor." Such as an eleventh-century piece of music, or the very copy of the book from which Dickens read on his American tour, or letters by Byron, Shelley, and Keats, or English caricatures, or manuscripts that were unfinished when their authors died.[131]

A greater marvel was the fact that the collector read and knew his books. "He is more than a collector," observed one magazine editor. "He is a reader and a student."[132] "He is a studious reader," wrote another, "taking a portion of each day for the perusal of the works of his favorite authors. He often reads until 2 or 3 o'clock in the morning."[133] Or, as it was summed up by another writer, "He is on intimate terms with his treasures, inside and out, having as intelligent a conception of the contents of his rarest books as he has of their market value. . . . Mr. Huntington follows his own unconventional bent in his readings, but he usually gets hold of the best. He seems to have an instinct for a good book."[134]

Thirteen

BEGINNING A NEW LIFE
1911–1914

COLLIS KEPT TELLING his friends that he was going to retire from business and enjoy a new life, but he never did. Business was his main enjoyment. Edward said that he was going to give up business at the age of sixty, and he did. He had developed other pleasures before he turned over the active control of his business enterprises to his associates.

It is amazing that Edward was able to take this step. In the course of a single decade, his net worth had risen from about $1 million in 1900 to $55 million by the end of 1910. It is true that $12 or $15 million had come from Collis, but Edward had made the rest. And making money, once you learn the trick, is hard to give up; it is in fact addictive for most people. Moreover, Edward had come to be regarded, in regional myth and legend, as a hero—as the one person who was mainly responsible, by his business activities, for the unparalleled growth and burgeoning development of Southern California. Hardly anyone would be able to turn his or her back on such an emotional gratification.

But Edward did not require such evidences of success to support his self-esteem. He had already begun, as we have seen, to devote greater creative attention to books, art, and nature and to get an increasing satisfaction from those interests. However, despite his involvement with books and other interests, he was often lonely. He always had several close friends whom he saw regularly, and these relationships were deeply important to him. But he was a family-oriented person whose marriage had become increasingly unhappy until it was terminated by divorce in 1906, and the feelings of the four children were divided between the two parents. Howard tipped more toward his father, Clara and Marian strongly toward their mother, and Elizabeth leaned toward both though perhaps a little more toward her mother. There was a lack in Edward's emotional life.

The new life that this chapter describes had several main features. One was the explosion of his activities in the acquisition of books so that he became, within this short space of time, perhaps the most important book collector in the United States. Another was the burst of acquisitions in the field of English paintings that brought him into the forefront in that field of endeavor and provided a focus for his art collection. Another was a series of problems and challenges with which he had to deal as part of ordinary living. Finally, there was his marriage to Arabella, which had a profound and far-reaching influence on almost everything that he valued in the remaining thirteen years of his life.

The first spectacular book purchase that Edward made was the acquisition of the E. Dwight Church Library in April 1911. In 1910, he had bought and studied the library's seven-volume catalog. Church—the head of Church and Dwight, manufacturers of baking soda—had founded his library during the twenty years before his death in 1908; although it contained only 2,133 volumes, they were especially choice and rare. Its treasures included the original manuscript of Benjamin Franklin's *Autobiography,* the unique copy of *The General Lawes of Massachusetts* (1648), twenty-two incunabula, twelve Shakespeare folios and thirty-seven Shakespeare quartos, first editions of Milton's *Comus* and *Lycidas,* and a host of fine early Americana (fifteen hundred items, including the *Bay Psalm Book*). George D. Smith was given the task of selling the collection. Smith first tried the Library of Congress, and then the state of New York, but both were slow to act. (Worthington Ford, the curator of manuscripts at the Library of Congress, declared that the manuscript of Franklin's *Autobiography* should be in the national library since it ranked after the Declaration of Independence and the final draft of the Constitution as the most important document in

American history.) Smith then turned to Huntington, and Edward bought the entire library on April 8, 1911, for $1,250,000.

The sale was widely reported in newspapers and magazines. Over one hundred accounts were published in the month of the sale, and they describe the library with a sense of awe. A long editorial in the *Los Angeles Herald,* under the title "Mr. Huntington's Purchase," exhibited strong local pride: "Not every Los Angelan appreciates the full value of the new distinction that will come to this city when Henry E. Huntington brings here the wonderful Church collection of rare tomes and manuscripts which he has just bought in New York." In the description of the library, the reader was told that "next to the duke of Devonshire Mr. Huntington now has the finest collection of Shakespeareana in the world, and his Americana is second to no other library." In conclusion, it was asserted that Huntington had "laid the foundation in this city of a museum that in the specialty which this collection will give it, can probably never be approached in America."[1]

The purchase of the Church library was a turning point in Edward's career as a book collector. It put him in the big time and focused public attention on his collection. If he felt a compulsion to live up to the exaggerated claims made for his collection, he soon had another chance. Two weeks after he had bought the Church library, the auction sales of the Robert Hoe Library began at the Anderson Galleries in New York, on April 24, 1911. They continued, in various increments, through November 22, 1912. On April 10, 1911, the president of the Anderson Auction Company had congratulated Edward on buying the Church library: "I had hoped that it would be sold by us by auction, but it is really much better that you should have it, if the Library is to be kept intact, at least the absolutely unique collection of Americana, by far the most important in the world." He went on to say that "I hope this will not prevent your being a buyer at the sale of the Hoe Library. Now that you have taken such a great place among the world's collectors you should not miss certain items in this sale, which for all time will stand in the foreground and give special distinction to the fortunate libraries which include them."[2]

The Hoe library was thought of as the finest private collection in the United States. It had been formed by Robert Hoe (1839–1909), the head of the family firm that manufactured printing presses, during the period 1880–1908, when numerous great foreign collections were being broken up and sold at auction, and when leading English dealers like Quaritch and Maggs were setting aside their choicest books for him. As a result, Hoe had some twenty thousand titles in his library when he died in 1909. Hoe had been an important figure in the New York book and art world: he was one of the founders, and the first president, of the Grolier Club and a founder of the Metropolitan Museum of Art. He published a series of careful bibliographic catalogs of his collection between 1903 and 1909, with a special foreword by his fellow collector and friend Beverly Chew, who said that the Hoe library was "the finest the country has ever contained."

The preview of the collection was a big New York social event. Arabella came with Archer; Mrs. John D. Rockefeller, Jr., was there, along with Joseph Widener, Mrs. William F. Havemeyer, and a host of others. The sales were held in the auditorium of the Anderson Galleries at Madison Avenue and Fortieth Street, and it was crowded with the fortunate 450 persons who had been given tickets of admission and assigned seating. The group was described as "the most representative of prominent bibliophiles ever congregated in this country and perhaps in any country. Men and women were there in about equal numbers."[3] Mrs. William K. Vanderbilt, Jr., appeared carrying her toy spaniel with a bell on its collar; the dog sat quietly on the chair next to hers, but it created a minor sensation every time it moved and broke the quiet with the ringing of its bell.[4]

Sidney Hodgson had come from London to act as auctioneer for the event, and many dealers from London, Paris, Frankfurt, and elsewhere were there. At the outset, women were asked to remove their hats so that everyone could see the treasures being offered, and all but three laughingly complied.

The star attraction of the collection was a copy of the Gutenberg Bible, on vellum, complete in two volumes. It was offered on the first evening. Hodgson gave a short explanation in his well-modulated English accent and asked for bids. A voice in the rear said, "A hundred dollars," and everybody laughed. "Ten thousand dollars," said Frank H. Dodd, and they applauded. Bidding moved quickly, and it was soon clear that there were four serious bidders: Dodd, Bernard Quaritch, Joseph Widener—representing his father, P. A. B. Widener of Philadelphia—and George D. Smith, sitting in the middle of the front row, next to Huntington, for whom he was bidding. Dodd dropped out at $31,000, and Quaritch at $33,000. Then Widener and Smith moved by thousands to $41,000, then by five hundreds and then by two hundreds. "Forty-six thousand dollars," said Smith. "Forty-seven thousand dollars," said Widener. "Forty-eight thousand dollars," countered Smith. "Forty-nine thousand dollars" came back from Widener, after a perceptible pause. "Fifty thousand dollars," said Smith immediately, and there was no retort. After a few moments Hodgson said, "This is the last chance you will have to purchase this book. Do I hear any advance?" There was silence. Hodgson then tapped the block with his hammer and said, "Sold for fifty thousand dollars." The auditorium broke into wild applause. "Let's see the purchaser! Let him stand up!" someone shouted. Smith stood up briefly, Widener pushed his way from his seat near the center of the first row and left, and the auctioneer announced, at the request of Smith, that the real purchaser was Henry E. Huntington, who did not rise. The applause was renewed, louder and more prolonged than before. The English dealers and assistants stared perplexedly about them at the clapping audience, and one said to another in an aside, "How very strange, don't you know!"

To the Americans, it wasn't strange at all. Everybody there knew that a new record had just been set. Fifty thousand dollars was twice the highest amount ever before paid for a book. And this was, moreover, a very special book—the Gutenberg Bible, the first book printed from movable type.

All the New York and nearby newspapers featured these facts and a full account of the auction in their next issue, in long and detailed stories.[5] Virtually every newspaper and magazine in the country communicated the details of the sale to its readers, lest anyone be left in ignorance. Enlightenment was spread from Fargo, North Dakota, to Macon, Georgia, from Jacksonville, Florida, to Spokane, Washington, from Oshkosh, Wisconsin, to Marion, Alabama, from Niagara Falls, New York, to Tucson, Arizona. I have seen more than five hundred long clippings on the subject, in a search that has been more desultory than comprehensive.[6]

In a few days, moralists began to write about the wickedness of spending so much money for a book when there was so much human need in the world. The *Chico (Calif.) Enterprise* gave Edward a partial break, however, and said that "Henry E. Huntington will squeeze half way through the needle's eye if the Lord will let him. The day after he paid $50,000 for the Gutenberg Bible he donated $25,000 to the half million dollar Los Angeles Y. M. C. A. fund."[7] Edward's friends also found ways to tease him. Epes Randolph in Tucson wrote to him in New York, "I have known for many years that you were sadly in need of the influence imparted by a constant use of Holy Writ, but I did not suppose you would feel the need of $50,000 worth of it 'in a bunch.' Notwithstanding the necessity for this sudden awakening, your old friends think just as much of you as ever and are anxious to see you. When are you coming out?" Edward replied gravely, "I note what you say about Holy Writ. I certainly should not have paid $50,000 for that Bible if I had not needed it very much." He went on to say, "I found out, after I had purchased it, that I could buy one for 10¢, the contents of which would probably have done me as much good as the one I have. So you can imagine how chagrined I felt that I had paid $50,000 for one."[8]

Many people reacted to the news of the sale of the Gutenberg Bible by trying to turn it to their advantage. Some brought old Bibles to the Anderson Galleries and asked to have them sold for big prices.[9] Others brought old Bibles to their local newspaper offices for marketing advice: Mrs. George Sussex of Galesburg, Illinois, carried her family Bible printed in 1653 to the *Evening Mail* office, and the paper reported that "much interest is being manifested at the present time throughout the country in old bibles" because of the Hoe sale.[10] A great many people wrote directly to Huntington and offered him their treasures, among them numerous old Bibles, and various prayer books and collections of sermons. He was also offered the complete works of Josephus in German, a volume of Cowper's poems (sent with thirty-two cents postage due), the issue of a newspaper reporting the assassination of Abraham Lincoln, the second edition of the *Life and Memoirs of the Rev. William Guthrie* (1705), an 1822 book on dentistry, "some very old and rare china," and a multitude of other objects in the fifty such letters that were sent to him within the first six weeks after the Gutenberg purchase. One offer was sent "c/o the late Collis P. Huntington, New York

City, N. Y." and it was duly delivered, though not by the routing suggested. Many wrote Huntington that "I would not sell it but I need the money very bad," many asked for a statement of the worth of their treasure, and others sought the name of any other possible buyer if Huntington refused this great opportunity. This was Edward's first experience with a public that wanted to turn his collecting activities to their advantage.[11]

When the Hoe sale concluded in November 1912, 14,585 lots had been sold for a total of $1,932,056.60. Smith had bought more than $1 million of the total, mostly for Edward. The sale was dominated by Huntington, who got what he wanted. There were many disappointed bidders, including Miss Belle da Costa Greene, J. P. Morgan's librarian. When she lost the St. Augustine *De Civitate Dei* (1470) to Smith at $2,700 (over her $2,500), she rose quickly and flounced out of the room "as if the subsequent proceedings interested her no more."[12] The next day, when she lost Blake's *Milton* at $9,000 (over her $8,500), "she, like the London, French and German buyers, went to the anteroom. 'This sale is disgraceful,' she said to a group. 'It isn't benefiting the real booklovers. The prices being paid here are making America a laughing stock among nations.' "[13] And, to emphasize her view, she was reported to have "wagged her gray feathers in angry disappointment."[14] A few days later she told a reporter that "the prices that are being paid for rare books at the Hoe sale are perfectly ridiculous. They are more than ridiculous," she continued, "they are harmful. They establish a dangerous precedent. It has hardly been an auction at all. Buyers have come from all over Europe and are getting nothing."[15]

Huntington obviously had obtained many desirable books at the Hoe sales. He had made twenty full pages of notes in pencil about books of special interest to him and had bought a wide variety of material.[16] His purchases included three early sixteenth-century manuscript Books of Hours, *Venus and Adonis,* the first three Shakespeare folios, five of the eight Shakespeare quartos sold, John Winthrop's *Declaration* (1645), and a lot of William Blake, including a presentation *Poetical Sketches, The Songs of Experience,* the illustrations for the Book of Job, Blake's annotated copy of Lavater's *Aphorisms on Man,* and a three-page manuscript letter.

The London *Times* had predicted that the Hoe sale would be "the greatest event of its kind in the annals of book auctions,"[17] and that view was frequently expressed after the event. A *New York Times* editorial said that "this is, assuredly, the most important book sale of its kind ever held."[18] The *American Art News,* in an editorial entitled "A Phenomenal Book Sale," called it "the greatest book sale probably ever held in Europe or America"; and the *Boston Transcript* called it "the most important in the history of book auctions" and went on to say that "no other sale ever held has been notable from the fact that one man bought more than half the total offerings."[19]

The principal New York newspapers took the occasion to appraise Huntington as a book collector. The *Times,* in a full-page story in a Sunday issue under the heading "Henry E. Huntington Leaps Into Fame as a Book Collector," concluded that "it is more than probable that if he keeps up the pace he has set he will soon own one of the finest book collections ever accumulated." The *Herald* said, "Mr. Huntington has been in the ranks of the bibliophiles for many years. . . . In the opinion of experts he will soon have the largest and most valuable private library in this country." The *Tribune* concluded that he "bids fair to become one of the greatest bibliophiles the world has known."[20]

April 1911 was a good month for Edward. In addition to the Church library and the first purchases at the Hoe sales, he also bought the Russell Benedict Collection of eight hundred pamphlets for $25,000. This purchase reveals one of Huntington's fundamental principles in collecting: specialize, and buy to your strength. The Church library excelled in early Americana; the Benedict collection was therefore especially desirable to him, because its eight hundred pamphlets dealt with the American Revolution and deepened and enriched his fine holdings in this area.[21] This collecting principle would later endear Huntington to scholars, who are usually specialists by practice and who delight in being able to explore their area of special interest without having to travel too much.

The Huth sales began in November in London, and this occasion provided another opportunity for specialized buying. The Huth library was rich in Shakespeareana, and Edward studied the catalog with care and made two pages of pencil notes headed "Shakespeare Items in

Huth Library I do not possess." The list included twenty items, like the second edition of *Venus and Adonis,* the sixth edition of *Romeo and Juliet,* the first edition of *Richard II,* the second edition of *Hamlet,* and so on.[22] Both George D. Smith and Bernard Quaritch acted for Huntington, who was able to get most of what he wanted for about $150,000 in the course of the nine parts of the sale, between 1911 and 1920.[23]

In 1911 Edward heard that Beverly Chew might be willing to dispose of his splendid collection of early English poetry. Chew was a New York banker who like Huntington had been born in upstate New York, less than two weeks after Huntington. Chew was a man of discriminating taste, a friend of Robert Hoe, sometime president of the Grolier Club, and one of the most respected collectors of his time. His collection of early English poetry contained only about sixteen hundred volumes, but it was a very choice collection, centering on the seventeenth century. It included the more obvious things such as fourteen editions of *Paradise Lost* and five of *Paradise Regained* and also amazing collections of about twenty other poets, such as fifty-four titles by George Wither, thirty-five by John Cleveland, and thirty-three by Edmund Waller. There was also a significant amount of late sixteenth-century material like Shakespeare and Spenser and strong collections of eighteenth-century writers like Pope, Gay, Goldsmith, and Prior. Characteristically, Edward thought carefully about this collection before taking steps toward acquiring it. He made twenty-one pages of pencil notes recording the Chew books and his parallel holdings. He found he already had about one-third of the books in the Chew collection, but he decided to try to acquire the whole collection.

Edward talked at length with Chew, and they agreed on a price. The next morning Edward went to Chew's apartment in New York to close the deal and give him a check in payment. Chew met him at the door and said, "I have not slept a wink all night for thinking about parting with my books." Huntington was touched by the grief of a fellow book lover and replied, "If that is the way you feel about parting with your books, Mr. Chew, I will not take them; but if at any time you decide to dispose of them, I wish the first opportunity of acquiring them."[24] In less than a year, Chew decided that he would part with these books and start a new collection; on October 19, 1912, he wrote out a receipt to Huntington for $230,000 as payment "in full for my library of old English literature." Chew, like Edward, had an affectionate regard for his books. Both shared with other collectors the feeling that books were friends. When Herschel V. Jones, the great Minneapolis collector, decided to sell his library at auction in 1918, he concluded the introduction to his catalog with these words: "For me the time of parting has come. I bid these volumes an affectionate farewell."[25]

One other spectacular purchase was made during these years. In January 1914 Huntington bought for $750,000, through George D. Smith, two magnificent collections from the Chatsworth library of the duke of Devonshire. One was the Kemble-Devonshire plays, comprising some 7,500 plays and 111 volumes of playbills, and the other was the Devonshire Caxtons, which comprised 25 volumes printed by William Caxton, the first English printer—about a third of his entire output. The wonderful play collection—begun by the actor John Philip Kemble and augmented by the dukes of Devonshire—gathered more than 90 percent of the English plays recorded for the period 1660 to 1800. Other notable books included a sixteenth-century manuscript of the Chester plays, the original manuscript of Bale's *Kynge Johan,* authors' manuscripts of several sixteenth-century plays, the first quarto of *Hamlet*—of which there were only two copies, the other one, at the British Library, lacking the title page—and the four folios and fifty-seven quartos of Shakespeare.[26]

The head of the Bernard Quaritch firm in London wrote to Edward about this acquisition in terms that reflect the best-informed opinion of the quality and value of the Devonshire collection, of the standing of Huntington's library, and of the repute of Huntington as a book collector:

> May I be allowed to offer you my heartiest congratulations on your purchase of the Devonshire plays and Caxtons. It is undoubtedly a momentous purchase, and will not only greatly strengthen your already large collections by adding many volumes that otherwise would be quite unprocurable, but it will raise the value and utility of your library above that of any other private library in the world. I am ex-

tremely glad that the books have gone into the possession of one who can appreciate them, and recognises their intrinsic value.[27]

Between 1911 and 1914, Edward also made significant purchases at twenty-eight other auction sales in New York and London.[28] He bought many smaller collections, like the John Quinn collection of 121 authorial manuscripts of Victorian writers such as Meredith (twenty-one items), Swinburne (twenty items), Morris (twenty-four items), and the Rossettis (forty-three items). The Lincoln Collection of Ward Hill Lamon, Lincoln's law partner in Illinois and his closest personal friend in Washington, included many autograph Lincoln documents and thousands of contemporary letters. And the Grenville Kane Collection added 170 Washington letters, documents, surveys, and maps to Edward's library.[29] Moreover, he was always on the lookout for choice individual items like the very rare Browning *Pauline*, or 427 pages of Robert Louis Stevenson manuscripts.[30]

Thus he assembled, in a short period of time, a library that was described, in 1914, as "above that of any other private library in the world." Perhaps this was an exaggeration. But Edward was moving in this direction.

In 1911, the same year that Edward entered the ranks of major book collectors by buying the Church library, he purchased three major Gainsborough paintings and came into the big time as an art collector.

During the four years before 1911, he had spent around $100,000 a year divided equally between pictures and books. But the big time costs big money. In 1911 alone, he spent about $2.5 million for pictures and books, again about equally divided, and about $1 million during each of the next three years.

In early 1911 he had continued to buy pictures from art dealers in New York, usually for relatively modest amounts, such as a Gerard painting for $4,000 from Edward Brandus, an English school portrait of a lady for $8,000 from Edward Burrus, and a Nattier portrait for $60,000 from Knoedler. He reached a bit higher to buy a *Portrait of an Ecclesiastic* by Velazquez from the Ehrich Galleries for $92,000. It proved not to be authentic, but he had already traded it in on other pictures long before that discovery was made.[31]

Edward took pleasure in the paintings he had acquired by this time. In an interview with Otheman Stevens in July 1911, he said, "I believe I have about fifty important canvases." It is interesting to see what he mentioned: "There are three Sorollas, and others by Harpigny, Del Mazo, Tiepolo, Sir Peter Lely, Sir Joshua Reynolds, Sir Thomas Lawrence, Zaloaga, Daubigny, Israels." He went on, "I also have a Velazquez, did you know that? Yes, I have a Corot, and paintings by Coello, Nattier, a Jules Breton—well, there are too many to name; you'll have to see them for yourself."[32] This assortment of artists was heavily weighted in the direction of contemporary popular taste, with a little push in the direction of Spanish artists, probably by the influence of Archer through his mother, Arabella. Some of the pictures Edward owned would now be thought of as good, some as not so good, none as stunning; but the group does not seem to have had any strongly defined organizing principle.

By 1911, prices on the art market had gone up dramatically. A full-page story in the *New York Times* for June 18, 1911, headed "Paintings Bought for a Song, Sold for Fortunes," recited the names of many popular artists whose works "cost but little a few years ago" and had now taken "sudden leaps." English pictures were bringing especially high prices.[33] At this time, the art market in the United States was dominated by wealthy collectors like Henry Clay Frick, P. A. B. Widener, Mrs. Jack Gardner, and foremost, so far as Huntington was concerned, J. P. Morgan the elder, who was acknowledged to have the greatest American collections of Old Masters and English paintings. Morgan was accustomed to spending big money; as early as 1907 he had bought from Duveen eleven paintings and five other art objects from the Kann collection for $1,275,000.[34] It is likely that Morgan's eminence in collecting paintings as well as books gave some inspiration to Edward's competitive spirit. In any event, he was not dispirited by the situation.

In August 1911 the great turning point took place in Edward's art collecting. That was when he bought, from Joseph Duveen, three stellar paintings by Thomas Gainsborough—*Edward, 2d Viscount Ligonier,*

Penelope, Viscountess Ligonier, and *Juliana, Lady Petre.* They directed the painting collection toward major English works of art and established a level of quality. It is true that he had already bought in 1908 through 1910, as we have noticed, a painting by Raeburn, one by Romney, two by Lawrence, and one by Reynolds, though the last one proved later to be a studio copy of a painting in the National Gallery in London, but these five were relatively minor examples. The three Gainsboroughs were major works of art.

Edward had been in New York up until July 13, 1911, and so had Arabella. On that day he left for Los Angeles and she sailed for Europe.[35] Apparently they had an understanding that she was to look at the paintings that Duveen had bought from the Wertheimer collection. On July 24 she cabled Edward that she had seen the paintings: "Best are three pictures which you must not miss namely two full length Gainsboroughs Man and Wife magnificent finest possible price £110,000 [Lord and Lady Ligonier] also large Romney with two figures beautiful women price £65,000 [Lady Clifden and Lady Elizabeth Spencer, the "Spencer Sisters"]. There is also full length Gainsborough beautiful woman [Lady Petre]" for seventy-five thousand pounds, which Duveen would reserve if Edward bought the other three. "Answer me immediately," she concluded.[36]

Edward decided to buy the three Gainsboroughs rather than the two Gainsboroughs and the Romney, and on August 1, 1911, Duveen wrote from London to Edward in Los Angeles that "you will of course ere this have had confirmation of the purchase, by Mrs. Huntington on your behalf of the pictures from the Collection of the late Charles Wertheimer." The three Gainsboroughs were "simply wonderful. No words of mine can do them justice. . . . When you see the pictures themselves I am positive that you will be more than delighted with your purchases." He concluded that "Mrs. Huntington came in again yesterday just before leaving for the cure, and had a final look at the pictures. She went away quite happy, and said she was so pleased that she had been able to secure them for you."[37]

There were long and enthusiastic newspaper accounts of this purchase; I have seen more than two hundred clippings about it.[38] The price was normally given as $1 million, but as usual some exaggeration was involved. According to Duveen's invoice, the price agreed on for the three was $775,000—rather less than the $925,000 that Arabella had quoted at an exchange rate of one pound to five dollars—but still a big-league figure.[39]

From this transaction, we see the confidence Edward had in Arabella's artistic and business judgment. He who insisted on making the decisions himself even about the details of transactions felt free to follow her instincts. It was undoubtedly Arabella who led Edward to his close association with Joseph Duveen. Two years earlier he had bought the five Beauvais tapestries through Duveen, but the three Gainsboroughs were the first of his major purchases of paintings from him. Edward liked to have one dealer he felt full confidence in: for books, it was George D. Smith from about 1908 until Smith died in 1920, then A. S. W. Rosenbach; for pictures, it was Duveen from this time on. Duveen was a supersalesman. He was well informed and fluent, he could generally get the art objects that a special client wanted, he would make almost any effort to satisfy such a client, and socially he was acceptable in his grace and courtesy. He was also self-confident and self-assured to the point of arrogance, except toward his special clients, to whom he was deferential to the point of obsequiousness.

Perhaps the greatest significance of Edward's purchase of the three Gainsborough paintings was that it turned the collection from what had been an assortment of paintings in the taste of the times to an integrated collection of high-quality English paintings of the Georgian period. There is no documentary evidence that explains this decision, but neither Arabella nor Duveen would have been likely to advise it. It seems to have been Edward's own instincts at work: he was a specialist by nature, and English paintings would complement and enrich the primary focus of his book collection on British literature.

Once the direction had been established, Edward was eager to proceed. Soon after the three Gainsboroughs had been acquired, he bought from Duveen, for $270,000, the other painting Arabella had praised in her cable—Romney's graceful portrait of the daughters of George, fourth duke of Marlborough, *Caroline, Viscountess Clifden, and Lady Elizabeth Spencer,* a painting that Edward generally called the "Two Sisters."

He was generous enough to lend these four most recent acquisitions—the three Gainsboroughs and the Romney—for the dedication of the new Museum of Art in Toledo, Ohio, in January 1912. They graced the large western gallery of the museum and were singled out for special comment in the newspapers.[40]

In 1912 Edward bought two minor Hoppner portraits (*Mrs. Munroe* and *Duchess of Gloucester*) from the Fischer Galleries in New York and one Romney (*Two Sisters,* of Sarah Siddons and Fanny Kemble) from Lewis and Simmons of New York.[41] His major purchase of the year, however, was another stunning Gainsborough portrait, *Anne, Duchess of Cumberland,* from Scott and Fowles of New York for $200,000.[42] When Edward returned to Los Angeles in May 1912, he told Otheman Stevens, "I have secured since I was here what I think is the most beautiful Gainsborough in existence, the portrait of the Duchess of Cumberland, which gives me four by that artist."[43]

Edward's major art acquisitions in 1913 were two magnificent full-length portraits by Sir Joshua Reynolds: *Jane, Countess of Harrington* and her mother *Mrs. Edwin Lascelles (Lady Harewood).* He bought these from Duveen for $735,000, from the collection of the earl of Harrington. The stories that reported this purchase emphasized that he now owned twenty full-length English portraits.[44] He kept going for more. His major acquisitions in 1914 were two large, handsome Romney portraits, one of *Jeremiah Milles* and the other of *Mrs. Jeremiah Milles,* bought from Duveen for $415,000.[45]

In this relatively short period of four years, the art collection had been defined and had made a magnificent beginning. Already Edward had acquired at least nine English paintings of major standing and another dozen of worthwhile importance.

Edward's friends considered his gardens an outdoor parallel to his art treasures. His friend Otheman Stevens wrote in 1911 that "what his house at that estate contains in treasures of art, his grounds more than duplicate in priceless and strange plants."[46] He was asked to exhibit at horticultural shows specimens of tropical and subtropical flowers, plants, trees, and shrubs; he agreed, but did not compete for the prizes.[47]

Edward urged Hertrich to do experimental planting to try to develop new crops for California. In October 1913 he was budding five thousand avocado plants that he had grown from seed, and the experiment was a success. In 1914 he had the largest planting in the United States—four acres—of the subtropical fruit *Feijoa sallowiana*—a South American shrub ten feet tall with tasty fruit like the guava, the size of an egg—and they expected it to be grown all over Southern California within a decade; but this experiment was not a success. The main impact of the gardens on those who then saw them, however, was from the extensive decorative planting. Eight thousand pansies were planted in October 1913 and another ten thousand the next month. Two thousand cyclamen were bought at one time, as at other times were three thousand English daisies, two thousand shrubs for the canyon, ten thousand bulbs, and so forth.[48]

The first two areas on the ranch that had been developed into gardens became the Lily Ponds and the Cactus Garden. Landscaping continued over the next four years; of special note were the building of the Japanese Garden in 1911 and 1912 and the acquisition and planting of a large number of cycads in 1913 and 1914.

Edward was not happy with the canyon just to the west of the Rose Garden. It had a dam, a reservoir, and a tangle of vines and undergrowth on its steep banks. Edward decided, in consultation with Hertrich, that the area should be transformed into a Japanese garden, with the plants and landscape features typical of such a garden. In the summer of 1911 the first efforts were made to plan the garden and acquire the materials. Hertrich was given the responsibility for the development, but Huntington kept his usual control by requesting weekly reports and letters when he was out of town.

The search for suitable material was at first fruitless. A breakthrough came in August 1911 when they bought a Japanese tea garden located on the corner of California and Fair Oaks in Pasadena, complete with a large collection of Japanese plants and garden statuary and a Japanese house; the tea garden had been an unsuccessful commercial venture, and the owner was quite willing to dispose of it for $12,000. This purchase provided many of the basic features for the Japanese Garden, though the plants had to be boxed and the house taken apart before being moved the three miles to their new location.

Throughout the autumn of 1911, Hertrich had a crew of seventy men at work on the project. They knocked down the old dam, drained the reservoir, graded the site, built a series of ponds, and brought a large number of big stones from the San Gabriel Mountains; they created a waterfall, an overlook, a full-moon bridge, and a nailless bell tower; and they prepared the soil for planting. They put in the material from the tea garden, obtained azaleas and camellias from Japan, and planted wisteria, iris, and a multitude of small trees like Japanese dwarf cherries, peaches, and almonds. The house was reassembled on the site, and a Japanese family lived in it at first to take care of the garden. By March 1912 the job was completed and photographs were sent to Edward in New York. He was "tremendously pleased" with this "great achievement" and thought that it would be "a joy forever."[49]

The Japanese Garden, with its group of stone images of the Buddha placed around the grounds, provided an opportunity for some satirical fun. In a story entitled "Corner on Idols" in *Pennsylvania Grit* that was widely copied elsewhere, it was said that

> H. E. Huntington of Pasadena, Cal., has done a foolish reactionary thing. He has bought 57 idols, brought them from their original Japanese temple, and installed them in his grounds so that he can worship Buddha in seclusion. How much better it would have been if he had got statues of some of the American idols and put them up so that the populace might worship. He could have several political favorites, Mammon, two or three baseball heroes, several moving picture cowboys, a ten-foot statue of an American silver dollar, a leading vaudeville actress, an aviator, a fat hog from Chicago, Kansas City and Omaha visitors, and statues of a bull moose, an elephant and a donkey.[50]

As early as 1905, Edward was considering the suggestion of Myron Hunt that a formal Italian garden be constructed around the house that he was thinking of building. But he gave up the conventional plan of an Italian garden in favor of a grouping of rare, primitive plants that had flourished during the time of the dinosaurs, plants that grew so slowly that they might take many hundreds of years before they reached their maximum height of perhaps a dozen feet. These were the cycads, somewhere between palms and tree ferns in appearance but not botanically related to either. They are rare because they are difficult to propagate, require a generation of growth to become a reasonable specimen, and will grow outdoors only in tropical or subtropical climates. Few are in cultivation. Buying cycads was a little like specializing in Gainsboroughs or incunabula.

Edward became keenly interested in cycads in 1909, and he made a special trip from New York to a nursery in South Orange, New Jersey, to look at a group of fifteen rare specimens. He bought them on the spot for $4,823.25 and wrote to Hertrich, in his characteristic understatement, "I think we have a nice lot of plants." They were soon on their way to San Marino in a freight car with daily telegraphic tracers and a special arrangement to prevent the car from standing on a siding in Kansas City.[51]

More cycads came from Belgium, England, San Francisco, and Rutherford, New Jersey, in 1913 and 1914. Hertrich made a trip to Mexico and brought back some choice specimens. Two other prominent local men were competitors in collecting cycads, Edward L. Doheny of Beverly Hills and Louis Bradbury of Duarte. Bradbury had been collecting them for some years and had accumulated a valuable group in his travels in Europe and Asia. In 1913 he decided to sell his collection. Doheny made an offer that was turned down. Edward authorized Hertrich to try to buy it, and Hertrich succeeded in making the purchase for $8,000. When Hertrich called on Bradbury to close the deal, he prudently took two wagons and six men with him and left them out of sight a block away. As soon as the final agreement was reached, Hertrich signaled for his men to bring the wagons up and they carried the most valuable plants to the ranch right away, lest Bradbury—like Beverly Chew—change his mind overnight.[52]

With that purchase, the collection was essentially complete. In four years, they had acquired specimens of some fifty species, about half of all that are known to exist. They were planted mainly around the new residence, particularly around the large covered porch on the east side. Edward had designed this large space so that he could sit, walk, or entertain there and enjoy the world of nature at close range; Hunt had been obliged to use double columns around the porch to keep the scale human. Now the rare cycads could be part of Edward's immediate view. Others were planted in the new Japanese Garden and on a slope near the house that later became the Subtropical and Jungle gardens.

During these years, Edward was away from Southern California much of the time, but his thoughts were often of the ranch. On his travels he bought a fine pair of iron gates from England for the main entrance to the ranch; the gates had been originally installed at Beddington Park, Surrey, by Sir Nicholas Carew in 1714.[53] Edward asked Hertrich to send him a weekly account, preferably written on Saturday, of the weekly developments in the gardens. Edward wrote regularly to Hertrich, and several letters from Paris to the ranch typify Edward's interest. His secretary wrote Hertrich in June that "your letters are a source of great interest to him and he is always looking forward to receiving the next." Edward suggested, in July, that the eucalyptus trees be topped and that bees be obtained for pollination, and he sent three packages of rare seed for experimental work. After traveling around in Europe, in October he wrote: "I tell you, Hertrich, I have seen no place as nice as the ranch."[54]

Meanwhile, Edward sustained a number of blows in his personal and public life. One that hit Edward deeply was the "nervous collapse" of his son Howard in the summer of 1911. Howard and his wife, Leslie, were at the Hotel Virginia in Long Beach for a short rest when Howard collapsed, on July 25. Edward was notified in Los Angeles and went there immediately in a special Pacific Electric car to take them to their home in Pasadena, where they were met by Dr. E. A. Bryant and a nurse. The problem was diagnosed as nervousness and poor health caused by overwork, popularly called a nervous breakdown. Edward and Leslie sat up all night with Howard, and a long rest was planned to help Howard's recovery. His work as general manager of the Los Angeles Railway had to be taken over by an assistant. After three months of rest, Howard and Leslie took a five-month trip abroad to France, Italy, Germany, and England and returned to Pasadena in April 1912. He was still not entirely recovered; during a further leave of absence they spent some months in the East and early in 1913 he was ready to resume work.[55]

Howard's illness meant that Edward felt extra personal and business responsibilities. He stayed on in Los Angeles and spent the mornings in his office; by September he felt that Howard was out of danger and he could return to New York to take care of responsibilities there. Howard's illness troubled him for many reasons, not least because Howard had come to harm by following in the footsteps of his hard-working father.

An allied problem was the public controversy about the operation of the electric street railways. In 1911 and for the next several years there were heated arguments against the electric railways, with mass meetings and frequent newspaper stories and editorials. The chief complaints were the congestion that they caused on the streets, overcrowding in the cars, the unfairness of giving long franchises for too little money, the refusal of the companies to issue free transfers from one system to another, and the five-cent fare—three cents was thought to be enough. Many citizens favored municipal ownership of the street railways and all utilities. There were literally thousands of newspaper stories on these subjects during the years 1911 to 1914.[56]

The halcyon days were over, and Huntington found himself criticized and denounced as a dictator. One editorial maintained that "Huntington and others of his ilk have had things their own way altogether too long, and it is time they were shown that they really do not own ALL the city and ALL the people in it."[57] Bitterness began to creep into the remarks about him, as demonstrated in this Christmas letter to Santa Claus published over his name in 1913: "Saint Nicholas: Please put the Los Angeles Railway company ahead of all others on your visiting list and bring three or four million straps, suitable for hanging innocent persons who have just parted with 5 cents. Also bring blanket franchise for four track lines on Main, Spring and Broadway and make it a capital crime for anybody to walk or ride in an automobile. Could use the Mona Lisa in my private art collection. H. E. Huntington."[58] Although the common attitude toward him was still praise for his past accomplishments, the controversy about the electric railway was a reminder of the transience of public fame.

Edward tried to stand above the controversy and say that he was retired and others were running the railways, but he could not avoid involvement. When a new city ordinance was proposed in August 1911 limiting franchises to twenty-one years, Huntington responded that he "was through with railroad building in Los Angeles. Under this new ordinance railroad building is impossible." Further, "only the city itself could successfully operate a street railway under the provisions of this ordinance."[59] In the next month he wrote a public letter recognizing the rights of the public and attempting a reconciliation, but Dunn took a hard line on his behalf with the city council that the city did not have the right to regulate fares or examine company books.[60] Matters were not improved when Edward fell in with the strong anti-trades-union stand taken by Harrison Gray Otis and preached in the *Los Angeles Times*. The essence of Edward's position was his adamant objection to anyone telling the owner of a property how that property should be managed.[61] The idea of property was, of course, central to Edward's career as a businessman. To him, everything of tangible value was a property, and he was a dealer in properties. He did not think this way about art, books, and manuscripts, however: they were property not to make a profit from but to keep and cherish.

Another problem was Arabella's health. She had been feeling badly through the winter of 1910/11. It turned out that she was suffering from acute appendicitis, and an appendectomy was performed by Dr. W. B. Coley and his assistants in her New York house on May 3, 1911. She recovered well but slowly, and it was not until July 13, 1911, that she felt well enough to go to Europe for a further rest.[62]

A couple of events that happened in Southern California during these years deserve mention. One was the incorporation of San Marino as a city of the sixth class on April 12, 1913. Its area was 3.5 square miles, bounded on the north by Pasadena, on the west by South Pasadena and Alhambra, on the south by Alhambra and San Gabriel, and on the east by San Gabriel Boulevard. Edward was by far the largest property holder of this area and the payer of 75 percent of all the taxes. He had arranged a meeting with the five other large property owners to discuss the establishment of a municipality to prevent the adjoining towns from extending their borders and taking over this property. They agreed, and an election was held: the proposal was carried by 126 to 5, with those against said to be associated with Alhambra. The total population at the time was 519, including one child born the day before. Three citizens, including George S. Patton, were elected as trustees.[63]

Everyone involved succeeded in having a little fun out of this procedure. In advance, Patton had written to Edward giving him the names of the proposed trustees, all strong conservatives. "You will notice," Patton wrote, "that this is a straight Socialist ticket, and a number of the citizens have suggested that in case the new City is incorporated, that you will be very likely to offer your residence as the public City Hall and Library." Among the many advantages to this plan was that "your wine cellar would make a safe and satisfactory depository for the public records. This, however, is merely by way of suggestion and not a threat." Edward replied to the wine cellar idea that "I am inclined to think a smaller, dryer place would be more suitable and less likely to overtax the capacities of the city officials."[64] Right after the election, the three trustees met for dinner at Patton's house and elected him the first mayor. A public outcry alleged that Patton had used the bribery of an elegant dinner prepared by his imported chef to get himself elected. One neighbor "was elected town marshal because his new Fiat would do for a patrol wagon." Another who had been found guilty of speeding was "duly named deputy marshal and speed officer." Finally, a telegram was sent to Huntington "notifying him that he was duly elected chief taxpayer." In due course Huntington contributed a lot on the corner of Huntington Drive and San Marino Avenue and paid for the building and landscaping of a city hall there, instead of in his own house and wine cellar.[65]

The other local event of interest was Edward's takeover and completion of the hotel that had been begun on twenty-three choice acres of Oak Knoll property a couple of miles from his house and near where he had built houses for his children. General M. C. Wentworth initiated this hotel venture in 1906 and got as far as building 163 rooms and opening them for a short time in 1907. But Wentworth ran out of money, his company became insolvent, and the big pile of white stone lay there incomplete for five years, with claims of more than half a million dollars on it. Finally, in January 1912 the sheriff conducted a foreclosure sale and the hotel was bought by the Southern Trust Company for $156,000.[66] A real estate company representing the owners tried for a long time to get Huntington to take it over, but he refused. At last, in September 1912 his building instinct got the better of him and he made an offer for the property. "If I get the property," he said, "I will complete the hotel and make the whole property what it should be, no matter what the cost may prove to be." He said that he would add some adjoining acreage of his own "for the proper beautification of the land. . . . My purpose would be to make the grounds assume an equal degree of landscape beauty to that I have endeavored to create on my own home place nearby." He was not trying to make money by investing in a hotel: "What caused me to finally give the matter consideration and to make the offer I have made, is the desire to remove from the view the unsightly barrack-looking blot that the property now is; it is offensive to the eye, and speaks a silent but powerful rebuke to the detail of beautiful progress which otherwise marks that entire region."[67]

His offer was accepted. He hired Myron Hunt to redesign the building, inside and out, to add floors and make a 360-room hotel, with a capacious garage and chauffeur quarters and two dozen cottages for those who preferred privacy. Hunt also designed a covered bridge and the landscaping, and Hertrich was allowed $50,000 to plant the grounds. As usual, Huntington kept a close eye on the work. In May 1913, while he was looking at the outside improvements, a tourist bus came by with a tour guide and megaphone. According to the newspaper account, the guide told his tourists: "This is the famous Hotel Wentworth, recently purchased by Henry E. Huntington and re-named the Huntington! Yonder is Mr. Huntington—the man in the soft hat and the gray suit of clothes. Take a good look, for he's a real millionaire." It was said that Huntington ordered the auto road, which had gone right by the entrance, to be moved back two hundred yards.[68]

Work proceeded well, and the hotel was described as the most lavish ever built, with three-quarters of a mile of rose pergolas, fifteen thousand pansies in one bed, a gymnasium, a theater, and two elegant suites on the ground floor, the Huntington Suite and the Presidential Suite. The hotel opened on January 4, 1914, with much fanfare. Special trains brought guests from New York and Chicago.[69] All the society leaders of Southern California wanted to be there, and demand was so great that three affairs had to be scheduled with the maximum of six hundred at each one—a reception, a dinner, and a late supper, with the ladies in their best gowns and jewels. Edward was not present, but his friend Otheman Stevens wrote that "there were ample thoughts of him; in this his latest addition to the serenity of joy hereabouts he has builded with his usual wisdom; he has transformed a sore spot on the smiling face of nature into a beauty spot."[70]

In the decade ending in 1910, Edward's net worth had gone up remarkably—from $13 to $16 million (including the $12 to $15 million from Collis's estate), to some $55 million. From 1911 to 1914, the increase was more modest, from $55 million to $67 million. These figures of net worth include, of course, the cost value of his books, art, tapestries, and furniture; at the end of 1914, these were carried on his balance sheets at a total of some $7.5 million, as compared with $1.5 million at the beginning of 1911—for an increase of $6 million.[71]

During these four years, the event of surpassing importance—so far as this biography is concerned—was the marriage of Henry Edwards Huntington and Arabella Duval Huntington in Paris on July 16, 1913.

After Collis's death in 1900, Edward spent a good deal of time in New York in connection with the business affairs of the estate, and he had rooms at the Metropolitan Club. Edward and his family—particularly his sister Carrie, his mother, and his children—had often been guests at the C. P. Huntington house. They continued to be entertained occasionally by Arabella after Collis's death. After the divorce of Edward and Mary in March 1906, rumors began to circulate that Edward and Arabella were going to be married. Each of them forcefully denied these rumors. When Arabella was interviewed in her home in early April 1906, she said, in a story with a dateline of New York, April 5, that the report was absolutely untrue:

> "Why, as you see," said the handsome woman, who was dressed in a magnificent black lace gown, with a pendant of pearls and small diamonds hanging from a chain about her neck, "I am still in mourning for my husband, and my thoughts naturally are very far removed from matrimony. And, besides, Mr. Huntington is my late husband's nephew, and only a few weeks ago was divorced from his wife. Why,

none of us know, for it came as a surprise to us all. Mr. Huntington is now in his California home, I believe, and has not been in this city for a long time, and if it is said that we are engaged I can only answer that we are not, nor have we any such an idea. It is really too painful to discuss under the circumstances."

A further response came from Los Angeles on April 6: " 'Huh!' said Henry E. Huntington today, when he was shown the New York dispatch intimating that he is going to marry the widow of C. P. Huntington. He said it so vigorously and it was accompanied with such a laugh that his glasses fell off. 'Absolutely without foundation,' said Mr. Huntington. 'It's on a par with other stories that are told about me.' "[72]

The rumors of their impending marriage continued periodically for the next few years after 1906. In 1909 there was a burst of newspaper stories on the subject: I have seen 165 clippings reporting the rumor from the eleven days May 9 to 19 alone. The uniting of two major fortunes and the thought of an aunt marrying her nephew especially appealed to reporters; and the construction of a mansion by a single man was taken as virtual proof that he was planning to be married. The two parties continued to deny the rumors.[73] Typically, in 1910 Edward, in Los Angeles, said, "There is not a particle of truth in the report. I have been denying it on an average of once in six months for the last six years"; Arabella, in New York, said that "there was no truth, whatever, in the report."[74]

Although the early relations with Arabella on the part of Edward's wife, Mary, and their daughters, Clara, Elizabeth, and Marian, had been cordial, by 1908 their feelings toward Arabella were bitter, and we can reasonably think that they were at least suspicious of the relations between Edward and Arabella. In July 1908, Mary was in Germany with Marian and Clara, on their way to the baths in Austria at Kopp's Königsvilla when, as Marian wrote to her sister Elizabeth, "I read in yesterday's Herald that Aunt Belle is at Kopp's Konigsvilla. We were all so upset about it that none of us slept last night. Poor little Mother! I feel so sorry—she had planned it all out and now she is perfectly miserable and yet feels she can't give up the cure particularly for Pegg's sake. Of course we'll go to another hotel if we can, but every room is taken months ahead and we may not be able to."[75] Two days later Mary also told Elizabeth of the bad prospect: "Our greatest worry now is the unpleasant feature that awaits us in Franzensbal: as Mrs. C. P. H. is stopping at Kopps Königsvilla which you can readily understand will be most embarrassing and unpleasant. We think we shall go to another Hotel if old Kopp will release us from our Reservations—but he is a mean skinflint creature, that I don't believe will consider it for a moment. We'll let you know later how it comes out."[76]

Two days later, it came out all right, as Marian wrote to Elizabeth from Kopps Königsvilla, where they had four rooms: "Aunt Belle never leaves her rooms (except to take a bath) and is in another building and as this is by far the best hotel—Mother decided to stay here. See peace and quiet reigning." Marian added, however, that their mother was "exactly like a small naughty child" as she refused to do whatever the doctor ordered, including removing her corset and going to bed for an hour after the bath.[77] All was not entirely well, however, according to a letter from Mary to Howard's wife, Leslie, who wrote to Elizabeth on August 6, 1908: "Had a letter from your Mother today and she seems to be quite unhappy over the fact that Aunt Belle is at the same Hotel in Franzensbal and that is very awkward for them all. I am so sorry."[78] A cryptic comment by Arabella in a letter to Carrie in about 1909 reveals the hurt that Edward felt: "I am sure everything will come out all right and I tell Edward not to mind the present state of affairs for the world judges one about right in the end. I am sorry for Edward simply because the others have been so disagreeable. Fortunately he is a man and can stand bad treatment."[79]

Whatever knowledge there was within the family of the relationship between Edward and Arabella was repugnant to the daughters, though apparently not to Howard and Leslie. Leslie and Howard were in Paris in February 1912 as part of his recovery from his nervous collapse, and they apparently heard that Edward and Belle were planning to be married. Leslie wrote to Clara that "I was surprised to hear it, but it will be lovely for you all. When is Father to be married?"[80]

After Leslie and Howard returned from Europe, they spent some time in Oneonta. Leslie wrote a long letter to Elizabeth in California on December 1, 1912, and marked it at the top "Please burn this letter" with the last two words triply underscored. Fortunately for us, Elizabeth did not carry out the instructions, as it contains a lovely behind-the-scenes view of Edward as at least some of his children saw him, and an open account of how they perceived his affection for Arabella:

> Father was here for two days at Thanksgiving time. Came Thursday & left Saturday so your letter came too late to give him your hug. He looks splendidly. I never saw him look so well—as handsome as a young "sprig" and full of life. We wanted to keep him longer, but he said he had to be home (in N. Y.) Sunday A. M. and go to Church with Aunt Belle. Oh, Betty, I wish you could hear him on the subject of Aunt B. He is apparently madly in love with her—does nothing but talk about her. He went to a reception here the other night and said to me afterwards—"if you should see Aunt Belle, don't tell her that I went to the ball, as she never likes me to go any place without her." I simply roared, right there—I couldn't help it. It did seem so absurd. He said they are to be married this winter—"surely." I asked him why she put it off, if she intended marrying him, and he said "Oh Belle puts off everything." Poor Father!! He spends every afternoon, dinner, and evening with her. He looked so dudish when he arrived, the other morning. Had a cutaway on. He said that was only his morning suit. That he changed 3 times a day. A certain colored cutaway, in the A. M.'s. A black cutaway for afternoon. And a dress suit every night for dinner at Aunt Belle's. Howard and I nearly fainted. I told him he was a complete revelation to me. But it's all so funny, though I can't help laughing when I see him. Howard and I look like old farmers beside him.[81]

This letter was probably distasteful to Elizabeth. She did not enjoy hearing people make jokes about her father, even though the comments—as here, on the formality of his dress—were good spirited; and she probably was not glad to hear that her father was "madly in love" with Belle, who was supplanting her own mother, whom she sincerely loved, and also herself, who had long been given reason to feel that she was supreme in her father's affection.

The wedding did not take place in the winter. In the spring, Belle went to Europe. In April, Edward applied for a passport for the first time; he described himself as age sixty-three, five feet ten and a half inches tall, with high forehead, blue eyes, straight nose, large mouth, prominent chin, white hair (bald), fair complexion, and oval face. In May, Edward made his long-delayed visit to Europe on a North German Lloyd steamer in the company of his new secretary, Robert T. Varnum. In due course they went to Paris, and there Edward and Arabella were married on July 16. First there was a legal wedding in the mayor's offices, and then a small church wedding performed by the Reverend William G. Allen at the American Church in the rue de Berri. Archer and his wife, Helen, were present, along with Clara Hatzfeldt from England, and Belle's companion and two friends from Paris. With Edward were his secretary, Robert Varnum, and Baron Randolph Natili, an old Southern Pacific friend of Edward and Collis.

Before leaving the United States, Edward had not told any of his family about the proposed wedding. Even Howard and Leslie were astonished when they first read the news in the papers. Three days before the wedding, Edward had written to Carrie in Oneonta and broken the news of the forthcoming event to her. "I cannot tell you how happy I am, my dear Sister," he wrote, "and I hope to make up for all I have lost and again have a home, and a home such as I never had. Belle is so good and kind to me, and I know she will make my life a very happy one. She is now suffering from a hard cold caught day before yesterday. With very much love to you, one and all, ever your affectionate Brother."[82] On the day of the wedding, Edward sent Carrie a cable: "Married today Belle sends love Edward."[83] Four days later he wrote her again with details of the wedding and his happiness: "I can never tell you," he began, "how very happy I am. Belle is so sweet. Good and kind, wishing me to have the best of everything. Which is something so entirely new to me. I am very sure, my dear Sister, I am going to be very happy in our new life. In fact, I feel that I am just beginning to live."[84] Carrie wrote a warm letter of congratulations, and he responded with thanks for the knowledge that "you wish me all the happiness in the world." He thought of the marriage as a culmination of all his wishes. "Now, my dear Sister," he wrote, "all that I hoped for has come to me. And Belle and I are so very happy. She has never seemed so free of care and responsibility, and looks years younger."[85]

When Elizabeth heard the news, she vented her feelings in a letter to her mother. "I have been thinking of you so constantly, sweetheart. I know from the way I feel how horribly you feel over father's affairs. It's no marriage at all to me. It's very hard to lose the respect for a parent. I feel the loss. The whole thing is very, very repulsive to me, and we just won't talk about it. Try as hard as we can to think of all the lovely things in our lives." And she concluded with expressions of love for her mother: "I believe, dearest, you have so much knowing just my love for you, dearest. And then to think that you have three other chicks who love you equally well, and no one can help loving you who's in their right senses."[86]

Edward wrote to Elizabeth on August 2 and told of the pleasure he and Belle were having in traveling around Europe, his sense of the Swiss countryside, and their plans for returning to the United States. The letter made no reference to his feelings about Belle, and it began as usual "My darling daughter" and ended "ever your affectionate Old Daddy."[87] In the meantime, both Elizabeth and Brockway had written to Edward; we can know the contents of their letters only from Edward's replies to them, written in Paris from the Hotel Bristol on September 2—they saved his letters, but he did not keep theirs. Elizabeth's sentiments were a very painful shock to him, and his letters reflect his reaction on this important topic so well that they deserve full quotation. To Elizabeth he wrote:

> My darling daughter
>
> I have received your letter of the 12th and I am surprised, pained, and grieved at the language. "If your wife, daddy, is a sensible woman, she cannot expect us to be friendly, and the sooner you realize that, the easier and better for us all." That is very strange language to come to me from you, who has furnished you with every comfort in the world, and who has never had a thought that has not been a loving one. I regret more than I can tell you that you should have that feeling, but you [can] certainly never expect any treatment from me that is not the same as you treat my wife. She does everything in the world to make me happy, and I never dreamed that such happiness could be. And I cannot understand why you should be so cruel, especially to

one [Belle] who has never had anything but kindly thoughts of you. She has always spoken of you kindly.

Your affectionate Father[88]

Brockway had written a kinder letter to Edward, and this was Edward's reply, which gives another view of his feelings about Elizabeth and his overriding loyalty to Belle as his new wife:

My dear Brockway

I thank you very much for your kind letter and I cannot tell you how much I regret Elizabeth's course. It cannot help creating much misery for us all. There is no reason in the world why she should not be nice to her Aunt Belle, who has never done a thing in her life to injure her, and would only be too glad to be nice to her. I have not told Belle about it and shall not do so, at least at present. I hope Elizabeth will change her mind and see how very foolish and cruel it would be to carry out her intentions. Again thanking you, I remain

Your affectionate Father.[89]

These family tensions were not communicated to the public, but the world at large was informed about this wedding to an almost unimaginable extent. Hundreds of newspapers from every nook and cranny of the United States gave full details about the two principals and their marriage.[90] The main themes were the marriage of a rich widow to her late husband's nephew—a typical headline reads "Bride Is an Aunt of Husband"—and the reunion of a large fortune under such headlines as "Wedding Reunites Huntington Fortune."[91] This second theme has been perpetuated ever since and has become a legendary truth—though it is, of course, entirely untrue.

Arabella asked to have only brief note taken of their marriage, and George E. Miles, a former newspaperman in Edward's New York office and once Collis's and then Edward's private secretary, was given the job of limiting the publicity. He wrote a confidential letter to them in Paris soon after the wedding and sent them clippings from a few papers. "I hope, Mrs. Huntington," he wrote, "you will not be disappointed at the failure to procure short news notices of your marriage. Unfortunately (?) you are two notable millionaires and when you take radical action it becomes an event and events are the stock in trade of our journalistic friends. You will, I am sure, give me credit for doing my best in your interest and doing it with pleasure." He told of having gone around to all the New York papers and asked to read the reporters' notes or writeups, correct mistakes, "curb to some extent the splurge," and give them material "about your mutual great interest in art & books & all that sort of thing." He asked them to "understand how utterly impossible it was for me to suppress, or curtail as much as I wanted to, the matter to be published."[92]

Many newspaper writers were attracted by the idea of a woman marrying her nephew, and for six months this thought was squeezed for all the fun that could be found in it. Here is one early example:

MARRIAGE MIXES UP RELATIONSHIP OF HUNTINGTONS
He Becomes:
His Own Uncle.
Nephew of His Wife.
Brother-in-Law of His Mother-in-Law.
Great Uncle of His Own Children.
Step-Grandfather of His Own Children.

And She Is:
Her Husband's Aunt.
Cousin of Her Adopted Daughter.
Sister-in-Law's Daughter-in-Law.
Step-Mother of His Own Great Nieces.
And in Case She Has Children She Will Be Their Aunt.[93]

After the wedding, the newlyweds stayed a few days at the Hotel Bristol in Paris and then took an automobile trip to southern France and Switzerland for their honeymoon. After they returned to Paris, Edward leased the Chateau Beauregard for a term of years from Baron de Forest. Edward described it with delight to Carrie as "a most beautiful place of four hundred acres on the highest ground around Paris," only forty minutes from the Hotel Bristol in Paris and seven minutes from Versailles. He concluded his letter by saying, "Belle joins me in love."[94]

They returned to New York in October, and several newspapers took occasion to praise Arabella as a model citizen. After making her customs declaration, she told the customs officer, "My foreign purchases amounted to $40,000 and here is my check for $20,000 duty if you find my figures correct." It was the largest declaration of the year, and the inspector said, "If all passengers were like Mrs. Huntington there would be no need for us."[95]

Edward moved into the big Huntington house at 2 East Fifty-seventh Street, and they took up home life together. Howard and Leslie visited them for several weeks in November, and plans were made for the first time Edward and Belle would be in the new house in San Marino. Society circles in Southern California prepared for a whirl of activity. Leslie was to see to the preparation of the house for their arrival, including the removal of coverings from all the paintings and the furniture, preparation of the library for daily use, and provision of all the big fireplaces with logs.[96]

After several postponements, they arrived on the morning of January 23, 1914, in two special cars. They were accompanied by Edward's secretary, Robert Varnum, Belle's companion, Carrie Campbell, and eight servants. En route they made a brief stop in Huntington, West Virginia—named for Collis—where Belle announced that she was going to present a statue of Collis worth $200,000 to the city as a tribute to him and that it would be erected on the plaza near the new Chesapeake and Ohio depot.[97]

They were met at the station in Pasadena by Howard and Leslie with their three children, Elizabeth, Harriet, and Margaret. "There's grandpa's engine coming around the corner," Margaret shouted as the train came into view. When they got off, Edward "was beaming and looking happy and healthy." Belle was wearing a Parisian tailored suit of finest black serge, a black hat, and a heavy black veil. They were driven by automobile to the new house. Belle kept her arm around Margaret, who was celebrating her sixth birthday that day.

On arrival for this momentous first visit, a forty-foot flag was flying on the flagpole to announce that they were in residence for the first time. They were driven for ten minutes around the grounds to enjoy a first view of all the gardens. They got out at the entrance to the house, and Belle walked through the plantings surrounding the house. They entered through the front door, and "Mr. Huntington seemed as pleased as a boy as he showed her through the magnificent libraries," the drawing rooms, and all the rest of the house. Belle's "delight at the wonderful vistas, and her appreciation of the matchless house were made evident," Otheman Stevens felt, "by her face and words." She looked at everything carefully, even "the marble tiled kitchen" where "she stopped at each closet to inspect the humblest of the cooking instruments." They spent a quiet day together at the house, and in the evening Howard and Leslie came back as their guests for dinner.

Edward and Belle had been surrounded by reporters at the station. She "secluded herself" from them, and the reporters rounded up all the usual questions for him about business conditions and the future of Southern California: he was, as always, confident and optimistic. At nearly sixty-four, he was perceived as having "the appearance of a man of 50 years." When asked for his advice to young men on the management of domestic finances, he replied, "I should tell the young man to go slowly and let his wife handle the pocketbook." He reiterated his affection for Southern California: if he were offered, as a choice of a lifetime of "twenty years in New York and ten years here, I should choose Southern California." He added that "after Mrs. Huntington is here a few weeks, she will succumb to the spell and will be as rabid as the rest of us." When asked whether they were planning any big social events, he responded, "No, we are plain people, you know, and balls and similar events do not appeal to us."[98]

And so it proved. Mostly they stayed quietly at home, and the greater part of their entertaining was of family members. Carrie and her husband came down from San Francisco and visited them for almost a month beginning on February 28; there were family trips to Riverside and Santa Barbara during this time, and Carrie's two children, ages sixteen and seventeen, were with them at the ranch for a week. The one major social event in their honor was a dinner at the California Club on February 23, 1914, for one hundred guests, given by Mr. and Mrs. William E. Dunn and Dr. and Mrs. E. A. Bryant. Howard and Leslie helped receive the guests. The club was handsomely decorated with spring flowers, a fancy dinner was served, and there was music afterward by Tandler's Quartet. Leslie wrote a glowing account of the occasion to Elizabeth: "It was gorgeous, and I had lots of fun. . . . Father had a beautiful time and looked so handsome." His enjoyment may have been partially attributable to the fact that he did not have to speak. Leslie's main way of telling about a social occasion was to describe the women's clothes or jewels: "Aunt Belle wore 7 strands of pearls (each one as big as your thumb nail). Her entire front was covered with them! Her dress was covered with black diamonds. She told me it cost a ransom in itself. Oh me! Such a life." The next Sunday Howard and Leslie had Edward and Belle and half a dozen others to their house for luncheon, and for the christening afterward of their two youngest children.[99] Edward attended a banquet for four hundred in honor of Secretary of the Treasury William G. McAdoo and Secretary of Agriculture David Franklin Houston; both spoke, and Edward was seated with them at the center of the head table.[100] The Jonathan Club gave a high-jinks stag party in honor of Edward's marriage; the entertainment included a toe dance by a very old man weighing three hundred pounds.[101]

Many society people in Southern California and in San Francisco were deeply disappointed by the lack of social activities. It had been hoped that there would be exclusive social affairs at the new house.[102] The sad news was even reported in New York that "society throughout California saw very little of the Henry E. Huntingtons during their visit, which ended in the same unostentatious manner in which it commenced three months ago." Social leaders "who wanted to entertain for them met with little encouragement."[103]

The only business that Edward is reported to have engaged in was signing his name 17,300 times on a series of new bonds issued by the Huntington Land Company, and he did this work in his library and on his porch with the aid of secretaries and Billy Dunn.[104]

In February, Clara had written to Elizabeth that "Father's place must be beautiful, but I doubt if he will ever be allowed to spend much time there, as she [Belle] does not like the country and is frank to maintain she doesn't like California."[105] In April, after less than three months in Southern California, Edward and Belle suddenly left to go to New York and on to Europe. Edward wrote to Carrie that "we are hurrying away as Belle has had a telegram from Archer saying they would sail on the 18th" and Belle wanted to see them in New York before they left.[106] On leaving San Marino, Edward said, "We have enjoyed our stay here immensely, for I have reduced business engrossment to a minimum and time for enjoyment to a maximum." And he added, "I fear that I shall not be able to return to my home here for something like a year."[107] Earlier in their visit, he had said, "I am done with business and business cares for good. The future years belong entirely to my wife, and will be dedicated to the pursuit of the peace and rest our advancing years make desirable."[108]

Howard and a few select friends went to the railroad station to see Edward and Belle off: "Looking the picture of health, Huntington briskly boarded his car after bidding his son and friends farewell."[109] The new life had begun.

Fourteen

WHEN EDWARD AND ARABELLA were married in 1913, we know—from Leslie's account to Elizabeth—that Edward was "madly in love" with her. And we know from his own letters to his sister and to his daughter with what joy he anticipated their marriage, how happy he was, how he perceived Arabella as good and kind, how he looked forward to having a real home, and how their union was to be a culmination of all his wishes (see chap. 13).

Two months after the wedding, his friend Baron Natili, who had been his chosen witness, confidently wrote Edward, "I know, my dear, your life is now one ceaseless song of happiness, and I know also that it will flow onward and onward unceasingly and 'as bright as the Iris'. I unite you both in one loving embrace of sincerest friendship."[1]

What was this woman like at the time that she made such a decisive impact on Edward's life? We can get clues from a consideration of her early life, her personality and human relationships, her health problems, her style of life, and her increasing prominence as an art collector. From these several points of view, we can perhaps understand a little better the special appeal that Arabella had for Edward when they were married in 1913 and the influence she exercised on the rest of his life.

Some facts about Arabella's life have so far been irrefutable. For example, that she gave birth to her son, Archer, on March 10, 1870. That she and Collis P. Huntington were married by the Reverend Henry Ward Beecher in the parlor of her house on West Fifty-fourth Street in New York on July 12, 1884. That she and Henry E. Huntington were married by the Reverend William G. Allen at the American Church in Paris on July 16, 1913. That she died in her house on East Fifty-seventh Street in New York on September 16, 1924.

Other facts about Arabella, particularly about her early life, have eluded searchers after truth. When and where was she born? What was the story of her early "marriage" to a Mr. Worsham? Who was the father of her son Archer? We are attracted by mysteries, and several popular writers have obliged by supplying full accounts of her early life.[2] I do not know the answers to all the questions, but I will give a brief account of her early life based on the facts I do know and the early opinions I have reason to value. For the sake of brevity—and in view of the fact that the matters in question are not crucial to an understanding of Huntington's life—I will not try to give the full arguments for and against other views.

The inscription on the Mausoleum asserts that Arabella was born at Union Springs, Alabama, on June 1, 1850. Since Edward wrote to Archer for this information, we may assume that it represents Archer's understanding of the matter. There is reason to believe that she was in fact born later than 1850. In the settlement of Collis's estate in the surrogate court in New York, the stipulations that were "deemed true and correct" included the statement that she "was born in 1852." In the return for federal estate tax filed after her own death, her age at death was recorded as seventy-two, placing her birthdate in 1852. However, in the legacy return by the executors for Collis's estate, filed in 1903, her age at the time of his death in 1900 was given as forty-five, placing her birthdate in 1855. In 1891, Collis declined the request of a friend who sought to have Arabella adopt his daughter by saying that she was "only about 37 years of age" and "would hardly care to adopt your daughter as you suggest, as she has a son already." "About 37" in 1891 would have placed her birthdate at "about 1854." While Elizabeth was visiting Arabella in New York in 1905, she wrote to her fiancé, Brockway Metcalf, that Arabella "was married the first time when she was fourteen. That seems so young, doesn't it?" It that were true, she would have been born about 1855. My guess is that she was born in 1852, was almost eighteen when Archer was born, and was seventy-two when she died.[3]

As to her place of birth, Richmond, Virginia, seems most likely. Members of her family had lived in Alabama and Texas, but her parents, Richard Milton and Catherine J. Yarrington, are reported to have come to Richmond in 1850. Arabella's full name was Arabella Duval Yarrington. She had two brothers, John Duval and Richard Milton—of whom we shall hear more later—and two sisters, Elizabeth Page and Emma. In 1859 her father died and was buried in Richmond and her mother supported the family by running a boardinghouse. In the later 1860s Mrs. Yarrington moved her family to New York, and after a short time most of the Yarringtons moved on to San Marcos, Texas, in Hays County, between Austin and San Antonio.[4]

There are two versions of Arabella's life leading to the birth of her son, Archer, in 1870. One is that she married a Mr. Worsham of Richmond, went with him to New York, where Archer was born, and that Mr. Worsham died soon thereafter. Efforts to identify Worsham or to locate a marriage license or birth certificate have not been satisfying. The usual candidate is John A. Worsham, the owner of a gambling parlor in Richmond who moved his activities to New York. A Mr. De Worsion was living with the Yarringtons when the United States Census for 1870 was taken in June; a garbled census entry lists Bell De Worsion, John De Worsion, and an infant De Worsion as living in the Yarrington house on Bond Street. Later that year John A. Worsham the gambler moved back to Richmond and lived with his wife Annette—to whom he had been married since at least 1866—until she died in 1874 and he in 1878.[5]

The other version—told by Archer to his second wife's nephew—a close friend and reliable witness—has it that Archer was Collis's son. Collis met Arabella, according to this version, while staying at the Yarrington boardinghouse in Richmond in about 1868 and brought her to New York to look after his invalid wife, at which time they fell in love and had a child. Her claim that she was married to Mr. Worsham was purely a cover-up to legitimize Archer in the public view.[6]

Arabella stuck to the Worsham story. She used the name "Belle D. Worsham" exclusively in correspondence and legal documents—including her many letters to Collis—from 1870 until she and Collis were married, and she had the monogram "BDW" embroidered on her household effects, some of which (like card table covers) are still extant. It is possible that the wrong Mr. Worsham has been the subject of close scrutiny. However, the version with Collis as the father depends entirely on what Archer told his wife's nephew, presumably what he had learned from his mother; there is no other evidence to support it. It is a wise child who knows his own father, and a mother may be excused for trying to make her son happy. I suppose that most people would feel more comfortable believing that Collis was Archer's father, since comfort is an important element of belief. I am not sure where the truth lies, but the Worsham version seems more likely.

Arabella's life after the birth of Archer is recorded in a good many letters. A private letter, unindexed in Collis's papers, sent from "B. D. Worsham" in New York to Collis, also in New York, is of special interest in revealing something about the spirit of her relationship with Collis. It was written on November 10, 1871, when she was probably nineteen years of age and Archer twenty months old:

> Mr. Huntington
>
> I am so worried that I dont know what to do, and I am going to ask your advice and assistance again. I have received another letter from home [in Texas] stating that my little boy is still very sick, and mama thinks I had better come on as early as possible. I am ashamed to ask you but you have been so kind that I shall impose on your good nature again. I want you to give me a ticket to Texas, and assist me in getting the family back here in the spring, for I know they will starve out there. I am asking a great deal Mr Huntington but you are the only friend I have in the world. If you will do this for me I shall never be able to express my gratitude, but if you can think of anything that will be better for me to do, I am perfectly willing to agree to any proposition you may make.
>
> Respectfully
> B. D. Worsham[7]

A remarkable letter, almost incredible if this is the mother writing to the father of their sick child.

In the 1870s, Belle began trading in real estate and securities in New

York on her own account. Presumably she made her start with capital supplied by Collis. She seems to have decided her transactions on her own, however, and she increased her funds successfully. In 1877 she bought four lots on Fifty-fourth Street for $156,000; the next year two more followed for $33,000, and in 1880 she purchased another two for $27,500, leveraging her funds with mortgages. She sold a part of these properties to William H. Vanderbilt in 1883 and the remainder to John D. Rockefeller in 1884 for a grand total of a little over $2 million.[8] She had a securities account in Collis's office, as did many other friends and relatives: in 1880, for example, she bought a thousand shares of Central Pacific stock at a market value of some $80,000 and in 1881 five hundred shares of Chesapeake and Ohio stock worth about $40,000, which she turned over quickly at a profit. She was scrupulous in sending checks—drawn on her account at the Metropolitan Trust Company in New York—to cover her purchases.[9] When she had need of legal counsel—as she did with mortgages on her properties and rental agreements—she dealt with Collis's attorneys, Bangs and Stratton, and often corresponded with them through Collis.[10] She and Archer were in Texas in 1877, and she went to Europe in the summer of 1877, presumably with Archer—as we learn from a cable from Collis to her in Paris. When she returned, Collis took care of her customs bill, and she sent him her check in repayment, along with a letter of thanks.[11]

This brief summary of her activities during her early life would be incomplete without remarking on one matter that was presumably striking to all who met her: her appearance. She was extraordinarily beautiful. A small oval painting made during these years reveals a lovely appealing face and soft dark hair parted in the middle and brushed to either side. She is shown attractively dressed, with a black lace scarf over the white collar of her dress.

When Edward's daughter Elizabeth was visiting Paris in 1901 with her mother, she wrote her father that "we luncheoned with Aunt Belle today." She put into a single sentence the essence of her perception of Belle: "I never saw anyone with so much magnetism." Elizabeth was a bright young woman of twenty. Archer, age thirty-one, was also present at the lunch along with his wife, Helen. Elizabeth went on to say that

"Archer has it [magnetism] too. He took us for an automobile ride and I never had so much fun in my life."[12]

Four years later, Elizabeth wrote to her fiancé, Brockway Metcalf, from New York that Aunt Belle was coming for tea the next day and that Elizabeth "will be glad to have a little chat. She is dear—very responsive and a very cultivated woman." She mentioned three qualities she wished to have, apparently still thinking of Belle: "I'd like to be beautiful. I would like to be magnetic. I would like to be witty."[13] Elizabeth wrote to Brockway again the next day to report on the visit. "Aunt Belle came to tea," she wrote, "and she is so sweet. She is very romantic herself, though she certainly wouldn't give one that impression at a glance." Belle told Elizabeth that she had her heart set on giving them a Tiffany tea set ("one that Tiffany only made one of a year") for a wedding present; Elizabeth was a little doubtful that she would like the floral design of the chrysanthemum pattern; "but, ginger, she has such excellent taste am sure I wouldn't tire of it. And dear, isn't she sweet to want to give it to us." Brockway had not met Belle, and Elizabeth assured him that "she is dear. Know you will like her. And bright."[14]

Another view of Belle is available in her own letters to Edward's sister Carrie. In reading them, we should keep in mind that Carrie and Elizabeth were probably the two women closest to Edward in temperament and affection. Ten of those letters have survived, all written in Belle's hand, between 1888 and 1909.[15] Carrie was midway in age between Belle and Archer, and she was a close friend and correspondent of both. She and her mother often visited Belle and Collis in New York, and Carrie was married in their house in 1896, with Collis giving the bride away.

Belle's letters to Carrie reveal a friendly, direct, and spontaneous nature, with special affection for family members. "Kiss Harriet for me," she writes. "I am very fond of her." At first she signed herself, "Affectionately, Aunt Arabella," but that soon became "Affectionately, Belle." She regularly urged Carrie to come for a visit, and she shared the little details of daily life, like her enjoyment of riding her bicycle in good weather in the country and the continuing interest of Collis, whom she called "Papa," in wall building. She told about the marriage of Clara and Prince Hatzfeldt in London in 1889, including the visits of the German nobility and the dinners, one of which was "at the house of that very ogre Mr. [Leslie] Stephen"—whose daughter, then seven, would achieve fame as Virginia Woolf. "You can imagine all this is slightly tiring. I never want to marry off another girl. Thank fortune Archer is a boy."[16]

After Collis's sudden death in August 1900, she grieved for many years. In December 1900 she wrote Carrie that "I find it very hard to realize that I shall never see or hear that dear face and voice again. Time as yet has helped me very little, but I get through the days one by one."[17]

Her family grieved with and for her. Harriet wrote to Carrie in September 1900 that "my heart aches for dear Belle. I do want to see her more than I can tell. I have her in my heart a great deal of the time, nights as well as day. Give her my dearest love." She had not written herself because she did not have the "words that would or could express my love and sympathy for her loss as well as mine also. You know how much I loved your uncle."[18]

Five years later, Elizabeth told Brockway that Belle's planned trip to San Francisco to close up the house there for good was, in prospect, "a hard trip for her because she and uncle Collis were last there together."[19] Belle remained anxious for some time. She worried especially about Archer, who had appendicitis in 1902: "Fortunately his strong constitution and willpower saved him and now in the interval it is not so very serious. Still I cannot help feeling dreadfully worried, for I have had all the sorrow and anxiety that I can possibly bear."[20] In 1909, she wrote to Carrie, before going away, that "it is like death itself to leave. I am not well, and every one thinks this trip will help me." She felt abandoned: "Do write to me, Carrie Dear, and tell me all the news. You will be the only one who will take the trouble to write."[21]

She came to express more and more firmness and resolution in her letters to Carrie. She believed that self-control could be obtained by personal effort. Less than a month before Collis's death, she wrote to Carrie: "You remember the Indian or Hindoo Philosophy—well there is something in it. You can obtain self control that no loss nor disappointment can make you suffer. You can give up any thing—and it makes you considerate, unselfish, and forgiving. I need all this and so I am going on with it."[22] She felt that others should follow this prescription. "What is the trouble with Edward," she wrote to Carrie in 1902. "I heard he was well and strong and having a gay time in Los Angeles. [A touch of envy in this comment?] Give him my love and tell him to get well. All his troubles are imaginary. With his power to live, work, and do good, nothing should trouble him. I will try and write him on some business matters tonight."[23]

With her strong nature, she wanted to have things match her conception of how they should be, sometimes to the point of obsessiveness. When Edward was supervising work on the San Francisco house of Collis and Belle in 1896, Collis sent from New York endless lists of detailed requirements about plumbing, sewers, windows, moving things, and the like. "Belle, you know," he wrote in explanation, "is exceedingly particular."[24] This trait did not bother Edward, as he was the same way—and so was Collis—when it came to any project in which he was closely involved.

After Collis's death, Belle did not always have her wishes fulfilled. A year after Collis's death, Edward wrote to Carrie that "Archer is at home [with Belle] all of the time. Is very nice to me, but I fear Belle has few things her own way, as you know he is very arbitrary."[25] Belle traveled with Archer and Helen for long periods of time in Spain, France, and Italy. Early in 1902, Lucy Cone Gayles, a New York friend of Belle's, wrote Edward about how things were going for Belle in Rome with Archer and Helen. Carrie Campbell, Belle's secretary, had written her saying that "Mrs. Huntington is far from well—nervous, depressed, and homesick." Mrs. Gayles went on to say that Carrie Campbell "never mentions Archer nor Helen. I fear neither of them are any comfort to dear Mrs. Huntington. They are too selfish. I wish they would stay in Europe and let her come home."[26] A few months after Belle returned from Europe, George E. Miles—the ex-secretary of Collis and Edward, now in the New York office—wrote Edward about a business call he had made on her at her house. "I had quite a long talk with Mrs. Huntington the other day and thought she was both looking and feeling better, although the same causes and effects that you know about are still ruling, and ruling still in disagreeable ways."[27]

Archer's wry sense of humor was sometimes hard on his mother.

Helen wrote to Carrie about Archer's Christmas gift to his mother in 1896 of a marmoset—"an odd little beast: no larger than a rat, with a tail like a squirrel, a face like an Irishman, and the temper of the Evil One himself." Helen wrote of Belle, "I wish you could have seen her face when he was presented—such real horror and dismay—such a forced and sickly joy! However, he made a lot of fun all Xmas day and after—so fulfilled his mission."[28]

Archer was the focus of his mother's deepest affection, and she showed her love in many ways. One was financial. She began establishing trusts for him in 1897, and within the next two years she had set up five at the Union Trust Company of New York with a total value of half a million dollars—a worthwhile sum for a young man still in his twenties.[29] That sum was doubled in value by the legacies under the will of Collis, after his death in 1900.[30]

Her thoughtfulness was evident in the fact that she always gave the members of the Huntington family, like Harriet and Carrie, gifts at Christmas, and she brought presents from Europe for the children. In 1905 Elizabeth reported to Brockway from New York that "Aunt Belle sent to mother . . . a huge bunch of American Beauty roses" to welcome her to New York and that "they are more perfect than ours in California have been the last five years."[31]

Her generosity was most conspicuous in her major philanthropic gifts, all of which were either in memory of Collis or in furtherance of an interest of Archer's. Her benefactions in honor of Collis during these years included $250,000 to the Harvard Medical School for the Collis P. Huntington Laboratory for pathology and bacteriology; to the Tuskegee Normal Institute, she bequeathed Huntington Hall (a dormitory for girls) and the Collis P. Huntington Memorial Building for the academic departments; to the Hampton Institute, she bequeathed the Collis P. Huntington Memorial Library; to the City of San Francisco, she deeded her Nob Hill property (valued at $275,000) for a park or children's playground named for Collis—and, as she sharply wrote to the mayor, to "be used so far as possible for the pleasure of the women and children of San Francisco" and not "as a loafing place for undesirable citizens."[32] Her principal gifts in support of Archer's interests included, in 1909, land in New York at 156th Street and Broadway (valued at $250,000) for a new home for the American Geographical

Society; and, in 1910, Velazquez's portrait of the Duke of Olivares, which she had bought the year before for $400,000, to the Hispanic Society of America.[33]

She was also generous with herself. The seven-strand pearl necklace that so impressed Leslie when Belle wore it to the dinner at the California Club in 1914 was indeed large and impressive. Belle had bought it in 1906, and it consisted of 497 large pearls in strands of from 47 to 93 pearls each; the pearls weighed more than eleven grams each, or a total of more than twelve pounds just for the pearls.[34] She bought many other expensive pieces of jewelry for herself. For example, from Tiffany in Paris she bought in 1903 about a dozen items—like a diamond corsage ornament, a black pearl scarf pin, and a black pearl and diamond bracelet—for some $55,000, and on occasion a grander piece, like an emerald and diamond brooch in 1912 for $20,000.[35] She always wore elegant designer clothes of silk or fine wool, often with fur, and always in black after Collis's death. She was usually described as "handsome," but we recall the problem of obesity with which she struggled, losing more than fifty pounds in 1896–97 (see chap. 7). Photographs of her in newspapers, after Collis's death in 1900 when she was nearly fifty, reveal a rather heavy woman with broad shoulders, broad hips, and prominent lower cheeks.[36] In 1907, she bought a mansion in Paris for her use. It was an historic eighteenth-century building on the avenue Gabriel, with many trees and gardens, once occupied by the Empress Eugénie and later rebuilt by Baron de Hirsch. While it was being thoroughly renovated for her use, Belle retained the Royal Suite at the Hotel Bristol.[37] She, Archer, and Helen did not travel light when they went to Europe. When they returned to New York in 1910, the party had three hundred pieces of baggage.[38]

There were occasional rumors that Arabella had been "socially ostracized" by Mrs. Leland Stanford in San Francisco.[39] After Collis's death the rumor was repeated that, in San Francisco and New York, "exclusive society had turned a cold shoulder to her in other days."[40] What gave life to these rumors was the bitter hostility between Mrs. Stanford and the Crockers on the one hand and Collis on the other just before and after the death of Stanford, Collis's manipulation to make himself president of the Southern Pacific, and his remarks about politics that were taken as adverse reflections on Stanford. Mrs. Stanford and the Crockers did whatever they could to thwart any recognition that might come to Collis or Arabella. Collis, Mrs. Stanford, and the Crockers vied with one another in vindictiveness, and Arabella was caught in the crossfire. In fact, she does not seem to have relished what was called high society. She was content to live quietly and enjoy the society of family and a few close friends. One New York paper perceived this when it reported, in 1908, that "Mrs. Huntington's tastes are quiet and her mode of living has been rather reserved."[41]

She did not show much interest in social issues of the day. When she returned to the United States from Europe on November 2, 1909, she was interviewed about her reflections on women's suffrage, which was becoming an important public question. " 'Have you become interested in "votes for women"?' she was asked. 'Not very much,' she replied with a smile; 'though I believe that in the cases of property rights and educational matters women should vote. Yet I am a large property owner, and manage my own estate, but I do not think I would vote if I could.' "[42]

Not everyone was charmed by her. James Henry Duveen, art dealer and cousin of Joseph, told of a telephone conversation with her shortly before World War I in which she screamed at him in what he suggested was an ill-mannered way. She responded, in "an icily cold voice: 'What do you dare to insinuate?' 'I will insinuate,' I said, 'and even state categorically, that Mrs. Huntington allows herself manners which even the Empress of Germany cannot afford!' " With that, he hung up on "this haughty and ill-mannered millionairess."[43] She had an imperious side and sometimes seemed rude or arrogant.

Public perception of Arabella differed from the view of those who had personal contact with her. An obituary notice observed, probably accurately, that she was "thought a rather haughty woman, keeping herself aloof from the herd." But the account goes on beyond the public view: "In reality she was very warmhearted and sympathetic. To her intimates she unbent to an amazing degree. These, and members of her immediate family, knew her as a true woman, feminine to the core."[44]

Nearly all Belle's letters include a comment about her own poor health. Here are samples from four of her first six extant letters to

Carrie: "I have been ill with neuralgia" (1888); "I have been ill for several days—not allowed to eat anything but hope soon to be well" (1893); "I am not well—have had a cold that won't go away—I cannot go out" (1900); "I was very seriously ill for several days" (1901).[45]

Her friends and relations confirm that she was frequently ill. Carrie Campbell wrote in 1902 that she was "far from well—nervous and depressed," and in the next year reported that "she has been very ill again" and unable to reply to a letter from her lawyer.[46] In 1903 Edward wrote his mother that Belle "has been troubled much with Rheumatism and tried the hot oven treatment that you were so successful with but got very little benefit from it."[47]

Belle had recurrent health problems during the sixteen years she and Collis were married, from 1884 to 1900, as I have earlier outlined (see chap. 7). And they continued. She had to postpone her trip to Europe in the spring of 1909 because of ill health, and in October she returned hastily from France to the United States because of the threat of appendicitis: "I returned because I did not want French physicians attending me, preferring to be taken care of by an American physician in whom I have great faith."[48] As it turned out, an operation was not required, at least not for almost two more years, when it was performed by American physicians in her own home on May 3, 1911 (see chap. 13).

She frequently suffered from "hard colds," as she did—according to Edward's report—just before their wedding (see chap. 13). And on most of her trips to Europe, she spent time taking "the treatment" at baths; even on their honeymoon in 1913, Edward reported to Carrie that they were going "to Lausanne where we will remain two or three weeks for Belle's treatment."[49]

Her most serious physical problem was her poor vision. I have already given an account of her partial blindness in the 1890s, the visits to specialists in the United States and Europe, and the conclusion that she could retain some vision but that her condition was irreversible (see chap. 7). About 1903, her secretary began writing her personal letters for her, and in a few years had to write them all. She continued to have limited vision for the rest of her life.

In 1910, when a blue Persian carpet was being laid in the salon of her Paris house, "she loudly insisted," according to the art dealer Edward

Fowles, "that it was not blue—but black! I now appreciate that she was suffering from an advanced stage of glaucoma, and was therefore unable to perceive certain colours." Fowles went on to tell of his dealing with her:

> As far as I could judge, she seemed to spend the greater part of her day seated at a card table in this immense room, which was palatial in its loftiness, but wholly bereft of comfort.
>
> I later discovered another extraordinary fact: that she was practically blind. It was, apparently, for this reason that she customarily walked arm-in-arm with her Scottish companion, Miss Campbell. From time to time, she asked me to write out the cheques with which she made her payments to tradesmen. I would sit at her desk, find the brass key that opened it, take out the cheque book and, when I had filled it in as directed, place her hand in the correct position for her signature. On such occasions, she would sometimes unbend a little; her austere bearing, accentuated by the very thick glasses which she always wore, became a trifle less formidable. She had been thrown on her head from a bicycle when a young woman, and it had affected her eyesight. She confessed to being able to see vaguely—as though through a heavy mist. Sometimes she would remove the heavy glasses and throw her head back so that her fine complexion and beautiful teeth could be admired. Everything was arranged for her convenience: her handbag was attached with a very fine steel chain to the belt which encircled her waist; inside the bag, her keys were similarly attached.[50]

In 1922, Belle's financial officer wrote to the United States Treasury Department that she could not sign a certain document as she "does not see well enough to write."[51] The next year, A. Hyatt Mayor—the nephew of Archer's second wife, Anna Hyatt—had lunch privately with Belle in the New York house and reported her showing him her picture gallery. As they stood in front of "this Vermeer," she told in detail about how she had acquired it in a Paris collection. "We were standing, I remember very well," recalled Mayor, "in front of a Reynolds. The Vermeer had been moved after she lost her sight." He said that "her deep gray gaze, like Uncle Archer's, imposed and alarmed. But she saw nothing, for glaucoma had blinded her before there were remedies."[52]

One anecdote seems to contradict the view of her poor vision. The art dealer Germain Seligman told of a visit Belle paid to his business in 1923. He showed her a little Falconet statue of Venus:

> Looking at me reproachfully through thick-lensed glasses, she said, "You really shouldn't go to so much trouble for me. You know my sight is so bad that I can hardly see anything." Whereupon she leaned forward for a closer view of the little figure, not over a foot high over all, and exclaimed, "What a lovely thing. Isn't it a shame that the little finger on the left hand is broken!" I couldn't help bursting into laughter, as I congratulated her on her bad eyesight, for the whole hand was not over a half inch long. Almost before I did she threw her head back in a hearty laugh.[53]

The anecdote can probably be understood more accurately as an example of her vivacity than of her good vision: she could see a bit at very close range through her "thick-lensed glasses," and her tactile sense was intact. Her inability to see well except at close range probably created the public perception of her as a haughty woman who held herself aloof.

Her poor health doubtless contributed to her occasional depression. She sometimes described herself as nervous and depressed. Or she begged Carrie to bring her two small children to stay for a while in New York: "The children will cheer me up."[54]

After Belle and Collis were married, they sent out an engraved Tiffany wedding announcement with the following somewhat unconventional text:

Collis P. Huntington,
Arabella D. Worsham,
Married,
Saturday, July twelfth, 1884.
New York.[55]

They had been married in the parlor of Belle's house at 4 West Fifty-fourth Street at ten o'clock in the morning by the Reverend Henry

Ward Beecher, whose church Collis had attended and with whom he had a cordial relationship. Mrs. Beecher and a friend of Beecher's were waiting in the next room, and the friend later recalled that Beecher, in speaking of the match of Arabella and Collis, said "he believed she would make Mr. Huntington an excellent wife. She was just the woman for him."[56]

Collis's first wife, Elizabeth, had died of cancer about nine months earlier. Collis had known Arabella and other members of her family—the Yarringtons—for at least the preceding ten or fifteen years. Two of her brothers had been working for Collis for some years.

John D. Yarrington had various jobs with Collis's railroads. He was a conductor, and he became the superintendent in charge of several divisions, most notably the Lexington Division of the Chesapeake and Ohio Railroad beginning about 1880. There are dozens of business letters extant between him and Collis, both before and after the marriage of Collis and Belle.[57] Yarrington answered Collis's queries on the value of property, how to reduce expenses, and how to increase earnings. In the 1870s, he sent Collis $50 a month from West Virginia out of his salary to be invested for him. "Kind Friend," his letters began, and they ended "Gratefully yours."[58] In his replies Collis made an occasional reference to his family, such as this one on January 2, 1880: "I saw your mother a few days since, and she said your brother Richard and sister Belle were quite well."[59] And Yarrington frequently sent regards to his family through Collis: "Kindly remember me to my folks if you see them soon."[60]

John Yarrington had about the same level of responsibility as did H. E. Huntington at that time, and there was a little competition between them. Yarrington wrote to Collis in January 1887 on returning to Kentucky after a visit to Belle and Collis in New York: "I have heard several rumors which make me feel like Mr. H. E. Huntington desired to operate the River Road when it is finished, and I feel like again requesting that you kindly consider my claim to operate it." He made his claim in terms of length of service and an implied promise: "Kindly remember my long and faithful service. While you did not promise me when I was there that I should have that Road, I thought you meant as much." Moreover, he adds a word in favor of Edward's other abilities. It was because he was "satisfied Mr. H. E. H. can be of more service to you otherwise" that he ventured to put himself forward. "Please excuse my having said anything on the subject if it is not pleasant to you."[61] The River Road was a new line between Ashland and Covington, Kentucky; Edward was in charge of constructing it, and he agreed about its operation. "I presume you will want it managed," he wrote to Collis, "by Capt. Yarrington, as the two roads can be run jointly and save some expenses."[62] Edward continued to run the Kentucky Central.

John Yarrington continued his effective railroad career through the 1880s, and he was also an investor in land—some jointly with Edward, some jointly with Belle—a buyer of railroad bonds, and inventor of the Yarrington station signal. Illness forced him to give up work for a few months in 1886 and go to the Yarrington family home in San Marcos, Texas, for a rest, but he was soon back and in 1887 was made second vice-president of the holding company called the Newport News and Mississippi Valley Company, and in charge of the Big Sandy Railroad. When Collis decided in 1890 to reduce his railroad investments in the East, Yarrington sold his securities at Collis's suggestion and resigned his position as second vice-president on May 1, 1890. Edward was temporarily elected to the position in his place. Yarrington bought the Lakeview Stock Farm in Lexington, Kentucky, and spent a decade breeding, training, and selling horses. When Collis died in 1900, John Yarrington was one of only twenty persons invited to attend the family funeral at the Huntington house in New York.[63]

Richard M. "Dick" Yarrington, another brother of Belle's, also had business connections with Collis. As early as 1878 he was supervising lumber deliveries in Austin, Texas, only twenty-five miles from the Yarrington home in San Marcos.[64] In the 1880s, he was managing a farm owned by Collis in Valhalla, Westchester County, New York, that included cows and chickens.[65] He was part owner, with Belle, of Belle Farm in Hays County, Texas, near San Marcos; this plot of some two thousand acres had been deeded to "Mrs. Belle D. Worsham," but three of the sixteen lots were marked on the official map as belonging to R. M. Yarrington.[66] He also had an investment account in Collis's office; Collis provided free advice, brokerage service, and security-holding facilities in his New York office for a number of relatives and friends. Richard owned $4,000 in Newport News bonds and $11,000 of the Big Sandy bonds; like his brother, he sold the latter at Collis's suggestion.[67]

After the wedding of Belle and Collis, Belle's mother was a regular visitor in their New York home. Indeed, she appears to have lived mostly with them for the remaining five years of her life. Willard's wife, Marie, provided an interesting sidelight on Mrs. Yarrington and Belle in her account to Harriet of an October 1885 visit she paid to the Huntingtons at their country house in Throggs Neck, Westchester County, with her daughter Edith, then a little under three. "I did not allow Edith around," she reported to Harriet, "unless someone asked to see her. Mrs. C. P. H. said one morning, 'Marie, I think it is a shame the way you keep Edith out of sight. I never see the child unless I ask for her.' Mrs. Yarrington spoke up and said, 'I think she is very sensible not to have the child always stuck under a person's nose. That is the way I brought my children up—to be kept in the nursery until they were asked for. But I notice mothers as a rule do not do so now.' Mrs. Yarrington and I became very good friends. In fact, she grew quite confidential before I left."[68] One wishes that Marie had shared some of Mrs. Yarrington's confidences, but at least her account gives a hint about Belle's early family life.

In July 1889, while the family was in the country at Throggs Neck, Mrs. Yarrington became ill and, after a short time, died. She was carefully attended by the Huntingtons' physician, who made "extraordinary efforts" on her behalf. When the bill came, Collis characteristically complained that his charges were excessive. The physician countered by saying that "you are, I am certain, aware that almost all of my time was taken up in attendance upon the deceased lady; that, by request, I neglected my business in New York City and elsewhere in order to devote myself especially to this case. And that my extraordinary efforts were recognized and appreciated, at the time, by every member of your family."[69] But Mrs. Yarrington had died, and that was reason enough for Collis to complain.

A family member of Belle's who was very much alive was her son Archer. He was fourteen when his mother married Collis, and he took full part in family activities. Collis adopted him, at least informally, and always spoke of him as "my son." Two years before the marriage, Collis undertook to find a suitable tutor for him. Collis asked his friend Caroline G. Reid—Mrs. Sylvanus Reid, who was just trying to start a college in New York—for advice, and she wrote to five persons to try to line up some likely candidates.[70] Collis wrote the candidates, Belle made her choice, and Collis informed them of her decision. The mother of one of the unsuccessful candidates sent her deep regrets to Collis that her son had not been chosen.[71] Archer's education was carried on under the direction of a series of tutors, and his mother joined him in at least some of the sessions. It was perhaps in this manner, coupled with her frequent trips to Europe, that she gained the reputation for learning and fluency in foreign languages. His tutors included a professor of Arabic at Yale and other distinguished academic scholars, and Archer showed particular proficiency in modern and classical European languages. After the marriage of Belle and Collis, Archer traveled with them to Europe, and he spent much time there on his own, especially in Spain, searching with the aid of assistants for books and manuscripts relating to the history of the Moors in Spain and to the Spanish hero the Cid. He bought the eight-thousand-volume Spanish library of Professor W. I. Knapp of the University of Chicago for $21,000 and combined it with his own collection.[72] He published a volume of poems in 1894, a history of the Moors in Spain, an edition of the *Poema del Cid* in 1897, and other studies. He was given honorary master of arts degrees by Yale in 1897 and Harvard in 1904, honorary doctorates by Columbia in 1907 and 1908, and membership in Spanish academies. In 1904 he founded the Hispanic Society of America and gave it land, a building, and an endowment.[73] When he was twenty, he was made a life member of the New-York Historical Society. Collis offered him, before he was twenty-five, the Newport News Drydock and Shipbuilding Company to manage, but Archer declined on the ground that he had no taste for business.[74]

Archer was a handsome, athletic man of six feet four inches and 260 pounds. He took an active part in sports. When he was sixteen, he was given a sailing schooner, the *Elfin,* and a membership in the New York Yacht Club.[75] His allowance for personal expenses when he was in his early twenties was $1,000 a month.[76] In 1895 he married, in London,

Helen Manchester Gates, the daughter of Collis's youngest sister, Ellen, and Isaac Gates, Collis's business associate and office manager. She was talented, sharing her mother's interest in writing. She had earlier married Thomas B. Criss, a young associate of her father's and Collis's; she and Criss had had a child, whom she gave up to its father in connection with their divorce and her emotional breakdown. In 1895 Helen had gone to London with a companion, and Archer with Collis and Belle; to everyone else the wedding, in St. George's Church, Hanover Square, was a surprise. When they all got back to New York, Collis bought the Waterbury Mansion in Pelham Park at $200,000 for the young couple.[77]

Archer lived an active life, traveling, reading, writing, and working for and supporting worthy activities like the American Numismatic Society (president, 1905–10) and the American Geographical Society (president, 1907–11)—in addition to his prime love, the Hispanic Society of America.

He was extremely important to his mother. He spent a lot of time with her in New York, in the country, and in Europe, and she had a deep admiration for him.

But her expressions of affection for Archer struck some people as slightly comic. Edward Fowles, the art dealer, recounted his first meeting with Archer in Belle's Paris house in about 1909, when Archer was thirty-nine and Belle about fifty-seven: "I met her son quite unexpectedly. One day, when I was upstairs, she thrust her head out of a door and called out 'Where's my baby?' To my surprise, a heavily bearded man ran up the stairs, shouting in response, 'Here I am, Mamma.' It was Archer Huntington, her son by her first marriage."[78]

After Belle and Collis married in 1884, they began to live the life we think of as typical of very rich Americans of their time. They lived lavishly at each of their several regular residences, traveled extensively and regally, and availed themselves of the very best goods and services.

Belle left her own house at 4 West Fifty-fourth Street and moved into Collis's establishment at 65 Park Avenue, which she did not like—"gloomy old 65," she called it. Both of them did a good deal of buying, selling, and swapping of real estate in the next few years. Belle had recently renovated and redecorated her house on West Fifty-fourth Street in an extremely elaborate and expensive style; she then sold part of her land to William H. Vanderbilt for $60,000 and swapped her house (valued at about $600,000) with John D. Rockefeller for nine lots on Fifth Avenue and Seventy-second Street. Her house was occupied until 1938, when it was torn down to make space for the garden of the Museum of Modern Art. (Three rooms of the house are on exhibit in museums; John D. Rockefeller, Jr., gave her bedroom and dressing room to the Museum of the City of New York and her Moorish parlor to the Brooklyn Museum.)

Among other real estate transactions, Collis deeded the house at 65 Park Avenue to her; she bought the country estate of Frederick C. Havemeyer called the Homestead with a hundred acres of land at a cost of several hundred thousand dollars after alterations and redecoration. Collis bought a house at 5 West Fifty-first Street and she improved it before they gave up on living there and sold it to Andrew Carnegie. Collis bought six lots on Fifth Avenue and Fifty-seventh Street; Belle bought the Colton house on Nob Hill in San Francisco for $275,000; and he bought Pine Knot Lodge in the Adirondacks as a summer retreat and had a small railroad named the Raquette Lake Railway built to serve them and their several neighbors, including J. P. Morgan, who was of the "decided opinion" that the bonds of their railway company "should be engraved."[79] All of this was accomplished in less than eight years.[80]

They decided to build their own mansion on the Fifty-seventh Street lots, and architect George B. Post was engaged to add another palace to this area of Vanderbilts, Whitneys, and the like. The work moved along under Belle's watchful attention, which Post occasionally objected to. He wrote to Collis about her direction to alter the paneling in the staircase. "The change suggested will throw much of the panelling out of centres as far as the axis of the staircase is concerned," Post said. "The result will be unarchitectural and therefore inartistic. Of course I am prepared to do whatever Mrs. Huntington wishes but in self-protection would like a written order."[81] They approached the distinguished Elihu Vedder to paint the ceiling decorations. Vedder wrote somewhat apprehensively to his friend Annie Fields (Mrs. James T. Fields), "I am to meet the formidable Mrs. Huntington." However, they met and agreed, and his work was a notable feature of the building.[82] The exterior of the palace, a heavy Romanesque masonry structure, was almost universally condemned for its homely exterior design, and Collis lived there only reluctantly. But they moved in, and this mansion became their city place. Collis said that "Mrs. Huntington and I talked over the plans and told the architect, Mr. Post, what we wanted, and he elaborated our ideas. Of course I left most of it to Mrs. Huntington. The only room in the house where I am in supreme control is my library. That will be fixed up according to my notions."[83] The house featured a bathing pool for Arabella, with water that went first through a filter and was then mixed with a spray of cologne, "making its limpid sweetness as long drawn out as the bather cares to have. The name of the bath at home is 'Diana's Pool.'" Flowers surrounded the pool, with palms along the steps down to it. The flooring was marble with inset strips of blue tile, but Turkish rugs were laid entirely around the pool "for fear the chill of the marble should penetrate the white fur slippers of the bather." It was called "the most famous bath in the world, a bath known in Europe as well as in America."[84]

For country life, they went to the Homestead, and for rough living to Pine Knot. They also maintained a house on Nob Hill in San Francisco, and they traveled to Europe frequently. Wherever they were, they lived in style. On board ship, they normally occupied the Royal Suite. Her dutiable purchases abroad were heavy, and on nearly every return to the United States she set a record for the year in duty payments: in 1910 she paid $48,000 duty on clothes, personal effects, and small art objects.[85] In San Francisco, the regular household staff included nine full-time persons headed by a butler and a housekeeper, with salaries of $307.50 per month plus room and board.[86] In the East, after Collis's death, she had nine automobiles registered in her name in 1907—the largest number of licenses that had ever been granted to one individual in New York.[87]

The activity most relevant to the later life of H. E. Huntington was the acquisition of works of art. In the thirty years between Arabella's marriage to Collis in 1884 and her marriage to Edward in 1913, Collis and she formed an art collection of major importance. By the time of

Collis's death in 1900, theirs was one of the three or four most highly regarded private collections in the United States, and the art in the San Francisco house alone was said to be "by long odds the most valuable west of Chicago."[88] Edward was thoroughly aware of the steps they were taking to form this important collection, and their work provided a model for him, as his uncle had been a model for him throughout his business life.

Collis's first major recorded art purchase was Albert Bierstadt's large and impressive landscape painting *Donner Lake,* which he bought from the artist in 1873. "I am sure myself," Bierstadt wrote Collis, "that it is by far the best picture I have painted"; and even so he offered it to Collis for $20,000—$5,000 less than his "standard price for a large picture." Bierstadt, a longstanding friend of Collis's, hoped the Donner Lake picture would "prove a pleasant reminder of our joint work," and he was glad that Collis liked it.[89] Twelve years later Bierstadt saw the picture on exhibition in the Metropolitan Museum and was shocked at how yellow it had become—he hardly recognized it as his own coloring. He got permission from Collis to restore it to its original state, "without cost to you."[90]

Collis also had a close relation with Carleton Watkins, the premier photographer of Western scenes in the nineteenth century. Watkins had gone with Collis from Oneonta to California in 1849 and had learned photography in 1854; Collis was his main financial backer through most of his career while he was making his superb photographs of the Western landscape and trying to sell them in his San Francisco shop.[91]

Collis bought pictures from various dealers: three from Knoedler in New York in 1875; one from George W. Huffnagle in New Hope, Pennsylvania, in 1880; and several more from S. P. Avery in New York in 1879, 1880, and 1881.[92] These were all relatively minor purchases, like a Fromentin painting for $2,300 and two drawings by Copley Fielding at $250 each. Nevertheless, by 1880 his collection had gained some repute. George Barrie, the Philadelphia publisher of *Art Treasures of America,* edited by Edward Strahan, wrote to Collis on August 12, 1880, and said that "Mr. Collins informs me that you have an important collection. Would you kindly permit Mr. Strahan and me to see it at your convenience?" And in the next year, Barrie sent Collis a copy of their book and asked him to make corrections in it.[93]

I have not found any records of purchases of pictures by Arabella before she and Collis were married. Her major attention may have gone to the interior decoration of her houses, including furniture and wall hangings, which are the chief features of the Moorish parlor and the other rooms that have been preserved from her West Fifty-fourth Street house. After their marriage, she bought a few pieces on her own, including a group of Japanese art objects from C. T. Marsh and Company in 1890, two Boucher paintings from S. Chatain in Chicago in February 1893, three watercolors by Alfred Parsons through the American Art Association in New York in September 1893, and eighteen pictures by Meryou, Bartolozzi, Henderson, Ward, and others from H. Wunderlich in New York in August 1900.[94] She commissioned Roxina E. Sherwood in 1892 to do a portrait of her for $1,000 and a watercolor of Archer reading for $300; Belle returned the portrait with the request that her eyes be made darker and brighter, and the artist "improved" them as much as possible without making them "look unnatural."[95]

Their other art acquisitions between 1884 and 1900 all seem to be associated with Collis. He bought a number of recent French paintings from Durand-Ruel, Harnett's *Ease* from the person who had commissioned it, C. Hublin's *Reflection,* and a good many watercolors directly from such artists as L. Chialioa in Paris and R. M. Shurtleff in New York.[96] At the end of their trip to Europe in 1889, Collis wrote to Gates that he had bought "a few pictures, one or two pieces of old furniture and some tapestry" as well as two large modern paintings.[97] In 1892 he bought Gérard's *Josephine,* said to have been owned by Napoleon, from Gumps in San Francisco, and in 1898 two paintings by G. B. Piazzetta that he gave to Golden Gate Park in San Francisco.[98] A few individuals offered him paintings, like Gouverneur Morris, who suggested letting him have his Rico, Eastman Johnson, and Coomans at less than his cost because he had to give up his house.[99]

Doubtless Arabella was involved in most of the purchases, though the records do not mention it. One dealer, Albert G. Sudlow, made it plain that he was interviewed by the two of them together when he came to show them some glassware and paintings in 1896. "Where formerly Mrs. Huntington had been gracious and kind," Sudlow wrote to Collis, "she was only coldly polite" at "the time of my second visit to your house"—which led him to conclude "that someone had been assailing my character," like "some envious dealer."[100] They turned down many works attributed to famous painters, like Bennison's offer of a Rembrandt and a Van Dyck from Prague, Ehrich's collection of Dutch and Flemish paintings, a Raphael *Enthroned Virgin with Child,* and a Ribera.[101]

Collis's office kept a cumulative record of the money paid to dealers for paintings after January 19, 1872: the amount was $80,000 by 1880, $287,000 by 1889, $386,000 by 1891, and $582,000 by 1895.

An inventory of the art objects in the San Francisco house made in April 1897 includes some 245 pictures. Most of them were of little consequence. There were, however, etchings by Bonheur, Israels, Millet, Rubens, Gainsborough, and Lawrence. There were about fifty paintings, the best of which were hung in the music room, including two by Murillo valued at $75,000 each, one Hamilton at $50,000, one Gérard at $75,000, one Greuze at $50,000, one Daiz at $40,000, two Schneiders, two Rousseaus, and one Verboeckhoven. Edward made a list of the paintings in 1899 for insurance purposes and valued them at $638,500.[102]

The paintings that Collis liked best were hung in the New York house. The gems of the collection were on the walls of a large gallery. "It was Mr. Huntington's custom after breakfast," a friend reported, "to go into the art gallery and spend an hour with his pictures. There he received the men he wanted to talk with intimately. Nothing pleased him better than to find some one with a soul for color and art to whom he would show the treasures of his collection."[103] Those treasures included Lawrence's *Nature* (sometimes known as *The Calmady Children*) and Vermeer's *Lady with a Lute.* (Collis had never heard of Vermeer when he was shown the picture in Paris, but he liked it so much he bought it on the spot for two thousand francs.) The collection also had a large Corot and a Daubigny. Among the other works then highly valued were de Neuville's *The Spy,* Vibert's large narrative painting *The Missionary Story* (an early favorite of Collis's), Troyon's *The Lane,* Rico's *The Woodcutter,* von Pettenkofen's *Hungarian Peasant Wagon,* Heilbuth's *San Giovanni Laterano,* and Baudry's *Fortune and the Child.*[104]

Various friends asked to bring family members or visitors to see the collection. In 1885, John Leonard of the National Bank of Commerce asked leave for his wife and a friend to come; in 1886 Lottie Bushnell asked for a card for a couple—the bank president and his artist wife—from Bradford, Pennsylvania, and A. J. Hodder wanted a group of women artists and his wife to be admitted. In 1887 M. H. Fuller of the Union League Club sought to bring a friend from Paris, and George Foster Peabody asked permission for his esteemed friend the Honorable J. Fletcher Moulton, QC, MP, the "very distinguished scholar and connoisseur of art," to see the San Francisco collection.[105]

Museums began to ask Collis to lend pictures for special exhibitions. In 1891, the Portland Museum of Art in Maine asked to borrow three or four modern French paintings for a summer exhibition; in 1893 the Union League Club asked for Lawrence's *Nature* for a special exhibition; and for the World's Columbian Exposition in Chicago in the summer of 1893, the Huntingtons lent a Breton and a de Neuville.[106] However, Collis declined to lend the Lawrence *Nature* to the Guildhall in London for a show of British art in 1894 or 1895, despite a special request from the lord mayor of London, on the grounds that he did not want it to cross the Atlantic again.[107]

Collis and Belle both took pleasure in the collection. Collis said that "I have only two extravagances—I buy books and pictures. My greatest pleasure is in reading books; my next is in looking at my pictures."[108] It was widely reported that Collis personally selected the paintings in the collection and that he showed artistic discrimination in his selections.[109] The *New York Times* reported that

> Mr. Huntington did not buy his pictures through any individual dealer or under the advice or influence of any dealer, as so many large picture collectors of New York have done. He had a natural taste, which he cultivated by frequent studies of the pictures in museums and galleries.
>
> He was fond of attending large picture auction sales personally, and his tall, spare figure and the fine head, always covered with a small black silk skull cap, were familiar to all the art dealers and the public. . . .
>
> He seemed to be proud of his acquisitions and of the fact that he knew sufficient of the subject to be able to buy intelligently.[110]

It was often said that he was "an intense lover of art" and that he learned a great deal as he went along; "his knowledge grew with his experience, and if in the earlier stages of his work as a collector of art works he was imposed upon, he afterward bought pictures the merit and genuineness of which may not be questioned."[111]

Undoubtedly both Collis and Arabella learned from going to auctions, from reading books on art, and from the many dealers with whom they did business. They were not under the special tutelage of any one dealer, as Belle and Edward were with Joseph Duveen. (Belle was buying from J. J. Duveen as early as 1887, when Duveen returned a check that Collis had sent to cover Belle's account because she had already paid it herself.)[112] Collis also had a long relationship with the director of the Metropolitan Museum of Art, L. P. di Cesnola. Cesnola gave Collis and Belle private showings of important new acquisitions, and he persuaded Collis to buy material for the museum, like a collection of Greek antiquities for $3,000. He suggested that Collis buy for his "new house a genuine authentic oil painting by one of the great old masters of Italy Carlo Maratta"; Collis bought it for $5,000 but then gave it to the museum instead, an act for which Archer was elected "Patron of the Metropolitan Museum of Art in perpetuity." Before the new wing was opened in 1894, no provision had been made for what was to go into one picture gallery; Cesnola felt free to ask Collis for the loan of fifty or sixty of his "best pictures" and added, "I know Mrs. Huntington for my sake will favor my application to you."[113] It is easy to see why Collis in his will left all of the pictures in the collection to the Metropolitan Museum, after giving a life interest to Arabella and to Archer.[114]

It is not easy to see what Belle's role was in the formation of this collection. In 1909, after she had become a celebrated collector on her own, a syndicated newspaper story by E. J. Edwards assigned her an important early role: "Before the death of her husband she was his teacher in matters of art, and inspired him to set about making the collection which he started late in life."[115] I have found no evidence to support this view, which seems more like a well-deserved but somewhat irrelevant tribute to her standing as a collector in 1909. My impression is that she and Collis worked closely together to form the collection, though Collis carried on most of the decision-making correspondence. The collection legally belonged to him and he could and did dispose of it in its entirety in his will. That Collis received the public attention for the collection was mostly because of his great wealth and prominence and partly because of the gender discrimination of the times. The collection would now be thought of as having been large and important in reflecting the taste of the times, with its heavy concentration on Barbizon pictures, but not a major collection: it had only a few star pictures, like the Vermeer and possibly the Murillos, the Lawrence, and a few others.

After Collis's death in 1900, Belle increased the collection along its established lines by purchasing pictures, furniture, tapestries, and decorative objects. The collection suffered a major blow in 1906, when virtually everything in the San Francisco house was destroyed by the fire that followed the earthquake. The house, on 1020 California Street, was scarcely damaged by the earthquake itself, which struck between five and six on the morning of April 18: a pedestal was broken, a bust thrown down, and a few minor art objects harmed. At about eleven o'clock soldiers took over the area and required the inhabitants to leave. Soon afterward the fire reached the Huntington house, and it was destroyed between one and two o'clock. Edward arrived in San Francisco two days later, checked on the welfare of all family members, and investigated all family properties. Later he learned that several pictures had been cut from the frames, removed from the California Street house, and put in the hands of Miss Eleanor Connell in Oakland for safekeeping. Edward got Burke Holladay, Carrie's husband, to recover them and have Gumps pack them in San Francisco and ship them to Belle's New York house. The paintings saved were a Morland, a Van Marcke, a Troyon, and Turner's *A Street in Carthage*. Edward thought they should be insured for $75,000, but Belle had the insurance canceled. She was troubled that other pictures might have been stolen from the house, and Edward wrote to her in Paris and reassured her that this was not the case: "I am thoroughly satisfied that no pictures were taken from the house except those you received. I investigated the matter thoroughly and found from an outside party as well as Mrs. Foley [the housekeeper] that she did not leave the house until 11 am when she and all others in the neighborhood were driven away by the authorities and soldiers placed in charge to guard same. At one pm the house was in flames. Mrs. Foley locked all doors when she left."[116]

Arabella spent considerable time in London and Paris and formed a closer acquaintance with several art dealers, but chiefly Joseph Duveen and Jacques Seligmann. From them she learned about buying pictures and other art objects—and discovered for herself the spite, greed, and jealousy that existed among dealers. In 1910, Seligmann wrote her a bitter four-page letter in response to Duveen's criticism of some furniture Belle had bought from Seligmann: "Excuse me when I have to mention Mr. Joe Duveen's name, though I feel his conduct is reprehensible and it ought to be beneath my dignity to occupy myself with him. . . . Mr. Joe Duveen ought to be above petty jealousy; he seems unhappy that Mrs. Huntington buys something from Mr. Seligmann. . . . If Mr. Joe Duveen attacks the quality of the furniture, it is simply because he would be highly pleased, if you would return it to me, as this would give him a chance to sell you something else in its place."[117] She kept the furniture, and she continued with both dealers. It was through Duveen, however, that she was able to bring real distinction to her collection.

The turning point was the sale of the Rudolph Kann Collection in Paris in 1907. When Kann died and left his magnificent collection of tapestries, paintings, furniture, and other art objects to his three sisters and one brother (instead of giving it to the Louvre, as the art world had expected), the collection had to be sold to effect a distribution.[118] It was widely regarded as the greatest collection in private hands at the time. Duveen was able—with the help of Gimpel and Wildenstein, and after fancy maneuvering within the Duveen firm—to buy it for some $5 million. Although the collection had 161 paintings as well as other art objects, Duveen was particularly attracted by the eleven Rembrandts and the Boucher tapestries. Special customers were allowed the privilege of seeing the collection and buying the choicest items, as Duveen's tactic was to sell the most notable objects at very high prices to recover his costs quickly. Benjamin Altman bought four of the Rembrandts, while J. P. Morgan took eleven paintings and five other art objects for $1,275,000. Belle was right along with these two preeminent collectors.

She was brought to the Duveen Paris galleries by the Hungarian Count Baltazzi, who, according to the history of the Duveen firm, was given ten thousand pounds for interesting her in the Kann collection.[119]

Her actions fully repaid Duveen for his gift to Count Baltazzi. She spent about $2.5 million. Her purchases were splendid. The paintings that head the list are, in our estimation, probably Rembrandt's *Aristotle Contemplating the Bust of Homer* (then known as *The Savant* or *Portrait of a Savant with a Bust of Homer*) and *Portrait of Hendrickje Stoffels,* Hals's *Young Kooijmanszoon van Ablasserdam* and *Portrait of a Lady,* and Roger van der Weyden's *Madonna and Child* (then called *Virgin and Child*). The wisdom of her choices is supported by the opinions of some connoisseurs that the Rembrandt *Aristotle* is now the most famous painting in the Metropolitan Museum of Art in New York and that the Roger *Madonna and Child* is the most important painting in the Huntington Art Collections in San Marino. She bought almost all of the eighteenth-century French paintings in the collection, including works by Boucher, Fragonard, Greuze, Nattier, Watteau, and half a dozen others. She bought a large number of spectacular pieces of French furniture, almost all of it Louis XV—desks, consoles, writing tables, commodes, a fire screen, a sofa—with sumptuously rich detailing. She also acquired such important objects as a bronze bust of Louis XV by Lemoyne, a Louis XV clock, Chinese porcelain ewers, a Meissen lion and lioness, and a pair of Dresden statuettes.[120] It was two years later, in 1909, that Edward bought the five Beauvais tapestries from the Kann collection.

With Belle's Kann purchases, her collection took a new direction, and she was held in much higher esteem as a collector. Her Paris collection was extolled in an article in the *New York Times,* and in 1909 she was described elsewhere as one of the three great collectors of paintings in New York—the other two being J. P. Morgan and Benjamin Altman.[121] The Union League Club of New York exhibited eleven of her paintings in January 1909, including two by Hals and a Vermeer, Reynolds, Lawrence, Romney, Rembrandt, Troyon, Corot, Rousseau, and the Lathrop portrait of Collis. At the important Hudson-Fulton exhibition at the Metropolitan Museum in 1909–10, her collection was as fully represented as that of any other collector.[122]

Her reputation as a collector also soared in England. The first issue of *The Connoisseur* in 1908 began with a fifteen-page article with twenty illustrations about her collection, which was described respectfully as "rapidly assuming formidable proportions." The writer, J. Kirby Grant, singled out six paintings (by Troyon, Lawrence, Romney, Reynolds, Hals, and Vermeer) from her pre-Kann collection as "masterpieces that take high rank in the *oeuvre* of their creators." Now, "Mrs. Huntington's collection has gained new strength, and, indeed, has become one of historical importance, through an influx of priceless and unique works of art and craftsmanship from the great Rodolphe Kann Collection." Five paintings were described and pictured—the two by Rembrandt, the two by Hals, and the Roger—as well as ten pieces of furniture and seven objects of art. Her new additions were "pieces of such importance and universal fame that their departure from the Old World will be regarded as a calamity by students and art lovers in England and on the Continent of Europe."[123] She had become a major force in the world of art.

Fifteen

EARLY SUMMER OF 1914 was not the best of times for visiting Europe, and for the Huntingtons it was very nearly the worst of times.

Edward and Belle left California for the East on April 10, 1914, and arrived in New York in time to see Archer and Helen off. May 4, Edward wrote Carrie that "Helen and Archer arrived in Paris safely after a very pleasant trip." Edward reported that he was "in the hands of the Dentist and am feeling well again"; not so Belle: "she does not feel able to write," but Edward enclosed her check for $1,000 for the expenses of Carrie's daughter Helen for her first year at Wellesley.[1]

Soon both Edward and Belle felt well enough to travel, and on May 16 they left for Paris on the *George Washington* in a suite with five extra rooms to occupy their Chateau Beauregard just outside of Paris near Versailles.[2] The chateau had been the subject of several hundred letters and cables since they had taken a lease on it on October 13, 1913. A hundred-page inventory of all furnishings and objects was made and approved, with each item valued. Repairs, decorating (painting, curtains, upholstery), and improvements (a septic tank, drinking water installation, new bathrooms, roofing, new floors) all had to be planned and authorized—at a cost of about $100,000 to Edward. New staff was recruited and hired, thirteen for the inside and nineteen for the outside.[3]

Belle had had much experience renovating large residences, and she took pleasure in having their palace near Paris fixed up to her taste. But it fell to Edward to work out the details. Dozens of pages of pencil notes in his hand specified where household furnishings were to be relocated, what materials should be brought from or sent to New York, what servants were needed or had been hired (with salaries); he also prepared letters to lawyers and bankers and French governmental agencies, sketches of rooms to be altered, and full household cash accounts for the operation of the establishment with its farm and stables.[4]

The house was habitable when they arrived, but bad news soon followed. First came the assassination of the Austrian archduke in Sarajevo on June 28, the turmoil of the following month, and the declaration of war on August 3 by Germany against France, with Russia fulfilling its treaty commitment in support of France. Then they heard that Helen and Archer were being detained in Nuremberg and "treated atrociously," partly because they were foreigners and partly because of what Edward called Archer's "almost exact resemblance to a certain Russian grand duke and his having a lot of road maps in his car."[5]

Edward immediately cabled his New York office that Archer and Helen were being held and mistreated: "Communicate with State Department at once and do everything possible to relieve them without regard to cost." Edward also got his friend Theodore Shouts in Paris to intercede, and Shouts sent a telegram to Brand Whitlock, the United States minister in Brussels, on behalf of "Mr. and Mrs. Archie Huntington my warm personal friends" and also cabled Leon Pepperman, an influential businessman in New York, that "Huntingtons here in great distress about Archie and wife. See Tumulty [President Wilson's secretary] in Washington at once and cable me result of conference." Pepperman assured Shouts on August 13 that "Secretary of State doing everything possible. Has cabled Ambassador Gerard. Also all consuls Germany." The diplomatic pressure worked, and Helen and Archer were released.[6] On August 23, Edward wrote Carrie that "our hearts were much gladdened last Friday on receiving a telegram from Archer saying they had just arrived at Amsterdam and were well. You can imagine how Belle felt. All these days of anxious waiting. She could get no natural sleep and was ill with worry. Write her a letter for she loves to hear from you." He told Carrie that they had "lost nearly all the servants from the place" but were "getting along nicely now. . . . The shops are opening up in Paris, but I seldom go in." He concluded with a revealing thought: "I don't know when we shall return but wish I were back now."[7] Archer and Helen returned safely from Amsterdam to London.

Shortly before war was declared, Edward and Belle had decided to take an automobile trip to Germany, traveling by easy stages. "The day before war was declared," as Edward told the story, "we were at Nancy on our way to Germany. As we were starting, an American drove to the hotel and told us to turn back. Though no declaration had been issued, war signs were all around us, troops were forming and preparations for entrenchments were to be seen." They returned to the Chateau Beauregard. "It was not long before French troops came to our place near Versailles and camped; I must say the discipline was wonderful; not a soldier picked any of the fruit, and the officer would ask our permission to drill in certain places and showed us every consideration. They took our horses, cattle and grain, but gave us orders for their value at good prices."[8] On August 15, Edward received a request for help from the Committee on Relief in the American Embassy in Paris for persons in destitute circumstances; he sent twenty-five hundred francs. Two days later, he gave twenty thousand francs for the purchase of an ambulance.[9]

Edward was ready to go home, but Belle preferred to stay in France, "declaring that she did not think there was any danger." After Archer and Helen reached London, Archer became concerned about his mother staying on in France, and he engaged Elbert E. Martin—an agent of Walton H. Marshall, managing director of the Vanderbilt Hotel in New York, who had sent Martin to Europe to help Americans get home—to return to Paris and persuade his mother to leave. Archer gave Martin a letter to his mother and another to her banker in Paris, Morgan, Harjes and Company, to release her money, jewels, and securities to him. It took Martin a good while to persuade Belle to leave. "The Minister of War and Ambassador Herrick are both personal friends of mine," she told Martin, "and they would have advised me had the danger been great." She thought it over for two days and then, toward the end of August, agreed to leave. It took three days to pack her thirty-five trunks and two motorbuses to transport the trunks to the railway station. In the meantime, Martin went to the banker and collected the valuables, said to be worth $400,000, and carried them himself in a small valise.[10]

The Huntingtons' automobile had been commandeered by the military, but Duveen came to the rescue. Martin urged Duveen on with a note from the Hotel Ritz saying, "Dear Mr. Duveen, Germans are within 50 miles and the Banks have shipped all gold away. Please hurry. Leaving tonight if possible. Hastily, Elbert E. Martin."[11] Duveen borrowed an automobile from the British Embassy and drove with the Huntingtons to Le Havre, where with "his formidable powers of persuasion" he managed to get them exit visas and berths on a British ship bound for England. "For which prompt action," as Edward Fowles wrote in his memoirs, "they were eternally grateful."[12]

Edward and Belle arrived safely in London on September 2 and put up at Claridge's, where Archer and Helen were also staying, then engaged a car and driver to get them around London and sent a cable about their arrival to the New York office. This news was widely printed in United States newspapers. The *Los Angeles Examiner* announced on September 5 that "apprehension felt by friends here over the safety of H. E. Huntington and his wife, who have been in France since the war began, was set at rest yesterday by the receipt of word that the local capitalist and Mrs. Huntington had reached London in safety."[13] Their friends in France had also been concerned for their safety at the Chateau Beauregard. Jacques Seligmann wrote to Belle soon after they left to say that he had been deeply concerned about their staying in the country: "When I heard that you had left I was quite glad to know that you and your dear husband were safe."[14] Archer tried to give Martin $1,000 for his successful efforts, but Martin declined and "informed him that I had been sent to London by Mr. Marshall to do exactly those things. Mr. [Archer] Huntington laughed and said he would invest the money in my name."[15]

Edward and Belle did not tarry long in England. They took passage for New York on the White Star line's *Adriatic* sailing on September 17. The last thing Edward did in England was buy a copy of the first edition of Bunyan's *Pilgrim's Progress* at auction. "I thought I had lost it," he said, "but my agent got it at last. You know this book fad is the only hobby that grows on you and keeps you agitated all the time."[16]

Edward was interviewed by an International News Service correspondent before they sailed, and his remarks were widely printed: " 'It's a long, long way to Tipperary,' " he is reported to have said, "and 'it's a long, long way to Southern California,' but now, as always, 'my heart's right there.' I have always said I lived only for the day to come when I can drop everything and just go to Southern California and stay there the rest of my life. To my mind it's the greatest place on earth and I've yet to meet anyone who has been there who doesn't agree with me."[17]

But it was New York to which they returned, and to the house at 2 East Fifty-seventh Street. After Edward had given up his rooms at the Metropolitan Club, his pictures and books—stacks of them covering the furniture and the floor—were provided a good home at East Fifty-seventh Street. In the autumn, shortly after their return from Europe, Edward went right back to working on his books.

Carrie and Burke, after visiting in Oneonta, had been invited to come for a stay with Belle and Edward in the autumn. Burke, in his initial diary entry after arrival, reported that "we found them both there and well. Edwards was in the midst of sorting and cataloguing his great library in the east rooms on the second floor. The finest private English library in the world and containing the finest lot of Americana: also the great Gutenberg Bible."[18]

It was a "family Christmas" in 1914 with Belle and Edward, Carrie and Burke, and Helen and Archer. A welcome telegram came on December 24 from Elizabeth and Brockway, addressed to Edward: "The heartiest good wishes from all of us. May Christmas be a very happy one for you and Aunt Belle and many happy New Years. Lots of love, Elizabeth and Brockway."[19] From this we can see that Elizabeth had gotten over enough of her anger to include "Aunt Belle" in the greetings. In fact, the family relations were gradually restored to their earlier cordiality.

It became evident to Edward early in 1915 that he needed help to put his growing collection in order. He thought of the splendid catalog of the E. Dwight Church Library, now his, that had been compiled in seven stout volumes by George Watson Cole, now sixty-four years old, just six months younger than Edward and from a small Connecticut town near Oneonta, though he had moved to Hollywood, California. When Belle and Edward next went to California in the spring of 1915, Edward talked with Cole about him becoming Edward's librarian. Cole was interested, and they parleyed about the job. The $6,000 a year that Edward offered suited Cole, who later suggested in a letter that a stenographer and two or three young women assistants ought to be adequate as help. Edward responded, on July 17, 1915, that "the only obstacle is the employment of women which for reasons of my own I object to. I know that in employing men the cost will be more, and I presume this is your principal reason for employing women. I hope you will not object to this or think I am too set in my idea. I do not think, aside from this idiosyncrasy of mine, you will regret taking up this work. I certainly intend giving you a free hand, and I shall be most happy to know that you accept." Cole was pleased to accept and said, on August 4, that he could "cheerfully comply with" Edward's "suggestion that young men be employed." He explained that "the greater part of my work of this nature has been done with young women for assistants. I have always found the latter willing, teachable, and efficient; but can certainly find for the service young men who are bright, alert, and intelligent."[20] Edward's insistence on male library assistants was doubtless a reflection of the fact that he, and Collis as well, had employed only men as secretaries, office managers, and bookkeepers, to whom they felt able to speak freely and whom they often had as traveling companions. The practice of engaging male staff members was perpetuated in Edward's library as long as he lived.

Cole came to work as librarian on October 1, 1915, and within six weeks he and Edward had assembled an initial library staff of six men and were busy organizing the books and manuscripts in rooms set aside for their use on the second floor of the house. The staff was assembled with special advice from Wilberforce Eames, the great bibliographer and librarian at the New York Public Library, and James I. Wyer, director of the New York State Library in Albany. In addition to Cole, there was Chester Cate, the head cataloger; he had been in charge of cataloging Americana under Eames at the New York Public. The assistant catalogers were Herbert Wm. Denis, Robert M. McCurdy, Leslie E. Bliss from the New York State Library, and Charles C. Knapp from the copyright bureau of the Library of Congress. Edward was personally involved in their recruitment and selection; in writing to Wyer on November 13, 1915, he listed the staff and said that "possibly later I may add one man more, whom I shall import from the Pacific Coast. As you see, you have been of very great use to me with your suggestions, for which I am very thankful to you."[21]

The library staff was assembled none too soon. They had thousands and thousands of rare books and manuscripts in front of them, mostly in unsorted piles, to organize and catalog. New purchases put them further and further behind. Within the next four years, Edward bought more than a dozen additional collections of remarkable importance, all described in the first issue of the *Huntington Library Bulletin*.[22] A few words about four of these purchases can give some sense of Edward's interests.

In December 1915, with the library staff in place, he bought for $750,000 the library of Frederick R. Halsey, a Wall Street broker who had spent thirty-five years collecting twenty thousand rare volumes of English and American literature from Shakespeare through Stevenson. The collection was especially rich in Elizabethan poetry and prose and in such nineteenth-century writers as Shelley (twenty first editions), Dickens, Meredith, Poe (including the *Tamerlane* of 1827, often described as the rarest of all first editions in American literature), Melville, and Longfellow. The Chicago literary magazine *The Dial* warmly joined in the chorus of praise that greeted this acquisition, but added that Huntington "ought to be entitled to a few weeks' vacation from collecting and railroading in order to become acquainted with his books." Little did they know that acquainting himself with his books was his main occupation.[23]

In 1916, Edward bought the Britwell Court Americana in London for $350,000. It was a small but very choice collection of some four hundred pieces of early Americana, including thirteen incunabula, a number of unique books, and a large collection of early Latin voyages. Quaritch told Edward that "this is probably the most important collection of such books that has ever been offered for sale in England" and "I am quite sure that you will find this sale is one of the greatest opportunities that you will ever have of adding really important books to the Americana side of your collection." Who could resist such an appeal? Although the material had already been cataloged for sale by auction at Sotheby's, Edward arranged to have George D. Smith buy the whole collection for him en bloc.[24]

The most spectacular acquisition of these years was the Bridgewater House Library, a family collection begun by Sir Thomas Egerton in Queen Elizabeth's reign and continued by his successors, the earls of Ellesmere and earls and dukes of Bridgewater. Its forty-four hundred volumes and twelve thousand manuscripts included key medieval material (the Ellesmere Chaucer manuscript, for example), important manuscripts of the sixteenth and seventeenth centuries (like Donne and Jonson), and twenty-five hundred manuscript plays of the eighteenth and early nineteenth centuries. Edward paid $1 million for the collection in 1917, and in the same year it was transported by steamer in 101 large cases across the Atlantic to New York, despite the threat of German submarines.[25]

In 1918, Edward acquired the extensive library of literary and historical manuscripts collected by the St. Louis manufacturer William K. Bixby. It contained large groups of letters by several dozen people (three hundred by Hawthorne, for example); manuscripts of poems and novels by Burns, Thoreau, Harte, and a dozen others; and private papers, such as Major André's journals and Shelley's notebooks. For this collection, Edward paid $400,000.[26]

For most of these major purchases, from the time of buying the Church library and the Hoe sales onward, Edward relied mainly on George D. Smith, the New York dealer who was widely regarded as the leading American bookseller. A. Edward Newton in 1918 called Smith "the greatest bookseller in the world"—a person who "has sold more fine books than perhaps any two of his rivals."[27]

Edward also bought books from other dealers—from Quaritch in London, and from sixteen additional dealers in the United States in 1918 alone. He even bought a set of the *Encyclopedia Britannica* from Sears Roebuck in 1916, for $58.88.[28] He also turned down books offered him by dealers, even a book for which the offering letter began, "Dear

Mr. Huntington: This is the most valuable book in the country and probably in the world . . . [The original tablets of the Ten Commandments? No—] the military manuscript written in 1465, in which is mentioned, for the first time, the use of gunpowder in connection with artillery."[29] Private persons were also offering him their book treasures, like "four old maps" and "a very odd Hamlet" written by an Irish priest in the nineteenth century.[30]

There was a competitive edge to his collecting. In June 1919, he asked Cole for a note of his holdings of plays and masques printed before 1700, as recorded in W. W. Greg's bibliography, in comparison with the holdings of the British Museum. Cole was happy to report that his total of 906 "as against the Museum's 922 is not bad. You are to be congratulated on making such a fine showing." Two months later Edward wrote Cole from California about eleven books in this category that he had just bought, and he added that "it makes quite a reduction in the number of plays I have to secure to be even with the British Museum." His desire was also for absolute completeness. He went on to say that "I should like to have you send me a list of all the Shakespeare plays lacking. Place the list on my desk and send me the duplicate."[31]

The library staff was busy cataloging his books. Edward agreed that they should first work on the English books printed before 1640.[32] They needed the *Catalogue of Printed Books* of the British Museum for reference purposes, and Edward heard that the Library of Congress had a duplicate set. He wrote about it to Herbert Putnam, the distinguished librarian of Congress, and their dealings are a reminder of a simpler and more innocent day. Edward offered to buy the extra set "if you are willing to dispose of it." And he added the alternative that "possibly there might be an exchange for duplicate Americana which I have and which you do not." (Oh, for the day when you could offer to fill the LC's needs in Americana out of your duplicates!) Putnam was sorry that they could not spare their extra set, because it was being used in the reading room as a supplement to the card catalog. But he wrote to an English dealer who owed him a favor and asked him to locate a set for Huntington, who was grateful.[33] Still there were details of British Museum books that needed examination, and Edward wrote to Quaritch in London and asked whether they would allow F. S. Ferguson—an assistant in the firm, later a well-known bibliographer and reviser of the Pollard and Redgrave *Short-Title Catalogue*—to do research for him at the British Museum. Quaritch agreed, saying that "he is my most valued assistant" but that he could "devote his spare time on Saturdays to your work and I shall grant him such further facilities as I am able." Quaritch suggested that Edward pay Ferguson ten shillings (about $2.50) an hour for his services, which at that time was good pay.[34]

One episode unsettled the operation of Edward's library staff in the autumn of 1917. Half a dozen of his early Americana books were stolen, apparently by a staff member. According to newspaper stories—on which everyone concerned refused to comment—Edward was offered a book for $2,000 by a New York dealer and recognized it as his own copy. This led to a search of his library and verification that his copy was missing, along with a few other books, which were recovered from the dealers to whom they had been sold. Suspicion lighted on Cole's secretary, Herbert M. Holden, who had not been at work recently because of illness. Private detectives were engaged to try to solve the case. Holden called on Cole on September 27, 1917, and later the same day wrote him a farewell letter saying that he was "tired of life anyway," that he wanted to "save you and Mr. Huntington the expense of hounding me any farther," and that "I want to say how sorry I am that in my uncontrollable temper I offended you by telling you of the many things that so embittered me at the library against every-one." And he concluded, "Perhaps—or likely I am insane." Holden disappeared and was never heard of again. Edward declined to have charges pressed against him.[35]

It became evident, once sorting and cataloging were under way, that Edward had accumulated duplicate copies of numerous books as a result of acquiring so many complete collections. More than three-quarters of the Britwell Court Americana, for example, duplicated his own holdings, but he had gladly bought the whole collection to get the other one-quarter.

In early 1916, he decided to begin disposing of his duplicates because, as he told his staff members, "they should go back in circulation" and become available to other collectors. Accordingly, he made an arrangement with the Anderson Galleries in New York for them to publish catalogs of his duplicates and offer them for sale by auction at their new galleries at Park Avenue and Fifty-ninth Street.[36] The first sale was held in March 1916. Over the next eight years Anderson put out fifteen catalogs of his duplicates: 8,121 lots were offered in the course of forty-three separate sessions.[37]

The sales catalogs were not shy in their evaluative remarks. The preface to the first (March 1916) asserted, "For many years Mr. Henry E. Huntington has been the largest individual buyer of rare books in the world." The preface to the second (November 1916, catalog 1251) claimed that the books included constituted "the finest collection of modern French books that has ever been offered for sale, either in this country or in Europe, and it is extremely unlikely that there will ever be another sale of the same high character." The preface to the third (January 1917, catalog 1269) began, "This is the finest collection of Americana ever offered for sale in this country or Europe." These sentiments were echoed and extended in newspaper stories, with more than a hundred long and glowing accounts of the sales.[38] A particularly influential story appeared in the *New York Times* for January 16, 1917, just before the third auction, under the heading "Say Huntington's Is Finest Library"; the article reviewed his principal en bloc purchases since 1911 and concluded that Huntington "now has the finest private library in the world."[39]

The sales created a great deal of public interest, and the prices held up well. Edward was described as being "an interested spectator" at the sales.[40] In the first year and a half, after almost half of the sessions, more than $400,000 had been realized.[41] Some of the prices now look like bargains, however. Among Hawthorne first editions, for example, *Twice-Told Tales* brought $8.50, *The Scarlet Letter* $20, *The Blithedale Romance* (the Halsey copy) $1, *Tanglewood Tales* (the Halsey copy) $3, and *Septimius Felton* (the Hoe copy) $5.[42] On the other hand, many lots fetched high prices, particularly the early Americana and the English plays.

Public interest focused on the first edition of Milton's *Comus* (1637), which came up for sale on February 5, 1918, as lot 595 of part 7. The catalog emphasized that this was the Bridgewater copy, that *Comus* had been written for and first performed before the Earl of Bridgewater, that this was the probable "dedication copy," that it contained several contemporary textual corrections (perhaps by Milton), and that the Bridgewater crest was impressed in its leather binding. The title page was reproduced as the frontispiece of the catalog, and the entry was boldly headed "The Greatest Milton Volume Ever Offered: The Dedication Copy of 'Comus'." It brought $9,400, and the newspaper stories about the sale featured it.[43] Many people have since thought that Huntington was foolish or ignorant to have sold the so-called dedication copy with corrections that might have been by Milton. In defense of Huntington it can be said that there is no basis for calling this the "dedication copy," whatever that means, or for thinking that the corrections were by Milton. Moreover, the Bridgewater crest was added when the book was rebound about 1800, and Edward had two other fine or finer copies. He initially included a second copy of *Comus* in the April 1918 sale but withdrew it to present it to the Elizabethan Club of Yale, of which he was a member. At the beginning of the sale, on April 26, 1918, the auctioneer announced, "Unfortunately, Mr. Huntington has no more copies of 'Comus' either to sell or give away."[44] Several club members sent him grateful letters, which pleased him "very much, and I am glad to have the Comus in a place where it is so appreciated." The Yale librarian brought the copy to New York and asked him to inscribe it, which he did, though he did not write in his own rare books and manuscripts or affix bookplates to them—in fact, he had no bookplate. After disposing of these two copies of *Comus,* he still had the splendid Church copy for his own library.[45]

The duplicate sales were successful, and Edward used the money to buy more books. Among the buyers of the duplicates was Beverly Chew; he displayed his loyal affection for his first loves by buying back many of the books he had sold to Edward several years before. When Chew died in 1924, it was reckoned that over 15 percent of his collection consisted of the very copies he had sold to Huntington and then bought back. They are affectionately known as Chew-Huntington-Chew copies.

Soon after Edward established his library in the house at 2 East Fifty-seventh Street in 1915, he began to receive requests from scholars and students to use his material. Hundreds of letters arrived during the period 1914–19; a few examples will suggest the nature of the requests and his responses. Academic readers will probably recognize most of the requesters as well-known scholars of their time.

Professor Tucker Brooke of Yale was an early user of the library. In November 1914 he asked to examine the anonymous sixteenth-century play *Common Condicions,* and Edward was happy to show it to him. The next month he asked Edward if he might come down from New Haven on a Saturday to examine the Marlowe quartos; when the answer was cordially affirmative he responded, "I thank you most heartily for your kind permission to see your library on the morning of December 30th. I will reach New York at about ten o'clock on that morning and will make my way at once to your house. Believe me, Yours very gratefully, Tucker Brooke." In the next years he made frequent trips to the library, and Cole and Edward both wrote him about new books they had received of interest to him, about copies elsewhere, and about variations among different copies. But when he asked, in 1916, to have Marlowe's *Edward II* sent to him in New Haven for study, Edward felt he had to refuse: "I find I will have to make it a rule not to let books leave the library or office of Mr. Cole, but I should be very glad to give you the privilege of examining Marlowe's Edward II, or anything else you may desire to see, at Mr. Cole's office."[46]

Many other professors wrote and visited the library, and a table was set aside for their use. Carleton Brown of Bryn Mawr asked for help in compiling a register of Middle English religious or didactic poems, and he was sent a transcript of the cards of all likely material; he found seven items of interest and came to the library to see them.[47] Herbert L. Osgood of Columbia and Charles U. Spencer of Princeton came to examine Robert Hunter's *Androborus,* the first American play.[48] Samuel C. Chew of Bryn Mawr came to see the Byron and Swinburne collections; he modestly explained that "I am doing some special research in those fields."[49] Henrietta C. Bartlett examined all the Shakespeare quartos in making, with A. W. Pollard, her ambitious census of Shakespeare plays in quarto, and both Edward and the library staff answered dozens of queries from her about details of the copies and locations of others.[50] Chauncey Brewster Tinker of Yale asked about Boswell letters in the collection, and he was sent photostats of a group in the Loudoun Papers.[51]

Students also used the material. Thomas O. Mabbott, while a sophomore at Columbia, got permission to see four rare Poe items; and he came back as a senior to look at Poe manuscripts.[52] Henry Ten Eyck Perry, while a graduate student at Harvard, sought to examine some writings of the Duchess of Newcastle in connection with his dissertation, and Edward agreed to have him do so "at any time during your stay in New York."[53] Catherine Oakes, an undergraduate at Wellesley, was not allowed to have a seventeenth-century book mailed to her, but she did come to New York to consult it.[54]

Requests to have rare material sent away from the library were declined. Maude E. Cryder asked to have the manuscript of Thoreau's *Walden* mailed to her at the University of Chicago, and Hardin Craig asked to have the Chester manuscript of medieval plays sent to him at the University of Minnesota.[55] Edward did not like to have any of his rare books or manuscripts leave the library. In 1919, he did allow the Grolier Club of New York to include some of his Blake items in an exhibition; when Edward A. Forbes, the director of the Fogg Art Museum at Harvard, asked him to allow his things to go on to Cambridge with the rest of the show, Edward agreed reluctantly, only after Forbes had assured him that he and Paul Sachs, the prominent collector, would personally transport the materials in a stateroom on the train and that he would insure them for $250,000.[56]

He was generous about having his material photographed for study or illustration. Ashley H. Thorndike of Columbia was given a photograph of the title page of the play *Messalina* (1640) to show the appearance of the stage in his book on the theater, Thomas W. Edmondson of New York University was given a photograph of a manuscript letter by Defoe and permission to publish it, and R. W. Chambers of University College London expressed gratitude to Edward for having sent a photostat of the notes of the Ashburnham manuscript of *Piers Plowman*.[57]

Edward also supplied photographs to other libraries. He provided the American Antiquarian Society in 1916 with copies of the three early American almanacs (1646, 1647, 1648) that they lacked. He provided the Massachusetts Historical Society with their nine missing issues of the Boston News-Letters for 1754–55 in 1918, and the director responded, "I need hardly add that the example you give in thus furthering historical studies is one worthy of all praise." The next year they were supplied a photograph of the unique copy of the Massachusetts General Laws (Cambridge, 1648).[58] In 1917, Falconer Madan, the head librarian at Oxford, wrote Cole, "seldom have I received a more welcome letter than yours of Nov. 23, accompanied by 12 photographs and first rate technical descriptions, in which you announce the accession to the great Huntington Library of some unknown Oxford pieces of 1585–6. I am really greatly obliged to you and to Mr. Huntington for allowing me to have such full information."[59] A photostat of the *Muses Gardin for Delights* (1608) was sent in 1917 to E. H. Fellowes in England for his edition of English lutenist songwriters.[60] In 1919, Edward went in with ten American libraries to exchange photostats of rare early Americana, and the project got under way with fourteen Huntington items.[61] Edward wanted to exchange with Folger photographic copies of Shakespeare quartos so that "Shakespeare scholars should have all the texts possible in the pursuit of their investigations." Cole wrote to Folger, "Should this idea strike you favorably Mr. Huntington would be very glad to have you select such titles as he has that you would be willing to take in exchange for such as he may choose from those that you possess." Folger was complimented but embarrassed and said, "I do not see how I can comply with it at this time. I am less familiar with my books than I would like to be, because I have been compelled, as fast as they were secured, to pack them up and put them away in storage for safety, often without adequate examination."[62] Scholars grumbled at the inaccessibility of Folger's copies. A. W. Pollard wrote Cole from London in 1919 that he hoped Huntington would buy the Mostyn plays rather than have them "shut up in one of Folger's inaccessible boxes. I find it hard to be in Christian charity with a man who has had the [unique] 1st edition of Titus Andronicus for some years and hasn't published a facsimile or at least an accurate reprint of it. I can't complete my Shakespeare work without it & he locks it up in a box!"[63] Folger was eager to have the Shakespeare Bookcase—made of pieces of wood from places connected with the life and plays of Shakespeare— that Huntington had bought in 1916 through George D. Smith for

$6,000, with a hundred-volume edition of Shakespeare with thirteen thousand extra illustrations, and Huntington wanted the *Titus Andronicus;* but they were never able to effect an exchange or a sale.[64]

Edward was averse to the idea of letting other people issue facsimiles or reprints of his unique or very rare books. "My idea is," he wrote Cole, "to produce these things ourselves the first chance we have." He envisioned a series of publications under some kind of program. Cole wrote to Pollard, who had asked to have the Malone Society issue facsimiles of some of Huntington's plays, that "Mr. Huntington is very liberal in his views and wishes to make his treasures of service to the public but in just what form it remains for him to say." Edward did want the plays to be available, and he told Cole that "if we do not [issue a series of publications ourselves] we can take the matter up with Mr. Pollard again."[65]

The attitude of scholars toward Huntington is epitomized in two letters to him from Professor Albert C. Baugh of the University of Pennsylvania. On August 2, 1919, Baugh asked Huntington if he might work on two of his fifteenth-century manuscripts, explained in detail what his project was intended to achieve, and added, "I have ventured to write you about the matter because of your sympathetic interest in serious scholarship and research." Two months later, in thanking Edward, Baugh wrote that "your generosity in permitting scholars to enjoy the opportunities which your marvellous collection affords is universally known." Moreover, "it is well known with what a high ideal and public-spirited conception you have gathered together this greatest private library in the world."[66]

In the course of these five years, Edward began to receive increasing acclaim as a collector of rare books and manuscripts. His collection multiplied in size and importance through the acquisition of some seventeen en bloc purchases as well as by the steady flow of individual books and manuscripts to his library. His new status was recognized in a series of thoughtful accounts and evaluations of his collection. Three or four of these stories can give the flavor of his extended reputation, as well as some sense of the public attitude that confronted him and with which he had to deal.

Early in 1916, the *Boston Evening Transcript* published a full-page story, by George H. Sargent, under the heading "Henry E. Huntington and the Treasures in His Greatest of All Private Libraries," with a picture of Huntington, four illustrations, and a box listing thirteen "gems" of his collection. It used to be, the story began, that J. Pierpont Morgan was the standard for the comparison of private libraries: "That time has passed. Today the finest private library in the world is that of Henry E. Huntington, at No. 2 East Fifty-seventh Street, New York." Moreover, "it has been surpassed by very few in the history of book collecting." Huntington learned by studying books; with counsel from dealers and friends "he soon learned to separate the wheat from the chaff." He was "having his fun," and at the same time "his services should be recognized" as "a conservator of literature." The "gems" listed included the Gutenberg Bible, the Caxtons, the Shakespeares, the Bay Psalm Book, and Franklin's *Autobiography*.[67] This story was read with approval as far away as London; there *The Sphere* concluded that the story "describes, probably with accuracy, as the greatest of all private libraries, that of Mr. Henry E. Huntington," and it listed ten of the "gems" to show its range and quality.[68]

In 1917, the *New York Times* carried on the *Boston Transcript* theme with a full-page story with picture under the heading "Huntington Now the Premier Book Collector." The lead sentence was "To Henry E. Huntington belongs, par excellence, the title of Prince of Book Collectors." The public was said to be interested in knowing who was number one, and this story fully satisfied that interest: "Mr. Huntington takes place as the first bibliophile in the land."[69] The story was widely copied, and more than three months later it was reprinted in the *Toronto Star*.[70]

The most elaborate story was Elizabeth Miner King's article in five parts, each of two or three columns, that appeared May 9 to 14, 1918, in the *New York Evening Post*. The city editor wrote to Cole and asked that King be allowed to visit the library. Cole replied that he had showed the letter to Huntington, who "is quite willing that such a paper or series of papers be prepared"; Cole agreed to give her "free access" to their catalogs and to let her examine any books she wanted to describe. The result was a careful account of the main collections and a loving description of many choice items, all on the general theme that America now had the greatest private library in the world. "In the honor of possession, England, France, Germany have given way to America. The Huntington Library now contains some of the world's greatest books of which there are no counterparts anywhere; or of which there are only one or two copies in the national or university libraries on the Continent or here. America is the richer because of the Huntington Library."

Huntington was presented as a true book lover: "For seven hours every day, with possibly an exception of one day, Mr. Huntington looks over his new acquisitions, compares editions, reads, inspects, and takes pleasure in his books. In his devotion, he says, with Samuel Rogers: 'When a new book comes out, I read an old one.' "

The five articles gave a brief account of Edward's progress as a book collector, reported on the main collections, described a few of the "remarkable manuscripts," and told of the "Crown Jewels" of the library. Readers were made aware of the wonder and glory of the Gutenberg Bible, the Ellesmere Chaucer manuscript, the first book printed in England, the traveling book collection of Queen Elizabeth's lord chancellor, the first edition of *Hamlet* (of which only one other copy is known), the Bay Psalm Book, the manuscript of Franklin's *Autobiography*, the manuscript letters of Thomas Jefferson, and a dozen other rare and choice items—which were made to seem important to each and every American.[71]

In December 1919, the *New York Sun* feature editor, Eustace Hale Ball, asked for an interview, and Edward gave him a tour of his library. He did what he enjoyed most: showing things to a visitor and reading passages from them. Edward showed this visitor a dozen items that were lying on a table next to his desk, including Shakespeare's sonnets, a Ben Jonson play, the Gutenberg Bible, *Pilgrim's Progress,* and the Ellesmere Chaucer. He turned the pages of the Chaucer to show the illuminations. "And on this page, as you see," he said, "is the only known genuine portrait of Chaucer, riding on his little nag." The reporter recalled "the delighted twinkle" that lighted his eyes as he picked up one book after another:

> "This is the journal of Major André, written before and after his capture by Washington's men. See—here are his maps and data which cost him his life." He turned to the other book.
> "This is the autographic genealogy of the Washington family, writ-

ten by the first President while he was in office. Here are more of his reports and personal letters."

"And here is the first galley proof of the Constitution of the United States—the corrections made by the 'fathers' are these scratchings in ink along the borders. This was sent back to the printer and finally became the basic law of the Republic."

He turned to another table to draw forth from an exquisitely hand tooled leather case a single page of manuscript. It was Robert Burns's original script of "To Mary in Heaven."

Ball's articles, which were based on this interview and further study, carried on the theme that the collection was the "Greatest Private Library in the World." It also included a more personal note, however, as intimated by the headline "Huntington Leads Book Lovers." He was presented as

> strangely dissimilar from many millionaires in these days. . . . He is so unassuming, modest in his vocation of collecting millions and his avocation of collecting rare volumes that outside the circle of his intimate friends and employees little is known of his individuality. . . .
> Mr. Huntington, whose extensive purchases of famous books during the last decade and a half have astounded the world, represents a type essentially American in appearance, demeanor, philosophy and purpose. Sartorially he is the immaculate and modestly dressed man of real affairs. In manner he is soft voiced and shy almost to the point of apparent timidity in the presence of strangers.
> Six feet in height, broad shouldered as an athlete, his gentle but keen eyes sparkling with intensive vision, his is a figure not soon to be forgotten. His knowledge of bibliography is at once profound as that of a college professor and as keen as that of the shrewd master of business affairs that he still is, despite his modest claim of "having retired from active work."[72]

This story was reprinted within the next month in many newspapers, including the *Pittsburgh Telegraph* on December 30, 1919, the *Kansas City Star* on January 2, 1920, and the *Morning Union* of Springfield, Massachusetts, on January 18, 1920.[73]

These stories provoked a fresh rash of letters to Edward, typified by one from Charles V. E. Starrett of Chicago: "Dear Mr. Huntington," he began. "Because you are the greatest book collector in the world, and I am probably the humblest (although far from the least enthusiastic and sincere) I write you." He told about his own collection, English literature of the 1890s, "but English literature of every age delights me." He wanted a catalog of the Huntington collection, and "frankly, too, I should like to have among my letters a letter from you." He concluded, "Forgive my impertinence in writing." Edward replied that he could not send him a catalog, since he had as yet only a card index. "You are right," he added, "in saying that all periods of English literature are interesting. While I have been specializing in the earlier periods, of late we have been acquiring much from the later writers."[74]

Edward had not been particularly happy to have such a profusion of articles published about him, partly because he thought them unbecoming when the country was engaged in war, and partly because of his innate modesty. Edward replied on July 1, 1918, to Harvard librarian George Parker Winship, about the five articles in the *New York Evening Post,* that "I regret very much that they were published: in fact, I was quite disgusted with them. Just at present, I do not think it is an opportune time to publish articles of this sort."[75]

Edward had been a key person in San Francisco in the 1890s. He had been regarded as the person mainly responsible for the development of Southern California in the first decade of the twentieth century. Now he was being described as the world's greatest book collector. It was a kind of public acclaim that he did not seek and did not really enjoy. But he enjoyed his books.

The private life of Edward and Belle in New York was quiet. Their guests were mainly family members: Archer and Helen, Carrie and Burke when they were in the East, Ellen and Edwin Gates, occasionally Carrie's children and Belle's siblings and their children. The main social events were lunches and dinners at 2 East Fifty-seventh Street, and frequent visits to the theater.[76] On special occasions there were parties. For Thanksgiving Day 1917 the seven who were in town went up to the Gates house at 11 West Eighty-first Street. Ellen—younger sister of

Solon and Collis, age eighty-two—wrote a loving, nostalgic account of the dinner and evening, "remembering the dear absent faces which we miss so much" and laughing "as we drew our chairs closer together at the dinner table." She reported that Belle "was in her merriest mood and talked earnestly about the great questions which are agitating the world at this time." They took special pleasure in the children, "our evening passed all too swiftly away," and soon "the fiesta was over."[77]

Edward took pleasure in showing friends around the library. Visitors included Wilberforce Eames of the New York Public Library; Worthington C. Ford of the Massachusetts Historical Society; Arthur Lord, president of the Club of Odd Volumes of Boston; James Hillhouse, an attorney from New Haven; and Lucius Wilmerding, a collector from Tuxedo Park. They all expressed delight at what they saw, and they doubtless shared Worthington Ford's sentiment that "it is not only the size and nature of the collections which are impressive, but the spirit of the owner, who is a trustee for its future permanent usefulness to mankind."[78] Occasionally, Edward showed groups of friends around. The Authors' Club of New York visited on December 18, 1919, and several members sent their thanks and appreciation; Gardner Teall wrote that "it was, indeed, a treat to be able to examine, leaf by leaf, so many treasures that could not help but awaken joy in the heart of a bibliophile."[79]

Edward belonged to many clubs and societies with bookish interests in and around New York. He had become a member of the premier book group, the Grolier Club, in 1911. He also became a life member of the Bibliographical Society of America, and of the Bibliographical Society of London. He was elected a fellow of the American Antiquarian Society, and he even paid his five dollars a year to Professor Charles G. Osgood to be a member of the Concordance Society.[80] In these groups, he was valued as a real book lover. When the secretary of the Grolier Club sent him notice of their annual meeting in 1919, he added: "If you have not set aside this evening for our meeting I would urge you, as Secretary of the Club, to try to lay aside any other engagement you have—and come. The President is specially anxious that the real lovers of books should be present at this our thirty-fifth Annual Meeting."[81]

The club in New York that he probably enjoyed the most, however, was the Hobby Club. This was a group of men who met about four times a year for dinner at the house of a member; after dinner the host was expected to hold forth on his hobby, even to "ride his hobby horse." Edward was one of the original members of the group, which began in 1911 with thirteen people present; over the next decade, it increased to about thirty-five members. Its members (and the hobbies they pursued) included George A. Plimpton (early schoolbooks), Phoenix Ingraham (Thackeray and Stevenson), John C. Tomlinson (sundials), Edwin R. Seligman (economic history), W. P. Trent (Defoe), John Quinn (recent art and literature), S. V. Hoffman (astrolabes), Edward T. Newell (coins), and Albert Gallatin (Japanese scroll pictures), as well as Beverly Chew, A. Edward Newton, and others. There was a menu printed by Tiffany for each meeting; it listed the wines and often something relevant to the program. Sometimes the former were spectacular: on February 12, 1915, 1886 Rüdesheimer Berg was served with the oysters, 1865 sherry with the green turtle soup, 1904 Bollinger Special Cuvée with the lamb, and 1815 Prince of Wales port with the coffee, followed by 1825 South Side madeira, Old Green Chartreuse, and 1808 Otard brandy. On April 23, 1914, the members were offered, among other things, an 1888 Chateau Lafitte and an 1811 Grande Fine Champagne caves du Duc d'Aumale. Edward was a regular host. On December 16, 1915, he gave an eight-course dinner with the menu printed on vellum. On December 6, 1917, his dinner was in honor of their fellow member from St. Louis, William K. Bixby.[82] He invited Bixby to give the talk that was the prerogative of the host. Bixby demurred a little, saying, "I always enjoy a dinner more when the other fellow is doing the talking" and that at best he could give "a rambling talk" about his interests. Edward replied that "we know, whether a formal address or a rambling talk, what you have to say will be most interesting." Bixby spoke about his collection of autograph letters. Edward passed out facsimile copies of a manuscript poem by Eugene Field called "Dear Old London" and—with a smile—the title page of the Psalms of David (London, 1660) inscribed by James Boswell in 1763: "I bought this for twopence at Greenwich when I was walking there with Mr. Samuel Johnson."[83]

A fellow member of the Hobby Club, Henry Howard Harper, later recorded in his reminiscences an account of Edward's behavior at club meetings. His account is also an admirable summary of Edward's human qualities. Huntington "was a voracious bibliophile—the prince of book and manuscript collectors," Harper wrote. "In his home, he was also a princely host—gracious, attentive, unassuming, easy to converse with, and seemingly as naive as a mid-Victorian swain. Always deferential, he assumed no airs of superiority. The least conspicuous guest at his table shared his attention equally with the most distinguished. While absorbed in conversation with one, without the slightest inattention he could listen intelligently to all the others who were within hearing." Harper was greatly impressed by Edward's deep sense of calm: "I never saw him exhibit the least passion or irritation. If he agreed, he usually nodded; if he disagreed, he merely smiled—seldom disputed."

Harper thought Edward gave the best dinners and was "the club's chief epicurean Maecenas." But he did not avail himself of the chance to talk: "Mr. Huntington being of a very retiring nature usually appointed some other member to entertain his guests. Mr. Huntington was always an attentive listener, and such a perfect host that he seemed to relish even the most vapid homilies on antique coins, old glass bottles, or whatever comprised the orator's hobby. I have seen half the listeners drowsing or whispering, while Mr. Huntington was as alert as a boy at his first circus."[84]

As a host, Edward was a good provider of wines even though he himself drank only in moderation. He kept well-stocked cellars; in January 1919 alone, he bought in New York twenty-five cases of claret and sauternes, twenty cases of sparkling burgundy, twenty cases of sparkling chambertin, and ten cases of dry Cliquot champagne. Some of this was shipped to San Marino, but he also bought there ten cases of California champagne.[85] His family, friends, and other guests were amply provided for.

Among the other personal matters he dealt with at this time was the disposition of the home place in Oneonta. By 1917 it was no longer being used by family members for vacations, and Edward bought the other interests from his sisters Carrie and Leonora. He offered them any of the furnishings they wanted; as for himself, as he wrote to Carrie, he wanted only one thing: "I would like Mother's scrap books as they relate largely to my wanderings." Then he bought two contiguous pieces of property and gave the whole thing, including all the books, to the city of Oneonta, in memory of his father and mother, to be used as a city library and park. He paid for the necessary improvements to the property to make it effective, provided more books, and added a trust fund to cover its operation and maintenance. His hope was that "the only thing required of the city is to furnish light and water." The gift was gratefully accepted by the city, and the newspapers wrote editorials about "His Munificent Gift" and praised him as "a book lover with intense filial devotion—what more suitable gift could he make his native city than a beautiful library in a park setting in the heart of the city of his nativity and in fact upon the site of his birthplace and boyhood home."[86]

They took no trips to the Chateau Beauregard during these years because of the war. However, they maintained in residence a steward and a housekeeper, a small staff, and an attorney in Paris, and Edward handled a never-ending flow of bills, correspondence, problems, and questions. The annual rental was about $35,000, and the additional expenses amounted to at least that much again.[87] Edward never complained, as Belle wanted to keep the residence. Archer and Helen ventured to go to Europe in 1917; they stayed at the Chateau Beauregard several times in October and November and enjoyed their visits.[88]

Of the various offers and requests that came to him in New York in these years, two are perhaps worth recording. One was received in 1919 from a real estate agent, who asked whether Edward would be willing to lease the house at 2 East Fifty-seventh Street "for business purposes," with the understanding that it could be used "practically without alteration." Edward replied stiffly that "the proposition would not interest me. The house is not for lease for any purpose."[89]

The other was an offer in 1918 to Edward for him to buy Monticello, described as "the historical home built by Thomas Jefferson, two miles from Charlottesville, Virginia." It was suggested that he could easily make it his residence. Or, if he preferred, he could use it as a convalescent home for soldiers, under the supervision of the American Red Cross. It was hoped that he would ultimately give it to the United

States as a museum or a memorial. He did not find this offer hard to turn down.[90]

Several events troubled the composure of Edward's and Belle's lives during these years. Both suffered frequently from "hard colds" that kept them in their rooms for a week or two at a time. Typically, Edward wrote early in September 1915 that "Mrs. Huntington has been ill for the past two weeks so that I have been up at the house most of the time."[91]

Later that month, Edward came down with a serious illness and was incapacitated most of the next six months. The attack began on September 27, 1915, when they were in the country at Throggs Neck. He had severe chills and was confined to bed with high fever and inflammation of the prostate, bladder, and kidneys. In the second week of October, his regular physician, Dr. William B. Coley, Jr., brought him by ambulance to 2 East Fifty-seventh Street, and two or three days later he became worse, with a temperature of 104 degrees. He was attended constantly by four physicians for two weeks and, according to Dr. Coley, was "in a very serious condition; at one time almost desperate."[92] Edward was quite aware of the seriousness of his illness. The next February, he said, "I almost died last October."[93]

The news got into all the papers that Huntington was "dangerously ill in New York" and that he was to have a major operation. Carrie packed her bags in San Francisco and held herself in readiness to leave for New York.[94] Billy Dunn sent an anxious telegram on October 14 from Los Angeles to C. E. Graham in the New York office: "What is the character of proposed operation? You will understand that our anxiety arises from personal affection and I am very desirous to keep well informed." Graham replied on October 15, after chiding Dunn for not having sent his message in code, that "as near as can ascertain operation for enlarged prostate and possible abscess thereon but as fever has entirely disappeared operation has been postponed. If improvement continues will not take place. Chief [HEH] feeling much better this morning, temperature normal, indicating to my mind that if there was an abscess it has broken and passed away. Will keep you posted." A week later Graham told Dunn, "Chief is feeling fine."[95]

On November 4, Dr. Coley reported that Huntington "has remained, and will for a long time remain under constant medical supervision" and must desist "for many months to come from work of every description. Unless he absolutely abstains from business, my colleagues and myself have advised him and his wife that we cannot be responsible that he remains alive long. For the next twelve months if not for a longer period, he is always to have an able physician in daily attendance upon him." He might recover more quickly in California, Dr. Coley thought, because of its "warmer climate."[96]

On January 4, 1916, Edward was examined by three eminent physicians in New York. Dr. J. Bentley Squier, professor of urinary surgery, found that he had an "infected condition of the bladder and prostate gland evidenced by the discharge of pus therefrom," that an operation might be needed on short notice, and that he needed "absolute quiet, free from nervous strain." Dr. Graeme M. Hammond, a neurologist, found that he had pus in his bladder and that he should desist from work and not be subjected to any anxiety. Dr. Charles L. Dana, professor of nervous diseases, also found him "suffering from a badly swollen prostate gland" that might require surgery at any time and that he "should not be subjected to any extraordinary nervous strain in his present condition."[97]

At last, in March 1916, Edward was judged to be well enough to seek a warmer climate. Edward and Belle arrived in California on March 11, accompanied by a physician, Dr. L. C. Williams, who stayed with Edward constantly while he was away from New York.

The grave warnings pronounced by the three eminent New York specialists hung over his head for the remaining eleven years of his life. His friends tried to mitigate them a little, however. The sculptor Frederick MacMonnies wrote in New York in April 1917, "I trust your health will improve with the approach of fine weather. It seems to me from a visualist's observation that if you could free yourself at once from the wear and tear and noise of New York you would find your own robust health at once. If I see rightly, you are only suffering from medicines and doctors."[98] And from Houston came many long letters of support and advice from Harry L. Fagin, who had the good fortune to own 5.5 percent of the original Texaco stock. "Dear, good friend of mine,"

Fagin wrote in early 1919, "I cannot but think that the real cause of your distemper—as Emerson was wont to put such things—is rooted in your THOUGHTS, in your reactions against present world conditions." Edward replied, "I am much better than I was when Mr. Graham wrote you, and with another trip to California in the near future, my thoughts, my happiness and health are most wholesome. Then, with a good doctor, I hope to come out all right." Fagin was delighted that he was "coming in good shape. . . . [I] knew you would be all right when you were once more in our beloved California. That is, dearly beloved friend, likewise our Mecca." When Edward's physical therapist in California, William Madsen, heard from his physician that surgery was being contemplated, he wrote Edward that he had a splendid body and should avoid the knife; he spoke approvingly of his bowling alley but deplored the lack of a gymnasium. He urged Edward to have, instead of surgery, "physical activity in the form of games," as "the enjoyment" would lead to his "general benefit."[99]

Illness was accompanied by other troubling events. Edward's brother Willard died suddenly on September 27, 1915, at the age of fifty-nine. Willard was with two friends in a chauffeur-driven car in the country near Oneonta; the car went down a fifty-foot embankment when the driver tried to pass a wagon, and Willard was thrown from the car and killed instantly. Edward was so ill at the time that he could not be told the news for several days; in the meantime, Belle sent a telegram to Carrie's husband, Burke, asking him "to do everything as Edward would want it." Willard's body was taken back to San Francisco and buried alongside that of his wife, Marie, who had died several years before.[100]

Another troubling event was the divorce of Archer and Helen. They had been married in 1895, had traveled extensively in Europe with and without Belle and Edward, and had been constant social companions of Belle and Edward in New York. Early in 1918, when Archer and Helen were in England, she separated from him. Family tradition has it that she put a note on his dressing table to say that she was leaving him. Their friends did not know until May that they were separated. They were divorced a few months after Harley Granville Barker and his wife, actress Lillah McCarthy, had been divorced. Then Helen and Granville Barker were married in London on August 31, 1918. He was forty-one years old, a theater manager, playwright, essayist on Shakespeare, and lecturer.[101] Archer came home alone.

Another death in the family was that of Edward's first wife, Mary Alice Prentice Huntington, on April 23, 1916, at the age of sixty-four. She died at her home in San Francisco, 32 Maple Street, after an illness of several weeks. Her three daughters supported one another in their loving sorrow for her.[102] While we have no record of Edward's feelings about her death, it is hard to think that he too did not grieve with his daughters at the death of the woman who had been his wife for thirty-three years, sharing a variety of hardships and joys.

An awkward and unpleasant development in the autumn of 1915, when Edward was seriously ill, was a lawsuit brought against him by his secretary, Robert T. Varnum. We recall that it was Varnum who had gone with him to Europe in 1913 and stood with him when he and Belle were married in Paris. He had been Edward's confidential secretary since July 3, 1911, and his services were, as he claimed in his suit, "of a peculiarly delicate and personal nature and of immeasurable value to said defendant." Varnum had succeeded George E. Miles, who had been secretary for Collis before Edward, after practicing law for twelve years in New York. Varnum left his job as secretary after about ten months—"for good and substantial personal reasons," he said in the suit—and resumed the practice of law on April 30, 1912. In the autumn of 1912, Edward offered him an annual salary of $10,000 ($4,000 more than his earlier salary) and living expenses while away from home, and Varnum took up the job again on December 1, 1912. All went well until about two years after the marriage. Then the situation became difficult and finally intolerable when they were all in California in 1915. According to Edward's testimony, Varnum

> exhibited irritation, bad temper, and ill-will, performed his services in an unwilling and objectionable manner, and was not considerate in his deportment and actions, and so conducted himself as to annoy and offend the defendant and his wife, and to become personally objectionable to them, and during the Spring and early Summer of 1915, while in California, frequently absented himself from the house of the defendant for days at a time without excuse and without defendant's permission, and neglecting the duties of his position.

Edward told his attorneys that Varnum took off for long weekends without permission and had a daily horseback ride "during best working hours of the day," and that "his almost constant manner during the time we were in California was surly and sulky and of the kind most irritating and least possible to describe." Things did not improve when they returned to New York. At Throggs Neck, Varnum "committed numerous acts and omissions, which were extremely distasteful to the defendant." The New York papers assumed that Varnum had offended Arabella. In July, Varnum asked for a leave of absence for six weeks to visit his wife in California. He then either quit or was discharged, depending on which testimony one accepts. In any event, he left the job, and Edward paid him his salary until December 1, 1915. Varnum brought suit for $86,540 with the claim that he had an appointment for life and had been wrongfully discharged. The case was settled out of court; Varnum received $22,500 on January 29, 1917, and signed a general release.[103] It was unpleasant for Edward to be involved in litigation against a person who had been a close associate.

Edward was involved in a second, less personal, lawsuit, also beginning in the autumn of 1915. It turned on the authenticity of a painting that he had bought from the British firm of Lewis and Simmons with a guarantee that it was a picture by George Romney of Mrs. Siddons and her sister Fanny Kemble. Edward hung it in his rooms at the Metropolitan Club, and a friend roused his suspicion by saying that it did not look like a Romney to him. When the experts whom Edward consulted expressed doubt, he asked to return the painting and get his money back. Lewis and Simmons refused, and a suit was instituted by Edward's London solicitors, Guedella and Jacobson. The case was heard in 1917 in the Royal Courts of Justice before the Honorable Justice Darling. By deposition, Edward was asked whether he was an art connoisseur. His reply was straightforward, and it deserves attention as his own view of himself as an art collector:

> No; not in the sense of being a literary or artistic critic. I am not a specialist. I do not know what is authentic from what is not authentic. If, for instance, I was shown a very clever copy or forgery, or if I was shown a picture of the same school, I would not necessarily know

whether it was by the master or by the pupil. Nor would I be sure in many cases whether the picture was painted in the better period or the worse period of a certain master's life. When I buy pictures I have to rely upon the honesty and straightforwardness of the art dealer who sells them to me. Until this case I have never had any trouble with any art dealer in this respect. I am accustomed to giving exceptionally big prices for the paintings which I buy, and therefore I expect and require to have sold to me only pictures of the very best quality.

The trial featured the testimony of art experts who gave opposing views, as well as what was considered witty repartee between the justice and counsel on such topics as whether Mrs. Siddons was in fact knock-kneed. The London newspapers and magazines gave the trial great play. The chambers were crowded by people who thought the trial better than a matinee, and members of all circles of society were intensely interested in it. Huntington was told, "Your name has become a household name in this country." More seriously, it was described as "the most important art case that has ever been fought in this country." Among the host of experts who testified, the curator of the Liverpool Art Gallery, the director of the London City Corporation Art Galleries at the Guildhall, and the curator of the Shakespeare Memorial Gallery all emphatically declared on the last day of the trial that the painting was an authentic Romney. Then Dr. George C. Williamson presented a preliminary sketch of the painting from the Archives of the Royal Academy, signed with the initials of Ozias Humphrey, after which it was concluded that the painting was by Humphrey and not Romney. The case was decided in favor of Edward in May 1917, and he received his money back plus his costs of the trial. The painting was offered by Lewis and Simmons to the National Portrait Gallery, but it was refused on the grounds that it was not of sufficient historical importance.

These two years of uncertainty and tension for Edward had sparked a good deal of levity in Britain; perhaps the controversy took people's minds off what was going on just across the English Channel. Since Edward was sent all the clippings, it is worth quoting one short passage, from *John Bull* for June 2, 1917, as a sample of what he read:

Dear Judge—It would have been surprising if so illustrious a humorist as your Lordship had not had the time of his life in Huntington *v.* Lewis and Simmons. The case set the town agape; it rivalled all the *matinées,* reduced the afternoon concerts to nought, and made the ha'penny papers worth a penny. I know a man who was one of the audience every day, and he told me he would not have missed the week's amusement even if it had cost him a guinea a seat, instead of—oh, no, *not* the policeman! And now that Messrs. Lewis and Simmons have to pay back the £20,000 to Mr. Huntington with interest and all the costs of the lawyers and the experts—oh, those experts!—your Lordship will probably agree with me that the question was as much "When is a joke not a joke?" as "When is a Romney not a Romney?" 'Tis a merry world, m'Lud. Think you not so?[104]

One further distressing event was a theft from the house at 2 East Fifty-seventh Street. On December 4, 1915—while Edward was still ill— a man claiming to be a detective on the New York police force inspected the house to prevent burglaries and carried away a vase valued at $400, under his coat. All 690 detectives from all precincts of the force were lined up to see whether the butler or the maid could identify the thief. They could not, but all the New York and Los Angeles newspapers carried full stories of the event, usually with an implied criticism of this method of trying to catch a thief of a minor object for a man whose art collection was said to have a value of $5 million.[105]

Upon retiring from business in 1910, Edward made a valiant effort to withdraw from the entrepreneurship by which he had become wealthy. He no longer allowed himself to actively start, merge, and sell companies or to acquire large tracts of land and develop them at a profit to himself and, as he thought, for the benefit of society.

His withdrawal from active business management virtually ended the rapid increase in his net worth. It had soared from $13 to $16 million in 1900 (including his inheritance from Collis) to some $55 million at the end of 1910, and then grown more modestly to $67 million by 1914. By the end of 1919, the increase was only to $69 million.

He still had a fortune, however, and he chose to manage it, along with Belle's separate fortune and the trust funds he had established for his children, and the additions he kept making to them. He was always saying that he left all the business matters to his associates, but in fact he retained a good deal of the decision making in his own hands.

He was, however, careful to avoid the spotlight as the owner of anything that received a lot of publicity. The Newport News Shipbuilding and Drydock Company, for example, which had been founded by Collis and was now owned jointly by Edward and Belle, was very active during World War I in building ships for the navy. The battleship USS *Pennsylvania* was launched on March 16, 1915, with about as much public notice as one could imagine. Among the speakers was Secretary of the Navy Josephus Daniels, and the ship was touted as the greatest warship in history. She was christened by Miss Elizabeth Kolb, who was chosen by the governor as "the sweetest girl in Pennsylvania." Every detail about the ship, those responsible for it, and those who were present was fully reported in the newspapers. I have seen 300 stories that came out on the day of the launching, and another 350 from the laggard papers that did not get the news out until the next week or two. Two people who were not present at the launching and who were never mentioned in any of the news reports were Mr. and Mrs. H. E. Huntington, the owners of the shipyard that made the ship. Edward and Belle did make occasional visits to the shipyard, however. Edward became much interested in the training of the apprentices in the twenty different technical trades that were needed there. Edward encouraged the establishment of extra study classes for them on company time, and even a program for especially meritorious ones to have two years of college training. On his visits, Edward always wanted to hear about the apprentice program and could hardly wait before asking, "Now tell me about the apprentices." They learned of his special interest and began a custom of sending him a telegram on his birthday, which he always acknowledged with a word of encouragement. Belle also showed an apt understanding of the shipyard operations and, according to the engineering director, "was a woman of remarkable economic instincts and was capable on occasions of giving very sound advice."[106]

Edward had made spasmodic efforts to sell the shipyard, first for $15 million, then $20 million. In 1917, a tentative offer was communicated from Graham to Edward in California. Edward replied that "Mrs. Huntington is very much opposed to selling it, but I think perhaps if I were on the ground I might induce her to do so." He told their agent that "Mrs. Huntington has a sentimental interest in the Yard. Possibly, when I return, if all the conditions are satisfactory, I can persuade her to sell."[107] But he could not. In 1918, there was another flurry of activity, with many letters and telegrams to and from Edward, the secretary of the navy (who wanted the government to take it over), Homer L. Ferguson (the president of the company), and Camille Weidenfeld, who was trying to act as a broker for the sale. Arabella put her foot down with a telegram to Graham that "Weidenfeld evidently misunderstands our position. Make him understand distinctly that he must drop the matter." The negotiations continued for a while, but no sale of the shipyard was effected during the lives of Edward and Belle.[108]

Edward's method of doing business at this time often irritated the people who were closest to him and in charge of the different enterprises. When money was tight, for example, he was extremely reluctant to allow them to raise the necessary cash for operations by selling any of the bonds they had on hand. When Dunn sold some bonds to raise cash, Edward told him that "I do not want any more of my bonds sold at any price." Dunn reminded him of a conversation in which Edward had fully authorized the sale. Edward replied that "very likely you did make the suggestion that you mention, when you were in New York, but I did not remember having agreed to it; however, it is all right." Likewise, bad feeling arose between Dunn and Graham as they tried to carry out wishes that Edward never fully articulated. In response to Graham's criticism, Dunn replied, "Please let it percolate through your mind slowly that I certainly am no more responsible for this unfortunate condition than you are." Later, in response to Graham's explanation that he had submitted a letter to Huntington and that it had been based on a careful analysis of the situation, Dunn said, "Permit me to say that if you and Mr. Huntington think that was a careful analysis of the situation then it is no wonder you have both been sick."[109]

At this time, Edward was director of as many as seventy-five companies, though many of them were subsidiaries. The companies included those in which he had a major interest but some others as well.

He was chairman of the board of the Chesapeake and Ohio Railway, for example, and also on the board of the Hocking Valley Railway Company.

The cards concerning the monthly meetings of the directors of these two corporations on February 15, 1919, can serve as emblems for Edward's basic concerns at this time. On the front of each card was the announcement of the meeting of the directors of the corporation. On the back of the C & O card, Edward made a list of American writers of special interest to him at that time. The list began with Jonathan Edwards and Benjamin Franklin and ended with Walt Whitman and William Dean Howells. In all, there were nineteen names, with asterisks next to Emerson, Hawthorne, and Longfellow and a question mark by Bryant. On the back of the Hocking Valley card, he made a list of eleven English writers: Chaucer, Spenser, Raleigh, Shakespeare, Bacon, Milton, Hobbes, Bunyan, Locke, Swift, and Fielding.[110] This businessman's attention was not focused on business.

Sixteen

THERE WAS NO PLACE THAT Edward was more enthusiastic about
than Southern California. When he was there, he expressed delight in
being there. When he was away, he expressed regret in not being there.
The expression of these feelings—which are probably the most recurrent motif in his remarks about any place during the last thirty years of
his life—can be epitomized by quoting once more what he told the
news correspondent in London in 1914, just after he and Belle had
escaped from France: "I have always said that I lived only for the day to
come when I can drop everything and just go to Southern California
and stay there the rest of my life. To my mind it's the greatest place on
earth and I've yet to meet anyone who has been there who doesn't agree
with me."[1]

After his remarriage in 1913, one might have expected him to follow
this deeply expressed desire, particularly since his new residence was
now completed to his discriminating satisfaction, fitted out with such
splendid objects as the Beauvais tapestries and the Gainsborough paintings, and surrounded by rare plants and beautiful gardens, all in what
was thought by many to be the most gorgeous setting in Southern
California.

As it turned out, he spent relatively little time in Southern California
from 1914 to 1919. He and Belle came out every year, but they spent only
a little more than a third of their time at their California home. In 1914,

they were there about two and a half months, from the end of January to early April, before they had to hurry back to say good-bye to Archer and Helen. In 1915, about four and a quarter months, from the middle of February to latter June. In 1916, a little over six months, plus half a month in Paso Robles, from the middle of March to latter September. In 1917, about six months, from early April to early October. In 1918, about three and a half months, from early August to latter November. And in 1919 about four months, plus a month in Paso Robles, between latter April and latter September. Natives—and more recent immigrants as well—may notice with surprise that they came more in the summer months, and very little from December through March.

There were doubtless many reasons they did not spend more time in Southern California during these years. The attraction of the Chateau Beauregard was not one, since they did not venture back to France during wartime. But they did spend a third of their time in Southern California during these six years, and this chapter is an effort to give some account of that life.

The quiet social life that the Huntingtons had established during their first visit in early 1914 continued through these years. They had frequent guests for lunch or dinner, but these were mostly family members—Howard and Leslie—or friends like the Pattons and the Dunns, or the Bannings, Bixbys, and Bryants. Carrie and Burke came down from San Francisco to visit them every year, and the visits usually extended to about two months; Edward had Myron Hunt design and build a house for them nearby on Rosalind Road, and they moved there permanently in 1919 and became a regular part of the family circle. Whenever family members came from out of town for a visit, Edward usually met them at the railway station with his car and driver and took them out to the ranch.

Once in a while the Huntingtons entertained visiting dignitaries. When the secretary of the navy, Josephus Daniels, and his wife stopped briefly in Los Angeles in August 1919, the Huntingtons gave a small tea for them. Edward drove out with them from Los Angeles, along with the mayor. He first took them on a stroll through the gardens and then showed them a selection of his choice books and manuscripts. Then

Belle presided over a tea in their honor, served on the loggia for a select group of guests.[2]

The loggia, or large covered porch on the east side of the house, was one of Edward's favorite spots. It was furnished informally with rattan chairs, sofas, and a swing, and it was the place the family liked to gather in the warm weather. The surrounding trees had not grown very tall, and it commanded a spectacular view—in smog-free air—of the San Gabriel Mountains to the north, Old Baldy and its associates to the east, and the fertile San Gabriel Valley and the distant Whittier Hills to the south. When newspaper reporters came to interview Edward, he often received them there. Otheman Stevens told of finding him, in 1917, "seated in a swinging chair on the broad, classic, portico of his San Marino home, with the vista of the San Gabriel, the most lushly serene and beautiful valley in the world, stretching for miles on either side, finally merging its radiance of cultivation and domesticity in the rosy tinted hills."[3] Garden writer Ernest Braunton thought that the foothill section of the San Gabriel Valley, where the Huntington house was located, was "the finest land the sun shines on." He told of sharing a joy in the views from that spot with Edward:

> Few know that this man of gigantic business affairs is an intense lover of nature. The world knows that he, with the aid of a staff of experts, is chasing rare and ancient books, but the writer has stood beside him on the heights at San Marino when he called attention to the golden rays of the setting sun as it tinted the hilltops and treetops and spoke of the deepening purple shadows cast by the hills and oak trees on his great estate. He stood for some minutes thus, "at the end of a perfect day," and as we turned to leave it he said: "I never get tired of that scene with its changes at the close of the day, and I have looked at it many times."[4]

The house itself was widely commended as complementing the beautiful scene. "I hesitate to use the word 'magnificent' in describing Mr. Huntington's residence," wrote Porter Garnett in *Sunset* magazine, "for the term may so easily convey a wrong impression. Standing white and long and low against its background of soaring mountains, it attracts the eye by reason of its classical reserve, stateliness and dignity. Through its possession of these qualities, rather than the quality of showy splendor, it may be said to be the most truly magnificent residence in the whole of California."[5]

Edward delighted in the house and the environment. " 'I would never go away from this place,' he said with beaming eye as he viewed the most beautiful vista of the most beautiful valley in the world, the San Gabriel, 'if I didn't have to look after things in the East occasionally.' "[6]

While in Southern California, Edward enjoyed himself thoroughly. He took long walks through the grounds nearly every day and admired the progress of the planting, which included—in addition to the rare trees and shrubs—thousands of specimens of annual and perennial flowers, like stock, penstemon, iris, and phlox. A number of other buildings had been constructed along with the residence, and they gave him pleasure, too—a bowling alley and billiard room, a large stable, a spacious garage, and a superintendent's office. He often sat on the loggia and read while enjoying the view. Croquet was the outdoor game of choice, played in the North Vista, especially when grandchildren were visiting. The servants had their own croquet grounds, and Belle saw to it that their equipment was replaced whenever it began to show signs of aging. Another pleasant outdoor activity was visiting the large aviaries behind the house: they had been finished in 1915 and housed many varieties of tropical birds. Edward usually spent the afternoons in his library with his books: reading, studying, getting to know them better. There was sociability with Belle and family and guests at lunch and dinner; these were formal meals taken in the dining room with black tie and long dresses and plenty of serving men (four even when the two dined alone). In the evening, cards were usually played whenever interested guests were there; auction bridge and hearts were the favorite games. They lived on a regular schedule: Edward's breakfast was brought to him at eight, lunch was at one, dinner at seven, and the evening entertainment concluded about ten.

When Edward woke up in the morning, he was full of good spirits and wanted to sing. He taught his valet, Alfonso Gomez, a song that he and Collis had sung together years before:

Here's to good old whiskey,
   drink it down, drink it down;
Here's to good old whiskey,
   drink it down, drink it down.
Here's to good old whiskey,
   'cause it makes you feel so frisky,
Here's to good old whiskey,
   drink it down, down, down.

As soon as Alfonso appeared in the morning, Edward began the ditty and insisted that Alfonso join in. The duet amused Edward mightily, and he began the day laughing. His friends and the servants thought of him as "a great kidder," and he got a lot of laughs out of silly, harmless jokes like the "good old whiskey" song. Or his dealings with John Gomboltz, the electrician whose job it was to break in Edward's new shoes. Gomboltz, whose feet were just the size of Edward's, would wear a new pair for two weeks, turn them over to Edward, and get the old pair as a reward. Edward sometimes went down to the basement and chatted with the people at work there. He would ask Gomboltz, with mock solemnity, "Well, how are my shoes?" and then add, with a smile, "Walk very carefully; don't spoil them, don't drop any grease on them." Later, Gomboltz went up to the pantry and "had a great laugh" when he told the other servants that "the old man came downstairs and told me not to spoil those shoes."

Edward's bedroom suite was on the southeast corner of the house on the second floor. It included the pleasant corner room with a view over the San Gabriel Valley to the south and of the foothills and Mount Baldy to the east (the room that has been used since the 1970s for "conversation" paintings), the next major room toward the west overlooking the south terrace, and the small rooms between them, which were used as his dressing room and bath. Belle's suite, later converted into a period room called the Quinn Room, was adjacent to the corner room on the east side of the house, which she and her companion occupied.[7]

Belle ran the house. She was the "real master of the house," according to Alfonso. "What she says, goes." She was independent-minded. Once when a friend of hers asked why they kept as many as fifteen cows for only themselves and their servants, she bridled and said, "No friend of mine, regardless of how frank, or no relation of mine will ever try to teach or explain how I shall run and conduct my home." She concluded her remarks by saying, "I'm not here to discuss—I want friends to play cards." In addition to independence, privacy was also important to her. She repeatedly told Edward that "I don't want any visitors in the house" who are not friends. "Whoever comes to my front door has to be my friend, coming for a cup of tea or for lunch." One evening three gentlemen called on Edward to talk business, and he received them in a parlor. When the call continued toward bedtime, Belle learned what was going on. She told Alfonso to "go downstairs and tell those three gentlemen that it's quarter to eleven and that Mrs. Huntington wishes that Mr. Huntington should be in bed right away, so they can leave." When Alfonso hesitated, she took his hands and said, "Alfonso, I'm the boss of this mansion. You tell Mr. Huntington that I want him to go to bed and tell those three gentlemen that I said for them to go home." Within one minute, they left.

The servants considered the Huntingtons kind and generous employers. People on duty on Sunday were always taken for a ride by the chauffeur so that they could have a pleasant break. On Christmas and other holidays, the servants were given the day off to be with their families and relatives. "Let them be free," said Belle to Edward. "You and I can spend the rest of the day in our rooms with a little applesauce, a little spinach, or a cup of soup. Let them have a good time." The Huntingtons gave generous cash gifts to the servants and treats to all their children. Belle went to visit the employees and families at their homes, and she had a cup of tea with them. Whenever the Huntingtons returned from a time away, the staff members were invited to come and visit individually with Belle, and she always asked about each member of their families.[8]

The Huntingtons socialized mostly with family members—at Howard and Leslie's house, and later at Carrie and Burke's—or with close friends like the George Pattons and the Billy Dunns. Once in a while they went to a small lunch or dinner at a gathering place like the California Club. Edward belonged to many social clubs. He continued his membership in the Bohemian Club in San Francisco, which he had joined in 1903. In Los Angeles, he had long been in the Jonathan Club, the California Club, and the Sunset Club, and frequently was president of the first two. He was also a member of most of the country clubs, including the Los Angeles, the Annandale, and the San Gabriel, as well as the Pasadena Polo Club. But Edward and Belle were not particularly active in the social gatherings of these associations.[9]

Occasionally Edward and Belle would take a day trip in the area. They might drive to Santa Monica, for example, to have lunch with a friend and look at the property that Belle had inherited from Collis— the high point opposite and overlooking the pier. Then they would proceed up the beach for several miles but return home in San Marino by 6:00 P.M., in time to dress for dinner. Other day trips included Mt. Lowe and Long Beach. In June 1915, Edward took Burke Holladay by train to the Big Creek Dam in Fresno County; they walked up to the dam to see Huntington Lake, where the Huntington Lake Lodge was being built. Edward and Burke spent the night in a tent house and returned home the next day by train. A more ambitious trip involving the whole family was to Paso Robles by train, where they stayed two weeks in May 1916 and a month in June 1919 at the Paso Robles Hotel. Edward and Belle both took "the treatment" of mud baths nearly every day, but Edward said that he did not feel any better at the conclusion than he had at the beginning.[10] When Belle and Edward left San Marino for New York in June 1915, they went by way of San Francisco to visit the Panama-Pacific International Exposition, held to commemorate the opening of the Panama Canal the year before; they stayed for several days, in company with Carrie and Burke, and with Elizabeth and Brockway. "They all enjoyed it greatly," according to Burke. Then Belle and Edward went on to New York.[11]

Their time in Southern California was marred by the periods of illness that plagued both Edward and Belle. Edward suffered from a bladder disorder that was treated by having him catheterized twice a day. Edward's valet was trained in the procedure by Dr. Ernest Bryant, and Edward thought that Alfonso was more skillful at it than the physicians were. The treatment took about forty-five minutes: Edward had it between 6:00 and 7:00 A.M. and between 10:00 and 11:00 P.M. every day. This practice went on every day for the last fifteen years of his life. Alfonso was happy that after the morning treatment Edward "was on the go all day long, feeling fine" and that after the evening treatment "he slept like a baby"—thanks in part to his daily sleeping tablet. Belle was extremely solicitous about Edward's health. If he sneezed, Belle had Alfonso "go upstairs and get his shawl and cover Mr. Huntington's head because she was afraid that a little draft might kill him." Edward said, "Well, I don't feel that I'm living in a private home, I feel I'm living in a hospital. Half of the time I'm always covered, head to nose, on account of the colds." Alfonso observed that "Mrs. Huntington thought he was just like a baby."[12]

As for Belle, her vision gradually got worse, she needed support in walking, and her hearing became impaired. Her companion helped her and read the newspapers to her every day. Mrs. Schwerin, the wife of a railway official, came twice a week to read to her more extensively, and Belle said that "nobody can read books aloud like Mrs. Schwerin does." In April 1917 Belle had the misfortune to break her leg: after being the guest of honor at a ladies' luncheon downtown at the California Club, she fell and fractured her leg just above the ankle while coming down the steps leaving the club. The fall also had an adverse effect on her vision. A little over a year later she had another accident when leaving a luncheon given by Mrs. Hancock Banning at the California Club: this time her hand was crushed, though not fractured, when her chauffeur closed the door of her car while her hand was resting on the sill.[13]

The greatest detriment to their joint pleasure in Southern California, however, was the fact that Belle simply did not like being there. Clara was right in her estimate, shortly after their marriage, that "I doubt if he will ever be allowed to spend much time there, as she doesn't like the country and is frank to maintain she doesn't like California."[14] She repeatedly told Alfonso how much she disliked Southern California. The heat bothered both of them. In June 1917, Edward suffered from heat prostration during a particularly hot spell and had to stay in bed for a week.[15] Once when Belle became ill from the heat, she called out, "Edward, I can't stand any more. You've just killed me. Alfonso, we're leaving for New York in two days. If Mr. Huntington wants to stay in California, let him stay, we'll go alone." Edward heard her outburst and quietly told Alfonso, "Pack my things. Let's go." Alfonso packed Edward's bags and they all left. Later Alfonso observed that "Mr. Huntington would never say a word or anything to upset Mrs. Huntington. He took her as the real boss of the place. He did everything she said." Heat or no heat, she said, "I don't like Los Angeles." Alfonso observed that "Mr. Huntington was in love with Los Angeles and she knew it, and every time she came to California it was just to please Mr. Huntington." Another time Alfonso said that "Mr. Huntington would have liked to stay here in California all year round and never move, but she wouldn't allow him to do such a thing."

It is likely that Belle's real reason for disliking California was because Archer was not there. In New York, Belle and Archer were with one another a great deal: they had lunch together nearly every day, and he always met her at the railroad station when she arrived. Many people said they had never known a woman so in love with her son as she was. Their family physician, Dr. Coley, said, "Never, never in my medical profession have I seen a woman so affectionate to her son." When they were together, she treated him like a baby, squeezing his arms and frequently kissing him. And she was always buying presents for him. Edward said, "It's wonderful how Mrs. Huntington loves her son Archer." Burke Holladay observed that "her ruling passion was mother love for her son." And Archer returned his mother's affection. When Edward once asked him what he wanted for a present, he replied, " 'The only present that I want is to have a rich and loving mother, beautiful mother' and he got up from his chair and he kissed her a dozen times and that made Mrs. Huntington alive again because she was crazy about him." Every year they asked Archer to come to California when they were there, and every year he refused. The house they had built for him did not draw him to California. When he said that he was too big to be comfortable in a sleeping car berth—he was six feet five inches and weighed over 260 pounds—they offered to send their private car with a special bed built for him. But he never came to California, and his absence probably had a good deal to do with Belle's wish not to be there either.[16]

Edward made substantial additions to the art collection during these five years. One way to sum these additions up is to say that the collection, which was mainly housed in San Marino, nearly doubled in its book value, from about $4 million to $7 million. Paintings comprised the major part, and they rose from $2.6 to $3.9 million; the other art objects—tapestries, bronzes, furniture, and sculpture—increased from $1.5 to $3.1 million. For comparison, we can recall that the books and manuscripts, mainly located in the New York house, nearly tripled in value, from $2.2 to $5.9 million, thanks to the stunning acquisitions reviewed in the preceding chapter.[17]

Among the paintings that he bought at this time, four deserve special note. Two good Romney paintings were acquired, *Penelope Lee Acton* in 1916 for $325,000 and *Susannah Lee Acton* in 1917 for $175,000, as well as two good Lawrence paintings, *Mrs. Cunliffe-Offley* in 1917 for $170,000 and *Emily Anderson (Little Red Riding Hood)* in 1918 for $230,000.[18]

The other art objects acquired can be represented by several major examples of European art—material that supported the role of the Beauvais tapestries that he had bought in 1909 and strengthened that feature of the collection at a high level of quality. In 1915 he bought two large carpets, woven in the Savonnerie factory in the late seventeenth century for the Grande Galerie of the Louvre, from P. W. French and Company in New York for $110,000. Like the three great Gainsborough paintings that Edward had bought from Duveen in 1911, these had been in the Charles Wertheimer Collection; they had gone from there to J. Pierpont Morgan and had become available again in the sale, after his death, of part of his collection. An even more splendid acquisition from the Morgan collection was a group of twenty-two Renaissance bronzes, bought in 1917 for $320,000. In 1916, Edward bought seven pieces of French eighteenth-century sculpture—featuring Clodion and Falconet—for $330,000, and in 1918 a suite of French furniture in Beauvais tapestry for $380,000.[19] These acquisitions, for about $1.1 million, along with a number of fine pieces of eighteenth-century French furniture, formed the nucleus of a strong supporting collection of French art. But the collection as yet had no individual pieces of star quality. It is interesting to consider how it came about that Edward's acquisitions of books and manuscripts during these years seemed to surpass his acquisitions of paintings and other art objects. The war limited dealings in all foreign material, of course, with greater limits on material that was in continental Europe. Edward's principal agent for books and manuscripts, George D. Smith, was in New York, while his principal agent for art works, Duveen, was centered in London and Paris. Finally, one could buy only what was offered for sale, and the owners of significant collections of books and manuscripts had, as it turned out, more reason to want to sell, or were more encouraged to do so. Edward had spectacular opportunities in the book and manuscript line during these years, and it is not surprising that there were not comparable opportunities in the art market.

Other opportunities could offer themselves in the future. In the meantime, Edward and Duveen were coming in closer contact, and Edward was moving toward becoming his preferred customer, that person who was first to be offered the very best that could be found. Duveen was a great salesman, prone to exaggerate the importance of whatever he had to sell, a master of rhetoric, and full of tricks to catch a customer. But he had a great eye for fine pieces of art, and he used his talents with abandon to procure fine things for his preferred customer, always at a big profit to himself. A few short passages from the many letters between Edward and Duveen during these years can perhaps offer some insights about their relationship and about Edward's role as an art collector at this time.

When Edward especially enjoyed a new work of art, he often told Duveen, who shared the enjoyment. In response to Edward's pleasure with the Savonnerie rugs, Duveen said, "Your remarks about the Savonnerie rugs make me feel very happy. They must indeed look great and I can see in my mind's eye what a wonderful effect they create." He was equally glad with Edward about the furniture with the Boucher tapestry covers and expressed the feeling that they were "the finest tapestry set in this country." Sometimes Duveen opened his treasury of hyperbole to try to convince Edward when he was hesitant about making a purchase. Duveen asserted that Romney's *Penelope Lee Acton* was "the finest Romney in existence. There is nothing like it in my opinion in England or anywhere in the world." It was not only "the finest Romney in existence but also one of the most beautiful pictures of the English School." When Edward had a small Houdon bronze in his house on approval and was considering sending it back, Duveen begged him to keep it: "It is much too fine to leave your house." And he proceeded to a little discourse on aesthetics. The library room with the large Beauvais tapestries needed just such a dark touch. "I cannot help thinking," Duveen wrote, "of the mise-en-scene of a beautiful ballet in which the color effect of the most wonderful shades of pinks, yellows, pale blues, etc., is heightened by the introduction of a few men in black costumes. The introduction of these darker notes has always had the approval of great artists in their conceptions. You have an example of such a stage setting in your library, having regard particularly to the Boucher tapestries. Please therefore do study out this theory with regard to the Boucher Room with Mrs. Huntington, as I am sure it will appeal to you both." Throughout these years, Duveen became more and more drawn to the Huntingtons and came to prefer them in offering art objects. In 1916, Henry Clay Frick heard that Duveen was buying an important Romney and asked him for it. Duveen explained to Edward that "I told him I had given you the first refusal, and indeed I told him I had given you the first refusal of any great English painting we might acquire. I must say that he was very charming about it and said I was quite right." Duveen kept Huntington's needs in mind, and in 1918 he anticipated the following years when he said, "There may be a chance of getting something great for you."[20]

In this stage of building the art collection, Belle's judgment was a big factor. She had an important collection of her own, and her taste was valued. Jacques Seligmann wrote to her from Paris in 1916 that "nobody understands works of art in America better than you do. Do not believe that I say that in order to flatter you, this really is my opinion. The proof is that you have got the most wonderful collection, which anybody can see." And Mitchell Samuels of P. W. French and Company told her in 1918 that "I cannot get over your wonderful memory for recognizing everything you have only once seen. For a person who claims to have poor eyesight, you are a marvel. For the last ten years you have never failed to recognize immediately any object you have previously seen."[21]

While in California, Edward befriended a sculptor, Prince Paul Troubetskoy. Archer had first sponsored his coming to the United States and acted as his patron in New York. Troubetskoy came to Pasadena in 1917 and did life-size clay busts of the two Huntingtons, which were cast in bronze. Edward thought well of his work and characterized him as "one of the finest sculptors in the world." He bought several of his small bronzes for the art collection and, as president of the Harrison Gray Otis Memorial Association, got Troubetskoy the commission to do a bronze statue, in heroic proportion, of Otis.[22]

The true collector is always at work. When he was in California, Edward was engaged part of the time in activities that led to his great achievements in collecting books and manuscripts reviewed in the preceding chapter. In addition, he was always stepping into bookshops. In one week in June 1916 he bought W. H. Hudson's *Green Mansions* for $1.50, an *Historical Atlas of Modern Europe* for $1.50, a *Handbook of Modern French Sculpture* for $2, and *Breathe and Be Well* for $1.[23] He was known to have all sorts of books. The general manager of his Los Angeles Railway Company, G. J. Kuhrts, wrote him in 1919 asking whether he had "an extra set of the Harvard Classics. If you have, I would appreciate it very much if you would donate it to the Los Angeles Railway Technical Library" for the use of employees.[24] Edward picked up a few collections in California, like the James T. Armstrong Collection of wood printing blocks, reputedly the largest in the world, and the A. S. Macdonald Collection of some four thousand items of Californiana, many of them great rarities.[25] It took a good deal of haggling with the agent before Edward was able to close the deal on the Macdonald collection for $15,000 in bonds and $10,000 in Los Angeles real estate. Soon afterward Macdonald wrote Edward saying, "I wish to congratulate you upon the acquisition of my 'Californiana'. It is a source of much satisfaction to me to have the library pass into the hands of one who I know fully appreciates its value and have it become one of the important units in the creation of the largest collection of Americana in existence." And he spoke as one book lover to another when he concluded, "I trust you will derive as much pleasure in the possession of these volumes as I have enjoyed in gathering them."[26]

As the quantity of books and manuscripts increased in the New York residence, it became evident to Edward that he had to make more extensive provision for housing them and the increasing library staff.

He had sent fifty thousand volumes to the San Marino house, but both sites were getting crowded. In September 1916 he told reporters that he had decided to bring all of his books and manuscripts to San Marino and that he would probably construct a library building there to house them.[27] This was just a year after he had engaged Cole as his librarian. It was also after such major acquisitions as the Church, Chew, Devonshire, and Halsey collections; but it was before the Bridgewater House Library, the Bixby, and the many collections he was able to acquire in the 1920s.

One year later Edward wrote formally to Myron Hunt about plans for the library. "As you know," he wrote on October 30, 1917, from New York, "I am planning to build a Library at the San Marino Ranch. I think you said your fee would be 6%. If you are coming East, I should like to go about with you to visit some of the library buildings here, to get some ideas for the one I am to erect."[28] Hunt went to New York the next month and visited fifteen or twenty libraries, often in company with Edward. He took particular note of the New York Public Library, the Library of Congress, and the John Carter Brown and John Hay libraries at Brown University in Providence. He also consulted George Parker Winship, the Harvard librarian who had earlier been head of the John Carter Brown Library. Edward asked Rosenbach to send him plans of libraries he thought well of, and Rosenbach supplied him with a package of plans on November 28. Hunt got back to Los Angeles in the middle of December after an absence of five weeks, and he set to work immediately on the project.[29]

By January 11, 1918, Hunt had completed twelve pages of preliminary sketches, including watercolors of the west and front elevations, which he sent to Edward. He had provided some four thousand square feet of closed space for book stacks divided into three floors with stacks seven and a half feet high, a large room called the Main Reading and Exhibition Hall, a founder's room, rooms for administrative purposes, and a planting plan for the surrounding area. Edward's first reaction was unfavorable. He wrote Hunt from New York, on February 5, that "I do not like the facade of the plans of the Huntington Library. It looks altogether too 'squatty', lacking the dignity I want it to have. This plan has been up in my library in front of me for some while, and I have tried my best to like it but can't. The more I look at it, the less it appeals to me." Two weeks later he sent Hunt some further comments about the proportions of the building, the size of the windows, and the arrangement of the columns. Hunt replied that he would offer "another scheme for exterior proportions and treatment."[30]

Hunt had also sent a copy of his preliminary sketches to Winship for comment, and Winship responded with two long letters. Hunt sent a copy of each reply to Edward right away. In the first, Winship lamented the lack of space for lectures and small classes and argued that the community "should be kept interested in the institution as something more than merely a place to take strangers to"; he proposed that a man "of the highest repute" should be hired each year to give lectures to the community. Winship thought the general layout thoroughly admirable for "handling the stream of transient passers-through," the throngs of invited guests, and the "occasional student investigator." In the second letter, Winship said that they were overestimating the number of serious students who might want to use the library and that it would be better to have the attendant who was supposed to supervise them be rather a janitor to keep watch over the visitors and point out items of interest. He warned against the normal appointment of "a retired clergyman or a discarded professor" to the position, advising that they talk about themselves too much, but suggested instead a retired butler, a pensioned coachman, or a superannuated bank messenger, any of which would be "likely to have quite as much general intelligence and more sense about kinds of people, than those usually selected for such places").[31] Such was the advice from Harvard, where Edward's son and nephew had gone.

Another suggestion came to Edward at this time that would have eliminated the need for a library building altogether. R. U. Johnson of the American Academy of Arts and Letters in New York suggested that the library be given to the academy and housed in the building to be erected on the lots that Archer had donated. "The Academy is likely to be a great influence," Johnson concluded, in helping to "build up the ideals of the Country against all forms of Bolshevism and lawlessness." Edward replied mildly that "regarding the future of my library, arrangements have already been made to present it to the state of California."[32]

Hunt went back to his drawing board and worked out alternate plans. He took his new plans to New York in the spring, and they settled most of the details when Edward was in California that summer and autumn, from August 3 to November 26, 1918. One of Edward's major requirements was that the building be made as fireproof as possible through the use of steel and concrete rather than flammable materials. In the winter, Edward approved the plans in principle. Then on February 21, 1919, Hunt was able to send him a copy of the working drawings, the specifications, and a long letter about all of the decisions on details, with special attention to the lighting. Hunt made frequent reference to what Huntington had said about this or that detail, with full explanation of any deviations from his wishes. In the planning and construction of the library building, Edward was really in control, he acted like the owner, and he tried to get just what he himself thought best after taking into account the views of the architect.[33]

There were still problems in the way of starting construction. First there had been the war, then shortages (such as of steel) caused by the war, and then an increase in the cost of labor and materials to a degree that Edward thought excessive and that caused him to defer any building. And some opposition developed within Edward's own circle of closest associates. Dunn sent Edward a telegram on March 13, 1919, that the news of the forthcoming construction of the library "is causing us untold trouble"; they were trying to get the railroad commission to raise fares because the company was losing money on its operations, and "all this extravagant library talk makes the situation almost unbearable." Hunt was taking bids as if construction were about to begin, and Dunn asked Huntington to contradict this impression. Edward dutifully replied that, at that moment, he had no idea of "building library and can't understand Hunt's taking bids."[34]

The problems were in due course solved. In August 1919 Edward felt able to tell Otheman Stevens, "Yes, I shall build the library I have contemplated. These books of mine in value to the world of thought are a great responsibility; if seriously damaged, and of course if destroyed, they could not be replaced and the loss would thereby be irreparable." He went on to express, in a single sentence, the essence of his feeling about his library. This sentence also admirably summarizes his whole general sense of responsibility for his possessions: "I feel it is my duty to give them a safe and proper home, for the owner of such things is really little more than a trustee and his responsibility is far greater than attaches to ownership of articles which there is some reason for regarding as purely personal."[35]

Excavation of the site began about the middle of August 1919, and the *Los Angeles Times* proudly announced that it was "progressing rapidly under the personal supervision of Mr. Huntington."[36] The foundations were in by the end of September, and work moved along smoothly. Construction was completed in a little more than a year. There were the usual number of problems that had to be solved in the course of construction. One example can serve to show who was in charge and where his heart lay.

Bronze doors were especially designed and cast for the front of the library building. Hunt wanted to use the signs of the zodiac as emblems on the doors. Edward insisted that the emblems should be the symbols or marks that early printers had used to identify their work. He gave a list of twenty-two such marks, arranged in order of his preference, beginning with the device of William Caxton, the first English printer.[37] His wishes were carried out. After the building was completed, when someone wanted to take a photograph of Edward, he liked to stand in front of the bronze doors with the printers' marks all around him.

The creation of the Huntington Library, Art Gallery, and Botanical Gardens was probably the greatest accomplishment of Edward's life. The legal document that formalized this creation was signed on August 30, 1919. It was preceded by a good deal of careful thought as to what disposition should be made of the ever-growing collection of rare books and manuscripts, of paintings and other objects of art, and of the gardens with their rare plants. And a number of his friends felt free to offer him a great variety of advice—ranging from wise to absurd—on the subject.

The idea that these personal possessions should be made useful to the public in some permanent form was long in Edward's mind, even when the collections were in their earliest stages. In 1906 he said, "I am going to give something to the public before I die."[38] The principle was clear to him, and he frequently described himself, in the manner quoted in the preceding section, as "a trustee" whose responsibility for his books and manuscripts and art objects was "far greater than attaches to own-ership of articles which there is some reason for regarding as purely personal." The method by which he could "give something to the public" became clear to him only gradually in the course of these years.

Various people encouraged him in several different ways to carry out his wish to "give something to the public." In 1906, George Ellery Hale was seated next to Edward at a banquet at the Hotel Maryland in Pasadena. Edward told Hale, an astronomer serving as director of the Mt. Wilson Observatory and active at Throop College, about his col-lection of rare books and art. Hale told Edward of his plan to develop a research center in Pasadena, and how well a library would fit into this scheme.[39] In 1910, Edward's friend Baron Natili urged him to allow the public to see his paintings. "You have the right to own paintings," he told Edward firmly, "but you have no right to deprive the world of the enjoyment of them."

Natili was seconding the comments of Otheman Stevens, who, in asking Edward about allowing the public into his ranch, had been bold enough to say that "no one has a moral right to shut up beautiful paintings where they cannot be enjoyed." Edward responded that he had had bad experiences with the public at his ranch: "Individually people are ladies and gentlemen, but collectively the public forgets other persons' rights. I had the ranch open for some time, and the place, the trees and the flowers were frightfully abused and I had to have the gates locked." He mused further about making the pictures available to the public: "What you say about pictures has some basis; I have not thought the matter over yet, but I will, and probably some suitable plan can be arranged. I am not selfish about pictures; in fact I enjoy having other people enjoy anything that I enjoy." He concluded his response by remarking, "I cannot say definitely about such things, but I shall think it over." Baron Natili was not quite satisfied, and he pursued the topic by adverting to the set of five Beauvais tapestries that Edward had bought the year before: "To shut that up, away from where people of taste and perception could see it, would be appalling. Do not do it, Edward." But Edward would not be pushed to agree to anything that he had not thought through thoroughly and to his satisfaction. "I will think it over seriously," he responded. Nothing more yet.[40]

In the summer of 1911, when Edward came to Southern California from New York with his new secretary, Robert T. Varnum, he was met in San Bernardino by Otheman Stevens, who rode the rest of the way in with him. Edward was in a frolicsome mood, and he began by interviewing Stevens: "Tell me all about politics and the cholera in New York," Edward began, "and who is going to be mayor." As they passed a walnut grove, Varnum asked why the nuts were so large and Edward responded that "a little farther on I'll show you some trees, improved ones, which grow the nuts ready to eat, and on every twig where a nut grows you will see a nutcracker growing as well." After Edward had answered Stevens's question about what new paintings he had bought, he added, "You'll have to see them for yourself." To which Stevens responded, "Then you have decided to be decent about your art possessions and let the public have a chance to enjoy them?" Edward answered, "Why, certainly; I am not a man who holds that personal possession of a beautiful piece of artistic creation carries with it the right to seclude that work. But this is a matter to which I have not given any attention, as the place is not ready. When the time arrives some plan will be put into effect whereby those who value such things can see them." This answer represented an advance over his open-minded, noncommittal reply of the year before.

Before 1911 and 1914, several events occurred that had a bearing on the future use of his collections. In 1912, a group of friends organized the Pasadena Music and Art Association and elected Hale as president and Huntington, who attended the organizational meeting on June 12 with George Patton and Howard's wife, Leslie, as a director. They described their mission as the promotion of "the interests of music, painting, sculpture, architecture, and the kindred arts in Pasadena."[41] In 1913, Edward and Belle were married, and we have already seen how bitterly she opposed having anyone except their friends enter their home to see the pictures or the books. In February 1914, Harrison Gray Otis wrote a long letter to Edward urging him to open his grounds to the public; he offered to have a plan drawn up to incorporate any restrictions that Edward wished to make and assured him that it would delight thousands and gain widespread credit for Edward.[42]

In 1914, Edward thought it prudent to make a new will after his remarriage, and he consulted with his personal attorney, Albert C.

Crutcher, and with Dunn. He signed his new will on March 28, 1914, with Crutcher, Dunn, and S. M. Haskin as witnesses. He left generous legacies and trust funds to his relatives—$4 million to Belle, $1 million to each of his children and to Carrie, one-half million to Willard and Leonora, and lesser sums to others. He left all the paintings, other art, books and manuscripts, and the home property of five hundred acres to Belle for her lifetime and then to the County of Los Angeles "to be by said municipality perpetually maintained as a museum, park and library for the use and benefit of the public"; if, however, the county failed to maintain the property "as a public museum, park and library," then it reverted to his heirs-at-law. With this document, Edward had settled on a way of establishing a permanent institution for the benefit of the public without its intruding on his and Belle's privacy; but the institution would not exist until after he and his wife had died, and then it would be under political control and without any specific mission. Nevertheless, a major step had been taken.

In the next month, when Hale was in New York, he spent an afternoon with Edward touring Archer's Hispanic Museum. In the course of the afternoon Edward told him of his decision to give all of his art, books, and home property to the County of Los Angeles for them to establish a museum, park, and library. The next day Hale wrote him an ardent five-page typed letter in response to what Edward had said. Hale congratulated him warmly on his generous decision and spoke expansively of the future central role of California in the development of art in America; he took exception to the thought of having "political leaders" in charge, as they do not have the necessary "judgment and taste." Hale suggested, instead, the Pasadena Music and Art Association as trustees, with Mrs. H. E. Huntington and Archer to be added to the board. Two weeks later, when Hale told a close friend about this letter, he called it "an argument . . . to prove that he should give them to the Art Association, and afterwards almost repented having sent it. But when I got home I found a very friendly letter saying he found some of the suggestions 'most excellent,' and would consider them. So perhaps no harm was done. If he would only leave the whole thing to the Association with an ample endowment, I should be more than delighted." When Hale reviewed this episode in his biographical notes, he said: "Realizing the menace inherent in political control I took my life in my hands and wrote him a letter . . . pointing out the dangers of leaving such unique and valuable books, manuscripts and objects of art in the hands of characteristic American politicians, who could not be expected to have adequate appreciation of their possibilities." He summed up Edward's response as "non-committal." Edward's reply, on April 20, 1914, was very brief and rather cool; he did say that "some of your suggestions are most excellent and I will take them under consideration."[43]

Hale did not wait for the results of that further consideration. On May 11 he sent Edward a ten-page letter arguing in favor of making his institution "of real international importance" so that students and scholars would flock to it from all over the world to copy his pictures and study his books. It should be housed in "a perfect copy" of the Parthenon—"a Parthenon in Pasadena, containing your pictures and books, would be in what is essentially a Greek setting," and it could be done for three or four million dollars, including copies of all the sculpture; then the Erectheum could be built, and then an art school. Since more original manuscripts would be needed to work on, the cheapest way to get them would be to organize archaeological expeditions to Egypt. Hale related his own experiences in starting international projects and offered to organize an international board for Edward. The letter arrived in New York shortly before the Huntingtons began their ill-fated trip to Europe, and Edward did not reply until after their return, in October. "I have given the suggestions some thought," he said in a rather cool, polite note. "I am not ready to reply yet but it is quite possible that you have planted a seed." Hale was pleased and did not consider it quite possible that he had *not* planted a seed—which turned out to be the case.[44]

Almost two years went by before there was any more action. Then on March 22, 1916, Hale wrote Edward and asked to see him to discuss the reorganization of the Pasadena Art and Music Association, and on the same day Hale wrote him two other letters, each of four pages: in the first, he reviewed recent developments in Pasadena—at Throop, at the observatory, in music and art—and expressed the need for a Huntington Institute with its own trustees to coordinate all these activities;

in the second, he urged a reorganization of the Pasadena Art and Music Association as the Huntington Institute of Arts and Letters with a scholar of international reputation at its head, an International Advisory Council with members like John Singer Sargent, Joaquin Sorolla, Archer Huntington, Sir Sidney Colvin, and others who would rank with the best of their kind in Europe or America.[45]

Hale did not send either of these letters. Instead, he went to call on Edward on the evening of March 27, and the next day sent him a five-page letter outlining "a concrete plan embodying the general principles we discussed." The Huntington Institute of Art, Letters, and Science would be formed and endowed to supervise and extend all the work in Southern California; the Huntington residence would be the museum; the proposed library would be the locale for literary work, including small rooms as studies for writers and scholars, with a large general meeting room, and a terrace or roof garden with a view. Work in chemistry could go on at Throop, astronomy at Mt. Wilson, and other fields could be developed. Concerts and art exhibits would be organized, and popular lectures given by leading authorities. Archer Huntington would be chairman of the trustees and other trustees would be people like Senator Elihu Root of New York, Professor Henry Fairfield Osborn of the American Museum of Natural History, and Charles L. Hutchinson, the Chicago banker. Edward responded on April 22 with a brief and noncommittal note in which he said that he thought he did not care to merge with the Music and Art Association but the mode of organization of trustees was "in line with my ideas and I hope, with the aid of Mr. Archer Huntington to develop and formulate some such plan."[46]

In May, Hale wrote to Archer to ask if they could meet to discuss plans for Edward's library. Archer politely replied that he did not wish to discuss Edward's plans with Hale: "I think he has a pretty clear idea of what he wants to do, and as intelligent and active men generally make their plans far in advance of action, no doubt there could be no better person to consult than the author of them. Do you not think that you should have a talk with him rather than with me in view of the facts? He has accomplished the impossible in making the collection, which would seem to qualify him for its disposition." He expressed appreciation for Hale's interest and concluded that "I am keenly interested in the great undertaking."[47]

Another two years went by without any further general talks about the organization of the institution. When Hale heard in early 1918 from Henry M. Robinson, the Los Angeles banker and a friend of Edward's, that Edward had made the decision to build a library and that Myron Hunt was at work on the designs, Hale wrote to Hunt and told him of the space needs that followed from his earlier discussions with Huntington "about the proper utilization of such a building . . . by prominent scientific and literary men who may be visiting Pasadena in connection with the work of Throop College or other institutions": a large terrace overlooking the valley "where a man might sit and write in fine weather"; a series of private rooms that would be "kept for the exclusive use of such men as Alfred Noyes, Arthur Noyes, Dr. Millikan, Professor Kapteyn, or other really eminent men while they are at work in Pasadena"; and general space for assemblies. Hunt prudently sent the letter on to Huntington and assured Hale that Huntington planned to have the library "accessible to scholars and their convenience considered." Hale was delighted and asked Hunt to show him his sketches as the work progressed: "I can imagine no greater satisfaction than to spend my declining years on the terrace or loggia, reading a fine old book and reveling in the pleasures of the imagination."[48] Which sounds more like a retirement home than a research institute.

During the next year and a half, Edward consulted with his lawyers about the form and substance of a legal document that would establish the kind of institution he wanted. The necessary document, in the form of a trust indenture, set up an institution comprising "a library, art gallery, museum and park." Its object, quoted directly from the California statutes authorizing such institutions, was the "advancement of learning, the arts and sciences, and to promote the public welfare," and it was named the Henry E. Huntington Library and Art Gallery. Five trustees were appointed: Howard E. Huntington (Edward's son), Archer Milton Huntington (Belle's son), W. E. Dunn and George S. Patton (Edward's two closest friends and colleagues), and George E. Hale, the astronomer who had shown such interest in this whole concept, even though most of his ideas were not adopted. Edward and

Belle retained, during their lifetimes, control of the trust property, the appointment of trustees, and the power to modify the trust. Merger with any other institution was prohibited; if a merger was attempted or the trust invalidated, the real property and securities were to go to Huntington's heirs-at-law and the contents of the buildings to the Metropolitan Museum of Art. The powers and duties of the trustees were specified in some detail, but the purposes were stated only in a general way as "to provide the means for encouraging and carrying on the above mentioned work [i.e., "advancement of learning, the arts and sciences, and to promote the public welfare"] within the State of California, and by otherwise doing such things as may be necessary to fully carry out the object of this grant." This indenture was signed on August 30, 1919, by Henry E. Huntington and Arabella D. Huntington in the presence of W. E. Dunn. The trust property consisted entirely of Huntington's personal possessions; his wife signed only to give the assent of a spouse to his gift.[49]

Edward's institution had been established. It met the several conditions that were important to him. The indenture enabled him to "give something to the public" while he was still alive. It provided him the continuing responsibility for getting it under way. It allowed him to maintain whatever privacy he and Belle wanted. It was drawn in sufficient generality so that he could have the gratification of shaping it to the needs and conditions that he might later envision. Its future governance was put in the hands of reliable relatives and close friends who were in tune with his interests and purposes. And its general future was secured against merger or radical change in purpose. There was much more to do to define its job and to make it effective, but the necessary first step had been taken, and this step was greeted with widespread enthusiasm.

In the course of Edward's life in Southern California, the first decade of this century proved to be the most fruitful period of his business career. His entrepreneurial activity in street railways and real estate had proceeded at a hectic pace, with the acquisition, reorganization, and extension of the street railways, and with the purchase and development of large areas of real estate. These were indeed years of growth and prosperity in Southern California: Edward was quite properly considered the one individual most responsible for its burgeoning, and he was widely acclaimed as its hero.

Many things changed in the years that followed. Edward's retirement from aggressive control of his business affairs in 1910 made a gradual but decisive difference in the conduct of his affairs. The colleagues to whom he turned over the active management of his businesses included C. E. Graham in New York and in Los Angeles his son Howard, George S. Patton, William E. Dunn, and George J. Kuhrts. They were all competent people, but they were not willing or able as managers to run the risks that Edward had earlier taken as owner.

Another change was a new form of competition for the street railway—the jitney bus. In 1914 and 1915, automobiles began to be used in most American cities as passenger carriers. ("Jitney" was carnival barkers' slang for "nickel.") They attracted much attention, including a newspaper column called "Jitney Bus News" and many doggerel verses, such as the following two from 1915:

> The jitney bus is all the fuss
> In L.A. town today;
> Five cents will easily carry you
> Most anywhere you say.

Reaction to them soon became adverse, especially when women began to be drivers. The jitneys could be blamed for anything.

> Why is Europe fighting?
>   Nations in a fuss;
> Don't know how it started,
>   Blame the jitney bus.

Efforts were made to pass ordinances to control them; Edward was asked his views about jitneys, and his comments were published under the heading, "Henry Not Worried About Em! Oh, No!" He was quoted as taking the high ground and saying, "My policy has always been 'live and let live,' so I have nothing to say about any repressive measure about the 'jitney' feature of transportation. However, I am inclined to think the 'jitney' will not long endure because it is impossible for any large number of the drivers to make any money, counting their machines, cost of maintenance and time."[50] The jitney drivers returned the compliment to Edward. One of them wrote to the paper about where the public's transportation money was going: "Does it go over to Italy and France and England for pictures the size of a jitney sign at $100,000 a throw?" Or "does it haul a private railroad car or train all over the country?"[51] There were also increasing grumbles about the service on the street railways. After an ordinance was passed in 1917 to regulate jitneys, the *Los Angeles Examiner* published a long editorial headed "Now, Mr. Huntington, Adequate Service, Please"—now that the alibi of the unfair competition of jitneys was out of the way.[52]

Another change was the increasing movement toward unionization. Edward's strong anti-union stand had worked adequately in the 1890s in San Francisco and in the earlier years of the twentieth century in Los Angeles. Now labor had more power. In 1918, the employees of the Los Angeles Railway Company formed a union and in the autumn threatened to strike.[53] In September, Howard left his job as general manager in favor of war service and went to San Francisco to be in charge of the Emergency Fleet Corporation there; the railway problems in Los Angeles were left in the hands of Dunn and Kuhrts.[54] Dunn sent Edward a telegram on December 2 that he feared a strike and exhorted him not to "buy any books or pictures" as they would be in a tight financial situation. Edward replied with the same reaction he had had in San Francisco in the 1890s: "I would discharge every agitator, and see to it that they never have another day's work with the Railway Company. We always have treated our men fairly, and now when it comes to a fight,—if it is a fight, I want you to stay with them to the finish. I can hardly bring myself to believe, however, that we will have much trouble."[55] They did, however, have a strike and trouble. In June, July, and August of 1919 there were arguments between the union and the railway, and the strike began on August 16. There were mobs and riots toward the end of August, unsuccessful arbitration, and partial restoration of service in September and October, but the strike was not called off until November 19.[56]

During these years, there was a growing feeling in Los Angeles in favor of municipal ownership of public utilities and the street railways. Edward, as the owner of the Los Angeles Railway, the Pacific Light and Power Company, and the Ventura County Power Company, was deeply involved in the complex bargaining. In 1915, 1916, and 1917, an agreement was worked out by which Southern California Edison Company and Edward's utility companies would merge, Los Angeles would obtain ownership of the city electrical service, and Edward would be the majority stockholder of the Southern California Edison Company. Edward accepted the terms of the agreement in a long telegram on December 5, 1916, in which he expressed the belief that it would "be of benefit to the building up of all of Southern California" and that it would "have a very beneficial effect upon the prosperity of Southern California."[57] Municipal ownership of the street railways was not consummated, however. In 1919, it no longer seemed such a desirable commercial activity, and advisors warned the city council that it would create an annual deficit of $3 million and that electric transport would soon be replaced by gasoline-driven vehicles.[58]

The tight money period during and just after the World War made the operation of Edward's businesses difficult, especially since they were not, on balance, making a profit from operations during these years. The expansion of his ownership of properties had been financed mainly by the issuance of bonds and other forms of indebtedness, and most of the time his securities were then used again as collateral for further loans and notes. This kind of expansion through the leverage of debts multiplies the profit in a successful operation, but it also multiplies the chance of being wiped out by even a short-term failure.

These were difficult years for Edward's businesses. I have already alluded in Chapter 15 to the bad feelings between Dunn and Graham created by their competition for the limited financial resources. Just before Dunn went away for a week's vacation in 1915, he wrote Edward a letter that is both a clue to the pleasant quality Edward admired in Dunn and also a reminder of the financial problem before things got bad:

> You have been enjoying two or three years vacation and I regard it as important that during my absence you be at your desk in the office

from 9.00 a.m. to 5.00 p.m. I am generally at the office myself at half past seven in the morning, but by reason of the fact that you live so far out in the country nine o'clock will be considered sufficiently early.

During my absence, if you hear of anyone having any money, please get it without fail. If, on the other hand, you should hear of any one wanting money, kindly follow my invariable rule, and dodge him.

I am satisfied if you will devote the same careful attention to business that you have to your ranch and your library, you can readily pull us out of all our troubles before my return.[59]

The financial situation soon became more serious, however. Edward's short-term solution of using funds that were committed to other purposes put both Dunn and Graham in hot water, and they objected strenuously. "You have lost all interest in us," Dunn wrote to Edward in September 1915, "and write only perfunctory letters." In the next month he said, "Please don't send any more telegrams to the effect that we won't build any additional railroads. I fully agree with you and we are not going to build any." In May 1918 he explained the absolute need for $1.2 million and added, "Do not give me any other advice, for I do not need it."[60] Edward was fixed in his position and replied that "I see you have an insane idea that we shall be able to send money from New York. I am not joking when I tell you it will be utterly impossible to send you a dollar." But he did send several suggestions as to how Dunn might go about trying to raise money in Los Angeles.[61]

By 1918, money was very hard to raise in Los Angeles. Dunn summarized the situation for Edward in a letter of June 4, 1918, saying that the Liberty Loans had absorbed much of the available cash, that banks refused to lend substantial amounts of money, that real estate was worth only half its prewar valuation and was not salable, and that Edward had apparently forgotten the real facts about the very transactions to which he had referred. Edward replied the next week by saying that conditions were worse in New York.[62]

Edward refused to raise cash through selling off some of his assets, which would reduce the threat of a collapse of his enterprises. He ran the risk of collapsing, as did some enterprises of the late 1980s and early

1990s, such as Eastern Airlines, Pan American Airways, and Donald Trump. It turned out to be a good venture.

Edward continued to be highly valued in the business community of Southern California, even though he was relatively inactive. When the first transcontinental telephone call was made from Los Angeles to New York on May 6, 1915, Edward was one of the three people chosen to speak on what was regarded as a momentous occasion—the other two were the mayor and the owner of two newspapers. Edward, who was featured in the pictures and stories of the event, laughed and talked with C. E. Graham in his New York office for several minutes about current business matters.[63] And when the twenty officers and directors of the Chamber of Commerce of the United States paid a two-day visit to Los Angeles in 1919, Edward was the person chosen to greet his fellow businessmen.[64]

He concerned himself about the employees of his companies. In 1914, he sent a personal check for $10,000 to enable all who worked for the Los Angeles Railway Company to go to Redondo Beach for the annual picnic, with entertainment, sports, a ball game, and visits to any of the beach amusements; Edward's gift covered all the expenses, and working schedules were arranged so that ten thousand people went.[65] The next year he gave a recreation clubhouse for employees as a personal Christmas gift; it had a dance floor with space for seven hundred couples, a motion picture theater, a card room, a kitchen, a swimming pool, and a gymnasium.[66] In 1917 he directed two voluntary increases in the salaries of all street railway conductors and motormen.[67]

He also concerned himself with public affairs. Soon after the United States entered the World War, in April 1917, an American Red Cross campaign was begun to raise funds to aid our troops. The Los Angeles chapter had a goal of $1 million. When Edward agreed to head the local campaign and be chairman of the executive committee, the newspapers expressed total confidence that the goal would be reached. Edward gave a good start to it himself by making a personal contribution of $100,000.[68]

Alfred G. Walker, who began working for Edward as a clerk in 1903 and rose to become president of the Huntington Land and Improvement Company, said that Edward was "loved and respected by all who worked for him. He was interested primarily in the development of Southern California and the welfare of her people. He owned the Los Angeles Railway till his death, and though it operated at a loss, he refused to raise the nickel fare. His tenacity was shown in other businesses in which he lost money but would not give up because he felt they were benefiting the area."[69]

Although Edward spent only a small fraction of his time in California during these years, he never failed to express his love of the area. When he arrived at his residence in 1915, he "made a dash for the wide portico that overlooks the loveliest valley in the world, and breathed contentment. Waving his hand toward the vista, he said 'There's nothing like that in Europe, nor anywhere else in the world.'" When he arrived two years later, he exclaimed, "Oh, California is delightful! I shall never tire of it. If it were not necessary that I go to New York I should never leave California."[70]

The public perception of him was doubtless responsive to his own outlook: "His step is that of a still vigorous man [in 1916, at age sixty-six] and his eyes shine with the zest of physical enjoyment in life."[71] The man who had been a hero in the previous decade for his accomplishments in the development of Southern California was now valued for his moral qualities. He was the "kindly looking man who lords it so genially at San Marino," and "one of the most modest men in the country." And his accomplishments were being recognized as epochal: "His name must ever flourish brilliantly in the history of the state."[72]

His presence at public ceremonies was taken as a sign that they were important. When the American Bankers Association gathered in Pasadena in 1915, the top bankers from all over the country attended, including such celebrities as Thomas Fortune Ryan, the financier who controlled Congo diamond fields, tobacco firms, and a life insurance company, and Charles Warren Fairbanks, the vice-president of the United States under Theodore Roosevelt; at the banquet, Edward was seated in the place of honor even though he did not speak. The newspaper stories focused on him and on the fact that he and Ryan spent their time chatting about orchids.[73] When the Los Angeles Transportation Association met in 1916, all the top people were present, and

Edward was invited to be their guest: "To Henry E. Huntington fell the honor of being given a spontaneous, heart-felt ovation at the close of the meeting, during which, as he rose to his feet for a moment, the entire assemblage sprang up and saluted him with a long-drawn-out cheer."[74]

The public perception of the nature of his special competence also began to change. Earlier, questions addressed to him had to do mainly with such particulars as where he was going to build the next street railway extension or what important paintings or books he had recently bought. Now, questions were about more general issues: How will the war in Europe come out? What effect will military service have on our young men? When will the hard times be over? Can we count on long-term prosperity for Los Angeles? These and a hundred other general questions were addressed to him, and he was treated with the respect due a wise elder statesman. He took the questions seriously, and his answers reflected his positive, optimistic attitude. As to the war, in 1917 he replied that "no one knowing anything about American character and capacity can have any doubt about the result. War is a big job, but we are a big people and are accustomed to attending efficiently to big jobs." As for military service, he responded in 1917 that "military training will take our young men during the time when they are building up character and forming the traits that will distinguish them through all their lives. It will give them poise, self confidence and will make them understand the great value of discipline." As for hard times and long-term prosperity, in 1916 he said, "I have no doubt that the hard times are behind us and that we may look forward with increased confidence to Los Angeles' future prosperity, as to which there cannot be a shadow of doubt."[75] His answers were always treated respectfully. An editorial in the *Los Angeles Times* began: "The opinions of Henry E. Huntington always carry weight in this community. He has done so much for Southern California and is so keen and able a financier that when he speaks the people listen."[76]

But Edward was not, in fact, eager for publicity. On September 5, 1918, the Associated Press wrote him and asked for permission to do an article on his library. Here is his answer: "Dear Sir: In answer to your letter of Sept. 5th, I would say that I do not care to have any articles published at present about the Library. Yours truly, H. E. Huntington."[77]

It was the gift of his library and his art collection to the public that brought a great burst of publicity and created the most profound public perception of him. The day after the establishment was announced, each of the major newspapers in Los Angeles devoted a full page with many pictures to the story. The lead in the *Los Angeles Times* was this: "The largest individual contribution for the advancement of literature and art ever made in the West was announced yesterday, when Henry E. Huntington, railroad magnate and world-renowned art and book collector of San Marino, recorded a trust indenture in which he gave to the public his private library, which is said by authorities to be the finest in the world." After a review of the growth and contents of the collections, the story concluded that "Mr. Huntington's remarkable bequest is without precedent and it gives promise that in the near future Los Angeles will become of world-wide importance in the field of art and letters." The *Los Angeles Examiner* went back to his business career, "where he has been a spirited example of genius of capacity and executive success. Now he is found to have been actuated by a massively great altruistic idea, in comparison with which his millions, his tremendous business, pale into insignificance. For what will grow from that library, and that gallery will far exceed in import to the country and thereby to the people, and to the founder himself, any and all material victories which his brain has carried through to profit."[78]

The next day the editorial writers reflected further on the meaning and significance of this gift. "The munificence of Henry E. Huntington," began the *Los Angeles Express,* "must form the theme of world-wide praise and wonder." And it concluded, "We believe that no one person in all recorded time ever made a single gift so splendid and costly a contribution to the enrichment of his community." The idea that Edward was a benefactor of the public was central to the editorial reflections. The *Los Angeles Times,* after speaking of the high cost of so many of his purchases, asserted that "the world now knows his reason for purchasing so many thousand rare volumes. It was for the public of California that he was buying. He was bringing in reach of the people a wealth of literature that could be secured in no other way." The cost, reported to be $20 million, was "a vastly greater sum than was represented in the sum that gave to the public Stanford University. Its educational value to a community without literary ancestry is beyond estimate." The editorial concluded that "for centuries the Hunting-tons have been illustrious in English history. By this peerless bequest Henry E. Huntington adds luster to a name that is now inalienably linked with the industrial development of the Far West."[79]

Many individuals added their reflections to this public perception. Walter Lindley of Boston wrote to Edward that "no monument that a man can build could exist longer and reflect more credit than this great library. Its influence for intelligence and education will be far reaching and profound." George Ellery Hale told Edward about the "universal interest" that had been created by "your great gift."[80]

Various organizations also joined in the loud praise. The board of directors of the Los Angeles Public Library recorded "its profound recognition of the great benefit that will be conferred upon the intellec-tual life of Southern California, and of the state at large, by your magnificent gift. It is impossible to over-estimate the influence that will radiate from such a collection as the Huntington Library . . . forming a Mecca for scholars and students from all parts of the country." And the senate of the state of California adopted, by unanimous vote, a resolu-tion thanking Huntington for establishing the institution and praising its holdings and its noble purposes.[81]

On September 18, 1919, the trustees of the Henry E. Huntington Library and Art Gallery met for the first time. William E. Dunn was chosen as chairman, George S. Patton as vice-chairman, and Howard Huntington as treasurer. The other members were Archer M. Hunting-ton and George Ellery Hale.[82] The institution was under way.

Seventeen

LIVING THE NEW LIFE
1920–1924

THE HUNTINGTONS HAD THREE attractive places in which to live, once the Great War was over and the immediate postwar adjustments were complete. There was Edward's palatial residence in Southern California, Belle's mansion in New York, and the Chateau Beauregard near Versailles, which they had leased for ten years just after their marriage in 1913.

Where to live? Belle did not like Southern California and Edward did not greatly like New York or France. In the preceding six years, from 1914 through 1919, they had spent, we recall, a little more than a third of their time in California; they spent the remainder in New York, except for three and a half months in France just as the war began.

During the five years from 1920 to 1924, they compromised and lived in Southern California for about half of the time. They took trips to France in 1920 and 1921 and stayed in the Chateau Beauregard a total of about half a year; the remainder of their time, about two years, they were in New York.

Edward's basic feeling about where he preferred to live can be quickly and fairly epitomized by several brief quotations from his letters from San Marino. He wrote to Duveen in 1922 that "I am more than ever persuaded that this is the only place in the world to live." In the next year he wrote to a fellow collector in Toledo, Ohio, A. J. Secor, that "I shall soon have to go East for a month or so, but hope to make the stay there as short as possible." In 1923 he wrote to Duveen that "we expect to leave in early June,—Mrs. Huntington anticipating it, and I regretting it." To an old friend he explained that "of late years I spend as little time as I can in the East. The Library and Art Gallery here occupy a great deal of my attention, and so many more of my interests are in this part of the country. We came this year in October and will probably spend not more than a month in New York." In actuality, it turned out to be four months in New York. Edward spoke openly to his valet and his business associates about his preference: Alfonso reported that "Mr. Huntington would have liked to stay here in California all year round and never move." And Frank Griffith, the general manager of his Huntington Land and Improvement Company in Los Angeles, wrote him in 1920 in New York that "I hope your European trip will not be as unpleasant as you anticipate."[1]

Edward was extremely responsive to weather: he associated good health and feeling well with fine weather and thought that Southern California had the finest weather of any place in the world. For a person who had suffered from occasional bouts of illness through most of his life and who had a hard time getting rid of a common cold, this association was important in his preference for where he lived. His health seemed to him to flourish when he was in California, and with it his natural optimism.

In early January 1922, Edward wrote from California to C. E. Graham, the head of his New York office, that "we have been here a week and I am already much improved, thanks to the wonderfully springlike air and warmth. Here everything is progressing well: I have been in town only once and then only for a short time." Graham replied that "I was quite sure that upon your arrival in California, your health would immediately become better." Edward's private secretary, George Hapgood, confirmed these facts to Graham: "All going well here and everyone is getting better. Mr. H. is on a diet and has lost seven pounds in less than a week. Has improved very much." After Edward had been in California for about three weeks, he wrote to Duveen that "we are enjoying our home here, and the bright sunny weather has already done both of us a world of good." In mid-January he wrote to C. Weidenfeld in New York that "it is needless to say that we are enjoying the Ranch.

19. Edward on the porch of the Patton house in November 1903, between George S. Patton and his wife. On the left, standing, is George S. Patton, Jr., who later became a general in the U.S. Army. Seated to his right is the elder Patton's sister, Susan Patton. On the right is Hancock Banning.

Reinforced concrete residence in course of construction for Mr. H. E. Huntington on his Los Robles Ranch, located in the garden spot of the world, the San Gabriel Valley.

Hunt & Grey,
Architects.

C. Leonardt,
Contractor.

20. The Huntington residence in San Marino, the "garden spot of the world," 1909–10. (*Opposite, above*) Scaffolding in place. (*Opposite, below*) The construction crew in front of the partially finished building. (*Above*) The completed building, viewed from the Desert Garden.

21. (*Above*) Edward at the reservoir on the grounds.

22. (*Below*) Edward with Elizabeth's young daughter, Mary.

23. (*Opposite, above*) Arabella as a young woman. (*Below*) Arabella in San Francisco in the 1890s, after her marriage to Collis.

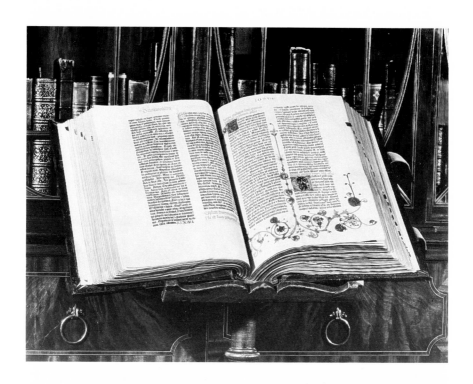

24. (*Opposite, above*) One volume of Edward's copy of the Gutenberg Bible.

25. (*Opposite, below*) A planting of cycads near the loggia of the residence.

26. (*Above*) Edward standing in front of the bronze doors to the Library. Printers' marks are used as decorative emblems on the doors.

27. Oswald Birley's portrait of Edward, 1924.

28. Birley's portrait of Arabella, 1924.

29. Gainsborough's *Blue Boy,* acquired by Edward in 1921.

30. Parody of the *Blue Boy,* attacking the Volstead Act (*Life* magazine, 1922).

31. (*Above*) Aerial view of the grounds in 1921, with the residence in the center and the Library above it and slightly to the right.

32. (*Opposite, above*) Edward and the Library staff in front of the new building, 1922. Edward (in the center, wearing a dark hat) is flanked by librarian George Watson Cole (holding his hat) and Chester Cate, who succeeded Cole as librarian.

33. (*Opposite, below*) Newspaper cartoon showing Edward and fellow collector Herschel V. Jones discussing recent acquisitions (*Los Angeles Times,* March 27, 1920).

34. Receiving the crown prince and princess of Sweden, 1926.
(*Above*) Showing them an exhibit in the Library. (*Opposite, above*) The
dining room set for a meal in their honor.

35. (*Opposite, below*) A portion of the Exhibition Hall / Reading
Room. Scholars worked at the tables except when visitors were
admitted to see the exhibitions.

36. The Mausoleum, erected by Edward on the site chosen by
Arabella.

It has done wonders for me, and now that the cool spell is over we are again having weather like May in the East."[2]

Edward made observations like these over and over again. In November 1922, shortly after returning to California from New York, he told L. B. Lewis of Indianapolis, in thanking him for the gift of a book, that "California has done wonders for me and with the fine weather we have been having ever since I arrived, I have never felt better in my life." In the next month he told Leroy Clark, a business friend in New York, that "we are having delightful weather here, and with the birds singing and the flowers out it seems far away from the bad storms we read that you are having. More and more I am impressed that this is the only place to live,—not only for this season, but for the rest of the year as well." Edward was a genuine California booster. When a New York friend wrote him about going to Florida because he had not felt well and "this wonderful climate has done its work," Edward responded that he was glad for his recovery; "I might add that if you had come to California instead of Florida you would have recovered much sooner." When Edward was not in California, he grumbled constantly about the unpleasant weather and expressed surprise if it did not adversely affect his health; "I am glad to say," he wrote from New York in August 1923, "that the disagreeable weather we have been having does not seem to affect my good health,—but it is needless to say that I am eager to get back to a climate which everyone seems to consider faultless throughout the whole year."[3]

The two trips that Edward and Belle made to France in these years were both in late summer. In 1920, they left New York at the end of July and returned in late October; in 1921, they left in early July and again returned in late October. They traveled with an entourage that consisted of Edward's private secretary, George Hapgood; his valet, Alfonso Gomez; Belle's companion, Carrie Campbell; her maid, Jeanne Riefer; her butler, McGilvray; and a servingman, Temple. They all traveled in first class, and six cabins were reserved for them at a cost of about $7,500 one way. The male attendants were required to wear blue suits, and other first-class passengers struck up friendships with them after being table companions. One lady became enamored of McGilvray the butler. An Italian opera star, Mme Tetrazini, spent time with Alfonso, held his hand, gave him her address in Rome, and asked him to come to see her; Alfonso got $50 from an agent for asking her to sign an endorsement, but he never saw her again. These misapprehensions amused Edward and Belle, and they teased Alfonso about his new lady friend.[4]

Their time at the chateau was quiet and uneventful. The chateau was handsome, well-appointed, and commodious, with six caves for wine, one for fruit, and eight extras. A large, active farm surrounded it with lovely views. Edward was surprised when there was good weather and wrote to Graham that "we have had delightful weather most of the time."[5] Belle was not enjoying herself because of pain from the ankle that she had broken the previous fall. As Edward reported it to the wife of his old secretary, George Miles, in the middle of their time in France, "Mrs. Huntington has suffered a great deal with her ankle this summer and I think likely she may have to have the bone broken and reset before it is ever right."[6]

Edward was basically unhappy there without his books and other things that interested him most. There were also many local problems to deal with, and he felt the burden of constant decision-making concerning servants and a multitude of other details involved in the operation of the chateau. Before they had left New York in the summer of 1920, he had convinced Belle to give up Chateau Beauregard if they could sublease it for the remainder of their ten years. After they arrived at the chateau, she changed her mind. Edward wrote to Duveen, who was at Vichy taking the treatment, and asked for his help. Duveen replied, on August 26, 1920: "I perfectly understand the position as regards Beauregard. I am not at all surprised that Mrs. Huntington is loath to leave such a beautiful place, but I feel certain that she must realize in these days, when the servant question is so difficult, that the place would become a source of worry and burden to you both." He thought that a good alternative would be for them to stay in a deluxe hotel in Paris, "in a beautiful suite of rooms without all these worries." He concluded, optimistically, that "I have no doubt you will be able to persuade her to return to the decision she had taken in New York, of removing her works of art and re-letting the Chateau." He thought it would be best to sell off the objects that were in the chateau: "I am of the opinion you should have the things sold in the name of Mrs. Huntington." He believed they ought to be easy to liquidate: "Of course, if we could get Mr. Gulbenkian interested, then we could sell part of the things to him and also get some money back for what has been spent."[7]

Edward was not able to persuade her to give up the chateau. The financial obligations that would still fall on them from their ten-year lease were barriers to her. So Edward wrote again to Duveen to see if there was a way around this obstacle: "You said when you were here that you knew of a gentleman who you thought would like to purchase Beauregard. At the time Mrs. H was very much opposed to giving it up, but there is no doubt in my mind I can persuade her to do so if conditions can be made easy. And you with your persuasive language can assist me." Edward's idea was that the buyer could get better terms from the owner, Baron de Forest, if the transaction took place subject to the lease: "As you well know, Mrs. H is very fond of the Chateau, and there is certainly no more beautiful place in France and I quite agree with her." But Edward felt that he could not continue to come to France because of his "large and varied interests in America."[8]

But that plan did not work out either. In October 1920, Edward wrote to Cole in New York to tell of their sailing date to return home; he concluded, "You may be sure that I shall be glad to again be in the midst of things that interest me more than anything over here."[9]

Edward felt it his duty to settle all problems in matters for which he was generally responsible. The chateau was managed by a steward, Constant Welker, and Edward had an attorney in Paris, Donald Harper, who looked after his legal affairs. When Edward was away, he got about a letter a week from one or the other of them, always full of questions. What amount to give as a New Year's present to each of the thirty-two staff members? Accept the government's offer for hay at 5.58 francs per quintal? What to do with the dog that Archer left there last year? Repair or replace the roof damaged by the hurricane? Who would substitute for Welker while he was recovering from his stroke? Appeal the government claim for income tax? And so on. Household help was hard to get, and the cry for higher salaries was constant. The overall costs were indeed rather high. In the dollars of that time, the rental under the lease was about $35,000 a year, the French income tax on foreigners with a residence in France added another $35,000 a year, the net cost of the operations of the chateau property averaged about $68,000 a year, and about $100,000 had been spent on repairs, decoration, and improvement before they moved in. And always there were new expenses, like the demand of the French agricultural officers to set right the many faults of the farm.[10]

At the end of their second visit, in 1921, Belle agreed to give up the chateau, even though the lease still had two years to run and there was no buyer. She shipped eight van loads of furniture and household goods back to the United States, seven to the country place in Westchester and one to 2 East Fifty-seventh Street. When they were getting ready to leave, Edward wrote to Graham that "I shall be glad to get home again."[11] Many details remained to be settled, however, even after they left. Valuable possessions needed to be sold or disposed of, including agricultural implements, four horses, a pony, and three automobiles. A survey and inventory had to be made and a claim by the owner for damages negotiated—and settled for some $10,000. And there were extended dealings about three missing objects—a Turkish chandelier, a Louis XV table, and a bronze decoration—which the owner claimed the Huntingtons had sent to the United States. Negotiations with Baron de Forest and the French government dragged on for a couple of years after Edward and Belle had left the chateau for the last time.[12] In July 1923, Edward wrote to his lawyer in Paris, "I shall be very glad to have this whole situation cleared up, so that I will have no further connection with the Chateau."[13] At last the problems were resolved, and they never returned to France.

Their time in New York during these years was not during the most attractive seasons. They spent all or a good part of every summer there, and two years they were there for the months of November through February. They were not there at all during the spring, or during the most appealing part of the autumn. Edward found plenty of reason to complain about the weather. In 1922 he wrote to Cole in San Marino that since their arrival at the beginning of July "we have had nothing but rain. The house is comfortable, however, and with much to do, it is not unbearable, although it is not California." Somewhat later he reported to Dunn, "All going well at No. 2, and while the weather is abominable, it does not bother me very much,—in fact I have never felt better in my life than I do now"—at the age of seventy-two and a half. Hapgood wrote Dunn an account of how things were going from the secretary's point of view: "Weather here is atrocious,—but I am glad to say that Mr. H. seems to thrive on it. At first he did not sleep well on account of the noise, but now he feels better, he says, than for a long time, and as well as he ever felt. He keeps very busy and perspires freely,—that may have something to do with his good health."[14]

He went irregularly to his downtown business office, which comprised about a third of the thirty-first floor of the Adams Express Building at 61 Broadway (Exchange Place and Trinity Place). His enterprises headquartered there included the Chesapeake and Ohio Railway, the Newport News Shipbuilding and Drydock Company, and the Old Dominion Land Company. Edward shared a large corner office of some five hundred square feet, with three windows on one side and two on the other, with C. E. Graham (his chief assistant) and Livezey of the Newport News Company, while Adams and the clerks were in adjacent space. When he sold his interest in the C & O to the Van Sweringens in 1923, they moved the headquarters to Cleveland. In 1924 he did not renew the lease and in the autumn of that year, after Belle's death, he broke up his New York office and divided the files, and Archer took the papers concerning his mother's financial affairs.[15]

Belle did not go to the office, but C. E. Graham transacted her business for her, either by calling on her at the residence or by correspondence. Her accounts were kept meticulously separate from Edward's. She was credited with all of her capital gains and the income from her properties and securities, and she was charged with the taxes, salaries, and maintenance of her private properties. But the costs connected with their joint residences in New York, France, San Marino, and Westchester were charged to Edward's account; these costs included the books, art, statuary, and gardens at the San Marino Ranch. Her main expenses were for clothes, jewelry, art, and gifts—especially to Archer, to his interests, and to memorials for Collis.[16]

Edward and Belle lived a quiet, gracious, well-regulated life at home, with occasional guests, especially Archer and other family members. There was a profusion of cut flowers throughout the house, and they ate well, especially seafood and fresh vegetables. Their principal suppliers for food were Park and Tilford and Bloomingdale's, from whom they received ample quantities of truffles, alligator pears, fresh ginger, Roquefort cheese, and delicacies; they needed large amounts of caviar, since Archer—according to Alfonso—would "eat enough caviar for six people." They went to the theater occasionally, and they frequently passed a few days during the hot weather at their country place at Throggs Neck in Westchester County. Edward was a life or annual member of some three dozen clubs—about half of them in New York—but he did not spend much time in their activities during these years.[17]

The main activity that occupied Edward's attention when they were in New York was dealing with his books—reading the old ones, as always, becoming familiar with the new ones, and thinking about the next ones. As he wrote to Dunn in Los Angeles, "I wish to get out of active business and fool away money on books and other things that give me pleasure."[18] The library was located in the New York house until the autumn of 1920, while the library staff cataloged the ever-increasing collection; then the move to the partially completed building in San Marino began. The arrangements illustrate Edward's penny-pinching instincts. His first inclination was to save money by having the staff pay their own way to California and asking Wells Fargo to transport his library at greatly reduced rates. Cole remonstrated that the men could not afford the expense and that "better work will be done by them, if all the expenses of moving are taken from their shoulders." The president of Wells Fargo told Edward that they could not legally give reduced rates to anyone. Edward then agreed to pay for the transportation of the household effects of the staff provided they delivered their goods to the freight car, and for the move of the staff and their dependents provided they came in parties to get the reduced group rate. He warned them that "housing will be a great problem" and that the weather in September—when they were to arrive—is "the worst of the year. I am sorry that they had to come then because I want them to be favorably impressed on their first visit." His natural generosity finally overcame his niggardliness, however: he had a series of small cottages built for the staff a few blocks from the library, and the ten transplanted Easterners—with thirteen adult dependents and nine children—were soon at work unpacking, sorting, and continuing the cataloging.[19]

One other bookish matter that engaged his interest during these years in New York was the establishment of the library that he had given to the city of Oneonta "as a perpetual memorial to Solon Huntington and his wife Harriet Saunders Huntington for the use of the People of Oneonta by Their Son Henry Edwards Huntington." The library and surrounding park (his childhood home, at 67 Chestnut Street) were formally opened to the public on July 8, 1920, but he had given the property in 1917, after buying out the interests of his siblings. The intervening three years were devoted to a thorough renovation of the house and grounds. He concerned himself with every detail: the type of flooring, the furnace, the furnishings, the boulder for the memorial plaque, the shrubbery, the fencing, and so forth. If a couple of weeks went by with no report on progress, he wrote to the city engineer to ask for word on any "point that you think may be of interest to me." In fact, he regarded the whole project as something "of interest to me," as he did the building of his San Marino residence, and his gardens, and his book and art collections, and everything that he built. He gave about five hundred books from the family residence and funds for many more; when the library opened, it had some twenty thousand volumes on the shelves. Edward could not go for the opening, as he and Belle had just returned from Southern California and were busy getting ready to go to France. The president of the library trustees, A. B. Saxton, wrote him in the autumn and asked him to come for a reception in his honor, but he had to decline as they had just gotten back from France and he was not well. He said that he would like to come "to meet old friends and to see the Park and Library." He added that "it gives me much pleasure to feel that Oneonta is enjoying what used to be my old home, and I hope that the Huntington Park and Library will prove to be, for years to come, a means of recreation and improvement for both mind and body."

The library flourished, and Edward kept in close touch with the librarian, Elizabeth W. Blackall. The circulation increased greatly to about ten thousand volumes a month, a children's story hour was established, and boys' reading clubs formed. "So often I think, Mr. Huntington," she wrote, "you should hear the unsought tributes so often paid the library and park to have any conception of what your thoughtful and well-planned gift really means to this community and its daily life. It is a center comparable, certainly, to the churches in its influence, and is, in its absolute democracy, even further reaching." He continued to guide its development, and in 1922 he gave $200,000 for an endowment fund.[20]

At last, Edward was able to go to Oneonta for a reception in his honor at the library on July 19, 1923. He stood in front of the fireplace in what had been his family living room, and the guests were presented to him. He was able to see the results of all the effort to create something for the public, and he was delighted with what he saw. A couple of weeks later he wrote to James M. Lee—another Oneonta native, then head of the journalism program at New York University—that "my trip to Oneonta was most delightful, and the Library and Park have turned out beyond my expectations. Altogether I had a delightful time there,— the reception at the Library contributing considerably to this."[21]

A major event in their lives during these years in New York was Archer's remarriage in 1923 to the sculptor Anna Hyatt, five years after his divorce from Helen Gates. Anna's nephew, A. Hyatt Mayor, told the story, which he knew from firsthand knowledge, of the courtship and marriage of Archer and Anna, and his story is important to Edward's life because of Archer's absolute centrality to Belle and, by association, to Edward. Archer's "illegitimacy scarred him with a compulsion for secrecy" throughout his life, Mayor began. Archer's distrust turned to misery when Helen abandoned him:

> In a torment of mortified rejection, he threw himself into gluttony
> and kept awake for work around the clock with black coffee and
> cigars. One of his frantic throng of projects was to have a medal
> struck for William Dean Howells, for which he asked my aunt, Anna
> Hyatt, to design the sketch. She saw him as a wounded animal that
> had retreated into the thickets to die. His instant perception under-

stood her simple wish to help, and he asked her to marry him. Though she found herself, in her mid-forties, in love for the first time, she hesitated.

She did not want to give up her simple way of life for the social life of the wealthy:

> Thus divided by doubts and loyalties, she went as usual for the summer of 1922 to Annisquam, Massachusetts. There one night at three or four in the morning, she woke my mother and said, "Harriet, Archer is dying. I know it. I must go to him." And she was gone before breakfast. She found him in a hospital, bloated to some 400 pounds. He simply said, "I want to die. Overeating is more gentlemanly than shooting myself or jumping out of a window." When he once again begged her to marry him, she said yes. He lost over 100 pounds, and they were married in her studio at 49 West 12th Street, on March 10, which was the birthday of both.

Young Mayor, less than a year out of Princeton, and Anna's mother were the two witnesses, and Mayor was given the task of reporting the marriage to the newspapers after the married couple, aged fifty-three and forty-seven, went off in their 150-foot yacht for a cruise in the Caribbean. Archer's remarriage did not alienate him from Belle and Edward, but thereafter they all saw one another much less frequently. New York would no longer be the same for them.[22]

Edward felt entirely comfortable only in Southern California. When he and Belle returned to the ranch from New York in March 1920, he wrote to Cole in New York that "the change has done wonders for me, and I am feeling almost myself again."[23] So much gave him delight: the views, the walks around the gardens, the birds, his books and manuscripts, the art, and the cordial relations with their relatives, friends, and staff.

They had guests nearly every day for lunch or dinner or both. Edward's sister Carrie and her husband, Burke, were the most frequent, often bringing their children, Helen and Collis, recent college graduates. They often saw Howard and Leslie and their children. Elizabeth and Brockway came down often from San Francisco to visit, sometimes with their children. The George Pattons and the Billy Dunns were the most frequent of the other visitors. We should notice that these guests were almost all relatives and friends of Edward rather than of Belle. There were occasional distinguished visiting guests like the Admiral and Mrs. Edward W. Eberle and Sir Gilbert Parker. A few business associates were houseguests, like Homer Ferguson, as well as dealer friends like Joseph Duveen.[24]

Edward found great pleasure in visiting the aviary and communing with the birds. He went every morning and often also in the late afternoon. He liked all the birds, but his valet, Alfonso, reported that "there was one white bird with a big head" that Mr. Huntington especially liked: "There was a bench put up there for Mr. Huntington to sit down and see this bird." Normally, the bird went back and forth, back and forth on its perch, talking very loudly and paying no attention to anyone. But "when Mr. Huntington went, and he sat on that bench, that bird stopped, and he sat on the center of a stick talking" to Mr. Huntington.[25]

Belle was not able to walk very far; whenever she ventured out, the gardeners were instructed to leave their tasks, no matter what they were doing, as she did not wish to see them.[26] Inside the house, she especially enjoyed the animals. She was very fond of her small dog, Buster. He lay on her long flowing skirt when she was at the dining table. When bedtime approached, Buster would leave Belle, go upstairs, and lie on her bed waiting for her. Buster loved Belle, but he didn't like anyone else, not even Edward. Buster came to an unhappy end: he was killed by one of the police dogs that accompanied the watchman outside of the house. The watchman was supposed to keep the dogs chained, but one got loose and that was the end of Buster. Belle had the carpenter make a coffin, and she had Buster buried in the Rose Garden. For months thereafter she went every afternoon and put a rose on his grave site.[27]

Belle had another pet, a green parrot also named Buster. The parrot used to sit on her shoulder every afternoon while she was being read to and conversing. It developed a vocabulary of about a hundred words that it could speak in a voice so like Belle's that everyone mistook it for hers. When the bird began talking upstairs in the afternoon—and it would talk for an hour—Edward joined the servants on the ground floor and they all marveled at the mimicry. The parrot disliked everyone except Belle and bit them whenever it had a chance. Once it escaped from its cage and drew blood by biting Edward on his finger and Alfonso on his head. One of its favorite messages, delivered in the evening when the parrot was upstairs and the family downstairs, was: "Edward, Edward, hurry up! Come up here! Go to bed!" Most men would probably be discomfited by this exposure of their domestic arrangements. But when Edward heard this speech, even when he was with guests, he laughed heartily and thought it a great joke. The parrot outlived Belle, and Archer took him over.[28]

Edward and Belle were formal in their domestic life. When they were together, they always had a valet or a butler present with them or in the next room with the door open between them: "We have no secrets," she said. They always dressed for dinner, whether they had guests or were alone, and their dress was on the formal side for all occasions.[29]

Belle set the standard for their appearance. She was always handsomely dressed and well groomed. Alfonso felt that she "dressed like a queen," always in long dresses that looked like wedding gowns, always in black after Collis's death in 1900: "She was so beautiful as she came down the stairway and walked down that long hall into the dining room."[30]

Edward enjoyed being neatly and inconspicuously dressed, in a conservative style. Gray was his principal color; outdoors, he wore a straw hat in hot weather and a gray fedora the rest of the time. After their marriage, Belle set a somewhat higher standard for him. Alfonso felt that Edward "was very proud of himself in neatness; he was a very neat man, always cleaning, cleaning, cleaning." He did not, however, like to wear new shoes or new clothes; the electrician broke in his shoes, but there was no one to break in his clothes so that he would feel comfortable in them. He would have ten or twelve cutaway coats, all new, but would choose instead to wear an old one. Belle said, "Alfonso, don't let Mr. Huntington go down for breakfast with that old coat." But Edward "said that was his best friend because he felt comfortable and it didn't bother him." The same with pants, beautiful striped pants without cuffs. (Edward felt that cuffs were "only a wastepaper basket, all the dirt goes there.") Belle remonstrated to Alfonso when Edward was not wearing new pants. Alfonso replied that Edward changed his pants twice a day and that they were good pants. Belle responded: "No, they don't look neat enough. You know Mr. Huntington. I'll tell you one thing, Alfonso. I want to tell you in front of him. [It was II P.M., in a bedroom.] You should not pay attention to Mr. Huntington. Before he married me, he came here like an angel. His tie was new and the shoes were new, everything just like an angel. But now that we are married, he comes in with old pants. I don't like it. I want things for him always new."

Alfonso tried to cool her off by saying, "Those pants are all right, Mrs. Huntington." And Edward observed, "Your old shoes and your old clothes are your best friends." But Belle was not appeased: "'That might be your idea, but I want Alfonso not to pay attention to you. You wear what Alfonso gives you from now on. From now on, whatever clothes he lays there'—and she said the same thing about underwear and things like that—'whatever clothes Alfonso lays out for you, you put them on. Not what you want. I want you to look just like you did when you first married me.'"

Edward was not offended. Indeed, he could find a joke in almost everything and thought that the world was big with jest. Before leaving for New York, he put his four newest pairs of pants in a bureau (over Alfonso's protest), locked the drawer, and secreted the key. When they returned and unlocked the drawer, they found that moths had eaten into all the pants: "So Mr. Huntington laughed and said, 'Oh, I see. I should have left them outside to get air.'" He called in the electrician to burn the remains so that his misdemeanor would go undetected.[31]

Belle's favorite painting in the house, according to Alfonso, was Raeburn's *Master William Blair.* Alfonso noticed that she looked at this picture every night before she went to bed, standing close to it and peering at the face through her thick glasses. He asked her several times why she liked that picture so much. One evening, after sending Edward upstairs, she told him: "'Archer Huntington. The eyes are Archer Huntington.' And she started crying."[32]

Edward and Belle shared a taste for orange juice, from trees on the ranch, freshly prepared by Alfonso in a glass squeezer. They had it themselves for breakfast, and it was served at luncheon when they had guests. They drank so much of it that the housekeeper decided to buy an electric juicer. But Belle felt that the juice it made was too sour, and they had to return to Alfonso and the glass squeezer.[33]

Edward and Belle often took short walks outside in the late afternoon. One beautiful clear afternoon she suggested they take a long walk to a hillock north of the house, more than a quarter of a mile away. Edward and Belle were alone, with Alfonso along to keep watch over Buster. When they got to the hillock:

> Mrs. Huntington stood there in the center of the place and she looked at the house—you could look straight to this house, the big house—and she said to Mr. Huntington, "You know, we are doing so much. I hope it won't be soon. I hope you will live many years yet and I hope I live many years yet, but we're talking so much about it, we've got to make a decision where we want to be buried. Don't you think this would be a nice place to be buried? Edward, I would like to be buried here, right here where I have my shoes." And Mr. Huntington said, "Yes." So Mr. Huntington made a little sign in the ground with a little stone, and he didn't say any more.[34]

There in good time their mausoleum was erected and they were buried on that spot.

Among the houseguests was Homer Ferguson, head of the Newport News Shipbuilding and Drydock Company. Ferguson came on business, but Edward invited him to stay in the house and occupy the bedroom next to his own. They had a cordial friendship, but Ferguson explained the assignment of his room by saying, "I'm right next to the Chief, and just because I sing in the shower and he likes to hear me."[35]

Joseph Duveen was a more frequent guest. Sometimes he came with pictures that Edward had already bought, sometimes with pictures he wanted Edward to buy. One morning at breakfast he told Edward that he had had an invitation from Pola Negri to go to a party at the Ambassador Hotel to meet some movie stars, but he didn't want to go. Edward told him that he ought to go to see how those stars compared with his favorite beautiful women in paintings, like Lady Hamilton. "How much money are they worth?" asked Duveen. "Well, the movie people are making all the money," replied Edward. "Can the movie people buy a painting from me for a million dollars?" asked Duveen. "Well, maybe some of the producers might want to have one," said Edward. "I don't know, I don't know about the movie stars, they won't want to go broke." So Duveen accepted at Edward's urging, and off he went with his secretary and personal valet in a cloud of fragrance, as Edward had gotten Alfonso to sprinkle cologne on Duveen's clothes.

At breakfast the next morning, Duveen regaled Edward with an account of the beauty of the evening, of the lights, of the gorgeous stars covered with diamonds and pearls. The conversation among the stars was, in his opinion, not so good, however: "the only thing they were talking about was did this girl make this movie, did that girl make that movie, and how beautiful she is, and how old she is." Edward asked, "Well, did anyone kiss you?" Duveen replied, "Well, some did, but let's not talk about those things." Better to talk business. "Some of the movie stars approached me and they asked me if on the next trip when I come to see you I can bring them some paintings, nice paintings, about $150 to $250, to hang over their fireplaces, to have in their homes in Beverly Hills." With which Duveen concluded, "That was terrible! Now, Mr. Huntington, you made me waste one solid evening, doing that kind of stuff."

Edward was greatly amused at the frustration of the single-minded man who only enjoyed making money and who could not savor the social comedy of the evening. On the following mornings when Duveen came down for breakfast, Edward would say, "Well, do you have any more movie invitations?" Duveen succeeded in laughing, but it was hard and he did not want to talk about it any more.

Duveen did like to talk, and the Huntingtons delighted in hearing him discourse, freely, openly, and appealingly. And loudly, so that he could be heard all over the house. He was candid about his profits, and he brought along his papers to show Edward exactly how much he was going to make on a transaction. He was also generous with the servants. He asked Edward what he thought of tipping the servants, and Edward said, "Well, I think it's wonderful." Duveen said, "I make $½ million from you. I should take care of these poor creatures." When he was ready to leave, he went around the house and handed each servant an envelope containing fifty or one hundred dollars.[36]

The project that engaged Edward's interest most extensively in Southern California during these years was his library: completing the building, finishing the cataloging of the books and manuscripts, putting it in order so that it could be most useful to scholars, and preparing an exhibition of choice materials that could be open to the general public. The progress of the library was the topic he most often wrote about to his friends. In 1920, he told Dr. Coley that his attention was focused on the library, "the work on which grows more interesting every day." In 1923 he wrote Dr. Coley that "the Library is now in a most interesting stage, as the books are being put in the stack, the large room being finished, and the new books unpacked." In 1924 he wrote to John W. Ensign in West Virginia that "my interests here keep me busy, and the Library and Art Gallery, one might say, is just in embryo, as neither has been opened formally to the public as yet, so you can readily imagine in what a varied way my time is taken up."[37]

Progress was slower than Edward had hoped. When the staff arrived in the autumn of 1920, they had to work in the basement of the new library building. Early in 1921 the finishing touches were put on the structure, and the grass for a lawn in front began to come up. But much still remained to be done on the interior and in the cataloging. "There is more work about the preparation," Edward said expansively, "than any one could understand; there is the job of placing the books, but the big delay is because of cataloguing. We catalogue in more detail than is used in any other library; every page of every book is inspected to verify its being a perfect copy, and the indexing includes every fact about the volume."[38] One of the catalogers wrote to a friend that "Mr. Huntington is very anxious to finish the final cataloguing of the English literature to 1640, and the early Americana, as soon as possible." The progress was slow, however, because "he buys so heavily all the time that the staff has to spend pretty much all its days in temporary cataloguing of new material."[39] Edward was busy urging them on and supervising, and in 1923 he said, in self-mockery, "This library keeps my nose to the grindstone; I hardly have a moment to myself; I'm working about as hard as I ever did, but this time it is real enjoyment and thrills I get from my efforts." When asked when the library would be open to the public—one of his great ambitions—he replied, "I wish I knew; I'd like to open it tomorrow."[40] But Belle was bitterly opposed to admitting the public. "I don't want to live in a public institution." Once he suggested that they adopt a different living style and open the place to the public. Her answer was simple: "No." While she was alive, she wanted the house and the library to be private. "When we pass away," she said, "then let the students and public appreciate what you have done, which will please me an awful lot." He respected her wishes, and during her lifetime the public was not allowed in.[41] Even when they were not in residence, any friend who wanted to come on the grounds had to get a pass from his Los Angeles office under rigorous rules. When a woman asked the librarian for permission to visit the gardens and write an article on them for an Eastern magazine, Edward absolutely refused: "My policy has been," he wrote Cole, "to keep it as private as possible."[42] In the meantime, however, thoughts were running through his head about making it public as soon as he could.

Edward's secretary, George Hapgood, generally played golf on Fridays, the day Edward went to his office in Los Angeles to attend to business. Sometimes Edward was driven downtown in his black Locomobile, and sometimes he went back and forth on the trolley; when he did the latter, he enjoyed standing on the platform and talking with the conductor to learn what was going on. He shared an office with Billy Dunn, and on the walls was a photograph of Collis, Edward, and a newsboy on the streets of San Francisco, and other photographs of Collis, Howard, several old friends, and Huntington Lake. Edward talked over all business and financial matters with Dunn, and they always had lunch together at the California Club. He brought herb tea and bottles of mineral water from home, and his secretary, Miss Emma Quigley, prepared refreshments for them; Edward called the mineral water their "cocktails."[43]

A threat to the street railways arose in 1923 when two proposals were put before the public to authorize a bus system to operate its buses parallel to the street railways for a ten-cent fare as opposed to the five-cent fare allowed the street railways. Edward wrote a long article, published in several papers, opposing the proposals on the grounds that it was unfair competition—the buses were allowed a larger fare and were not responsible for street paving, maintenance, or taxes—and that it would destroy the street railways. He wrote a persuasive argument, in which the facts, history, and consequences were all presented. Toward the end he took a personal stand: "You know when one has grown up with a city, has great confidence in its future, acted on that belief, found his hopes coming true, is proud of the result and perhaps almost a little vain about it, one cannot help but have a tremendous desire that no great mistake should be made in any public policy of importance to that city." He ended with a call for cooperation.[44] But the key personal comment about his perception of the success of the area was his admission that he was "perhaps almost a little vain about it." The proposals were both defeated, on May 2, 1923, by votes of some forty-five thousand to forty thousand, and a cooperative arrangement was made between the buses and the street railways.

On the whole, however, Edward was not very involved in the active management of his street railways, utilities, or land companies. He did see to it that Christmas bonuses were given to employees—$60 to each person employed more than six months, with extra awards for special efficiency or courtesy, at a total of about $100,000 a year.[45] He took the opportunity in 1924 to write a long letter to the mayor of Los Angeles, George E. Cryer, about the installation of traffic lights; he gave a description of how they worked on Fifth Avenue in New York and included a copy of the New York traffic regulations. His interest bore fruit: the material was turned over to the Los Angeles Traffic Commission, which went to work on the topic and sent him copies of their findings.[46]

Edward's business interests extended all over the Los Angeles area, not only in street railways and utility companies but also in real estate. It is a mistake to think that his land holdings were mainly in the general vicinity of his residence. In fact, only about 20 percent were in the San Gabriel Valley, with the remainder all around the Los Angeles area. And his real estate holdings were extensive. Everything that was available for sale was held by his Huntington Land and Improvement Company. On January 1, 1924, its real estate inventory covered twenty-five pages, with a total asking price of just over $20 million and a book value of over $10 million.[47] He liked to keep up with his various enterprises even when he was out of town. He asked A. G. Walker, the general manager of the Huntington Land and Improvement Company, to write him twice a month to keep him posted, and he asked Hertrich to write him every Saturday about developments on the ranch.[48]

But the spirit of his office work during these years can perhaps best be epitomized by the coupon-cutting contests between Edward and Dunn. Each contestant would place on his table a stack of fifty bonds with coupons of a date to be cut off and submitted for payment. Edward had Miss Quigley as his assistant, and Dunn had A. G. Walker. At a signal, Edward and Dunn began cutting coupons, one from each bond, and their assistants put the coupons in one pile and the bonds in another. The winner was the one who was the first to finish cutting his pile of fifty. The contest went on amid much laughter and merriment. At the conclusion, the bonds were returned to the vault and the coupons to a shelf. The coupons were not submitted for payment because the company could not afford to pay and still keep the five-cent fare. Edward preferred to keep the five-cent fare, but he derived great fun from the contest.[49]

Everything we say or do doubtless reveals to the perspicacious our nature as human beings. But it is probably through our relations with other people that what we are like becomes more understandable. I hope that readers have all along been deciding what kind of person H. E. Huntington was at different times of his life and on different occasions. The pages that follow offer material on the relations that he and Belle had with a variety of people during these years, and readers can have the pleasure of deciding what each of them seems to have been like in these various experiences.

In the privacy of their home, Edward was seen most intimately by his personal valet, Alfonso Gomez. For the last sixteen years of his life, from the time that Edward woke up in the morning until he went to bed at night, Alfonso was at hand, shaving him, giving him his catheter treatments, laying out his clothes, helping him bathe and dress. "I went to Mr. Huntington in the morning," said Alfonso, "and he got dressed and he was singing and he was pleasant all day long and he was pleasant to everybody."[50] Alfonso spoke often of the fact that Mr. Huntington was "a great kidder. You know, he was always kidding."[51] "In his private life, among friends, he wanted light, he wanted joking, he didn't want to discuss business, never."[52] Mr. Huntington especially liked his secretary, George Hapgood, because—according to Alfonso—"he was always funny" and Mr. Huntington "wanted me to tell something I saw funny."[53] Mr. Huntington laughed a great deal, and he enjoyed mimicry or a joke, even at his own expense, like the parrot telling him to come to bed. Alfonso thought that people in general liked Mr. and Mrs. Huntington "because they were human. They were the most human people. You learned to love them because they were so plain."[54]

Otheman Stevens, a dear friend of Edward's, felt that "the spirit of fun was dominant with him." Once when Stevens came to his house to call on him and had to wait a while for him in his library, he noticed the guest book, in which visiting dignitaries had inscribed messages. Stevens scribbled a verse in the book about the institution that Edward was founding. When Huntington arrived, Stevens said, "I haven't wasted my time, for in your guest book I have written a verse about you, and I think it is not bad poetry. . . . [Huntington's] face at once grew contorted with pain, and he put his head on my shoulder, sobbing, and finally moaned, 'My dear Steve, I never thought it would come to this. To think that you would come into my house, sit down, and write poetry. How could you bring yourself to do me such a wrong.' And then he stood up and roared with laughter." On another occasion, Stevens sent him a manuscript volume from India written on bark in a language that no specialist had been able to identify. Huntington acknowledged it, tongue in cheek: "Dear Steve, Thank you for the poem in the Ahsamese dialect, which I have placed with my other Oriental manuscripts in the Library. I think the lyric strains of this very beautiful poem should be accompanied by soft chords on the lute or theorbo. Did you notice the false quantity in the third line of the fifth stanza?" Stevens was delighted.[55]

Edward enjoyed mimicry. Once he was in the Duveen Brothers shop with Edward Fowles, a junior partner, who thought that "the affable H. E. H. was very fond of a joke." Joseph Duveen arrived in the shop and, in Fowles's account, "immediately began to extol the merits of a wonderful picture he had just purchased in London. 'Wait a minute,' H. E. H. exclaimed, rising to his feet, 'I will give you the works.' Waving his arms, he shouted at me, 'The greatest picture I have ever owned! It's simply stupendous,' in mimicry of Joe's sales talk. He sat down again, laughing uproariously."[56]

He was not always genial, however. To a man who had cleaned his pictures three years before and had offered to clean them again, he wrote: "Dear Sir: In reply to your letter of April 9th, I would say that after my last experience of having you clean the Lawrence, I do not wish you to clean any more pictures for me."[57] To a Pasadena real estate firm that had asked whether he would lease his house in San Marino for the winter to a client of theirs, a childless lady who would be an excellent tenant, he replied, "I do not believe that I can lease my home, but perhaps you might get the First Presbyterian Church of Pasadena"—which was perhaps paying back one absurdity with another.[58]

At his office, his secretary, Miss Emma Quigley, and his best friend, Billy Dunn, saw him the most. Edward inspired strong loyalty in his whole staff, according to Miss Quigley, because he sought to know and give support to each of them individually. She found him simple, direct, approachable, democratic, and courteous. He had a capacity to grasp a situation with little explanation. The staff felt at ease with him and "had lots of fun." They were made to feel free to talk with him about anything, and he seemed immensely interested. When a task needed to be done, he always asked people to help him with it; he never summoned them with a buzzer and gave them orders. Miss Quigley thought that Dunn was Edward's most trusted associate, advisor, and confidant. Edward never did anything important of a business nature without talking it over with Dunn, and he had absolute confidence in him. "I've never heard one man speak as highly of another man in all my life," she observed.[59]

Edward once told Alfonso that he had had only four "real friends," but Alfonso did not reveal who they were.[60] Dunn must have been one. A good guess as to the others would be George Patton, Epes Randolph, and his uncle Collis. But Edward had a large number of friends all through his life, and kept in touch with a great many of them. Passages from the letters of several old friends can suggest something of his relationships. J. L. Murphy wrote him from Atlanta that "I hope the years have dealt as kindly with you as with me, and that you still wear the cheery smile of the days in Kentucky."[61] M. L. Akers, after stopping to see Edward in both New York and San Marino, sent him a photograph of the house he had once occupied in Louisville "some thirty years ago"—then in a community of the leading families, now a run-down neighborhood of shops and garages.[62] I. N. Phipps reminisced about the time "you, Randolph and I sat down in the cabin of the mountaineer, Blair, there at the confluence of the Devil's Fork and the North Fork of Licking that July evening long years ago, to the tempting corn-pone, corn on the cob, and thick strips of utterly fat bacon a-float in a miniature lake of hot white grease."[63] An old railroad colleague, J. C. Stubbs, expressed pleasure on learning that Edward was "feeling so young and fit. Keep it up and you may pass the four score mark in a gallop! I think you deserve a long life and a happy one—if any man does."[64]

Edward was approachable, and he made new friends all the time. Noel T. Arnold, for example, called on him at home in 1920 because he and his wife wanted to buy one of the vacant lots nearby and build a house on it. Edward received him, and they spent a delightful hour together, though Edward was not in the least interested in personally selling lots. Edward put him in touch with the Huntington Land and Improvement Company, and Mr. Arnold bought the two acres he wanted. While the house was under construction, Edward would walk over to find out how they were coming on. After it was completed, they had an occasional dinner at one another's houses. Once they invited him to come for lunch with Ruth Draper, a friend who was in Los Angeles doing her one-person show. Edward went to her performance with them, "laughed heartily at her impersonations, as of the elderly New England woman at an art exhibition," and enjoyed a backstage visit with her afterward. The Arnolds met Belle only a couple of times: she was not well, they were told, and mostly stayed upstairs. Their first impression of her was of "sternness and austerity," which they attributed to her poor hearing and limited vision.[65]

This was not at all the impression that Belle made on the people who knew her better. Howard's wife, Leslie, who had lunch with her nearly every day when she was in San Marino, found her "always very much alive" and stated that "she always seemed to be very alert and always capable of entertaining and meeting people most graciously under all conditions and at all times." Another friend in Los Angeles, Alberta Johnston Denis—a society person who said that "I had no more intimate friend than she was, nor, I am very sure, had she than I"—spent much time with her. They read together about once a week from "new books, and new plays, in which last, Mrs. Huntington was much interested," with Mrs. Denis doing the reading "because of good eyes and a voice that would not tire." They "discussed all these from every point of view, and enjoyed our afternoons in each other's company." In Mrs. Denis's view, Belle had "a rather splendid personality" and "a forceful dominating intellect." One of Belle's closest friends in New York was Harriet Crocker Alexander, the daughter of Collis's partner Charles Crocker, who felt that "Mrs. Huntington was a woman of unusual intelligence and mental vigor." She had "the keenest interest in everything about her, and nothing seemed to escape her mind. She talked animatedly about paintings, California, the topics of the day, real estate transfers, charities, and so on." Her "whole attitude up to the last time I saw her was that of one who keenly enjoyed life." Finally, a word about her from George D. Hapgood, Huntington's private secretary, who lived with them from 1917 on, and with whom she discussed many personal and family matters. He was of the opinion that "she was a woman of the highest intellect and attainments. . . . She was deeply interested in matters of art and art collections," and "she became intensely interested in Mr. Henry E. Huntington's plans for the library and art gallery and the collection he was making for the same, and that no acquisition was ever made to his art collection without her advice and approval."[66]

The common themes that run through these perceptions of Belle are that her mind was bright and lively and strong, that she was keenly interested in what was going on around her, and that she was responsive to other people. It was doubtless in some such way as this that Edward perceived her.

Edward enjoyed reading to his friends passages from books and manuscripts that he had recently acquired. To the Arnolds he read passages from the letters of the Civil War general George E. Pickett to his wife, LaSalle Corbell Pickett. They were delighted with his reading and observed how he threw himself into the performance and was so moved by some events that the tears came into his eyes. He also corresponded with Pickett's aged widow and sent her an occasional check, and later a small pension, to help with her living expenses.

He also read to friends from newly acquired manuscript letters of Robert E. Lee to his cousin "Markie" (Martha Custis Williams). Here are a few sentences from one of the passages that greatly appealed to Edward and that he read to Otheman Stevens in October 1923. The letter was written on January 22, 1861, shortly before the beginning of the Civil War, when Lee was a U.S. army officer stationed at Fort Mason, Texas: "God alone can save us from our folly, selfishness & short sightedness. . . . I fear that the country will have to pass through for its sins a fiery ordeal. . . . There is no sacrifice I am not ready to make for the preservation of the Union save that of honour. . . . I still hope that the wisdom & patriotism of the nation will yet save it." Another Lee letter that Edward enjoyed reading to friends was one written to Markie shortly after the end of the war about his affection for Traveller, the horse that he had ridden throughout the war.[67]

Edward's relations with his children also reveal something about him at that time. He had a deep love for each of them, and he often tried to express his feelings by means of gifts. He was generous; his birthday and Christmas presents were usually about one thousand dollars for each, he established substantial trusts for each one of them—each trust, all in bonds or preferred stock, was increased from $300,000 to $550,000 during these years—and he helped each with their special wishes, like buying a house or spending a long period abroad. He was in close touch with Howard and his family until Howard died in 1922, but demonstrated little personal warmth. Of his daughters, he saw Elizabeth most: she came down from San Francisco, sometimes with her children. He saw Clara and Marian infrequently, though they all wrote to one another. The coolness the daughters felt toward him after his marriage to Arabella never went away entirely. They made a point of addressing their letters only to Edward, and the thank-you notes from their children were to "Dear Grandfather and Aunt Belle." Marian and Clara sometimes complained about the lack of his interest in them; in 1920, for example, Clara reproached him for his inattention to her son David: "You see, Daddy, he is nine years old, and to the best of my recollection you have never written him a letter."[68] In 1923, Elizabeth wrote to thank him for a visit she and her family had made to the ranch: "Larry [her son] said you looked like Santa Claus only you weren't dressed like him." She continued that "I do want the children to have some love and regard for you and how can they if they never see you? So I feel it's right for them to come down sometimes. Neddy [her son Edwards Huntington Metcalf] is so particularly fond of you. He has a heart as big as all outdoors." And then she summed up her sense of lack in the expression of feelings between them and on the part of her father: "Same old thing on both sides of the family. We none of us can show our affection." And she concluded with an allusion to what her father had said about her sister: "Don't be hard on Peggy [Clara]. She needs our kind thoughts, really. I know what I say."[69]

Edward's relations with the members of his library staff were friendly and cordial. He often walked through the area where they worked and chatted with them. One new member was surprised at his friendliness and wrote him this note: "Dear Mr. Huntington—I was so much surprised at the precious greeting this morning, that I don't know whether I said anything intelligible. I was very much pleased. This is a good time to say that I have thoroughly enjoyed my work in your library ever since I joined the staff. I wish you the utmost satisfaction in your developments of the coming year. Sincerely yours, Clifford B. Clapp."[70] Another staff member wrote to a friend and urged him to seek a position with them. Many books were being bought, he said, and a lot of cataloging was needed: "While Mr. Huntington is disposed to be fairly liberal in the matter of salaries, he does not throw away his money in big chunks, as some outsiders seem to think; nevertheless I think none of us now members of his staff can complain of his treatment of us in the last three years."[71] Edward took a personal interest in the staff; when cataloger Leslie E. Bliss's mother died, Edward wrote him a warm, sympathetic, understanding letter and concluded, "I realize that it comes doubly hard just at this time, when you are worried so much about your little girl."[72] Edward tried to help them when they were in need. In 1919 he heard that his ex-secretary, George E. Miles, was having a serious health problem: he wrote to Graham in New York that "I hope, as I know you will, do everything to cheer him up. I want you to spare no expense in getting the best medical advice, as he is thinking a good deal of the cost. I will take care of that."[73] In 1923 he sent a telegram to Graham when he heard that Belle's old butler "McGillivray is in bad mental state caused by his business anxiety. See him immediately and find out what amount would be necessary. Wire me immediately. He has been in family twenty-two years and we cannot let him go to pieces."[74]

Edward was friendly and informal with all the people who worked for him. Alfonso reported that, wherever Edward went, he always shook hands with the workmen and asked about them and their families. Alfonso reported that the workmen were "all crazy about him."[75] He especially valued those who were meticulous in carrying out their duties. Miss Quigley reported on one occasion when Mr. Huntington went early in the morning to the carbarn of his railway company in downtown Los Angeles. The nightwatchman was still on duty and would not let him in. "I'm Mr. Huntington," Edward said. "That may be," said the nightwatchman, "but I do not know you and cannot permit you to enter the building as my orders are to permit no strangers to enter." Edward turned away, and the nightwatchman later worried what the consequences would be for himself if indeed it was Mr. Huntington to whom he had refused admittance. The next day he received from the general manager a letter of commendation, which had been sent to him at the direction of Mr. Huntington.[76]

Edward felt free to impart advice, privately, to those who worked directly for him. Saving money was one of the key doctrines that he urged on all of his helpers. He distrusted people who didn't save something out of their earnings, no matter how small those earnings were. He urged one of the house servants to break the habit of letting her money slip away and, instead, save little by little. "Anna," he said, "when you get $25 together, bring it to me, and I'll put it away for you and pay you 5 percent on it. Bring me more money and when you have saved up $100 I'll buy a bond or some stock for you." She tried. "And before Anna knows it she's the owner of a gilt-edged bond bought with the money that used to slip through her fingers. It is not what you earn, but what you save that counts."[77]

Aside from urging his staff to save money, the two most recurrent themes in his advice to his staff about their behavior can be called the principle of trusting others and the principle of spontaneous personal action. He once summed up these principles in talking with Alfonso: "I worked with my uncle, Collis P. Huntington," Edward began, "and I never went to college. I learned a lot of things in life and I learned to trust people. I want you to trust people all your life." Even if one or two people are mean or do dirty tricks, he said, don't be discouraged and don't condemn people in general. As for spontaneity, he urged Alfonso to do good things for others on impulse: "When your mind tells you it's time to do a good deed—do it." Mrs. Huntington, he said, "does things on the spur of the moment. That is what I want you to do."[78]

In the matter of trust, we can consider Edward's dealings with Robert Booth, the man who looked after Mrs. Huntington's horses. Mr. Huntington, Booth said, "is a wonderful man. Other men wouldn't even look at you. I'm a colored man. For some people, you're just a slave. But not Mr. Huntington. He's kind and no matter where he is I always come in to see him." Once a soldier on crutches came to Booth's room and asked him for help in getting to Chicago. Booth appealed to Mrs. Huntington, who had a meal prepared for the soldier and gave the money for his fare. When Booth got back to his room, he found that the soldier had stolen his overcoat, razor, and other belongings before he left: "Mr. Huntington held Robert Booth's hands and said, 'Don't worry—those things will happen as long as the world is in existence. Whatever you lost, Mrs. Huntington will replace for you. I do not want you to close the door to anybody. We keep on doing the right part."[79] For another instance, Edward's German masseur complained one day about someone setting fire to his garage, saying, "You know, you can't trust anybody." According to Alfonso, Huntington "was shocked, jumped up, said that only one man deserves the blame not everybody." The masseur came back the next day to apologize, but Huntington didn't want to mention it any more—it was finished and forgiven and the case was closed.[80]

In the matter of spontaneity, Edward had the habit of saving five-dollar gold coins, and he kept them in a cabinet in his bathroom. One day he asked Alfonso how many he had. The answer was thirty-five. "Well," said Edward, "something came into my mind this morning. Give one to each of the servants." And it was done.[81]

Side by side with these principles of trust and spontaneity, however, was his propensity for penny-pinching, which led him to complain to his doctors and tradespeople about their excessive charges. He disputed with Dr. Coley about the charges for going to California for a month and argued with the people who sold them eggs—why ninety cents a dozen when they were sold elsewhere for forty-eight cents? He complained to the ice company about a bill for $95.40 for ice for their residence in July 1922: he "cannot understand how we could possibly use that much ice in one month, and particularly in view of the fact that in June 1921 our ice bill was only $40, and in July 1921 $21." But his care worked both ways. In 1921 he wrote to his shoe supplier that "I duly received your bill in the sum of $38.70, covering three pairs of shoes and some shoe-laces. My recollection is that I bought four pairs of shoes. If I am correct in this, will you kindly send me corrected bill, and oblige."[82]

In 1923, the Huntingtons decided to have their portraits painted, and the arrangements for these paintings—how they dealt with other people, how they envisioned themselves, how others saw them—can serve as a final example from which we can derive some sense of what they were like as human beings.

Having their portraits painted was Edward's idea. At first Belle opposed it, on the grounds that "she was too old to be painted again." They argued it out in front of Alfonso, who reported that she said, with the logic of desperation: "If we are painted now, it will look as though we want to open this house to the public right away. We hope it will be a long time yet" before we die and it goes "to the nation." At last, however, she agreed.[83] Edward then asked Duveen for advice about who should be chosen as the portrait painter. Duveen suggested the English painter Oswald Birley, and Edward asked Archer for his opinion of Birley. Archer replied by telegram: "Have just talked with Duveen regarding Birley's portraits. I strongly advise have your portrait done by this man, whose work I have seen. He is keen."[84] After many more letters and telegrams, Birley was engaged for a fee of $6,000 per painting, including all expenses, with each to pay for his or her portrait, and with acceptance contingent on the satisfaction of the subject.[85]

Birley came to California to do the portraits, with sittings in their residence. He painted Edward first: it took six sittings, according to Alfonso, "and it was complete, it was perfect, and they were very pleased." Birley proceeded with Mrs. Huntington, who sat in a chair on a platform in the large drawing room. "Mrs. Huntington sat one time, and she got very tired and she got up and she told him to stop." She said, "Edward thinks I'm a young girl, that I can sit down there for hours without fainting." Maybe other people "can sit for long hours, but not me." Later, when the first full sitting had ended, the painting of her face was complete:

> Mrs. Huntington took her eye glasses and she started to look very closely at the painting. (She didn't see very well, but she could see up close with her extra glasses. She could see where it was wet.) She looked at the painting, and she got very upset. She didn't like it. So she called him [Birley] and I was present. She said, "You are a great master, you are a great painter; you painted Mr. Huntington very well, as he is today. You took all my wrinkles away, you have made me young. Why, the people will call me a fool. You scratch that painting off and start over again."

So he did. "He painted Mrs. Huntington a second time—he painted her exactly as she was. Well, when the painting was finished, Mrs. Huntington was quite pleased." Birley returned to England and left the two paintings. One evening a week later, Belle took Alfonso into the room where the portraits were hanging, and, after pledging him to secrecy, had him take down the portrait of her "and she turned it on the other side and wrote 'I give this picture to my dear son, Archer Huntington.'"[86]

The two portraits were taken to New York for inclusion in an exhibition of thirty-five of Birley's portraits in early 1924 at the Duveen Galleries. The exhibition was widely reviewed, and the Huntington portraits were given special attention. The *New York Herald Tribune* reviewer thought that, in the portrait of Belle, "Mr. Birley has surpassed himself as the interpreter of character and as the craftsman"; the *New York World* reporter thought that her portrait was done "honestly and without flattery" and that Birley "seems to challenge the camera to go him one better."[87] The editor of *Art News* offered a more elaborate reading of the two Huntington portraits:

> The portrait of Henry E. Huntington is a masterpiece of character delineation. The artist has portrayed a keen man of finance who yet possesses as one of his major traits a passionate appreciation of the aesthetic; you see here the man who could strive to make money in order that he could spend millions on millions for paintings and rare books. Mr. Birley's picture in this instance is an historical document for which the nation is deeply indebted. And as its pendant is the portrait of Mrs. Huntington, attired all in black, with large eyes that placidly look through the beholder from their place of vantage behind big horn-rimmed spectacles—a woman of great power of mind, of insight and of character.[88]

Like most viewers, the critic read Birley's portraits. And, through them, he interpreted the man and the woman who were being depicted, in the way that they chose to present themselves to the world.

Eighteen

THE PUBLIC ESTEEM IN which Edward was held reached its highest point during these years. Building on a decade of notable book and art acquisitions, he bought during these five years a dozen paintings of the first importance, including Gainsborough's *Blue Boy* and Reynolds's *Sarah Siddons as the Tragic Muse.* The former was widely touted in the press as the greatest picture in the world after the *Mona Lisa.* His new acquisitions were more and more widely publicized, and every new purchase was described and lavishly praised. For his library, he bought about fifty significant collections of books and manuscripts, extended the focus of his collection, brought the library to a much higher level of professionalism, and encouraged the wider use of his materials by scholars.

The role of the Huntington Library and Art Gallery was developed and extended in a series of adaptations of the original plans so that it could serve as a prime source of material for scholars and a cultural center for the public. This new role was widely acknowledged as an important step in the cultural development of Southern California.

As a result of these developments, Edward became a public figure of wider prominence. He had long been valued as the business leader who had contributed most to the development of Southern California, and now a further dimension was added to this view. Now he was taken to be a principal enhancer of the intellectual and cultural life of the area, and many honors and distinctions were bestowed on him.

All of these events and conditions, which led to success and acclaim, have to be understood as the public side of the private life that we observed in the preceding chapter, with its various human joys and satisfactions and limitations.

Of all the works of art that Huntington acquired in his lifetime, none created a sensation like the purchase of Gainsborough's *Blue Boy*. Partly this was because the picture had been widely praised, and partly because it sold for more than any painting had ever before brought.

Edward had been interested in this picture for twenty years. In 1901 he bought a color print of it, as well as one of *Sarah Siddons as the Tragic Muse* and the *Pink Boy*, from the New York dealer William Schaus. Two years later, in another group of color prints, he got a further reproduction of the *Blue Boy*. Gainsborough had been, for a decade, at the center of his collection. We recall that it was the purchase in 1911 of three star Gainsborough paintings—*Edward, 2d Viscount Ligonier, Penelope, Viscountess Ligonier,* and *Juliana, Lady Petre*—that had been the turning point in the development of his collection and set its future direction in terms of school and quality. And in 1912 he added Gainsborough's *Anne Duchess of Cumberland.*

The *Blue Boy* was often thought of as Gainsborough's greatest painting. In 1896, Bernard Berenson urged Mrs. Jack Gardner to make an offer to the Duke of Westminster for the *Blue Boy* and for Reynolds's *Sarah Siddons as the Tragic Muse* to give preeminence to her collection. She did not want the latter picture, but she agreed to offer $150,000 for the *Blue Boy*. Berenson told her that "I doubt whether, in the whole realm of possible purchases there is such another prize." But her offer was turned down and she was told that the painting was not for sale.[1] In 1916, a gossip columnist in the *London Daily Mirror* reported, under the heading "Mr. Huntington's Pictures," that "I hear that Mr. H. E. Huntington, the famous American millionaire, has the finest collection of the English school of pictures in the world. He has not got the Duke of Westminster's great Gainsborough, 'The Blue Boy,' though the Duke has refused an offer of eighty thousand pounds [about $320,000] from a well-known dealer. I hope that picture will never leave England."[2]

In 1921, Edward and Duveen discussed the possible purchase of the *Blue Boy,* and Edward agreed that he would be willing to pay about

$600,000 for it. Duveen went to work. He parleyed with the owner, and in due course he was able to buy it from the Duke of Westminster, who was badly in need of cash at that time. Duveen was able to include in the deal, for the same purchase price, Gainsborough's *Cottage Door* and Reynolds's *Sarah Siddons as the Tragic Muse*.[3]

After the accumulated dirt and varnish had been removed from the *Blue Boy,* it was again blue instead of the green it had become. Edward agreed to exhibit it in the National Gallery in London for three weeks before it left England. The exhibition opened on January 2, 1922, and crowds of people came every day. There was a queue outside the building, and another to get into room 25, the largest room in the gallery, where it was hung. It took half an hour to make one's way to the picture, and hawkers did a flourishing business outside selling copies of it. In the three weeks, almost one hundred thousand people came to see the picture, an average of five thousand a day. The English newspapers carried daily stories about the exhibition. Initially, the feeling expressed was of wonder and delight at the picture. The tone soon changed to sadness, however, and the newspapers reflected the feeling with such headlines as "Good-Bye to the Blue Boy," "The Passing of the Blue Boy," "The Lost Masterpiece," and the lament of "the mourning crowds" that the picture was going to "the land of freaks and freedom." A large demonstration was mounted in Trafalgar Square, in front of the main entrance to the National Gallery, to protest the loss of the picture. At the end of the exhibition the London *Times* published a sentimental account of a last visit to the picture called "A Farewell." It began, "We have been to say good-bye to a boy who is leaving England, in a day or two, for ever. He received us dressed in a beautiful blue satin suit." In speaking of the great crowds there, "one or two of us had tears in our eyes, we hardly knew why." The speaker explained to the boy that "he was going because we have not enough money to keep him" and that it was "not indifference or lack of love. . . . He gave us one of his shy smiles, and we felt sure that he understood." Duveen sent Edward in San Marino a large collection of the various clippings, and Edward replied: "Thank you for the clippings which you have so kindly sent me, and it has given me much pleasure to read them. I see that the Blue Boy has bidden 'Goodbye' to London, and we all will hope that its subsequent trips pass without serious incident." Andrew Mellon also sent Edward a copy of the London *Times* "Farewell," and Duveen sent Edward a dozen copies of a popular song called "The Blue Boy" when it was published in England.

After the exhibition closed, the *Blue Boy* was placed in a waterproof covering inside a steel box within an iron-bound wooden case. It was brought by two of Duveen's staff members as hand luggage and carried at night by van from London to Southampton and then on a night ship to France for shipment by the French Line to New York, to avoid the ad valorem freight tax imposed by the British steamship companies. Later, Wilhelm von Bode, the long-time director general of the Berlin Museum, expressed a continental view about the departure of the painting: "Any one who a decade ago had even hinted at the possibility of Gainsborough's 'Blue Boy' making its way across the Atlantic to become the central gem in the Huntington collection would have been thought mad. He might as well have suggested the uprooting of England's century-old oaks, or the removal of the Rock of Gibraltar. And yet the impossible has happened."[4]

Edward had agreed that the picture could be exhibited for three weeks in New York at the Duveen Galleries for the benefit of the Fifth Avenue Hospital. The public showings began on February 23, 1922, some 11,000 people came to see the picture, and the hospital gained about $15,000. Newspapers all over the United States covered the exhibition as did many magazines. As the *New York Post* reported about the opening day, "There was something of the reverence of one of the quiet chapels of a mediaeval cathedral" on the part of the "art lovers who lowered their voices to a whisper after the first instinctive 'Oh!' that greeted the first sight of the heralded painting. It was better than they had hoped." The hyperbole used in the descriptions of the picture began with the first sentence of the leaflet that the Duveen Brothers gave to each gallery goer: "With the possible exception of Leonardo's 'Mona Lisa', no picture in the world has received more notice or attention than Gainsborough's 'Blue Boy'."[5] This thought was endlessly paraphrased and amplified in newspapers and magazines. The media were equally mindful of the fact that this picture had cost more than any picture ever had before in the history of the world. "Some $640,000" to "nearly $1 million" was the range of the expressions generally used. In fact, Duveen's bill reveals that Huntington was charged $728,800 (£182,200) for the *Blue Boy*.[6] We recall the great excitement in 1911 when Huntington paid $50,000 for a copy of the Gutenberg Bible—more than had ever before been paid for a printed book. Likewise, the sale of the *Blue Boy* set a new standard in the realm of paintings, and it excited the interest of many Americans, whether they cared for paintings or not.[7] Extreme popularity is never complete until the object of attention is used in unrelated ways. An example involving the *Blue Boy* was its use in attacking the Volstead Act of 1919, which prohibited the sale of intoxicating liquors in the United States. The old *Life* magazine ran a full-page picture of the *Blue Boy* with Andrew Volstead's face substituted and the caption that "Mr. Huntington only paid $640,000 for Gainsborough's 'Blue Boy.' Uncle Sam's 'Blue Boy' has already cost him $169,026,727.24—and will cost him about $100,000,000 a year—*until he gets rid of it.*"[8]

When the New York exhibition concluded, the *Blue Boy* was again packed and brought in the drawing room of a train as baggage with Duveen and his helpers. From Chicago, Duveen sent a reassuring telegram to Edward in San Marino: "Arrived here safely leaving eight oclock tonight the Dear Boy is very well Regards."[9] On March 21, the *Blue Boy* arrived in Southern California, and Edward was at the station to meet the train. The reporters peppered him with questions. Before the arrival, one said that he had heard the picture was coming under the surveillance of an armed guard: " 'I am very glad to know that he will arrive safely,' laughed Mr. Huntington, adding, 'I do not mean to be unromantic, but it is as simple as shipping a sack of potatoes.' " Another wanted to know, "When will the general public be invited to see the 'Blue Boy'? 'I don't know,' replied the Sage of San Marino, 'but the "Blue Boy" is going to be a permanent resident in the Southland and the people will certainly be given a chance to look him over.' " Earlier, he had been asked whether it was true that the *Blue Boy* was to "occupy a whole room, all to himself, in the Huntington home." Edward replied that "these things cannot be decided until he gets here," and he added with a little irritation that "the to do over this is worse than that preceding a royal wedding." Newspapers all over the United States had had stories, often with a picture of the *Blue Boy,* about the two exhibitions, the transatlantic voyage, and the transcontinental trip. At last it was safely in the Huntington residence in San Marino, after a truly remarkable show of public interest.[10]

The *Blue Boy* box was opened up in the main hall of the house on the afternoon of March 21, with Edward and a few others present, including Carrie and Burke. The next day it was hung in the large drawing room so that it could be seen in a good light.[11] Edward very much enjoyed looking at it. About a week after it got there, he wrote to Jacques Seligmann in New York that the *Blue Boy* "arrived safely and is, I think, my greatest picture and the one I take the greatest delight" in. His next sentence reveals the ultimate reason for his drive to acquire good things: "I am sure it will prove to be as great an attraction to future generations here."[12] He seems to have thought more about those "future generations" than he did about himself.

Edward also acquired the two other paintings that Duveen had bought from the Duke of Westminster, Reynolds's *Sarah Siddons as the Tragic Muse* for $151,200 and Gainsborough's *Cottage Door* for $325,000. The three paintings thus cost Edward about $1.2 million. In addition, he bought fourteen other important British paintings during these five years, for a little over $3.5 million. They included two by Gainsborough, five by Reynolds, three by Romney, two by Hoppner, one by Turner, and one by Raeburn. Among these were such popular favorites as Reynolds's *The Young Fortune Teller,* Romney's *Lady Hamilton in a Straw Hat,* Raeburn's *Master William Blair,* and Turner's *The Grand Canal: Venice.*

Edward told Otheman Stevens that his ambition to own beautiful paintings began when he was a very young man. He admired, in a home, a French painting that particularly appealed to him, and he said that "from that moment I determined that I would surround myself some day with works of similar quality and learn about them, for that painting gave me such remarkable satisfaction, and enjoyment, I realised that a man would be wise to acquire such surroundings."[13] A crucial feature in making a decision to buy a painting was always whether it truly appealed to him or not. He summed up his attitude to a reporter in 1924 when "in speaking of the acquisition of great pictures, Mr. Huntington confided the information that he never purchases a picture without he likes it personally"—no matter what "value it may have in the eyes of others. He doesn't care to have a painting in his collection that he doesn't like personally."[14] And it was a principle he put into practice. When Duveen was trying to persuade him to buy Reynolds's *Strawberry Girl,* he sent Edward a photograph of the painting and an ecstatic description of it as "one of the greatest and most beautiful gems by the master"; "its coloring I cannot describe—it is all so wonderful." But it did not appeal to Edward. "I have no doubt," he told Duveen, "but that the picture is fine in color, but it is not one that I would care to purchase: the girl is too simple."[15]

Edward's art purchases during these years were not limited to paintings. He acquired a dozen miniature portraits, nearly three dozen Chelsea porcelain figures, and a few more bronzes. These were not trivial purchases: the Chelsea figures, for example, were both good and expensive, at a cost of about $680,000.[16] Garden statuary was added, such as four bronze statues, a fountain, MacMonnies's bronze *Bacchante,* Anna Hyatt Huntington's pair of Great Danes in stone, and thirty-one seventeenth-century stone figures from Padua. All of them were placed on the grounds.

He also continued to buy art objects for the library, either for their historical value (like nineteen paintings of Indians by Carl Moon, plus Moon's collection of 250 photographs of Indians) or because they represented authors in the collection (like marble busts of Thackeray and Sterne, or paintings of Tennyson and Milton). He acquired likenesses of historical personages like Robert E. Lee and Abraham Lincoln in bronze, a marble bust of Benjamin Franklin, paintings of Martin Van Buren and General Sutter, one of Benjamin Franklin appearing before the Privy Council, and four portraits of George Washington—by Gilbert Stuart, Charles Willson Peale, Rembrandt Peale, and Charles Peale Polk.[17]

He could not buy all of the art that was offered him. We can perhaps reconcile ourselves to the fact that he declined Rembrandt's *Titus,* a Van Dyck, an El Greco, a Titian, and a Velazquez.[18] He explained, in turning down the Titian, that "the important pictures in my collection are of the English School only,—those relating to historical or literary subjects are placed in the Library, not the Art Gallery, and while these are important, I do not feel as free to spend as much on them as I have to get so many more of that nature." But a twinge of regret comes from his declining the Gainsborough sketchbook with 329 drawings in it, the Romney sketchbook with many pen and pencil sketches and drawings, the eighty Burne-Jones pencil drawings for the wood engravings in William Morris's Kelmscott Chaucer, and even the contemporary portrait of Oscar Wilde by Harper Pennington.[19]

As his collections developed, he became more rigorous in turning down art and books that were outside his fields of interest. Moreover, he was spending so much during these years that he often said he felt poor. He insisted on preserving his capital and spending only income or funds that derived from business mergers or planned sales of real estate. Most of the time his financial managers had a hard time projecting enough income to pay the bills for art and books and extending the notes for payment as they came due. His secretary, Emma Quigley, said, "There was a stock phrase in Mr. Huntington's Los Angeles office, 'We're in mourning,' which meant that HEH had sent a large bill for books or art for them to pay, which sometimes meant considerable difficulty in laying hands on the necessary amount right away." In the New York office, the expression used under a comparable situation was "We're poor now." Indeed, they had great difficulty much of the time during these years. Edward left the problem to his managers, and could even resort to a little joke when they complained. "Once when it was particularly difficult," Miss Quigley said, "Mr. Dunn telegraphed HEH that he was unable to raise the necessary amount. HEH replied, 'Have you thought of the banks?'"[20]

Edward did his part by declaring occasional moratoriums on the purchase of art or books. In 1924 he wrote from San Marino to Duveen, who had suggested that he might come for a visit, "While I shall be very glad to see you if you are coming to California, I have my doubts as to buying any more pictures, as I feel I should not purchase any more until I have paid for those I already have." In the autumn of 1924, Edward owed $2 million to Duveen, and his managers were having a hard time finding money to cover the notes as they came due.[21]

During these five years, the library also grew at a fast pace. Edward spent a great deal of time reading catalogs of books and manuscripts from dealers and for auction sales. He corresponded endlessly about material that might be available, and he used agents to locate and purchase collections for him. George D. Smith, who had been the agent he depended on the most from 1911 onward, died of a heart attack in March 1920. Smith was sitting in his shop at 8 East Forty-fifth Street in New York, talking with a man who had recently supplied him with some books, when he suddenly collapsed and died on the spot. Cole wrote to Edward, who was in San Marino, that "the death of George D. Smith came on us like a thunder-clap out of a clear sky. The public press has had many articles concerning him and his career. He was a most remarkable man and his place in the book world cannot well be filled."[22] Edward's time in San Marino was, as his secretary, George Hapgood, wrote to Cole, "marred of course by the sad news of Smith's death. Mr. H. feels it keenly."[23]

Smith's death was a great loss to Edward, who had long relied on his knowledge of books and on his honesty. Although Smith was only fifty when he died, compared to Edward's seventy, Smith had spent his whole life in the book trade: he had a superb knowledge of scarce and valuable books, and his geniality opened doors for him. The newspaper accounts praised him as "the greatest bookseller in the world" (A. Edward Newton), "the greatest book dealer the world has ever known" (Mitchell Kennerley), "a man you couldn't help liking" and "generous to a fault and endlessly good natured" (a fellow book dealer). Privately, the collector W. K. Bixby wrote to Cole that "I doubt whether there was a man in the country that knew more about rare books from either a commercial or collecting standpoint." Unlike Edward, he did not bother with the contents; "I don't read books," he said. "I buy 'em." And he was a great help to Edward in getting the material he wanted in the treacherous commercial world of the book.[24]

After Smith's death, Edward began to use A. S. W. Rosenbach as his principal agent at auction sales. It was not a new relationship. Edward had begun buying from and through him in 1911; from a modest beginning of $3,000 a year, his annual purchases rose to over $100,000 by 1919. Rosenbach—Abe, or Rosey, as his friends called him—was different from Smith: he had a Ph.D. in English literature from the University of Pennsylvania with a dissertation on Elizabethan drama, he knew a good deal about the insides of the books he sold, he was a salesman by nature, and he, like Duveen, was not content with a modest profit or a supporting role.

After Edward had studied and annotated auction catalogs, he frequently discussed with Rosenbach the books that appealed to him. Rosenbach had a good sense of the market, he went to the major sales in New York and London, and he could carry out Edward's detailed wishes in person. E. H. Dring, the head of the Quaritch firm in London, politely complained in 1924 that Huntington had not, for some years, "entrusted me with your commissions for the London sales"; Edward politely reassured him that he had no personal feelings against the firm but that he used Rosenbach because "my opportunity for consultation was better with him than with others so far away."[25] Rosenbach was able to buy to advantage at the auctions, in part by arranging in advance with the likely bidders to insure that they did not bid against one another. The way he juggled his clients in taking or withholding their bids for popular items at the Christie-Miller sales in 1923–25, for a typical example, was a marvel of manipulation. He wrote to Huntington on February 4, 1924, that "I can ask Mr. Folger, Mr. W. A. White, Mr. Clawson and Mr. Pforzheimer to refrain from bidding on the items in which you are interested. This has always worked so satisfactorily to you, keeping the prices down and avoiding all American competition."[26] His influence extended to institutional libraries; he wrote Huntington that "I arranged with Mr. Edgar H. Wells, who bought for Harvard College, for him to refrain from bidding on the ones you especially wanted."[27] Later, Rosenbach could write to Huntington that "the Britwell Sales are now over and I secured for you nearly every lot at very reasonable prices. I do not think there was a single bid from America as I arranged all that before I left, so there was absolutely no competition from our side of the water."[28] About an earlier sale, Rosenbach wrote Huntington with boyish enthusiasm that "I permitted Dring of Quaritch to purchase a few books for the British Museum and Sir Leicester Harmsworth."[29] In reporting to Huntington about the price level of his purchases, Rosenbach was almost always able to say something in self-praise, like "these are most reasonable prices and I must congratulate you on obtaining them."[30]

Rosenbach was a true enthusiast about the books he had for sale.

About the King-Haney-Ellsworth portolan map of America of 1501–02, he said, "It is without doubt the finest piece of early Americana that has been *ever offered for sale.*" Of the English manuscripts from T. Fitzroy Fenwick, he said, "This comprises the finest lot of early English poems and prose that has ever been offered for sale." About the Duke of Veragua's Columbus collection, he said, "It is the most desirable collection in existence from an American standpoint and absolutely priceless."[31]

Whenever he could, he made big profits on the turnover. Several examples from his own records might include the Phillipps incunabula, which Rosenbach bought for $92,593 and (before the deal was closed) sold to Huntington for $150,000, with Rosenbach retaining the ones that Huntington already had—about 5 percent of the total. Or the Battle Abbey records, which Rosenbach bought for $18,000 and sold to Huntington immediately for $50,000. Or a group of twenty fifteenth-century manuscripts, which had cost Rosenbach $50,000 and which he sold to Huntington for $92,000, while retaining six of them for himself.[32] (Rosenbach made even greater profits from sales to other collectors: in 1922 he sold to Folger for $50,000 a copy of the Shakespeare First Folio for which he had paid $8,600 two months before.[33]) Rosenbach was sometimes reluctant to have Huntington know the extent of his profits. Once when a shipping clerk in Rosenbach's New York shop was packing some fifteenth-century books for shipment to San Marino, he inadvertently enclosed the bills from the dealers from whom Rosenbach had bought the books. When the blunder was reported to Rosenbach, he first raged and swore, and then overcame his fear of flying enough to go by plane to get there before the shipment did. With help from Huntington's secretary George Hapgood—and a gift of a thousand dollars to him—Rosenbach was able to recover the incriminating bills and return to New York in peace.[34]

Part of Rosenbach's salesmanship included sending interesting books as gifts to Huntington: for Christmas 1922, he sent the printed memoirs of a professor at the University of Virginia with a manuscript letter laid in from Thomas Jefferson appointing that man to his professorship; in the autumn of 1924, he sent the recent books by Gamaliel Bradford; for Christmas 1924 he sent a Stevenson Christmas card; and for Huntington's seventy-fifth birthday in 1925 he sent "a naughty but thoroughly characteristic letter of Lady Hamilton." Huntington acknowledged each present with delight. "You seem to have the faculty of always sending books," Huntington wrote him, "which prove to be most interesting." After reading them and showing them to friends, he put them in his library.[35]

Huntington was not taken advantage of by Rosenbach, however. He was aware of the tricks of the book and art trade through long association with many dealers, he had a good sense of market value, and he was always inclined to bargain and ask for a special price for an old customer and the "usual discount" for his library. When he paid high prices for art or books, it was because he thought he was getting his money's worth in a commercial marketing situation governed by supply and demand.

Early in 1920, a friend sent Edward a letter by Aaron Burr as a gift for his library. In his reply, Edward said, "As you know, the founding and building of this Library is now the controlling interest in my life: your appreciation of this as shown in your gift, pleases me very much."[36]

The major expansion of the collections in his library continued to take place through en bloc purchases of other collections or other libraries. During these five years, he bought forty-seven collections of substantial importance, seventeen of them with Rosenbach as his agent, the other thirty directly from the owners or through one dealer or another.[37]

These collections greatly enriched the library by giving it greater depth, from medieval manuscripts to twentieth-century writers. The collections included a total of more than 300,000 books and manuscripts, but numerical reckoning gives no sense of the range or importance of the material, which extended from 66 royal charters before the year 1245 to 2,410 incunabula, to 40 treaties between whites and Native Americans or between warring "Indian" tribes, to 296 letters by John Greenleaf Whittier.

In these acquisitions there was less emphasis on the display item, which is of primary interest because of its extreme rarity, public recognition, or high monetary value, and more emphasis on large groups of related material, of primary interest for their contents or their elucidation of other matters. Scholars use both classes of material, but the latter sort provide resources for more types of research. In this sense, the Huntington Library became much more of a scholar's library during these years.

A few words about several of these collections can perhaps give a little more sense of Huntington's attitude toward collecting. He was eager to buy the rich collection of Lincoln material that had been put together by Judd Stewart, which included over twenty-seven hundred printed pieces and many manuscripts: a lot of Lincoln letters, including the one to the parents of Colonel Ellsworth, who was the first person of note to be killed in the Civil War; the proof copy of the first Inaugural Address; the resolution for the Thirteenth Amendment abolishing slavery, signed by all the members of Congress; and many manuscript notes by Lincoln. After the death of Stewart, Edward approached his son about buying the collection. The son was at first willing and they agreed on a price, but then he declined out of respect for the memory of his father. Edward responded with an understanding that reflects his own experience in collecting: "The labor and love which your father put into gathering and preserving the collection has endeared it to you more than perhaps any mere money could make up for. Such being the case, I think I would rather that you did not sell to me at this time, much as I would like to join the collection with my library. Some other time, perhaps a year or two later, if you do not decide to present it to Yale, we may talk over the matter again." Two years later, after the son had distanced the collection from his feelings about his father, he agreed to sell the collection to Edward, who paid what he had earlier offered, $62,500.[38]

Edward's purchase of the massive collection of Virginiana assembled over a period of fifty years by Robert A. Brock reveals in a somewhat different way his feeling for collectors and collections. After buying the collection, he wrote to Brock's daughter that "I can imagine how you must have felt in parting from this library with its many close and loving associations going back through your whole lifetime; but I feel sure it will always be a comfort and satisfaction to you that it has fallen into good hands where it will receive the best of care and be kept intact." He invited her to come to San Marino to see the collection "after it is properly placed on the shelves of the library ready for use." He felt that a collection was a little like a member of the family. "When I secure a valuable and worthy collection such as this, I am always desirous of a biographical sketch of the man who made it," he said, and he asked her for an outline of her father's "literary life and career."[39] Similarly, when he bought Walter U. Lewisson's collection of Washingtoniana comprising some twelve thousand items, he asked Mr. Lewisson to send a photograph of himself: "It has been in my mind," he wrote, "to obtain and preserve wherever possible photographs of the men like yourself who have formed parts of the Huntington Library."[40] And it was not only the personal identity of the collector that mattered to Edward but also the collector's knowledge of books. When Edward gave his check to Beverly Chew for his collection, he is reported to have said: "I should take the greatest pleasure in writing another for the same amount if you could only transfer to me the knowledge you have of these books."[41]

The extent of Edward's acquisition of large collections was a source of puzzlement to some people. In commenting on his purchases at the Britwell Court sale, Edmund Gosse declared from his influential weekly "pulpit" in the London *Sunday Times* that "Mr. Henry Huntington, of Los Angeles, is a book-collector on a royal scale. He is bent on gathering together the noblest library of old English books in the world. He collects pictures, too, with magnificent profusion, but his books are what he most delights in, and he proposes, when he is satisfied with their number, to build a matchless library, and present the whole to the State of California. It is only in the United States that people do these things."[42]

We tend to pay special attention to the en bloc acquisitions, especially when they include spectacular items. Edward's own attention was much more focused on the search for single books and manuscripts. He read and studied booksellers' catalogs constantly, checked what he wanted against his own holdings, and ordered the missing ones that he thought reasonably priced. For example, in the five months between April and August 1921, he sent 120 orders for books listed in the catalogs of sixty different booksellers; the orders were relatively small, $75 on average, with his total purchases amounting to about

$9,000.[43] He made endless lists of books on cards or sheets of paper, in pencil or in ink, of books that he wanted, was trying to buy, or had recently bought.[44]

Sometimes he bought a lot of books from one catalog; from Quaritch's catalog 369, in 1922, he ordered sixty-one books; eight had been sold, but he got fifty-three, for some $15,000.[45] He was able to get fourteen autograph letters from the catalog of the George D. Smith estate sale for $480.50; he obtained several by signers of the Declaration of Independence, including two by Francis Hopkinson for $20.[46] Since he was a good customer, dealers tried hard to give him what he wanted; when his order from Maggs catalog 429 was received in January 1923, the Major André letter and two other items he asked for had already been sold; but Maggs contrived to get them back so that he could have them.[47] Sometimes it worked the other way: when Huntington objected that Smith had bought Tottel's *Miscellany* for Pforzheimer, both Smith and Pforzheimer explained the arrangement that Pforzheimer had agreed not to bid on other books for the sake of this one; Edward immediately wrote to Pforzheimer that "I am very glad that you have the copy of Tottel's *Miscellany,* and as soon as Smith told me the circumstances, I could not take the book myself, as you were entitled to it."[48] And sometimes he gave something up when he thought another bidder had a better right to it. He bought at auction in 1923, for one thousand dollars, the 1867 letter from Edwin Booth to Ulysses S. Grant asking for the return of John Wilkes Booth's body to their mother. Members of the Players Club in New York, founded by Edwin Booth, wrote him that they too had bid a thousand dollars for it, to go with their Edwin Booth letter given out to the public after Lincoln's death, and asked if they might have it after his lifetime. Edward replied that "I myself think that The Players Club is more entitled to the Edwin Booth Letter than the Library" and he returned it to the dealer "with instructions to relinquish my claims on it in favor of the Club."[49]

Edward thoroughly understood the ways of dealers, including their use of hyperbole. Rosenbach and Duveen were notable practitioners of this style, but it was in general use. Maggs could tell him, by cable, that they could offer him "the most astounding collection of Americana in the world."[50] Walter C. Wyman of Chicago offered him what was " 'far and away' the finest collection ever in the market of documents relating to Early New York and the Atlantic Coast. . . . The collection is priceless."[51] Charles Sessler of Philadelphia frequently used such expressions as "the most magnificent and finest collection of original manuscripts which I have ever had."[52]

A few of the books that Edward was buying individually at this time were exceedingly rare, like the unique copy of Shakespeare's *Venus and Adonis* (1599).[53] More usually, they were worthy books like the first edition of Darwin's *The Origin of Species* (1859) in the original cloth for $22.79 from a dealer in New York.[54] Or books to fill in the gaps of his collections of modern authors like Yeats, Stevenson, Kipling, or Conrad; he made detailed notes on their books missing from his collection, such as a full page of thirty-one items headed "Robert Louis Stevenson Lacking."[55] As always, his inclination was to add to strength. For example, in 1921 and 1922 alone he increased his collection of Yeats, which he had begun in 1904 with *The King's Threshold,* by fifteen books and one manuscript; Stevenson, begun in 1905 with *Prayers at Vailima,* by twenty-six books and five manuscripts; Kipling by forty-six books; and Conrad by twenty-five books.[56]

He also had the good fortune to have an offer from Clarence Brigham, the librarian of the American Antiquarian Society, to pick up pre-1640 books for him while traveling on vacation in Europe and visiting provincial book shops; Brigham got almost a thousand books at modest cost, and Edward insisted on paying his personal expenses and giving him an honorarium.[57] Edward also kept in touch with a number of writers, like John Drinkwater and Bliss Carman, and fine printers like John Henry Nash, whose work he admired and whom he knew personally; they corresponded and sent him their work. Edward acknowledged a book from Carman, for example, by saying, "I can not tell you how much pleasure the reading of it has given me."[58] And when Nash arranged to have one of his books, *Old California* (1924), dedicated to him, Edward was delighted that such a "beautifully done" book with "subject matter of great merit" should be dedicated to him; the author had said he was "the most worthy person to dedicate an art book to, for the reason of your great work in collecting art and literature."[59]

In the course of this rush of buying, Edward also declined many things that were offered him. For a few examples, in 1922 he refused the authorial manuscript of Arnold Bennett's *Old Wives Tale.* The next year, when offered a collection of a hundred unpublished autograph letters from Ruskin to John Allen, he simply said, "I am not interested in buying them." And when offered the manuscript of Chesterfield's *Letters to his Son* for twelve thousand pounds and commission, his telegraphic answer was, "Not interested in Chesterfield Collection. Price exorbitant."[60]

He was also buying many scholarly reprints of early texts, like all the publications of the Roxburghe Society, the Hakluyt Society, the Camden Society, and all 149 volumes of Tudor Facsimile Texts.[61] And when he bought current scholarly books, as from the Yale University Press, he said, "I want first editions only." In a postscript he added, "I notice that the copy you sent to me of World Power and Evolution is dated 1920. Can you not get me a 1919 copy?"[62] (If you get a first edition of *Venus and Adonis,* hadn't you better get first editions of scholarly books too?)

But the type of material that he was buying is epitomized in the public mind by a cartoon published in the *Los Angeles Times* in 1920. It shows Huntington and a fellow collector, Herschel V. Jones. The caption reads: "Henry E. Huntington and Herschel V. Jones, who publishes the Minneapolis Journal and collects rare books, are talking shop out in San Marino."

> Huntington: "*I've* just picked up Eve's diary."
> Jones: "Oh! That reminds me, *I* got hold of 'The Log of the Ark,' by Noah, the other day."[63]

In fact, Jones was in the process of selling his collection. As Huntington remembered it, Jones came to him and said

> "H. E., you've several duplicates in your library I'd like to have. Will you let me look them over?"
> "Of course." I said to give him the run of the library, and then while his collection was being sold, and he had quit as a collector, he bought a number of my duplicates.
> A man may quit cigarets or cocktails, or money making, or anything else he likes, except collecting.[64]

During these years, even after there was a considerable library staff and an extensive library building, the collection of books and manuscripts was still very much Huntington's personal library. He himself decided on almost all acquisitions—en bloc purchases and rare or expensive things, of course; but also minor needs and all the books of the modern writers. The librarians often checked catalogs and indicated items that were missing in the collection, but it was Huntington who generally authorized purchases. Occasionally he suggested that Cole use his own judgment about lesser acquisitions, and the librarians were free to buy reference books needed in connection with cataloging. When the collecting of western material began, Leslie E. Bliss spent a lot of his time traveling throughout the West in search of books and manuscripts of western Americana and Mexican interest. Huntington would give him an advance of several hundred dollars, and Bliss would buy a great deal of material, usually at an average of less than a dollar an item.[65] As for all the rest of the purchases, Huntington had to approve each bill before it could be paid. As Bliss wrote to the dealer Walter C. Wyman in Chicago, "Mr. Huntington is a man who wishes to make all important decisions himself." And to the New York dealer James F. Drake, Bliss wrote that "I rarely ever make any recommendations to Mr. Huntington with regard to manuscripts."[66]

Although Edward felt that the first job of his library staff was to catalog the collection, he was glad to have their suggestions about acquisitions. When he gave Cole the list of modern authors, he said that they were writers "all of whose works, it seems to me, we should have"; but he added, "I should be glad to have you make any additions or other suggestions. I should like lists of what we need to make our collections complete."[67]

A vignette portraying Huntington at work with his staff is contained in a letter to Bliss, when he was away on one of his trips, from Robert Schad, a library assistant:

> Mr. Huntington has sent for me several times for different little matters and we have gone over several catalogues. He made what I considered very generous bids in the Kipling and Dickens and Thackeray sales and I wrote the order Saturday. I called his attention to your rec-

ommendations in the last Drake catalogue again and he ordered practically everything including the Stevensons and Kiplings. We went
over the Sauer books once and he put aside a great many as being too
highly priced but he wants to go over some of them again.[68]

The library acquisition program also felt the force of his moratoriums when his debts exceeded his income. In 1921, he wrote to Cole that
"I do not wish to purchase any books except what I have given orders
for." In 1922, he sent a telegram to a dealer saying that he was "intend-
ing to take vacation from buying books." In 1923, he told Cole that "I
do not wish to order another book for the Library or the catalogue
room"; when Cole sent him a list of some choice things six weeks later,
he replied, "While the items seem desirable, I am too poor to think of
buying the Milton manuscript."[69] Fortunately for the library, these
pauses in buying lasted only a few months at a time, until the debts
were taken care of in one way or another.

For Edward, the process of cataloging seemed to drag on endlessly. In
1924, he told Mitchell Kennerley, president of the Anderson Galleries,
that "we still are very busy at the Library, and I do not think that we are
any farther along in the cataloging than we were a year ago." But he was
still content. As he had earlier written to Kennerley, "The Library
meets all my expectations and the staff is hard at work on the new
material I brought with me. They all seem happy and contented in
their new homes."[70]

In the meantime, scholars were using the library more and more, and
some of the names of the users are still familiar. J. S. P. Tatlock, then at
Stanford, came down for the summer of 1922, and he found it so useful
that he returned for the summers of 1923 and 1924. Each time he
brought a couple of graduate students or young instructors with him,
and he thought the library "a great boon to graduate and research work
on the whole Pacific coast."[71] John M. Manly of the University of
Chicago came for several winter months, to spend half of his time on
pre-Shakespearean drama and the other half on golf. He asked, "Could
I find lodgings and board for my sister and myself at reasonable rates in
the neighborhood of the Library, and finally is there a golf course to
which I could secure admissions on reasonable terms?" He was sent an

outline of the holdings in pre-Shakespearean drama, an offer of admission cards to two golf courses, and a promise of lodging and board for the two of them.[72] Chauncey Brewster Tinker of Yale wrote to get information on manuscript letters by Boswell, and Wilbur L. Cross—known affectionately as "Uncle Toby" at Yale because of his interest in *Tristram Shandy,* and later governor of Connecticut—sent a letter to Huntington that was the ultimate in tact in inquiring about Sterne manuscripts: "May I have your permission to inquire of your Librarian about such manuscripts as you may have?" "Certainly," was Huntington's answer.[73] Amy Lowell wrote, at the suggestion of John Livingston Lowes, in connection with her life of Keats, to ask about Drayton's *Endimion and Phoebe* (1595) and the possibility that Keats might have seen this book before writing his *Endymion;* a staff member drew up a three-page memo for her, and she was pleased.[74] R. H. Griffith wrote a dozen letters from the University of Texas with inquiries about details concerning Pope, Davenant, and Byron.[75]

There were other ways in which the library began to contribute to the advancement of learning. Herbert Putnam, the librarian of Congress, asked Edward whether he would let him have photographs of manuscripts needed to fill in the Library of Congress collections of similar materials; Edward was entirely agreeable.[76] The librarian of the Bancroft Library asked for permission to print the early California letters of Father Kino, and Edward was willing.[77] He also consented to the request by Robert G. Cleland of Occidental College to publish extracts of the Sutter Papers in his history of California.[78] And the Huntington series of facsimile reprints was begun in 1920, with the unique copies of two pre-Elizabethan plays—Henry Medwall's *Fulgens and Lucres,* and William Wager's *Enough is as good as a feast*—each with an introductory note by Seymour De Ricci, each published in New York in two hundred copies at five dollars each. They were welcomed by scholars and libraries and highly praised in the London *Times Literary Supplement* in a long article that congratulated Huntington, thought that it was "a mark of a true sportsman" to pay ten or fifteen thousand dollars for a play and then let everybody have a copy of it for five dollars, and concluded that "the pangs with which some English scholars view the exportation of rare books to the United States should be much alleviated."[79]

The library also did a lively business by correspondence with scholars in England. J. Dover Wilson, the distinguished British Shakespeare scholar, frequently sent long lists of variant readings to be checked against the Huntington copies.[80] And A. W. Pollard, the keeper of printed books at the British Museum, sent numerous letters and proofs asking detailed questions about pre-1640 books, for which he was compiling the short-title catalog. When Edward sent a copy of the check list of his pre-1640 books, Pollard thanked him warmly and offered him "congratulations on the splendid library you are getting together with such astonishing speed."[81] Pollard was certainly aware of the "contest" advertised in the press between Huntington and the British Museum, with such comparisons as this one in the London *Times,* happily reprinted in the *New York Post:* "It is only by owning more copies of the poems than Mr. Huntington that the museum collection of Shakespeare first editions holds its own. In the plays Mr. Huntington has been adjudged, if anything, a trifle stronger."[82] No matter how these matters are judged, by 1924 the Huntington collection had indeed taken shape as a research library of real importance.

The public acclaim of the Huntington Library and Art Gallery began in 1919, when the first indenture was signed establishing the institution in the state of California for the benefit of the public. Commendation of the institution and praise for its founder increased to an almost inconceivable degree during these years. This acclaim revealed a deep strain of idealism cherished by people of the time and an eagerness to believe that society could be essentially improved by the altruistic acts set in motion by one person.

Since this form of idealism is no longer very common, it is worth reminding ourselves that it was a belief deeply held in those times. Here is a typical statement: "The value of the gift is greater than one dares estimate. Not the money worth, although that is incalculable, but its power for good, the inexhaustible benefits. Generations to come will enjoy the benefaction. It will educate and uplift, bringing happiness."[83] Huntington himself shared this view of the power of books and art. In thanking the Los Angeles Chamber of Commerce for their appreciation, he said, "Looking ahead, even in the near future, I feel that the

Library and Art Gallery will prove a means of pleasure and instruction to the people of California, and in the far future, as this wonderful country becomes more and more a factor in the growth of the Nation, I trust that this place of mine will play its part in the development of better men and women, and in this way, better citizens."[84]

All of the public response to Huntington's gift came spontaneously, without any public relations manipulation, and with limited participation on the part of Edward, who disliked publicity. One of his friends, Frank A. Miller of Riverside, complained that Edward declined to accept public credit for having given $15,000 to build a road up Mt. Rubidoux, where an Easter service that touched many people was held: "You insist on doing everything in such a quiet way and not allowing anybody to do anything in recognition, and by doing it this way I fear you miss knowing the effect of what you are doing."[85]

Several widely publicized events kept the institution in the public consciousness between 1919 and 1924. One was the construction of the library building in San Marino, commencing in August 1919 and continuing for the next couple of years. Another was the transfer of his books and manuscripts from New York to California, beginning in the late summer of 1920. The third was the signing of three deeds, on April 8, 1922, by which he transferred ownership of his books and manuscripts, art, and the San Marino Ranch to the trustees of the Huntington Library and Art Gallery. These events all validated or gave concrete form to the institution he had established. They created such a wide and deep response that only a few examples can be offered in order to suggest the public and private reactions to this new institution and to its founder.

When the construction of the library was under way, the excitement about the meaning of this new development for Southern California began. In the spring of 1920, various distinguished people were asked to explain it. George Ellery Hale told a gathering of Southern California librarians that "the Huntington library will be the means of bringing students to Pasadena and Los Angeles from all over the world." It is of such significance, said Hale, that "I doubt if the real importance is realized by the people of Southern California or of the United States at large."[86] Herschel V. Jones, the book collector and Minneapolis publisher, publicly described the library as "the greatest English collection in the world"; "Los Angeles will be the center" for scholars and for laymen, and "the Huntington library will be perpetuated for 1000 years to come and will continue through that period the name of Henry E. Huntington."[87] The editorial writers took pains to try to explain the significance and value of the library. A long editorial in the *Los Angeles Express* began, "Among the really great educational institutions of the State of California, and more particularly of the Southland of California, will be the notable library which Henry E. Huntington has planned and is rapidly bringing to completion on his estate known as San Marino on the outskirts of Pasadena." The library is "a splendid structure, one of the best of its kind in existence"; its "collection has no rival anywhere in the world" and "it will stand for all time an imperishable monument to a man who has held to a noble ideal and a benefaction worthy of a masterful man's appreciation of the highest art."[88]

In the late summer of 1920, when the move of the library to California began, the eastern papers all reported it "with deep regret"—much as the British papers spoke of the departure of their native art objects for the New World.[89] The Los Angeles papers reported the move with great pride: "If you are not interested in books and minds and ideas, you may not think this library means much to Los Angeles and Southern California." In fact, it means "the coming here of the great intellects of the world, it means the creation here of new literature, of new thoughts, of new dynamics of ideas." It would attract "the creative minds of literature" and no longer would American writers and scholars have to "take enforced pilgrimages to either Paris or London for their material of research."[90]

The editorial writers went to work to celebrate the move. In the *Los Angeles Examiner,* an editorial was headed "A Grand Public Spirited Move to Make This a Library Center." "The time is near," it began, "when people from all over the world will be coming to Los Angeles to see and consult the treasures not to be found in other places in the United States or Europe," all because of "the taste, public spirit and liberality of Henry E. Huntington. . . . The Huntington Library will be something to which our people may point with appreciation and just pride for all time to come."[91] The *Los Angeles Times* devoted a full column to its editorial on the subject, simply titled "The Huntington Library." It was praised as

> another magnificent addition to the cultural resources of this section.... Hundreds of the best scholars of this continent will come here every year to take advantage of the contents of that library. Out of it will grow many literary works of practical interest to America.... We will also produce writers of greater merit because of the material which will be at hand.... And from it all California will benefit. By our contact with such a library we will come to a more wholesome way of looking at books, learning to value those which ring true and touch life and to waste but little time with those which are merely mental gymnastics or the diversions of phrase-spinners.... [It] will be a wonderful asset [for] the motion-picture capital of the world: we will have better American plays, since it will be easier for producers to get the facts about and the spirit of America. The story of California will be available for reproduction through the motion picture as never before.... The gift, indeed, is one of the most valuable which any commonwealth has ever received.[92]

There were also many feature articles, with pictures. The headline of the one in the *New York World* magazine section by John Farrar almost tells the whole story: "World's Greatest Private Library: Henry Huntington's Fabulously Precious Store of Books, Once in New York, Are Now Being Housed in a Palatial Library on the Pacific Coast." This story was adapted in various places, and even converted into an editorial in the *Toronto Mail*.[93] This tradition was carried on in various accounts, like the long essay by George H. Sargent in the *Boston Transcript* ("World's Finest Private Library in Trust for All"), which maintained that "the formation of the Huntington Library is, without doubt, the greatest bibliothecal achievement of the twentieth century" and argued that three important factors made it possible: "the discriminating taste and ability of Mr. Huntington," "the means he possessed," and the unparalleled number of libraries that came on the market during these years.[94]

The most copied feature story was one written by John Daggett for the *Los Angeles Times*. It was copied because it was based on an interview with Huntington and offered some choice quotations by him; the interview had also included a conducted tour of the library and several readings by Huntington. One of the quotations was a response to the interviewer's natural American question about the cost of some of his books:

> "Please do not mention any monetary figure in connection with any book or painting which I have acquired," he requested yesterday and a request from those firm-set lips inspires the respect of a command.
>
> "I say money has nothing to do with it," he continued. "True values can only be expressed in eons of time, by the march of centuries to come and by the uplift of humanity."
>
> Then abruptly he turned and gazed thoughtfully down into the heart of the San Gabriel Valley, as if regretting that he had said so much. Mr. Huntington is a man of few words when sensing an interview, but is delightedly outspoken when discussing the books he loves, his rare pictures or his garden with its old sculpture.

One other remark that has been often quoted was his answer to the interviewer's question as to whether he had ever thought of writing his autobiography. "No, never," he replied. "I have been approached regarding a biography, but I do not want that. This library will tell the story. It represents the reward of all the work I have ever done and the realization of much happiness. I say, I do not want any biography." This comment reveals the depth of his belief that his library was both the consummation of his life's work and his reward and source of happiness. What he understood "a biography" to be was one of those popular short sketches with a photograph, written to order for, say, $1,000 and printed in a group of "famous Americans"—the kind of thing that Collis had paid for about himself and that Edward, along with most other wealthy people, had been solicited about. These comments about money values versus true values and the library as his biography were widely quoted in places like the *Boston Transcript* and a New York magazine for book lovers called *The Biblio*.

But the main part of Daggett's interview, so far as Edward was concerned, was doubtless showing and handling the Harte editions and the

Fort Sutter manuscripts and the like, and reading many excerpts from a book about the first efforts of some great writers. He also conducted a walking tour to show where the book vault would be, and the reading room, and the bindery, and all the rest.[95]

While the library was the focus for estimates of what Huntington's benefactions would mean to the future of California, the prospect of the art was not ignored. The California Art Club, for example, sent Huntington a letter of appreciation in January 1922. "The artists of California feel very much indebted to you," they wrote, "for bringing these wonderful art treasures to our beautiful Southland. You are helping California make a history for herself that will always live. We want you to know that we feel you are assisting the development and growth of local art by bringing to us these beautiful canvasses that time has rendered famous."[96]

The public interest in these matters was renewed and multiplied when it became known that Huntington had signed three deeds, on April 8, 1922, conveying to the trustees the library and all its contents of books and manuscripts, the surrounding property, and the residence and all its art. He had, in fact, legally transferred all this property to the trustees earlier, on November 30, 1921. His personal balance sheets reveal that the books and manuscripts transferred had a value at cost of some $7.4 million, the art of $8.4 million, and the real property of $1 million, for an initial book value of $17 million. All acquisitions after this time were paid for out of Huntington's personal funds during his lifetime but transferred immediately to the trustees. As a consequence of these transactions, Edward's personal net worth declined considerably during these years, from about $67 million at the end of 1920 to about $40 million at the end of 1924.[97]

When the signing of the deeds became known in April 1922, all the major newspapers in Southern California printed long stories about this transfer, which they considered "the most important step in the turning over of this greatest collection and library for the use of the public."[98] The *New York Times* devoted two columns to the announcement, and the Paris edition of the *New York Herald* observed in an editorial that "of the various kinds of immortal fame, that which rests upon personal benefactions to learning or art or social well-being is perhaps the clearest, as it is the most deserved. The donation to the public by Mr. Henry E. Huntington of his very notable collection of books and works of art, together with the buildings in which they are housed at San Marino, Cal., is an instance of the noblest and most durable use which a man may make of his wealth and his superior taste and culture."[99] These sentiments were echoed in Boston, London, Philadelphia, Hartford, Savannah, Oakland, Buffalo, Detroit, and places in between. Praise came even from San Francisco; in an editorial entitled "A Western Asset," the *Examiner* admitted that "as San Franciscans, we could wish that the Huntington Library were in this city rather than in Los Angeles. But as Westerners, we can rejoice that such a notable collection . . . is housed in an institution in the west. . . . The Huntington Library is one of the world's great archives. It is something to be more enthusiastic about than even oil wells."[100]

Edward received letters in praise of his gift from a multitude of friends. Herschel V. Jones even extended the library into a university; he wrote that he had a vision of "Huntington University surrounding the great library you have installed. . . . I pictured it as the greatest university in this country. The middle west will turn to the far west in the future when that university is a fact."[101]

Edward's own sense of his gift is clearly stated in a letter to John P. Green of the Pennsylvania Railroad Company: "In giving my library to the State of California, I feel that I am really giving it to the nation." As a collector, he felt himself a temporary custodian of the collections made by others, and he had a concern for their feelings, which he shared: "Those men who have devoted so much time to making the various collections which I have bought would undoubtedly feel it a matter of great satisfaction if they could know that their labors and their devotion will be, in the future, of such help to those who will use the Library for the ends for which I have meant it. Furthermore it should appeal to them, as it does to me, that the collection is there for all time,—never to be dispersed."[102]

The public and private acclaim of Huntington's institution went on and on. "The most outstanding cultural endowment of modern times" was one of many rhetorical flourishes. And the resources of history were ransacked for comparisons. Dr. Moore of the University of California asserted that "the Huntington Foundation is as important to the world as the founding of the Alexandrian library, and the Medici collection at Florence." Rosenbach asserted that the creation of Huntington's library was "a greater achievement than the building of the pyramids or the Panama Canal." (Too bad to neglect the Great Wall of China.) The *New York Sun* maintained more modestly that "when the State of California is enriched with the Huntington Library it will be enriched as is no other country in the world, not even Italy with its Vatican and Laurentian collections."[103]

This report can be appropriately concluded by reference to two popular articles, widely distributed all over the United States. Arthur Brisbane devoted one of his syndicated columns in December 1924 to a glowing description of "Huntington's Noble Gift." The *American Weekly,* which was included in hundreds of newspapers, had a two-page spread late in 1922 on this subject, with many pictures. "What may justly be said," it began, "to be the most potentially beautiful, inspiring gift ever made by an individual to a people is the Henry E. Huntington Foundation, at San Marino, a suburb of Los Angeles, in Southern California. . . . By some authorities the Foundation has been termed the 'most outstanding cultural endowment of the century'." The story concludes: "When one ponders the significance of this gift to the people; when imagination pictures what beautiful ideas, what great works, what wide culture to those who otherwise would have no introduction to the world of art, to the realm of genius, will spring from this wealth of knowledge, its potency is realized. For all future generations will have at their command this library, the art collection and the smiling gardens."[104]

The institution soon became a model for others, and thus provided an opportunity for the sincerest form of flattery. In 1922, H. C. Folger asked to see a copy of Huntington's documents forming his institution for his own guidance in establishing the Folger Library, and J. P. Morgan felt inspired by Huntington's example and borrowed copies of the Huntington Trust Indentures when he was establishing the Morgan Library. In 1923, William A. Clark, Jr., asked to bring his architect for some visits to help in planning the Clark Library, and they came often.[105]

The acclaim lavished on the library and art gallery soon brought Huntington himself into the spotlight. Elsewhere in the world he was frequently described as the greatest book collector of all. An essay in the *Philadelphia Inquirer* began as follows: "Henry E. Huntington, of Los Angeles and New York, is the most important leader of the book lovers." In London, "A Literary Letter" in *The Sphere* began: "By far the greatest book collector—and, indeed, picture collector—in the world is Mr. Henry E. Huntington of New York and Los Angeles."[106]

A major shift took place in the basis for which Huntington was best known in Southern California. "Hereabouts we have thought Mr. Huntington's fame was to rest on his business accomplishments," the *Los Angeles Examiner* reported in 1921; "on what he has done for Southern California in building railways and developing huge expanses of land." All of that important activity, "creative of tremendous material benefits as it has been, is insignificant when compared with this library. For from its mass of books will be created new thoughts, new knowledge, and thought as the one imperishable, ever productive effort of mankind."[107]

A variety of new honors began to come to Edward. On March 12, 1923, the senate of the state of California passed a resolution of thanks and gratitude to him for establishing the Huntington Foundation. It fully described the library, the art collection, and the botanical gardens in the highest terms of praise and concluded that this benefaction was, "in its extent and educational and artistic values to the American people, one of the greatest gifts of an individual to a state or nation in all recorded history," and the people of California and the United States were "thus provided with artistic, literary and botanical facilities that are equal to the best and highest provided in the cultural centres of the world." The senate commended the donor "as a benefactor who is deserved well of his state and his nation."[108]

There were also many personal expressions of gratitude from individuals, schools, and societies. An editorial in the *Los Angeles Express* in 1924 summed up the public reaction to Huntington for his gift by saying that people felt "the sense of very personal gratitude, as if each Californian knows himself to have received the magnificent legacy. So it becomes his individual possession, and the acknowledgments addressed to Mr. Huntington contain the warm note, that intimate word of man to man for a benefit gratefully received. . . . Such by right should be the people's thanks for the great gift. It is personal. It is individual. It is for each of us. And none before us has been so richly endowed."[109]

Edward also received many honorary degrees. New York University gave him an LL.D. degree in December 1920, with a citation that particularly commended his "liberal spirit and discriminating taste" in forming "a treasure house of learning, where scholars from all lands shall find enrichment for the thought of all mankind."[110] He received another LL.D. degree, this time from the University of Southern California, on April 3, 1924.[111] In May 1924 he got an LL.D. degree from the University of California at Berkeley, and he and Belle spent a week in San Francisco, his first visit there in three years, the first for her in nine years; while Edward went over to Berkeley to get his degree, Belle visited the park she had given the city in honor of Collis and watched the children at play.[112] In the next month, Occidental College gave him an LL.D. degree "for creation of the Huntington Library and art collection."[113] And on October 10, 1924, he was formally inducted into membership in the Phi Beta Kappa Society in the Alpha Chapter at William and Mary College; he had actually been made a member three years earlier, but it was only at this time that he took part in the initiation ceremonies.[114]

Various other honors came to him. The Sunset Club of Los Angeles devoted one of their meetings in 1922 to a symposium in his honor and in appreciation for "the greatest gift to a people ever made by an individual for the promotion of culture and scholarship."[115] The American Institute of Architects awarded him its Certificate of Honor in 1923 for the Huntington Library.[116] He was elected president of the Pasadena Music and Art Association in 1920.[117] In San Francisco, he was made an honorary member of the Book Club of California "in admiration for your unparalleled service to Letters," as well as an honorary member of the Booksellers' Association of the San Francisco Bay Counties, while from Boston came honorary membership in the book collectors' society, the Club of Odd Volumes.[118]

He became acquainted with a good many well-known people. Herbert Hoover sent him, in 1922, a presentation copy of Agricola's *De re*

Metallica, which he and Mrs. Hoover had translated, and Edward was appreciative.[119] He had a cordial relationship with Andrew W. Mellon, they visited one another in Washington and in California, and they corresponded, each sharing his plans for the future of his art collection with the other.[120] He and Theodore Roosevelt, Jr., exchanged some lively letters about books and children, and Roosevelt came to see the collection in New York.[121] Baron Rothschild spent a happy afternoon with Edward in his library in California and cordially invited him to visit the family place near Paris.[122] And there were many others, some of whom are still generally remembered, like Harry Houdini, William G. McAdoo, and David Belasco.

Edward began to be regarded as a truly eminent person, as a man of great achievements. But was this the complete story? Perhaps not. Harry Chandler, the head of the Times-Mirror Company in Los Angeles, wrote to him in 1923 to suggest that the present is not the final judge:

> You have achieved a wonderful record in the great things you have done at San Marino. You have erected a more lasting monument than all the railroads and the other physical creations of the age. I do not think the people of this neighborhood and of this country yet begin to appreciate it,—in fact I doubt if even you with all your far-sighted vision are able to realize the full magnitude of the accomplishment. That knowledge will only come to the generations of the future."[123]

Nineteen

THE DARK SIDE OF FAME
1920–1924

THE ACCLAIM THAT CAME to Edward during these years, from both public and private sources, does not seem to have changed his view of himself. He continued to behave with his usual quiet modesty. There was, however, a dark side to his life, most of it private and observable only to those who were close to him. The illnesses that had been plaguing him grew worse, and his uncertain health gave an uneasy tone to his activities during these years. Problems arose among his business associates and subordinates, as well as among the members of the library staff, and he seemed to be at a loss to solve them. His associates and children thought they noticed a general diminution in his powers, and they were afraid that he might have some kind of a breakdown. Demands were made on him as a consequence of his public acclaim, and often he found it difficult to respond to them; he tried, however, and his efforts were often a burden for him. In addition, several of his closest friends died—notably his dear son, Howard, and his two associates, Epes Randolph and Billy Dunn. But the darkest event of these years was the death of Arabella in 1924. Her loss left a shadow over him for the rest of his life.

Edward rarely made it through a spell of bad weather without catching a cold, and it was even harder for him to get rid of one. His recurrent prostate and bladder problems had become life-threatening in the autumn and winter of 1915–16 (see chap. 15). During these years he had to be catheterized regularly at least twice a day. His New York physician, Dr. William B. Coley, Jr., saw him frequently, traveled with him when necessary, and prescribed medicaments for him. He often prescribed strychnine tablets and a digitalis mixture: "I enclose prescription for some fresh Digitalis mixture," he wrote. "It contains some Strychnine so when you are taking it you can leave off the Strychnine Tablets. The weather is very depressing and it will brace you up and be a good thing for your heart." Dr. Coley had sought a second opinion about this treatment, from Dr. Evans, who agreed with him.[1]

Edward continued to have frequent illnesses. In January and February 1920 he was in bed for several weeks with a severe case of flu, and the physicians were afraid that he would develop pneumonia. Elizabeth heard that he was ill and wrote him solicitously on January 8: "I was so sorry to hear you had been ill—we presume the same old trouble." The trip to California had to be delayed until the middle of March, and Dr. Coley went out with him—at a charge of $1,527.95—and put him in the hands of Dr. Bryant. By the end of March, Edward wrote to Dr. Coley in New York that "I have been gaining every day, and feel quite myself again. I have engaged a masseur who is to start at once, and will take suggestions from Dr. Bryant so as not to make the treatment too strenuous."[2]

The following December, when they were back in New York, Edward wrote to Carrie that they hoped to start out for California soon after January 1, and he said, "I am well except my usual winter cold which I am hardly ever free from here. New York certainly is not the winter climate for me and I fear it will sometime lay me out." In early January, he had "a slight attack of his old trouble," his secretary Hapgood wrote to Cole, "and the starting time has been postponed a bit." He was in bed for a couple of weeks. On January 18, Hapgood wrote Dunn, "Mr. Huntington has been quite ill"; on January 24, he reported, "he sits up today for a couple of hours, but he is still quite weak, and, to add to other troubles, has had a little gout in his ankle." On January 28, Hapgood told Dunn that "Mr. Huntington has asked me to write you a line to say that he is still confined to his bed but that he hopes to get away soon. Between the attack of his old trouble which came on just two weeks ago, and a slight cold which he caught notwithstanding the attention of two nurses and two doctors, he has had a rather hard time. Mrs. Huntington has not been up to the mark either so you can imagine that the winter has been rather hard for them." In early February he was "gaining slowly, owing to a cold which he contracted after he was getting over his first attack," but it was not until the middle of the month that he was able to go downstairs, and on February 21 he said, "I am now taking up the correspondence which I have had to neglect during the last five weeks in which I have been sick." At last, in the middle of March, he was well enough to travel to California.[3]

Dr. Coley wrote on May 31 that he was delighted with the report of his progress and offered to come any time needed: "Just wire me." Edward replied on June 8 that Dr. Coley need not come: "I have gained much in weight, and feel better in every way." Dr. Coley urged him to exercise: "I think the croquet will be a great help as it will keep you outdoors and gives you just about the right exercise." Also, he should not travel without a doctor: "With your trouble, you never know when an attack may come out of a clear sky."[4]

Edward had regular urinalyses, which were not reassuring. On August 14, 1922, and September 18, 1923, they revealed the signs of infection: "very many white blood cells," pus, and cells shed from the lining of the bladder.[5] These results would suggest possible obstruction in the bladder and trouble with the prostate, but physicians were then limited in the treatments at their disposal.

When Edward coughed in San Marino, it was heard in New York, at least by Duveen and Rosenbach. In 1923 Duveen sent a telegram: "So sorry to hear you have been unwell sincerely hope you getting better." And in 1921 Rosenbach wrote to Herschel V. Jones that "for your private ear, Mr. Huntington has been quite ill during the last week, and it has worried me considerably. There are very few collectors today, and Mr. Huntington has been a great prop to the market."[6] Business first, naturally. Nearly all of the letters to Edward at this time made reference to his health. Some of his older friends took a happier view. One longstanding friend, when he saw a picture of Edward in 1921, wrote:

> Please accept my sincere congratulations on your apparent good health and physical stamina. When looking at this picture, I see the same Huntington that I went to work for at Trimble, Tennessee, just

forty years ago this October, and how well I remember what tremendous physical strength you possessed. For you were about the only man on the job that could lift clear of the ground one of those five foot terracotta joints that were used in culvert construction. And you appear today sturdy enough to perform the same feat. Congratulations and may you live and enjoy health and strength for many years to come.

In thanking him, Edward said, "I hope that your strength and health of body is as vigorous as your memory and may continue so for years to come."[7]

During these years, Edward was continually coping with illness. Many of his and Belle's activities were limited by the vicissitudes of his health; several times he had to postpone a visit to Berkeley to receive his honorary degree, for example. Belle planned a large family luncheon for February 27, 1924, on the occasion of his seventy-fourth birthday, and many of his children and grandchildren were present. Because of his illness, it was only at the last minute, however, that Edward was able to get dressed, come downstairs, and put in an appearance.[8]

When Edward formally retired from the active management of his businesses in 1910, he seems to have felt that they would continue to operate effectively under the policies he had established and in the directions he had pointed them. He thought that his business managers—and his librarians, too, after he had formally established a library—would be able to operate with continued success under such occasional guidance as he chose to give them; he thought he could give directions about specific details that interested him and could ignore all matters that did not engage his attention. He was not entirely correct in his expectations.

Edward's principal business managers during these years were William E. Dunn in Los Angeles and C. E. Graham and E. A. Adams in New York. The toughest problem they faced was finding the money to pay Edward's bills. They sent him regular projections of the income and expenses, always noting the unfavorable gap between the two. He generally treated these projections and deficits in a cavalier fashion. In June

1921, for example, Dunn outlined the needs of the Los Angeles Railway Company for the next nine months, including notes coming due, other expenses, and income, with a net deficit of $1 million; he enclosed a letter from Rollins and Sons, suggesting that the Huntington Land and Improvement Company issue bonds to provide the necessary cash. Edward replied: "I have read your letter, and also copy of letter from Rollins & Sons to you in regard to financing, and to me the whole thing is laughable. I do not propose to issue any more long term bonds for the Huntington Land & Improvement Company." Instead, he suggested that Dunn simply delay paying the outstanding bills, let the vouchers accumulate, and buy nothing new like "rails, equipment, or anything else." Two months later, Dunn wrote him in distress that although "I know you do not like to get letters" on this subject, they had an absolute minimum need of $700,000 to $800,000 before December 1. Edward's reply repeated his injunction to spend less money: "I do not mean this letter to be any criticism of the management as I am as much responsible or perhaps more, but we shall be obliged to reduce expenses as I cannot carry the Los Angeles RR to the injury of my credit." He told Dunn that he was sending the correspondence to Graham: "I hope between you something can be done to meet the emergency. Now my dear Billy, don't for a moment think that I am placing any blame on your shoulders for I am not."[9]

Similar problems recurred concerning book bills, money to pay the federal income tax, interest due Duveen and Rosenbach on loans for earlier purchases. The sale of the Chesapeake and Ohio stock to the Van Sweringens of Cleveland in October 1922 for $7 million helped temporarily.[10] But always there seemed to be a new need for money and always Edward passed it on to his managers for solution. Sometimes they complained, as when he offered to take back from the estate of George D. Smith $427,000 in Safety Insulated Bonds. Graham objected that he had no obligation to do so: "Just because Mr. Smith squandered the fortune which he made, is no reason why you should go out of your way to help the Estate." There was no market for the bonds, and Mrs. Smith was hysterical. After a month of controversy, Edward signed an agreement, over Graham's protest, to buy the bonds back.[11]

Edward's subordinates found it increasingly difficult to do business with him. When Graham complained to Dunn in 1920 that he couldn't get accurate facts from Edward, Dunn replied, "He never tells me any more than he does you, and when he does tell me anything it is generally wrong." He concluded, "I want to suggest to you that you, as well as the writer, are growing old with a probable increase of blood pressure, and might just as well give up the idea that we can ever get much satisfaction out of the Chief on any subject." Graham had the same experience. In 1923 he was in Los Angeles for a week; he wrote back to Adams, "Spent yesterday afternoon at the Ranch, but it was not very satisfactory, as to business."[12]

Edward's business associates had even more difficulty dealing with Belle. Adams had to call on her in New York to arrange the details for a train trip to the South, and he found her exceedingly perverse. He wrote Graham that "Mrs. Huntington was in very fine humor this morning, and found fault about everything and everybody in every particular." She was slow in paying her bills, and Mitchell James of P. W. French & Company appealed to Graham to get "something on Mrs. Huntington's account. I have written her once or twice, but I know how little Mrs. Huntington pays attention to correspondence, and am sure a request to you will have a speedier response." Dunn also found it hard to deal with her in Los Angeles and apologized to Graham about his inability to get an acknowledgment from her concerning a government claim for additional taxes: "In view of the fact that it is very hard work for me to get communications from Mrs. Huntington even here, I am not surprised. I rather think they will be in New York within a few weeks and you can have an opportunity of trying your luck there."[13]

There was also some disharmony among Edward's closest associates. Earlier, in 1918 and 1919, bad feelings had arisen between Dunn and Graham when they were trying to carry out Edward's somewhat unarticulated wishes (see chap. 15). By 1921, Dunn felt he "had been pretty badly knocked to pieces" because of his work, and he told Graham that "I have been knocked out myself with a nervous breakdown, and although I have come to the office every day, I am taking treatments for it and am improving steadily." Edward urged him to go away on a trip with Mrs. Dunn and a physician to recover. There were also problems in the New York office. Adams wrote Edward that Graham was treating him unfairly and that Graham was having surreptitious business meetings with their lawyer; finally, he felt that Graham was so hostile to him that he did his work for Edward at home rather than in the office.[14]

In his dealings with his business associates, Edward grew to be somewhat forgetful. On October 23, 1923, he asked Graham why he had never sent him a deed, requested in a letter of May 9, for a strip of land he wanted to give to the city of San Marino; Graham replied that he had responded to the request on May 15, had sent the deed on May 21, and that Edward had executed it on July 23. Occasionally Edward became confused about the complications of shifting securities. On July 12, 1922, he sent twenty Annandale Land Company bonds to his New York office, and on July 14, 1922, he donated them to the Huntington Memorial Library in Oneonta; then on April 10, 1924, he directed that those same bonds be returned to Los Angeles to be exchanged for a new issue, having forgotten that he had given them away.[15]

Edward's daughters felt he had lost more of his powers than natural aging would account for. Marian wrote to Elizabeth that "Father himself has failed so." Marian wrote more explicitly to her other sister, Clara (Peggy): "Peggy dear I'm worried about Father. At his age and in his health—he bore up at the time [of Howard's death] but I think now—I am afraid—the break will come."[16]

During these years the library was in transition from the status of a private collection of books and manuscripts to a major institutional library. The transition was accompanied by problems, and Edward was involved in all of them. He retained the principal responsibility for acquisitions, as we saw in Chapter 18. He also continued his role as the decision-maker for all matters affecting the library, and only gradually, by inaction, gave increasing leeway to the librarians. They all felt that the main job of the library staff was to catalog the books and manuscripts and put them on the shelves in usable order. This had to take place before the library could be formally opened to users, and the process seemed dreadfully slow to everyone except the library staff.

The trustees felt that the progress within the library left much to be desired. In October 1920, Dunn, as chairman of the trustees, wrote to Edward in New York that "affairs at the library are, I suppose, going along all right, but it looks to me as though the mess will never be untangled, and I sincerely hope you will come out here yourself at the earliest possible moment and take charge of the situation." When Edward replied that he could not come, Dunn responded in November that "I was much disappointed to learn that you do not expect to come out until early next year. I hope you will be able to change your mind and come within the next few weeks, as I am very anxious to have a conference with you over our many troubles." But Edward did not change his mind, and Dunn went to New York to see him several weeks later.[17]

The essential difficulty was a management problem: Edward did not delegate authority to his subordinates. It was a little like Collis's running the Southern Pacific in the 1890s from New York, but this time there was no nephew in California authorized to get things done. In 1923 the trustees remonstrated further with Edward. At the insistence of George Patton and Henry M. Robinson, Dunn wrote to Edward in September about their dissatisfaction: "The only thing that seems to be suffering from 'dry rot' here is the Library. Patton and Robinson both called my attention to it, and finally I went out to the Library yesterday and stayed some time. Cole was not there, but I called a regular meeting of the Board for Saturday morning, and I think before you get this we shall have waked them up." The trustees were pressing to open the library "in the comparatively near future." Dunn's appeal to Edward on behalf of the trustees was that "I think your attention should be given to bringing that about." In the meantime, Dunn said, "I will not disorganize your staff or hurt anyone's feelings, but I am certainly going to wake things up out there. Hertrich is the only man out there who has real good judgment and horse sense. You have given him charge of almost everything there, and I do not know but that you will have to make him Librarian before you get through." Dunn urged Edward to authorize him or Hertrich to get the necessary furniture, finish up the library, and prepare a plan to open the library "for study within the next few months" and with visiting days for the general public.[18]

Edward's reply expressed lukewarm agreement, but not in a way to suggest that he was going to give his attention to bringing about the objectives: "I note what you say about the Library, and very likely they need stirring up a little." In response to the plan for visiting days after opening the library for study, he said, "I should like to do as you suggest, but Mrs. Huntington will have to be consulted and I think no one would have as much influence in that line as yourself." He passed over the furniture suggestion by saying, "As to installing furniture, it would be well, but I have not yet decided just what to build, but we will consider that when I return."[19] So not much happened in response to the trustees' suggestions.

In this state of indecision, strains arose among the library staff. In 1920, one member of the staff was about to be fired, but he appealed to Edward to be allowed to resign so that he could get another job, and Edward agreed.[20] A young cataloger complained to the librarian that his work was boring, routine, and mechanical, and the next year he wrote to Huntington and suggested that they carry on staff research work in bibliography; Edward declined, on the grounds that "the big task now is making the Catalogue and getting the books on the shelves."[21] But Edward continued his old habit of watching the little details. In driving by the houses occupied by the library staff, he thought that the one occupied by Dr. Bendikson "looks terrible" and he directed that the occupant be told that "we are not satisfied with the way he is taking care of his place, and that if he does not wish to see to it, we shall have to have it done and add to his rental. He ought to realize that his lack of care is very bad for the neighborhood and in a way reflects on us"; six months later Edward was still dissatisfied with Bendikson's lawn care, and the maintenance of it was given to Hertrich and the cost added to the rent.[22]

A staff problem that cut deeper was the Philip S. Goulding affair. Cole had hired Goulding, who was head cataloger at the University of Illinois Library, in 1917, and he joined the staff in New York. He took over cataloging from Chester M. Cate, who had recently joined the U.S. Army Hospital Corps. Goulding thought that he had been hired as head cataloger, but Cate was given his old job back when he returned in 1919 from military service. Goulding complained to Cole, who told him in 1920 that he and Cate were equals. In 1923 Cole sent a three-page report, presumably prepared by Cate, telling Huntington of the errors that Goulding had made in cataloging and in ordering books that turned out to be duplicates. Then on December 31, 1923, Huntington issued a memo to the staff in which he announced that all cataloging was under Cate. The next day Goulding wrote an incensed letter to Huntington, who was in San Marino, in which he gave his side of the story, declared that a great injustice had been done him, and asserted that the "order has taken away all the real joy I have felt for my work." Edward responded on January 4, 1924, by saying that Goulding's letter should have been sent to Cole, and that he was "very much surprised at the contents." He denied that there had ever been any intention of having Goulding become head cataloger and stated that Goulding was apparently suffering from a series of misapprehensions. Edward sent the letter on to Cole with a note that repeated his sense of Goulding's misapprehensions and observed that "from its tone Mr. Goulding will be a disturbing element in the staff which can not be permitted." Goulding responded to Huntington on January 6, 1924, declaring that Huntington had not addressed the substantive points at issue and concluding that "I know the incident has been a shock to the whole staff. Has it never occurred to you what will be the effect on their attitude toward their work when they see that a man who has given honestly of his best is suddenly deprived of his rightful position, while one who has persistently defrauded the library of its due, in the matter of time at least, is rewarded by advancement?" Goulding resigned from the staff at the end of the month; Edward told his business office that "you may add to the salary check of Mr. Goulding two-fifths of a month's salary. He is resigning January 31st."[23]

Goulding's wife, Helen L. Plummer Goulding, added a bitter farewell on February 2, 1924. First, she wrote a long letter to Huntington that began, "It seems a cruel thing to hurt a fellow-being who has never done anything to you or for you but good. You have had neither a legal nor a moral right to treat my good husband as you have done, and aside from your outrageous injustice to him, your treatment of Mr. Cole has been unpardonable, and will be resented by every person in the library world who knows him and his work, for they know that he is the one who has really put your library on the map, so to speak." She then took direct aim at Huntington:

> You are an old man, Mr. Huntington, with not many more years to
> look forward to. Have you never thought of those last days or hours

on your couch, when you will have to realize that in a short time you must go out alone into the great Unknown, and give an account of your every action to the Maker you have ignored? There will be no evading of questions then as now. When that time comes, you will realize too late that all your power and material possessions amount to nothing in view of what you might have had—the heartfelt respect and love of your fellow-men and women, which would have brought you real happiness and satisfaction in your declining years.

She concluded by saying how glad they were to be leaving the library, and how sorry she was for those staff members who had to remain "in an atmosphere which I am pretty sure is distasteful to them."

Mrs. Goulding had enough hostility left to write a letter on the same day to Cate and denounce him for "the underhanded ways of a mere cheat to work injury to another man." She alleged that he had hurt Cole and misrepresented her husband, lost the respect of his colleagues, and "placed a stigma on the library and the profession."[24]

A few months later, in June 1924, it was decided, in a conversation between Cole and Huntington, that Cole should retire and be succeeded by Cate as librarian. There had never been much warmth between Edward and Cole; Edward and Cate, on the other hand, enjoyed a spirited correspondence with one another: Cate wrote Edward often while he was in the service, once sending a ten-page letter describing minute and amusing details of army life. On September 23, 1924, Cole and Cate wrote separate memoranda to the library staff about the change in librarians at the end of that month: Cole spoke of being seventy-five years of age, having been librarian for nine years, and wanting rest and freedom in his home on nearby Lombardy Road; Cate asserted that he would try to live up to Cole's high standard. In November, Edward gave Cole about ten thousand dollar's worth of bonds and wrote out in his own hand a receipt, which Cole signed, for payment "in full of all services to be rendered as Librarian Emeritus." After he retired, Cole brought visitors over to the library from time to time, but that perquisite was limited after a few months. On January 23, 1925, Cate wrote Cole, with a copy to Huntington, that "in accordance with the wishes of Mr. Huntington, the Library is no longer open to visitors except by my permission. I am accordingly regretfully obliged to request you to discontinue your practice of bringing visitors here without my previous knowledge."[25]

Cate's librarianship did not last many months. On May 19, 1925, he killed himself. He drove his car to a deserted area nearby, got out, and put a bullet in his temple. Several weeks before he had been charged by a sixteen-year-old boy from Monrovia with having committed improper acts and assault on a minor; he had been arraigned on May 8, pleaded not guilty, and was freed on bail. Rather than face trial, he shot himself. He was thirty-five years old.[26]

Edward's business activities and his library made reasonably satisfactory progress during these years. But these tensions, disharmonies, and human tragedies limited Edward's sense of achievement.

Many members of the public feel it their privilege as citizens to write letters to famous people, and Huntington was overwhelmed by letters on almost every imaginable topic. Unlike most public personages—politicians and people in the entertainment world, for instance—he did not have the staff or machinery to cope with this deluge of correspondence, and he did not find a way for others to handle it for him. So he dealt with it as best he could, by himself, with the aid of his one secretary. It was part of the price he had to pay for the fame he did not much want anyway. A very few examples of this mass of letters to Huntington may give some hint of the problem and why he, as an older "retired" man, found it such a burden to be torn between being a decent person responding to the needs of others and a person committed to giving his undivided attention to his own concerns.

Many of the letters were straightforward appeals for money, occasioned by newspaper stories telling of Edward's gifts to the public. "We have read in the paper," wrote Mr. and Mrs. Charles Shook, "that you are giving so much to the American people. We thought we would write and ask you if you would please help us out. We have been down and out for the last 5 years, we have lots of sickness, and we thought you would please give us something"—and so on for another page or so. Some writers were more specific: "I read in the paper that you give art works worth millions of dollars to the public, so thought I would write you if you could do me a favor and send me five hundred dollars so I can go to a Sanitarium to take treatments for my nerves." A young school teacher in Massachusetts wrote that he needed to get married and go abroad to further his career; he could not finance both, but he could if Huntington would just give him two thousand dollars—"⅟₃₇₅₀ of the price of 'Blue Boy' or ⅟₁₇ the price of a first folio." A resident of Ventura, California, wrote to congratulate him on his philanthropy and added: "Mr. Huntington haven't you more wealth than you will spend while you are on this beautiful earth? Can't you give me some to build me a new house, please?" Some are sad letters. One from a woman in Northern California said, "I seen in the Illusterated Daily News where you had bought the Bust of George Washington, an old Relic. I have some Whittelings made by my Father in 1892. there are some 80 pieces of the Different Kinds of woods of Oregon"—and she wondered whether he would help her out by buying them.[27]

Many letters came from people in severe need. A former serviceman with a wife and a two-year-old son worked in the fields near San Diego for three dollars a day and was in distress; they needed two hundred dollars for a well and a pump, and they wrote to him because he was "famous as a philanthropist." A family that moved to Los Angeles two years before was about to have their household effects taken from them and sold at auction; the wife had heart trouble, the children had no food: "I have read of your kindly acts, and decided to put my cards upon the table and write." Sometimes an object was offered for sale to remedy the distress. An eighty-four-year-old man offered "a very curious rock which I found in New York state that weighs seven pounds. . . . I don't expect to live much longer, I am sick and you can have it very cheap." A woman offered him "an old map of New York State printed in 1846" and the autograph of U. S. Grant: "Are they worth $250 to you. My Husband and I are old and our means are small. This would buy us warm winter clothes. We have not had a new suit for 9 years."[28] Sometimes Edward sent money in response to the appeals, but he always responded sympathetically and with understanding.

Many people scratched their heads to find a way to appeal to him. If your name was Huntington—and there seemed to have been thousands of them—perhaps you were kin. So Davis Huntington of Wellington, New Zealand, asked whether they might not be related and requested the capital to start a small business: "I would let nothing stand in my way until success was mine! (That is the true Huntington spirit, is it not?)" William Marvin Huntington of Cortland, New York, wrote the "pre-eminent living member" of the Huntingtons to say that he had completed one year at Yale but needed $1,200 a year to finish the Sheffield Scientific School at Yale; his "security is my word and note of honor."[29]

Not everyone was pleased by what Huntington had done. Cuyler Reynolds of Albany, New York, congratulated Edward in 1922 for having given his art collection to the public, but he complained bitterly that it was wasted in California: "How few of us can go to California. I hardly believe the people out there care. Give each one a Ford and he will keep out of a gallery. Over here the museums are crowded every Sunday. The West, in 50 years, when able to stop to appreciate art, will have its mind on radios and aeroplanes, or a newer discovery. Why not reserve art for New York and Boston? It will be 100 years (or never) before California knows an Old Master."[30]

People whom Edward had been acquainted with in the past always received careful attention. W. O. Paxton, with whom he had been associated in Kentucky, became ill, lost his job, and asked for help; Edward promptly gave him a substantial loan. When Paxton had a breakdown and could not work, Edward gave him further financial help. When Mulford S. Wade, an old friend, asked for his support in getting the job of assistant treasurer for the Southern Pacific Company, he replied immediately—though the letter had come in the middle of Belle's final illness and he had not left the house for some days—that "of course you know I will do all I can to further your interests," and he did.[31]

Even those who had met him only briefly got responses to their requests. Thomas Dickson met him at a reception at the Oneonta Library; when Dickson was laid off his job at the age of forty-three with a wife and children, he asked Edward to "please send $75 or even $50 for food" and to ask the president of his company, Mr. Lorce, to take him back: "Send me a check immediately and either call or write to Mr. Lorce to have me reinstated immediately." Characteristically, Edward wrote him a long, sympathetic letter, enclosed a check for $50 and explained that he could not appeal to Mr. Lorce: "In the first place, it would do no good, and secondly, I could not ask him to do anything for me that I would not do for him." Dickson continued to ask for help: his wife was pale and haggard, "I do not eat enough to keep a bird alive," he needed $50 to pay his insurance, and so on. This went on for a couple of years, with Huntington sending him several checks; he then told Dickson he could help no more. But Dickson would not take no for an answer and kept writing grumbling complaints in hopes that Huntington would have a change of heart. At last Huntington's secretary tried to still Dickson: "Mr. Huntington has not asked me to write this letter, but as his secretary, I feel that he has been annoyed long enough."[32]

Many people sent Edward things for his enjoyment—and their own satisfaction. Reynold Ahleem sent him a series of his own poems in 1921 and 1922; "The Swan" concludes "I'll cease to roam, and reach my home, / My blest, sweet home some day." M. J. Keane of Liverpool, England, billed on his letterhead as "Metaphysician," sent him a copy of his book *The Wisdom of the West* with his autograph, since "your wonderful collection of books would not be complete unless you had one of mine," and with the request that Huntington "kindly let me know if you like the book." Lewis McKenzie Turner from Baltimore sent his recent poem "Processional," as well as a duplicate of his manuscript *The Youth of the World,* touted by its author as "an answer in full for reasons why the world has no solution for its many problems." Mrs. Lillian Gibbs-Keys of New York told him of her public lectures and asked him to "endow" her lecture on "Ideal Married Life" at $5,000 so that it could be given one hundred fifty or two hundred times a year. Robert Seeger wrote him from Pasadena saying, "I paint oil pictures and wish when you have time you would come and look at them and tell me what you think of them. I am only eleven years old and live on 2415 East Colorado in the rear." Edward generally took the time to look at the things sent him and to respond to the sender.[33]

Edward received many advisories on how to improve his physical health and his spiritual future. C. W. McMorron, "International World Traveled Syndicate Newspaper Writer," told him how to increase his vision by the use of hot and cold towels, and in a dozen letters explained the merits of clam broth extract, egg cocktail, and bed rest. Dr. J. M. Petter sent him a long letter on how "to normalize any abnormal condition that ails you, or to keep you healthy and long lived." Bataille Loomis urged a visit "if you want to live longer and become younger and happier, you can do so—you need not die." The priestess of the Melkizedek Temple in Columbus, Ohio, sent him a card to sign so that she could send it to "the Lord Himself." Edward read all these letters and acknowledged most of them, but he declined to see the writers or to send them money.[34]

Edward was asked to take part in many new business ventures during these years, almost always with the promise of great success and vast riches. He always declined. Frederick C. Emery, president of the Aztec Consolidated Mining Company of Sonora, Mexico, wrote him on January 10, 1922, with a full account of their plans to reopen the Mexican silver mines and make much money, and asking him to invest in the venture. Edward refused, as he did all new business schemes: "I would not be interested personally as I am not going into anything new. As you probably know, I am spending all my thought now on the Library and Art Gallery."[35]

Similarly, he turned down all appeals for major contributions to good causes, even the missionary who said that he had prayed for him every day for the last seventeen years, held a meeting every night, slept in his car, and wanted only a lot and $10,000 for four mission buildings. The reasoning and style of his reaction to these many appeals are typified by his answer to the Reverend Harley H. Gill of Sacramento, who had asked him to contribute to the building of their church:

> There have been so many calls on me of late that I have had to make a fixed rule to confine myself to the charities and projects to which I am already pledged. I realize that many of the requests that come to me are most worthy, but it is, to my mind, more urgent to concentrate on the matters now in hand, the most important being the Library and Art Gallery which, at present, is taking considerable of my attention. I am sure you will understand my point of view, and I regret exceedingly that I am unable to assist in the Pioneer Memorial Church.[36]

Still the appeals poured in, and he bore the burden of dealing with them.

During these years, Edward's life was diminished by the death of a number of his friends and associates. Among those who were important to him were George E. Miles, who died in 1919 after having been the valued private secretary to Collis and then to Edward; Edward's older sister, Leonora, Mrs. Bradley W. Foster, who died in Huntington, West Virginia, in 1920; Edward's Aunt Ellen—Mrs. Isaac E. Gates, the mother of Helen—who died in 1920; and George D. Smith, Edward's favorite book dealer, who died in 1920. But the three deaths that struck him hardest were those of Epes Randolph in 1921, Edward's only son, Howard, in 1922, and Billy Dunn in 1925.

Epes Randolph had been continuously associated with Edward in railroad work since the 1870s. They worked together on construction and management in Kentucky and Tennessee, and Randolph was responsible for building the bridge over the Ohio River. Two years after Edward left to go to California, Randolph resigned and went west also. First he was based in Tucson as superintendent of the Arizona and New Mexico division of the Southern Pacific, and Edward sent Howard to be trained by him before going to Harvard. When Edward was developing Southern California, Randolph moved to Los Angeles in 1901 as vice-president and general manager of Edward's Los Angeles Railway and the Pacific Electric. In 1904 he had to go back to Tucson because his tuberculosis worsened, and there he continued as president of several smaller railroads. He and Edward maintained a close contact with one another. In 1921 he had a heart attack in his hotel apartment and died. Edward was in France when the news reached him, and his spontaneous reflection in a letter to Billy Dunn is deeply true: "I was terribly grieved by Randolph's death and never knew how much I loved him until he passed away."[37]

Then in March 1922, Howard died. He had never been in robust health since his nervous breakdown in 1911, and he became seriously ill during the six months before his death from what was reported to be a stomach ulcer but was apparently cancer. Although the physicians and the family were aware of his imminent death—with a physician and two nurses in constant attendance, and with artificial rectal feeding—the seriousness was not revealed to Edward. Burke Holladay explained in his journal that "we all feared he would break down" if he knew that Howard was about to die. But after a period of deliriousness, Howard died quietly on the afternoon of March 27, leaving a wife and six children.[38]

Edward was devastated. The death occurred six days after the arrival of the *Blue Boy*. Family and friends rallied to give him support. He received about a hundred letters and telegrams of sympathy, many of them full of warmth and understanding. A letter from his eleven-year-old grandson, David Huntington, away at military school, began: "Dear Grandfather, I am very, very sorry that Uncle died. I wish I could think of someway to make you feel better." The concern that Edward's friends felt for him is evident in their letters to other people. J. E. Brown of the Los Angeles Railway wrote to Graham in New York that "Mr. Huntington feels the loss of his son very keenly but he is bearing up nobly. My heart aches for him." Billy Dunn wrote to Homer Ferguson that "Mr. Huntington is taking the loss terribly hard, but is, I believe, pulling up a little all the time." G. W. Cole wrote to a friend that the death "of course, has been a severe blow to Mr. Huntington and we are all deeply in sympathy with him." One of Duveen's assistants, Adolfo Muller, wrote to the Roman Catholic archbishop in San Francisco that "Huntington's loss of his son was a very cruel unexpected sorrow for him and he is terribly oppressed." His daughter Marian wrote to her sister Elizabeth, "I hope you will tell me about Father. It is so pitiful at his age to lose his boy."[39]

Edward displayed his usual fortitude. Five days after Howard's death, he wrote to Jacques Seligmann in New York, "I have passed through great sorrow,—having lost my only son Howard, of whom you have heard me speak so often. The shock has been great, but I keep myself busy here, with the many things that are of interest to me, and I am glad that I have the comfort of work,—the building up of the Library and Art Gallery, which now absorbs a great deal of my time."[40]

Another hard blow came to Edward on August 22, 1925, when his closest and dearest friend, Billy Dunn, died of a stroke. Dunn had been his right-hand man for twenty-seven years, after having been the city attorney of Los Angeles and having formed a law firm. In effect, he was the chief operating officer of all of Huntington's enterprises in Southern California, and he was, we remember, the first chairman of the board of trustees of the Huntington Library and Art Gallery. Huntington trusted and admired him supremely. He made the following comments to Otheman Stevens right after Dunn's death: " 'Billy' Dunn was the most unselfish man I have ever known. . . . I soon learned his wonderful qualities, and in my affairs he became myself as far as handling them went. . . . I trusted his judgment when I would hardly rely on my own, and he never failed me. . . . His going leaves a great void in my life."[41] These deaths left large empty spaces in Edward's life.

The most distressing event in Edward's life during this period was the death of Belle, in New York, on September 16, 1924. Both of them had assumed, in the light of their medical histories, that she would survive him. He had had a series of life-threatening illnesses and an incurable continuing physical problem. Her poor eyesight and difficulty in walking and her neuritis were, by comparison, less critical, though she had begun in the spring of 1922 to have X-ray radium treatment for her eyes and hip.[42]

In December 1923, Belle became seriously ill while they were in San Marino, and she was in bed for more than a month. Edward sent letters and telegrams about her illness to several friends, and they were distressed. By the middle of January, a nurse was no longer needed and Belle was feeling much better. As Edward wrote to the Schwerins in San Francisco early in January, they felt that Belle would "be entirely well soon, although it is taking a long time to get back her strength wholly." She did recover in due course and carried on her normal social life for several months. According to Alfonso Gomez, the valet, she had frequent premonitions of her own death and, for example, told a luncheon group of ladies in the spring of 1924: "'I hate to go before Edward, but my time has come and my next trip to California, it will be in a box. I want you all to know I have no more time to live.' The ladies said 'Oh, Mrs. Huntington, don't talk like that; you're going to live. This place will be a private home to you for many years to come.' She said 'No.'" Edward and Belle and their retinue left for New York on June 16, 1924. Archer met them at the station and, again according to Alfonso, she said, "Archer, you will never have to be at the depot again to meet your mother. This is my last trip."[43]

Less than a month after their arrival in New York—on July 13—Belle became seriously ill, and Dr. Coley immediately came to see her. Three days later her temperature was 105 degrees and she had periods of unconsciousness, with a nurse in constant attendance and a doctor with her through most nights. Edward kept Dunn and others informed of the downs and ups of her illness by frequent letters and telegrams. Edward was with her constantly, and his secretary was pleased that "Mr. H. is standing the strain fairly well." She was given a series of four blood transfusions, oxygen, various remedies, X-rays of her entire body, and an operation for an abscessed kidney. From time to time, her temperature became normal and she was declared to be out of danger. Then she would become very ill again with a high temperature and pain. On September 7, 1924, Edward gave the following account of these weeks in a handwritten letter to George S. Patton in Los Angeles:

> My dear friend
>
> Eight weeks ago today Mrs. Huntington had a very hard chill and has been critically ill ever since. Twice in the meantime the Doctors informed me they did not think she could survive until morning. She was operated on last week and thank God there are strong hopes of recovery. No one can have the faintest imagination of my suffering. In her delirium her expressions were to take care of Edward. The last two or three days we see a marked improvement and the Doctors all have strong hopes of her recovery. God grant they are right.
>
> With much love to you and yours in which Mrs. Huntington would join could she realize I was writing. I remain
>
> Affectionately yours
> H. E. Huntington[44]

The hopes for her recovery were ill-founded. She had a bad spell at 10 A.M. on September 16, and she sank rapidly into unconsciousness. As she had wished, Edward and Archer were both at her bedside when she died at 6 P.M. The cause of her death was given as pneumonia. A funeral service was held two days later, with Dr. Milo H. Gates of the New York Church of the Intercession officiating.

Edward sent forty-six telegrams immediately after Belle's death to family members and close friends. He suggested to his daughters that they not come to New York. Howard's widow, Leslie, was already on her way with two children, and so were Carrie and Burke. Expressions of sympathy came from all those who had been sent telegrams. Letters and telegrams also came from William Randolph Hearst, Mrs. Winthrop Aldrich, Joseph Duveen, and Frederick W. MacMonnies, the sculptor, as well as from others like John Wesley Johnson, who described himself as "the colored pastor" and praised her "many unselfish deeds of charity." Dunn's telegram, sent to Edward the day after Belle's death, said, "You know without my saying it that my heart is with you. You can only do your best and carry on as she would have wanted you to." The responses were so numerous that Edward had to have an engraved card made, with a black border and black-bordered envelope, with the text "Mr. Henry Edwards Huntington gratefully acknowledges your expression of sympathy." These were mailed out, hand addressed, beginning six days after her death, to the several hundred persons who had sent letters or telegrams of condolence. He also wrote personal letters to many people. To Nora M. Larsen, the housekeeper of their home in San Marino, he said: "It is a great comfort to me to receive the wonderful tributes that are made to Mrs. Huntington, for we all know that none of them do only in part express her goodness and kindness, and I feel that they come really from the hearts of those who knew her. I wish at this time to express my appreciation of much you have done for Mrs. Huntington in the years we have been at the Ranch."[45]

Edward stayed in seclusion in the New York house for several weeks after Belle's death. He saw people who called on him, however, like Homer Ferguson and C. F. Bailey of the Newport News Shipbuilding and Dry Dock Company, who stopped in for a few minutes on the day following the funeral. "We found Mr. Huntington in his library," recalled Bailey, "perusing some of his books, which he loved to read." He began to read to them, though they felt uneasy about intruding on him. "Among other things he read to us excerpts from a book by Mrs. Custer, giving touching incidents in the life of General Custer." Hapgood wrote to a friend that "he is bearing the strain far better than one would think he would. . . . His general health is very good, or he would not have been able to stand the strain of the past two months at all. Mr. and Mrs. Holladay [Carrie and Burke] are with him, and the present plan is to go to California as soon as various business matters are settled." Edward was interviewed by N. P. Stedman for a syndicated press service story, and it was widely published. "Though Mr. Huntington has been under considerable strain since the death of his wife, he is bearing up well for a man of his age," the story reported. Edward was quoted as saying, "I have a strong will and can stand a lot. I am going back to California, and I suspect I'll find it pretty lonesome there without Mrs. Huntington, but I'll have my grandchildren about me."[46]

The main business matter that Edward had to attend to before returning to California was Belle's will. She had signed it on August 30, 1923, about a year before her death, with Archer as the executor; she added a codicil on September 5, 1923, making Edward coexecutor. On October 21, 1924, Archer and Edward appointed as their attorneys the New York law firm of Cadwalader, Wickersham and Taft, and gave them full powers. By the executors' report, the value of her estate was just short of $19 million; in the surrogate court settlement, $17 million came to the trustees after taxes. Archer was given most of the estate, valued at almost $15 million, including a $2 million trust fund, all her jewelry, paintings, furniture, books, and real estate, and all of her estate that was left after her specific trusts and legacies. She made substantial gifts totaling almost $1 million to two kinds of institutions: those that were of prime interest to Archer, such as the Hispanic Society of America, the American Geographical Society, and the American Numismatic Society; and those that Collis had been concerned with, such as the Hampton Institute, Woodlawn Cemetery, Museum of Natural History, and the Metropolitan Museum of Art. She gave trust funds and legacies to her brothers and their families totaling about three-quarters of a million dollars, a legacy of one-quarter million to Collis's adopted daughter, Clara, and small legacies to a goddaughter named for her, a nephew of Collis's named for him, her companion, and her principal household servants. Edward was not mentioned in her will, except by being named in the codicil as coexecutor. Neither were Edward's children, nor his sister, nor the Huntington Library and Art Gallery.[47] It is worth reiterating that she had given nothing to the institution during her lifetime: no art objects, no books, no money. The institution was entirely Edward's gift to the public.

Edward arrived in San Marino on October 28, bringing Belle's remains with him for interment. Hapgood wrote to Duveen the next day that it had been "a rather trying trip, but Mr. Huntington stood the strain better than I thought he would. The house seems desolate and it will be a long time before he becomes adjusted to the new conditions." He had the company of Carrie and Burke Holladay and their children, as well as of Leslie and her children. Elizabeth and Brockway Metcalf also came down to stay with him.

Edward wrote to a niece of Belle's on December 6, 1924, about his feelings:

> I have now been here a month, and you can readily realize how hard a time it has been for me. But fortunately there have been many things to keep me busy, and that has helped somewhat in keeping my mind from the sorrowful thoughts of my loss. The interment will take place shortly, on a beautiful knoll here at the Ranch, a location which your Aunt Belle and I selected some time ago. I shall shortly approve, with the cooperation of Archer, of a plan for a Greek temple to be erected there. Altogether, with the surrounding trees which your aunt so loved, it will be a resting place, fitting in its beauty and peace, for one whose character and loving disposition we all appreciated.[48]

Edward was especially restless in the days before the interment. His secretary wrote to Duveen, "When that is over I think he will feel more settled. His restlessness now is the only thing that causes any concern." After a brief service in the large drawing room, the interment took place on that "beautiful knoll" at ten-thirty on the morning of Wednesday, December 17, 1924, with family and a few close friends present. At the service, the casket was covered with a flower pall of choice roses, lilies of the valley, maidenhair fern, and, from the gardens, forty-three cypripedium and twenty-four cattleya orchids. At the interment, the bronze casket was enclosed in an outer case of cement. After the interment, Hapgood wrote that Edward "was very much depressed,—more than at any other time."[49] No wonder. A crucial chapter of his life had come to an end.

Twenty

THE QUIET TIME
1924–1927

WHEN EDWARD RETURNED to California from New York in November 1924, he hoped to stay there for the rest of his life. He gave up his business office in New York and resigned from most of his clubs. He did keep his membership in two book clubs—the Grolier Club in New York and the Elizabethan Club in New Haven. But he expected to spend his time pursuing his interests—books, art, and gardens—in the place he liked best in the world—Southern California.

Edward always found something to enjoy at the ranch, and he absorbed himself in its natural beauty all the more after Belle's death in New York. He wrote to Sir John Maxwell that "I want to stay here for the rest of my days. California is as lovely as ever, and the Ranch grows more beautiful all the time." When a friend in Oneonta expressed pleasure on reading about the ranch in a newspaper account that Edward had sent him, Edward responded, in the middle of February, "[I] wish that you could see it, especially at this time when it is at its best. The orange orchards show both the fruit and the flowers,—the roses are beginning to bloom again, and the fruit trees are a mass of color. With balmy, sunny days, do you wonder that I am enthusiastic about this part of the country?"[1]

The world of nature meant a great deal to him. Soon after getting back to the ranch, he replied to a letter from Elise Ferguson, the young daughter of Homer Ferguson, head of the Newport News Shipbuilding and Drydock Company. His letter reveals not only his love of nature, but also his optimism, his way of reading and interpreting paintings, and his affection for children:

My dear Elise:

I wish to thank you for your lovely letter which I enjoyed very much. Yes,—I hope, too, that you may some time come out here to see not only the paintings, but also many other lovely things in California. There are beautiful things everywhere, but it seems to me we have more here than in any other part of the world. Just now the roses are at their best: how would you like to see a white rose bush climbing a tree for over a hundred feet? I can show you that. Then there are roads with rose covered fences that stretch sometimes a mile. If you can not come in rose season there will be other things as beautiful.

I am glad you like The Blue Boy. He must have been a fine little fellow, and although we know little about him, he looks as if he did a lot of good in the world as he grew up. He will be here waiting for you, and also a beautiful little Scotch boy, painted by Raeburn, and I want you to meet him too. My kindest regards to your mother and father, but my love to you.

Affectionately yours,
H. E. Huntington[2]

This letter describes the world outside. On the inside, he was suffering from the death of Belle. Three months after getting back to the ranch and five months after Belle's death, he composed a careful description of his feelings to send to Sir John Maxwell. "In the long illness and death of my dearly beloved wife," he wrote, "I am so completely broken that I hardly know or care what is going on about me. The old saying that time is a great healer does not seem to apply in my case."[3]

The anniversary of her death was remembered by Edward, Archer, and various friends. On September 16, 1925, Courtenay De Kalb of the University of Alabama wrote, "On this date, the sad anniversary of the death of Mrs. Huntington, I am moved, on behalf of Mrs. De Kalb and myself, to send you our renewed sympathy for the great loss suffered, which we know must weigh heavily on your heart." Archer sent flowers, and Edward responded that "they were very beautiful, and were placed on Belle's grave on the morning of the 16th, with many other tokens from friends. I assure you I appreciated this and it helped me to get through a day of sad memories."[4]

Edward kept Belle's place at the dining table. "I want to feel that Mrs. Huntington is alive," he told Alfonso. "So we had to set a chair for Mrs. Huntington," Alfonso reported, "every day for breakfast, lunch and dinner—the same chair she used—but no one else could sit there."[5]

The dining table was in constant use. Despite his mourning, Edward had an active social life and entertained many houseguests. His three daughters spent several weeks at a time with him: Elizabeth came half a dozen times a year, often with her husband, Brockway, and one or two of their children; Marian visited twice a year, and Clara less frequently, as she was living in Europe. Edward's cousins from Oneonta, Mary and Ed Lewis, spent four or five months with him every winter. Duveen was there at least twice a year, sometimes with Lady Duveen, for a couple of weeks at a time; Rosenbach came about twice a year for a week or so, and so did Homer Ferguson. There were occasional guests for a night or two. Sometimes the house was full.

Local families and friends who lived nearby often visited back and forth for meals. First and foremost were Edward's sister Carrie, her husband, Burke, and their two children, now young adults, Helen and Collis. Howard's widow, Leslie, also came often, with their six children and her new husband, James Brehm. (She had remarried some two and a half years after Howard's death, to the disgust of Howard's sisters.) There were also many local friends, but the closest ones were Billy Dunn and George Patton and their wives.

Perhaps a clearer idea of the structure of Edward's social life can be gleaned from an outline of his activities during one typical season, like the spring of 1925. The Lewises were house guests during the whole period. Elizabeth and Brockway visited two times, for a total of four weeks; when they departed after their first visit, they left their youngest child, Larry (and his nurse), with his grandfather. Marian was there for three weeks. Homer Ferguson came for a week, Rosenbach twice for a week each time, and the Duveens once for a week. A hint about the kind of pleasure Edward enjoyed with his houseguests is contained in one of his letters to Duveen, in which he thanked him for a recent letter: "It was almost as good as a chat with you, bubbling with enthusiasm and exuberance."[6]

During this period Edward hosted about eight luncheons or dinners, with up to fifteen or twenty at the table. Edward went out for meals about an equal number of times. At home when there were no outside guests, in the evening they often played cards, hearts or bridge. When Duveen was in Paris, Edward wrote him teasingly that "we play Hearts as we used to, and with the experience we are getting, I fear you will have little chance against any of us when it comes time for you to make your trip in this direction. By the way, if you learn of any nice new simple game of cards over there, bring it along when you come and teach it to us,—you may have some chance then."[7]

Most of their entertainment was at home, but Edward went out with family and friends to a few shows. They saw Sheridan's *The Rivals* at the Biltmore Theatre, and *The Swan* and Shaw's *You Never Can Tell* at the Community Playhouse; they went once to Hollywood to see a matinée of *The Iron Horse* at Gramman's Egyptian Theatre, and another time there for a matinée of Charlie Chaplin's *Gold Rush*. They heard Ruth Draper's one-woman show at the Shakespeare Club in Pasadena.[8]

The house was attractive, and Edward enjoyed it along with his guests. *Sarah Siddons as the Tragic Muse,* in the main hall, could be seen immediately upon entering the house. *Blue Boy* was in the large drawing room, and next to it was *Pinkie,* after the latter was acquired in 1927. *Master William Blair* and *Lady Hamilton* were in the south front hall. The whole house was full of paintings, of course, but these were said to be Edward's special favorites. He usually saluted the *Blue Boy* when he left home and gave him a formal greeting on his return.[9]

Edward went across the lawn to the library every day to consult with the librarian and other staff members and to check on their progress. One staff member later said, in speaking of the large reading room, that "we can all call up a picture of Mr. Huntington marching through that room with his stick in hand, hat tipped up at the back and a cheery word for everyone."[10] He looked at the new books and manuscripts, and much of his intellectual interest was focused on his library and art gallery as an institution.

He did most of his reading in the library room in his residence. He read both alone and to guests. Although with friends he usually shared short passages from recently acquired books and manuscripts, one evening he read an entire book aloud to Carrie and Burke. People sent him their favorite books. When Rosenbach sent, in 1925, the new two-volume edition of Wilbur L. Cross's *The Life and Times of Laurence Sterne,* Edward expressed deep appreciation for it: "I know I shall enjoy it, and it comes at an opportune time as I am reading considerably and am tired of the light fiction everyone is thrusting upon me."[11]

He continued to enjoy the gardens, and he took pleasure in the flowers, in the development of the planting, and in playing croquet. Grandchildren were often with him, and they too enjoyed the outdoors, but more as a place where they could race about on the lawns and roll down the hill on the south side of the house. Elizabeth's children were very fond of him because of the fact that he liked to joke with them, and Clara's son David Huntington remembered him affectionately as "a very lovable 'old' man whose moustache tickled when he kissed me and usually smelled of bay rum." In addition to family and houseguests, a great many people came to see him, either for a meal or just for a visit. Some were collectors, such as his friends Herschel V. Jones, the Minneapolis publisher; Edward E. Ayer of Chicago, a principal early benefactor of the Newberry Library and first president of the Field Museum; and Arthur Secor, the president of the Toledo Museum. Other collectors who visited included Thomas W. Streeter, John Clawson, and Frank B. Bemis. New York financiers like Otto H. Kahn and Mortimer Schiff came to call, as did college and university presidents like Remsen D. Bird of Occidental, Aurelia H. Reinhardt of Mills, Frank Aydelotte of Swarthmore, John Grier Hibben of Princeton, and Clarence C. Little of the University of Michigan. Edward received many personages like William Randolph Hearst, British Ambassador Sir Esmé Howard, Lady Beaverbrook, U. S. Grant, Jr., Cecil B. De-Mille, John Drinkwater, and Albert Einstein. He showed each guest things that he thought might interest them in the residence and in the library. He received very appreciative letters afterward. Aurelia Reinhardt said that her visit was "one of the pleasantest of my life" and she appreciated his "cordial care that a passing guest might see and enjoy these precious creations of the human spirit which you have brought from distant lands to enrich the life of California." Clarence Little said that his "visit to the Pacific Coast would have been a failure if he had not had this privilege."[12]

A few visits were more elaborate. In June 1926, Mr. and Mrs. John D. Rockefeller, Jr., and their three younger sons, David, Winthrop, and Laurance, stopped by. Although they were traveling incognito as "Mr. John Davison and family," their progress was attended by numerous reporters. One of them asked Mr. Rockefeller if they planned to visit the Huntington book and art collections. "To my mind," he replied, "that is as wonderful an asset to a community as anything else in a civic nature that I can think of now. I certainly would regret it if I didn't see it. Is Mr. Huntington home now?" He was, and he welcomed the Rockefellers for a day in which he guided them around his estate. Edward later reported to Duveen that "I had a pleasant visit with the Rockefellers—there were eight in the party, which included Mrs. R. and the three younger sons. After seeing the house and the Library, they stayed to lunch, and altogether we had a most enjoyable time, and I was glad to have the opportunity to know Mr. R. better." Later he told Duveen that Rockefeller "takes quite seriously, as he should, the training of his children, and the three boys that were here were good types of American youths, and are being brought up in a most democratic way."[13]

In the next month, Crown Prince Gustavus Adolphus and Princess Louise of Sweden paid a royal visit of two nights to the Huntington establishment. They were shown around the collections and the estate, and a formal dinner was tendered them on one evening. Twenty-four were present, including the Holladays, with Carrie acting as hostess for the occasion, and the trustees and their wives; a seating chart was carefully made out in pencil by Edward and has been preserved.[14]

The vast majority of the visitors were not persons of public distinction, however, but Edward tried to receive them when he could. Cora Case Porter, who worked in the public library in Muskogee, Oklahoma, can serve as a single representative of a large number of people. While on a visit to Los Angeles, she wrote to ask whether she might come out with a friend to see the *Blue Boy*. Edward agreed and suggested two-thirty on Friday afternoon, June 26, 1925. She came, and went away with a happy memory.[15]

He sometimes turned down requests from people who wanted to

visit, often because he was not free or it was inconvenient. Sometimes he declined to admit people who wanted to treat his house as an art museum, like Hannah T. Jenkins, the retired head of the art department at Pomona College, who wanted to show his art to two of her visitors from the East. Often he declined requests to visit the library on the grounds that it would disturb the serious students and the staff work.[16]

Edward went regularly to his office in Los Angeles during these years except when he was ill. When Billy Dunn was alive, he and Edward had lunch together every day at the California Club. After Dunn died, Edward brought his lunch from home—cheese sandwiches in a tin box that had begun its life as a tea container—and ate at his desk.[17]

Edward's health had been relatively good through most of his first year back in California, with no ailment worse than a cold. In the summer of 1925, Burke Holladay thought he was "looking pale and thinner in the face," and Dr. Bryant soon afterward became concerned at the results of his urinalyses. In early October he was put to bed after an attack of his old prostate problem, and he agreed to consult with a specialist to determine whether an operation was indicated.[18] When Otheman Stevens heard that Edward was in bed, he wrote, "I hope you will soon be strong enough to sustain the shock of seeing me again without having to take to your bed and call on Dockie as soon as I go. I think if I could see you and discuss Labor Unions, Socialism, and Free Trade you would soon feel okeh."[19] But he did not soon feel "okeh," and Dr. Bryant's choice of a consultant was Dr. John B. Deaver in Philadelphia, Dr. Bryant having had his medical training at the University of Pennsylvania. Although Edward's trip to Philadelphia was not regarded as dangerous, Elizabeth and Marian came down to see him before his departure, and Carrie and Burke returned from San Francisco to be with him. Dr. Bryant told the family that Edward's general condition was so good that he could stand an operation very well should one be necessary. On October 19 Edward set out for Philadelphia in his private car with Dr. Bryant, Alfonso, and a nurse. En route, he wrote a letter to the impoverished Mrs. Pickett offering her a pension of $50 a month for life saying that "this is about the least I could do for the widow of that gallant soldier and Christian gentleman."[20] He confided to Alfonso his wish to create a memorial to Belle: he told him, with tears, "You know, Alfonso, there will never be another Mrs. Huntington and I would like to have her picture and I would like to have all the Madonnas that were hanging on the main floor and all the things there because that's what she loved the most." About the picture, Alfonso responded, "What will you do with it? She gave it to Mr. Archer." Edward replied, amid tears, "Mrs. Huntington died before me, which I didn't expect, and I want to make a special memorial for my wife."[21]

They got to Philadelphia on October 24 and went directly to the Lankenau Hospital, where Dr. Deaver began a series of examinations. Elizabeth and Marian were with him, and Dr. Bryant sent a telegram to Carrie and Burke to say that it was not necessary for them to come to Philadelphia. Elizabeth cabled to Rome for Clara, who responded with sympathy but seemed more interested in her own travels.[22] Telegrams were also sent to various friends.

Rosenbach, on his home ground, stood by and had special foods prepared as a relief from hospital fare. Duveen came down from New York to see Edward. One day during the observation period messages were sent to Rosenbach and Duveen that Huntington wanted to see them. When the nurse called them in, they found him lying on the bed in his hospital shirt, with head slightly raised and his arms extended. They sat stiffly on chairs on either side of the bed and tried to utter words of encouragement. Suddenly, Huntington turned to Duveen and asked, "Sir Joseph, do I remind you of anyone?" Duveen was nonplussed and answered, "Why, no, Mr. Huntington, I don't believe so." Then Huntington turned his head toward Rosenbach and said, "Tell me, Doctor, do I remind you of anyone?" Rosenbach was at a loss and muttered that he really did not know. "Well, gentlemen," said Huntington, still lying flat on his back with his arms outstretched, "I remind myself of Jesus Christ on the cross between the two thieves." Rosenbach and Duveen smiled weakly.[23]

After four days of examinations, it was decided that an operation should be performed, and on October 28 Dr. Deaver removed Edward's prostate gland. No mention was made of cancer, which by then had presumably spread beyond the prostate. On November 3, Rosenbach sent a telegram to Hapgood in San Marino: "Saw Mr. Huntington for the first time this morning and he is improving steadily. He will probably sit up in four or five days. His two daughters are here and they saw him for the first time today. Will keep you advised. Regards."[24] On November 5, Edward dictated a message to George Patton in reply to an affectionate letter from him: "I have only just been allowed to open my mail today for the first time. I am getting along fully as well as could be expected; as a matter of fact, a little better than could be expected."[25] Expressions of cheer came from many people. Carrie's letter contained a vignette of him back at home: "It is good to get such encouraging reports about you but I shall be truly happy when I see you again, seated in your own library, in front of your card table, dominoes spread out, snorting at long waists and short hair. I am not sure but that I would be willing to bob my hair if it would keep up your circulation." And she ended her message with "here's a world of love from us all, Carrie."[26] During the recovery period, Alfonso slipped away to New York and told Archer how much Mr. Huntington wanted the portrait of his mother and the madonnas for a memorial to her in the library; Archer sent Edward a telegram that he would give him the pictures he wanted.[27] Edward was a target for salesmen, even in the hospital. On November 6—the day after he was first allowed to open mail—an art dealer who lived two blocks from the hospital tried to sell him a Reynolds, a Rembrandt Peale, and a sixteenth-century Holy Family and asked to be allowed to bring photos of them to his hospital room; a secretary declined for him on the grounds that he was not allowed to take up business.[28]

Edward improved slowly, but after three weeks he was allowed to leave the hospital. On November 19 he left Philadelphia in his private car with Dr. Bryant, Alfonso, and the nurse and arrived home on November 24. He was brought to his house from the station in an ambulance and carried to his upstairs bedroom on a stretcher. He looked pale and thin and was weak, but he claimed that he felt fine. Dr. Bryant said that he should be able to get about within several weeks.

The recovery was a little slower than that, but within weeks he was sitting up every day. Edward received encouragement from many friends. On December 1, Otheman Stevens wrote him in the jocular vein that Edward so much enjoyed that "I haven't had the slightest apprehension about your recovery; I know how tough you are and how imperious is your willpower." So Stevens suggested a poker and jazz party: "What you need is a bit more observation of the spirit of the age, the Great God of Jazz. If I come across a good Charleston teacher I'll send him out to give you a course in the latest buck and wing steps."[29] Edward's optimism was tested a good deal during these weeks and months. "I hope to be up soon," he wrote a friend in December 1925, "and when I am up and about, I shall be better than for a long time." To Rosenbach he wrote on the same day, "I feel I shall be better than ever."[30] In January 1926 he was at last able to get up and walk around the second floor of the house every day, and he was gradually able to do more. All three of his daughters were there in February, as well as Mary and Ed Lewis, and on February 26 he wrote to Carrie and Burke, who were in Europe, "It helps a lot having the family here, and I have enjoyed them immensely. We play cards nearly every evening." He concluded that "the Ranch is looking its best, and I anticipate getting out to see it before long."[31] The problem was that the incision for his operation—"the wound" they always called it—did not heal properly: it would seem to be closed for two or three days, but then it would open again and yet again under the dressing.

In March, he invited his friends at the California Institute of Technology to have the organizational meeting of their active support group, the Caltech Associates, in his house. The house was thrown open for them, and the formal meeting took place in the large drawing room, with 180 people present. Robert Milliken, the chief executive officer at Caltech and a good friend of Edward's, gave a talk on cosmic rays. Unfortunately, Edward had to stay upstairs, but the meeting was successful in launching an important group.[32] Edward declined, during the same month, to allow Universal Pictures to come and take pictures in his house to incorporate in a movie featuring a duke's palace.[33]

He went downstairs for the first time on March 28, as he proudly reported to Carrie, and added that "I feel it will be soon when I shall be about as usual. . . . Naturally I am most anxious to get out as there are so many things I want to get at. . . . I am changing some of the roads about the Ranch, making some new ones and changing some of the old, and as I enjoy this sort of work especially, I am looking forward to getting out in the car and advising Hertrich about this." In June, he had an aerial photograph made of the ranch. He wanted especially to be out and around in view of the fact that, as he had written Carrie two weeks earlier, "We are having a wonderful season,—sunny and warm, with the flowers quite a bit ahead of the usual season. The girls [his daughters] enjoyed their stay here, and needless to say, so did I. Clara spent most of the time making a bas-relief of me, and I hope it turns out all right."[34]

Despite the slowness of his improvement, Edward was hopeful and optimistic. In April, he was able to go over the ranch in his car and plan the improvements he wanted carried out. He came downstairs for lunch every day. Elizabeth and Marian were there for a week in May, the Rockefeller visit was in June, that of the Swedish crown prince in July, and in August he went downtown for the first time. The wound kept reopening, and the doctors kept a catheter in him all the time. Still, he was cheerful and as active as he was allowed to be.[35] His attitude is typified by this letter to Thomas J. Kerr in New York, written on November 4: "I am glad to say that I am improving every day, and beginning to lead a more normal life, although I do not yet go to town as regularly as I used to. But I get out every day, and expect soon to be able to do as much as I please."[36] In January 1927, Dr. Bryant brought two specialists to examine Edward to see why the wound did not heal. They determined that it was caused by a flap of scar tissue and two growths, and they removed them by cauterization.[37] This procedure made no noticeable improvement in Edward's health.

He continued to live a moderately active life on the ranch. He enjoyed the affection expressed by his many friends and his sister and daughters. Frank Miller of Riverside urged him to come and hide away with them if he wanted some peaceful rest: "Please, dear friend, make use of us here if there is anything we can do to help you in any way."[38] The letters from Elizabeth were especially affectionate. Her messages to "My dearest daddy" always included warm and sincere expressions of affection, including "worlds of love" and "a big hug, dear" and "ever and ever so much love."[39] He was supported by all of these expressions of affection. But he was doubtless supported most of all by his own courage and optimism.

Edward continued a vigorous program of acquisitions during these years. He bought ten major paintings in 1925, 1926, and 1927, and they included several of those valued most highly by connoisseurs and the informed public. In 1925 he got Constable's great landscape *View on the Stour near Dedham;* Gainsborough's *Karl Friedrich Abel,* the chamber musician with his instrument; and Reynolds's *Georgiana, Duchess of Devonshire,* the fashionable lady in her garden. And in 1927 he acquired what has proved a popular favorite, Sir Thomas Lawrence's *Pinkie.* In addition to these four star pictures, he also acquired Gainsborough's *Mrs. Henry Fane,* Reynolds's *Theresa Parker* (and *Lavinia, Countess Spencer,* then attributed to Reynolds), and three valuable Romney paintings, *Mary, Lady Beauchamp-Proctor, Mrs. Francis Burton,* and *Lady Hamilton in a White Turban.* These ten paintings cost $2.7 million.[40] Edward was a little embarrassed at the amount of money he was spending for paintings. He told Otheman Stevens, as a secret, that he had paid $380,000 for *Pinkie* and explained that "I can not let the trustees know I have spent so much money. They would raise an awful row if they knew."[41] The trustees were trying to get him to increase the endowment of the institution, as we shall see, and the million-dollar bills for art substantially diminished the pot from which they were hoping to draw the future sustenance of the institution. Stevens had to carry the weight of this disquieting secret for some time.

The acquisition of a couple of these paintings involved negotiations that reveal something of Edward's feelings in his decision-making. Duveen offered him Reynolds's *Duchess of Devonshire* for $480,000, and Edward told him, in the first of a series of telegrams between the two, that he was not interested: "Doubt very much my ability to purchase any more pictures." He thought the price too high, and he was usually able to get Duveen to come down. Duveen then offered it to Mellon, who wanted to buy it. After Edward had thought about the picture, he expressed interest in it to Duveen without knowing it had been offered to Mellon. When Duveen told him of Mellon's interest and his willingness to try to persuade Mellon to take another picture, Edward told him to go ahead and sell it to Mellon: "If party wants it I would like to see him purchase." But Duveen went to Washington and persuaded Mellon to buy another painting instead. He cheerfully reported to Edward: "I returned last night from Washington having with my slight manipulative powers saved Reynolds Duchess to show you but have sold him Gainsborough Duchess instead." And Edward went ahead and bought the Reynolds painting for the asking price of $480,000, the largest price of any of these ten paintings.[42]

In the case of *Pinkie,* the situation with Mellon was reversed. Edward bought *Pinkie* from Duveen in the autumn of 1926. Duveen had first offered it to Mellon, who turned it down because he thought that the ensuing publicity would be injurious—that a public servant, secretary of the treasury, should spend so much money for one picture. After Edward bought it, the painting was kept on exhibition for two weeks in December at the Royal Academy in London at the request of the British government, and thousands of visitors came. Duveen brought the picture personally to San Marino in January 1927; en route he telegraphed Edward from Kansas, "Pinkie only fairly well last night crying for Grandpa but am taking greatest care of her until she returns home." Two months later, an embarrassed letter from Duveen to Edward began: "I am endeavoring to write you a letter which I find the greatest difficulty in composing." The problem was that Mellon had changed his mind about buying *Pinkie* and wanted to have it: Mellon saw in Pinkie a likeness to his own daughter, and "of all the pictures he owns he coveted this the most." Amid many flattering remarks about their friendship and the "admiration and esteem" felt by Huntington and Mellon for one another, Duveen asked whether Edward could make "a really magnificent gesture" and let Mellon have the picture. Edward responded, amid many expressions of admiration and friendship for Duveen and for Mellon and his deep desire to do something for both of them, that the painting did not belong to him but to the Huntington Library and Art Gallery. He would be willing to put the question to the trustees, but he knew that they liked the painting so much that they would be unwilling to part with it. The picture stayed in the collection.[43]

Edward was also buying a considerable number of other works of art at this time: an important group of British miniature paintings, a good many pieces of French eighteenth-century sculpture and French furniture and decorative art, a few Renaissance bronzes, and several Barbizon paintings. He studied art catalogs with care. He kept writing to Mitchell Kennerley, president of the Anderson Galleries in New York, to send him marked copies of art catalogs, which he read with close attention. Some "are in tatters," he wrote, and the ones on oriental rugs and porcelains "will complete my collection. I am very much obliged for all the trouble you have taken in preparing these for me, and hope I am not asking too much of you, but they are a source of much pleasure to me."[44]

Even more pleasure and deep satisfaction came from his completion of a special art collection as a memorial to Belle. This idea had been in his mind ever since her death, and he included in his will signed on August 1, 1925, a long paragraph about its establishment: in it he left $2 million to the trustees in case he had failed in his negotiations with Archer and had not otherwise established the memorial, with half of this amount to be used for acquisitions and the other half as endowment for it. The first step toward its fulfillment was Archer's willingness to contribute the Birley portrait of Arabella, and the nineteen paintings—they called them "Italian primitives"—that had hung in the hall at 2 West Fifty-seventh Street, which she had been particularly fond of. Alfonso's private visit to Archer had, in fact, been preceded by discussions between Edward and Archer, but Alfonso's account of Edward's deep feelings on the subject doubtless encouraged Archer to make the gift. These pictures were on loan to the Metropolitan Museum in New York, and Archer notified them that they now belonged to H. E. Huntington; in the winter of 1926, they were sent to San Marino.[45]

In the meantime, Edward had bought a great many other items— furniture, clocks, porcelain, and sculpture—at a cost of $1,858,000 to complete the collection.[46] He decided to dedicate the west wing of the library as the space for the memorial. In December 1926 he wrote to a friend, "I am going to fit up the west wing of the Library as a memorial to Mrs. Huntington. The idea has been in my mind for some time." He said there would be placed, in "the main part of one of the four rooms, the collection of Italian Primitives which used to be in the Hall at No. 2 East 57th Street, and which Archer Huntington has given to me in memory of his mother." In addition, "the collections will be mainly furniture, bronzes and the objects of art such as Mrs. Huntington loved to surround herself with. This will, in a way, supplement the collection in the house. The Italian Primitive room will be especially lovely, as I have the old red velvet for the walls,—that having come from No. 2 as well."[47] He gave a glowing description to Archer of the contents of the four rooms; and he was especially pleased to report the opinion of a few intimate friends who had seen it "that it is quite worthy, in its beauty, of the lovely character which we both loved."[48]

His lawyers drew up an indenture, which he signed on April 23, 1927, establishing "The Arabella D. Huntington Memorial Art Collection" as a "perpetual and fitting memorial." The west wing of the library was set apart for and dedicated to this purpose, and the trustees were given the duty "forever to keep and maintain said Memorial Collection in said west wing of said Library." The indenture concluded with a five-page list of the eighty-six objects that constitute the collection.[49]

The library also gained some important acquisitions during these years. Edward continued his practice of making en bloc purchases when he could, and he was able to get twenty-nine such collections in 1925, 1926, and 1927. He bought three collections of fifteenth-century printed books, a total of 2,148 titles. Among British historical papers, he bought the Stowe collection of some three hundred fifty thousand deeds, court rolls, letters, documents, and account books of the Temple, Grenville, Nugent, and Brydges families, from the twelfth through the nineteenth centuries, and the Hastings Papers, comprising fifty thousand pieces about the Hastings and related families, from the twelfth through the nineteenth centuries. He bought half a dozen collections that focused on the period of the American Revolution, a total of some five thousand letters and pamphlets. Many of the acquisitions were more specialized, like the papers of Elizabeth Montagu, the eighteenth-century "Queen of the Blue Stockings," including some twelve thousand letters to and from contemporaries; a collection of the letters of the leaders of the Women's Suffrage Movement in the United States; the papers of Jack London; and letters and manuscripts of Ambrose Bierce.[50] These acquisitions continued the tendency away from expensive single items, the "collector's preoccupation," to large groups of generally inaccessible background material, the "scholar's interest." He was still a voracious reader of dealers' and auction catalogs. In 1926, he said,

> I am buying modern books to a larger extent than I have in the past. My choice is confined to those modern authors who are likely to

"live" in the estimation of the public and of scholars; certainly there now exist writers whose works in the centuries to come will be of equal or more importance to the world than those of olden times. My aim is to make the library well rounded, giving students the earliest and the latest, as well as the between eras, of literature. The truly valuable works outside of scientific and abstruse studies, are those which truly reflect the humanity of the times in which they were written.[51]

The "earliest era" can be represented by his purchases of incunabula during these years. For the "latest era," in the Henkels auction sale of February 5, 1926, he picked out only two items, both by Ezra Pound—*A Lume Spento* (first edition, 1908, autographed by the author) and *A Quinzaine for This Yule* (first edition, 1908). He got them both, the former for $25 and the latter for $11.[52] For the "in between eras" perhaps William Blake can serve as an example. Edward began seriously collecting Blake in 1911, long before Blake became popular, and by 1923 he had gathered one of the premier assemblages of his pencil sketches, watercolor drawings, tempera paintings, prints, illuminated books, and manuscript letters.

Once in a while something was given up from the collections. In 1925 Edward discovered that he had acquired, in a lot of assorted material bought ten years earlier, the burial register of the Mission San Fernando. So he sent it back to Mission San Fernando, "to restore the volume to its rightful owner."[53]

The institution began to function more actively during these years. At first, the changes were modest. After Chester Cate died, Edward appointed Leslie E. Bliss as acting librarian on May 20, 1925. Bliss, one of the first persons hired by Cole for the library staff in 1915, later recalled his first impression of Huntington as "somewhat shy, and exceedingly gentlemanly, a very fine person." Bliss had done cataloging, had marked material in booksellers' catalogs for Huntington to consider, and had made field trips to pick up western Americana. In September 1926, after working hard to improve the spirit of the staff and get better work done, he was made librarian.[54]

Edward closely supervised the operations. As Carrie's husband, Burke, observed: "Mr. Huntington looked upon the institution as his creation, as a parent would look upon a child, and . . . it was his desire to look after its interests and manage its properties, as a parent or guardian would care for the separate property of a minor child." When Bliss felt in 1927 that they needed two additional staff members, he told Farrand that "after a brief but bloodless struggle Mr. Huntington has finally allowed me to increase the library staff to twenty-seven."[55]

Staff members felt a personal relation with Huntington. When a cataloger learned from the librarian that he was to have a salary increase, he wrote a note of appreciation to Huntington. "Dear Mr. Huntington: Mr. Bliss told me this morning that after the first of January my salary was going to be increased. I want to thank you for this, Mr. Huntington, and to tell you that I shall always try to merit your appreciation of my work. Sincerely, E. B. Sweetman." Shortly before Chester Cate died, he had expressed his feelings toward Huntington to a friend when he said, "There are times when I should just love to put my hand on his arm and call him 'Dad.'" Huntington was thoughtful toward staff members. After Cate's death, he sent a telegram to a friend of Cate's mother in Wakefield, Massachusetts: "Telegram bearing very great shock for Mrs. Cate will arrive shortly. Prepare her as gently as possible."[56]

Edward continued to help his staff manage their money. They could deposit their savings in an account at 5 percent interest until enough accumulated to buy a bond or stock; Alfonso Gomez was able to deposit from $30 to $60 a month in his account. Those in need of temporary cash could borrow sums that were paid off by payroll deductions; Hapgood, Bliss, Cate, and others availed themselves of this service, in amounts from $100 to $2,500. Edward even offered to lend money to a staff member who he heard wanted to buy a car, but the staff member decided not to do it and thanked Huntington profusely for his generous kindness. And on December 29, 1925, eighty-three members of the grounds staff signed a note of appreciation to him, with hopes that the new year would restore his health.[57]

The library was used more and more by scholars. Alice I. Perry Wood, associate professor of English at Wellesley College, wrote to thank Huntington "for your generous hospitality to students in making it possible for them to examine your literary treasures in most advantageous and beautiful surroundings." William Maxwell, professor at

the State College in Santa Barbara and a student of Elizabethan literature, wrote Huntington that it was a "very great privilege to avail myself
of the undreamed of opportunities your Library affords to one interested in problems of research. . . . I do not remember ever having been
in a Library where so much was done to place one quite at ease and to
furnish the student with interesting, valuable, and even unique data
bearing on his subject." Maxwell's plan was to spend his vacations at
the library "that I may make good use of the privileges you have so
unselfishly extended to students." The librarian felt that they could not
accommodate all who wanted to use the collections, and it was decided
that they would not receive undergraduates nor M.A. students unless
they had a special need; Ph.D. candidates, faculty members, and independent scholars were welcomed.[58]

The staff was kept busy in answering letters of inquiry. Hundreds of
pieces of correspondence passed between the staff and W. W. Greg
during these years, on a variety of bibliographical matters, mostly answering his detailed questions about Huntington copies, sending him
photos, and checking his proofs for him. Margaret Stillwell made several hundred inquiries about details of Huntington copies for her census of incunabula. Further details about incunabula were needed by the
editors of the *Gesamtkatalog* in Berlin, and a couple of hundred letters
went in answer to their queries during these three years.[59]

Edward authorized some important institutional changes during
these years. The character of the trustees had been altered somewhat
from the original group: when Howard died in 1922 he was replaced by
Henry M. Robinson, a lawyer by training and practice, and president
of the First National Bank of Los Angeles, and in 1925 Billy Dunn was
replaced by Robert A. Milliken, a Nobel prize-winning physicist, and
head of Caltech. Since Archer never attended any meetings, that left
George S. Patton, a lawyer and landowner, and George Ellery Hale, an
astronomer and man of ideas. Two lawyers and two scientists, and no
one of an historical or literary or artistic bent. And it was a time when
"scientific investigation" was gaining ground as a mode for literary and
historical scholarship.

In 1924 and 1925, several events encouraged a rethinking of the role of
the Library and Art Gallery. In 1924, the Carnegie Foundation under-

wrote the purchase of one of the plots of land surrounding the library for a small observatory for Hale's studies. Otheman Stevens wrote that "this, it is taken, is the first step toward providing other research institutions adjacent to the Huntington Foundation, where the library, the botanical gardens and the art gallery will be at hand to serve their part." He observed that the adjacent areas were "spacious enough to provide for any number of research institutions," and these would "form a center of learning and scientific investigation such as the world has never dreamed it was possible to create." He asserted that these steps fitted into "the definite plan H. E. Huntington has had in mind of making the Foundation a sort of post graduate university, in so far as provision for research studies is concerned."[60]

Edward received suggestions from a number of scientists along this line. Professor C. S. Sargent of Harvard's Arnold Arboretum urged him to establish a botanical institute with herbarium, library, and scientific botanist, asserting that this "would greatly benefit the world." Professor H. M. Hall of the Department of Botany at the University of California urged him on in scientific dealing with plants, and the director of the International Museum of Oology encouraged him to go into the field of scientific bird study.[61] In early 1925, there was a flurry of activity about establishing a southern branch of the University of California, and the "Huntington site" in Pasadena was one of the three locations most often discussed. Various people became excited at this prospect. The *Pasadena Star News* thought that Huntington's "great library would be the focal point of Pasadena as a seat of learning—a distinctive central unit in a great seat of learning, embracing the university, California Institute of Technology and other cultural institutions of the city." Various committees formed to press Pasadena's claims, and a friend suggested that Huntington give the land "as a tribute to your beloved wife as a memorial." When Edward looked into the matter, he concluded that the amount of land needed was so great that the university had better be on the Hastings ranch in West Sierra Madre. Robert G. Sproul, the secretary of the board of regents, found fault with the Hastings ranch site because it had no sewer connection, was hot in summer, and was smoky in winter from the smudge pots in the orange groves. Though the Pasadena area was not chosen for the location of the university, the affinity of the Library and Art Gallery with wider research efforts had been suggested.[62]

In 1925, the trustees felt that the purpose of the institution as stated in the original trust indenture of 1919 should be amplified and focused on research. To that end, Hale drew up a document entitled "Policies: The Future Development of the Huntington Library and Art Gallery," which was presented to the trustees, formally approved by Huntington on October 14, 1925, and thereafter kept along with the legal indentures. Reflecting recent events, this document of five printed pages presented a "unified scheme" for converting the Library and Art Gallery into a research institution. The premise was that "its value to the world will depend chiefly upon what it *produces*"; the materials in the collections were "instruments of research, and they should be utilized in the most effective manner in advancing and disseminating knowledge." All competent scholars would be free to use the materials, but the main work would be in the hands of a research staff, "original investigators of the highest caliber," drawn temporarily from leading institutions all over the world, "under the direction of a great and productive scholar." The research would focus on the "origin and progress of the civilization of the English-speaking peoples, with special reference to their intellectual development." The growth and progress of civilization would be central to the research effort, and future acquisitions would be governed by research needs. The general public would be served by providing exhibitions of selected objects. The document concluded with the following statement, written, signed, and dated by Huntington: "I approve the adoption of the above policy for the Huntington Library and Art Gallery."[63]

The trustees had already begun to look for "a great and productive scholar" to direct the institution. They first considered Max Farrand, a specialist in the history of the United States Constitution, who had recently at age fifty-six resigned his professorship of American history at Yale to supervise the fellowship program of the Commonwealth Fund. Milliken wrote and asked him to give a series of lectures at Caltech. Farrand declined but offered to stop by on a Commonwealth Fund trip to discuss the idea of a lecture series. He and Mrs. Farrand—Beatrix Cadwalader Jones, a noted landscape designer—came in January 1926 for a few days and soon realized that the real topic was the Huntington Library. Farrand met Milliken and Hale, visited the library (but did not meet Huntington), read and discussed the plan of research embodied in the document signed a few months earlier, and returned east.

On February 8, 1926, Huntington signed a new trust indenture to amplify and confirm the earlier indentures and to conform with the policy statement of October 14, 1925, with its unified scheme of a research institution. The 1919 indenture had defined the nature of the institution as "a free public library, art gallery, museum and park, containing objects of aesthetic, historic or literary interest." The 1926 indenture began a much longer definition of it as "a free public research library, art gallery, museum and botanical garden, containing objects of artistic, historic, scientific or literary interest, which library shall be for reference or research only." For the first time, provision was made in the new indenture for a director, research associates, and fellows ("scholars of exceptional ability"), and its object was broadened to include "research or creative work in history, literature, art, science and kindred subjects." The summary statement of the earlier objective, "to promote the public welfare," became "to conduct an institution of educational value to the public."[64]

When Farrand returned from a trip to Europe in June 1926, he was met in New York by Henry M. Robinson, who asked him to come to the library as the first research associate. Farrand agreed only to visit for two months in the winter, and he wrote Huntington that he thought it would be desirable for him to undertake a specific piece of research; he suggested a careful study of the Huntington manuscript of Franklin's *Autobiography,* looking toward a scholarly edition of that masterpiece.[65] The trustees wanted to make Farrand the director, but they also wanted to use the occasion of his appointment to get Huntington to commit the money to endow the research program and the institution. When Farrand arrived in December 1926, Robinson and Hale took him to meet Huntington, they discussed the desirability of having a specific research program, and Farrand was asked to draw one up. Over the period of the next few days he did so, with help from his wife. Farrand read it to the trustees and then again to Huntington and the trustees together. Huntington was pleased and asked for a budget, and Farrand provided two, a minimum and a maximum, with six or eight senior scholars and an equal number of junior investigators. When Farrand took his budgets to Huntington, he was first shown, in Huntington's usual manner, some art objects Huntington had under consideration and was read extracts from some recent purchases. When Huntington turned to the budgets, Farrand asked whether he wanted the minimum or the maximum. "Maximum, of course," was the answer. The cost? "$340,000," said Farrand. "Is that every year?" and Farrand said it was. Huntington asked whether Farrand realized that meant the income on $7 million, and Farrand said that he did. "Immediately and without hesitation Huntington said, 'You may have it' and later he added, 'My word is sufficient; it is as good as my bond.'" Farrand asked whether the plan of research interested him. "He hesitated just a moment," recalled Farrand, "then looked me straight in the eye and with the utmost simplicity said, 'I don't know what it is all about. I have confidence in my Trustees, who I think are an extraordinary group of men, and they tell me you are the best person for this job. I like you and I am going to do whatever you tell me to do.'" Farrand told him that, if he wanted the place to continue as "the influential institution that he dreamed of its being," as an active force even after a hundred years, he should provide $10 million more in endowment. "I don't know whether I have it," Huntington replied, and outlined the provisions yet to be made for the memorial hospital and for his children and relatives. "If there are sufficient funds," he added, "you shall have it." "Have you made, or will you make, such provision in your will?" He said, "I will."[66]

The trustees held a special meeting with Huntington present on February 5, 1927. They created the office of director of research, made it a matter of record that Huntington had agreed to increase the endowment so that the research department could have an annual budget of $400,000, and offered Farrand the directorship, to include general charge of the Library and Art Gallery and acquisitions. Farrand was in Cambridge, Massachusetts, and he spent an evening discussing the offer with three historian-friends, Charles Haskins, Arthur M. Schlesinger, and Edwin F. Gay. Farrand had misgivings about the program of research that he had hastily prepared, and his "mind was greatly relieved" when his friends approved it. He felt uncertain about accepting the job and giving up a life that he was planning to devote to research, but they urged him to take it.[67]

He accepted, and Huntington was delighted. Huntington wrote to his friend Professor Edwin R. Seligman at Columbia that "we are all very glad that the Trustees decided upon such a man as Dr. Farrand as Director: besides his qualifications as a scholar, his personality is so pleasing." Huntington made one of his typical little jokes to Henry M. Robinson about Farrand's stipulation that he be allowed to spend four months in the summer at their house at Bar Harbor, Maine. Robinson tried to reassure Huntington that Farrand would change that provision if it proved necessary. Huntington replied, "You don't understand; I am afraid if Farrand is away from here for four months at a time I will have to run that damned library again myself."[68]

So the new orientation to research was under way in the spring of 1927. Even before Farrand got there, the first research associate arrived and spent a month at the library. It was Frederick Jackson Turner, the American historian. Matters were handled personally; when Turner was ready to leave, Hale sent a note to Huntington asking him to give Turner a check for $500 as his stipend, and Huntington did so.[69]

Edward took steps toward providing the endowment that he was told the institution needed. In paragraph 18 of the will that he had signed on August 1, 1925, he had made a bequest of $2 million for endowment, and on April 28, 1927, he fulfilled that bequest in advance by giving $2 million in bonds to the trustees.[70] To fulfill the commitment to provide an annual income of $400,000 for the research program, he transferred land to the Huntington Land and Improvement Company—land that they would sell—in return for 5 percent bonds to the trustees. The total annual income from endowment was thus calculated to be $600,000, of which $400,000 was for the research program and $200,000 for "cataloging and upkeep of property."[71] Some other institutions were experiencing financial difficulties at this time. It was widely publicized in January 1926 that the Metropolitan Museum of Art in New York had had a deficit in 1925 of $432,900, with income of some $600,000 but with administrative costs of over $1 million.[72] But this fact apparently did not disturb Huntington. Neither did he take any steps at this time toward meeting Farrand's suggestion that an additional $10 million in endowment would be needed to insure that the institution would be an active force in the distant future.

For many years Edward had looked forward to opening his institution to the public. When Belle was alive, she bitterly opposed having outsiders in the house or in the library (see chap. 17). He had several ideas for allowing the public to see his things. As early as 1922 he told the mayor of Los Angeles, "It is my intention to add a gallery to my Library for the exhibition of pictures." He told the same thing to the California Art Club. After Belle's death, he considered building a smaller house for himself and opening the residence to the public.[73]

Gradually, more groups were allowed to visit. In 1924, the American literature class at the Alhambra School came to see a special exhibit and hear talks by staff members. The Los Angeles Library School came once a year with forty or fifty students for talks and to visit the stacks, and four hundred members of the California Library Association came in connection with their meetings. Every year several groups of Caltech students were shown around. The Shakespeare Club of Pasadena used the grounds to present "A Century of Fashion" before more than fifteen hundred persons. Still, Edward did not want any publicity, and he resolutely declined to allow feature writers, magazines, and newspapers to have special access to the institution.[74]

At last the time came when the institution was opened to the general public. By action of the trustees, and to Edward's special delight, the first day was Friday, March 18, 1925, with hours from 2:00 to 5:00 P.M. Two hundred tickets of admission were available, and people had to apply in advance to the librarian. A special display of choice rare books and manuscripts was prepared in the library. The books included the unique copy of the first set of American laws (1648) and the first Bible printed in colonial America (1663). The manuscripts included letters of Columbus, Washington, and Franklin. Those who had gotten tickets came and stayed until closing time. The librarian watched Huntington's reaction: "'He stood out on the lawn and watched the people attending the exhibit,' Mr. Bliss reported. 'He seemed very pleased.'"[75]

The newspapers published enthusiastic stories. The banner headline on the front page of the *Los Angeles Examiner,* for example, proclaimed: "Huntington Library Is Opened Without Ceremonies. 200 Inspect

Massive Gift on First Day. Priceless Documents Arranged in Cases About Great Hall. Donor Pleased at Interest." The report quoted Huntington: "My purpose in creating this foundation," he said, "was to make it for the benefit of the world." He went on to say that "it is for all people who may find use for it," and he was happy that "many students, writers and authorities on historical and literary matters" were already using it.[76] Every Friday afternoon the library was open to the two hundred people who had made reservations. It was a small beginning, but a real start for the Huntington Library and Art Gallery as a public institution.

The Mausoleum was another act of loving remembrance by Edward for Belle. In his ledgers it was always recorded as "Memorial Temple (Arabella D. Huntington)," and he normally referred to it as "the Temple" or "the Greek temple."[77] We recall that it was Belle who chose the spot where they should be buried, on a hillock a little north of the residence (see chap. 17). We should also remember that in 1894 she had built a mausoleum for Collis six years before his death at Woodland Cemetery in Westchester County, New York, at a cost of one-quarter million dollars; with its sixteen crypts, it was ample in size to accommodate Belle and Edward and others as well, but she chose to be laid to rest in California, with Edward.

The casket containing Belle's remains was temporarily interred in the general area she had chosen. Edward had been thinking about a suitable structure to erect on the exact site. He told his daughter Elizabeth that he wanted the building to resemble a Greek temple. He asked his secretary, George Hapgood, and curator Robert Schad to look for pictures of classical temples, and they brought him reproductions of the Temple of Love at Versailles, the Temple of the Sybil, and the Temple of Vesta at Tivoli. Hertrich had a draftsman prepare a rough sketch for a temple based on the Villa Borghese in Rome.[78] On the day after Belle's interment, Edward wrote to Rosenbach and told him that he was planning to build a small marble structure in the shape of a temple, about twenty-five feet in diameter, "above the spot where we have laid Mrs. Huntington to rest, and where in time I expect to be." He asked Rosenbach to see if he could find some books with pictures of such temples, either modern or of classical antiquity: "Knowing your versatility, I think you are able to do this for me better than any one else I know." Rosenbach went to several libraries in search of designs. He could not find any modern examples and Edward sent him a telegram saying that "what I want are sketches and books of old Greek temples not modern architectural books which I can get here." Rosenbach then sent him a three-volume book on Greece with slips at pages illustrating temples, and he brought reproductions and photostats of Greek and Roman temples when he made his next trip to California.[79]

Edward then consulted Duveen about an architect for the project. Duveen suggested John Russell Pope. When Edward showed interest in him and his work, Duveen responded from Paris with a cable phrased in his usual language of hyperbole: "Delighted you interested and again repeat he is greatest architect modern times and the only man for you."[80] In August 1925 Edward wrote to Pope about the project: "I have in mind to erect a mausoleum in the form of a Greek temple, and I am writing you in this preliminary way, as my idea is very indefinite. Of one thing only, am I sure—that is, that the structure must be earthquake proof. My plan is that it should be round, and of about twenty five feet in diameter. If you have any photographs of work you have done in this line, I should appreciate it very much if I might see them." Although Pope had done no similar work, the project appealed to him and he was glad to undertake it. He worked on it during the autumn and winter of 1925, and he and Edward corresponded frequently. Pope came to feel that "the entire monument" should "avoid as much architectural ornament as possible, relying instead on a purity of architectural proportion and for interest and expression of purpose on sculptural relief." Edward responded that "I quite agree with you" about relying on purity of proportion and sculpture. Pope was ready to start on working drawings in January 1926, but first he made a model in plaster of paris and shipped it to Edward in San Marino. It arrived in March, and Edward immediately sent Pope a telegram that he was "perfectly delighted" and wrote him a letter the next day that it was "a great work of art, and I have never seen anything in modern architecture which appeals to me more than this does. It is a great classic and just the type I dreamed of." Two days later Edward wrote to Carrie in

Paris about the arrival of the model and said, "Mr. Pope has accomplished wonders and it is just what I had in mind." Edward suggested to Pope that he consider Anna Hyatt, "who is now Mrs. Archer Huntington," as the sculptor for the low reliefs on the four panels: "Have you seen her Joan d'Arc in the French chapel of the Cathedral of St. John the Divine? If not I do wish you could see it. This is only a suggestion. I want to be frank with you, and you with me, as well, and what you care to write me is confidential, as mine is to you."[81]

Pope had also thought of Anna Hyatt as the sculptor, and he approached her. She demurred on the grounds that she had never done that kind of work and doubted her fitness for it. Edward also heard directly from Archer and Anna, who appreciated his wish but she felt that she should not undertake a form of sculpture in which she had had no experience. Edward wrote to Pope, "I can see how she feels about it especially in view of the affection she had for my wife, but I would not want to urge her to try something out of her sphere simply for sentimental reasons."[82]

After considering several other sculptors, Pope recommended John Gregory—because of the "poetic character" of his work—and Gregory accepted the commission. A general contractor, William C. Crowell, was chosen and work got under way in the winter of 1926–27. Edward visited the site and observed the progress. After the sarcophagus was in place, he pushed up against it with his cane and said to the contractor, "I guess that will hold me all right." He had some of his favorite trees planted—lemon eucalyptus around the site and evergreen elms and bay trees nearby.[83]

By the end of March 1927 the reinforced concrete work had been finished, and the marble was going up. Edward was thinking about the inscriptions for the tomb, and on April 8 he wrote to Archer, "I shall have to know, before long, the exact date of your mother's birth, and I have no record of it. Can you supply this?" (Surprisingly, even Edward did not know the year of Belle's birth.) He went on to say that "the more I see of this site, the more I am impressed with its beauty, and it proves again the good judgment your mother had in everything,—in picking out this lovely spot."[84]

The Mausoleum was not completed until 1929. The feeling of unity of style—and the complementary nature of the sculpture and the architecture—were especially pleasing to Pope.[85] He went on later to use this mausoleum as the prototype for his design of the Jefferson Memorial in Washington.

By early spring 1927, almost a year and a half had passed since Edward's prostate operation in Philadelphia. The wound never healed properly, and the cauterizing procedure did not have a permanent effect. Edward remained cheerful, however. He read a book every day, visited with Mary and Ed Lewis in the mornings, afternoons, and evenings, and welcomed his three daughters for a visit in February.[86]

By the end of March, however, Edward was not feeling well. Dr. Bryant was unhappy about the condition of his postsurgical damage, and on April 20 he sent a telegram to Dr. Deaver asking him to "come out here and fix it." Dr. Deaver preferred to have Edward come to Philadelphia because of the better facilities there, and Edward agreed to go.[87] He wrote optimistically to several friends about the forthcoming trip. He assured Duveen that "I am feeling well, for my general health is good, but as long as the wound has not wholly healed, it seems best to go on now and have it looked at." He told Rosenbach that he hoped to see him when he was there, that he wanted "to find out why the wound does not heal satisfactorily" even though "I am feeling very well." He assured E. A. Adams that he was feeling well but wanted to go now and find out about the wound before "the approaching hot season in the East" arrives. The president of the Southern Pacific personally saw to all the arrangements for the transport of his private car and sent a cordial telegram "to express the hope and expectation that you will have a comfortable trip and that you will return in due course in the happiness of renewed health and spirits."[88] Edward was accompanied on the trip by Dr. Bryant, Alfonso, and a nurse.

Alfonso reported that Huntington "was so well when he went in the private car to Philadelphia—he was singing and humming and happy-go-lucky. I never saw Mr. H. as happy." He was up at 7:30 every morning, and while dressing he sang such favorite songs as "My Old Kentucky Home" and "Carry Me Back to Old Virginny." He had three hearty meals a day, drank much lemonade, and ate cookies between meals.[89]

In Philadelphia he was taken directly to Lankenau Hospital on

May 4. Dr. Bryant thought he was "very cheerful and pleasant and did not worry or have any anxiety about his illness. He thought he was going to recover." He sat up and played hearts with Dr. Bryant. On the day of his arrival, a friend (presumably Rosenbach) sent him a book, *Abraham Lincoln in Peoria, Illinois* (1926), by B. C. Bryner. Edward enjoyed this account of the Lincoln-Douglas debate in Peoria in 1854, by a man who had attended it as a young boy. It was to be the last book that Edward read, though the last book he looked at before the operation was the *Short-Title Catalogue* of English books of the period 1475 to 1640—an area in which his own collection was preeminent.[90]

On May 4, he sent a letter to Mrs. Pickett in Washington to thank her for writing him. "I am to be operated on tomorrow, but there is very little danger of its not being successful," he said. "I do not know how long I will be in the hospital but probably not more than two or three weeks." He offered to stop to see her on his way home.[91]

Dr. Deaver performed the operation, and it was regarded as successful. It was painful, however. Edward told Burke that "he had suffered more than ever before in his life," and the aftermath was "very painful." For a short time he was considered to be in a critical condition, but then he rallied and began to gain strength. Carrie and Burke had arrived in Philadelphia on May 7 to be with him, Elizabeth came from Northern California to join them, and Marian got there on May 19. Rosenbach and Duveen called on him nearly every day, and they went over catalogs together. Homer Ferguson also visited him to discuss the shipbuilding company, and Edward planned to go to Newport News on his way home to California.[92]

Edward suffered occasional periods of delirium during which he attempted to rise and leave the hospital. Several specialists examined him and tried to reassure his relatives that they should not feel anxious if he did not recognize them. About ten days after the operation he became progressively weaker. Presumably the cancer had spread through his body. Rosenbach wrote to Bliss on May 17:

> For your private information, Mr. Huntington is really in a serious state. He does not respond to treatment and his temperature is around 101, showing some disturbed condition. He seems flighty at

times, which is also caused either by the wound not healing or some kidney condition. His heart and pulse seem strong and perhaps his enormous vitality will pull him through. He has two nurses who are looking after him most faithfully, and Dr. Bryant is, of course, with him all the time. Dr. Deaver, who performed the operation, is also making every effort for him, but it is his own vigorous constitution that must tell the tale.

On May 19 and 20 he could barely open his eyes, and he only dimly recognized Carrie. The entry for Saturday, May 21, in Burke Holladay's diary concluded: "Today Lindberg made his great non-stop flight New York to Paris, in 33 hours." The complete entry for the next day was: "Edwards is steadily sinking, has been unconscious now about two days. Dr. Deaver virtually told Carrie and me that there is no hope now."[93]

He died on the following day at 7:10, on the morning of May 23, 1927. At his bedside were Carrie and Burke, Elizabeth, Marian, and Dr. Bryant. According to a special report from Philadelphia to the *Pasadena Star News*, "His last known words were a call for his wife, who died several years ago, and whose memory was the closest thing to his heart. The end came peacefully with all of the relatives who were here in the hospital room. Mr. Huntington breathed a sigh, smiled faintly and closed his eyes." On the return for the federal estate tax, the cause of death was given as "bronchial pneumonia following operation."[94]

The report of his death was telegraphed by the news services to Los Angeles, and on the afternoon of the day of his death all flags were flown at half mast on all the buildings of the city and county of Los Angeles, and of the city of Pasadena.[95]

Edward's private car, with all the relatives who had been with him in the hospital, left Philadelphia on the morning of May 24, bearing his remains in a bronze casket. On arrival on May 28 at the station nearest San Marino, the car was switched to the street railway tracks and brought to the house by a Pacific Electric engine draped with black and bearing flags. The car was met in San Marino by the local troop of Boy Scouts, and by the staff of the library and of the botanical gardens. As the casket—piled high with roses, violets, lilies, and carnations—was transferred from the railroad car to a hearse, the Boy Scouts stood at attention while their bugler sounded taps and the engine bell tolled. The casket was carried into the library room of the residence, and the next day many friends called to pay their respects. Hundreds of people sent flowers and letters of sympathy.[96]

The funeral service took place in the library room at 11 A.M. on May 31, with about 150 relatives, close friends, and staff members present. At the same time, service on all the street railways in Los Angeles was temporarily suspended. Belle's portrait was placed near the casket. There was no music and no ritual; the minister, Reverend Robert E. Freeman of the Pasadena Presbyterian Church, read passages from Psalms 23, 90, and 123 and from Ecclesiastes and delivered a short eulogy on Edward's accomplishments. The active pallbearers, seven of the longest-tenured employees at the ranch, then carried the casket to a car, which drove to the grave site. There, in the presence of Edward's children and grandchildren, trustees, and household servants, the pallbearers lowered the casket into the temporary grave next to Belle's casket, and the two were covered with flowers. Mr. Freeman read a short passage from *The Pilgrim's Progress* and offered one final, brief prayer.[97]

In the last years of Edward's life, his net worth had moved gradually downward. It stood at about $70 million in the years just before 1920. The gift of his books, art, and real estate to the Huntington Library and Art Gallery toward the end of 1921 reduced his net worth to about $50 million, and from there it went down year by year as he bought and gave books and art to the institution. By the end of 1924, it was $40 million, and when he died it was about $32 million. These figures, prepared by Edward's careful bookkeepers and verified by his accountants, are doubtless a little low. When the executors made their official report of the value of his estate to the superior court of California, the grand total was $42.5 million, but with debts and expenses of $4.5 million for a net of $38 million.[98] The media are attracted by larger and rounder numbers. After his death, his worth was widely reported as $100 million, even after he had set up the Library and Art Gallery with gifts stated at $75 million.[99]

Edward himself thought that he might have very little money left when he died. Privately he communicated this fear to various friends. To one who was teasing him about his wealth shortly before he made his last trip to Philadelphia, he said, "The fact is I have very little left." He told both his sister Carrie and the head of one of his companies that "I shall die a poor man."[100]

His primary concern was to provide funds for his children. His will, signed on August 1, 1925, set up a $1 million trust fund for each of his three daughters and smaller trusts totaling about $1 million for Howard's children. Beyond those, $1 million went to his sister Carrie, $260,000 to sixteen other relatives, $95,000 to four friends, and $15,000 to two nonprofit organizations. He also left $2 million for a hospital in memory of Collis and Howard, $2 million as endowment for the Library and Art Gallery, $2 million to establish the Arabella Huntington Memorial should he not complete it, and $250,000 to construct the Mausoleum should he not cover those expenses. Finally, he provided that the residue of his estate—all that was left after fulfilling the specific bequests and trusts—should be divided into four parts: one part for each of his three living children and one part for Howard's children.

On December 25, 1925, he signed a codicil to his will in which he added a trust of $10,000 for his friend Mrs. Pickett, four bequests totaling $27,500 to nonprofit organizations, bequests of $1,000 to household servants, and some other minor changes. On April 25, 1927, he added a second codicil canceling the $2 million bequest for endowment of the Library and Art Gallery, the $2 million for the Arabella Huntington Memorial, and the $250,000 for the Mausoleum on the grounds that he had already made provision for these specific financial needs—as indeed he had done.[101]

He succeeded in satisfying his primary concern. The four children—including the three daughters and Howard's children—got about 85 percent of his estate, with the memorial hospital, other relatives, and friends receiving the other 15 percent. If we assume an estate of $38 million, that would mean about $8 million for the benefit of each child. But it took a long time for them to get anything. Four years after Edward's death, less than a quarter of his estate had been distributed.[102]

The question may be raised as to why he did not leave—as Farrand had asked and he had tentatively agreed—an additional $10 million for the endowment of the Library and Art Gallery so that they would be "the influential institution that he dreamed of." First, we must remember his overriding concern for his immediate family, his wish to provide for their welfare, and perhaps a touch of compensation for not having given them as much of himself during his lifetime as they may have wanted. And there was the model of Collis's will, in which the great majority of his estate was given to close family members and a relatively small amount to philanthropic institutions and friends.[103]

Moreover, Edward doubtless felt that he had already provided handsomely for his institution. His private financial secretary, C. E. Culver, testified that "when Mr. Huntington died he had given away, to Henry E. Huntington Library and Art Gallery, approximately one half of his fortune" in the total value of the books, manuscripts, art, buildings, real estate, and endowment. His attorney, James A. Gibson, reported that Huntington had during his lifetime given securities for endowment to the total value of $8.9 million and that since he had "picked the cream of his securities for this purpose, the market value is undoubtedly more." In addition, the trustees were free to sell three hundred acres of their land and add the funds received to the endowment.[104] Still, these benefactions for endowment did little more than cover his promise of an annual income of $400,000 for the research program and $200,000 for the other operating expenses.

He presumably felt that with good management the trustees could keep the institution active and influential. Edward had earlier thought that the net income from the sale of oranges and avocados from the ranch and its adjacent properties would supply much of the funding needed for the institution; during the period 1918 to 1920, the ranch did in fact show a net profit each year of nearly $100,000.[105] But this income was highly variable, and of course it declined as land was sold. Still, Edward seemed to think that the endowment he had provided would guarantee the future of the institution. He was accustomed to thinking in terms of low operating costs, such as thirty cents an hour as a good wage for workers on the grounds. Shortly before his last trip to Philadelphia, he told Otheman Stevens that the endowment of about

$8 million "was enough not only to maintain the Foundation, but to provide for what accessions of books and pictures the trustees may find advisable and to erect such additions to the library building as may be demanded."[106] This was an extremely optimistic view.

We have watched Edward's development through the whole course of his life. Let me offer, in summary review, a few reflections about the characteristics that seem to have been dominant in his life.

Some features remained constant throughout his life. One that we tend to think of as a rather routine virtue, but which was near the top for him, was his drive to work hard. Throughout his life, he devoted himself wholeheartedly to the task that lay before him, whether working in a hardware store, running a sawmill, laying railroad lines, managing properties, operating a small railroad, providing the essential management to guide the largest corporation in California through its most difficult times, developing Southern California through the creation and merger of street railways and improvement in the use of land, or building library and art collections and botanical gardens and creating an institution out of them for the benefit of the public.

His drive to work hard was always governed by a worthwhile goal that he wanted to achieve. The goal was always clear to him, and he was generally able to achieve it. When he was not able to achieve it—as in his desire to be made president of the Southern Pacific Company—he shifted to an alternate goal, which turned out to be a very much better one, and devoted himself to achieving it.

His two most significant accomplishments were both achieved by constant and intelligent drive. The lesser of the two was his significant contribution to the development and shaping of Southern California in its economic and sociological dimensions during the period 1900 to 1915. The greater of the two was collecting what can be considered the most important private library of its time on the broad theme of Anglo-American culture, acquiring a great collection of British art, building a set of botanical gardens, and creating out of all of them a research institution for the benefit of human knowledge and culture.

A commitment to hard work often has limiting corollaries. For Edward, focusing on work left him relatively little time to spend with his wife and children, to develop deep friendships, and to play. His children regretted his lack of time with them; and even when they were together, he was unable to be demonstrative in showing his deep affection. His closest friends were always business colleagues with whom he worked constantly. The nearest things to pure play for him were the evening card games, walks around the grounds, and his endless reading of books. But there was a leavening of play in most of his ordinary daily activities, with his preference for fun and merriment in dealing with his helpers and his daily tasks.

Another constant feature was his modesty and unassuming nature. He never put himself forward. He avoided giving speeches and often arranged for a friend or colleague to speak for him. He generally declined requests for special visits or information for those who wanted to write newspaper or magazine stories about him or his projects, and he allowed himself to be interviewed only if the writer was a friend or if he could not avoid it. But he was not antisocial or a lover of privacy: he enjoyed human contact, he liked to mix with his friends on social occasions or at his clubs, and he enjoyed talking informally with individual staff members or employees.

Such modesty usually results in a lack of public recognition. But that was not true in his case. The enormous amount of attention and acclaim he received would today seem like the splendid result of a massive public relations staff, or the natural right of a sports or entertainment star. On the other hand, this modesty did limit the amount of public support he could attract to the good causes he favored. If he had been a more aggressive and yet nonpolitical person, one can imagine the improvements he might have sponsored to benefit the cultural life of, for example, the people of Southern California, following the model of the intrinsic qualities of his institution: to bring, for instance, small, beautiful gardens and modest examples of good art and choice books to communities throughout the area and to magnify knowledge of and esteem for such matters.

Another obviously important characteristic was the clarity and alertness of Edward's intellect. He was always quick to grasp the essential meanings of what he read or was told, and he readily understood the implications of those meanings. His academic education was limited to what he got at the local public school in Oneonta before the age of seventeen. His later reading, though extensive, was not planned or organized with an objective in mind and did not lead him to deep knowledge. (It is surprising, perhaps, that he was a specialist in his professional activities and in his collecting, but not in his reading.) Academic people would probably think of him as relatively uneducated. His mind was not "disciplined," and he was not adept at "rigorous" thinking or dealing with abstractions. He displayed very little inventiveness or imaginative power and did not ask unusual questions or play with new solutions to problems. These limitations may have worked to his advantage in the context of his times and circumstances, as they may have led him to feeling quite comfortable in retaining a single-minded commitment to the job that he had chosen to follow through on until he had brought it to completion.

A social man, he was always open to and interested in people. But his interest was always in individuals. Unlike a politician, he was not attracted to large masses of people; and unlike a reformer, he was not drawn to groups burdened by injustice. His emotional interest went out to individuals with human problems, and his reaction tended to be sentimental. When his heart was touched, he responded with an expression of feelings, like simple words or acts of sympathy or tears.

His special talents and abilities probably did not exceed those of a large number of the people of his time. But he used his talents and abilities with great effectiveness, and at a time and under circumstances that were favorable to the style of his efforts. As a result, he achieved a great deal. He was essentially a builder—of railways, of trolley lines, of towns, and of a research institution. This was his form of creation.

After Edward died, many people wrote evaluations of his accomplishments and of him as a human being. Some of these estimates were extravagant in their phrasing. But many of them give us a considered view of how he was seen by his contemporaries. A brief review of a few thoughtful appraisals can perhaps give us a better understanding of how he was perceived in his own time, at the end of his life.

The world stands ready to praise famous men. Edward had his share of the world's attention during the last thirty-five years of his life. In San Francisco in the 1890s, he was recognized as a person of authority because of his management role in the most influential industrial corporation in California, the Southern Pacific Company. Soon after the turn of the century, he received the attention given to very wealthy men, thanks to Collis's bequest added to his own accumulation of capital. In the first decade of the twentieth century, he came to be considered the one person most responsible for the meteoric growth of Southern California. During the next decade, he came to be thought of as the greatest American book collector and one of the most important art collectors. After his establishment of the Huntington Library and Art Gallery in 1919, he was considered a great philanthropist who was freely giving the rich resources of art and learning to the people of the United States.

The world also stands ready to forget men who have been famous. At the end of Edward's life, earlier forms of recognition were readjusted. His management role with the railroads was no longer mentioned, and he was no longer credited with prime responsibility for the development of Southern California. These evaluations, though probably not forgotten, were subsumed into other perceptions of him.

Three general views of Huntington were prominent in the appraisals of him at or shortly after the time of his death. One had to do with the estimates of him as a collector and of the collections. A second was an evaluation of the purposes he had in mind in the use of his resources. A third was an appraisal of him as a human being—what he was like, what his deep drives were, and how he interacted with other people.

At the time of his death, Edward was widely regarded as the preeminent American book collector. In an essay in the *Atlantic Monthly* for October 1927, Rosenbach proclaimed, in a statement frequently repeated, that

> Mr. Henry E. Huntington was without doubt the greatest collector of books the world has ever known. Without possessing a profound knowledge of literature or of history, his flair for fine books was remarkable. His taste was sure, impeccable. The library at San Gabriel, California, which houses his wonderful collections, will be the Mecca of students for all time. No gift to a nation or to a state can ever equal his. America does not appreciate it to-day, but, as time spins its web and the world becomes better acquainted with the Huntington treasures, this fact will be adequately recognized.[107]

A long *New York Times* story after his death concurred that "Henry E. Huntington, who died last Monday, left behind him . . . the greatest private library ever assembled in the history of the world, and one that, in respect of items of the very first importance, is a match for many famous public collections." The *New York Herald Tribune* described him as "the donor to the public of a library and art gallery which many judicious authorities regarded as the finest private collection in the world." This view was shared by people with less impressive platforms. L. Kashnor, the proprietor of the Museum Book Store in London, sent condolences to Bliss after Huntington's death: "To speak of his qualities and other attributes is as impertinent now as when he was alive, but he was a great man in more ways than one. To bookmen he was the one great man who came in and overshadowed all other great bookmen. I wonder whether there will ever be another like him; it seems doubtful." Edward was also highly praised as a collector of art. Duveen said, "In my opinion you have the greatest eye for an English picture I have ever known in anyone." He was valued by many as a collector of both art and books. An editorial in the *Brooklyn Eagle* asserted that "Henry Edwards Huntington will be remembered as a connoisseur and collector of books and art objects."[108]

What did the public think about Huntington's use of his resources? The general view can be typified by the "Symbol of Good Citizenship" award he was given by the Los Angeles Chamber of Commerce two months before he died. Later, Arthur Brisbane devoted a syndicated column to Huntington under the title "A Good Man Dead." He said, "The nation, and the rest of the world, have cause to regret the death of H. E. Huntington yesterday. This son of California was a good American. He spent his fortune intelligently for the finest books and works of art. And he gave his collection and the magnificent estate which contains them to the people of California. No sane man grudges or envies a gigantic fortune to such a man as Huntington, who knew how to use money. The country honors him." B. C. Forbes in his syndicated column presented Huntington as a model American because he "proved, by hard, industrious work that he was made of the right stuff" and then went on to use his accomplishments to benefit the public. Forbes saw in the death of Huntington the end of "the era of individual achievement. We are now in the era of corporate achievement." The *Wall Street*

Journal devoted half a column to Huntington, praising his hard work and philanthropy. Because he was "among the world's great givers, . . . [he] will have lasting renown." The *Literary Digest* presented Huntington as an American Maecenas and praised him because he devoted his fortune "to public uses." The *Los Angeles Times* honored him for his leading role in "the cultural development of Southern California," while the *San Francisco Chronicle* praised him as "one of the most important contributors to the perpetuation of culture in the history of the United States." The *Los Angeles Mercury* valued his institution as "a perpetual source of learning, of beauty, of the best sustenance, of the most invigorating stimulus to the brain of mankind" and honored Huntington for "putting into the most material form, his love of his fellow man." Finally, an editorial in the *San Marino Tribune* expressed the wish that all schoolchildren should learn about Huntington as "a conspicuous example of achievement under American free enterprise, a citizen who arose to his high station through his own abilities and initiative," and who then gave all to the betterment of those of us who would come after him.[109]

How was he thought of as a human being? People most frequently perceived the simplicity and modesty of his manner. It was observed that on his birthday in 1927 the only guests for dinner were his cousins Mary and Ed Lewis, "for Mr. Huntington, quiet, unassuming and disliking ostentation, has no desire to do else but enjoy the society of intimate friends or relatives." When it was learned, after his death, that the hospital he was giving was a memorial to his uncle and his son, the immediate reflection was, "Here again is exposed the modesty, the total lack of egotism of the founder. But it is for the soul of Henry E. Huntington that the prayers of those healed at this institution of mercy will be uttered. He will be greater because he desired and consented to be less." His burial was similarly quiet: "With the simplicity that was his lifelong trait, Henry Edwards Huntington was yesterday laid to rest beside his wife, Mrs. Arabella Huntington."[110]

He was perceived as having "a remarkable sweetness of thought, and a most profound quality of affection." W. A. R. Goodwin, the president of William and Mary College, had once thanked him for being so open, for letting Goodwin have "an understanding of your deeper sympathies and deepest affections. You have not let the successes which have come to you spoil you, as they spoil so many successful men. You have not walled yourself about with barriers which shut out the human approach. We all felt this very strongly when you were here at the College." George Ellery Hale spoke of the openness with which Edward was willing to express his feelings: "His affection for his books and manuscripts was so intense that I have often seen tears come into his eyes as he talked of them or read aloud some favorite passage."[111]

How did people respond to him? Max Farrand felt that "his qualities even in brief association inspired personal affection." Leslie Bliss lamented that "the personal influence has left us with his departure, leaving a gap which cannot be filled." The minutes of his companies about "the death of our President and friend, Mr. Henry Edwards Huntington," record that "to all of us who have been intimately associated with Mr. Huntington, he was more than a leader, he was a friend, an adviser, and always a considerate and lovable associate." Even those who did not know him well were drawn to him. Theodore Irwin, whom he had known in Kentucky, wrote a friend, "I have just arrived here from California where I went from Arizona to stand beside the grave of my friend Henry E. Huntington, with deep sorrow. Next to my own father, I never admired any man more than Mr. Huntington." Alfonso Gomez's feelings toward Huntington are proof against the notion that no man is a hero to his valet: Gomez admired Huntington intensely, and in his will left $50 to buy a wreath of red roses to be placed on the tomb of Mr. and Mrs. Huntington.[112]

Public perceptions of Huntington can be summed up from the views expressed about him right after his death. The story in the *Los Angeles Examiner* appeared under the headline "Mankind Loses Friend" and asserted that "there will be a heavy sense of personal loss in the community over the death of Henry E. Huntington"; it predicted that "he will be treasured in the hearts of men for his good works." The *Los Angeles Times* claimed "it would be difficult to imagine a more satisfactory life than that lived by H. E. Huntington." He "represented the highest type of American—vision, financial genius and high idealism. And withal great kindness." Finally, on the day of his funeral service and burial, the *Los Angeles Examiner* concluded, "It was a fitting end to a life that had accomplished all its aims: first that of accumulating the means, then of wisely directing those means to a gift to all humanity that must fructify during the centuries to come into results that will forward the highest hopes of mankind."[113]

All of these views reflect a remarkably consistent perception of Huntington. They feature a person of vision and idealism, of practical accomplishment, of kindness and affection, and of concern for humanity. Doubtless such a person could be totally realized only in myth. But it was in this direction that the actual life of Huntington moved.

NOTES

I. GROWING UP IN ONEONTA

1. Details of the ancestors are in *The Huntington Family in America* (Hartford, Conn.: Huntington Family Association, 1915).

2. The conversation preceding the operation is given in "Statement of M. S. Wade," HEH MS 19/1(9).

3. Curtiss, Candu and Stiles to Dr. Saunders, November 6, 1838, HEH Correspondence, box 1; Solon to Harriet, April 25, 1840, HEH Correspondence, box 1.

4. HEH Correspondence, box 1.

5. *Oneonta Star,* June 28, 1906.

6. October 29, 1857, HEH Correspondence, box 1.

7. Willard V. Huntington, *Oneonta Memories and Sundry Personal Recollections of the Author* (San Francisco: The Bancroft Company, 1891), 36–37.

8. Henry Saunders to Harriet, August 25, 1855, HEH Correspondence, box 3; Collis P. Huntington to Solon, September 19, 1855, HEH Correspondence, box 3.

9. Ellen M. Huntington, January 18, 1852, HEH Correspondence, box 2.

10. I have also taken a few general details about Oneonta in the 1850s from the memories of Mrs. Caroline Watkins Strong (who was born there in 1834), as recorded in the *Oneonta Herald* for September 25, 1924, HEH MS 9/10(39).

11. HEH Correspondence, box 4.

12. HEH MS 20/. The following inscription by his sister Carrie appears on

the top of the book: "Child's Book of Mr. H. E. H. Used by him when a child."

13. December 25, 1856, HEH Correspondence, box 3.
14. HEH Correspondence, box 5.
15. HEH Correspondence, box 5.
16. Henry Saunders to Harriet, August 6, 1864, HEH Correspondence, box 5.
17. Henry Saunders to his wife, April 24, 1862, HEH Correspondence, box 4.
18. Huntington, *Oneonta Memories,* 48.
19. HEH Correspondence, box 4.
20. April 24, 1862, HEH Correspondence, box 4.
21. Huntington, *Oneonta Memories,* 47, 83.
22. Sample bills dated September 25, 1857, HEH Correspondence, box 4.
23. The accounts in the preceding paragraphs are drawn from Huntington, *Oneonta Memories,* 89–90, 91–92, 110–11, 111–13.
24. Otheman Stevens, "Memories of H. E. Huntington," Huntington Biographical File, HEH 19/3.
25. Huntington, *Oneonta Memories,* 72–74.
26. HEH Correspondence, box 1.
27. HEH Correspondence, box 1.
28. A summary account of the trip and Collis's early years in California is contained in David Lavender, *The Great Persuader* (New York: Doubleday, 1970), 6–47.
29. HEH Correspondence, box 2.
30. January 1, 1853, HEH Correspondence, box 3.
31. Undated receipt, HEH Correspondence, box 3.
32. There is a rich store of letters from Collis to Solon for this period in HEH Correspondence, boxes 3, 4, and 5. Letters of the following dates are of special interest: June 28, 1851; March 28, 1852; February 14, May 31, and September 14, 1853; July 30 and October 15, 1854; July 31 and September 19, 1855; and January 3, August 19, and December 30, 1856. Lavender gives a full account of this period, *Great Persuader,* 33–281.
33. The letters from Collis to Solon in the preceding passage are all in HEH Correspondence, boxes 2 and 3.
34. Jacob Dietz, Joseph Hudson, and Egbert Sabin were the purchasers, for a total of $2,025. January 3, 1853, HEH Correspondence, box 3.
35. May 29, 1862, HEH Correspondence, box 4.
36. *Los Angeles Times,* February 23, 1912, HEH MS 7/4(27).
37. July 24, 1870, HEH Correspondence, box 6.

38. March 3, 1924, HEH MS 42/5.
39. January 31, 1924, HEH MS 42/5.

2. TOWARD INDEPENDENCE

1. Sunday, October 10, 1869, HEH Correspondence, box 6.
2. The quotations in the preceding three paragraphs are all from the letter of February 17, 1870, HEH Correspondence, box 6.
3. HEH to Harriet, February 24, 1870, HEH Correspondence, box 6.
4. February 3, 1870, HEH Correspondence, box 6.
5. Recollections of George W. Safford, to whom HEH told the story, HEH Biographical File, HEH MS 19/3.
6. The quotations in the preceding five paragraphs are all drawn from a long letter to Harriet, May 16, 1870, HEH Correspondence, box 6.
7. HEH to Harriet, July 24, 1870, HEH Correspondence, box 6.
8. HEH to Harriet, July 31, 1870, HEH Correspondence, box 6.
9. June 13, 1870, HEH Correspondence, box 6.
10. HEH Correspondence, box 6.
11. June 13, 1870, HEH Correspondence, box 6.
12. HEH to Harriet, July 5, 1870, HEH Correspondence, box 6.
13. July 5, 1870, HEH Correspondence, box 6.
14. August 10, 1870, HEH Correspondence, box 6.
15. July 1870, HEH Correspondence, box 6.
16. HEH to Harriet, October 5, 1870, HEH Correspondence, box 6.
17. HEH to Harriet, July 5, 24, 1870, HEH Correspondence, box 6.
18. HEH to Harriet, August 15, July 5, 1870, HEH Correspondence, box 6.
19. July 18, 1870, HEH Correspondence, box 6.
20. HEH to Harriet, July 31, August 10, 1870, HEH Correspondence, box 6; *Oneonta Herald,* August 17, 1870.
21. I. E. Gates to Rhoda Dunbar, March 3, 1871, HEH Correspondence, box 6; Ellen Gates to Rhoda, March 1871, HEH Correspondence, box 6.
22. I. E. Gates to Solon, September 6, 1870, CPH Papers, ser. 2, reel 1; I. E. Gates to Dr. Fitch, September 6, 1870, CPH Papers, ser. 2, reel 1.
23. July 1870, HEH Correspondence, box 6.
24. HEH to Harriet, June 13, July 5, 31, August 15, 1870, HEH Correspondence, box 6.
25. July 24, 1870, HEH Correspondence, box 6.
26. HEH to Harriet, April 13, 17, 1871, HEH Correspondence, box 6.
27. HEH to Harriet and Solon, May 20, 28, 1871, HEH Correspondence, box 6.

28. CPH to HEH, CPH Papers, ser. 2, reel 9.
29. Leonora to Caroline, August 20, 1871, HEH Correspondence, box 6; CPH Papers, ser. 2, reel 9.
30. The quotations and references in the three preceding paragraphs are from two letters from Edward to his parents, May 20 and 28, 1871, HEH Correspondence, box 6.
31. September 18, 1871, HEH Correspondence, box 7.
32. HEH to Harriet, September 26, 1871, HEH Correspondence, box 7.
33. HEH to Harriet, September 4, August 22, September 12, 26, October 30, 1871, January 31, 1872, HEH Correspondence, box 7.
34. On joining the church, HEH to Harriet, May 20, 28, September 12, 1871, HEH Correspondence, boxes 6, 7. On his religious feelings, HEH to Harriet, August 22, September 12, October 30, 1871, January 5, 1872, HEH Correspondence, boxes 6, 7.
35. HEH to Harriet, July 16, 1871, HEH Correspondence, box 6.
36. HEH to Harriet, January 31, February 5, 1872, HEH Correspondence, box 7.
37. HEH Correspondence, box 7.
38. CPH to HEH, May 18, 1871, CPH Papers, ser. 2, reel 9.
39. HEH Correspondence, box 7.
40. HEH Correspondence, box 7.
41. CPH to HEH, April 26, 1872, CPH Papers, ser. 1, reel 4; CPH to HEH, January 18, 1873, CPH Papers, ser. 2, reel 2.
42. CPH to HEH, March 28, May 20, 1872, CPH Papers, ser. 2, reel 9; CPH to HEH, January 2, 11, 1873, CPH Papers, ser. 2, reel 2.
43. CPH to HEH, CPH Papers, ser. 2, reel 2.
44. CPH Papers, ser. 2, reel 2.
45. HEH Biographical File, April 18, 1873, HEH MS 19/3.

3 . TRIAL AND ERROR

1. Mary to Harriet, February 9, 1874, HEH Correspondence, box 7.
2. Richard Franchot to Edwin Gates, April 8, 1873, CPH Papers, ser. 1, reel 5.
3. Edwin Gates to HEH, May 23, 28, 1873, CPH Papers, ser. 2, reel 2.
4. CPH to Huntington & Franchot, June 10, 1873, CPH Papers, ser. 2, reel 2.
5. CPH to Huntington & Franchot, April 8, 1873, CPH Papers, ser. 2, reel 2; July 23, 24, 1873, CPH Papers, ser. 2, reels 2, 35.
6. *Pasadena Chimes* 6, no. 14, HEH MS 16/2(2).

7. April 3, 6, 1874, CPH Papers, ser. 2, reel 9; June 10, 1874, CPH Papers, ser. 1, reel 6.
8. June 10, 1874, CPH Papers, ser. 1, reel 6.
9. S. P. Franchot to R. Franchot, June 25, 1874, CPH Papers, ser. 1, reel 6.
10. CPH Papers, ser. 1, reels 6, 7; CPH Papers, ser. 2, reels 2, 9, 33.
11. July 1, 1874, CPH Papers, ser. 1, reel 6.
12. July 12, 15, 1874, CPH Papers, ser. 1, reel 6.
13. June 25, 1874, CPH Papers, ser. 1, reel 6.
14. July 14, 1874, CPH Papers, ser. 2, reel 33.
15. July 2, 1874, CPH Papers, ser. 1, reel 6.
16. August 23, 1874, HEH Correspondence, box 8.
17. N. V. V. Franchot to Robert Schad, May 4, 1929, HEH Biographical File, HEH MS 19/3; Robert Schad to Caroline H. Holladay, October 31, 1938, HEH Biographical File, HEH MS 19/3.
18. HEH to CPH, October 11, 1874, CPH Papers, ser. 1, reel 7.
19. Huntington & Franchot to CPH, October 16, 1874, CPH Papers, ser. 1, reel 7.
20. CPH Papers, ser. 1, reel 7.
21. HEH to CPH, September 26, 1875, CPH Papers, ser. 1, reel 8.
22. HEH to CPH, October 8, 1875, CPH Papers, ser. 1, reel 8.
23. HEH to CPH, December 6, 1875, CPH Papers, ser. 1, reel 9.
24. CPH to HEH, December 11, 1875, CPH Papers, ser. 2, reel 10.
25. HEH to CPH, December 21, 1875, CPH Papers, ser. 1, reel 9.
26. Clara Prentice to CPH, April 7, 1876, CPH Papers, ser. 1, reel 9; HEH to CPH, April 9, 1876, CPH Papers, ser. 1, reel 9.
27. HEH to Harriet, May 18, 1876, HEH Correspondence, box 8.
28. CPH to Willard, November 29, 1875, CPH Papers, ser. 2, reel 10; Gates to Willard, January 14, March 9, May 8, 1876, CPH Papers, ser. 2, reel 2.
29. CPH to Willard, December 7, 1876, March 31, 1877, CPH Papers, ser. 2, reel 2.
30. CPH to Willard, November 5, 1878, November 27, 1880, CPH Papers, ser. 2, reel 35.
31. Harriet to Carrie, February 14, 1880, HEH Correspondence, box 11.
32. Mary to Harriet, March 19, 28, 1879, HEH Correspondence, boxes 10, 11; Harriet to Carrie, February 4, 1878, HEH Correspondence, boxes 10, 11.
33. Mary to Carrie, January 4, 1879, March 18, 1880, HEH Correspondence, box 11; Mary to Harriet, March 19, 28, 1879, HEH Correspondence, box 11.
34. Mary to Harriet, September 12, 1877, HEH Correspondence, box 10.

35. Mary to Carrie, February 4, 1879, HEH Correspondence, box 11; Clara Prentice to CPH, March 24, 1881, CPH Papers, ser. 1, reel 22; Mary to CPH, June 29, 1878, CPH Papers, ser. 1, reel 15.
36. Mary to Harriet, March 19 and 26, 1879, HEH Correspondence, box 11; Mary to Carrie, January 4, 1879, HEH Correspondence, box 11.
37. Mary to Harriet, March 19, 1879, HEH Correspondence, box 11; Mary to Carrie, March 16, June 18, 1879, HEH Correspondence, box 11.
38. Gates to Willard, January 8, 1876, CPH Papers, ser. 2, reel 10.
39. All the letters quoted or referred to in the two preceding paragraphs are in CPH Papers, ser. 2, reel 35.
40. Willard to Harriet, June 22, August 22, 1879, HEH Correspondence, box 11; Willard to Carrie, March 23, 1880, HEH Correspondence, box 11.
41. Willard to Harriet, December 12, 1879, HEH Correspondence, box 11.
42. CPH Papers, ser. 1, reel 23.
43. April 8, 1881, CPH Papers, ser. 2, reel 35.
44. August 10, 1881, HEH MS 9/1.

4. WORKING ON THE RAILROAD

1. HEH to CPH, August 15, 18, 23, 24, September 3, October 27, 1881, CPH Papers, ser. 1, reels 23, 24, 25.
2. HEH to CPH, August 21, 1881, CPH Papers, ser. 1, reel 24.
3. Hillhouse to CPH, June 9, 1882, CPH Papers, ser. 1, reel 28.
4. CPH to Hillhouse, June 16, 1882, CPH Papers, ser. 2, reel 21.
5. Hillhouse to CPH, June 20, 1882, CPH Papers, ser. 1, reel 28.
6. Echols to CPH, September 19, November 1, 1882, CPH Papers, ser. 1, reels 29, 30.
7. CPH to HEH, September 8, 1884, CPH Papers, ser. 2, reel 22.
8. CPH to HEH, July 6, 1883, CPH Papers, ser. 2, reel 21.
9. HEH to CPH, May 16, 17, 18, 1882, HEH MS 9/44.
10. HEH to Edwin Gates, April 18, 1882, HEH MS 9/44.
11. CPH to HEH, October 30, 1881, CPH Papers, ser. 2, reel 21.
12. CPH to HEH, September 23, 1881, CPH Papers, ser. 2, reel 21.
13. HEH to CPH, September 23, 1881, CPH Papers, ser. 1, reel 24.
14. HEH to CPH, January 18, February 28, 1882, CPH Papers, ser. 1, reels 26, 27.
15. See, for example, letters to CPH, April 17, November 18, December 6, 1884, CPH Papers, ser. 1, reels 36, 38.
16. HEH to CPH, November 2, 14, 1882, CPH Papers, ser. 1, reel 30.

17. HEH to Harriet, October 20, 1882, HEH Correspondence, box 14.
18. Echols to CPH, March 6, 1883, CPH Papers, ser. 1, reel 31.
19. Echols to CPH, January 5, 1883, CPH Papers, ser. 1, reel 30. Also April 2, 9, 12, 1883, CPH Papers, ser. 1, reel 31.
20. CPH to HEH, January 13, 1885, CPH Papers, ser. 2, reel 24.
21. CPH to HEH, June 2, 1884, CPH Papers, ser. 2, reel 24.
22. CPH to HEH, October 17, 1881, CPH Papers, ser. 2, reel 21.
23. Harriet to Carrie, November 25, 1881, HEH Correspondence, box 13.
24. HEH to CPH, December 5, 1881, January 4, 1882, CPH Papers, ser. 1, reels 25, 26.
25. HEH to CPH, February 24, 1882, CPH Papers, ser. 1, reel 27.
26. Mary to Harriet, August 29, 1882, HEH Correspondence, box 14.
27. CPH to Willard, September 13, 1881, CPH Papers, ser. 2, reel 35.
28. Willard to Harriet, November 16, 1881, HEH Correspondence, box 13; Harriet to Carrie, November 25, 1881, HEH Correspondence, box 13; CPH to Willard, November 18, 1881, CPH Papers, ser. 2, reel 35.
29. Marie to Harriet, August 17, 1882, HEH Correspondence, box 14.
30. CPH to Willard, January 23, August 30, 1883, CPH Papers, ser. 2, reel 35.
31. HEH to CPH, August 18, 1882, CPH Papers, ser. 1, reel 29; Echols to CPH, August 24, 1882, CPH Papers, ser. 1, reel 29.
32. Mary to Carrie, October 16, 1882, HEH Correspondence, box 14.
33. HEH to CPH, October 5, 1882, CPH Papers, ser. 1, reel 29.
34. Echols to CPH, December 18, 1882, CPH Papers, ser. 1, reel 30.
35. Mary to Harriet, February 8, 1883, Metcalf Add. MSS.
36. CPH to HEH, March 19, April 6, 1883, CPH Papers, ser. 2, reel 21.
37. CPH to Abbott Robinson, September 4, 1883, HEH Correspondence, box 15.
38. HEH to CPH, September 18, 1882, January 15, 1883, CPH Papers, ser. 1, reels 29, 30; CPH to HEH, January 10, 1883, CPH Papers, ser. 2, reel 21; HEH to CPH, January 15, 1883, CPH Papers, ser. 1, reel 30.
39. HEH to CPH, May 18, 1882, CPH Papers, ser. 1, reel 23; HEH to CPH, December 1, 1882, HEH Correspondence, box 14.
40. HEH to CPH, June 12, 1882, HEH MS 9/44.
41. HEH to CPH, June 12, 1882, CPH Papers, ser. 1, reel 28.
42. Echols to CPH, December 23, 1883, CPH Papers, ser. 1, reel 34.
43. CPH to HEH, April 22, 1884, CPH Papers, ser. 2, reel 22.
44. C. W. Smith to CPH, June 15, 1885, CPH Papers, ser. 1, reel 40.
45. HEH to Holmes Cummins, December 2, 1882, CPH Papers, ser. 1, reel 30.

46. HEH MS 7/6(1); Harriet to Edward Pardee, January 5, 1885, HEH MS 638.
47. Kittie W. Bushnell to CPH, December 26, 1879, CPH Papers, ser. 1, reel 18. Also letters by May Butterfield, Clara Howard, Belle Sarsfield, and others.
48. Theodore Irwin to Robert Schad, September 12, 1929, HEH Biographical File, HEH MS 19/3.
49. CPH to HEH, September 20, 1884, CPH Papers, ser. 2, reel 22.
50. C. W. Smith to CPH, March 21, 1885, CPH Papers, ser. 1, reel 40.
51. C. W. Smith to CPH, March 25, 1885, CPH Papers, ser. 1, reel 40.
52. CPH to HEH, March 21, 1885, CPH Papers, ser. 2, reel 24.
53. CPH Papers, ser. 1, reel 40.
54. C. W. Smith to CPH, May 5, 1885, CPH Papers, ser. 1, reel 40; CPH to HEH, May 7, 1885, CPH Papers, ser. 2, reel 24.

5 . RUNNING A RAILROAD

1. C. W. Smith to CPH, July 2, 1885, CPH Papers, ser. 1, reel 40.
2. CPH to Gates, March 30, 1884, CPH Papers, ser. 1, reel 35.
3. C. W. Smith to CPH, April 21, 1885, CPH Papers, ser. 1, reel 40.
4. CPH to HEH, May 27, 1885, CPH Papers, ser. 2, reel 24.
5. CPH to HEH, May 30, 1885, CPH Papers, ser. 2, reel 24.
6. C. W. Smith to CPH, June 4, 1885, CPH Papers, ser. 1, reel 40.
7. CPH to HEH, June 4, 8, 1885, CPH Papers, ser. 2, reel 24.
8. CPH to HEH, September 16, December 2, 1885, CPH Papers, ser. 2, reel 24.
9. CPH to HEH, January 7, 1886, HEH MS 30/17.
10. W. C. Wickham to CPH, January 29, 1886, CPH Papers, ser. 1, reel 41.
11. HEH to CPH, December 22, 1886, HEH MS 10/1.
12. HEH to CPH, April 23, 1887, HEH MS 10/1.
13. HEH to Gates, June 8, 1887, HEH MS 10/1.
14. HEH MS 9/16.
15. CPH to HEH, December 2, 1890, CPH Papers, ser. 2, reel 25.
16. HEH to CPH, March 3, 1887, HEH MS 10/1.
17. HEH MSS 9/54, 9/13, 9/27.
18. HEH MS 7/6(1).
19. HEH MSS 9/18, 14/2, 19/5.
20. Book bill, November 28, 1892, HEH MS 25/5.
21. Small notebooks, c. 1885, HEH MS 14/40, and HEH Correspondence, box 16.

22. Marie to Harriet, October 21, 1885, HEH Correspondence, box 16.

23. Carrie to Harriet, March 1, 1889, HEH Correspondence, box 17.

24. Carrie's journal, vol. 3, HEH Correspondence, box 195.

25. CPH to Gates, July 2, 1887, CPH Papers, ser. 1, reel 45.

26. CPH to Gates, September 11, 1889, CPH Papers, ser. 1, reel 48; Belle to Carrie, October 20, 1889, HEH Correspondence, box 17. For many newspaper accounts of Prince Hatzfeldt and the wedding, HEH MS 7/7(1).

27. HEH MS 7/6(1).

28. August 15, 1890, HEH MS 7/6(1).

29. HEH to Harriet, December 9, 1888, HEH Correspondence, box 18.

30. HEH to Harriet, March 20, 1891, HEH Correspondence, box 19.

31. W. L. Baldwin to HEH, May 21, 1891, HEH MS 9/20.

32. W. L. Baldwin to HEH, December 12, 1890, HEH MS 9/15.

33. CPH to HEH, April 2, 14, 19, June 30, 1886, CPH Papers, ser. 2, reel 23.

34. CPH to HEH, August 18, 23, 25, November 5, 8, 1886, CPH Papers, ser. 2, reel 23.

35. CPH to HEH, January 31, 1887, HEH MS 30/17.

36. Gates to HEH, August 8, 1887, CPH Papers, ser. 2, reel 23.

37. CPH to HEH, August 27, 1887, CPH Papers, ser. 2, reel 23.

38. CPH to HEH, May 18, 1888, CPH Papers, ser. 2, reel 23.

39. CPH to HEH, August 13, 1888, CPH Papers, ser. 2, reel 25.

40. HEH MS 38/2.

41. CPH to HEH, September 6, 12, 1888, CPH Papers, ser. 2, reel 24.

42. CPH to HEH, November 16, 1888, CPH Papers, ser. 2, reel 24.

43. CPH to HEH, March 17, 1889, CPH Papers, ser. 2, reel 25.

44. HEH MS 38/2.

45. HEH MSS 10/1–2, 9/1–54; CPH Papers, ser. 2, reels 22–25.

46. CPH to HEH, September 30, 1891, HEH Correspondence, box 20.

47. Five from the period 1891–92 are included in HEH MS 11/5(3).

48. CPH to HEH, November 18, 1887, CPH Papers, ser. 2, reel 25.

49. CPH to HEH, May 13, 1886, CPH Papers, ser. 2, reel 25.

50. CPH to HEH, September 17, October 16, 1886, CPH Papers, ser. 2, reel 22; CPH to HEH, September 4, 1886, September 3, 13, 1887, CPH Papers, ser. 2, reel 23.

51. CPH to HEH, November 28, 1887, CPH Papers, ser. 2, reel 23.

52. HEH to CPH, November 6, 1886, HEH MS 10/1.

53. HEH MS 30/17, p. 458.

54. HEH to Gates, October 12, 1885, CPH Papers, ser. 2, reel 31; HEH to CPH, February 27, 1888, HEH MS 10/2; HEH MS 9/15.

55. Gates to HEH, October 12, 1885, CPH Papers, ser. 2, reel 31; December 15, 1890, HEH MS 9/15.
56. HEH Correspondence, box 19; HEH MSS 9/15, 11/1(3).
57. HEH to A. T. Sabin, December 18, 1891, HEH MS 9/17.
58. Yarrington to CPH, March 30, 1886, CPH Papers, ser. 1, reel 42.
59. CPH to HEH, July 23, 1886, CPH Papers, ser. 2, reel 16.
60. HEH MS 9/43.
61. HEH MS 10/2 (1890).
62. The letters in the four preceding paragraphs are all in HEH MS 30/22. Other relevant letters are in HEH MS 9/18.
63. HEH MS 9/25.
64. HEH MS 20/.

6. GOING TO CALIFORNIA

1. HEH MS 16/6.
2. April 9, 1890, CPH Papers, ser. 1, reel 48.
3. For a brief account of these events, see Lavender, *Great Persuader,* 359–62.
4. CPH to A. N. Towne, December 21, 1891, HEH MS 30/23.
5. CPH to W. H. Mills, July 18, 1891, HEH MS 30/22, p. 43.
6. CPH to Mills, August 19, 1891, HEH MS 30/22, p. 132; Mills to CPH, June 14, 1892, CPH Papers, ser. 2, reel 33.
7. C. F. Crocker to CPH, May 5, 1891, CPH Papers, ser. 1, reel 49.
8. Crocker to CPH, August 13, 1891, CPH Papers, ser. 2, reel 29.
9. CPH to Crocker, August 19, 1891, CPH Papers, ser. 2, reel 29.
10. Mills to CPH, December 15, 1891, CPH Papers, ser. 1, reel 50; Crocker to CPH, December 22, 1891, CPH Papers, ser. 1, reel 50.
11. Leland Stanford to CPH, March 13, 1884, CPH Papers, ser. 1, reel 35.
12. Mrs. Stanford to CPH, August 23, 1881, CPH Papers, ser. 1, reel 24.
13. CPH to Towne, August 4, 1891, HEH MS 30/22, p. 88.
14. CPH to Towne, December 22, 1891, HEH MS 30/22, p. 215.
15. CPH to Towne, December 22, 1891, HEH MS 30/23.
16. Ben C. Truman to CPH, October 10, 1890, CPH Papers, ser. 1, reel 48.
17. Truman to CPH, April 26, 1890, CPH Papers, ser. 1, reel 48.
18. *Oakland Enquirer,* July 3, 1891, HEH MS 16/6.
19. *San Francisco Star,* November 19, 1892.
20. Hutchinson to CPH, April 5, 1892, CPH Papers, ser. 1, reel 50.
21. Stubbs to CPH, October 10, 1892, CPH Papers, ser. 2, reel 33.

22. *San Francisco Examiner,* November 1, 1891.

23. Interviews with HEH in *Pasadena Star,* October 25, 1909, HEH MS 16/2(2); *Los Angeles Sunday Times,* May 9, 1909, HEH MS 7/10(16); *Los Angeles Examiner,* May 29, 1909, HEH MS 7/10(16).

24. S. J. Ross to CPH, June 18, 1877, CPH Papers, ser. 1, reel 12.

25. J. DeBarth Shorb to CPH, April 30, 1878, CPH Papers, ser. 1, reel 14; CPH to Shorb, May 9, 1878, CPH Papers, ser. 2, reel 11.

26. CPH to Gates, April 7, 1892, CPH Papers, ser. 2, reel 33.

27. Crocker to CPH, December 23, 1889, CPH Papers, ser. 1, reel 48.

28. HEH to CPH, July 22, 1892, HEH Correspondence, box 21.

29. CPH to N. T. Smith, treasurer of the SP, May 2, 1892, HEH Correspondence, box 20.

30. CPH to HEH, June 2, 1892, HEH Correspondence, box 21; HEH to CPH, June 7, 1892, HEH Correspondence, box 21.

31. CPH to HEH, June 2, 22, 1892, HEH Correspondence, box 21.

32. For example, Mills to CPH, June 26, 1892, CPH Papers, ser. 2, reel 33; CPH to HEH, July 7, 1892, HEH Correspondence, box 21; Mills to CPH, August 10, 1892, CPH Papers, ser. 1, reel 51.

33. HEH to CPH, November 28, 1892, HEH Correspondence, box 22.

34. CPH to HEH, November 16, 1892, HEH Correspondence, box 22.

35. Stow to CPH, December 22, 1892, CPH Papers, ser. 2, reel 33.

36. HEH to CPH, June 29, 1892, HEH Correspondence, box 21; CPH to HEH, July 5, 1892, HEH Correspondence, box 21.

37. HEH to CPH, June 6, 1893, HEH Correspondence, box 25; HEH to CPH, July 15, 1893, HEH Correspondence, box 27; HEH MS 7/6(1); *Cincinnati Enquirer,* July 17, 1893, HEH MS 16/11.

38. HEH to CPH, July 16, August 8, 1892, HEH Correspondence, box 21.

39. *Santa Cruz Surf,* July 21, 1892, HEH MS 7/10(43).

40. HEH to Harriet, June 7, 1892, HEH Correspondence, box 21; Mills to CPH, February 15, 1893, CPH Papers, ser. 1, reel 51.

41. Mills to CPH, January 12, 1893; R. D. Carpenter to CPH, January 17, 1893; Mills to CPH, January 25, 1893; Stow to CPH, February 1, 1893; Mills to CPH, February 3, 4, 1893. All in CPH Papers, ser. 1, reel 51. CPH to Mills, January 11, 1893, CPH Papers, ser. 2, reel 33; CPH to Stow, January 25, 1893, CPH Papers, ser. 2, reel 33; CPH to HEH, January 14, February 6, 1893, HEH Correspondence, box 23; HEH to CPH, January 19, 1893, HEH Correspondence, box 23.

42. Mills to CPH, November 22, 1893, CPH Papers, ser. 1, reel 52; HEH to CPH, December 2, 1893, HEH Correspondence, box 30.

43. Mills to CPH, January 18, May 11, 1893, CPH Papers, ser. 1, reel 51.

44. H. H. Markham to CPH, July 3, 1893, CPH Papers, ser. 1, reel 52; CPH to Markham, July 6, 1893, CPH Papers, ser. 2, reel 34.
45. HEH MS 7/10(43).
46. HEH MS 16/11.
47. CPH Papers, ser. 1, reels 51, 52; HEH Correspondence, boxes 26, 27.
48. Willard to Harriet, April 11, 1887, HEH Correspondence, box 16; CPH to Willard, June 27, July 10, 1893, CPH Papers, ser. 2, reel 34.
49. CPH to Willard, May 9, 1894, CPH Papers, ser. 1, reel 53.
50. HEH to CPH, July 14, 1893, HEH Correspondence, box 27.
51. Post to CPH, October 24, 1893, CPH Papers, ser. 1, reel 52.
52. CPH Papers, ser. 1, reels 51, 52; HEH Correspondence, boxes 26, 27.
53. HEH to CPH, March 19, 1893, HEH Correspondence, box 24.
54. HEH to CPH, April 20, 1893, HEH Correspondence, box 25; CPH to HEH, April 25, May 17, 1893, HEH Correspondence, box 25.
55. *San Francisco Daily Report,* September 14, 26, 1893, HEH MS 16/11.
56. August 10, 1893, HEH Correspondence, box 28.
57. *San Francisco Daily Report,* October 7, 1893, HEH MS 7/10(1).
58. *San Francisco Chronicle,* December 8, 1893; *San Francisco Call,* December 8, 1893; *San Francisco Examiner,* December 8, 1893. All in HEH MS 7/10(1).
59. Crocker to CPH, January 9, 1894, CPH Papers, ser. 1, reel 52; Speyer & Co. to CPH, March 3, 1894, CPH Papers, ser. 1, reel 52.
60. *San Francisco Daily Report,* March 19, 1894. Also *San Francisco Bulletin,* March 28, 1894; *San Francisco Call,* March 28, 1894; *San Francisco Examiner,* March 29, 1894; *San Francisco Chronicle,* March 29, 1894. All in HEH MS 7/9(2).
61. Gates to CPH, April 5, 1894, CPH Papers, ser. 1, reel 53; CPH to Gates, April 10, 1894, CPH Papers, ser. 1, reel 53.
62. HEH to CPH, June 27, 1894; CPH to Towne, June 27, 1894; CPH to HEH, June 29, 1894. All in HEH Correspondence, box 33.
63. *San Francisco Examiner,* July 29, 1894, HEH MS 7/8(2).
64. *San Francisco Examiner,* July 1, 1894, HEH MS 7/8(2); *San Francisco Call,* July 2, 1894, HEH MS 7/8(2).
65. *San Francisco Examiner,* July 2, 1894, HEH MS 7/8(4).
66. *San Francisco Call,* July 4, 1894, HEH MS 7/8(4); *Oakland Times,* July 6, 1894, HEH MS 7/8(4).
67. HEH to CPH, July 2, 1894, HEH Correspondence, box 34.
68. HEH to CPH, July 6, 1894, HEH Correspondence, box 34.
69. HEH MS 7/6(1).
70. *Oakland Times,* July 7, 1894, HEH MS 7/8/9.

71. *San Francisco Examiner,* July 7, 1894, HEH MS 7/8/8.
72. *New York Tribune,* July 7, 1894, HEH Correspondence, box 34.
73. HEH to CPH, July 13, 1894, HEH Correspondence, box 34.
74. HEH to CPH, July 14, 1894, HEH Correspondence, box 34.
75. HEH to CPH, July 21, 1894, HEH Correspondence, box 34.

7. BECOMING A CALIFORNIAN

1. HEH to CPH, November 7, 1895, HEH Correspondence, box 44.
2. *San Francisco Chronicle,* January 4, 5, 1897, HEH MS 7/1(29).
3. *Los Angeles Herald,* December 15, 1899, HEH MS 7/1(45).
4. Dates of HEH's travels are often included in E. B. Holladay's diaries for 1890–1901, HEH MS 53/2.
5. HEH to CPH, November 9, 1897, HEH Correspondence, box 60.
6. CPH to W. H. Mills, April 28, 1896, CPH Papers, ser. 1, reel 53.
7. HEH to CPH, November 1, 1897, HEH Correspondence, box 60.
8. HEH to CPH, November 27, 1897, HEH Correspondence, box 61. For a few other letters relating to the infighting, see HEH to CPH, December 27, 1897, HEH Correspondence, box 62; CPH to HEH, July 2, 1898, HEH Correspondence, box 65; CPH to HEH, July 7, 1898, HEH Correspondence, box 66; CPH to HEH, March 9, 1899, HEH Correspondence, box 70.
9. HEH to CPH, November 9, 1897, HEH Correspondence, box 60.
10. CPH to HEH, November 8, 1897, HEH Correspondence, box 60.
11. *San Francisco Examiner,* March 22, 1896, HEH MS 7/10(1).
12. *San Francisco Examiner,* April 7, 1896, HEH MS 7/10(1).
13. *San Francisco Examiner,* April 8, 1896, HEH MS 7/1(26).
14. *San Francisco Examiner,* April 11, 1896, HEH MS 7/1(26).
15. *San Francisco Examiner,* April 13, 1896, HEH MS 7/1(26).
16. CPH to W. H. Mills, April 28, 1896, CPH Papers, ser. 1, reel 53.
17. *San Francisco Examiner,* January 30, 1898, HEH MS 7/1(35).
18. See, for further details, the *San Francisco Examiner* for January 31, February 1, 2, 9 (3 stories), April 14, 21, 24, 1898; *San Francisco Call,* February 2, 1898; *San Francisco City Argus,* February 5, 1898. All in HEH MS 7/1(35).
19. A full account of this complex episode is contained in Stuart Daggett, *Chapters on the History of the Southern Pacific* (New York: Ronald Press, 1922), 370–424.
20. Most of them are collected in HEH MS 50; others are in HEH MSS 7/1(26), (37).

21. *San Francisco Examiner,* February 7, 1896, HEH MS 50/.
22. *San Francisco Call,* January 27, 1896, HEH MS 50/.
23. HEH MS 50/.
24. CPH to HEH, January 22, 26, February 3, 1896, HEH Correspondence, box 46.
25. *San Francisco Examiner,* April 7, 1896, HEH MS 7/1(26), p. 107.
26. HEH MS 50/.
27. HEH MSS 13/16/2, 13/16/9.
28. *San Francisco Bulletin,* April 19, 1894, HEH MS 7/10(1); *San Francisco Examiner,* April 22, 1894, HEH MS 7/6(1).
29. HEH to CPH, June 24, 1895; HEH to Harriet, June 15, 1895; HEH to Gen. Hubbard, July 13, 1895. All in HEH Correspondence, box 42.
30. HEH Correspondence, box 49.
31. HEH Correspondence, boxes 51, 52.
32. CPH to HEH, October 2, 1897, HEH Correspondence, box 59; HEH to CPH, October 15, 1897, HEH Correspondence, box 59.
33. HEH to CPH, October 30, 1897, HEH Correspondence, box 60.
34. *San Francisco Call,* May 6, 1897, HEH MS 7/1(31).
35. *San Francisco Examiner,* October 1, 1895, HEH MS 7/1(22).
36. *San Francisco Examiner,* November 25, December 2, 1895, HEH MS 7/10(1).
37. Details of Carrie and Burke's activities are drawn from E. B. Holladay's diaries, 1890–1901, HEH MS 53/2.
38. E. B. Holladay, Diaries, April 25, 26, 27, 1898, HEH MS 53/2.
39. HEH to Burke Holladay, January 28, 1897, HEH Correspondence, box 54.
40. E. B. Holladay, Diaries, January 22, February 4, July 17, 1897, HEH MS 53/2.
41. HEH to Mary, September 25, 1896, HEH Metcalf Add. MSS.
42. Mary to HEH, August 6, 1899, HEH Metcalf Add. MSS.
43. Helen Huntington to Carrie, November 1897, HEH Correspondence, box 61.
44. Clara to Harriet, June 26, 1897, HEH Correspondence, box 57.
45. Ellen Gates to Harriet, July 18, 1897, HEH Correspondence, box 57.
46. E. B. Holladay, Diaries, HEH MS 53/2.
47. *San Francisco Argonaut,* December 24, 1900, HEH MS 7/10(2).
48. January 28, 1895, HEH MS 13/16/5.
49. San Francisco newspapers, November 5, 1899, HEH MS 7/6(1).
50. April 23, 1900, HEH Correspondence, box 80.
51. December 26, 1900, HEH MS 13/16/20.

52. Charles G. Saunders (Boston) to HEH (SF), July 3, 1900, HEH Correspondence, box 82.
53. *San Francisco Examiner,* November 18, 1900, HEH MS 7/1(42).
54. HEH to Harriet, June 18, 1896, HEH Correspondence, box 50; HEH to CPH, July 28, 1896, HEH Correspondence, box 51.
55. B. A. Worthington to CPH, January 29, 1896, HEH Correspondence, box 46; G. E. Miles to B. A. Worthington, March 24, 1896, HEH Correspondence, box 47; CPH to Edwin Gates, April 11, 1898, CPH Papers, ser. 1, reel 54.
56. Carrie to Burke, August 1897, HEH Correspondence, box 58; Harriet F. Saunders Douglas to HEH, July 26, 1897, HEH Correspondence, box 57; Archer to Carrie, December 17, 1897, HEH Correspondence, box 62; Clara to Harriet, August 3, 1897, HEH Correspondence, box 57.
57. CPH to HEH, December 2, 1897, HEH Correspondence, box 61; G. E. Miles to HEH, October 2, 1897, HEH Correspondence, box 59; HEH to Miles, October 8, 1897, HEH Correspondence, box 59.
58. Helen Gates to Carrie, November 7, 1897, HEH Correspondence, box 60; CPH to Gates, April 11, 1898, CPH Papers, ser. 1, reel 54.
59. G. E. Miles to Edwin Gates, July 12, 1895, CPH Papers, ser. 1, reel 53; Helen to Carrie, November 1897, HEH Correspondence, box 61.
60. CPH to Gates, June 12, 1895, CPH Papers, ser. 1, reel 53; CPH to HEH, November 3, 1897, HEH Correspondence, box 60; CPH to Gates, April 25, 1898, CPH Papers, ser. 1, reel 54; Harriet to Carrie, June 1, 1896, HEH Correspondence, box 49; Harriet to Carrie, May 31, 1899, HEH Correspondence, box 71; Miles to Gates, March 23, 1898, CPH Papers, ser. 1, reel 54.
61. HEH MS 31.1.1.13.
62. For a discussion of Doxey, see Robert Ernest Cowan, *Booksellers in Early San Francisco* (Los Angeles: Ward Ritchie Press, 1953), 51–59. Also, Madeleine B. Stern, *Antiquarian Bookselling in the United States* (Westport, Conn.: Greenwood Press, 1985), 142–43.
63. The records of purchases from Doxey, Miller, and other booksellers during this period are in HEH MSS 25/5, 13/16/3, and 14/7.
64. HEH MS 53/2.
65. Carrie to Harriet, February 1896, HEH Correspondence, box 47.
66. HEH MS 25/5.
67. HEH MS 11/1(4).
68. December 10, 1897, HEH Correspondence, box 62.
69. October 31, 1898, HEH Correspondence, box 69.
70. C. F. Crocker to CPH, January 13, 1887, CPH Papers, ser. 1, reel 44;

Crocker to CPH, March 14, 1887, CPH Papers, ser. 1, reel 45; Crocker to CPH, December 23, 1887, CPH Papers, ser. 1, reel 46.

71. CPH to Gates, April 13, 1888, CPH Papers, ser. 1, reel 46.

72. *San Francisco Examiner,* April 12, 1893, HEH MS 7/10(1).

73. HEH to CPH, October 17, 1894, HEH Correspondence, box 37; CPH to HEH, January 14, 1895, HEH Correspondence, box 39; HEH to CPH, May 14, 1895, HEH Correspondence, box 44.

74. M. H. Sherman to HEH, December 12, 1895, January 24, 1896, HEH MS 11/4(1).

75. June 8, 1895, HEH MS 7/10(1).

76. *San Diego Union,* June 8, 1895, HEH MS 7/10(1).

77. *Los Angeles Herald,* July 28, 1895, HEH MS 7/10(1).

78. *San Francisco Examiner,* November 19, 1895, HEH MS 7/1(24).

79. *Los Angeles Evening Express,* November 6, 1897, HEH MS 7/10(1).

80. Concerning his California Club membership, see 1896–97, HEH MS 13/16/12. For correspondence with Shorb, see letters from HEH on November 1, 23, 25, 28, 1892, February 21, March 1, July 3, 1893, Shorb Collection, Huntington Library. Regarding possible new rail lines, see HEH to CPH, July 5, July 11, 1898, June 10, 1899, HEH Correspondence, boxes 65, 66, 71. Concerning the convention hall donation, see June 20, 1900, HEH MS 7/1(46).

81. *Los Angeles Times,* June 2, 1935, HEH MS 16/6.

82. *Los Angeles Herald,* June 28, 1898, HEH MS 7/10(1).

83. *Los Angeles Herald,* September 17, 1898, HEH MS 7/1(36).

84. *San Francisco Chronicle,* July 18, 1895, HEH MS 7/1; *San Francisco Examiner,* July 18, 22, 1895, HEH MS 7/1.

85. *San Francisco Examiner,* November 19, 1895, HEH MS 7/1(24).

86. HEH to CPH, July 22, 1897, HEH Correspondence, box 57.

87. CPH to HEH, August 7, 1897, HEH Correspondence, box 57.

88. HEH to Gen. Hubbard, August 19, 1897, HEH Correspondence, box 58.

89. HEH to CPH, August 26, 1897, HEH Correspondence, box 58.

90. HEH to CPH, August 24, 1897, HEH Correspondence, box 58.

91. HEH to CPH, October 28, 1897, HEH Correspondence, box 60; CPH to HEH, November 3, 1897, HEH Correspondence, box 60.

92. *San Francisco Examiner,* December 3, 1897, HEH MS 7/1(34).

93. CPH to HEH, November 26, 1898, HEH Correspondence, box 68.

94. HEH to SP Board of Directors, January 17, 1899, HEH Correspondence, box 70; HEH to SP Board of Directors, April 6, 1899, HEH Correspondence, box 71.

95. CPH to HEH, March 7, 1899, HEH Correspondence, box 70.

96. *San Francisco Examiner,* April 9, 1899; *San Francisco Chronicle,* April 9, 1899; *San Francisco Examiner,* April 10, 11, 19, 1899; *San Francisco Call,* April 15, 1899. These clippings and many others of similar purport are in HEH MSS 7/1(37), 16/4.

97. G. E. Miles to Edwin Gates, April 19, 1899, CPH Papers, ser. 1, reel 54.

98. *San Francisco Call,* September 23, 1899; *San Francisco Examiner,* September 26, 1899. These and a dozen others are in HEH MS 7/1(39).

99. B. A. Worthington to HEH, September 20, 1899, HEH Correspondence, box 73. About a dozen other letters of this sort are in HEH Correspondence, box 74.

100. HEH to CPH, October 24, 1899, HEH Correspondence, box 74; CPH to HEH, October 30, 1899, HEH Correspondence, box 74.

101. CPH to HEH, November 15, 1899, HEH Correspondence, box 75; HEH to CPH, November 15, 1899, HEH Correspondence, box 75.

102. CPH to James Speyer, December 9, 1899, CPH Papers, ser. 1, reel 54.

103. *San Francisco Examiner,* November 14, 1899, HEH MS 7/1(40); *San Francisco Chronicle,* November 14, 1899, HEH MS 7/1(40); HEH MS 7/1(40).

104. E. P. Ripley to HEH, November 18, 1899; HEH to CPH, November 22, 1899; CPH to HEH, November 27, 1899. All in HEH Correspondence, box 75.

105. HEH to Carrie, June 14, 1900, HEH Correspondence, box 81.

106. *San Francisco Examiner,* June 15, 1900, HEH MS 7/10(43). Other stories are in HEH MSS 7/1(41), (42), 7/6(1), 7/10(2), (43), 17/3.

107. HEH Correspondence, box 85.

108. The death certificate is in HEH Correspondence, box 85. Contributing causes of death recorded were cystitis and excessive heat.

8. UNCLE COLLIS

1. HEH to Harriet, August 19, 1900, HEH Correspondence, box 85.

2. The letters from which these excerpts are taken are all in HEH Correspondence, box 85.

3. Mary Lewis (a niece) to Harriet, August 17, 1900, HEH Correspondence, box 85.

4. HEH to Harriet, August 19, 1900, HEH Correspondence, box 85.

5. Harriet to Carrie, September 7, 1900, HEH Correspondence, box 86.

6. Arabella to Carrie, December 17, 1900, HEH Correspondence, box 87.

7. *San Francisco Bulletin,* August 14, 1900, HEH MS 7/1(42).

8. J. O'H. Cosgrave, *San Francisco Saturday Wave,* August 18, 1900, HEH MSS 7/6(2), 16/11.
9. October 22, 1887. Reprinted in *Sacramento Weekly Union,* August 17, 1900, HEH MS 16/11.
10. *Milwaukee Wisconsin,* August 18, 1900, HEH MS 7/10(2); *Newport News Daily Press,* March 1898, HEH MS 7/6(2). His maxims were reprinted in many newspapers.
11. The story is reviewed in various papers, such as the *San Francisco Call* for August 19, 1900, and the *Sacramento Bee* for August 16, 1900. HEH MS 7/1(42).
12. Inscribed Oneonta, July 20, 1900, HEH MS 7/6(2).
13. CPH to HEH, June 20, 1900, HEH Correspondence, box 81.
14. CPH to HEH, July 12, 1900, HEH Correspondence, box 82.
15. CPH to HEH, June 16, 1900, HEH Correspondence, box 81.
16. CPH to HEH, July 19, 1900, HEH Correspondence, box 83.
17. CPH to HEH, February 20, 1900, HEH Correspondence, box 78.
18. CPH to HEH, February 21, 1900, HEH Correspondence, box 78.
19. CPH to HEH, July 16, 1900, HEH Correspondence, box 83.
20. CPH to HEH, February 14, 1900, HEH Correspondence, box 78; HEH to CPH, February 20, 1900, HEH Correspondence, box 78.
21. HEH to CPH, June 28, 1900, HEH Correspondence, box 82.
22. HEH to CPH, June 11, 1900; CPH to HEH, June 16, 1900; HEH to CPH, June 23, 1900. All in HEH Correspondence, box 80.
23. HEH to CPH, February 8, 1900, HEH Correspondence, box 78.
24. CPH to W. H. Holabird, July 10, 1900, HEH Correspondence, box 82. CPH sent a copy of this letter to HEH.

9. ENDING THE PAST

1. CPH Papers, ser. 3, reel 23.
2. *Portland Oregonian,* February 19, 1901, HEH MS 7/10(3).
3. Estate Appraisal, Surrogate's Court, County of New York, October 10, 1902, HEH Correspondence, box 97.
4. Legacy Return, U.S. Internal Revenue Service, August 13, 1903, HEH Correspondence, box 104.
5. Agreement for Sale, January 31, 1901, HEH Correspondence, box 87.
6. *San Francisco Examiner,* August 25, 1900, HEH MS 7/1(42).
7. HEH to Harriet, April 14, 1901, HEH Correspondence, box 88.
8. HEH to Carrie, April 21, 1901, HEH Correspondence, box 88.
9. HEH to Harriet, April 28, 1901, HEH Correspondence, box 88.

10. HEH MS 7/10(44).

11. *New York World,* October 29, 1889, HEH MS 7/7(1); *San Francisco Call,* June 18, 1901, HEH MS 7/7(3); *New York Town Topics,* June 27, 1901, HEH MS 7/10(44).

12. *Boston Post,* August 18, 1900, with byline New York, August 17, HEH MS 7/10(2). Also in New York papers and many others, HEH MS 7/6(2).

13. *San Francisco Examiner,* February 19, 1901, and many other stories, HEH MS 7/10(3).

14. HEH MS 7/6(2).

15. *New York Town Topics,* April 11, 1901, HEH MS 7/10(44).

16. *San Francisco Examiner, San Francisco Bulletin,* June 15, 1900; *San Francisco Examiner, San Francisco Call, San Francisco Evening Post,* June 16, 1900. All in HEH MSS 7/10(2), (41), (43).

17. *New York Sunday Telegraph,* July 8, 1900, HEH MS 7/10(2).

18. See the papers for the period August 16 to August 29, 1900, HEH MSS 7/1(42), (47), 7/6(2), 7/10(2), 16/11.

19. *Arizona Daily Star,* August 28, 1900, HEH MS 7/6(2).

20. *Los Angeles Daily Times,* August 28, 1900, HEH MS 7/1(47).

21. *San Francisco Bulletin,* August 16, 1900, HEH MS 7/1(42).

22. J. C. Stubbs to HEH, September 12, 1900, HEH Correspondence, box 86.

23. HEH to H. Shainwald, September 25, 1900, HEH Correspondence, box 86.

24. HEH to H. M. Daugherty, Columbus, Ohio, September 24, 1900, HEH Correspondence, box 86.

25. M. H. Sherman to HEH, September 26, 1900, HEH Correspondence, box 86.

26. See papers for October 21 to 31, HEH MS 7/1(42).

27. *San Francisco Examiner,* October 21, 1900, *San Francisco Chronicle,* October 27, 1900, HEH MS 7/1(42).

28. *San Francisco Examiner,* November 10, 1900, HEH MS 7/1(42).

29. HEH MS 7/1(43).

30. Agreement, HEH Correspondence, box 87.

31. Don L. Hofsommer, *The Southern Pacific, 1901–1985* (College Station: Texas A & M University Press, 1986), 9–14.

32. HEH to Carrie, April 7, 1901, HEH Correspondence, box 88; HEH Correspondence, boxes 91–94; April 18–30, 1906, HEH MSS 7/2/3, 19/5.

33. HEH to Harriet, April 6, 1901, HEH Correspondence, box 88.

34. HEH to Harriet, May 19, 1901, HEH Correspondence, box 88.
35. Elizabeth to HEH, April 16, 1901, HEH Correspondence, box 88.
36. HEH to Elizabeth, May 22, 1904, Metcalf Add. MSS, box 1.
37. Marian to HEH, October 5, 1901, HEH Correspondence, box 90.
38. HEH to Elizabeth, December 10, 1905, Metcalf Add. MSS, box 4.
39. Elizabeth to HEH, April 23, October 1901, HEH Correspondence, boxes 88, 91.
40. Clara to HEH, October 27, 1901, HEH Correspondence, box 91.
41. Elizabeth to HEH, September 13, 1901, HEH Correspondence, box 90.
42. Letters to HEH, 1901, HEH Correspondence, boxes 90, 91, 92.
43. Howard to HEH, April 6, 1902, HEH Correspondence, box 94.
44. Howard to Harriet, March 21, 1903, HEH Correspondence, box 100.
45. HEH to Carrie, May 3, 1901, HEH Correspondence, box 88.
46. Mary to Elizabeth, December 21, 1901, Metcalf Add. MSS, box 1.
47. Elizabeth to HEH, October 7, 1901, HEH Correspondence, box 90.
48. Elizabeth to HEH, February 27, 1903, Metcalf Add. MSS, box 1.
49. Mary to Elizabeth, April 24, 1904, Metcalf Add. MSS, box 1.
50. Elizabeth to J. B. Metcalf, April 29, 1904, Metcalf Add. MSS, box 1.
51. *Los Angeles Times,* January 12, 1904, HEH MS 7/10(7); Howard to Harriet, January 15, 1904, HEH Correspondence, box 107.
52. HEH to Elizabeth, 1904, Metcalf Add. MSS, box 2.
53. Leslie to Harriet, July 25, 1905; HEH Correspondence, box 118; Elizabeth to Harriet, August 3, 1905, HEH Correspondence, box 119.
54. HEH MS 7/6(3).
55. Elizabeth to Brockway, October 3, 1905, Metcalf Add. MSS, box 3; Mary to Elizabeth, September 26, 1905, Metcalf Add. MSS, box 2.
56. Marian to Harriet, November 13, 1905, HEH Correspondence, box 119.
57. Elizabeth to Brockway, September 25, 1905, Metcalf Add. MSS, box 2.
58. For a few accounts of the visits: Marian to Harriet, October 11, 1904; Clara to Harriet, August 2, 1905; HEH to Harriet, December 24, 1905. All in HEH Correspondence, boxes 114, 118, 119. For some other accounts relating to Elizabeth: HEH to Elizabeth, June 30, December 10, 1905; Brockway to Elizabeth, October 28, 1905: Elizabeth to Brockway, December 1905; December 30, 1905, January 5, 1906. All in Metcalf Add. MSS, boxes 2, 3, 4.
59. HEH to Elizabeth, 1901, Metcalf Add. MSS, box 2.
60. HEH to Brockway, September 11, 1905, Metcalf Add. MSS, box 2.
61. HEH to Elizabeth, December 3, 1905, Metcalf Add. MSS, box 3.
62. HEH to Elizabeth, 1901, Metcalf Add. MSS, box 2.
63. HEH to Elizabeth, February 11, 1906, Metcalf Add. MSS, box 4.

64. HEH to Elizabeth, February 16, 1906, Metcalf Add. MSS, box 4.
65. Harriet to HEH, February 27, 1905, HEH Correspondence, box 117; HEH to Harriet, March 12, 1905, HEH Correspondence, box 117.
66. HEH to Elizabeth, May 22, 1904, Metcalf Add. MSS, box 1.
67. *San Francisco Chronicle,* March 22, 23, 1906, HEH MS 7/10(10); *San Francisco Examiner,* March 23, 1906, HEH MS 16/11; *Los Angeles Times, Los Angeles Herald,* March 22, 1906, HEH MS 7/4(15).
68. April 1, 1906, HEH MS 1/D/4(2).
69. Relevant material is contained in the newspapers cited in n. 67 and in *San Francisco Wasp,* March 31, 1906, and *Los Angeles Examiner,* July 30, 1906, both in HEH MS 7/10(44).
70. HEH to Elizabeth, March 22, 1906, Metcalf Add. MSS, box 4.

10. BUSINESSMAN OF SOUTHERN CALIFORNIA

1. *Los Angeles Examiner,* May 19, 1908, HEH MS 7/10(15).
2. *Los Angeles Herald,* December 20, 1908, HEH MS 7/10(15).
3. *Los Angeles Examiner,* October 26, 1910, HEH MS 7/2/6.
4. *Santa Barbara Independent,* May 30, 1905, HEH MS 7/4(6); *Los Angeles Express,* April 4, 1908, HEH MS 7/10(15).
5. *Los Angeles Examiner,* April 26, 1910, HEH MS 16/2(2).
6. HEH to Elizabeth, May 26, 1906, Metcalf Add. MSS, box 4.
7. *Los Angeles Record,* August 18, 1906, HEH MS 7/10(12).
8. *Los Angeles Times,* September 6, 1903, HEH MS 7/2/1.
9. *Los Angeles Express,* June 30, 1905, HEH MS 7/4(6); *Los Angeles Graphic,* December 2, 1905, HEH MS 7/4(12).
10. *San Diego Union,* August 1, 1909, HEH MS 16/2(2).
11. *Los Angeles Times,* February 23, 1902, HEH MS 7/10(4).
12. *Santa Barbara Independent,* May 30, 1905, HEH MS 7/4(6).
13. *Los Angeles Examiner,* May 27, 1908, HEH MS 7/10(15).
14. *Los Angeles Examiner,* May 29, 1910, HEH MS 7/10(18).
15. *Los Angeles Express,* October 1, 1903, HEH MS 7/2/1.
16. *Los Angeles Record,* July 7, 1905, HEH MS 7/4(6).
17. *Los Angeles Times,* March 16, 1909, HEH MS 7/10(16).
18. About fifty pages of such notes are preserved in HEH MS 11/1(3), folder F.
19. G. J. Kuhrts (Chief Engineer) to HEH, December 4, 1909, HEH Correspondence, box 126.
20. June 28, 1901, HEH Correspondence, box 89.
21. *Los Angeles Evening Express,* May 25, 1900, HEH MS 7/1(46).

22. Contracts for the sale, HEH Correspondence, box 77.
23. Incorporation, November 13, 1901, HEH Correspondence, box 91.
24. *Los Angeles Herald,* March 7, 1902, HEH MS 7/10(4).
25. *Los Angeles Times,* April 8, 1902, HEH MS 7/10(4).
26. *Los Angeles Times,* February 25, 1903, HEH MS 16/2(2).
27. *Los Angeles Express,* February 28, 1903, HEH MS 16/2(2).
28. *Los Angeles Express,* March 10, 1903, HEH MS 7/10(5); *Covina (Calif.) Argus,* March 14, 1903, HEH MS 7/10(5).
29. February 7, 1902, HEH MS 7/6(1).
30. Harriet to HEH, January 28, 1903; HEH to Harriet, July 5, 1905; Harriet to HEH, July 9, 1905; HEH Correspondence, boxes 99, 118.
31. C. E. Graham to George E. Miles, January 7, 15, 19, 1903, HEH Correspondence, boxes 99–101; E. A. Adams to C. E. Graham, March 17, 24, 28, April 24, 1903, HEH Correspondence, boxes 99–101.
32. *Los Angeles Herald,* April 1, 3, 4, 1902, HEH Correspondence, HEH MS 7/10(4); *Los Angeles Times,* April 2, 1902, HEH MS 7/10(4).
33. *Los Angeles Express,* February 28, 1903, HEH MS 7/10(5).
34. *Los Angeles Herald,* February 12, 1903, HEH MS 7/10(43).
35. HEH to A. B. Hammond, April 14, 1903, HEH Correspondence, box 101; Harriet to HEH, April 12, 1903, HEH Correspondence, box 101.
36. Agreement, May 7, 1903, HEH Correspondence, box 102; Hellman to E. Randolph, July 10, 1903, HEH Correspondence, box 103; *San Francisco Call,* May 8, 1903, HEH MS 16/2(2); HEH to Harriet, May 24, 1903, HEH Correspondence, box 102.
37. *Los Angeles Times,* May 21, 1903, HEH MS 16/2(2).
38. May to June 10, 1903, HEH Correspondence, box 102.
39. HEH to *Street Railway Journal,* January 28, 1904, HEH Correspondence, box 108.
40. Information supplied to *Poor's Manual of Railroads,* July 5, 1904, HEH Correspondence, box 112.
41. G. Harold Powell, January 25, 1904. In R. G. Lillard, ed., *Letters from the Orange Empire* (Los Angeles: Historical Society of Southern California, 1990), 19.
42. *Los Angeles Express,* December 23, 1904, HEH MS 7/10(7); *Riverside Daily Press,* April 11, 1903, HEH MS 7/10(6).
43. *Los Angeles Examiner,* December 8, 1904, HEH MS 7/4(5); *Santa Ana Blade,* March 28, 1905, HEH MS 7/10(8).
44. *Compton Press,* June 2, 1905, HEH MS 7/4(6).
45. *Los Angeles Times,* June 29, 1905, HEH MS 7/4(6); *Los Angeles Express,* April 8, 1905, HEH MS 7/10(8).

46. *Los Angeles Times,* September 17, 1905, HEH MS 7/10(9); *Los Angeles Examiner,* November 23, 1905, HEH MS 7/4(16); *Santa Ana Bulletin,* November 10, 1905, HEH MS 7/4(11).

47. *Los Angeles Examiner,* July 4, 1909, HEH MS 7/10(17); *Los Angeles Times,* July 5, 1909, HEH MS 7/10(17).

48. *Los Angeles Express,* April 8, 1905, HEH MS 7/10(8); *Los Angeles Herald,* July 3, 1904, HEH MS 7/10(7); *Alhambra Advocate,* September 30, 1905, HEH MS 7/4(10).

49. *Los Angeles Express,* July 5, 1905, HEH MS 7/4(6); *Los Angeles Evening News,* January 13, 1906, HEH MS 7/10(10).

50. HEH to Hellman, May 20, 1904, HEH Correspondence, box 110.

51. *Los Angeles Examiner,* December 10, 12, 1904, HEH MS 7/10(7); *Los Angeles Examiner,* February 7, 1910, HEH MS 7/10(18).

52. March 21–31, 1906, HEH MSS 7/4(11), (15), 7/10(11), (12).

53. *Los Angeles Graphic,* March 24, 1906, HEH MS 7/10(11); *Los Angeles Express,* December 27, 1906, HEH MS 7/10(11); *Los Angeles Graphic,* March 2, 1907, HEH MS 7/4(18).

54. *Oakland Tribune,* September 10, 1909, HEH MS 16/2(1).

55. *Los Angeles Times,* December 19, 20, 1904, HEH MS 7/10(7); *Los Angeles Examiner,* January 8, 16, 1906, HEH MS 7/10(7).

56. *Los Angeles Express,* December 6, 1904, HEH MS 7/10(7).

57. *Los Angeles Record,* February 19, 1903, HEH MS 16/2(2).

58. March to April 1906, HEH MS 7/10(11); *Los Angeles Herald,* September 2, 1906, HEH MS 7/4(17).

59. All Los Angeles papers, December 17, 1903, HEH MS 7/10(6); all Los Angeles papers, January 21, 1904, HEH MS 7/10(6); all Los Angeles papers, May 20, 1904, HEH MS 16/6.

60. *Los Angeles Examiner,* April 17, 19, 24, May 15, 1907, HEH MS 7/4(19).

61. *Los Angeles Herald,* June 1, 5, 1910, HEH MSS 7/10(18), 7/4(24), 7/2/5.

62. HEH MSS 2/1(1), (2).

63. *Los Angeles Times,* March 3, 1904, HEH MS 7/10(7).

64. *Los Angeles Graphic,* September 7, 1907, HEH MS 7/10(4); *Los Angeles Graphic,* May 16, 1908, HEH MS 7/10(15).

65. *Los Angeles Herald,* April 25, 1903, HEH MS 7/10(6).

66. For fuller details about the threats of strikes, see, for example, papers for March 29, 1903, April 29, September 6, 1906, December 4, 1910, HEH MSS 7/10(6), 16/6, 7/4(17), 7/10(19).

67. His actions are called "dictatorial paternalism" in an interesting essay by William B. Friedricks, "Capital and Labor in Los Angeles: Henry E. Huntington vs. Organized Labor, 1900–1920," *Pacific Historical Re-*

view, 59 (1990): 375–95. Friedricks is certainly right in describing Huntington as anti-union, but wrong, I think, in lumping all of his efforts on behalf of labor as "paternalism."

68. HEH to Committee of Trainmen, December 11, 1902, HEH Correspondence, box 98.

69. *Los Angeles Times,* March 29, 1906, HEH MS 7/4(12).

70. *Los Angeles Graphic,* January 1, 1910, and many other papers, HEH MS 7/10(17).

71. *Los Angeles Examiner,* January 12, 1910, HEH MS 7/10(17); *Los Angeles Times, Los Angeles Express,* January 11, 12, 1910, HEH MS 7/10(17).

72. *Los Angeles Examiner,* February 21, 1906, HEH MS 7/4(15).

73. *Los Angeles Times,* April 1, 1906, HEH MS 7/10(11).

74. See, for example, *Los Angeles Examiner,* November 10, 1910, HEH MS 16/2(2).

75. Incorporation papers, November 7, 1910, HEH Correspondence, box 127.

76. *Los Angeles Examiner,* November 9, 1910, HEH MS 7/4(24).

77. *Los Angeles Times,* November 8, 1910, HEH MS 16/2(2).

78. *Los Angeles Express,* November 11, 1910, HEH MS 7/10(18).

79. *Los Angeles Sunday Times,* November 13, 1910, HEH MS 7/10(19).

80. *Los Angeles Financier,* November 5, 1910, HEH MS 17/3.

81. *Los Angeles Examiner,* December 25, 1910, HEH MS 7/2/6.

82. *Los Angeles Times,* January 1, 1910, HEH MS 7/10(18).

83. HEH to J. M. Elliott, May 26, 1903, HEH Correspondence, box 102.

84. *Los Angeles Examiner,* May 10, 1910, HEH MS 7/4(24).

85. Reminiscences of Alfred G. Walker, HEH MS 19/4.

86. *Los Angeles Times,* April 1, 1902, HEH MS 7/10(4).

87. Patton to HEH, April 27, 1910, Patton Collection, Huntington Library, box 5.

88. For one example, see the six-page letter from Bicknell to HEH, July 30, 1903, HEH Correspondence, box 104.

89. *Los Angeles Examiner,* August 23, 1925, HEH MS 7/10(40).

90. For a sample of the smaller purchases during 1902 and 1903, for example, see HEH MS 1/FF/2.

91. *San Bernardino Sun,* November 7, 1905, HEH MS 7/4(11).

92. For a few examples from 1905 alone: *Los Angeles Herald,* April 2, 1905, HEH MS 7/10(8); *Los Angeles Times,* July 30, 1905, HEH MS 7/10(9); *Los Angeles Express,* August 1, HEH MS 7/10(9); *Long Beach Tribune,* August 31, 1905, HEH MS 7/4(10).

93. *Santa Monica Outlook,* August 4, 1905, HEH MS 7/4(9).

94. *Santa Monica Outlook,* August 21, 1905, HEH MS 7/4(10).

95. *Phoenix Enterprise,* August 3, 1905, HEH MS 7/4(9).

96. *Ventura Free Press,* August 25, 1905, HEH MS 7/4(10).

97. *Los Angeles Times,* July 30, 1905, HEH MS 7/10(9).

98. *Los Angeles Examiner,* August 22, 1905, HEH MS 7/4(10).

99. *Pomona Review,* August 22, 1905, HEH MS 7/4(10).

100. *San Bernardino Sun,* August 22, 1905, HEH MS 7/4(10).

101. *Los Angeles Herald,* August 22, 1905, HEH MS 7/4(10).

102. *Los Angeles Herald,* July 30, 1905, HEH MS 7/10(9).

103. Canceled cover dated January 27, 1906, HEH Correspondence, box 120.

104. *Los Angeles Examiner,* February 20, 1909, HEH MS 7/10(16).

105. December 31, 1901, HEH Correspondence, box 92; *Los Angeles Evening News,* January 16, 1907, HEH MS 7/10(13).

106. Clark and Bryan to HEH, March 20, 1905, HEH Correspondence, box 117; HEH to Clark and Bryan, March 27, 1905, HEH Correspondence, box 118.

107. *Los Angeles Express,* April 13, 1906, HEH MS 7/10(11).

108. *Los Angeles Herald,* December 11, 1904, HEH MS 7/10(7).

109. HEH to A. B. Hammond, June 9, 1904, HEH Correspondence, box 111.

110. *Los Angeles Times,* March 27, 1903, HEH MS 7/10(5).

111. HEH to Patton, March 9, 1905, HEH Correspondence, box 117.

112. *Los Angeles Times,* September 11, 1904, HEH MS 7/4(4).

113. *Los Angeles Examiner,* July 13, 16, 1905, HEH MSS 7/4(6), 7/10(9).

114. *Los Angeles Examiner,* July 16, 1905, HEH MS 7/10(9).

115. July 7–17, 1905, HEH MSS 7/2(2), 7/4(6), 7/6(1), (3), 7/10(9), 16/6.

116. E. B. Holladay to Harriet, July 13, 1905, HEH Correspondence, box 118.

117. See, for a typical example, *Los Angeles Herald,* July 12, 1905, HEH MS 7/10(9).

118. Clipping for July 11, 1905, with envelope of the same date, HEH MS 7/6(1).

119. *Los Angeles Examiner,* July 13, 1905, HEH MS 7/4(6).

120. Redondo Improvement Co., HEH MS 1/R/16.

121. *Los Angeles Times,* November 19, 1908, July 2, 1909, HEH MSS 7/4(22), 7/2(5).

122. *Los Angeles Examiner,* August 22, 1905, HEH MS 7/2/2.

123. *Los Angeles Examiner,* November 22, 1908, HEH MS 7/10(15).

124. HEH to Patton, July 29, 1904, HEH Correspondence, box 113.

125. HEH to A. B. Hammond, June 27, 1904, HEH Correspondence, box 112.

126. *Los Angeles Examiner,* May 23, 1912, HEH MS 7/4(27).

127. *Los Angeles Times,* May 9, 1909, HEH MS 7/10(16).

128. Register of Companies, November 1, 1907, Metcalf Add. MSS, box 5; Register of Companies, November 20, 1906, HEH Correspondence, box 121.

129. *San Antonio Daily Express,* March 5, 1904, HEH MS 7/10(43); *Los Angeles Times,* June 8, 1904, HEH MS 16/6; *San Francisco Call,* June 26, 1904, HEH MS 7/10(7); *Los Angeles Express,* June 28, 1904, HEH MS 7/10(7).

130. 1908–1910, HEH MS 16/2(2); September 17, 1908, HEH MS 7/10(15).

131. HEH to W. G. Kerckhoff, July 20, 1904, HEH Correspondence, box 113.

132. *Los Angeles Times,* June 22, 1910; *Los Angeles Herald,* June 22, 1910; *Los Angeles Graphic,* June 25, 1910; *San Francisco Globe,* June 24, 1910. All in HEH MS 7/10(18).

133. *Los Angeles Times,* April 4, 1903, HEH MS 16/2(1); *Los Angeles Herald,* April 10, 1903, HEH MS 7/10(6).

134. HEH to Patton, July 6, 1904, HEH Correspondence, box 112.

135. HEH MS 35/1–13; *Los Angeles Times,* May 9, 1910, HEH MS 7/4(24).

136. *Directory of Directors,* 1903–09, HEH MS 11/1(3).

137. August 18, 1903, HEH MS 11/1(3).

138. March 6, 1908, HEH Correspondence, box 124.

139. HEH MS 1/D/4(1).

140. HEH to Patton, July 27, 1903, HEH Correspondence, box 104; C. E. Graham to HEH, August 13, 1903, HEH MS 11/1(3).

141. Balance sheets, 1901–10. HEH MSS 11/2(1), (2). Related information is in HEH MS 11/1(1–3).

II. HERO OF SOUTHERN CALIFORNIA

1. *Los Angeles Herald,* December 27, 1898, HEH MS 7/1(36).

2. *San Francisco Wave,* July 14, 1900, HEH MS 17/3.

3. *Oneonta Star,* July 25, 1900, HEH MS 7/1(42).

4. Unidentified Los Angeles paper, 1902, HEH MS 7/6(2).

5. *Los Angeles Daily Journal,* March 20, 1903, HEH MS 7/10(5).

6. *Riverside Daily Press,* May 13, 1903, HEH Correspondence, box 102; *Riverside Enterprise,* March 24, 1903, HEH MS 7/10(5).

7. *San Pedro News,* August 2, 1904, HEH MS 7/4(4).

8. *Los Angeles Express,* January 20, 30, 1903, HEH MS 7/10(5).

9. *Los Angeles Herald,* July 3, 1904, HEH MS 7/10(7).

10. *Los Angeles Times,* November 26, 1904, HEH MS 7/4(5).

11. Alfred G. Walker, "Reminiscences," HEH MS 19/4.

12. *New York Globe,* June 25, 1904, HEH MS 7/10(7). And see *Los Angeles Herald,* July 23, 1904, HEH MS 7/2/1.

13. *Monrovia News,* November 12, 1904, HEH MS 7/4(5).

14. *Los Angeles Times,* May 8, 1904, HEH MS 7/10(7).

15. "New York Letter," by John Marthol, January 17, 1903, HEH MSS 7/10(5) and 16/2(2). Also in, for example, the *Richmond (Va.) Times, Lexington (Ky.) Leader, St. Paul (Minn.) Pioneer Press,* and *New Haven (Conn.) Union.*

16. *Chicago Star and Record-Herald,* August 26, 1905, HEH MS 7/10(9).

17. *New York Globe,* June 25, 1904, HEH MS 7/6(2). For a sample reprint, see *Alhambra Advocate,* August 12, 1904, HEH MS 7/4(4).

18. *Los Angeles Graphic,* August 19, September 16, 1905, HEH MS 7/10(9).

19. *Los Angeles Times,* January 1, 1905, HEH MS 7/6(3).

20. *Los Angeles Financier,* August 2, 1905, HEH MS 7/10(9).

21. J. B. Metcalf to Elizabeth Huntington, September 22, 1905, Metcalf Add. MSS, box 2.

22. HEH to James McLachlan, February 1, 1902, HEH Correspondence, box 93.

23. *Los Angeles Herald,* November 19, 1905, HEH MS 7/10(9).

24. *Los Angeles Times,* June 23, 1907, HEH MS 7/2/3.

25. *Los Angeles Herald,* November 10, 1910, HEH MS 7/4(25).

26. *Los Angeles Sunday Herald,* January 11, 1903, HEH MS 7/10(5).

27. *Los Angeles Express,* August 15, 1910, HEH MS 7/2/6.

28. *Los Angeles Herald,* April 4, 1903, HEH MS 7/10(6).

29. *Los Angeles Times,* August 24, 1904, HEH MS 7/4(4).

30. *Long Beach Daily News,* September 3, 1904, HEH MS 7/4(4).

31. *Los Angeles Herald,* November 19, 1905, December 13, 1906, HEH MS 16/2(2).

32. *San Francisco Evening Post,* May 3, 1904, HEH MS 7/10(7).

33. *Los Angeles Herald,* July 3, 1904, HEH MS 7/10(7).

34. HEH to Harry Chandler, December 31, 1906, replying to a letter of December 22, 1906, HEH Correspondence, box 122.

35. *Los Angeles Times,* January 12, 1902, HEH MS 16/6; *Los Angeles Herald,* January 12, 1902, HEH MS 7/10(4).

36. *Riverside Daily Press,* March 21, 1903, HEH MS 16/2(2); *Los Angeles Herald,* March 21, 1903, HEH MS 7/6(2); *Fresno Democrat,* March 28, 1903, HEH MS 7/10(5); and many other papers.

37. E. B. Holladay to Harriet, March 22, 1903, HEH Correspondence, box 101.

38. *Fresno Morning Republican,* May 19, 1903, HEH MS 7/6(2); *Fresno Evening Democrat,* May 19, 1903, HEH MS 7/10(6); *Los Angeles Times,* November 8, 1903, HEH MS 16/6; *Los Angeles Examiner,* February 22, 1904, HEH MS 7/10(7).

39. *Los Angeles Times,* June 22, 1905, HEH MS 7/10(8); *Los Angeles Examiner,* June 22, 1905, HEH MS 7/10(8).

40. *Los Angeles Times,* October 4, 1906, HEH MS 7/10(12); *Los Angeles Herald,* October 4, 1906, HEH MS 7/10(12); *Los Angeles Evening News,* October 4, 1906, HEH MS 7/4(17). The program is in HEH Correspondence, box 121.

41. *Los Angeles Express,* May 3, 1907, HEH MS 7/10(13); *Los Angeles Examiner,* June 16, 1909, HEH MS 7/10(16); *Los Angeles Herald,* June 16, 1909, HEH MS 7/10(16); *Los Angeles Express,* June 27, 1910, HEH MS 7/10(18).

42. *Los Angeles Examiner,* January 1, 1906, HEH MS 7/14(12); *Los Angeles Herald,* December 31, 1905, HEH MS 7/4(12).

43. *Los Angeles Times,* January 1, 1906, HEH MS 7/4(12).

44. *Los Angeles Times,* April 8, 1906, HEH MS 7/10(11).

45. *Los Angeles Times,* January 1, 1907, HEH MS 7/10(13).

46. *Los Angeles Times,* May 11, 1907, HEH MS 7/10(13).

47. *Los Angeles Herald Sunday Magazine,* December 20, 1908, HEH MS 7/10(15).

48. *Los Angeles Times,* January 1, 1909, HEH MS 7/10(16).

49. *Los Angeles Examiner,* December 26, 1909, HEH MS 7/10(17).

50. *Los Angeles Graphic,* May 18, 1908, HEH MS 7/10(15).

51. *San Francisco Argonaut,* January 22, 1910, HEH MS 16/2(3).

52. *San Francisco Evening Post,* March 25, 1910, HEH MS 7/10(18).

53. *San Francisco Chronicle,* October 3, 1910, HEH MS 7/10(19).

54. Ralph D. Paine, "H. E. Huntington an American Builder of Today," *The Outing Magazine,* 1906; Henry Shedd Beardsley, "Is Los Angeles the New York of the Pacific Coast?" *Leslie's Weekly,* March 22, 1906.

55. *New York Commercial,* May 17, 1905, HEH MS 7/10(8); *New York Town Topics,* March 1, 1906, HEH MS 7/10(44).

56. *St. Louis Daily Globe-Democrat,* November 25, 1906, HEH MS 7/12(12).

57. *Los Angeles Herald,* November 19, 1905, HEH MS 7/10(9).

58. *Los Angeles Times, Los Angeles Herald, Los Angeles Examiner,* October 25, 1909, HEH MS 7/10(17); *Pasadena Star,* October 25, 1909, HEH MS 16/2(2).

59. *Los Angeles Times,* November 13, 1910, HEH MS 7/10(19); *Los Angeles Times,* January 1, 1910, HEH MS 17/3; *Los Angeles Examiner,* December 25, 1910, HEH MS 7/2/6.

60. William B. Friedricks, *Henry E. Huntington and the Creation of Southern California* (Columbus: Ohio State University Press, 1992), 159. This study gives explicit details about the capitalizing, operating, merging, and disposition of Huntington's many companies in Southern California. It appeared after this manuscript had been completed; there seem to be no important contradictions between the two treatments.

61. *Los Angeles Herald,* August 18, 1906, HEH MS 7/10(12).

62. *Los Angeles Times,* May 11, 1907, HEH MS 7/4(19).

63. *Corona Courier,* October 15, 1904; *Anaheim Gazette,* October 20, 1904; *Los Angeles Record,* November 2, 1904. All in HEH MS 7/4(4).

64. *Los Angeles Spectator,* August 27, 1910, HEH MS 7/10(19).

65. *Los Angeles Evening News,* October 16, 1905, HEH MS 7/10(8).

66. *New York Evening Mail,* January 24, 1905, HEH MS 7/6(3).

67. *Los Angeles Evening News,* March 2, 1906, HEH MS 7/4(16).

68. *Huntington Beach News,* December 29, 1905, HEH MS 7/4(12).

69. *Long Beach Press,* September 23, 1905, HEH MS 7/4(10).

70. *Los Angeles Evening News,* January 17, 1906, HEH MS 7/4(15).

71. HEH MS 19/4.

72. *Pictorial American,* July 1907, HEH MS 7/10(28).

73. *Los Angeles Examiner,* October 2, 1906, HEH MS 7/10(12).

74. For other versions, see *California Independent,* March 1, 1906, HEH MS 7/4(16); *Los Angeles Times,* January 27, 1907, HEH MS 7/10(13).

12. CHANGING DIRECTIONS

1. *Los Angeles Herald,* May 31, 1905, HEH MS 16/6. This story was copied in various other papers, such as the *San Pedro News,* May 31, 1905, HEH MS 7/4(6).

2. *Compton (Calif.) Press,* June 2, 1905, HEH MS 7/4(6).

3. *Los Angeles Express,* September 9, 10, 1907, HEH MS 7/4(20).

4. *Los Angeles Express,* August 18, 1904, HEH MS 7/4(4).

5. Unidentified Seattle paper, April 30, 1902, HEH MS 7/6(2).

6. Bill, February 21, 1896, HEH MS 13/16/8.

7. *Compton (Calif.) Press,* July 7, 1905, HEH MS 7/4(6).

8. *San Francisco Examiner,* March 28, 1896, HEH MS 7/1(26).

9. *Los Angeles Sunday Times,* c. 1904–5, HEH MS 7/6(3).

10. Helen Holladay to Burke Holladay, May 1906, HEH Correspondence, box 120.

11. Frank A. Miller to William Crewdson, September 17, 1902, HEH Correspondence, box 96.

12. Elizabeth to HEH, September 27, October 1, 1902, Metcalf Add. MSS, box 1.

13. *Los Angeles Examiner,* October 4, 5, 18, 25, 1907, *Los Angeles Times,* October 5, 1907; *Los Angeles Evening News,* October 25, 1907, HEH MS 7/4(20). Also see HEH MSS 7/10(14), 7/2/3.

14. Harriet to HEH, January 28, 1902, HEH Correspondence, box 93.

15. Leonora (Mrs. B. W. Foster) to HEH, May 28, 1907, Metcalf Add. MSS, box 5.

16. The notes of her last words are in HEH Correspondence, box 120, folder 75. Representative newspaper accounts are in *San Francisco Chronicle,* June 22, 1906, and *Oneonta Herald,* July 5, 1906, HEH MS 7/10(44). See also *San Francisco Examiner,* June 28, 1906, HEH MS 16/6; *San Francisco Chronicle,* June 28, 1906, HEH MS 16/6.

17. *Los Angeles Times,* January 8, 1904, HEH MS 7/10(7).

18. Edith Jamison Lowes to HEH, September 16, 1919, HEH MS 31.1.1.29.

19. Carrie to HEH, May 1907, Metcalf Add. MSS, box 5.

20. For an example of a threatening letter, June 29, 1908, HEH MS 31.1.1.52.

21. *Los Angeles Herald,* December 5, 1905, HEH MS 7/4(16).

22. *Los Angeles Express,* November 28, 1905, HEH MS 16/11.

23. *Los Angeles Times,* April 15, 1905; *Los Angeles Examiner,* April 15, 16, 22, 1905; *San Bernardino Times-Index,* May 9, 1905. All in HEH MS 7/4(8).

24. *Los Angeles Times,* October 21, 1908, HEH MS 7/10(15).

25. Carrie to HEH, November 30, 1906, HEH Correspondence, box 121.

26. *New York Town Topics,* December 13, 1906, HEH MS 7/10(44).

27. *Los Angeles Examiner,* April 26, 1910, HEH MS 16/2(2). A short version was in the *New York Herald,* April 27, 1910, HEH MS 7/10(18).

28. Correspondence for November, December 1903, HEH Correspondence, box 106; *Los Angeles Examiner,* July 8, 1904, HEH MS 7/10(7).

29. *Los Angeles Express,* April 27, June 4, 1907, HEH MS 7/10(13).

30. *Los Angeles Times,* November 23, 1904, HEH MS 7/4(5); *Los Angeles Evening News,* October 31, 1906, HEH MS 7/10(12); *Los Angeles Examiner,* November 5, 1906, HEH MS 7/10(12).

31. *Los Angeles Times,* December 2, 1909. Stories about Aviation Week are in HEH MSS 7/10(17), (18), 7/2/5.

32. *Los Angeles Evening News,* November 20, 1906, and all other Los Angeles papers for the period November 12 to 21, 1906, HEH MS 7/10(12).

33. Correspondence between HEH and H. G. Otis, January 10–17, March 5–6, 1905, HEH Correspondence, boxes 115, 117; *Los Angeles Times,* November 29, 1905, HEH MS 16/11; *Los Angeles Herald,* December 22, 1905, HEH MS 16/11.

34. *Los Angeles Examiner,* December 21, 1910; *Los Angeles Herald, Los Angeles Daily Journal, Los Angeles Express,* December 23, 1910. All in HEH MS 7/4(25). *Los Angeles Graphic,* December 24, 1910, HEH MS 7/10(19).

35. *Los Angeles Evening News,* December 19, 1905, HEH MS 7/10(9).

36. *Los Angeles Examiner,* September 19, 1909, HEH MS 7/10(17).

37. *Santa Ana Blade,* December 29, 1905, HEH MS 7/4(12).

38. *Los Angeles Examiner,* April 9, 1907, HEH MS 7/4(19).

39. *Los Angeles Express,* September 4, 1906, HEH MS 16/11.

40. *Los Angeles Express,* October 21, 1908, HEH MS 7/10(15).

41. *Los Angeles Examiner,* April 26, 1910, HEH MS 16/2(2).

42. *Los Angeles Examiner,* January 23, 1905, HEH MS 7/4(6).

43. *Los Angeles Examiner,* November 27, 1908, HEH MS 16/3.

44. *Los Angeles Examiner,* November 28, 1908, HEH MS 16/3.

45. These and other representative papers are in HEH MS 16/3.

46. *Los Angeles Evening News,* November 27, 1908, HEH MS 7/24(22).

47. *Los Angeles Graphic,* September 4, 1909, HEH MS 7/4(23).

48. *Los Angeles Examiner,* April 26, 1910, HEH MS 16/2(2).

49. *Los Angeles Herald,* July 18, 1911, HEH MS 7/2/7.

50. *Los Angeles Examiner,* May 10, 1910, HEH MS 7/2/5.

51. Agreement, January 2, 1903, HEH Correspondence, box 99; Purchase Agreements, Los Angeles Land Co., May 16, 1903, HEH MS 1/I/1; Huntington Land and Improvement Co. Audits, December 31, 1911, HEH MS 1/EE.

52. *Los Angeles Examiner,* May 25, 1909, HEH MS 7/10(16).

53. *Los Angeles Examiner,* August 13, 1910, HEH MS 7/2/5.

54. Huntington Land and Improvement Co. maps, c. 1903–05, HEH MS 1/BB(3), (4).

55. *Los Angeles Times,* October 11, 1908, HEH MS 7/10(43).

56. HEH to Elizabeth, October 23, 1904, Metcalf Add. MSS, box 2.

57. HEH to Harriet, October 16, 1904, HEH Correspondence, box 114.

58. *Los Angeles Examiner,* January 17, 1904, HEH MS 7/10(7).

59. *Los Angeles Times,* May 25, 1909, HEH MS 7/10(16).

60. William Hertrich, "History of San Marino Ranch," 4, HEH Biographical File.

61. *Los Angeles Sunday Times,* June 7, 1908, HEH MS 7/4(22).

62. *San Francisco Call,* January 26, 1909, HEH MS 7/10(16).

63. Carrie to Harriet, March 31, 1903, HEH Correspondence, box 101. Also in Diary of E. B. Holladay, March 22, 1903, HEH MS 53/2.

64. Elizabeth to Brockway Metcalf, December 30, 1905, January 5, 1906, Metcalf Add. MSS, box 4.

65. Diary of E. B. Holladay, May 29, 1908, HEH MS 53/2.

66. HEH to Patton, December 31, 1904, HEH Correspondence, box 115.

67. HEH to Patton, January 3, 1905, HEH Correspondence, box 115.

68. HEH to Patton, January 16, 1905, HEH Correspondence, box 115.

69. HEH to Patton, January 23, 1905, HEH Correspondence, box 115.

70. HEH to Patton, February 20, 1905, HEH Correspondence, box 116.

71. HEH to Patton, March 3, 1905, HEH Correspondence, box 117.

72. HEH and Patton, December 23, 28, 31, 1904, February 6, 16, March 15, 28, 1905, HEH Correspondence, boxes 115–18.

73. Patton to HEH, January 4, 1905, HEH Correspondence, box 115.

74. HEH to Patton, January 23, 1905, HEH Correspondence, box 115.

75. William Hertrich, *The Huntington Botanical Gardens 1905–1949: Personal Recollections* (San Marino: Huntington Library, 1949).

76. Ernest Braunton to HEH, September 28, 1906, HEH Correspondence, box 121. See also his recollections in the garden column of the *Los Angeles Times,* November 13, 1910, HEH MS 16/10; Patton to HEH, October 20, 1906, HEH Correspondence, box 121; E. D. Sturtevant to Patton, October 29, 1906, HEH Correspondence, box 121.

77. *San Diego Union,* January 27, 1908, HEH MS 7/10(15).

78. HEH to Hertrich, March 18, 1909, HEH Correspondence, box 125; *Los Angeles Times,* August 17, 1908, HEH MS 7/10(15).

79. *Los Angeles Examiner,* June 21, 1909, HEH MS 7/4(23).

80. Hertrich, *Huntington Botanical Gardens,* 8–9.

81. Ed Fletcher to HEH, August 10, 1908, HEH Correspondence, box 124.

82. Morgan Ross to HEH, July 30, 1908, HEH Correspondence, box 124.

83. *Los Angeles Examiner,* November 27, 1908, HEH MS 16/3; Hertrich, *Huntington Botanical Gardens,* 38–39.

84. Hertrich, *Huntington Botanical Gardens,* 27–28; 1909 Chronology, Huntington Biographical File, HEH MS 19/3.

85. HEH to Hertrich, October 26, 1908, HEH Correspondence, box 124.

86. HEH to Hertrich, October 11, 1910, HEH Correspondence, box 127.

87. HEH to Hertrich, December 23, 1910, HEH Correspondence, box 127.

88. Patton to HEH, December 24, 1908, Patton Collection, box 5.

89. *Los Angeles Express,* May 24, 1909, HEH MS 7/4(23). For more examples: *Los Angeles Times,* January 1, 1909, HEH MS 7/10(16); *San Francisco Chronicle,* May 9, 1909, and twenty-seven other papers, HEH MS 16/7.

90. Details in the following paragraphs about building the residence are drawn from the reminiscences of Myron Hunt (November 21, 1927, May 8, 1928, February 1, 1930) and Charles E. Richards (June 19, 1928), all in HEH MS 19/3, and from Hertrich's recollections in *Huntington Botanical Gardens,* 2–4, 27–28, 30–31, 33–39, 53–54. Sources are given for quotations.

91. Myron Hunt, February 24, 1908, HEH MS 19/3.

92. Twenty-two letters, documents, and photographs in HEH Correspondence, boxes 125, 126, folder 15.

93. HEH to Hunt, July 22, 1908, HEH Correspondence, box 124.

94. HEH to Hunt, March 12, 1910, HEH Correspondence, box 126.

95. Hunt, November 21, 1927, HEH MS 19/3.

96. Duveen Brothers to HEH, December 9, 1909, HEH Correspondence, box 126.

97. Charles E. Richards, June 19, 1928, HEH MS 19/3.

98. Myron Hunt interview, February 1, 1930, HEH MS 19/3.

99. Duveen invoice, January 28, 1909, HEH MS 28/1.

100. Myron Hunt, Reminiscences, February 1, 1930, HEH MS 19/3.

101. Charles E. Richards, Reminiscences, June 19, 1928, HEH MS 19/3.

102. *Los Angeles Graphic,* August 21, 1909, HEH MS 7/10(17).

103. Samuel T. Clover, *Los Angeles Graphic,* November 27, 1909, Metcalf Add. MSS, box 6.

104. Otheman Stevens, *Los Angeles Examiner,* May 25, 1909, HEH MS 7/10(16).

105. 1907 note, HEH Correspondence, box 123.

106. Bill, June 11, 1904, HEH MS 25/5.

107. Dodd Mead, 1905, HEH MS 25/5; Walker and Stonestreet, May 19, 1905, HEH MS 31.1.1.48.

108. HEH to Dodd Mead, May 9, 1905, HEH MS 31.1.1.13.

109. Reminiscences of Isaac Mendoza, October 18, 1930, HEH MS 19/3; *Huntington Library Bulletin* 1 (1931): 36.

110. Reminiscences of Isaac Mendoza, October 18, 1930, HEH MS 19/3; *Huntington Library Bulletin* 1 (1931): 36.

111. *Los Angeles Examiner,* November 6, 1905, HEH MS 7/4(11).

112. S. and G. Gump Co. to HEH, September 16, 1905, HEH Correspondence, box 119; twenty-three letters and telegrams between Gump and HEH, HEH Correspondence, box 98.

113. HEH to William Schaus, February 2, 1907, HEH Correspondence, box 122; Schaus to HEH, February 4, 1907, HEH Correspondence, box 122; HEH to Knoedler, February 20, 1907, HEH MS 13/13/9.

114. H. H. Topakyar invoices, February 1907, Metcalf Add. MSS, boxes 5–6.
115. N. P. Chapin to HEH, February 26, March 2, 4, 13, 15, 1907, HEH MS 31.1.1.9.
116. G. E. Miles to HEH, March 15, 1906, HEH MS 31.1.1.32; HEH to G. E. Miles, March 26, 1906, HEH MS 31.1.1.32.
117. Catalog, October 15, 1906, HEH MS 16/5/3.
118. HEH to Elizabeth, December 29, 1907, Metcalf Add. MSS, box 5.
119. HEH's contemporary statement, HEH MS 31.1.1.40.
120. Duveen invoice, January 28, 1909, HEH MS 28/1.
121. April 15, 1909, HEH Correspondence, box 125. For Raeburn, HEH MS 19/3.
122. March 8, 1910, HEH MS 1/D/4(2); thirty letters and documents, HEH Correspondence, box 126.
123. Ehrich Galleries, December 29, 1910, HEH Correspondence, box 127; June 21, 1909, HEH Correspondence, box 125.
124. Partridge, Lewis & Simmons invoice, December 12, 1910, HEH Correspondence, box 127.
125. *Pasadena Star,* October 25, 1909, HEH MS 7/4(24).
126. Howard E. Morton, *Los Angeles Examiner,* May 17, 1909, HEH MS 16/2(1).
127. Invoices from Sessler, HEH MSS 31.1.1.41, 1/D/4(2); Reminiscences of Mabel Zahn, a Sessler associate, HEH MS 19/1(12); HEH to Sessler, June 2, 1909, HEH MS 31.1.1.41.
128. Catalogs bought February 3, 11, 1910, HEH MS 25/5.
129. W. Roberts, *Rare Books and Their Prices* (New York, 1896), HEH 20649.
130. *Los Angeles Examiner,* December 25, 1910, HEH MS 7/10(19).
131. *Los Angeles Examiner,* April 18, 1910, HEH MS 16/10.
132. *Los Angeles Financier,* May 16, 1908, HEH MS 16/11.
133. *Los Angeles Examiner,* May 26, 1909, HEH MS 16/2(2).
134. Samuel T. Clover, *Los Angeles Graphic,* November 27, 1909, HEH MS 7/10.

13. BEGINNING A NEW LIFE

1. *Los Angeles Herald,* April 16, 1911, HEH MS 16/3. The other clippings about the Church library are also preserved in this collection, as well as in Metcalf Add. MSS, box 6.
2. Emory S. Turner to HEH, April 10, 1911, HEH MS 31.1.1.2.
3. *New York Sun,* April 25, 1911, HEH MS 16/9.

4. *New York American,* April 26, 1911, HEH MS 16/6.

5. For examples, see *New York World, New York Sun, New York Telegraph, New York Times, Hartford Times,* all for April 25, 1911, HEH MS 16/9.

6. For examples, see HEH MSS 16/6, 16/9, 7/10(38–43), 7/2/6, 7/4(25).

7. *Chico (Calif.) Enterprise,* May 2, 1911, HEH MS 16/9.

8. Epes Randolph to HEH, May 2, 1911, HEH Correspondence, box 128; HEH to Randolph, May 8, 1911, HEH Correspondence, box 128.

9. *Boston Transcript,* May 3, 1911, HEH MS 16/9.

10. *Galesburg (Ill.) Mail,* April 29, 1911, HEH MS 16/6.

11. Offers are preserved in HEH MS 31.1.1.19.

12. *New York Herald,* April 25, 1911, HEH MS 16/9.

13. *New York World,* April 26, 1911, HEH MS 16/6.

14. *New York American,* April 27, 1911, HEH MS 16/6.

15. *Milwaukee Evening Wisconsin,* May 1, 1911, HEH MS 16/6.

16. HEH MS 7/10(38).

17. Quoted frequently, as in *Chicago Post,* April 24, 1911, HEH MS 16/6.

18. *New York Times,* April 26, 1911, HEH MS 16/9.

19. *American Art News,* April 29, 1911, HEH MS 16/6; *Boston Transcript,* May 6, 1911, HEH MS 16/6.

20. *New York Times,* April 30, 1911, HEH MS 16/9; *New York Herald,* May 7, 1911, HEH MS 16/3; *New York Tribune,* May 7, 1911, HEH MS 7/10(21).

21. *Huntington Library Bulletin* 1 (1931): 38.

22. November 1911, HEH MS 7/10(38).

23. Quaritch correspondence on the sale is in HEH MS 31.1.1.37; Purchases, 1912–19, HEH MS 25/4.

24. HEH's notes are preserved in HEH MS 16/5/1. For the conversation, see George Watson Cole, "Report of the Librarian," October 1, 1924, p. 22, based on MS reminiscences of Caroline Holladay, HEH MS 19/3.

25. Receipt, October 19, 1912, HEH MS 31.1.1.9; the Library of Herschel V. Jones, 1918, HEH MS 46/2.

26. *Huntington Library Bulletin* 1 (1931): 42–43.

27. Bernard Quaritch (E. H. Dring) to HEH, March 27, 1914, HEH MS 31.1.1.37.

28. A list of sales and dates is in HEH MS 25/2.

29. *Huntington Library Bulletin* 1 (1931): 40–42.

30. See the book bills arranged by dealer in HEH MS 25/1–6.

31. March 16, January 2, 30, April 17, 1911, HEH MS 28/1.

32. *Los Angeles Examiner,* July 18, 1911, HEH MS 7/10(22).

33. *New York Times,* June 18, 1911, HEH MS 16/7; *New York Herald,* May 11, 1912, HEH MS 16/7.

34. *New York Times,* December 11, 1912, HEH MS 16/7.

35. E. B. Holladay's Diary, July 13, 1911, HEH MS 16/2(2).

36. ADH to HEH, July 24, 1911, HEH MS 28/1.

37. Joseph Duveen to HEH, August 1, 1911, HEH MS 28/1.

38. HEH MS 7/10(38).

39. Duveen invoice, November 1911, HEH MS 28/1.

40. *New York Times,* January 17, 1912; *Philadelphia Item,* January 18, 1912; *Philadelphia Inquirer,* January 21, 1912. All in HEH MS 7/10(24).

41. Invoice for the Hoppners, December 31, 1912, HEH Correspondence, box 130; for the Romney, HEH MS 16/1(1).

42. *New York Sun,* February 24, 1912, and twenty other papers, HEH MS 16/7.

43. *Los Angeles Examiner,* May 23, 1912, HEH MS 7/2/9.

44. Duveen bill, April 7, 1913, HEH MS 28/1; *New York Herald,* April 25, 1913, HEH MS 16/7; *Los Angeles Examiner,* May 2, 1913, HEH MS 7/4(29).

45. Duveen bill, November 5, 1914, HEH MS 28/1.

46. Otheman Stevens, *Los Angeles Examiner,* December 28, 1911, HEH MS 16/7.

47. *Pasadena News,* March 18, 1912, HEH MS 16/7.

48. Hertrich to HEH, October 20, November 6, 1913, May 23, 1914, HEH Correspondence, box 131; HEH MS 6/15.

49. Correspondence between HEH and Hertrich, August 1911 through March 1912, HEH Correspondence, boxes 128, 129; *Los Angeles Tribune,* August 20, 1911, HEH MS 16/7; HEH MS 19/5 for 1911; William Hertrich, *Huntington Botanical Gardens,* 78–80. Hertrich's memory played him false in the dating of the project, which he gives as 1912–13 rather than 1911–12.

50. *Ogden (Utah) Standard,* November 7, 1912, from *Pennsylvania Grit,* HEH MS 7/10(38).

51. HEH to Hertrich, April 25, 1909, HEH Correspondence, box 125.

52. Letters between HEH and Hertrich, 1912–13, HEH Correspondence, boxes 129–31; bills for purchases, HEH MS 6/15.

53. HEH to J. Starkie Gardner, October 17, 1913, HEH Correspondence, box 131; *New York Times,* December 10, 1913, HEH MS 16/7.

54. Letters, June 10, July 8, October 5, 1913, HEH Correspondence, box 131.

55. *Los Angeles Times, Los Angeles Examiner, Los Angeles Herald, Los Angeles Tribune,* all for July 26, 1911, HEH MS 7/4(25); *Los Angeles Examiner,*

September 9, 1911, HEH MS 7/10(22); *Los Angeles Tribune,* April 7, 1912, HEH MS 7/2/9; *Pasadena News,* January 28, 1913, HEH MS 7/10(24).

56. For a few typical stories: congestion, *Los Angeles Examiner,* November 17, 1911, HEH MS 7/4(26); overcrowding, *Los Angeles Examiner,* January 15, 1912, HEH MS 7/10(24); franchises, *Los Angeles Record,* August 12, 1911, HEH MS 7/4(25); fares and transfers, *Los Angeles Herald,* March 14, 1912, HEH MS 7/4(27); public ownership, *Los Angeles Tribune,* June 21, 1913, HEH MS 7/10(25).

57. *Los Angeles Record,* August 16, 1911, HEH MS 7/4(25).

58. *Los Angeles Herald,* December 23, 1913, HEH MS 7/2/13.

59. *Los Angeles Herald,* August 12, 13, 1911, HEH MSS 7/4(25), 7/10(22).

60. *Los Angeles Tribune,* September 15, 1911, HEH MS 7/10(22); *Los Angeles Express,* September 15, 1911, HEH MS 7/10(22).

61. HEH to H. G. Otis, December 1, 1912, HEH Correspondence, box 130.

62. *New York American,* May 4, 1911, and forty-three other papers, HEH MS 7/10(21); *New York Sun,* July 13, 1911, HEH MS 7/10(22).

63. *Los Angeles Times,* April 13, 1913, HEH MS 7/10(25).

64. George S. Patton to HEH, March 21, 1913, HEH Patton Collection, box 5; HEH to George S. Patton, April 9, 1913, HEH Patton Collection, box 5.

65. *Los Angeles Examiner,* May 16, 1913, HEH MS 7/4(29).

66. *Los Angeles Express,* January 29, 1912, HEH MS 7/10(23).

67. *Los Angeles Examiner,* September 13, 1912, HEH MS 7/4(28).

68. *Los Angeles Express,* May 15, 1913, HEH MS 7/10(25).

69. *Los Angeles Herald,* January 3, 1914, HEH MS 7/2/13.

70. *Los Angeles Examiner,* January 9, 1914, HEH MS 7/10(26).

71. Balance sheets, HEH MS 11/2/1.

72. *Los Angeles Examiner,* April 6, 1906, HEH MS 7/10(44). Also in *Pasadena News,* April 6, 1906; *Seattle Times,* April 8, 1906; *Louisville Post,* April 18, 1906.

73. The May 1909 clippings are in HEH MS 16/11. Other accounts for the period 1907–10 are in HEH MSS 7/4(23), 7/10(13), (16), 16/2(1), (2).

74. *Los Angeles Times,* December 23, 1910, HEH MS 7/10(19).

75. Marian to Elizabeth, July 16, 1908, Metcalf Add. MSS, box 5.

76. Mary to Elizabeth, July 18, 1908, Metcalf Add. MSS, box 5.

77. Marian to Elizabeth, July 20, 1908, Metcalf Add. MSS, box 5.

78. Leslie to Elizabeth, August 6, 1908, Metcalf Add. MSS, box 5.

79. Arabella to Carrie, undated (1909?), HEH Correspondence, box 125.

80. Leslie to Clara, February 25, 1912, Metcalf Add. MSS, box 6.

81. Leslie to Elizabeth, December 1, 1912, Metcalf Add. MSS, box 6.
82. Passport application, April 16, 1913, HEH Correspondence, box 130; HEH to Carrie, July 13, 1913, HEH Correspondence, box 131.
83. HEH to Carrie, July 16, 1913, HEH Correspondence, box 131.
84. HEH to Carrie, July 20, 1913, HEH Correspondence, box 131.
85. HEH to Carrie, August 2, 1913, HEH Correspondence, box 131.
86. Elizabeth to Mary Huntington, July 25, 1913, Metcalf Add. MSS, box 6.
87. HEH to Elizabeth, August 2, 1913, Metcalf Add. MSS, box 6.
88. HEH to Elizabeth, September 2, 1913, Metcalf Add. MSS, box 6.
89. HEH to Brockway Metcalf, September 2, 1913, Metcalf Add. MSS, box 6.
90. There are more than two hundred clippings on the subject in HEH MS 38/2 alone, and many in other sources.
91. *Cincinnati Enquirer,* July 17, 1913, HEH MS 38/2; *New York Sun,* July 17, 1913, HEH MS 38/2.
92. George E. Miles to M/M HEH July 17, 1913, HEH Correspondence, box 131.
93. *St. Louis Republic,* July 18, 1913, and many other papers, all in HEH MS 16/11.
94. HEH to Carrie, September 5, 1913, HEH Correspondence, box 131.
95. *Los Angeles Tribune,* October 28, 1913, HEH MS 7/4(30).
96. *Los Angeles Herald,* December 11, 1913, HEH MS 7/4(30).
97. *Los Angeles Examiner,* January 21, 1914, HEH MS 7/4(30).
98. Full details of the arrival are in *Los Angeles Herald, Los Angeles Times, Los Angeles Examiner,* all for January 23, 1913; *Los Angeles Tribune,* January 24, 1913. All in HEH MS 7/10(26).
99. E. B. Holladay, Diary, February 28 to March 28, 1914, HEH MS 53/2; Leslie to Elizabeth, February 25, 1914, Metcalf Add. MSS, box 6. Newspaper accounts appeared in *Los Angeles Examiner,* February 24, 1914, HEH MS 7/10(26); *Los Angeles Times,* February 24, 1914, HEH MS 7/4(30).
100. *Los Angeles Times,* February 5, 1914, HEH MS 7/4(30).
101. *Los Angeles Examiner,* February 20, 1914, HEH MS 7/4(30).
102. *Los Angeles Herald,* April 10, 1914, HEH MS 7/10(26).
103. *New York Town Topics,* April 23, 1914, HEH MS 7/10(26).
104. *Los Angeles Times,* February 6, 1914; *Los Angeles Herald,* February 6, 1914; *Los Angeles Examiner,* February 7, 1914. All in HEH MS 7/4(30).
105. Clara to Elizabeth, February 21, 1914, Metcalf Add. MSS, box 6.
106. HEH to Carrie, April 8, 1914, HEH Correspondence, box 131.
107. *Los Angeles Examiner,* April 10, 1914, HEH MS 7/4(31).

108. *Los Angeles Tribune,* January 24, 1914, HEH MS 7/10(26).

109. *Los Angeles Herald,* April 10, 1914, HEH MS 7/10(26).

14. ARABELLA

1. Randolph Natili to HEH, October 4, 1913. HEH Correspondence, box 131.

2. Two worth mentioning are Stephen Birmingham, *The Grandes Dames* (New York: Simon and Schuster, 1982), 185–220; and James T. Maher, *The Twilight of Splendor* (Boston: Little Brown, 1975), 215–309.

3. Surrogate's court, HEH MS 39/1–2. federal estate tax return, HEH MS 37/1; legacy return, August 13, 1903, HEH Correspondence, box 104; CPH to W. N. Batchelder, July 14, 1891, HEH MS 30/21, p. 17; Elizabeth to Brockway, November 13, 1905, Metcalf Add. MSS, box 3.

4. Cerinda W. Evans, *Arabella Duval Huntington* (Newport News, Va., 1959); Maher, *Twilight of Splendor,* 249–57.

5. Maher, *Twilight of Splendor,* gives a full account of this version, based on a careful study of city directories, census reports, and other documents (pp. 246–57), and makes a central point of his interpretation of Arabella that she "lived with the burden of a lie."

6. A. Hyatt Mayor, *A Century of American Sculpture* (New York: Abbeville Press, 1980), 21–22.

7. B. D. Worsham to CPH, November 10, 1871, CPH Papers, ser. 1, reel 4.

8. Block 1269, lots 38–48, title search reports, HEH Correspondence, box 194.

9. CP stock, January 30, November 8, 1880, CPH Papers, ser. 2, reel 12; C & O stock, May 17, 1881, CPH Papers, ser. 2, reel 12.

10. For example, her letters of October 10, November 1, 4, 10, 1882, CPH Papers, ser. 1, reels 29, 30.

11. Texas, B. D. Worsham to CPH, January 28, 1877, CPH Papers, ser. 1, reel 11; CPH cable, September 18, 1882, CPH Papers, ser. 2, reel 13; customs bill, B. D. Worsham to CPH, April 12, 1883, CPH Papers, ser. 1, reel 32.

12. Elizabeth to HEH, November 3, 1901, HEH Correspondence, box 91.

13. Elizabeth to Brockway, November 12, 1905, Metcalf Add. MSS, box 3.

14. Elizabeth to Brockway, November 13, 1905, Metcalf Add. MSS, box 3.

15. These letters, from which I quote in the following three paragraphs, are in HEH MSS 418–26 and HEH Correspondence, box 125.

16. ADH to Carrie, October 20, 1889, HEH MS 419.

17. ADH to Carrie, December 17, 1900, HEH MS 422.

18. Harriet to Carrie, September 7, 1900, HEH Correspondence, box 86.
19. Elizabeth to Brockway, November 8, 1905, Metcalf Add. MSS, box 3.
20. ADH to Carrie, April 1, 1902, HEH MS 425.
21. ADH to Carrie (1909?), HEH Correspondence, box 125.
22. ADH to Carrie, July 20, 1900, HEH MS 421.
23. ADH to Carrie, April 1, 1902, HEH Correspondence, box 101.
24. CPH to HEH, June 4, 1896, HEH Correspondence, box 49.
25. HEH to Carrie, March 3, 1901, HEH Correspondence, box 88.
26. Lucy Cone Gayles to HEH, January 6, 1902, HEH Correspondence, box 93.
27. George E. Miles to HEH, April 7, 1902, HEH Correspondence, box 94.
28. Helen Huntington to Carrie, December 28, 1896, HEH Correspondence, box 53.
29. HEH MS 39/3.
30. HEH MS 24/5.
31. Elizabeth to Brockway, October 22, 1905, Metcalf Add. MSS, box 3.
32. ADH to Harvard, March 2, 1902, HEH Correspondence, box 94; HEH MS 7/6(2); May 24, 1903, HEH MS 16/11; February 17, 1915, HEH MS 7/4(32), Metcalf Add. MSS, box 24.
33. May 25, 1909, HEH MS 7/10(44); March 19, 1910, HEH MS 16/7.
34. May 18, 1906, HEH Correspondence, box 120.
35. Tiffany bills, 1903–12, ADH Papers, reel 4280.
36. *San Francisco Call,* August 15, 1900, photo by Taber, HEH MS 7/1(42), p. 73.
37. October 6, 1907, HEH MS 7/10(14); May 25, 1908, May 4, 1909, March 10, 1910, HEH MSS 16/11, 7/10(44).
38. *Los Angeles Examiner,* November 18, 1910, HEH MS 7/10(44).
39. *San Francisco Call,* May 4, 1896, HEH MS 7/1(27).
40. *San Francisco Chronicle,* November 29, 1900, HEH MS 7/1(43).
41. *New York World,* April 26, 1908, HEH MS 7/10(44).
42. November 3, 1909, HEH MS 7/10(44), contains accounts from many papers, including the *New York World* and the *Los Angeles Times.*
43. James Henry Duveen, *Secrets of an Art Dealer* (London: Robert Hale, 1937), 170–71.
44. *San Francisco Wasp,* January 24, 1925, HEH MS 16/3.
45. ADH to Carrie, HEH MSS 418, 420, 422, 423.
46. January 6, 1902, October 13, 1903, HEH Correspondence, boxes 93, 105.
47. HEH to Harriet, June 20, 1903, HEH Correspondence, box 103.

48. July 29, 1909, HEH MS 7/10(44); *New York Herald,* November 3, 1909, HEH MS 7/10(44).

49. HEH to Carrie, July 20, 1913, HEH Correspondence, box 131.

50. Edward Fowles, *Memories of Duveen Brothers* (London: Times Books, 1976), 68.

51. Graham to Treasury Department, January 11, 1922, HEH Correspondence, box 150.

52. Mayor, *A Century of American Sculpture,* 22–23.

53. Germain Seligman, *Merchants of Art* (New York: Appleton, 1962), 139.

54. ADH to Carrie (1902?), HEH MS 424.

55. A copy is in CPH Papers, ser. 1, reel 37.

56. The long statement of the unidentified friend is taken from the *Philadelphia Post* and printed in the *Des Moines Register,* December 21, 1900, and other papers. HEH MS 7/10(2).

57. See, for example, April 15, 1884, to April 22, 1885, CPH Papers, ser. 2, reel 24.

58. John D. Yarrington to CPH, December 30, 1879, and later, CPH Papers, ser. 1, reel 18.

59. CPH to John D. Yarrington, January 2, 1880, CPH Papers, ser. 2, reel 12.

60. John D. Yarrington to CPH, April 17, 1884, CPH Papers, ser. 1, reel 34.

61. John D. Yarrington to CPH, January 5, 1887, CPH Papers, ser. 1, reel 43.

62. HEH to CPH, November 2, 1887, HEH MS 10/1.

63. These details are elaborated in CPH Papers, esp. ser. 1, reels 46–48, 53, ser. 2, reels 33, 34. The funeral details are in Mary Lewis to Harriet, August 17, 1900, HEH Correspondence, box 85.

64. CPH to R. M. Yarrington, December 27, 1878, CPH Papers, ser. 2, reel 35.

65. CPH Papers, ser. 1, reels 40, 41, 43, ser. 2, reel 16, ser. 4, reel 2.

66. November 3, 1886, CPH Papers, ser. 3, reel 22.

67. CPH Papers, ser. 1, reel 47, ser. 2, reel 33, ser. 3, reel 4.

68. Marie Huntington to Harriet, October 21, 1885, HEH Correspondence, box 16.

69. D. W. MacNichol, M.D., to CPH, July 17, 1889, CPH Papers, ser. 1, reel 47.

70. Caroline G. Reid to CPH, May 20, 1882, CPH Papers, ser. 1, reel 28.

71. Mrs. A. J. Wiles to CPH, June 5, 1882, CPH Papers, ser. 1, reel 28.

72. December 3, 1894, CPH Papers, ser. 1, reel 53.

73. Beatrice G. Proske, *Archer Milton Huntington* (New York: Hispanic Society of America, 1963), 4–8.

74. *San Francisco Examiner,* August 10, 1895, HEH MS 7/10(1).

75. May 21, 1886, CPH Papers, ser. 1, reel 42.

76. February 1894, CPH Papers, ser. 1, reel 53.

77. October 14, 1896, HEH MS 7/6(1).

78. Fowles, *Memories of Duveen Brothers,* 69.

79. J. P. Morgan to CPH, November 27, 1899, CPH Papers, ser. 1, reel 54.

80. These transactions are more fully described in Maher, *Twilight of Splendor,* 264–81.

81. G. B. Post to CPH, June 29, 1894, CPH Papers, ser. 1, reel 53.

82. Elihu Vedder to Annie Fields, November 23, 1894, HEH Fields Collection, FI 4297.

83. *New York Tribune* (1890?), HEH MS 16/11.

84. Helen Ward, Ryman Newspaper Syndicate, unidentifiable New York newspaper, 1895, HEH Correspondence, box 42.

85. In 1902 her record duty payment was $34,000. *Los Angeles Examiner,* November 18, 1910, HEH MS 7/10(44).

86. February 1897, HEH Correspondence, box 55.

87. *Los Angeles Times,* March 9, 1907, HEH MS 7/2/3.

88. *San Francisco Chronicle,* July 12, 1908, HEH MS 16/7.

89. Albert Bierstadt to CPH, July 18, 1872, January 1, 17, 23, February 15, 17, March 6, 21, December 3, 1873, CPH Papers, ser. 1, reels 4, 5.

90. Albert Bierstadt to CPH, November 13, 27, 1885, CPH Papers, ser. 1, reel 41.

91. Carleton Watkins to CPH, February 3, 1877, CPH Papers, ser. 1, reel 44; HEH to CPH, June 13, 1896, HEH Correspondence, box 50; CPH to HEH, June 18, 1896, HEH Correspondence, box 50; *Oneonta Star,* November 10, 1970, HEH MS 16/2(1).

92. Knoedler, September 30, 1875, CPH Papers, ser. 1, reel 8; Huffnagle, March 15, 1880, CPH Papers, ser. 1, reel 19; Avery, April 17, November 18, 1879, April 30, 1880, March 17, 1881, CPH Papers, ser. 1, reels 17, 19, 22.

93. George Barrie to CPH, August 12, 1880, June 14, 1881, CPH Papers, ser. 1, reels 20, 23.

94. C. T. Marsh & Co., November 21, 1890, CPH Papers, ser. 1, reel 48; S. Chatain, February 12, 1893, CPH Papers, ser. 1, reel 51; American Art Association, September 1893, CPH Papers, ser. 1, reel 52; Wunderlich, August 1, 1900, HEH Correspondence, box 84.

95. Roxina E. Sherwood to ADH, March 1892, CPH Papers, ser. 2, reel 33.

96. Durand-Ruel, February 25, 1891; Harnett (James T. Abbe), January 20, 1891; Hublin (A. May Hassler), January 29, 1891; Chialioa, Decem-

ber 10, 1890, February 9, 1891; Shurtleff, April 23, 1891. All in CPH Papers, ser. 1, reel 49.

97. CPH to Gates, October 1, 1889, CPH Papers, ser. 1, reel 48.

98. Gump, October 3, 1892, CPH Papers, ser. 1, reel 51; Piazetta, December 1898, HEH Correspondence, box 69.

99. Gouverneur Morris to CPH, March 20, 1891, CPH Papers, ser. 1, reel 49.

100. Albert G. Sudlow to CPH, March 7, 1891, CPH Papers, ser. 1, reel 49.

101. Bennison, September 24, 1892, CPH Papers, ser. 1, reel 51; Ehrich, October 30, 1890, CPH Papers, ser. 1, reel 48; Raphael, January 15, 1892, CPH Papers, ser. 1, reel 50; Ribera, March 8, 1895, CPH Papers, ser. 1, reel 53.

102. About the inventory, April 1897, HEH Correspondence, box 56; for the list of paintings, HEH to CPH, July 5, 1899, HEH Correspondence, box 72; concerning value, HEH to CPH, October 26, 1899, HEH Correspondence, box 74.

103. CPH to HEH, October 2, 1897, HEH Correspondence, box 59; October 15, 1897, HEH Correspondence, box 59; J. O'H. Cosgrave, *San Francisco Saturday Wave,* August 18, 1900, HEH MS 7/6(2).

104. *New York Times,* September 1900, HEH MS 16/11.

105. Leonard to CPH, February 5, 1885; Bushnell to CPH, April 7, 1886; Hodder to CPH, August 16, 1886; Fuller to CPH, May 9, 1887. All in CPH Papers, ser. 1, reels 39, 42, 42, 45. Peabody, August 30, 1899, HEH Correspondence, box 73.

106. Portland Museum, April 22, 1891; Union League, January 23, 1893; Columbian Exposition, January 23, 1893. All in CPH Papers, ser. 1, reels 49, 51, 51.

107. To CPH, January 12, 1894, January 30, 1895, CPH Papers, ser. 1, reels 52, 53; from CPH, February 19, 1895, CPH Papers, ser. 1, reel 53.

108. Anecdotes about CPH, widely printed, as from *Philadelphia North American,* August 18, 1900, HEH MS 7/10(2).

109. *Los Angeles Times,* September 16, 1900, HEH MS 16/11; *San Francisco Chronicle,* July 12, 1908, HEH MS 16/7; *San Francisco Wave,* August 18, 1900, HEH MS 7/6(2).

110. *New York Times,* September 1900, HEH MS 16/11.

111. *San Francisco Chronicle,* July 12, 1908, HEH MS 16/7.

112. J. J. Duveen to CPH, March 9, 1887, CPH Papers, ser. 1, reel 45.

113. L. P. di Cesnola to CPH, March 26, 1887, April 3, 1888, February 25, June 15, 1891, June 16, 1894, CPH Papers, ser. 1, reels 45–53; June 17, 1891, HEH MS 30/1–23; CPH to di Cesnola, October 11, 1892, CPH Papers, ser. 2, reel 33.

114. CPH will, March 13, 1897, HEH Correspondence, box 56.

115. *Kansas City (Mo.) Journal,* November 21, 1909, HEH MS 16/7.

116. About the earthquake and fire, there are many family letters in HEH Correspondence, box 120, esp. HEH to E. B. Holladay, May 9, 12, 1906; E. B. Holladay to HEH, May 11, 18, 19, 1906; HEH to Arabella, August 12, 1906, HEH Correspondence, box 121.

117. Jacques Seligmann to ADH, February 20, 1910, HEH Correspondence, box 126.

118. *Catalogue of the Rodolphe Kann Collection* (Paris: Charles Sedelmeyer, 1907), pictures 2 vols., objets d'art 2 vols.

119. James Henry Duveen, *The Rise of the House of Duveen* (New York: Knopf, 1957), 236.

120. *New York Times,* November 24, 1907, HEH MS 16/7; "The Kann Pictures," *American Art News,* January 4, 1908. And see n. 123 below.

121. *New York Times,* March 19, 1909, HEH MS 16/17; *Hartford Times,* October 25, 1909, HEH MS 16/7.

122. *New York American,* July 24, 1909, HEH MS 16/7.

123. J. Kirby Grant, "Mrs. Collis P. Huntington's Collection," *The Connoisseur,* 20 (1908): 2–15.

15. THE NEW LIFE: EASTERN DIVISION

1. HEH to Carrie, May 4, 1914, HEH Correspondence, box 131.

2. HEH MS 12/2.

3. HEH MSS 12/9, 12/10, 12/1, 12/7.

4. HEH MSS 12/2, 12/7.

5. *Los Angeles Examiner,* February 12, 1915, HEH MS 7/4(32).

6. HEH MS 12/2.

7. HEH to Carrie, August 23, 1914, HEH Correspondence, box 132.

8. Interview with Otheman Stevens, *Los Angeles Examiner,* February 12, 1915, HEH MS 7/10(27).

9. August 15, 17, 1914, HEH Correspondence, box 132.

10. *New York Herald,* September 14, 1914, and a shorter version in *Los Angeles Times,* October 3, 1914, HEH MS 7/10(26).

11. HEH MS 12/2.

12. Fowles, *Memories of Duveen Brothers,* 87.

13. *Los Angeles Examiner,* September 5, 1914, HEH MS 7/4(31); also HEH MSS 7/10(26), 7/2(14).

14. Jacques Seligmann to ADH, Sept. 11, 1914, ADH Papers, reel 4280.

15. *New York Herald,* September 14, 1914, HEH MS 7/10(26).

16. *Los Angeles Times,* February 12, 1915, HEH MS 7/10(27).

17. *Los Angeles Examiner,* September 18, 1914, HEH MS 7/4(31). Also *New York American* and *New York Journal,* September 18, 1914, HEH MS 7/10(26).

18. Burke Holladay, Diary, December 8, 1914, HEH Correspondence, box 195.

19. Elizabeth and Brockway to HEH, December 24, 1914, HEH Correspondence, box 132.

20. Cole to HEH, July 19, 1915; HEH to Cole, July 27, 1915; Cole to HEH, August 4, 1915. All in HEH MS 31.1.1.10.

21. HEH to James I. Wyer, November 13, 1915, HEH MS 31.1.1.51.

22. *Huntington Library Bulletin* 1, no. 1 (May 1931): 43–56.

23. *New York Times, New York Herald, New York Sun, Los Angeles Examiner,* and some fifty other papers, December 31, 1915, HEH MSS 7/10(38), 7/2/19; *The Dial,* January 20, 1916, HEH MS 7/10(38).

24. Quaritch to HEH, June 30, 1916, HEH MS 31.1.1.37; newspapers for November 20, 1916, HEH MSS 7/2/20, 7/10(38).

25. Purchase agreement, February 21, 1917, HEH MS 31.1.1.42. Also HEH MSS 7/4(36), 16/3.

26. HEH MS 7/4(37).

27. A. Edward Newton, *The Amenities of Book-Collecting* (Boston: Atlantic Monthly Press, 1918), 36.

28. For purchases in 1917–18, HEH MS 4/2; for Sears, August 5, 1916, HEH MS 11/8/4.

29. January 18, 1918, HEH MS 31.1.1.36.

30. May 27, 1917, HEH MSS 31.1.1.40–41.

31. Cole to HEH, June 17, 1919, HEH MS 31.1.1.10; HEH to Cole, August 21, 1919, HEH MS 31.1.1.10.

32. HEH MS 31.1.1.22.

33. HEH to Herbert Putnam, June 10, 1918; Putnam to HEH, June 13, 1918; HEH to Putnam, June 24, 1918. All in HEH MS 31.1.1.47.

34. Quaritch to HEH, July 10, 1916, HEH MS 31.1.1.37.

35. Holden to Cole, September 27, 1917, HEH MS 31.1.1.21; *New York Times, Chicago Herald,* October 13, 1917, HEH MS 7/10(38); *Los Angeles Examiner,* October 24, 1917, HEH MS 7/4(36); Robert H. Dodd to HEH, November 20, 1917, HEH MS 31.1.1.13; HEH to Dodd, November 26, 1917, HEH MS 31.1.1.13.

36. February 1, November 22, 1916, HEH MS 31.1.1.26; Ludwig Bendikson, "Reminiscences," HEH MS 19/1(18).
37. The printed catalogs are classified as Z997 H52. HEH's personal copies, mostly priced, are classified as Z999 A63, catalog numbers 1269, 1308, 1309, 1365, 1406.
38. HEH MS 7/10(38).
39. *New York Times,* January 16, 1917, HEH MS 7/10(38).
40. *New York American,* December 11, 1917, HEH MS 7/10(38).
41. Summaries of sales are in HEH MSS 59/1–11.
42. Part nine, November 6, 1918, catalog 1365.
43. For example, *Los Angeles Examiner,* February 17, 1918, HEH MS 7/2/21.
44. HEH MS 7/10(38).
45. May 2, June 4, 1918, HEH MS 31.1.1.25.
46. Letters between HEH, Tucker Brooke, and Cole, 1914–19, HEH MSS 31.1.1.6, 31.1.1.22.
47. HEH MS 31.1.1.6.
48. HEH MS 31.1.1.34.
49. HEH MS 31.1.1.9.
50. HEH MS 31.1.1.3.
51. HEH MS 31.1.1.45.
52. HEH MS 31.1.1.29.
53. HEH MS 31.1.1.35.
54. HEH MS 31.1.1.34.
55. HEH MSS 31.1.1.11–12.
56. HEH MS 31.1.1.16.
57. November 23, 1915, July 7, 1920, November 1, 1919, HEH MSS 31.1.1.45, 31.1.1.14, 31.1.1.28.
58. January 26, 1916, HEH MS 16/10; September 27, 1918, HEH MS 31.1.1.16; March 14, 1919, HEH MS 16/10.
59. December 23, 1917, HEH MS 31.1.1.16.
60. HEH MS 31.1.1.1.
61. June 30, October 29, November 1, 1919, HEH MS 31.1.1.16.
62. November 17, 24, 1919, HEH MS 31.1.1.16.
63. March 15, 1919, HEH MS 31.1.1.36.
64. Letters between HEH and Smith, March 14, April 7, 24, August 26, September 2, 1916, HEH MS 31.1.1.42; *New York Times,* March 19, 1916, HEH MS 7/10(30).
65. Pollard to Cole, April 12, 1919, HEH MS 31.1.1.10; HEH to Cole, May 19, 1919, HEH MS 31.1.1.10; Cole to Pollard, May 26, 1919, HEH MS 31.1.1.36.

66. Albert S. Baugh to HEH, August 2, October 23, 1919, HEH MS 31.1.1.3.
67. *Boston Transcript,* January 5, 1916, HEH MS 7/10(38).
68. *The Sphere,* January 29, 1916, HEH MS 16/10.
69. *New York Times Magazine,* May 27, 1917, HEH MS 16/3.
70. *Toronto Star,* September 1, 1917, HEH MS 16/10.
71. Elizabeth Miner King, *New York Evening Post,* May 9–14, 1918, HEH MS 16/6.
72. Eustace Hall Ball, *New York Sun,* December 19, 28, 1919, HEH MS 38/2.
73. HEH MS 7/10(38).
74. Charles V. E. Starrett to HEH, January 31, 1918, HEH MS 31.1.1.42; HEH to Starrett, February 16, 1918, HEH MS 31.1.1.42.
75. HEH to G. P. Winship, July 1, 1918, HEH MS 31.1.1.50.
76. Burke Holladay, Diary, HEH Correspondence, box 195.
77. Ellen M. H. Gates, November 29, 1917, HEH Correspondence, box 138.
78. Eames, February 25, 1919, HEH MS 31.1.1.14; Ford, January 23, 1919, HEH MS 31.1.1.16; Lord, February 3, 1919, HEH MS 31.1.1.16; Hillhouse, December 10, 1918, HEH MS 31.1.1.21; Wilmerding, February 27, 1919, HEH MS 31.1.1.50.
79. Gardner Teall, December 19, 1919, HEH MS 31.1.1.45.
80. Grolier Club, January 1, 1913, HEH MS 4/2; Bibliographical Society of America, March 27, 1917, HEH MS 1/D/4(4); Bibliographical Society (London), HEH MS 31.1.1.34; American Antiquarian Society, September 28, 1914, HEH MS 31.1.1.1; Concordance Society, April 15, 1912, HEH MS 4/2.
81. Grolier Club, January 18, 1919, HEH MS 31.1.1.18.
82. Invitations and menus for the period 1911–17 are in HEH MS 7/1. Many newspaper clippings about the meetings are in HEH MS 16/2(1). Other information is in HEH MS 31.1.1.21 and HEH Correspondence, boxes 131–32.
83. W. K. Bixby to HEH, November 21, HEH MS 31.1.1.5; HEH to Bixby, November 24, 1917, HEH MS 7/1.
84. Henry Howard Harper, "Reminiscences," recorded January 25, 1937, HEH MS 19/1(7).
85. January 17, 23, 24, 30, 1919, HEH Correspondence, box 142.
86. HEH to Carrie, November 5, 25, 1917, HEH Correspondence, boxes 137, 138; November 1, 3, 5, 8, 1917, HEH MS 7/10(38).
87. For full details, see HEH MSS 12/1–30.
88. C. Welker to HEH, October 3, November 7, 1917, HEH MS 12/3.

89. Hess Real Estate to HEH, July 18, HEH Correspondence, box 143; HEH to Hess Real Estate, July 19, 1919, HEH Correspondence, box 143.

90. Amity F. Mayhoff (Mrs. Charles Mayhoff) to HEH, July 31, 1918, HEH Correspondence, box 140.

91. HEH to Frank Griffith, September 9, 1915, HEH Correspondence, box 133.

92. William B. Coley, Jr., November 4, 1915, HEH Vault Material, box 2.

93. HEH deposition, February 1916, HEH Vault Material, box 2.

94. For example, *Los Angeles Examiner, Los Angeles Tribune, New York American, St. Paul (Minn.) News,* October 16, 1915. All in HEH MSS 7/10(29), 7/4(33).

95. Dunn to Graham, October 14, 1915; Graham to Dunn, October 15, 1915; Graham to Dunn, October 22, 1915. All in HEH Correspondence, box 134.

96. Coley, November 4, 1915, HEH Vault Material, box 2.

97. Reports, January 5, 1916, HEH Vault Material, box 2.

98. Frederick MacMonnies to HEH, April 20, 1917, HEH Correspondence, box 136.

99. Harry L. Fagin to HEH, January 16, 29, 1919, HEH Correspondence, box 142; HEH to Fagin, January 20, 1919, HEH Correspondence, box 142; William Madsen to HEH, June 8, 1917, February 3, 1918, HEH Correspondence, boxes 137, 139.

100. Letters and telegrams about Willard's death, September 27, 1915, HEH Correspondence, box 133; ADH telegram to E. B. Holladay, September 28, 1915, HEH Correspondence, box 134; newspaper clippings, September 27, 28, October 1, 1915, HEH MSS 7/2/18, 7/10(29).

101. *New York Sun,* September 9, 1918, HEH MS 7/10(44); *Hartford Courant,* May 27, 1918, HEH MS 7/10(44).

102. Letters of Elizabeth, Clara, and Marian in Metcalf Add. MSS, box 6; *San Francisco Chronicle,* April 24, 1916, HEH Correspondence, box 135.

103. Correspondence between HEH and Carter, Ledyard, and Milburn, HEH Correspondence, box 135; July 23, 1915, box 133; December 13, 1915, box 134; March 28, 29, November 4, 1916, HEH MSS 16/11, 7/2/19, 7/10(30).

104. 1912–17, HEH MS 16/1(1); deposition, 1916; Guedella and Jacobson to HEH, June 9, 1916, HEH Correspondence, box 135.

105. December 8, 9, 1915, New York papers, HEH MS 7/10(29); Los Angeles papers, HEH MSS 7/2/18, 7/4(33).

106. March 16–31, 1915, HEH MS 7/10(27); C. F. Bailey (Engineering Director), "Reminiscences," HEH MS 19/3.

107. HEH to Graham, July 27, 1917, HEH Vault Material, box 3; HEH to Henry Noble, July 31, 1917, HEH Vault Material, box 3.

108. June through December, 1918, HEH Correspondence, boxes 139–41.

109. HEH to W. E. Dunn, January 5, 17, 1916, HEH Correspondence, box 134; Dunn to Graham, January 25, February 10, 1916, HEH Correspondence, box 134.

110. Announcements for February 15, 1919, HEH Correspondence, box 142.

16. THE NEW LIFE: WESTERN DIVISION

1. *Los Angeles Examiner,* September 18, 1914, and many other papers, HEH MS 7/4(31). Quoted in chap. 15.

2. *Los Angeles Examiner,* August 12, 1919, HEH MS 7/10(33).

3. Otheman Stevens, *Los Angeles Examiner,* May 7, 1917, HEH MS 7/4(36).

4. Ernest Braunton, "The Garden Beautiful in Southern California," *Los Angeles Sunday Times,* March 9, 1919, HEH MS 7/10(33).

5. Porter Garnett, "Stately Homes of California. VII. The Huntington Home at Oak Knoll," *Sunset,* June 1, 1914, HEH MS 16/6.

6. Otheman Stevens interview, *Los Angeles Examiner,* April 24, 1919, HEH MS 7/10(33).

7. Details of their everyday life described in the three preceding paragraphs are contained in many reminiscences, as of Collis Huntington Holladay and Margaret Huntington McLaren, both in HEH MS 19/3, and Alfonso Gomez, HEH MS 19/1(17).

8. The quotations and details in the two preceding paragraphs are drawn from Alfonso Gomez's reminiscences, HEH MS 19/1(17).

9. HEH MSS 19/5, 1/D/4(4).

10. Trips taken when Carrie and Burke were in residence are recorded in Burke Holladay's diary, HEH Correspondence, box 195.

11. Burke Holladay, Diary, June 24–26, 1915, HEH Correspondence, box 195.

12. Alfonso Gomez, Reminiscences, HEH MS 19/1(17).

13. *Los Angeles Examiner,* April 21, 1917, HEH MS 7/2/21; Gomez, Reminiscences, 19/1(17); *Los Angeles Herald,* September 19, 1918, HEH MS 7/4(37).

14. See chap. 8. Clara to Elizabeth, February 21, 1914, Metcalf Add. MSS, box 6.

15. *Los Angeles Tribune,* June 19, 21, 1917, HEH MS 7/4(36).

16. The quotations and details in the two preceding paragraphs are from Gomez, Reminiscences, HEH MS 19/1(17), and E. B. Holladay, deposition of December 6, 1927, HEH MSS 37/1–18.

17. Balance sheets, 1901–24, HEH MSS 11/2(1)–(3).

18. Invoices, January 24, 1916, February 9, March 21, 1917, August 8, 1918, HEH MS 28/1.

19. Invoices, September 28, 1915, March 6, 1916, February 9, 1917, August 8, 1918, HEH MS 28/1.

20. About the Savonnerie rugs, April 11, 1916, HEH Correspondence, box 135; about the tapestry set, August 26, 1918, HEH Correspondence, box 140; for the Romney, August 9, 1915, HEH MS 28/1; for the Houdon, April 11, 1916, HEH Correspondence, box 135; about first refusal, September 13, 1916, HEH MS 28/1; for "something great," August 28, 1918, HEH Correspondence, box 140.

21. Jacques Seligmann to ADH, December 5, 1916, ADH Papers, reel 4280; Samuels to ADH, February 16, 1918, ADH Papers, reel 4280.

22. *Los Angeles Examiner,* August 19, 1917, HEH MS 16/2(1); HEH to Frank Miller, December 30, 1918, HEH Correspondence, box 141; *Los Angeles Times,* November 23, 1918, HEH MS 7/2/21.

23. Invoice, C. C. Parker, June 1916, HEH MS 11/1(1).

24. Kuhrts to HEH, December 1, 1919, HEH MS 31.1.1.29.

25. *Los Angeles Times,* January 12, 1919, HEH MS 7/10(38).

26. Correspondence between Robert E. Cowen and HEH, 1916, HEH MS 31.1.1.11; A. S. Macdonald to HEH, May 3, 1916, HEH MS 31.1.1.29.

27. *Los Angeles Times,* September 28, 1916, HEH MS 16/10; *Los Angeles Herald,* September 28, 1916, HEH MS 7/10(30).

28. HEH to Myron Hunt, October 30, 1917, HEH Correspondence, box 137.

29. Myron Hunt to HEH, January 11, 1918, HEH Correspondence, box 138; A. S. W. Rosenbach to HEH, November 28, 1917, HEH MS 31.1.1.39; *Los Angeles Examiner,* December 17, 22, 1917, HEH MS 16/10.

30. Hunt to HEH, January 11, February 13, 1918, HEH Correspondence, boxes 138, 139; HEH to Hunt, February 5, 19, 1918, HEH Correspondence, box 139.

31. George Parker Winship to Myron Hunt, January 12, 28, 1918, HEH Correspondence, box 138.

32. R. U. Johnson to HEH, March 26, 1918, HEH MS 31.1.1.1; HEH to Johnson, March 27, 1918, HEH MS 31.1.1.1.

33. Myron Hunt to HEH, February 21, 1919, HEH Correspondence, box 142.

34. W. E. Dunn to HEH, March 1919, HEH Correspondence, box 142; HEH to W. E. Dunn, March 1919, HEH MS 31.1.1.14.

35. Otheman Stevens, *Los Angeles Examiner,* August 2, 1919, HEH MS 7/4(38).

36. *Los Angeles Times,* September 6, 1919, HEH MS 7/4(38).

37. HEH to Myron Hunt, 1919, HEH Correspondence, box 144.

38. HEH to William Hertrich, as quoted by Max Farrand, HEH MS 19/3.

39. George Ellery Hale, "Biographical Notes," recorded February 8, 1933, HEH MS 19/1.

40. Otheman Stevens, *Los Angeles Examiner,* April 26, 1910, HEH MS 16/2(2).

41. Mt. Wilson Observatory Collection, G. E. Hale Papers, Huntington Library, suppl. box 3.

42. Harrison Gray Otis to HEH, February 7, 1914, HEH MS 31.1.1.34.

43. G. E. Hale to HEH, April 17, Hale Papers, reel 19; HEH to Hale, April 20, 1914, Hale Papers, reel 19; Hale to Harry Manley Goodwin, May 6, 1914, HEH MS HM 28487; Hale, "Biographical Notes," HEH MS 19/1.

44. G. E. Hale to HEH, May 11, 1914, Hale Papers, reel 19; HEH to Hale, October 5, 1914, Hale Papers, reel 19.

45. G. E. Hale to HEH, March 22, 1916, and the two unsent letters of the same date, Hale Papers, reel 19.

46. G. E. Hale to HEH, March 28, 1916, HEH Correspondence, box 135; HEH to Hale, April 22, 1916, HEH Correspondence, box 135.

47. Archer Huntington to G. E. Hale, May 15, 1916, Hale Papers, reel 19.

48. G. E. Hale to Myron Hunt, January 4, 1918; Hunt to Hale, January 11, 1918; Hale to Hunt, January 19, 1918. All in Hale Papers, reel 19.

49. Trust indenture, Trustees' Files, Huntington Library.

50. *Los Angeles Record,* February 12, 16, 1915, HEH MS 7/4(32).

51. *Los Angeles Record,* October 24, 1916, HEH MS 7/4(35).

52. *Los Angeles Examiner,* June 9, 1917, HEH MS 7/4(36).

53. *Los Angeles Times,* August 11, 14, 1915; *Los Angeles Examiner,* August 11, 12, 1915; *Los Angeles Express,* August 14, 1915; *Los Angeles Record,* August 10, 14, 1915. All in HEH MS 7/4(37).

54. *Los Angeles Times,* September 7, 1918, HEH MS 7/4(37); *Los Angeles Examiner,* September 11, 1918, HEH MS 7/10(32).

55. W. E. Dunn to HEH, December 2, 1918, HEH Correspondence, box 141; HEH to Dunn, December 5, 1918, HEH Correspondence, box 141.

56. See, for example, *Los Angeles Times* for June 30, July 23, August 16, 17, September 23, 30, October 28, November 19, 1919, HEH MS 7/10.

57. Memo of agreement, December 30, 1915, HEH Correspondence, box 134; telegram, December 5, 1916, HEH Correspondence, box 136; *Los Angeles Times,* December 5, 1916, HEH MS 7/4(35); *Los Angeles Times,* April 17, May 23, 1917, HEH MS 7/10(30).

58. See, for example, *Los Angeles Examiner,* May 19, September 7, October 2, 1919, HEH MSS 7/4(38), 7/10(33).

59. W. E. Dunn to HEH, May 4, 1915, HEH Correspondence, box 133.

60. W. E. Dunn to HEH, September 18, October 16, 1915, HEH Correspondence, box 134; Dunn to HEH, May 24, 1918, HEH Correspondence, box 139.

61. HEH to Dunn, May 31, 1918, HEH Correspondence, box 139.

62. W. E. Dunn to HEH, June 5, 1918, HEH Correspondence, box 139; HEH to Dunn, June 11, 1918, HEH Correspondence, box 139.

63. *Los Angeles Herald,* May 6, 1915; *Los Angeles Express,* May 6, 1915; *Los Angeles Times, Los Angeles Examiner, Los Angeles Tribune, Pasadena Sun,* May 7, 1915. All in HEH MS 7/10(27).

64. *Los Angeles Times,* August 2, 1919, HEH MS 7/4(38).

65. *Los Angeles Times,* August 16, 1914, HEH MS 7/4(31).

66. *Los Angeles Herald,* December 9, 1915, HEH MS 7/2/18.

67. *Los Angeles Herald,* June 30, 1917, HEH MS 7/4(36).

68. *Los Angeles Tribune,* June 2, 18, 21, 1917; *Los Angeles Times,* June 17, 19, 1917; *Los Angeles Examiner,* June 18, 1917. All in HEH MSS 7/4(36), 7/10(31).

69. Alfred G. Walker, Reminiscences, HEH MS 19/4.

70. Otheman Stevens, *Los Angeles Examiner,* February 12, 1915, HEH MS 7/4(32); Stevens, *Los Angeles Examiner,* April 7, 1917, HEH MS 7/2/21.

71. *Los Angeles Examiner,* March 12, 1916, HEH MS 7/4(33).

72. *Pasadena Star,* June 5, 1915, HEH MS 7/10(29).

73. *Los Angeles Examiner, New York World, New York Mail, New York Journal,* and many other papers, March 6, 1915, HEH MS 7/10(27).

74. *Los Angeles Examiner, Los Angeles Times,* July 1, 1916, HEH MS 7/10(30).

75. *Los Angeles Examiner,* May 7, September 21, 1917, May 16, 1916, HEH MSS 7/2/21, 7/10(31), 7/4(34).

76. *Los Angeles Times,* April 9, 1917, HEH MS 7/10(31).

77. Associated Press to HEH, September 5, 1918, HEH MS 31.1.1.2; HEH to AP, September 22, 1918, HEH MS 31.1.1.2.

78. *Los Angeles Times, Los Angeles Examiner,* September 16, 1919, HEH MS 7/4(38).

79. *Los Angeles Express, Los Angeles Times,* September 17, 1919, HEH MS 16/10.

80. Walter Linley to HEH, September 23, 1919, HEH MS 31.1.1.28; G. E. Hale to HEH, October 8, 1919, Hale Papers, reel 19.

81. Los Angeles Public Library to HEH, October 16, 1919, HEH MS 31.1.1.29; California Senate Resolution, Metcalf Add. MSS, box 6.

82. *Los Angeles Examiner,* September 19, 1919, HEH MS 7/4(38).

17. LIVING THE NEW LIFE

1. HEH to Joseph Duveen, January 23, 1922, HEH Correspondence, box 150. HEH to A. J. Secor, May 5, 1923; HEH to Duveen, May 19, 1923; HEH to W. O. Paxton, May 5, 1923. All in HEH Correspondence, box 161. Alfonso Gomez, Reminiscences, tape G, HEH MS 19/1(17) (hereafter in this chapter referred to as "Gomez, tape __"). F. Griffith to HEH, July 24, 1920, HEH Correspondence, box 145.

2. HEH to C. E. Graham, January 10, 1922; Graham to HEH, January 16, 1922; George Hapgood to Graham, January 30, 1922; HEH to Joseph Duveen, January 23, 1922; HEH to C. Weidenfeld, January 16, 1922. All in HEH Correspondence, box 150.

3. HEH to L. B. Lewis, November 21, 1922, HEH MS 31.1.1.28; HEH to Leroy Clark, December 27, 1922, HEH Correspondence, box 157; Calvin W. Hendrick to HEH, April 14, 1924; HEH to Hendrick, April 21, 1924. All in HEH Correspondence, box 167. HEH to Hendrick, August 31, 1923, HEH Correspondence, box 162.

4. Gomez, tape E; Cunard to E. A. Adams, April 29, 1922, HEH Correspondence, box 152.

5. HEH to C. E. Graham, September 25, 1921, HEH Correspondence, box 149.

6. HEH to Mrs. Emma Miles, August 31, 1920, HEH Correspondence, box 146.

7. Joseph Duveen to HEH, August 27, 1920, HEH MS 31.1.1.14.

8. HEH to Joseph Duveen, undated, holograph pencil draft, HEH Correspondence, box 156.

9. HEH to G. W. Cole, October 4, 1920, HEH MS 31.1.1.22.

10. Full details on the operation of Chateau Beauregard, correspondence, and a complete account of expenses are contained in HEH MSS 12/1–30.

11. HEH to C. E. Graham, September 25, 1921, HEH Correspondence, box 149.

12. HEH MS 38/6.

13. HEH to Donald Harper, July 9, 1923, HEH Correspondence, box 147.
14. HEH to G. W. Cole, July 6, 1922, HEH MS 31.1.1.10; HEH to W. E. Dunn, July 25, 1922, HEH Correspondence, box 154; George Hapgood to Dunn, July 18, 1922, HEH Correspondence, box 154.
15. C. E. Graham to HEH, May 7, 1923, HEH Correspondence, box 161; E. A. Adams to HEH, October 25, 1924, HEH Correspondence, box 171.
16. HEH MS 1/D/5(3); C. E. Graham to ADH, October 31 and November 1, 1923 (for example), HEH Correspondence, box 162.
17. For house activities, HEH MS 38/11; for Archer and caviar, Gomez, tape F; for clubs, HEH MSS 19/5, 1/D/9.
18. HEH to W. E. Dunn, September 6, 1923, HEH Correspondence, box 162.
19. HEH to Cole, May 12, 17, June 2, 1920, HEH MS 31.1.1.10; Cole to HEH, May 27, June 7, 12, August 30, 1920, HEH MS 31.1.1.10; Cole to HEH, May 25, June 3, July 2, 1920, HEH MS 31.1.1.18.
20. Full details about the library are contained in HEH MSS 42/1–5 for 1917–25. Newspaper clippings are in HEH MSS 16/2(1), 7/10(39). A. B. Saxton to HEH, November 13, 1920, HEH Correspondence, box 146; HEH to Saxton, November 16, 1920, HEH Correspondence, box 146.
21. HEH to James M. Lee, August 8, 1923, HEH Correspondence, box 162.
22. Mayor, "Introduction: Brookgreen Gardens," *A Century of American Sculpture*, 23–24, 26. New York newspapers, March 10, 1923; *New York Town Topics,* April 5, 1923; *Los Angeles Examiner,* September 30, 1923; all in HEH MS 7/10(37).
23. HEH to G. W. Cole, March 27, 1920, HEH MS 31.1.1.10.
24. Many of these details are recorded in Burke Holladay, Journal, vol. 2, Metcalf Add. MSS.
25. Gomez, tape B.
26. Reminiscences of Max Gschwind, grounds foreman, HEH MS 19/3.
27. Gomez, tapes B, C.
28. Gomez, tape B.
29. Gomez, tape L.
30. Gomez, tape B.
31. Gomez, tapes K, L.
32. Gomez, tape C.
33. Gomez, tape I.
34. Gomez, tapes D, M, N.
35. Emma Quigley, "Reminiscences," HEH MS 19/1(1).
36. Gomez, tapes A, I.

37. HEH to Dr. Coley, April 1, 1920, April 14, 1923, HEH Correspondence, box 145; HEH to John W. Ensign, December 4, 1924, HEH Correspondence, box 172.

38. *Los Angeles Examiner,* October 11, 1923, HEH MS 16/3.

39. Philip S. Goulding to C. H. Lincoln, December 29, 1920, HEH MS 31.1.1.28.

40. *Los Angeles Examiner,* October 11, 1923, HEH MS 7/5(2).

41. Gomez, tape N.

42. HEH to G. W. Cole, December 16, 1920, HEH MS 31.1.1.10.

43. Emma Quigley, "Reminiscences," HEH MS 19/1(1).

44. *Los Angeles Record,* April 27, 1923, HEH MS 7/4(41); *Los Angeles Times,* April 29, 1923, HEH MS 7/4(41).

45. *Los Angeles Express,* December 14, 1924, HEH MS 7/4(42); *Los Angeles Times,* December 16, 1924, HEH MS 7/4(42).

46. HEH to George E. Cryer, July 5, 1924, HEH Correspondence, box 168.

47. Inventory, Huntington Land and Improvement Co., January 1, 1924, HEH MS 1/DD/2.

48. HEH to A. G. Walker, June 20, 1923, HEH Correspondence, box 161; HEH to William Hertrich, July 30, September 13, 1923, July 8, 1924, HEH Correspondence, boxes 162, 168.

49. Emma Quigley, "Reminiscences," HEH MS 19/1(1).

50. Gomez, tape N.

51. Gomez, tape G.

52. Gomez, tape J.

53. Gomez, tape B.

54. Gomez, tape H.

55. Otheman Stevens, "Reminiscences of HEH," July 11, 1929, HEH MS 19/3.

56. Fowles, *Memories of Duveen Brothers,* 71.

57. HEH to Herbert N. Carnur, May 6, 1920, HEH Correspondence, box 145.

58. HEH to Blankenhorn-Hunter Co., March 27, 1919, HEH MS 31.1.1.5.

59. Emma Quigley, "Reminiscences," HEH MS 19/1(1).

60. Gomez, tape L.

61. J. L. Murphy to HEH, December 27, 1920, HEH Correspondence, box 147.

62. M. L. Akers to HEH, July 22, 1921, HEH Correspondence, box 148.

63. I. N. Phipps to HEH, March 3, 1921, HEH MS 16/10.

64. J. C. Stubbs to HEH, January 14, 1924, HEH MS 31.1.1.44.

65. Noel T. Arnold, "Recollections of HEH," HEH MS 19/1(5).

66. From depositions made by Leslie G. Brehm, December 1, 1927; Alberta Johnston Denis, November 30, 1927; Harriet Crocker Alexander, November 18, 1927; and George D. Hapgood, December 6, 1927. All in HEH MSS 37/1–18.

67. Otheman Stevens, *Los Angeles Examiner*, October 11, 1923, HEH MS 16/3.

68. Clara to HEH, January 23, 1920, Metcalf Add. MSS, box 7.

69. Elizabeth Metcalf to HEH, January 23, 1920, Metcalf Add. MSS, box 7.

70. Clifford B. Clapp to HEH, December 26, 1922, HEH MS 31.1.1.9.

71. Philip S. Goulding to C. H. Lincoln, December 29, 1920, HEH MS 31.1.1.28.

72. HEH to Leslie E. Bliss, July 10, 1918, HEH MS 31.1.1.22.

73. HEH to C. E. Graham, August 12, 1919, HEH MS 31.1.1.18.

74. HEH to C. E. Graham, May 16, 1923, HEH Correspondence, box 161.

75. Gomez, tape D.

76. Emma Quigley, "Reminiscences," HEH MS 19/1(1).

77. HEH interview, *Los Angeles Times,* October 13, 1923, HEH MS 16/10.

78. Gomez, tape I.

79. Gomez, tape H.

80. Gomez, tape I.

81. Gomez, tape I.

82. For the masseur, January 6, 1920, HEH Correspondence, box 144; about eggs, June 23, 1924, box 168; about ice, August 8, 1922, box 154; about shoes, September 20, 1922, box 155.

83. Gomez, tape B.

84. Archer Huntington to HEH, February 1, 1923, HEH Correspondence, box 158.

85. HEH Correspondence, boxes 165–78.

86. Gomez, tape B.

87. *New York Herald Tribune, New York World,* March 30, 1924, HEH MS 16/9.

88. Peyton Boswell, *Art News,* March 22, 1924, HEH Correspondence, box 166.

18. ACHIEVEMENT AND ACCLAIM

1. Louise Hall Tharp, *Mrs. Jack* (Boston: Little Brown, 1965), 190–91.

2. *London Daily Mirror,* March 10, 1916, HEH MS 16/7.

3. An erroneous account of Edward's dealing with Duveen is contained in S. N. Behrman, *Duveen* (New York: Random House, 1952), 198–99. In

this account, a 1921 conversation is created between Huntington and Duveen in which Huntington is represented as a dolt who had never before heard of the *Blue Boy.*

4. HEH to Duveen, April 19, 1922, HEH Correspondence, box 151; HEH to Duveen, February 2, 1922, HEH Correspondence, box 150; clippings in HEH MSS 7/5(2), 16/7; Von Bode, *New York Times,* March 7, 1926, HEH MS 16/10.

5. "The Blue Boy," dated February 1922, HEH Correspondence, box 150.

6. Duveen invoice, November 21, 1921, HEH MS 1/D/5(3).

7. Newspaper and magazine accounts of the New York exhibition are in HEH MS 16/7.

8. *Life,* c. 1922, p. 7, HEH MS 16/2(2).

9. Duveen to HEH, March 18, 1922, HEH Correspondence, box 151.

10. Newspaper clippings are primarily in HEH MS 16/7, with more in HEH MS 7/4(40). The quotations are from *Los Angeles Times,* March 13, 22, 1922.

11. Burke Holladay, Journal, vol. 2, March 21, 22, 1922, Metcalf Add. MSS.

12. HEH to Jacques Seligmann, April 1, 1922, HEH Correspondence, box 152.

13. Otheman Stevens, "Reminiscences," July 11, 1929, HEH MS 19/3.

14. *Riverside (Calif.) Enterprise,* December 27, 1924, HEH MS 16/10.

15. Joseph Duveen to HEH, February 14, 1922, HEH Correspondence, box 150; HEH to Duveen, February 20, 1922, HEH Correspondence, box 150.

16. HEH MS 28/1.

17. HEH MS 28/1; *The Huntington Art Collection: A Handbook* (Huntington Library, 1986).

18. About Rembrandt, Van Dyck, and El Greco, Jackson Higgs to HEH, January 15, 1924, HEH Correspondence, box 165; about Titian, HEH to Mrs. Frank R. McMullin, February 15, 1923, HEH Correspondence, box 159; about Velazquez: C. H. F. Kinderman-Walker to HEH, April 11, 1923, HEH Correspondence, box 160.

19. About Gainsborough, Anderson Galleries to HEH, November 19, 1924, HEH Correspondence, box 171; HEH to Anderson Galleries, November 28, 1924, HEH Correspondence, box 171; about Romney, E. H. Furman to HEH, June 29, 1922, HEH Correspondence, box 153; about Burne-Jones, HEH to Philip Burne-Jones, December 6, 1920, HEH MS 31.1.1.7; about Wilde, HEH to B. F. Stevens & Brown, March 7, 1922, HEH Correspondence, box 150.

20. Emma Quigley, "Reminiscences," HEH MS 19/1(1).

21. HEH to Joseph Duveen, February 2, 1924, HEH Correspondence, box 165; HEH MS 28/1.

22. George W. Cole to HEH, March 11, 1920, HEH MS 31.1.1.10.

23. George Hapgood to George W. Cole, March 10, 1920, HEH MS 31.1.1.19.

24. Quotations are from a scrapbook about Smith's death, HEH MS 25/3. Other clippings, March 4–13, 1920, are in HEH MSS 16/3, 7/5(1). W. K. Bixby to G. W. Cole, March 10, 1920, HEH MS 31.1.1.5.

25. Quaritch (E. H. Dring) to HEH, July 1, 1924, HEH MS 31.1.1.37; HEH to Quaritch, July 14, 1924, HEH MS 31.1.1.37.

26. A. S. W. Rosenbach to HEH, February 5, 1924, HEH MS 31.1.1.39.

27. A. S. W. Rosenbach to HEH, May 27, 1926, HEH MS 31.1.1.39.

28. A. S. W. Rosenbach to HEH, April 7, 1925, HEH MS 31.1.1.39.

29. A. S. W. Rosenbach to HEH, March 15, 1922, HEH MS 31.1.1.39.

30. A. S. W. Rosenbach to HEH, November 24, 1922, HEH MS 31.1.1.39.

31. Rosenbach to HEH, January 21, September 27, 1923, February 5, 1924, HEH MS 31.1.1.39.

32. Leslie A. Morris, *Rosenbach Abroad* (Philadelphia: Rosenbach Museum and Library, 1988), 38–39.

33. *Los Angeles Times,* February 24, 1924, HEH MS 16/10.

34. Edwin Wolf II and John F. Fleming, *Rosenbach* (Cleveland and New York: World Publishing Co., 1960), 206–7.

35. Rosenbach to HEH, December 13, 1922, October 3, 1924, March 5, 1925, HEH MS 31.1.1.39; HEH to Rosenbach, December 23, October 3, 1924, January 24, 1919, HEH MS 31.1.1.39.

36. HEH to Mrs. Holder, May 28, 1920, HEH MS 31.1.1.21.

37. They are described in *Huntington Library Bulletin* 1 (1931): 56–85.

38. Roger E. Stewart to HEH, July 23, 1920; HEH to Stewart, July 24, 1920; bill of sale, signed May 12, 1922, HEH MS 31.1.1.43.

39. HEH to Elizabeth Brock, November 21, 1922, HEH MS 31.1.1.6.

40. HEH to Walter U. Lewisson, September 12, 1922, HEH MS 31.1.1.28.

41. *New York City Telegram,* July 26, 1924, HEH MS 16/3.

42. Edmund Gosse, *London Sunday Times,* January 4, 1920, HEH MS 7/10(38).

43. For the book orders, HEH MS 4/8.

44. A sample group of his lists is in HEH MS 16/5/5.

45. Quaritch catalogue 369, HEH MS 25/1.

46. HEH MSS 46/5–9.

47. January 31, 1923, HEH MS 25/2.

48. Pforzheimer to HEH, February 11, 1920, HEH MS 31.1.1.35; HEH to Pforzheimer, February 1920, HEH MS 31.1.1.35.
49. Francis Wilson to HEH, November 10, 1923, HEH MS 31.1.1.50; HEH to Wilson, November 19, 1923, HEH MS 31.1.1.50; HEH to Rosenbach, November 19, 1923, HEH MS 31.1.1.39.
50. Maggs to HEH, March 16, 1923, HEH MS 31.1.1.18.
51. Walter C. Wyman to HEH, October 25, 1920, HEH MS 31.1.1.51.
52. Charles Sessler to HEH, January 22, 1926. (Also September 15, November 14, 1924, February 14, September 29, October 10, 1925.) HEH MS 31.1.1.41.
53. *Los Angeles Times,* January 19, 1920, HEH MS 7/5(1).
54. May 24, 1922, HEH MS 25/5.
55. HEH MSS 25/4–6; about Stevenson, 1921, HEH Correspondence, box 149.
56. HEH MS 25/4.
57. March 22 to November 22, 1920, HEH MS 31.1.1.10; January 10, December 7, 1921, HEH MS 25/6.
58. A dozen letters between HEH and John Drinkwater are in HEH MS 31.1.1.13; HEH to Bliss Carman, December 28, 1920, HEH MS 31.1.1.8.
59. HEH to John Henry Nash, March 2, 1921, March 14, 1923, October 3, 1924; Nash to HEH, October 8, 1924. All in HEH MS 31.1.1.33.
60. Bennett, May 2, 1922, HEH MS 31.1.1.13; about Ruskin, June 20, 1923, HEH MS 31.1.1.26; about Chesterfield, December 16, 1923, HEH MS 31.1.1.14.
61. HEH MS 25/1.
62. HEH to Yale University Press, October 9, 1922, HEH MS 31.1.1.51.
63. *Los Angeles Times,* March 27, 1920, HEH MS 7/4(39).
64. Interview with Otheman Stevens, *Los Angeles Examiner,* March 30, 1920, HEH MS 7/10(34).
65. HEH MS 25/6.
66. Leslie E. Bliss to Walter C. Wyman, June 29, 1920, HEH MS 31.1.1.51; Leslie E. Bliss to James F. Drake, December 17, 1920, HEH MS 31.1.1.13.
67. HEH to G. W. Cole, November 23, 1920, HEH MS 31.1.1.22.
68. Robert Schad to L. E. Bliss, January 19, 1922, HEH MS 31.1.1.40.
69. HEH to G. W. Cole, June 23, 1921, June 3, July 21, 1923, HEH MS 31.1.1.10; HEH to James F. Drake, March 13, 1922, HEH MS 31.1.1.13.
70. HEH to Mitchell Kennerley, June 19, 1924, March 30, 1921, HEH MS 31.1.1.26.
71. J. S. P. Tatlock, July 25, 1922, October 25, 1923, May 26, 1924, HEH MS 31.1.1.35.

72. John M. Manly to HEH, July 15, 1924, HEH MS 31.1.1.30; HEH to Manly, July 22, 1924, HEH MS 31.1.1.30.

73. C. B. Tinker, November 7, 1923, HEH MS 31.1.1.45; W. L. Cross, December 12, 1924, HEH MS 31.1.1.11.

74. Amy Lowell, January 10, March 12, 1923, HEH MS 31.1.1.29.

75. R. H. Griffith, 1920–24, HEH MS 31.1.1.18.

76. Herbert Putnam to HEH, February 20, 1924, HEH MS 31.1.1.47; HEH to Putnam, March 11, 1924, HEH MS 31.1.1.47.

77. H. H. Bolton to G. W. Cole, April 24, 1923, HEH MS 31.1.1.5; Cole to Bolton, April 27, 1923, HEH MS 31.1.1.5.

78. Robert G. Cleland to G. W. Cole, February 20, 1922, HEH MS 31.1.1.5; Cole to Cleland, February 25, 1922, HEH MS 31.1.1.10.

79. About reprints, HEH MS 31.1.1.42; *London Times Literary Supplement,* March 4, 1921, HEH MS 11/10.

80. J. Dover Wilson, September 15, October 21, November 18, 1922, HEH MS 31.1.1.50.

81. A. W. Pollard, letters 1920–24, HEH MS 31.1.1.36; Pollard to HEH, February 2, 1921, HEH MS 31.1.1.36.

82. *New York Post,* October 9, 1920, HEH MS 16/10.

83. Editorial, *Los Angeles Express,* April 18, 1924, HEH MS 16/10.

84. HEH to J. D. Fredericks, January 8, 1923, HEH Correspondence, box 158.

85. Frank A. Miller to HEH, May 1, 1920, HEH Correspondence, box 145.

86. *Los Angeles Times,* February 8, 1920, HEH MS 16/10.

87. *Los Angeles Times,* March 25, 1920, HEH MS 16/10.

88. *Los Angeles Express,* March 29, 1920, HEH MS 16/10.

89. For example, *New York Post,* July 30, 1920, *New York Telegram,* August 1, 1920, *Philadelphia Ledger,* August 3, 1920, HEH MS 16/10.

90. *Los Angeles Examiner,* August 6, 1920, HEH MS 16/10.

91. *Los Angeles Examiner,* August 11, 1920, HEH MS 16/10.

92. *Los Angeles Times,* December 3, 1921, HEH MS 16/10.

93. John Farrar, *New York World* magazine, October 24, 1920, HEH MS 16/2(1); *Toronto Mail,* October 1920, HEH MS 16/10.

94. *Boston Transcript,* February 16, 1921, HEH MS 7/5(2).

95. John Daggett, *Los Angeles Times,* January 9, 1922, HEH MS 16/2(1); *Boston Transcript,* January 18, 1922, HEH MS 16/10; *The Biblio* 1 (February 1922), HEH MS 19/5.

96. California Art Club to HEH, January 16, 1922, HEH Correspondence, box 150.

97. About transfers, November 30, 1921, HEH MS 1/D/4(5); for net worth, HEH MS 27/2.

98. *Los Angeles Times,* April 9, 1922, HEH MS 16/2(1).

99. *New York Times,* April 8, 1922, *New York Herald,* Paris ed., April 12, 1922, HEH MS 16/10.

100. See newspaper clippings for April to November, 1922, in HEH MSS 16/10, 7/10(36); *San Francisco Examiner,* October 13, 1923, HEH MS 16/10.

101. Herschel V. Jones to HEH, April 11, 1922, HEH MS 31.1.1.25.

102. HEH to John P. Green, October 16, 1922, HEH MS 31.1.1.18.

103. For "most outstanding cultural endowment," *California Graphic,* November 15, 1924, HEH MS 17/3; Dr. Moore, *Chicago Examiner,* January 7, 1923, HEH MS 16/10; Rosenbach, *New York Times,* December 16, 1923, HEH MS 16/10; *New York Sun,* May 23, 1922, HEH MS 16/10.

104. Arthur Brisbane, *New York American,* December 16, 1924, HEH MS 16/10; *American Weekly,* 1922, HEH MS 16/7.

105. Rosenbach to HEH about Folger, April 17, 1922, HEH MS 31.1.1.39; Mitchell Kennerley to HEH about Morgan, January 14, 1924, HEH MS 31.1.1.26. W. A. Clark, Jr., to HEH, March 17, 1923; HEH to Clark, March 19, 1923; and many later letters. All in HEH MS 31.1.1.9.

106. *Philadelphia Inquirer,* June 19, 1923, HEH MS 16/10; *The Sphere,* July 29, 1922, HEH MS 16/10.

107. *Los Angeles Examiner,* April 21, 1921, HEH MS 7/4(39).

108. Senate Concurrent Resolution 27, May 12, 1923, HEH MS 17/2.

109. *Los Angeles Express,* April 18, 1924, HEH MS 16/10.

110. Citation, New York University, December 16, 1920, HEH Correspondence, box 146.

111. University of Southern California diploma, April 3, 1924, Metcalf Add. MSS, box 7.

112. *San Francisco Chronicle,* May 15, 1924; Metcalf Add. MSS, box 7; Gomez, tape G, HEH MS 19/1(17).

113. *Los Angeles Times,* June 15, 1924, HEH MS 16/2(1).

114. J. A. Chandler to HEH, October 10, 1924, HEH Correspondence, box 172.

115. *Los Angeles Examiner,* November 27, 1922, HEH MS 7/10(36).

116. Certificate, January 9, 1923, HEH MS 17/4.

117. *Los Angeles Examiner,* June 3, 1920, HEH MS 7/4(39).

118. Book Club of California, June 5, 1923, HEH MS 31.1.1.4; Booksellers' Association, May 12, 1923, HEH MS 31.1.1.5; Club of Odd Volumes, May 3, 1921, HEH MS 31.1.1.10.

119. HEH to Herbert Hoover, May 6, 1922, HEH MS 31.1.1.21.
120. Gomez, tape F, HEH MS 19/1(17); Mellon to HEH, April 16, 1924, HEH Correspondence, box 167; Mitchell Samuels to ADH, April 10, 1920, ADH Papers, reel 4280.
121. Theodore Roosevelt, Jr., to HEH, December 8, 1920, HEH MS 31.1.1.38; HEH to Roosevelt, December 15, 1920, HEH MS 31.1.1.38.
122. Baron Rothschild to HEH, June 7, 1922, HEH MS 31.1.1.38.
123. Harry Chandler to HEH, July 21, 1923, HEH Correspondence, box 162.

19. THE DARK SIDE OF FAME

1. Dr. W. B. Coley to HEH, 1920, HEH Correspondence, box 141.
2. Elizabeth H. Metcalf to HEH, January 8, 1920, Metcalf Add. MSS, box 7; Coley bill, April 1, 1920, HEH MS 4/2; HEH to W. B. Coley, March 26, 1920, HEH Correspondence, box 145; *Los Angeles Examiner,* March 15, 1920, HEH MS 7/4(38).
3. HEH to Carrie, December 18, 1920, HEH Correspondence, box 146; Hapgood to Cole, January 15, 18, February 3, 9, 19, 1921, HEH MS 31.1.1.19; Hapgood to Dunn, January 18, 28, 1921, HEH Correspondence, box 147; HEH letter, February 21, 1921, HEH Correspondence, box 147; *Los Angeles Times,* March 22, 1921, HEH MS 7/10(35).
4. Dr. W. B. Coley to HEH, May 31, 1921; HEH to Coley, June 8, 1921; Coley to HEH, April 21, 1922. All in HEH MS 31.1.1.11.
5. Reports for August 14, 1922, September 18, 1923, HEH Correspondence, boxes 154, 162.
6. Duveen to HEH, February 16, 1923, HEH Correspondence, box 159; Wolf and Fleming, *Rosenbach,* 141.
7. N. P. Garrett to HEH, October 18, 1921, HEH Correspondence, box 149; HEH to Garrett, November 3, 1921, HEH Correspondence, box 149.
8. Burke Holladay, Journal, vol. 2, Metcalf Add. MSS.
9. W. E. Dunn to HEH, June 15, 1921, HEH Correspondence, box 148; HEH to Dunn, June 23, 1921, HEH Correspondence, box 148; Dunn to HEH, August 31, 1921, HEH Correspondence, box 148; HEH to Dunn, September, 1921, HEH Correspondence, box 149.
10. About book bills, Graham to HEH, January 3, 1923, HEH Correspondence, box 158; about federal income tax, Adams to HEH, December 15, 1924, HEH Correspondence, box 172; about interest on loans, Graham to HEH, February 8, 1922, HEH Correspondence, box 150; about C & O stock, October 20, 1922, HEH Correspondence, box 156.

11. March 23, April 12, May 21, 22, 23, 25, June 11, 1923, HEH MS 31.1.1.26.

12. W. E. Dunn to C. E. Graham, October 26, 1920, HEH Correspondence, box 146; C. E. Graham to E. A. Adams, March 4, 1923, HEH Correspondence, box 159.

13. E. A. Adams to C. E. Graham, September 17, 1923, HEH Correspondence, box 162; Mitchell James to C. E. Graham, May 26, 1924, HEH Correspondence, box 168; W. E. Dunn to C. E. Graham, May 21, 1924, HEH Correspondence, box 168.

14. W. E. Dunn to C. E. Graham, May 6, 13, 1921, HEH Correspondence, box 148; E. A. Adams to HEH, November 15, December 5, 10, 1924, HEH Correspondence, boxes 171, 172.

15. C. E. Graham to HEH, October 29, 1923, HEH Correspondence, box 163; HEH to C. E. Graham, July 12, 14, 1922, April 10, 1924, HEH Correspondence, boxes 154, 166.

16. Marian Huntington to Elizabeth, April 11, 1922, Metcalf Add. MSS, box 7; Marian to Clara, April 18, 1922, Metcalf Add. MSS, box 7.

17. W. E. Dunn to HEH, October 26, November 3, 1920, HEH Correspondence, box 146.

18. W. E. Dunn to HEH, September 13, 1923, HEH MS 31.1.1.14.

19. HEH to W. E. Dunn, September 20, 1923, HEH MS 31.1.1.14.

20. Herbert W. Denio to G. W. Cole, July 15, 17, October 9, 1920, HEH MS 31.1.1.12; Cole to Denio, July 17, October 16, 1920, HEH MS 31.1.1.12.

21. Thomas Cowles to G. W. Cole, September 19, December 4, 1923; Cowles to HEH, November 17, 1924; HEH to Cowles, November 20, 1924. All in HEH MS 31.1.1.11.

22. HEH to A. G. Walker, February 17, 1923, HEH MS 31.1.1.24; Walker to Hertrich, March 19, October 12, 1923, HEH MS 31.1.1.24.

23. On Goulding's appointment, Goulding to Cole, July 31, August 8, 1917; Cole to Goulding, September 4, 1917; Goulding to HEH, January 1, 1924; HEH to Goulding, January 4, 1924; HEH to Cole, January 7, 1924; HEH to Hertrich, January 31, 1924. All in HEH MS 31.1.1.21, 31.1.1.18.

24. Helen L. Plummer Goulding to HEH, February 2, 1924, HEH MS 31.1.1.18; Helen Goulding to Cate, February 2, 1924, HEH MS 31.1.1.18.

25. Cole to HEH, September 30, 1924, HEH MS 31.1.1.10; HEH to Cole, October 6, 1924, HEH MS 31.1.1.10; staff memos, September 23, 1924, HEH MS 31.1.1.9; receipt, November 15, 1924, HEH MS 31.1.1.10; Cate to Cole, January 13, 1925, HEH MS 31.1.1.9.

26. *Pasadena Evening Post, Pasadena Star-News, Los Angeles Examiner,* May 20, 1925, HEH MS 31.1.1.9; library statement, HEH MS 31.1.1.9.

27. Shook, January 18, 1923; about the sanitarium, April 25, 1922; from Massachusetts, May 19, 1922; from Ventura, September 3, November 28, 1922; about the Washington bust, October 27, 1924. All in HEH MS 31.1.1.52.
28. From the former serviceman, June 27, 1924, HEH Correspondence, box 153; about losing household effects, October 30, 1922, HEH Correspondence, box 156; about the curious rock, June 14, 1921, HEH MS 31.1.1.52; about the old map, October 11, 1923. All in HEH MS 31.1.1.40.
29. Davis Huntington to HEH, December 18, 1922, HEH MS 31.1.1.52; W. M. Huntington to HEH, July 21, 1923, HEH Correspondence, box 162.
30. Cuyler Reynolds to HEH, April 8, 1922, HEH MS 31.1.1.52.
31. W. O. Paxton to HEH, January 5, 1924, HEH Correspondence, box 165; HEH to Paxton, January 19, 1924, HEH Correspondence, box 165; Mulford S. Wade to HEH, August 4, 1924, HEH Correspondence, box 169; HEH to Wade, August 4, 1924, HEH Correspondence, box 169.
32. Thomas Dickson to HEH, July 19, 23, 1923, July 13, 16, April 30, May 6, 1924, April 23, December 29, 1925, January 28, 1926, HEH Correspondence, boxes 162, 168, HEH MS 31.1.1.52; Hapgood to Dickson, December 6, 1924, HEH Correspondence, box 172.
33. Reynold Ahleem to HEH, June 1921, January 1922, HEH MS 31.1.1.52; M. J. Keane to HEH, May 17, 1924, HEH MS 31.1.1.25; HEH to Keane, June 12, 1924, HEH MS 31.1.1.25. Lewis McKenzie Turner to HEH, January 10, May 16, 1924; HEH to Turner, March 11, 1924; Lillian Gibbs-Keys to HEH, October 15, 1924; all in HEH MS 42/5. Robert Seeger to HEH, April 3, 1922, HEH MS 31.1.1.52.
34. C. W. McMorron to HEH, October 25, 1923, and many other letters, with negative replies from HEH, November 19, 1923, July 17, December 27, 1924; J. M. Petter to HEH, December 9, 1922; Bataille Loomis to HEH, March 12, 1924; HEH to Loomis, March 13, 1924; Priestess to HEH, April 8, 1924. All in HEH MS 31.1.1.52.
35. Frederick C. Emery to HEH, January 10, 1922, HEH MS 31.1.1.14; HEH to Emery, January 30, 1922, HEH MS 31.1.1.14.
36. Missionary to HEH, November 22, 1922, HEH Correspondence, box 156; HEH to Harley H. Gill, June 6, 1924, HEH Correspondence, box 168.
37. HEH to W. E. Dunn, September 1921, HEH Correspondence, box 149; Los Angeles Times, August 22, 1921, HEH MS 7/10(35).
38. Burke Holladay, Journal, vol. 2, March 27–29, 1922, Metcalf Add. MSS; Los Angeles Times, March 28, 1922, HEH MS 7/10(36); Los Angeles Examiner, March 28, 1922, HEH MS 7/4(40).

39. David Huntington to HEH, March 31, 1922, HEH Correspondence, box 151; J. E. Brown to Graham, April 10, 1922, HEH Correspondence, box 152; W. E. Dunn to Ferguson, April 3, 1922, HEH Correspondence, box 152; G. W. Cole to L. L. Mackall, April 4, 1922, HEH MS 31.1.1.30; Adolfo Muller, April 6, 1922, HEH Correspondence, box 163; Marian Huntington to Elizabeth, April 11, 1922, Metcalf Add. MSS, box 7.

40. HEH to Jacques Seligmann, April 1, 1922, HEH Correspondence, box 152.

41. Otheman Stevens, *Los Angeles Examiner,* August 23, 1925, HEH MS 7/10(40).

42. On her survival, HEH deposition, October 7, 1926, and E. B. Holladay deposition, December 6, 1927, HEH MS 37/1–18; on treatment, Leslie Huntington to Elizabeth H. Metcalf, April 27, 1922, Metcalf Add. MSS, box 7.

43. HEH to Joseph Duveen, December 8, 1923, January 11, 1924; R. P. Schwerin to HEH, December 11, 1923; HEH to Schwerin, January 8, 1924. All in HEH Correspondence, boxes 164, 165. Gomez, tape C, HEH MS 19/1(17).

44. Daily notes on the progress of her illness for the period July 13 to September 18, 1924, are contained in HEH Correspondence, boxes 168–70. George Hapgood to Hertrich, August 29, 1924, HEH MS 31.1.1.19; HEH to George S. Patton, September 7, 1924, Patton Collection, box 5.

45. The letters and telegrams of sympathy and responses are preserved in HEH Correspondence, boxes 169–70. HEH to Nora N. Larsen, October 1, 1924, HEH Correspondence, box 170.

46. C. F. Bailey to Robert O. Schad, September 25, 1929, HEH MS 19/3; George Hapgood to Annie V. Wright, September 30, 1924, HEH Correspondence, box 170; N. P. Stedman, October 7, 1914, HEH Correspondence, box 199; *Los Angeles Examiner,* HEH MS 7/10(39).

47. Her will is in HEH Correspondence, box 162, folder 43, and in HEH MS 37/1. For the appointment of attorneys, October 21, 1924, HEH Correspondence, box 171. For newspaper stories about her will, October 9, 1924, HEH MS 7/10(44).

48. George Hapgood to Duveen, October 29, 1924, HEH Correspondence, box 171; HEH to Kate W. Barton, December 6, 1924, HEH Correspondence, box 172.

49. George Hapgood to Duveen, December 13, 1924; Siebrecht's House of Flowers bill; Hapgood to E. A. Adams, December 29, 1924. All in HEH Correspondence, box 172. Burke Holladay, Journal, vol. 2, Metcalf Add. MSS.

1. HEH to Sir John Maxwell, March 4, 1926, HEH Correspondence, box 180; HEH to Henry Sanders, February 12, 1926, HEH Correspondence, box 179.

2. HEH to Elise Ferguson, May 5, 1925, HEH Correspondence, box 175.

3. HEH to Sir John Maxwell, February 1, 1925, HEH MS 31.1.1.31.

4. Courtney De Kalb to HEH, September 16, 1925, HEH Correspondence, box 177; HEH to Archer, October 8, 1925, HEH Correspondence, box 177.

5. Gomez, tape K, HEH MS 19/1(17).

6. HEH to Joseph Duveen, May 29, 1925, HEH Correspondence, box 176.

7. HEH to Joseph Duveen, August 10, 1926, HEH Correspondence, box 182.

8. Most of these details about social activities are drawn from Burke Holladay, Diaries, book 13, HEH MS 53/2. Some details come from the letters of HEH and his daughters, 1925–26, HEH Correspondence, boxes 171–77.

9. George Hapgood, Report on the Arrangement of Pictures, 1927–28, HEH MS 31.1.1.19; for his favorites, Emma Quigley, Reminiscences, HEH MS 19/1(1); Fred Hogue, *Los Angeles Times,* May 29, 1927, HEH MS 38/3.

10. R. B. Haselden, "Memo to the Director," December 1, 1928, HEH MS 19/3.

11. Burke Holladay, Diaries, book 13, September 27, 1925, HEH MS 52/2; HEH to Rosenbach, December 20, 1925, HEH MS 31.1.1.39.

12. Memories of Margaret Huntington McLaren, HEH MS 19/3, Elizabeth to HEH, December 23, 1926, Metcalf Add. MSS, box 8; David Huntington to James Thorpe, January 2, 1986. Correspondence with visitors, 1925–27, is in the institutional files, HEH MSS 31.1.1.—, and in HEH Correspondence, boxes 173–86. Aurelia Reinhardt to HEH, May 6, 1925, HEH MS 31.1.1.37; Clarence Little, November 15, 1926, HEH MS 31.1.1.42.

13. *Los Angeles Times,* June 22, 1926, and many other papers of June 21 and 22, HEH MS 38/2; HEH to Joseph Duveen, June 25, August 10, 1926, HEH Correspondence, box 182.

14. July 23, 1926, HEH Correspondence, box 182; July 23, 1926, HEH MS 31.1.1.44; newspaper clippings, July 20–30, 1926, HEH MS 7/10(41).

15. Cora Case Porter to HEH, June 22, 1925, HEH Correspondence, box 176; HEH to Porter, June 23, 1925, HEH Correspondence, box 176.

16. Hannah T. Jenkins to HEH, April 28, 1925, HEH Correspondence, box 175; HEH to Jenkins, May 1, 1925, HEH Correspondence, box 175; HEH to Mr. Stiles, April 5, 1925, HEH MS 31.1.1.43.

17. Emma Quigley, Reminiscences, HEH MS 19/1(1).

18. The details of the ensuing account of the trip to Philadelphia, the operation, and the return are based on Burke Holladay, Diaries, book 13, July 9, October 15 to November 24, 1925, HEH MS 53/2.

19. Otheman Stevens to HEH, October 16, 1925, HEH MS 31.1.1.43.

20. HEH to Mrs. Pickett, October 22, 1925, HEH Correspondence, box 177.

21. Gomez, tape B, HEH MS 53/2.

22. Clara Huntington to Elizabeth H. Metcalf, November 1, 1925, Metcalf Add. MSS, box 7.

23. Wolf and Fleming, *Rosenbach*, 234–35.

24. Rosenbach to Hapgood, November 3, 1925, HEH MS 31.1.1.39.

25. HEH to George S. Patton, November 5, 1925, HEH Correspondence, box 178; in answer to Patton from HEH, October 28, 1925, Patton Collection, box 5.

26. Carrie to HEH, October 30, 1925, HEH Correspondence, box 177.

27. Gomez, tape B, HEH MS 19/1(17).

28. Mary E. Dunlap to HEH, November 6, 1925, HEH Correspondence, box 178; and reply, November 10, 1925, HEH Correspondence, box 178.

29. Otheman Stevens to HEH, December 1, 1925, HEH MS 31.1.1.52.

30. HEH to John W. Ensign, December 30, 1925, HEH Correspondence, box 178; HEH to Rosenbach, December 30, 1925, HEH MS 31.1.1.39.

31. HEH to Carrie and Burke Holladay, February 26, 1926, HEH Correspondence, box 179.

32. HEH Correspondence, box 180; March 10, 1926, HEH MS 16/2(1); January 2, 1926, HEH MS 31.1.1.32.

33. March 23, 1926, HEH MS 31.1.1.46.

34. HEH to Carrie, March 13, 29, 1926, HEH Correspondence, box 180.

35. HEH Correspondence, boxes 180–83.

36. HEH to Thomas J. Kerr, November 4, 1926, HEH Correspondence, box 183.

37. Burke Holladay, Diaries, book 13, January 28–29, 1927, HEH MS 53/2.

38. Frank A. Miller to HEH, December 30, 1926, HEH Correspondence, box 184.

39. For example, letters from Elizabeth to HEH, Metcalf Add. MSS, boxes 7–8.

40. Invoices for these paintings are in HEH MS 28/1.

41. Otheman Stevens, Reminiscences, July 11, 1929, HEH MS 19/3.

42. Telegrams between HEH and Duveen, April 2, 6, 9, 14, 1925, HEH Correspondence, box 175.

43. Duveen to HEH, December 10, 1926, HEH MS 28/1; Duveen to HEH, January 29, March 29, 1927, HEH Correspondence, boxes 184–86; HEH to Duveen, April 13, 1927, HEH Correspondence, boxes 184–86. For a full newspaper account, *Philadelphia Inquirer,* June 2, 1927, HEH MS 16/7.

44. HEH to Mitchell Kennerley, April 26, June 4, 1926, HEH MS 31.1.1.26.

45. Correspondence between Metropolitan Museum and HEH, July 26, 31, August 9, 17, 1926, HEH Correspondence, boxes 182–83.

46. List of objects and cost, January 25, 1927, HEH Correspondence, box 184.

47. HEH to Mrs. Edwin J. Marshall, December 27, 1926, HEH MS 31.1.1.31.

48. HEH to Archer Huntington, April 8, 1927, HEH Correspondence, box 185.

49. Trust indenture, "Establishment of Arabella D. Huntington Memorial Art Collection," April 23, 1927, HEH Correspondence, box 187.

50. "Huntington Library Collections, 1925–27," *Huntington Library Bulletin* 1 (1931): 85–104.

51. Interview with Otheman Stevens, *Los Angeles Examiner,* March 13, 1926, HEH MS 16/10.

52. Lots 414, 415, Henkels Catalogue no. 1386, February 8, 1926, HEH MS 31.1.1.39.

53. May 1, 1925, HEH MS 31.1.1.14.

54. Leslie E. Bliss, Reminiscences, HEH MS 19/1(16); Bliss to HEH, June 11, 1926, HEH MS 31.1.1.5; *Pasadena Star News,* September 27, 1926, HEH MS 16/3.

55. Notarized statement, E. B. Holladay, May 1931, HEH Correspondence, box 189; Bliss to Max Farrand, April 9, 1927, HEH MS 31.1.1.15.

56. E. B. Sweetman to HEH, December 30, 1926, HEH MS 31.1.1.44; Margaret Stillwell, June 18, 1925, HEH MS 31.1.1.43; HEH telegram, May 19, 1925, HEH MS 31.1.1.22.

57. Loans for 1925–27, HEH MS 1/D/5(4); W. O. Waters to HEH, June 11, 1925, HEH MS 31.1.1.49; staff letter to HEH, December 29, 1925, HEH Correspondence, box 178.

58. Alice I. Perry Wood to HEH, May 25, 1927, HEH MS 31.1.1.35; William Maxwell to HEH, February 25, 1925, HEH MS 31.1.1.31; Leslie Bliss to G. E. Hale, December 3, 1926, HEH MS 31.1.1.19.

59. For Greg, HEH MS 31.1.1.18; for Stillwell, HEH MS 31.1.1.43; for *Gesamtkatalog*, HEH MS 31.1.1.26.

60. Otheman Stevens, *Los Angeles Examiner*, July 8, 1924, HEH MS 16/3.

61. C. S. Sargent to HEH, December 11, 1924, HEH MS 31.1.1.40; H. M. Hall to HEH, May 26, 1924, HEH MS 31.1.1.19; W. L. Dawson to HEH, May 17, 1924, HEH MS 31.1.1.12.

62. *Pasadena Star News*, February 14, 1925, HEH MS 7/10(40). For "a friend," February 22, 1925, HEH MS 31.1.1.52; HEH to Ralph S. Vanderhoof, January 30, February 3, March 2, 1925, HEH Correspondence, box 173; Robert G. Sproul, March 16, 18, 19, 1925, HEH Correspondence, box 174.

63. HEH MS 27/3.

64. HEH MS 27/3.

65. Max Farrand to HEH, July 21, 1926, Hale Papers, MS film 714, reel 19.

66. Max Farrand, "Recollections of H. E. H.," February 9, 1933, HEH MS 19/3.

67. Trustees minutes, February 5, 1927, HEH Correspondence, box 184; Hale Papers, MS film 714, reel 19; Max Farrand to Arthur M. Schlesinger, March 26, 1941, HEH MS 31.1.1.40.

68. HEH to Edwin R. Seligman, March 10, 1927, HEH MS 31.1.1.40; Max Farrand, "Recollections of H. E. H.," February 9, 1933, HEH MS 19/3.

69. G. E. Hale to HEH, March 9, 25, 1927, Hale Papers, MS film 714, reel 19; Hale to Turner, March 8, 1927, HEH Correspondence, box 185; Farrand to Hale, March 8, 1927, HEH Correspondence, box 185.

70. About the will, August 1, 1925, HEH MS 27/4; about the gift, April 28, 1927, HEH Correspondence, box 186.

71. Calculations and notes, January 20, February 8, 1927, HEH Correspondence, box 184; February 28, 1927, HEH MS 1/F/41(C).

72. *New York Sun*, January 19, 1926, HEH MS 7/10(41).

73. HEH to Mayor George E. Cryer, February 24, 1922, HEH Correspondence, box 150; HEH to California Art Club, January 16, 1922, HEH Correspondence, box 150; Gomez, tape G, HEH MS 19/1(17).

74. For the Alhambra visit, May 21, 1924, HEH MS 31.1.1.9; for Caltech and L.A. Library School, February 11, 1927, HEH MS 31.1.1.32; for the Shakespeare Club, November 15, 1926, HEH MS 31.1.1.42; for a feature writer, July 7, 1925, HEH MS 31.1.1.35; for a magazine, May 15, 1925, HEH MS 31.1.1.8; for a newspaper, August 17, 1926, HEH MS 31.1.1.35.

75. *Pasadena Star News*, February 26, 1950, HEH MS 19/3.

76. *Los Angeles Examiner*, March 19, 1927, HEH MS 16/2(1).

77. HEH MS 1/D/5(4).

78. Elizabeth to HEH, January 12, 1925, Metcalf Add. MSS, box 7.

79. HEH to Rosenbach, December 18, 1924, HEH Correspondence, box 172; Rosenbach to HEH, January 3, 29, February 2, 1925, HEH MS 31.1.1.39; HEH to Rosenbach, January 8, 1925, HEH MS 31.1.1.39.

80. HEH to Duveen, August 1, 1925, HEH Correspondence, box 177; Duveen to HEH, August 11, 1925, HEH Correspondence, box 177.

81. J. R. Pope to HEH, January 9, 1926, HEH Correspondence, box 179; HEH to Pope, January 14, 1926, HEH Correspondence, box 179. HEH to Pope, telegram, March 26, 1926; HEH to Pope, letter, March 27, 1926; HEH to Carrie, March 29, 1926; all in HEH Correspondence, box 180.

82. J. R. Pope to HEH, April 6, 20, 1926, HEH Correspondence, box 180; HEH to Pope, April 22, 1926, HEH Correspondence, box 180.

83. About sculptor selection, T. J. Young letter, July 2, 1928, HEH Correspondence, box 187; about the mausoleum contract and construction, HEH MSS 38/6, 19/4; Crowell Reminiscences, May 23, 1939, HEH MS 19/3; about trees, Hertrich notes, May 1939, HEH MS 19/3.

84. HEH to Archer Huntington, April 8, 1927, HEH Correspondence, box 185.

85. J. R. Pope to John Gregory, March 18, 1929, HEH MS 19/3.

86. Mary Lewis to her family, January 28, 1927, HEH Correspondence, box 184. Various dates and details in this section are derived from Burke Holladay, Diaries, book 13, HEH MS 53/2.

87. Dr. E. B. Bryant to Dr. J. B. Deaver, April 20, 1927, HEH Correspondence, box 186; Deaver to Bryant, April 20, 1927, HEH Correspondence, box 186.

88. HEH to Joseph Duveen, April 22, 1927, HEH Correspondence, box 186; HEH to Rosenbach, April 26, 1927, HEH MS 31.1.1.39; HEH to E. A. Adams, April 26, 1927, HEH Correspondence, box 186; William Sproule of SP Company, April 29, 1927, HEH Correspondence, box 186.

89. Gomez, tape N, HEH MS 19/1(17).

90. Dr. Bryant, *Los Angeles Times,* May 30, 1927, HEH MS 38/3; Gomez and Dr. Bryant, *Pasadena Star News,* May 24, 1927, HEH MS 16/6; about the *Short-title Catalogue,* Rosenbach, *New York Times,* May 24, 1927, HEH MS 16/6.

91. HEH to Mrs. Pickett, May 4, 1927, HEH Correspondence, box 186.

92. Burke Holladay, Diaries, book 13, May 7–8, 1927, HEH MS 53/2; *Pasadena Star News,* May 24, 1927, HEH MS 16/6.

93. Rosenbach to Bliss, May 17, 1927, HEH MS 31.1.1.39; Burke Holladay, Diaries, book 13, May 21–22, 1927, HEH MS 53/2.

94. *Pasadena Star News,* May 24, 1927, HEH MS 16/6; federal estate tax return, HEH MS 38/6.

95. May 23, 1927, HEH MSS 38/3, 16/6.

96. Burke Holladay, Diaries, book 13, May 24–29, 1927, HEH MS 53/2; HEH MS 38/3; Metcalf Add. MSS, box 8.

97. Burke Holladay, Diaries, book 13, May 31, 1927, HEH MS 53/2. *Los Angeles Times, Los Angeles Examiner, Pasadena Star News,* June 1, 1927, Metcalf Add. MSS, box 8.

98. For 1917–24, HEH MSS 11/2(3), 27/2; for 1924–27, HEH MS 1/FF/2; official estate report, September 12, 1928, March 24, 1929, HEH MS 38/6.

99. For example, *Los Angeles Herald Examiner,* May 27, 1927, Metcalf Add. MSS, box 8.

100. Otheman Stevens, *Los Angeles Herald Examiner,* May 26, 1927, HEH MS 16/6; notarized statements, Caroline H. Holladay and C. E. Culver, April 1931, HEH Correspondence, box 189.

101. Will and codicils, HEH Correspondence, box 186.

102. Distribution record, May 22, 1931, HEH MS 38/6.

103. Collis P. Huntington Will, HEH MS 7/6(2).

104. C. E. Culver, notarized statement, April 24, 1931, HEH Correspondence, box 189; James A. Gibson, *Los Angeles Times,* May 28, 1927, HEH MS 38/3.

105. William Hertrich, notarized statement, April 25, 1931, HEH Correspondence, box 189; orchard records, 1918–20, HEH MS 6/12.

106. Otheman Stevens, *Los Angeles Herald Examiner,* May 26, 1927, Metcalf Add. MSS, box 8.

107. A. S. W. Rosenbach, *Atlantic Monthly* (October 1927): 455–56. Reprinted in Rosenbach, *Books and Bidders* (Boston: Little Brown, 1927), and often quoted.

108. *New York Times,* May 29, 1927, HEH MS 16/10; *New York Herald Tribune,* May 24, 1927, Metcalf Add. MSS, box 8; L. Kashnor to L. E. Bliss, June 24, 1927, HEH MS 31.1.1.33; Joseph Duveen to HEH, May 23, 1925, HEH Correspondence, box 175; *Brooklyn Eagle,* May 24, 1927, HEH MS 16/10.

109. Los Angeles Chamber of Commerce award, February 27, 1927, HEH Correspondence, box 185; Arthur Brisbane, syndicated column, May 24, 1927, HEH MS 16/10; B. C. Forbes, syndicated column, May 26, 1927, HEH MS 16/10; *Wall Street Journal,* May 25, 1927, HEH MS 16/10; *Literary Digest,* June 18, 1927, HEH MS 16/6; *Los Angeles Times,* May 29, 1927, HEH MS 16/12; *San Francisco Chronicle,* May 1927, Metcalf Add.

MSS, box 8; *Los Angeles Mercury,* September 8, 1926, HEH MS 7/10(41); *San Marino Tribune,* May 23, 1927, HEH Correspondence, box 186.

110. *Los Angeles Examiner,* February 26, 1927, HEH MS 7/10(42); Fred Hogue, *Los Angeles Times,* May 29, 1927, Metcalf Add. MSS, box 8; Otheman Stevens, *Los Angeles Examiner,* June 1, 1927, HEH MS 16/6.

111. Otheman Stevens, *Los Angeles Examiner,* May 27, 1927, HEH MS 16/6; W. A. R. Goodwin to HEH, November 13, 1926, HEH Correspondence, box 183; G. E. Hale, *Los Angeles Times,* May 30, 1927, Metcalf Add. MSS, box 8.

112. Max Farrand to L. E. Bliss, May 24, 1927, HEH MS 31.1.1.15; L. E. Bliss to Henry Stevens, June 6, 1927, HEH MS 31.1.1.43; minutes, Huntington Land and Improvement Co., August 5, 1927, HEH MS 1/F/41(C); Redondo Improvement Co., August 5, 1927, HEH MS 1/R/12; Naples Extension Co., August 5, 1927, HEH MS 1/0/12; Theodore Irwin to C. William Buma, October 31, 1927, HEH MS 31.1.1.24; R. O. Schad to David Huntington, April 9, 1960, HEH MS 31.1.1.24; announcement, June 1960, HEH MS 20/.

113. *Los Angeles Examiner,* May 24, 1927, HEH MS 16/12; Harry Carr, *Los Angeles Times,* May 26, 1927, HEH MS 38/3; Otheman Stevens, *Los Angeles Examiner,* June 1, 1927, HEH MS 38/3.

PHOTOGRAPH SOURCES

All materials are from the Huntington Collections. Frontispiece, 61/2(3); fig. 1, 285/5(2) and 285/5(15); fig. 2, 61/2/3(1); fig. 3, 61/5/1(1); fig. 4, 61/2/12(1); fig. 5, 61/2/3(7); fig. 6, 61/4(9)(218) and 285/1(14); fig. 7, 61/2/9(102) and 61/5/1(6); fig. 8, 61/2/6(9); fig. 9, 285/1(21.1); fig. 10, 61/1(1); fig. 11, 61/2/13(B); fig. 12 (*Howard*) 285/7(2), (*Elizabeth*) 61/4(216), (*Clara*) 285/7(7), and (*Marian*) 285/7(27); fig. 13, 61/3/3(8607); fig. 14, 61/3(83); fig. 15 (*Patton*) uncatalogued; fig. 16, 7/10(8); fig. 17, 7/6(3); fig. 18, 31.1.1.42.3; fig. 19, 61/3(1); fig. 20, 285/10(166), 285/10(177), and 285/10(176); fig. 21, 107/4/8(105); fig. 22, 285/1(19); fig. 23, 61/2/1 and 61/2/2; fig. 24, Rare Book 92588; fig. 25, 107, box 4/9, p. 25; fig. 26, 285/1(10); fig. 27, 285/1(9); fig. 28, 285/4(5); fig. 29, Huntington Art Gallery; fig. 30, 16/2(2); fig. 31, 107, box 2/4, p. 35; fig. 32, 285/1(26); fig. 33, 7/4(39); fig. 34, 285/1(30) and 61/5(12); fig. 35, 107/26(3); fig. 36, 61/5/17.

Aviaries, San Marino Ranch, 373, 414
Aviation, HEH's interest in, 245–46
Aviation Week, 245–46

Baldwin, W. L., 80
Ball, Eustace Hale, 353–54
Balloonists, 245–46
Baltazzi, Count, 334
Barker, Harley Granville, 362–63
Barrie, George, 327–28
Bassett, J. M., 96
Baugh, Albert C., 351
Beecher, Henry Ward, 25, 27, 69, 307,
   319–20
Bendikson, Dr., 473–74
Berenson, Bernard, 435
Biblio, The, 458
Bibliographical societies, 356
Bierce, Ambrose, 97
Bierstadt, Albert, 327
Birley, Oswald, 431–33
Bixby, William K., 357, 442
Blackall, Elizabeth W., 412
Bliss, Leslie E., 342, 428–29, 451, 503–4,
   511, 527
Bode, Wilhelm von, 437
Books, 153–54, 164–65, 339–40, 369,
   524; about art, 133–34; as art, 266;
   about books, 269–70; British Museum, 344–45; cataloging, 265, 340–
   41, 344–45, 410, 411, 419–20, 452,
   471–74; clubs, 349, 356, 488; Collis
   and, 154, 330; dealers, 76, 131–32,
   262–81 passim, 284, 343–44, 380,
   442–51 passim; duplicates on sale,
   345–47; as gifts (personal), 10, 132–
   33; Gutenberg Bible, 270, 274–76,
   438; HEH reading, 10, 77, 132, 164–
   65, 264, 265–66, 270, 342, 353, 426–
   27, 485, 491–92, 523; in HEH's childhood, 9–10; HEH's last, 516; HEH's
   retirement and, 238, 249, 250, 262–
   81; offers refused, 449–50; reading
   aloud, 132, 426–27, 485, 492; records

of, 133; subjects of, 266; writers corre-
   sponding with HEH, 449. *See also*
   Library
Booth, Robert, 430
Borel, Antoine, 138, 189
Boruff, Fred L., 192
Boston Transcript, 278, 352, 457, 458
Bradbury, Louis, 288
Brand Ranch, Glendale, 199
Braunton, Ernest, 255–56, 372
Brehm, James, 490
Brigham, Clarence, 449
Brisbane, Arthur, 461, 525
British Museum, 344–45, 454
Brooklyn Eagle, 525
Brown, C. L., 75–76
Brown, J. P., 151–52
Brown, Juliet, 267
Bryant, Ernest, 376, 466, 494–95, 496,
   498, 515–17
Burgess, Gelett, 132
Bushnell, Kittie, 69
Business: Belle's, 309–10, 316, 374–75,
   409, 470; Collis-HEH relations,
   150–52; Collis's principles of, 30, 73,
   81, 82–83, 109; Collis's retirement
   ideas, 271; depressions, 104–6, 115,
   213, 223; *Directory of Directors*, 212;
   Harriman's qualities, 191; Huntington & Franchot, 36–45; HEH's
   broad interests, 209–14; in HEH's
   childhood, 15–16, 18; HEH's daily
   routines, 184–85, 237; HEH's early
   NYC job and, 24, 25; HEH's financial analysis skills, 83–86, 212–13;
   HEH's management style, 181;
   HEH's manufacturing companies,
   210, 211–12; HEH's mistakes, 212;
   HEH's in NYC, 409; HEH's opera-
   tional analysis skills, 76; HEH's people judgments, 86, 231; HEH's profit-
   maximization policies, 209; HEH's
   property examination skills, 86;
   HEH's public-private negotiations,

355; with HEH in Philadelphia hospital, 516, 517; at HEH's death, 517; and HEH's library, 503–4; and Howard's death, 481; illness, 243; marriage, 125, 132; in San Francisco, 376; in Southern California, 206–7, 224, 225, 254, 371, 375, 413–14, 439, 490, 492, 494

Holladay, Helen Huntington, 126, 129, 239, 336, 413–14, 490

Holladay, S. W., 132, 133

Hook Lines, 138, 186

Hoover, Herbert, 463–64

Hopkins, Mark, 92, 93

Hopkins-Searles SP interests, 92, 115, 117, 144, 160

Hotel del Coronado, 256

Hotel Wentworth (the Huntington), 292–94

Houghton, A. C., 257

Hubbard, Thomas H., 92, 117, 139, 141, 144

Hunt, Myron, 258–61, 287–89, 293, 371, 383–86, 392

Huntington, Arabella ("Belle"), 69, 164, 306–35; appearance, 310, 315, 415; and art, 283–84, 326–35, 381, 388, 406–7, 416, 426; art memorial, 495, 496, 501–2, 519; birth, 307–8, 514; burial, 417, 487, 512–15; Chateau Beauregard, 301–2, 315, 336–37, 359, 371, 403, 406–8; and Collis's death, 145, 147–48, 162, 312–13, 315; and Collis's will/estate, 156–57, 307, 314, 331; death, 307, 409, 465, 483–87, 489–90; domestic behavior, 415–17; Europe, 77, 78, 164, 166, 295–302, 313, 315, 323, 326, 333, 336–40, 405–8; health problems, 130–31, 291, 298, 312, 316–19, 360, 377, 406, 425, 483; HEH's daughters and, 295–300, 307–14 passim, 340, 427–28; HEH's ranch house planning, 259–60; in HEH's will, 389; and Hoe Library,

274; and Huntington Library and Art Gallery, 392–93, 420, 486; independent business, 309–10, 316, 374–75, 409, 470; jewelry, 315; marriages, 69, 148, 272, 294–309, 319–20, 324–25; mother, 322; NYC mansion, 98–99, 125, 325–26, 403; personality, 310–16, 319, 425–26; pets, 414–15; philanthropic gifts, 148, 314–15, 463, 486; portraits, 328, 431–33, 495, 496, 501; and San Francisco, 123–26, 312, 315–16, 325, 326, 332–33, 463; and shipbuilding company, 367–68; siblings, 87, 308, 320–22; social life, 302–5, 316, 355–56, 371–76, 410, 413–14; and son, 69, 306–15 passim, 322–24, 378, 412–13; in Southern California, 302–5, 370–78, 403, 413–26; and SP stock, 156–57, 163; will, 486

Huntington, Archer Milton, 69, 127, 306–15 passim, 322–24; and Anna Hyatt (second wife), 318, 412–13, 514; and Belle memorial, 495, 496, 501, 502; and Belle's death, 409, 483, 484, 486, 487, 489, 490; and Belle's parrot, 415; and Belle's portrait, 432, 495, 496, 501; birth, 306, 308, 309; and California, 378; at Collis's funeral, 147; in Collis's will, 156, 331; divorce, 362–63, 412; and Edith, 77; Europe, 78, 164, 166, 313, 315, 323, 336, 337, 338, 339, 359; father of, 307, 308–9; and Helen Manchester Gates (first wife), 323–24, 362; at HEH and Belle's wedding, 298; and HEH's health, 129; Hispanic Museum, 315, 323, 389, 486; and Hoe Library, 274; and Huntington Library and Art Gallery, 391–92, 402, 505; and Mausoleum, 514; in NYC with Belle and HEH, 340, 355, 378, 410; and portrait painter, 431–32; and Troubetskoy, 381–82; watercolor portrait, 328; and World War I, 337, 338, 339

church life, 10–11, 25, 27, 32–33, 76, 121; in Cohoes, 22–23; and Collis's death, 145–62; and Collis's will, 155, 156–60; colors, 226; death, 221, 517–18; divorce, 173–76, 201, 272, 294; domestic behavior, 415–17; engagement to Mary, 34; in Europe with Belle, 294, 297–302, 336–40; exercise for health, 129–30, 362; family affection, 7, 28–29, 61–62, 153, 165, 175–76, 427–28, 522; friendships, 22, 79–80, 127, 200–201, 243, 271, 424–25, 480–83; harassments, 193, 243–44; hard-working, 184–85, 237, 521–22; health problems, 102–3, 121, 128–30, 239, 313, 360–62, 376–77, 404, 465–68, 483, 494–98, 515–17; hero myth, 232–35, 271, 528; honorary degrees, 463; intellect, 522–23; lawsuits, 363–66; letters from public, 243, 476–80; listkeeping, 84, 133, 181; on marriage, 153, 171–72; marriages, 38, 153, 172–73, 272, 294–306, 317; modesty, 522, 526; mother's death, 21, 240–42; nonbusiness activities, 245–48; in NYC, 23–29, 34, 53, 164–65, 294, 302, 340, 355–61, 403, 408–13, 466, 483–86; NYC social life, 355–58, 410; in Oneonta, 1, 3–21, 46–51, 53–54; optimism of, 177–80, 497, 498; passport (first), 297–98; pennypinching, 431; personal behavior, 422–31; phrenology, 159; play, 522; portrait, 431–33; public honor and praise, 218–36, 399–402, 434, 462–63; remarriage rumors, 244, 294–95; retirement, 237–305, 366–69, 394, 468; in San Francisco, 76, 88–91, 97–145, 155–64, 332–33, 463; schooling, 9, 10, 20, 522–23; Solon's estate handled by, 79; in Southern California, 97–98, 134–38, 165–236, 361, 370–78, 403–5, 413–64, 486–521; Southern California social life, 264, 302–5, 371–76,

413–14, 490–94, 497–98; and temperance, 27, 40, 223; thefts from, 345, 366; on trust and spontaneity, 430–31; unworthiness theme, 33; and "vacations," 78; in West Virginia, 29–47; will, 388–89, 501, 509, 510, 519–20; women closest to, 311; and Yarrington brothers, 320–21. *See also* Art; Books; Business; Money; Nature; San Marino Ranch

Mills, D. O., 161, 162

Mills, W. H., 90–104 passim, 119

Milton, Richard, 308

Money: American Red Cross, 398; Archer's trust, 314; Aviation Week, 245–46; Belle's art purchases, 334; Belle's customs declaration, 302; Belle's estate, 486; Belle's philanthropy, 314–15; Belle's stocks, 156–57, 163, 310; borrowing, 18, 39, 40, 190; Chateau Beauregard upkeep, 359, 407–8; Collis's art purchases, 327, 329; Collis's estate, 155–60, 213, 314; cost of HEH's gift of library and art collection, 401–2, 518; debt leverage tactic, 18, 190; dependence on, 25; HEH's art purchases, 133, 262–68 passim, 281–85, 379, 435–41 passim, 499–501; HEH's assets, 212–14, 271, 294, 366, 378–79, 459, 518–19; HEH's capital accumulation, 67, 76, 86–88, 212–13; HEH's financial analysis skills, 83–86, 212–13; HEH's furniture purchases, 262, 267, 268, 379; HEH's garden, 258, 288; HEH's librarian, 341; HEH's library purchases, 43, 76, 133–34, 262–81 passim, 343, 382, 438–52 passim; HEH's management of, 79, 212–13, 396–98, 441, 468–69; HEH's Market Street Railway salary, 159; HEH's real estate deals, 199, 203–4, 207, 208–9; HEH's real estate value, 421–22; HEH's SP salary, 100, 159; HEH's SP stock sale, 163; HEH's staff and, 429–30, 504; HEH's support of relatives, 128, 166–67, 171, 174, 427; HEH's will, 388–89, 509, 510, 519–20; HEH's World War I relief, 338; Huntington Library and Art Gallery upkeep, 499, 509, 510–11, 518–21; inheritance taxes, 156; Los Angeles street railways, 138, 183, 187, 189–90, 194–95; Oneonta's library, 412; portrait painting, 432; public letters to HEH for, 476–80; railroad finances, 83–85, 105; San Francisco earthquake and fire relief, 163–64; San Marino Ranch purchase, 251; saving, 24, 27, 60, 429–30, 504; Varnum's salary, 363; Varnum's suit, 364; Willard's land investments, 198; after World War I, 396

Monrovia, railway, 188

Monsarrat, N., 57

Moral outlook: in Collis's business principles, 73, 83; HEH's, 11, 27, 40; and Huntington & Franchot, 40, 41

Morgan, J. Pierpont: art collection, 282, 333, 334, 379; librarian, 277; library, 352, 461; and Raquette Lake Railway, 325

Morse, S. F. B., 104, 125

Mt. Lowe Railway, 182, 229

Muir, John A., 169, 184, 225, 242–43

Muller, Adolfo, 482

Murphy, Blinker, 119, 124–25

Murphy, Francis, 223

Musfelder, Jules, 133

Nadeau tract, 198

Naples land companies, 199

Natili, Baron Randolph, 125, 298, 306, 387

Nature: HEH's love of, 238, 488–89; wild animal park, 248. See also Gardens; San Marino Ranch

Newbegin, John J., 132

New Orleans Daily States, 104

Newport Beach: HEH's land, 199, 205, 209; railway, 187, 188

Newport News Shipbuilding and Drydock Company, 367–68, 417, 485, 516

Newton, A. Edward, 343

New York: Cohoes, 22–23. See also New York City; Oneonta

New York City: Collis in, 20, 23–28, 34, 62, 77, 98–99, 106, 125, 324–26;

Grolier Club, 349, 356, 488; HEH in, 23–29, 34, 53, 164–65, 294, 302, 340, 355–61, 403, 408–13, 466, 483–86; HEH's library, 342–55; Hobby Club, 356–58; Metropolitan Club, 164–65, 264, 265, 294, 340; 65 Park Avenue, 20, 23, 26, 28, 34, 48, 50, 62, 77, 324–25; Sargent and Company, 23–26; weather, 408–9, 466

New York Commercial, 229
New York Evening Mail, 234
New York Evening Post, 352–53, 355
New York Globe, 219–20
New York Herald, 278, 459–60
New York Herald Tribune, 433, 525
"New York Letter" column (Marthol), 219
New York Post, 437, 454
New York Sun, 206, 353–54, 461
New York Sunday Telegraph, 160
New York Times, 278, 282, 330, 334, 352, 459, 525
New York Town Topics, 158, 229, 244
New York Tribune, 112, 278
New York World, 433, 457
Norris, Frank, 97
Northam Ranch, Long Beach, 199

Oak Knoll tract, Pasadena, 199, 203, 204, 258, 292–93
Oakland Enquirer, 96
Oakland Times, 110, 112
Octopus (Norris), 97
O'Melveny, Henry, 201
Oneonta: Harriet's burial, 242; missed by HEH from West Virginia, 32; HEH moving back to, 46–51, 53; HEH visits from West Virginia, 34; HEH visits from California, 127, 239; HEH's childhood in, 1, 3–21; HEH's letters from NYC about, 25; HEH's wife and children in, 46–51, 54, 61–62, 65–66, 122, 127, 164; Huntington Park and Library, 21,

358–59, 411–12, 471; population, 4, 15; public events, 13–15
Oneonta Memories and Sundry Personal Recollections of the Author (W. Huntington), 7
Oneonta Star, 216
Ord family, 125
Osgood, Charles G., 356
Otis, Harrison Gray, 93, 291, 382, 388
Outing Magazine, 229

Pacific Electric Building, 165, 233
Pacific Electric Railway Company, 182–98
Pacific Improvement Company, 138, 141
Pacific Light and Power Company, 210, 396
Pardee, Edward, 26, 27, 63, 127, 131
Pardee, Mary, 51
Pardee, Phoebe Huntington, 17
Park, wild animal, 248
Pasadena: and HEH's death, 517; HEH's land, 171, 199, 203, 204, 209, 258, 292–93; Oak Knoll tract, 199, 203, 204, 258, 292–93; SP, 135, 136. *See also* San Marino
Pasadena and Altadena Railway, 135, 216
Pasadena Board of Trade banquet, 227
Pasadena Music and Art Association, 388, 389–93
Pasadena Star News, 506, 517
Paso Robles, 376
Patton, George S., 165, 200–201, 375, 414, 424, 490; and HEH-Harriman struggle, 190–91; HEH's business turned over to, 394; HEH's letters to, 204–5, 209, 211, 213; and HEH's ranch, 252–53, 254–55, 258; and Huntington Library and Art Gallery, 392, 402, 472, 505; and San Marino incorporation, 292
Patton, George S., Jr., 200
Patton, Ruth Wilson, 200
Paulham, Louis, 246

Woman in Black, 243–44
Women: employment of, 341; jitney drivers, 394
Wood, Alice I. Perry, 504
Woolf, Virginia, 312
World War I, 337–39, 367, 385, 398, 400
Worsham, Annette, 308
Worsham, Arabella. *See* Huntington, Arabella ("Belle")
Worsham, John A., 308
Worthington, B. A., 142

Wyer, James I., 341, 342
Wyman, Walter C., 448–49, 451

Yarrington, Catherine J., 308
Yarrington, Elizabeth Page, 308
Yarrington, Emma, 308
Yarrington, John Duval, 87, 308, 320–21
Yarrington, Richard Milton ("Dick"), 308, 321–22